Vaudeville:

From the Honky-tonks to the Palace

VAUDE

FROM THE

HONKY-TONKS

KENNIKAT PRESS
Port Washington, N. Y./London

VILLE:

TO THE

PALACE

by JOE LAURIE, JR.

coauthor of

Show Biz: From Vaude to Video

VAUDEVILLE

Copyright, 1953, by Joe Laurie, Jr.
Reissued in 1972 by Kennikat Press by
arrangement with Holt, Rinehart and Winston, Inc.
Library of Congress Catalog Card No: 74-153225
ISBN 0-8046-1535-7

Manufactured by Taylor Publishing Company   Dallas, Texas

TO MY DAD—

who loved me when I couldn't even act—much less write

Foreword

Twenty years ago my friend Joe Laurie, Jr., told me that he wanted, more than anything else, to write the history of vaudeville. Assuredly he would be the one to do this work competently, for he had been a bright young star at the time when vaudeville and its glorious people brought us our happiest contacts with the world of entertainment.

Laurie, as almost everyone knows, is as clever as he is lovable, and when vaudeville engagements succumbed to the motion picture and to other factors of change, he turned his talents to radio. To no one's surprise, he became a star of the air. This success, together with Laurie's duties as a *Variety* columnist, coauthor of *Show Biz*, and special article writer, seemed to sidetrack the work on vaudeville history. But always there persisted in Laurie's mind the wish to do this history. Now it has been accomplished, and in these pages we can relive the days when the two-a-day artists brought us exciting glimpses—at moderate cost—of the stage.

Vaudeville folk were a clannish group, more down to earth and human, it seemed, than the remote geniuses of the legitimate stage. They had fewer swell heads than the ordinary run of actors, and they helped one another at all times. This loyalty and love which they had for their fellows somehow showed in their public work, and the audience felt a kinship with the gay visitors who called once or perhaps twice a season in the smaller cities.

When television suddenly came to our homes, vaudeville leaped back to our affections. There were reunions, so to speak, with many old friends such as Smith and Dale and Ed Wynn.

This definitive book by Joe Laurie, Jr., is not only of historical import, but gives us a correct view of an art that charmed our fathers and ourselves at a time when bickerings and greed and hatred and envy were not our principal characteristics.

Joe Laurie does not know it, but he is a shrewd psychologist, a gifted observer, and in terms of his own unstudied style a talented writer. And, of course, a grand little guy, a graduate of vaudeville in the best tradition.

GENE FOWLER

Take-a-Bow-Department:

A deep bow (and I hope an encore) to my friend and editor Bill Raney, for his indispensable help, advice, interest, and understanding for which I shall be forever grateful. And to my old and dear pal, Gene Fowler, for his encouragement of my scribbling, and a bend-of-the-knee to all those that have been booked-out-of-town, and from whom I learned so much about the business there's nothing like, SEZ

JOE LAURIE, JR.

Contents

2 THESE WERE THE KINGS, RULERS, AND CZARS OF THE NOW-FORGOTTEN KINGDOM OF THE TWO- AND THREE-A-DAY

3 PAGES TORN OUT OF OLD VAUDEVILLE

1 LEFTY'S LETTERS

Lights Dim–Curtain About to Go Up

This book was written with love and memories for all of Lady Vaudeville's children! To the boys and girls I played with for many years in the fun garden of show biz—VAUDEVILLE! With especial thanks to the Pilgrims of vaude who through pioneering in the honky-tonks and the free-and-easies made variety, and who later through their originality, breeziness, and freshness made vaudeville possible. They started in sawdust and floundered on velvet! They are entitled to the glory, living or dead, for they blazed the trail to make vaudeville the number one entertainment of a nation for nearly half a century!

It wasn't all fun. There are lingering memories of damp basement dressing rooms, layoffs, empty stomachs, long jumps for short dough (sometimes no dough), cancellations after the first show, terrible orchestras, amateur stagehands, lousy boarding-houses with cold rooms in winter and hot ones in summer, dirty day coaches with the smell of oil lamps swinging overhead, greasy grub, and, worse than all this, flopping. Of course, if you were a hit, all the other discomforts were forgotten. It all turned into a fairyland—a *fake* fairyland! For we were young and ambitious and gauged our happiness by applause and laughs!

When you finished serving your apprenticeship by playing every slab in all the whistle stops to all kinds of audiences from the ones that you thought were painted on the seats to the ones that applauded, laughed, stomped their feet, and whistled—and sometimes threw pennies!—your diploma was a full route sheet, play-or-pay contracts, good orchestras, able stagehands, good hotels, decent food, comfortable rooms, riding on plush, and playing the Big Time to reserved seats and maybe ending up at the Palace, on Broadway, with your name out in front, no matter how small. The only thing to top all this was the gathering in comradeship after the show to exchange laughs, dreams, and hopes!

3

There were many reasons for the passing of vaudeville. Pics at first helped vaude, and vice versa; then came talkies and radio. But the vaude termites started working when the ears of the managers became dulled by the clink of gold in the box office. Vaudeville dropped its manners and grosses when the "goose" became the coat of arms of its comedians. Brashness and vulgarity superseded talent and industry. On the part of management, there was hypocrisy and egotism. They beat down the opposition, starved the vaude actor, kidded him, made a spy of him on his fellow artists by dangling forty-week routes before his caved-in stomach. They had a blacklist that kept many a good act away from the big-time bills on which they belonged. And as they stalled the actor, the actor became stale. "We don't care if you copy anybody; is it cheap?" became the motto.

Pictures played to masses and classes; vaude played in a limited sphere. Picture houses with their tremendous seating capacities and continuous performances could outbid the vaude managers for the standard acts. The salaries became fantastic, through competition rising so high that even the most prosperous pic houses couldn't afford to pay them, but they did, until vaude was killed. It was then that they eliminated vaude and went back to straight pics, using acts only when they needed live attractions to help out a bad picture. Now TV has taken over what's left of vaudeville, but still it's a "picture under glass." It hasn't the warmth, the neighborliness, the friendliness, and the clasp and hug and closeness of vaudeville in the flesh! Progress? Maybe!

The vaudeville we knew from the turn of the century to 1932 when the Palace closed its stage door and practically tacked up a sign reading "Vaudeville Dispossessed," the real, honest, vital vaudeville of the old two-a-day of the Palace (and other big-time vaude) will never return. Real two-a-day vaude was a personalized business. The theaters were small; you could almost touch the actors on the stage. Their personalities reached over the footlights; you could see every change of expression; you could hear every word, catch every intonation. There was a free movement; no microphones got in the way!

The spirit of vaudeville will never die as long as there are ambitious kids jigging on cellar doors, doing acrobatics in barns, juggling apples, playing instruments in the school bands, harmonizing "Sweet Adeline," making faces in the mirror, putting on Dad's and Mom's clothes and "playing theater," and telling "jokes"! Every town and hamlet in the United States is a silo of future talent. Like reincarnation, vaude will keep coming back in other forms. But *big-time* vaude is now just a sweet memory!

I have been in almost every branch of the show biz (even owned a tent show that was to have Bob Benchley, Gene Fowler, Heywood Broun, Dorothy Parker, and Ben Hecht as actors, but it folded before they could even read their contracts). But my "brag" is vaudeville, not only because it was my cradle, but because I saw vaudeville feed every branch of the show biz with talented, starry-eyed children of smiles, knights of song and dance, contortionists, magicians, monologists, serio-comics, sketch artists, acrobats, minstrels, and even the freak act, the black sheep of the vaudeville family. They are all Lady Vaudeville's children—their father was Entertainment!

I feel I can tell you the story of vaudeville better through my two favorite vaudevillians, Lefty and Aggie.

Lefty and Aggie are a composite of all the great men and women that made the long march from the honky-tonks to the Palace, on Broadway and Forty-seventh Street, New York City (the last known address of vaude).

When the vaudeville they knew died, they too died a little. Through Lefty and Aggie's Blickensdorfer typewriter, their memories, and their hearts, they will try to recall the days of the two-, three-, four-, and even five-a-day. The days when actors weren't on an assembly line, when comedians didn't worry about tomorrow's jokes while telling them today, as they do in radio and TV in 1953. They will try to recapture the days when we all joined the parade to the golden stage door of the Palace: some of us tried hard to make it, and did; some fell by the wayside, because they didn't get the breaks which are so necessary to success in show biz; and many more quit because the journey was a little too long for them. They will try to recapture the days in vaude when we would all gather after the show for a session of shoptalk and laughs, instead of huddling with lawyers and business managers trying to figure a way to beat the tax or to keep more money with fewer ulcers!

The nicest people in show biz are the ones that are wriggling their way to the top; they listen to everybody and take everybody's advice until they click—then they seldom listen to anybody. But there is nothing more inspiring to an old-timer than to see a kid building his ladder to climb to the stars!

Lefty and Aggie were what they call "theatrical-trunk babies." Their mothers used the bureau drawers for cribs, and hotel towels for diapers. When the parents were on the stage the kids were baby-sitted by acrobats, comedians, tragedians, and song-and-dance men. They took their first bows at the age of two, did a "time step" at three, and, where the law allowed it, worked in the act at six. The New York *Clipper* was their McGuffey's Reader, and they learned geography through the day-coach windows and history by living it. They weren't educated but they are intelligent. When grammar and spelling were being passed around, they were busy rehearsing "off-to-Buffalo" or how to take a prat fall. They didn't want to be professors—they wanted to do a specialty in vaudeville.

Aggie was a good wife and did a good "straight" for Lefty. She could make her own costumes and press and mend Lefty's clothes when she had to. She could do plain cooking on a stove or a gas jet and stretch a buck over a week end by saying, "Go ahead and eat, Lefty, I ain't a bit hungry." Lefty was a good husband, always fixing up the act and making daily rounds of the agents and booking offices. His wants were few. As long as Aggie looked good, with "decent threads," and he kept fairly busy, had a pack of cigarettes, and could afford a nip now and then he was happy. But most of all he wanted someone to talk to about show biz and have laughs.

They were the kind of people that shared their little flat and little food with pals waiting for a break. They were church people (any church) and said their prayers every day in their own church, the Theater. That's a pretty religious place, that "first entrance." It's there that you see the boys and girls crossing themselves and kissing mezuzahs (the Commandments in Hebrew in a tiny case) —and asking The Almighty to make them a hit! Being a hit meant they could take care of their parents, or maybe a crippled sister or brother, or poor relatives. Lefty and Aggie saw that their kids got good schooling and became decent citizens. And they were proud but disappointed when they turned out to be doctors, lawyers, or engineers instead of actors.

They never asked what your religion was or even noticed your color. They weren't prudes or reformers. If you had talent, a good story, or were just good company, that was your ticket to get in the magic circle of performers. They'd get up from a sick bed to play a benefit, and sometimes would even give their most prized possession—part of their routine—to someone who was trying to get started. Lefty and Aggie are real nice folks. They're show folks, who loved show biz as show biz loved them.

Lefty was the kind of guy who was stuffed with unimportant info. He could tell you where he played in 1890 and who was on the bill and how they got over. He could tell you what time he took a train out of Rock Island for Milwaukee twenty-five years ago. He could tell you the first names of the managers, orchestra leaders, stage managers, doormen, and even the spotlight man in every theater he ever played in. He could tell you how much excess he paid in Des Moines and the salary of every act. He knew every boardinghouse and theatrical hotel and the laundries that ruined his cuffs. He knew the real names of most of the actors and what they did before they went into show biz. But he never knew who was President. If he did know, it was because there was a gag about him. "Can the President do a wing like this?" "I never knew a President that could even do a time step." He kidded because he had to pay taxes and had to give his kids to the army and navy. And if you caught him away from his gags, he could even give you a good idea how the government should be run.

Lefty and Aggie knew the right guys and the chiselers. They would give a good artist his due even if they disliked him personally. "He is a great performer on the shelf (stage), but personally he is a louse—he stole a gag from a friend of ours."

Lefty and Aggie have young hearts with a white-haired memory, but even they couldn't mention all the standard acts that were in vaude, because it would make this book look like a telephone directory. Everybody was important in vaudeville, from the guy that opened the show in Pratt Falls, Montana, to the headliner at the Palace on Broadway! Those he mentions are no more important than those he left out, so if your name isn't in this book, it isn't because you weren't important, or that Lefty and Aggie didn't remember you, but because they just couldn't get it out of their hearts in time for printing. SEZ

Vaude-willingly yours,

JOE LAURIE, JR.

Exit Laughingly

Vaudeville was first started in the Garden of Eden! Adam was the first to do a specialty act—he ate an apple! His audience was Eve and the Snake; they sat in the tree and applauded. No doubt Eve and the Snake even laughed (snakes didn't know how to hiss until a gallery was built in the tree). When Adam ate the apple he must have laughed too, and so the apple stuck in his throat, and that's where folks have carried the apple ever since. That made Adam a sort of freak act, and when they were thrown out of the Garden of Eden, they went out as a man-and-woman act on the first road tour in the world's history, and it also marked the first cancellation!

Cain and Abel were the first two-man act. Cain was the straight man, hitting Abel with a club instead of a newspaper. Noah did a circus act with a special attraction: his son was a Ham.

Then came the tribes, and when one primitive clansman would dance a bit better than the others or make himself understood in pantomime, he became the medicine man, the origin of the headliner. This was followed by the jesters with their caps and bells, who made kings laugh as they turned handsprings; they were the first comedy acrobats. Then came the bards with their lyres and their songs and stories. They preserved history with their voices. They were the first minstrels. Aaron did a magic act when he turned an ordinary shepherd's staff into a snake, while Moses was an illusionist, splitting the Red Sea and walking the Children of Israel across it.

Solomon did a singing act using his own material, the Song of Solomon. Jonah did a tank act, while Joseph must have done a quick-change act with his coat of many colors. Nero did a violin solo, Daniel a lion act, and David a sharpshooting act with his slingshot.

So, you see, vaudeville started when the world began. God must have laughed when he saw the first man; he must have looked as funny then as he does now. So it all started with a laugh, and it sort of became a slogan with the children of vaudeville—"Exit Laughingly"!

Lefty's Idea of How It Started

Dear Joe,

Me and Aggie read that stuff of yours how you figured vaudeville started in the Garden of Eden. It was a bit corny, but we got a laugh out of it.

At that, you are as near right as a lot of these professors who have been writing stuff in books about how and when it started. You know me and Aggie have been around a long time; in fact it was Aggie that dug down into her grouch bag for the twenty-four bucks to pay off the Indians for the Island of Manhattan! I read a lot of stuff these pen-pushers wrote about vaudeville (of course skipping the big words) and find a half a dozen opinions.

Some say that vaudeville is as old as drama itself. When the Greeks presented their classic plays, strolling players were doing vaudeville stunts. Some say the name Vaudeville came from a valley in Normandy, the *Val de Vire*, while others say she was christened on the banks of the Seine centuries ago. Her sire (that's the professor's word; you certainly know it ain't mine) is supposed to have been a Fuller (who like guys in those days took his name from his job, that of fulling the earth). Each evening his workers gave *virevaude* or *vaudevire* or *vire vire* entertainment. Then another professor sez it started in the eighteenth century with a pop form of entertainment of light dramatics, consisting of pantomime, dances, songs, and dialogues written in couplets (that sent me to Webster). *Vau-de-vire* was the name given to the convivial (the last one means something like getting stewed) songs of the fifteenth century. Then still another long-hair sez the name originated with a literary association as the *Companons Gallois*, i.e., boon companions or gay comrades in the Valley of the Vire or Virene in Normandy. The most famous author of these songs was Oliver Basselin. When in the seventeenth century the term had been applied to satiric verses current in the towns, it was corrupted into its present form either from *vau-de-ville* or *voix-de-ville*. Don't blame me for this, Joe, I just copied what I read. I personally think it's bunk! Only those professors have a way with words that can make you believe almost anything.

I do know there were quite a few guys in America who claimed they coined the word "vaudeville." In 1871 there was Sargent's Great Vaudeville Co., billed from the National Theatre in Cincinnati, played at Weisiger's Hall, at Louisville, Ky., and he claimed that was the first time the word was used instead of "variety" (which was what vaudeville was called originally). M. S. Leavitt, a great showman, also claimed that he was the first to use the word "vaudeville," as did John W. Ransom, who claimed he used it while Keith was still a candy butcher in a circus. So it's a case of "put up your dough and take yer cherce." I do know that originally it was called Variety (which it was), then Vaudeville, Advanced Vaudeville, Refined Vaudeville, Progressive Vaudeville. And when it was almost dead they called it Glorified Vaudeville!

I claim that vaudeville was started by guys showing off. When a guy figured he could sing, dance, juggle, do flip-flops better than the other guy (and that goes for the first guy to throw a javelin that hit its mark), he took it to the public who were always willing to pay for the best in entertainment. Then some smarty came along and put the different acts together and called it variety, and when it got on a paying basis they called it vaudeville, to get away from the word "variety," which meant, in the early days, a stag show.

We know there were a lot of minstrel shows during the Civil War and there was a lot of talent roaming around the country "buskin'." Now here's another word that professors hop on and give you a half a dozen double-talk meanings. I went to Webster, who says (and I'm copying it, kid), "Busk—a nautical term to 'cruise as a pirate,' 'to search everywhere,' 'to beat about.' " And in my opinion that's just what the amateurs have always done. The show folks called it "buskin'," not because it's the name of a shoe that the legits wore when they played Romans, but because the guys "cruised around" to find a place for their talents. A saloon was the natural place to go to, as the customers were looking for entertainment. Most of the customers were sailors and no doubt started to call these guys "buskers," and then the performers got to saying, "I'm going buskin' tonight." Now, Joe, this is my own idea how it was called "buskin'," and I am entitled to it as much as the professors!

A "busker" sang or danced, then passed the hat or picked up his "throw money." They got so that they even hired a shill to start throwing a few coins to kinda start off the collection.

The saloonkeepers noticed that the customers liked this side entertainment and stayed in the place buying more drinks. Some of the smarter ones added a little stage and a piano player, then added boxes with curtains, so the big spenders could have a little privacy (for an extra charge, of course), hostesses, and, naturally, gambling tables. These places were soon known as "free-and-easies" or "honky-tonks," giving low-down stag entertainment. They spread from coast to coast. Some were elaborate, charging admissions, while most were just gambling houses and saloons providing entertainment. You would enter the bar, pass the gambling tables, then enter the "hall."

It's funny how they practically use the same idea today in Las Vegas. You can go there, live at a first-class hotel, eat great food, and see blue-chip entertainment for less than it costs any place in the world. But—to get to the powder room you must go via the Casino where all the gambling tables are, and there are very few (especially women) that can resist dropping a few bucks while en route. It is all done in first-class style and lawfully, but it's the old honky-tonk idea, in plush and without hostesses!

The honky-tonks used many hostesses working the boxes. These gals worked on commission, sitting with the customers to get them to buy drinks. They would drink with the customers but would usually get tea that looked like whisky and was charged as whisky to the sucker (if you can call a guy with a lot of dough a sucker). They still use the trick today in spots that use hostesses. The gals got a check for every drink ordered, which they cashed at the end of the night's work. To make the girls more attractive to the "Johns," the management had them open the show with a song and a simple dance. They dressed in soubrette costumes, short skirts and low necks. This, of course, made them actresses and more desirable to the Johns. Some of the girls would take turns doing a single and would get throw money, adding to their commissions.

The gals soon got wise that they could make more and easier money while singing than by sitting with the Johns all night guzzling bad tea and worse booze and getting pawed. Their percentage on drinks was small, about 20 per cent tops for wine and a smaller percentage for liquor and beer. They started telling their friends not to spend their dough on booze for them but to throw the money

to them when they were on the stage singing. It was a common
sight to see a gal singing a heart-rending ballad while picking up
coins (the same as the kids did years later at Amateur Nights).

It didn't take long for the owners to get wise to what was going
on. They passed a rule that it was unladylike and unprofessional
to have the performers pick up the throw money, so to save embar-
rassment *they* would pick it up and give the girls 20 per cent of the
take. That ended one of the first theatrical rackets and turned
saloonkeepers into managers!

The honky-tonks, free-and-easies, and museums were really the
future vaudeville's cradle for talent. In these places they played to
all types of audiences, sometimes doing fifteen shows a day. As long
as there was a customer buying, he had to be entertained. The
comedians wrote their own stuff, the song-and-dance men wrote
ditties and created new dance steps. The show usually followed a
set pattern: Opening chorus by the "ladies" (the start of chorus
girls), then came the song-and-dance men, musical mokes, two-
men acts, quartettes, contortionists, etc. Nearly everybody knew
how to plunk a banjo. The show would finish with an "afterpiece"
in which the entire company took part. (That's how many acrobats
learned how to talk.) These afterpieces were practically ad-libbed
sketches. The boys would talk it over at the first rehearsal, and from
then on it was a case of every man for himself. In this way these
skits became familiar to the actors, and so when someone would
say, "Let's do 'Slim Dempsey' or 'Ghost in the Pawnshop'" or
dozens of others, they all knew the general layout and it was just
a case of what part you'd play. Many actors became known for certain parts in afterpieces. And some of these afterpieces became
classics in vaudeville and on the legitimate stage. "The Bathing
Girls," sometimes called "Dr. Holcomb," a particularly dirty skit
which Denman Thompson wrote and played in honky-tonks, became the famous legit play, "The Old Homestead," which played
on Broadway and toured the country for many years—100 per cent
pure! It made Thompson rich and famous. Another pretty dirty
afterpiece called "The Book Agent," which the famous team of
Evans and Hoey played in honky-tonks, later became "A Parlor
Match" in the late 1880s, and was a big success all over the country.

Some of the girls who made their debuts in show biz as hostesses
and singers became very good performers, and many married actors.
They would do a double act and play the regular variety theaters,

and in the slack season go back to the "wine rooms," where the missis would work the boxes between shows to add to the family income. Some of the greatest stars of yesteryear, both male and female, got their start in honky-tonks!

In the '70s and '80s there were hundreds of museums, honky-tonks, and beer halls. Some theaters were permitted to serve beer. (In later years Hammerstein's Victoria, on Forty-second Street and Broadway, and the Metropolitan Opera House were the only two theaters in New York City with bar licenses.) It was a rough, lusty, booming, guzzling time. People were seeking amusement wherever they could find it. People were learning how to play. And, brother, in those honky-tonks you sure could play, from dice to wine, women, and song.

One of the best of the old free-and-easies of the early days was Harry Hill's on Houston and Crosby streets in New York. Besides presenting specialty acts he ran an athletic club with boxing, club swinging, bag punching, walking contests, and song and dance and drama. Owney Gagan's at Bowery and Hester streets would also stage boxing bouts, with Owney himself meeting all comers, whom he quickly knocked out. It was later discovered that he had the "difference" in the form of a small horseshoes in his glove. If the opponent was tough, he would back him against the backdrop, where an assistant hit the guy on the konk with a bung-starter from behind the drop, saving Owney the $25 offered anyone who could stay three rounds with him.

Jack Berry's Varieties on Greenwich Street, the Alhambra at 124 West Twenty-seventh Street, Spencer's at Bowery and Houston streets, the Aquarium on Broadway and Thirty-fifth Street (away uptown in those days), the Brighton, where Will H. Fox, who later became the first comedy pianist in vaude, played piano and where Joe E. ("I Wonder Who's Kissing Her Now?") Howard would audition songs. Nigger Mike's, where Irving Berlin performed as a singing waiter and Jules Saranoff played the violin. The White Elephant, a tourist joint, a novelty place—the rooms were dressed in mourning and the tables were caskets. Hartigan's Saloon at Chatham Square, where General Grant was a customer when in town. Charlie Pinkunelly owned Paresis Hall on the Bowery (Jake Isaacs was the bartender), Fred Fleck was the alderman of the district, and the guy outside writing calling cards in a fine Spencerian pen for 25 cents a dozen was Al Woods, who later became one of the great Broadway producers and took both these gentlemen into his organization. But Koster and Bial's at Twenty-third street west of Sixth Avenue was the tops in wine rooms, playing the best imported and domestic acts. (Williams & Walker started here in their first New York appearance.) It was the "class" of all the wine rooms in the country.

There was a regular circuit of honky-tonks in the West, not organized, but the performers laid out their own routes, writing direct to the managers for time. The usual route of a recognized performer was to open at Salt Lake and finish up in New Orleans. The jumps were pretty big, so they'd book themselves for five to six weeks in each place. When an act arrived, he would get a handful of checks good at the bar (they were charged to him), and many performers got into the management so deep that the management had to keep them for a few extra weeks so they could collect the monies owed. A good spender (and gambler) was always booked back. They do the same today in the top night clubs in the country where gambling is allowed. Many of our present-day headliners are also gamblers and many times leave their salary (and sometimes I.O.U.s) at the gaming tables. The management practically gets its entertainment for free with this kind of guy.

George Munroe's People's Theatre was the stand in Salt Lake City (he also ran the Novelty in Ogden). Gordon and Richard's Comique in Butte, Montana, was the next stop. Here they used to put the afterpiece on at 7 A.M., and the miners, dinner pails in hand, stopped off for a shot of liquor and entertainment on the way to work. At Helena, Chicago Joe ran the Coliseum. Then they'd go to Great Falls and Missoula, and then on to Spokane at Big Bertha's Casino and Comique. Big Bertha weighed about 450 pounds, was a smart operator, and had a great joint. Her show would start at 7 P.M. and finish at 2 A.M., when the men in the afterpiece would take positions on the stage and ad-lib for an hour about topics of the day. This gave the gals another hour to collect commissions. At 3 A.M. everybody lined up and sang "Auld Lang Syne" after eight straight hours of entertainment. The late John Cort, the famous Broadway manager, producer, and theater owner also owned honky-tonks in Seattle, Portland, and Victoria, B.C.

Frank Nelson ran the Comique in Tacoma. From there the performers went to Frisco, the New York City of the West. (And you know I'm a New Yorker, but the old Frisco was at times even better than New York. They always loved actors and actors loved Frisco.) The Wigwam was one of the few variety places that was sort of family style and about the only one in the West at that time (about 1886) that didn't run a wine room. Walters, who had a lot to do with the Orpheum Circuit's beginning, ran it. Later a guy by the name of Meyers, who was supposed to originate the crack, "Well, if you're a comedian, now's your chance to make me laugh," ran it. He'd tell you this when you told him your salary— and in an empty barroom!

There was a bunch of honky-tonks in Frisco. The greatest of them was the Belle Union, that had a rep in those days like the Palace on Broadway many years later. Anybody that made good there had a free ticket to any honky-tonk in the country. The shows at the Belle Union were strictly stag and would have made even Minsky blush. Junie McCree and Johnny Ray (John and Emma Ray) were great favorites there. Another well-known spot was the Cremonde. They were the only two houses where the girls were allowed to mingle with the audience. There were a lot of smaller honkies in the city, like Theatre Comique, White Elephant, Bottle Koenig's, Eureka Hall, Bottle Meyer's, Elite, Olympic, and many more. When actors finally got out of Frisco (which no performer wanted to) they went to the Perry Brothers' Club Theatre in Los Angeles (one of the greatest money-makers in the West), Joe Bignon's in Phoenix, Arizona, Sherwood's Mascot in Galveston, Texas, then the Camp Street Theatre in Dallas, which was run by Belle Houston and George Woods. Woods also ran the hotel and you had to stop there if you wanted to play his theater. He disliked Hebrew comedians, but his audience liked them and insisted on his booking them. He had a cute way of getting even with any Hebrew performer that played his place. He would serve pork at most of the meals. Joe Welch told me that he wanted to get even with him by stealing the towels in the hotel, but the guy didn't have individual towels, just a roller towel in the hall. After a week it looked like crepe!

The famous Swor Brothers and Tom Beeson (father of Lulu Beeson, who won the Fox Medal for buck dancing) got their start at the Camp Street Theatre in Dallas, their home town. Fanny Prestige ran the Academy in West Superior, Wisconsin. She was a big blond character who wore a sealskin coat over a Mother Hubbard and eight-carat diamond earrings. Then there was the Parlor

Theatre, Duluth, Minnesota, which was practically a store with
the front window shuttered. They were not allowed to serve liquor
in a place of amusement in Duluth, so they got this store next door
to the bar, made a hole in the wall, room enough for one guy at
a time to go through during intermissions. They also had a midnight closing law, so the actors liked to play this place because it
was easy work and a lot of "fun"!

Besides these honky-tonks, there were also hundreds of museums
throughout the country where, besides the freaks and curio halls,
there usually was a small theater. Because of the small stage, they
only played small, stand-up acts. Aerial wire walkers and animal
acts couldn't play these places; in fact jugglers had to be careful
not to throw their balls or clubs too high, as there was very little
headroom. Some places played one-act dramas. An actor once said,
"When we played a war drama, everybody had to be privates, because a general's epaulets couldn't get through the first entrance!"
After the show in the Main Hall, they'd sell a five- or ten-cent
ticket for the "theater," a 125-seater. Some had a few reserved seats
(10 cents extra), while the rest of the audience stood up. To do
fifteen or twenty shows a day was just a walkover. Some of the top
museums were Austin and Stone's and Pilling's in Boston, Epstein's
on Randolph street in Chicago, Wonderland in Minneapolis and
Wonderland in St. Paul, Avery's in Cincinnati, Conners' in Alle-
gheny, Pennsylvania, Davis's in Pittsburgh (he later became one
of the great two-a-day vaude managers), Brandenberg's in Philadelphia, Huber's on East Fourteenth Street in New York City, and
of course the Eden on West Twenty-third Street, which was high-
class and ran a higher grade of entertainment. The ones I mentioned were the tops of the museum circuit, show biz kindergartens
preparing talent for variety houses.

Now, Joe, these honky-tonks and museums were doing plenty
good missionary work for future vaudeville. Besides training future
greats, they made the people amusement conscious. But it was
pretty low and raw entertainment, catering mostly to stag audiences. So it was on July 31, 1865 (I wasn't there but Aggie was,
ha ha), that a great guy, a singing clown in a circus (yeh, clowns
used to sing and talk in the old circus shows) figured that variety
should have a real theater where ladies and gentlemen and children
could attend without being ashamed. So on that day he opened
Tony Pastor's Opera House at 199-201 Bowery, New York City.

He had gas footlights, and when they turned them on the auditorium was filled with the smell before the stagehand would come out and light the foots with a long wax taper. The smell of gas tangled with that of oranges, apples, cigars, pipes, and cigarettes. But the audience didn't mind, and the actors never complained about gas hurting their voices. In those days they received small salaries and had no temperament. Besides, gas was like an oxygen tank compared to the air inhaled in honky-tonks, wine rooms, and museums. And remember, too, they had no union!

Tony Pastor's was a big hit, and so was another circus guy, who started out as a candy butcher, Benjamin Franklin Keith, who laid the cornerstone in Boston for what was to become the greatest vaudeville circuit in the world!

When Pastor and Keith started, it was a sort of catch-as-catch-can business. It was nothing like the fine organized biz that it later became. Anybody that could sing, dance, whistle, bend in the middle, do a flip-flop, or play an instrument joined the ranks of the variety "artists," as they called 'em later, but we called 'em all "Preformers." If you liked a guy, you called him "cull" or "bo." They came from all walks of life, lured by adventure and the glamor of the stage and most of all the dough! The dough meant more to the guys and gals at that time than applause, although the more applause you got, the more dough you got. But most of the variety actors (and that goes for all other actors) came from poor families. Their fathers had to get up maybe at 6 A.M. to get to work, so being able to sleep until noon had a great appeal (besides the applause), and being an actor was much nicer work than being a truck driver, a factory hand, a clerk, or a laborer. Earning $25 to $75 a week (a banker's salary in those days) and being able to sleep late, dress flashily, and get applause were hard to resist.

There were lots of chances in those days to sneak into show biz. There were free-and-easies, store shows, museums, showboats, burly shows, dramatic shows, medicine shows, wagon shows, and minstrel shows using variety acts and specialties. The field was large and there was room for nearly everybody with or without talent. The managers had nothing to lose. They paid a small wage (you furnished costume and music) and could cancel you any time they pleased, so there was nothing to lose in giving an amateur a chance. The ones with talent and originality and ability soon became the standard and headline acts (as in any biz), the mediocre ones were used as fill-ins, and the no-talent guys grabbed anything they could get and tried to hang on as long as possible. You know, being an old performer doesn't make you good. We had a hell of a lot of bad old performers! It's like the time Joe Jefferson (who made Rip Van Winkle famous) was walking along Broadway with his son, and as they passed an elderly gentleman Jefferson nodded. "Who was that?" asked Junior. "That is an old amateur who has been in the theater for many years," said his old man.

The salaries, as I said, weren't much in those days, but it took very little dough to live. Many of the acts did light housekeeping in little flats and others lived in boardinghouses where for a buck you could get three meals a day and a room with a window. And there were kind-hearted landladies who "carried" you when you were laying off. And then there were the guys who lived in furnished rooms for three bucks a week (with a skylight and no window, a buck and a half) and depended for their meals on the free lunches served in the saloons, and some of them were better than they served in the boardinghouses. The better paid actors used to live at the Morton House or the Union Square Hotel on Fourteenth street and Fourth avenue.

The big worry was wardrobe for both street and stage wear, as a good "flash" (prosperous appearance) on and off made the act more valuable. Many of the actors would invest their surplus(?) dough in on-time jewelry. The favorite hunks of ice were a large sunburst for the women and a horseshoe pin for the men. They were practically *musts*! They didn't mind if the stones were yellowish, as long as they were large and made a great flash when the spotlight hit 'em! Jewelry was considered a good investment: it made managers think you were loaded and during the "at liberty" periods you could hock 'em!

The early ranks of variety performers were made up mostly of Irishmen, and there were also a lot of Germans, but very few Hebrews! The performers were mostly out for laughs, before and after shows. They kept to themselves because the legits wouldn't mix with these crazy troubadours. For many years there was a strained feeling between the dramatic actor and the variety actor, because the dramatic actor felt he was playing down when he played vaude (they soon got over that when the grouch bags got filled). The variety actor was always a carefree guy with very little dignity. He was a bohemian who liked to mix with fighters, bookmakers, bartenders, jockeys, gamblers, wine agents, and gals from the oldest profession, all of whom, like himself, were looking for adventure and laughs. It was the spirit of fun among the variety artists and minstrels that started a small group to organize a club which they called the "Jolly Corks." It was organized for their own fun and entertainment. Soon many more actors joined, and then they admitted some laymen, and in a short time it became the greatest benevolent organization in the United States.

They changed the name from the "Jolly Corks" to the "Benevolent Protective Order of Elks"!

It was Tony Pastor and Keith and all the "Jolly Corks" who did more for vaudeville than anyone in the history of our biz. And so you see, Joe, why I don't care what the professors say how it all started and how it got its name, it makes interesting reading, but to me and Aggie it was these guys that started vaudeville on its way to become the nation's number one entertainment for almost half a century!

But let's not forget that the free-and-easies and honky-tonks and museums were the incubators of the talents that made vaudeville. They didn't have any fancy names like *vau-de-vire*, but me and Aggie figure that variety is what it always was and always will be, no matter what fancy names you give it.

Thought you'd like to read the rules of an old honky-tonk that me and Aggie saved for just an occasion like this. Here 'tis.

RULES FROM AN OLD HONKY-TONK

1 Ladies must be dressed and in the boxes by 7:30.
2 No vulgar language allowed in green room, boxes, or dressing rooms.
3 Ladies and performers must turn down the gas every time they leave the dressing rooms.
4 All lady performers must wear tights.
5 Ladies are not allowed to smoke during the show.
6 Performers are expected to give and take one-week notice.
7 Performers late for an act will surely be fined.
8 Anyone so under the influence of liquor as to neglect an act or turn will surely be fined.
9 Absence or late for rehearsal without satisfactory excuse will

be fined; 15 minutes' grace allowed; rehearsal call whenever required.

10 Performers are required to do as many acts and specialties as required by manager.

11 Ladies must settle up before dressing.

12 Lists of props for specialties and acts must be handed in at first rehearsal.

13 Ladies are allowed only two packages of cigarettes nightly.

14 Male performers are not allowed around the bar, in the green room, or boxes.

15 Performers must costume themselves according to the requirements of acts or specialties.

16 Ladies are not allowed to run each other down to the customers in the boxes.

17 Performers must keep their dressing rooms in good condition and hang up their wardrobe.

18 Performers are not allowed to guy or laugh in acts or turns.

19 Performers are obliged to take one business encore.

20 The above rules and regulations will be strictly enforced.

STAGE MANAGER

SEZ

Your pal,
LEFTY

And They Called 'Em Dumb Acts!

Dear Joe,
Being a "dumb act" in the days of variety and vaudeville was really rough. They were the acts that didn't talk, like acrobats, bicycle acts, jugglers, etc. They usually opened or closed a show. We used to describe an opening act as "They see 'em sitting down," and a closing act as "They see a lot of haircuts," because

the opening act would be on when the people were arriving and during the closing act the audience would start leaving to avoid the crowds. (They later used pics to chase the audience.)

In Europe the dumb act was respected and was usually a featured act and many times a headliner. In America it was many years before a dumb act was headlined or featured. Houdini was one of the first to be headlined, followed by terrific box-office attractions like Cinquevalli, May Wirth, Kara, Poodles Hanneford, Joe Jackson, and the Rath Brothers. Most of the great dumb acts were Europeans, because they had the patience to work for hours, weeks, and years to perfect their specialties. The Americans wanted to "do it fast." The foreign troupes had apprentices who worked for years for just room and board, a few clothes, and maybe a buck or two for spending money. The owner of the act would send the kid's parents a few bucks a week, which they were glad to get while their kid was learning a "profession."

When vaude took the count, the dumb act was in a better position to adjust itself than any other type act. First, because many of them had saved their dough (the majority of them were not high-priced acts) and had a trade or a side business; some had farms. They realized that a guy depending on eyes, legs, arms, muscles, and physical condition couldn't last very long. Being sight acts, they didn't have to depend on languages, and so could play almost everywhere in the world, in circus or on stage, which talking acts couldn't do. Most of the dumb acts came from the circus.

We have a lot of guys and gals in show biz today that started out as a dumb act and have become fine actors and great comedians. Fred Allen started as a juggler, as did Jimmy Savo, whose billing was, "Juggles everything from a feather to a piano." And another juggler that did O.K. was W. C. Fields. Cary Grant was a stilt walker with the Loumas Troupe; Victor McLaglen, an Oscar winner in pics, was an "understander" in an acrobatic troupe; and another fine stage, radio, screen, and TV actor was a top-mounter with the famous Dollar Troupe—Conrad Nagel. Charley Grapewin, a vet vaude stage and screen actor, was a parachute jumper in a circus. Burt Lancaster, a fine pic star, was part of the acrobatic act of Nick Cravat & Burt Lancaster. If you remember seeing a couple of acrobats billed as Prevost & Brown, "Watch the Corkscrew Kid," it was Joe E. Brown who was the Corkscrew Kid. Another one of our famous comic stars who started as an acrobat was

Bobby Clark; he and his late partner Paul McCullough started out
as kids with a circus. There was a kid who started out doing a
trapeze act with his family's rep show, then became a star in all
branches of show biz, the famous "Cap'n Andy" of *Show Boat*,
Charles Winninger. Joe Cook, the man who made the Four Hawaiians famous, started as a club juggler. Tom Mix, the most
famous of all the cowboy actors, did a sharpshooting act. Roger
Imhof (Imhof, Conn & Corinne, whose sketch, "The Pest House,"
was one of the biggest laugh-getting acts in vaude) was a clown
with the Miles Orton Circus.

Gus Sun, who at one time booked more theaters than B. F.
Keith, was originally a juggler. Another foot juggler by the name
of Levantine didn't do so bad either. You heard of him as F. F.
Proctor, the one-time partner of B. F. Keith. George Hamid was
a tumbler, and a good one, with an Arab troupe, and finished up
owning the Steel Pier at Atlantic City, also some carnivals and
circuses. Charles T. Aldrich started as a tramp juggler, then did one
of the first protean acts, became a fine actor in many Broadway
shows, and is now living in retirement on his large Lakewood, New
Jersey, estate. Guy Weadick (Weadick & LaDue), who originated
"The Stampede" act and whose late wife was a champ lady roper,
is now retired in Arizona. Ernst London (Four Londons, a great
casting act) owns an apartment house in New York. Ben Beyer
(Ben Beyer & Brother) a pioneer international comedy bicycle act,
owned a garage and real estate in Miami Beach, Florida, and is
now retired. McClellan & Carson started out as a skating act and
became a fine comedy talking act in big-time vaude. Stan Stanley
worked on a trampoline and became a fine talking comic. Ann
Codee, originally with her two sisters in an acrobatic act (Three
Athletas), became a straight woman for her husband, Frank Orth
(Orth & Codee), and then took over the comedy chores of the act,
which played all over the world (they did the act in five different
languages). William & Joe Mandell were just a regular straight
acrobatic act, but soon became one of the best comedy talking acts
in vaude. Jack LaVier did a monologue on a trapeze. Mitchell &
Durant worked together as a comedy acrobatic act, split after
twelve years, and Durant became a fine comedy monologist both
here and abroad, using one-line gags mixed with great falls.

Knockabout acrobats, bag punching, boxing, wrestling, and walking acts were some of the early dumb acts in variety. Club swinging

was very popular in the early '8os and '90s; there were contests all over the country. The late Gus Hill, one of the pioneer burlesque producers, won the Fox Medal Championship (via *Police Gazette*). He traveled all over the country with his variety and burly shows, challenging the local boys to a club-swinging contest. He would build these contests up by letting the local boy win and giving him a medal (he carried a trunkful), then in a few weeks would play a return date to try and win it back (which meant another jammed house), and this time Gus would win; and so he see-sawed through the country, changing championships and medals weekly, playing to jammed houses. He became a very wealthy man. Club swinging was judged by "free swinging, grace, formation, and smoothness." One of the first to swing clubs was Walter Brown, champ oarsman. They were then called "Kehoe clubs" because a guy by the name of Jim Kehoe made them (which is fair enough). We always called them Indian clubs, and I don't know why. Nellie Clark was the first lady club swinger and DeWitt Cook was the first to do a juggling act with Indian clubs—instead of swinging them!

Me and Aggie had a lot of friends among the jugglers. We liked 'em because many of them had a good sense of humor and anyway we figured any guy that wants to be a juggler has something the matter with him enough to make him interesting. Among jugglers they don't judge each other by the salaries they get. They each stand out in their own particular line. We think Cinquevalli (from England) was the greatest showman of the juggling fraternity. He didn't do hard tricks, but spectacular ones. He was a fine gentleman and a great juggler. He was also a fine violinist (never used it on the stage, but would play for me and Aggie and the rest of the bill after the show). Kara, of course, was the greatest object juggler in the world. He would manipulate more objects of different weights than any other juggler. That's a very tough thing to do in juggling. He missed a lot, but his tricks were so hard you expected him to miss. Harrigan, "The Tramp Juggler," did a tramp comedy juggling act long before W. C. Fields (in fact W. C. stole Harrigan's make-up and tricks when he first started). Later Harrigan became a fine monologist and gave up juggling. W. C. Fields without a doubt was the greatest American comedy juggler, even long before he started to talk (excuse me, Fred Allen and Jimmy Savo).

Billy Cromwell was the fastest juggler. He worked without stalling and hardly made mistakes. The Cromwells did a swell act; Billy worked as a "lady" and the other Cromwell was the comic. Salerno was a great object juggler. He claimed (I believe) to have originated the picture sliding down his forehead (I don't know if it is so). But I do know he was great when he threw an envelope in the air and as it came down he would cut the edge off with a scissors. This later was faked by many jugglers.

Chinko was one of the first to juggle eight balls, which was a record for a time. Then along came Amerous Werner, a German who juggled ten, throwing one ball in the air at a time. That caused plenty of "Ah's" until the Max Wesseley Troupe came along and Max juggled sixteen balls, which is a record that still stands as far as I know! The Five Mowatts were really great double-club jugglers, as were the Juggling Normans. Some years later came the Three Swifts (still going), who were and are as good as or better than any club jugglers around. They all worked fast. The passing of clubs between two of the boys swiftly while one walks by, just missing one of the clubs by a hair, was done many times, but not as expertly as by the Three Swifts!

Friscarry was a terrific hat juggler; he did four hats at one time with *one* hand. I have never seen this trick done since. From Australia some new ideas of club juggling were brought over by the Kelso Brothers. Their toes would touch clubs and throw them in position for juggling. They later replaced Clark & McCullough in burlesque and did comedy dancing and talking and were very successful. Griff was a very funny British-talking juggler. He was what I would call the Will Rogers of juggling, making sarcastic remarks about his juggling and about things in general. He was assisted later by his son George. He also did a bit of ventriloquism with a skull which he called Poor Richard. He was made up as a clown in white face, and certainly made good in America.

The Morton & Jewell Troupe were the first jugglers to put singing in their act. Selma Brattz was the greatest of the lady jugglers; she did stuff that only men were supposed to do. Anita Bartling, Maybell Fonda, Elly, the youngest gal juggler, and Raquel were all fine lady jugglers. Charlene & Charlene did violin playing with juggling and real good fiddlin'. Sylvester Schaffer was the greatest one-man talent (of the dumb acts) that I or anybody ever saw. He did juggling, sharpshooting, drawing, animal training, acrobatics, magic, wire walking, dancing, whips, roping, and anything you could mention—and did them all very well. A remarkable man. His act ran from one hour to an hour and a half.

Tom Hearn, "The Lazy Juggler," was a very funny man, as was La Dent, who was the first to have a sign on a screen reading "Swearing Room," and when he would miss a trick he would go behind the screen. (Many copied this bit.) Paul La Croix was the greatest with the bouncing hats and Emerson & Baldwin were fine club jugglers. Sparrow, "The Mad Juggler," caught apples thrown at him by the audience on a fork in his mouth. The Zanettos also claimed to be originators of this bit—anyway, they all finished with a rotten apple (planted with a stooge) hitting the comic on the head. The Zanettos worked on a battleship, juggling life preservers, knives, and catching the turnip (you see, some of them were clever enough to switch from apples to turnips). In 1894 the Hoppers (tramp act) caught oranges on a fork. So Aggie and me figure they were all originals with different fruits.

There were many claimed to be originators of dancing while juggling. H. M. Lorette seems to me to be the first according to the records, but there were plenty of good ones, like Alburtus & Weston, and Paul Dupont, whom me and Aggie played with on the S. & C. Time when he first came over from France, and a few more who claim being the first dancing jugglers. It really doesn't matter; they all danced while juggling. Among the comedy jugglers were Herbert Lloyd, who when he missed a trick said "No good, Napoleon," and H. M. Nelson, who kept emptying a small water jug throughout his act. Pollard shot pool and scored on rings of the portieres; he also had a funny line of talk. Edwin George was a very funny man, too, and a good juggler; you must remember him trying throughout his act to put a hat on a cane he was balancing on his head. Finally, after a lot of misses, he would put the hat on the cane and say, "This is the way it looks when it's done!" Billy Kincaid, Clever Conkey, Frank Hartley were all funny men and good jugglers. Kashima had pool pockets on his jacket and caught the balls in the different pockets. The Glockers juggled water jugs. Van Cello and Mary did foot juggling; Mary handed him the stuff and looked very pretty. Elverton was a baton spinner. Paul Conchas was the greatest of the heavyweight jugglers and had a comedy assistant named Neuman who was just one of the greatest of all comedy assistants.

General Ed Lavine was a great comedy juggler. Bedini & Arthur were assisted by Eddie Cantor—his first stage job. Christy (Christy & Willis) was one of the first talking jugglers. Moran & Weiser I thought was one of the funniest and most original of all the hat-juggling acts. The Original Barretts (Harry was the original thrower of boomerang hats), Johnson, Baker & Johnson, and Johnson & Baker were all hat throwers, but I still claim that nobody was funnier or better than Moran. Les Kiners Moulin balanced musical instruments borrowed from the orchestra. Bob Ripa (English) was à la Rastalli (from Italy), Serge Flash worked à la Felovis but they were all really great acts. Rastalli was in a class with Kara and Cinquevalli. Max Cincinnati was considered Europe's greatest juggler.

The Baggesons were a swell comedy act, juggled and broke plates, and were the first ones we ever saw do the flypaper bit (while holding an armful of plates which his wife throws to him, his other hand gets stuck on flypaper, and he tries to get rid of it while holding about 100 dishes; well, just imagine)! There was a guy called Rebla who had a jerky style of juggling three balls (before W. C. Fields). Rich Hayes, who worked for Rebla at one time, was a very funny man in his own right and a fine juggler. Robertus & Wilfreds introduced returning balls by reverse english, but it was originated by Alexander & Evelyn. Selbo was the first to spread clubs. Morris Cronin was first to do sliding clubs, George Swift was first to kick up clubs with his feet, and Stan Kavanaugh was one of the greatest and funniest with the spread clubs.

While I am telling you about jugglers, I must tell you a true story about my favorite show biz clown, Eddie Carr, of Conlin, Steele & Carr, who also played his own comedy sketch for many years. There was a certain (I just won't get sued) Spanish juggler who was brought over here by Martin Beck to play the Orpheum Circuit. He landed in New York, was met by the circuit representatives, and was immediately shipped to Minneapolis where the Orpheum tours started. He couldn't speak or understand a word of English and was assigned to dress with Eddie Carr. This juggler was the headliner, but because the show was a big one and there were very few dressing rooms, he had to share one with Eddie, who didn't speak or understand a word of Spanish, but greeted the gentleman with the universal language, a bottle of good rye which was hidden behind the make-up mirror. As it happened, it was the start of a fine friendship, because the juggler liked rye too! Carr tried to make him understand with gestures, etc., that they were going to be together for fourteen weeks and he would teach him English while getting Spanish instruction in return. A few drinks and they were buddies! Carr roomed with him, ate with him, and was with him every minute, while the rest of the troupe couldn't get near him.

In a week or so the Spaniard would come into the company car on getaway day and greet the troupe with, "Goot heeving," or "Goot morin," etc. But Carr would take him to their drawing room. The man was really a big hit (he was one of the great jugglers of our time). They got to the Orpheum in San Francisco about eight weeks later, and I must tell you that Frisco's Orpheum was comparable to the Palace in New York. It had one of the greatest subscription lists of any theater in the country; subscriptions were handed down in the family, and the audience was not only the finest in San Francisco but in America. So on opening day the Spaniard was a tremendous hit, and to the surprise of everybody on the show, he stopped the music, walked slowly to the footlights, and in his best-taught Eddie Carr English, said, "Laddis and gentlemans, for my next treek I weel juggle billard kue (showing a billiard cue), billard bowl (showing billiard ball), and (showing a vase) *peese pot!*" (Remember, this theater wouldn't allow you to say cockroach.) There was a moment's silence, and then—oh well, just figure it for yourself.

Martin Beck and Mr. Meyerfield ran backstage in nothing flat and canceled the guy immediately—by the way, he never did get to do the trick; he got scared with the terrific laugh he got. Beck, besides canceling him, wanted to punch him in the nose. Backstage it was just a young riot—the actors and stagehands didn't dare laugh (that is, in front of Martin Beck). Well, it was finally straightened out when they found out that Eddie Carr rehearsed the poor guy for eight weeks and told him it would be a big "heet"! It was. Everybody looked for Eddie, especially the Spaniard—with a dagger! But Eddie, after hearing how his gag got over, went out talking to bartenders. Carr got baek on the bill when everybody got the humor of it (even the Spaniard), and because Eddie's brother-in-law happened to be a very powerful manager, Mike Shea of Buffalo! And he started doping what else he could do to keep the actors laughing. We in vaude called him Peck's Bad Boy . . . a terrific guy with a great sense of humor.

Allez OOP! Acrobats and acrobatics started way back when court jesters did rollovers and handsprings for kings! They carried on through history until variety shows came along; in fact they started shows and also closed them—even when it was called vaudeville! Me and Aggie don't go along with "he's a dumb acrobat"—because we met plenty of 'em, and they may have been uneducated from a schooling standpoint, but me and Aggie would listen to many of 'em tell about their travels all over the world through many a bottle of beer and it was fascinating listening. Most of 'em came from poor families (as most of us did) and were apprentices for short dough, and even when they got their own acts continued getting short dough because acrobats were a dime a dozen. European troupes would come over, get a flat and sleep five high, cook a stew for the gang—and rehearse the rest of the time. But they were real nice guys.

Many acrobats in vaude resent being called acrobats; I don't know why, but they like to be classed in their own particular field of acrobatics. But to me and Aggie anybody who puts his feet in the rosin box (except dancers) is an acrobat and there is certainly nothing to be ashamed of. There are really many angles of acrobatics: tumblers, trapeze, bar acts, trampoline, strong acts, casting acts, barrel jumpers, high kickers, leapers, equilibrists, roman rings, stilts, ladder acts, flying rings, revolving ladder, perch, risley, wall scaling, rolling globes, contortionists, wire walkers, bareback riders, etc. I can't mention all of these sons and daughters of the rosin box; it would be like calling the roll in the army. So I'll mention just a few sort of ad-lib.

Angelo Armento and his brother, who were Mexicans, were the greatest tumblers; Angelo was a lightning tumbler. Henry Bolden, who worked with the Hassel Benali Troupe, was considered the greatest Negro acrobat in show biz. Acott & Bailey were also great Negro acrobats. They played very little over here, but went to Europe, where they were a sensation, and stayed there. Mazetti Troupe of ten had a kid who was the first to do a real triple somersault—he was only fourteen years old and was imported by the Barnum & Bailey Circus. Now in 1953 he is working in pics under the name of Richard Talmadge (he doubled for years for Fairbanks, Sr.). The Judge Family were one of the first to juggle human beings . . . great! Bush Bros. were the funniest of the bounding-bed (trampoline) acts; for a finish one of the boys did seventy-five somersaults in the bed. The big laugh throughout their act was when one kicked the other in the mouth and he kept spitting out his teeth (beans). Seymour & Dupree had a great act: O. G. Seymour would jump over the head of his wife, Katie, then over an upright piano. The Seven Bracks were a great risley act.

Speaking about risley work (that is, juggling people with the feet), nobody seems to know how it ever became known as risley work. I was sure that it was named after the person who originated it—it must have been hundreds of years ago—maybe even before anybody was called Risley.

Rice & Prevost were the greatest of all American comedy acrobats. Eddie Prevost would fall in the pit. His brother Howard was one of the first to develop a double somersault without a springboard. Boganny's Lunatic Bakers jumped in and out of ovens. The Three Rianos made up as monkeys and were great. Collins & Hart were the burlesque strong men, holding each other up on a finger (one of them was on a wire)—one of the veteran teams of comedy acrobats. Bert Melrose with his falling tables was a riot in vaude for many years. In "The Briants" (Walter and Paul) act "The Movers" Walter handled Paul like a dummy until the finish. It was one of vaude's big comedy acts. Paul's dummy mask was made by Walter, who was a very fine sculptor. LaVeen & Cross and Bellclaire Bros. were class acrobats. Caron & Herbert originated the diving into the backdrop, which would come down and the audience would see stage hands playing cards, a gal fixing her stocking, etc., all supposed to be a surprise to them—and they all acted as if it was an accident. A very big laugh and of course many acts copied it. Welsh, Mealy & Montrose, comedy acrobats, were real funny. "Scream" Welsh was a character; before going on stage he would screw his large diamond stud on his underwear so he wouldn't lose it. An Englishman who once dressed with him, when asked back in London what he thought of the American acrobats, said, "They wear the dirtiest underwear and the largest diamonds I have ever seen."

Marceline, the famous clown, and "Slivers" Oakley, another famous clown (both committed suicide because they couldn't get work) were really tops. Toto, who made his entrance on the stage in a toy auto with his dog Whisky—the car was so tiny you wouldn't think you could get a dog in, much less a man—was a standard vaude act for years until he went blind. Luke Wilson did a bar act at the age of seventy-two; he was originally with the "Span of

Life" (they were on a wire), where three men made a chain to rescue a gal from a roof fifteen feet away. Alex Patti & Brother created a sensation when Alex went down a long flight of steps on his head. One night at Joel's Restaurant Tom McNamarra, the cartoonist, ribbed him that it was a fake, and that he had the stairs or his head padded. After a few drinks Alex got so angry he said, "I will show it is not a fake." He went to the top of the iron steps in Joel's and came down on his head step by step. There was no damage to the steps or his head. The Gee-Jays were a standard acrobat act. The Three Keatons, Joe, Myra, and Buster, were one of the real great knockabout acrobatic acts. Buster became a big star in pics and is still going great on TV. And of course George & Dick Rath, billed as the Rath Brothers, held a feature spot in the *Ziegfeld Follies* and became a headline act in vaude. They were swell-built guys and did slow lifts (many others did this type work, but they didn't have the class or showmanship of the Rath Brothers).

The tops of the wire acts were the Carmen Troupe, who were first to use five people on a tight wire, and the Youngman Family, who were the first to do a back somersault with umbrellas on a tight wire. Cadieux (from Pawtucket, Rhode Island) was just great doing a bounding-wire act. Juan Caicedo was the best bounding-wire act from Spain. Kartella (his right name was Julian St. George) was in the opinion of wire walkers without a doubt the greatest slack-wire act in the world. He did what they called impossible tricks, like doing a handstand on the seat of a unicycle on a slack wire and standing on a kitchen chair bouncing four balls while balancing on wire, and for a finish stood on his head on wire playing a clarinet. Could you ask for anything more? The Eddy Family, swell. Don & Lora Valadon were tight- and slack-wire cyclists. Lora did her famous "slide for life" from the balcony to the stage, and was billed as "Mile-a-Minute" Lora. A fine artist. And of course the one and only Bird Millman was the tops of 'em all!

Among the comedy bicycle acts me and Aggie liked Charles Ahearn & Co. and Ben Beyer & Brother, who in 1935 booked themselves for a month's stay at the Scala in Berlin for 1936. They figured by that time the Hitler regime would be defunct. (P.S.: They didn't play it.) Ralph Johnstone originated the trick of jumping his wheel up and down stairs, gripping the saddle with his thighs and not, as many supposed, holding on the handle bars; he also turned a somersault with a wheel. He became one of the pioneer stunt pilots of an airplane and gave me and Aggie our first trip in a plane. We had to have our hearts examined before we went up; after he gave us a few thrills in the air is the time they should have examined our hearts. Poor Ralph died when his wing broke off 400 feet in the air. A great guy and a pioneer in trick bicycling and airplanes. There were the Original Six Kaufmans; Cycling McNutts; Hill & Sylvany (unicycles); Calotta, who looped the loop; Fred St. Onge & Co., who used all kinds of wheels and were pioneers in bicycling acts; the Brothers Soncrant, who rode buggy wheels; the Royal Polo Team, who played polo on wheels; the Cycling Brunettes, La Salbini, who juggled while dressed in skin tights riding a wheel—she was a beautiful gal with a beautiful form, so who cared if she juggled or not?

And the greatest comedy act on or off a bicycle was the pantomimist Joe Jackson. When he first showed his act at a theater out of town, the manager sent in a report to the booking office: "A funny act, but he can't ride a bicycle." The funny part of it was that Joe was once a racing rider. Joe Jackson died after taking his bows at the Roxy Theater. He died a hit, like he always was. His son is now doing his act, and doing it very well, but there was only one Joe Jackson!

There were many great aerial acts, but there are a few that were great in vaudeville: Aerial Budds, Lohse & Sterling, Six Flying Vanvards, Break-a-way Barlows, Alcide Capitaine, who was known as "the perfect woman and aerial queen," Flying Martins, Dainty Marie, who did a strip tease on rope and flying rings, Harry Thriller, who balanced on a chair and broom handle on the trapeze, the Jungman Family, and of course C-H-A-R-M-I-O-N, who was a headliner, and Lillian Leitzel, who was the greatest; she did forty revolutions by one hand. She met an untimely death when she fell while performing in Copenhagen. A wonderful artist.

The casting acts were always thrilling to watch. They had two uprights set about 20 feet apart, one man on each cradle. They'd throw humans from one to another, some doing single and most always finishing with a triple somersault (worked with a net). Some worked without a net until the law was passed compelling nets to be used. Some of the real greats in this line were the Four Lukens, the Casting Dunbars, the Four Londons, the Duffin-Redcay Troupe, and the Four Readings.

The horizontal bar acts, straight and comedy, were always good for a laugh and a thrill. There were a lot of them in the early days of variety, but then they seemed to die out except in circuses. But a few came back on TV and were a real novelty. Newell & Shevett did the longest twisting somersault ever done, Graggar Bros. did great falls, LaMoyne Bros. did a swell triple-bar act, as did the Camille Trio. The Artoise Bros. were the only ones doing triple over bars. Mason & Bart and Rice, Scully & Scott also did great comedy bar acts.

Skating, both roller and ice, was very well represented in vaudeville by Earl Reynolds & Nellie Donegan, who were a stand-by in vaude for many years. (Earl Reynolds is now a state senator in Indiana.) There were Steel & Winslow, Van Horn & Inez, Sprague & McNeese, Coogan & Bancroft, Beeman & Anderson (one of the best), Athos & Reeves (Percy Athos is now a producer in London) El Rey Sisters, Roy Harrah (great), the Nathano Bros., and Paul Garret. Did you know that Jim Barton, the great comedian, started in show biz as a skater? (Barry & Barton.) Sandy Lang (now a wealthy toy manufacturer in Chicago) and his girls were a standard act for many years on the Big Time. The Sakatells and Anderson & Revell were great names on the marquee.

But all the old-timers agree that the Three Whirlwinds—three Chicago kids, Frank Weisner, a truck driver (still around) and Harry Avers and Buddy Carr, truck mechanics—who wore rink-skating white pants and shirts and used a handmade mat, were the tops. They came to the theater without music and just said to the leader, "play anything you can play fastest." They had no technique, and without regard to life and limb this amazing trio miraculously slam-banged their way to the Palace, New York, in the first six months of their try-in in show biz. They made the Earl Carroll *Vanities* by the end of the year, then the Strand Roof with top billing and several command performances in Europe, and oblivion in three short years! You just know they must have been great to have accomplished all this. Buddy Carr, now fat and forty, a bartender, sez, "The thing I know less about is skating."

Roller skating was one of the real big crazes that hurt show biz for a time. There were thousands of large arenas, especially in the West and Southwest, and one of the largest skating rinks for Negroes only at Fort Worth, Texas. In 1907 there was an ice skater named Roamin; he would freeze water and skate on a block of ice

5 feet square; he said he had a secret that would revolutionize the artificial ice business. Don't know what ever became of him.

There were hoop rollers, who were always entertaining and interesting. Everhart was called the "Christopher Columbus of Hoops"; Ollie Young and April were one of the best acts, as were J. Francis Wood and the Nicholas Nelson Troupe. The Kratons (Negroes) had the finest novelty hoop act. It was a "Hoop Village" with a "drunken hoop." Colored hoops denoted different characters, all woven into a story. The drunken hoop was a scream. Eugene Adams was the greatest of his time, in this line.

Variety and later vaudeville was just packed with bag punchers, as bag punching was being taken up by many people for home exercise. The Seebacks were the champs and winners of the Fox Medal, and they were a standard big-time act for many years.

Strong-man acts were liked mostly by women, who admired the physique and the strength of the strong men, but the men in the audience (especially the tiny skinny guys) resented them and felt like they were being shown up. The greatest of the strong men and who received the most publicity was Sandow, who was managed by Flo Ziegfeld, later the famous Ziegfeld of the *Follies*. But there were many strong-men (and women) acts who made the tour of the big- and small-time circuits year after year. Martha Farra, a little 120-pound woman, held an auto with twelve men in it while lying on her back on a board of nails. Alba was another strong woman. Apollo lifted a half a dozen men on a piano. Bertish had a 250-pound cannon ball fall on his body. Wilfred Cabana lifted an auto, while Fred Carrol (Englishman) bit spikes in half. The Francelias were a man-and-woman act. He would hold her by the hair with his teeth while he did a cakewalk. Ben Meyer lifted a man with his teeth and walked up a tall ladder. Joe Bonomo did a strong act in vaudeville before he worked in pictures. Orville Stamm was a small man but did a fine strong act. Strong-man acts were booked because they could put on a good publicity stunt in front of the theater, usually with two teams of horses (or autos) trying to pull the strong man apart. The horses would actually pull against each other (via a gimmick). The strong men all did mostly the same routines, driving big spikes through a plank with their hands, bending iron bars, biting spikes, and lifting many people and objects.

Me and Aggie were on our way to play a date in Allentown,

Pennsylvania, in a day coach and had trouble trying to open the car window. A big handsome guy (with a thick German accent) offered to help us. He struggled with it for ten minutes and couldn't budge it. The trainman came along and raised the window in a few seconds. When we got to the theater all the acts were on stage for music rehearsal and to our surprise there was the big German. When he saw us he quickly came over and said, "Blease dunt say nodding about de vindow on de train. I am de strong man on de bill here."

Boomerang throwing was a novelty for a while in vaude. Van & Belle were pioneers of the boomerang acts, and Rawson & June threw boomerangs and javelins. Many of them did other things besides boomerang throwing, as the one thing became very monotonous. The Australian Waites also did whip cracking, and the Three Scotch McGradys threw booms and also did arrow shooting and acrobatics.

Tank acts (swimming and diving) were a great attraction in the old museum days and later played variety and vaude houses. One of the first was Enoch, "The Man Fish" who while in a tank of water placed a pail over his head and sang, also played trombone under water. Some ate bananas, etc. But it was Annette Kellerman who really started the "water nymph" and diving acts. She was the first to wear a one-piece bathing suit, which caused a sensation and received plenty of publicity. She had a beautiful figure and when the water hit that tight-fitting black suit . . . B-R-O-T-H-E-R! She was a great box-office attraction for many years. When Keith stole her from William Morris (who discovered her), Morris engaged Rose Pitnof, a fifteen-year-old girl who swam from Charleston Bridge to Boston Light and was a local sensation, but as you know it takes more than fifteen years to develop a figure like Kellerman's, and Rose couldn't combat Kellerman at the box office. Another big attraction was Odiva and her seals. She swam in a tank with a seal and duplicated all of the seal's swimming tricks. You could easily tell Odiva from the seal, for she wore a one-piece bathing suit over a swell figure.

There were many diving acts swimming into vaudeville once Annette Kellerman broke the dam: Maude & Gladys Finney, the Six Water Lillies, Lottie Mayer. The Berlo Sisters had a fine act; at the finish their mother (real mother), about sixty, got up on stage from the audience to save her daughters, and—yep, you guessed it—fell in the tank fully clothed. (A big laugh, of course.) Gertrude Hoffman in her big act of imitations did a burlesque of Kellerman and finally dived in the tank on a wire.

One of the oddest tank acts was Sam Mahoney, an Arctic swimmer. He swam in a tank of ice, and for a finish he would sit on a cake of ice and tell the audience about the beauty of physical culture and deep breathing, etc. I forget the rest of his act, because by that time Aggie had my "longies" ready. Tank acts were expensive, as a crew had to go a week ahead to put up the tank. We played with many of them where the tank leaked and the dressing rooms in the basement were flooded. That's how we learned that Ivory Soap floats but Stein's make-up doesn't!

Sharpshooters were always an attraction in vaude, especially after a war. Stage sharpshooters never place a human life in jeopardy, so when you see the marksman shoot a ball from off the head, etc., it is really an optical illusion, because the ball is actually placed from a foot to a foot and a half above the head, but to the back of the subject, giving the audience an upward range of vision. And sharpshooters use what they call splash bullets that spread, and so it isn't very hard to hit the resin balls and pipes, etc. When they shoot at objects held by humans, they use a specially prepared bullet that can't inflict an injury. But still they have to be excellent marksmen. Pauline Cook & May Clinton were among the first women sharpshooting acts; they played musical instruments by shooting at the keys. Benny Franklin was the youngest. Others were General Pisano, the Randalls, Corrigan & Vivian, Chevalier de Louis, Cook & Madison (who did a comedy sharpshooting act). In the Two Vivians' act, he shot an apple off his partner's head, and Miss Vivian played the chimes by shooting from the balcony. Henry & Alice Taylor shot through a tube and also at swinging targets. The Ioleen Sisters did sharpshooting while swinging on a wire, as did Kit Carson. The Deda Vells had a French gal that was really great. Jack Texas Sullivan did gun fanning—old Western stuff where they filed off the triggers and pushed back the hammers with their thumbs, in that way being able to fire quicker than by using a trigger. That was O.K. on the old guns, but today the trigger works faster than any gun fanner can do it. St. Ferdinan Thetron used revolvers instead of rifles and was real great. Due to an accident where an empty shell hit a lady in the eye as it jumped from the gun, many managers barred sharpshooting acts for a long time.

I must tell you the story about a certain Frenchman (again I refuse to be sued, so I won't mention his name) who did a great sharpshooting act. He didn't understand or speak much English, but a performer on the bill (at the old Hippodrome) told him he should explain his opening trick to the audience, which was shooting off his wife's wrap as she stood on a raised platform, and when he shot off what looked like the buttons of her wrap she was revealed in tights and really looked beautiful. The "buttons" on the wrap were really tiny white rubber balls with black dots painted on them which made them look like large buttons from the front of the house. You can imagine the surprise of everybody, stagehands, actors, musicians, management, and audience, when this Frenchman, who had been doing his act without a word for two weeks, stepped down to the footlights one matinee, stopped the music, and in broken English said, "Laddies & Gentlemens, I weel now proceed tu shoot the balls off my wife!" When they explained to him what he had said, he took all his guns and went hunting for the actor who taught him the speech. He never found him!

There were roping and whip acts, strictly Western stuff. Clinton & Beatrice, "Chuck" Haas, the Chamberlains (who did lasso and whips), Fred Lindsay, and the Shephards were great whip manipulators; Jack & Violet Kelly also did a good whip act. Shield & Rogers (one Indian and one cowboy) did roping; La Due, Guy Weadick's wife, was a champ roper. Then there was a guy by the name of Will Rogers, who started with a rope, a horse, and an assistant, then started doing a single and became the greatest monologist of topical topics of our time. But he was really a great roper too and never gave it up.

There were hundreds of contortionists during the heyday of variety, usually coming from the circuses and museums. Among the best was Zeeda, billed as "The Snake Man" (Zeeda & Hoot, known before as Dilla & Templeton). Mercer Templeton and his brother Jimmy (Templeton Bros.) became great contortion and straight dancers. There were Byers & Herman, Herman & Shirley (Herman was the "Dancing Skeleton"), Ben Dova (still doing great on TV), the Le Grohs, Demonio & Bell, and Yuma.

Years ago Yuma couldn't get in to see J. J. Murdock (then the manager of the Masonic Temple in Chicago) for bookings. He had himself packed in a small box and delivered to Mr. Murdock's office. When J. J. opened the box, Yuma came out dressed as a devil. Murdock was scared into booking Yuma for a week at the Temple. H. B. Marinelli, one of the top European and American booking agents, started in show biz as "The Boneless Wonder." And did you know that the great Houdini started as a contortionist and trapeze artist in Appleton, Wisconsin? The first contortionist on program records was Walter Wentworth, who started back bending in 1872. (You know there were front benders and back benders and just a few that could do both.) Of course the man that outlasted all the old-time contortionists was the late Ferry, "The Frog Man," who worked at the age of eighty.

I must put posing acts among the dumb acts, because for a long time they were part of variety bills. It was way back in 1875 that the manager of the Comique, New York, was in trouble with his posing groups. Judged to be unchaste by the puritan minds yelling about the female form in skin-fitting silken tights, some managers threw a cloak over the gals. At the Comique, "The Rock of Ages" tableaux was posed by young beauties in fleshings, and this scandalized people. The *Clipper* wrote:

"Matt Morgan's statuary
Think our police a bore
Which makes each statue wary
To wear a little more."

These, of course, were almost all gone and transferred to burlesque when vaudeville took over for real. Instead of the old-time tableaux with no beauty, there came to vaudeville some really beautiful posing acts. William Edirette with horse and dog was billed as "The Act Beautiful," and it was. Also Andree's Studies (in china and ivory), Brenck's Bronze Horse, Neptune's Garden, Maxim's Models, Frank Stafford & Dog (a beautiful act; Frank did some fine whistling too), Weston's Models, Marble's Gems, the Five Golden Graces, who posed with golden tint on their bodies, the Frey Trio, in wrestling poses. Maude O'Dell, in 1908, was the first strip teaser, posing instead of dancing, or I should say walking, in time to the music; she would pose, and after each pose she would wear less clothes, and didn't start with much. It got pretty bad and the police made her put on more clothes. Three Seldon's Living Pictures, Seldon's Venus, and in 1906 Hathaway's

Indian Tableaux, "Love and Revenge of American Indians," and a few more were really artistic and brought novelty to vaude bills. There were a few gals who posed in the nude, but were painted with gold leaf . . . and on them it looked good!

I almost forgot to mention a guy who started in show biz as a dumb act and hit the jack pot of international fame and fortune— Charlie Chaplin.

And they called 'em "dumb acts"—Ha ha, SEZ

Your pal,

LEFTY

The Last Eight Bars Forte– Professor!

Dear Joe,

The song-and-dance men have always been the life blood of vaude. In the early days of variety they were the top guys, but later on they were looked upon like a "club fighter" in the fight racket. They had a half a dozen on every bill. To hear a legit or "talking" act say the word "hoofer" was the new low in sneers! But to me and Aggie (who started as hoofers), they always represented real vaude more than any other kind of an act. They had a certain fire and ambition through the years that no other kind of performers ever had. They took the racket seriously and were always talking about their act. They'd get up in the middle of a meal in any restaurant and show you a step they'd "originated"; they'd show you a new(?) step in front of the Palace, New York, or the Palace in Keokuk.

An honest-to-God hoofer really believed that his act meant more on the bill than the headliners! If it didn't get over, he had a million alibis. "The music was bad" was sure-fire, and there were many more, like "Our spot was bad," "My partner is lousy," "There was no rosin box," "We were breaking in new shoes," "I just got over 'newmonyeh' and I couldn't get my breath," "We didn't have

our new threads (suits) on," or "We were working in new suits
and it *boddered* us." Mostly it was the music that got the blame,
and as an ex-hoofer I'll say they were right 95 per cent of the time.

Me and Aggie in all our years of show biz hardly ever saw a
dancing act (even if it was a hit) that didn't come off fighting.
We've seen 'em hit each other with wooden shoes, yell, scream,
faint, and go through the regular temperamental routines of hoofers; but there was one team of dancers (and good ones too) with
whom we played for many years and never saw them do anything
but kiss each other when they came off stage. They were the Gliding O'Mearas, two swell micks that came from Double-Fifth (that's
Tenth Avenue), and little Timmy, who didn't weigh 110 pounds
with anchors in his hands, would punch Joe Louis in the nose if
he thought he had a beef. I don't know what he did to his sweet
wife when he got her in the dressing room, but when a couple of
micks (especially hoofers) can control themselves like they did
through the years of hoofing, me and Aggie sez, "More power to
'em."

Now I don't say the other hoofing acts were wrong when they
went through their temperamental routines, because me and Aggie
know what it is to have your music loused up and the audience
helping it along by no clapping, and you're sweating and outta
breath and—oh, hoofers have a million legit excuses! As I said, me
and Aggie were hoofers once, but I left no marks on her—my Aggie
is a quick healer! All I can say is that hoofers are honest-to-God
children of vaudeville—and they're awful nice people when they're
not dancing!

Many of the low-down hoofers reached the heights. I say
"hoofers" for anybody that ever dipped his feet in a rosin box and
gave the tempo to the orchestra leader by stomping before he made
his entrance. I don't care if they wore ballet skirts or wooden shoes,
they were all hoofers! There were a lot of different style dancers.
Clog, pedestal, sand, soft-shoe, buck and wing, acrobatic, skirt,
rough-house, neat song-and-dance, legomania, eccentric, rough
wooden-shoe, cane, rope-skipping, chair, roller- and ice-skating,
cooch, Hawaiian, ballet, toe, Russian, Salomé, Scotch, apache, ballroom, Texas Tommy, grizzly bear, turkey trot, cakewalk, shimmy
and jazz, tap, Charleston, black bottom, low-down, varsity drag,
sugar-foot strut, adagio, big apple (also little pear and little peach),
Lambeth walk, and so many many more. I just wanted to let you

know the terrific competition in the dance line. I didn't mention bubble, dove, or strip-tease dancing, because they never belonged or ever got in vaudeville, thank God!

Vaude had many crazes, but there were more dance crazes than any of the others. In 1890 Carmencita appeared at Koster and Bial's. She did the fandango, a sort of a waltz done with castanets, which had steps like the tango but was not done to the same tempo. The comics of the day burlesqued this dance, as they did all others. The Spanish craze lasted for a couple of years. Before, most dancing had been done in ballet costumes with short skirts, which were lengthened to the ankles when the "skirt dance" came in.

After about three years of seeing medium and ankle-length costumes, the customers got to longing for a peep at the undraped figure, so when Loie Fuller, dressed in a full-length transparent skirt, came into the spotlight with her "serpentine" dance, Miss Fuller and the dance jumped into favor. Closely following the serpentine came the "fire dance," with cheap electrical effects. The "butterfly" and other variations of the serpentine and fire dances were also popular. In these dances all the gals did was practically pose in transparent gowns and a guy from the orchestra pit would throw different colored slides on them, like fire effect, butterflies, etc. The gal had two long sticks to which the bottom of the gown was attached, and she would wave the sticks while the slides were thrown on the gown and it would make a pretty effect, but you saw *nothing!* It really wasn't even a dance!

High kicking was the next craze. Evelyn Law and Charlotte Greenwood were great in this line. With the high kicks came the splits and different forms of legomania that lasted for about four years, and then gradually settled down to a standard form of vaudeville dancing.

One of the biggest crazes in dancing was the hootchy-kootchy. It was first introduced by Little Egypt at the Chicago World's Fair of 1893 as a specialty in the Nautch Village. Ayesha brought the "*dances du venture*" to vaude and burlesque. In 1894 at Coney Island, New York, there were fifteen to twenty "cooch shows" running full blast, each claiming to have the original Fatima, another sensational dancer of the Fair. One of these dancers later became a vaude headliner as "Rajah" (she danced holding a chair in her teeth at Huber's Museum, when Willie Hammerstein discovered her there and booked her, which started her on a big-time career).

Little Egypt was engaged to entertain at the Seeley dinner given in honor of Herbert Seeley, a nephew of P. T. Barnum. Someone blew the whistle to Captain Chapman (known as the Czar of the Tenderloin in the '90s), and just as Little Egypt was ready to pull off a few nifty wriggles, Chapman with a flock of bulls broke in and pinched everybody. The raid was front-paged and Weber & Fields put on a burlesque of it in their show. This put the cooch on the map. Although it didn't get much headway in vaude, it found plenty of ground to work on in burly. They called it the "Oriental Fantasy" and "Egyptian Serpentine" and other fancy names, but it was still the cooch! (It was many years later when they added the grind and bumps to it . . . anything to further *art*!)

In 1908 the phoniest craze to hit vaude was the "Salomé dance." This came to vaude via grand opera. Oscar Hammerstein produced it for a single performance at his Manhattan Opera House. One after another the single women of vaude started to do the Salomé dance. Gertrude Hoffman was the first in America. Willie Hammerstein sent her over to London to see Maude Allen do it there and she came back and did an imitation which was a sensation. (Ruth St. Denis claims she did the dance in Paris in 1906—which no doubt is true, but she didn't get the publicity.) Gertrude Hoffman stayed at Hammerstein's for many weeks and then went on the road, managed by Morris Gest, who started as a ticket speculator at Hammerstein's, then became press agent and scout for Willie, and later became one of Broadway's most famous producers (*Miracle*, etc.). It was Eva Tanguay who really busted things wide open for Salomé dancers, when she discarded all seven veils. Ada Overton Walker, wife of George Walker of Williams & Walker and a great dancer, put it on with Creatore's Band, which added a string section to play for her. Malcolm Scott, an English female impersonator, did a burly Salomé around empty whisky bottles. Lind?, another female impersonator, had an act called "Who Is It?" He did a Salomé and never took his wig off at the finish. The Marco Twins (a tall and a short fellow) also did a funny burly on it, as did hundreds of other comics. Julian Eltinge, the greatest of all female impersonators, did a beautiful version of Salomé.

In Pittsburg there were prayers said by the community for the saving of the soul of Miss Deyo of the Weber & Fields Co., which was playing there at the time. Mlle. Froelich was hooted off a Yonkers stage with her Salomé. Velaska Suratt did a mild version.

Vera Alcore performed it at Huber's Museum, while Lotta Faust danced it in *The Girl Behind the Counter*. Managers in Ohio, West Virginia, Pennsylvania, and Kentucky banned the dance. The Orpheum Circuit barred it from their bills. While all the Salomés wore veils, showed figures in gauze skirts, and danced in bare feet, La Sylph, a contortion dancer who did the nearest thing to the real dance, wore fleshings to the neck! The craze lasted for about five years and gradually died out, not only because of the ravings of the reform elements but because it was overdone and was no longer bringing returns at the box office!

In 1915 ragtime was the rage and all the shoulder-shaking, wriggling, and finger-snapping epidemics, such as the grizzly bear, bunny hug, Texas Tommy, and various "trots," arrived in vaude by the carload. Craze after craze came along and was taken up and then forgotten, then after a decade or so revived. (They're sneaking in the Charleston on TV right now.) Ballroom dancing went over big, with the Castle walk, maxixe, fox trot, one-step, and turkey trot. These made way for the shimmy. Bee Palmer & May Gray (later known as Gilda Gray), who were introduced to New York by Sophie Tucker, were the greatest exponents of the quiver shoulders. Ballin' the jack, toodle-oo, Charleston, black bottom, and jitterbug were all crazes, as well as control, acrobatic, adagio, apache, Hawaiian, ballet, and tap dancing. It was a long cry from the essence, sand jig, clog, buck and wing, sailor's hornpipe, soft-shoe, Irish jig, Highland fling, pedestal clog, and the cakewalk. But a new set of feet were doing them.

The cakewalk was really one of the great dance crazes, not only on stage but off stage as well. It was originally known as the "chalk-line walk," danced by Negroes with pails of water on their heads. The couple who spilled the least water were declared the winners. It later was called the "prize walk," then the "cakewalk wedding," which showed all stages of meeting, flirtation, courtship, engagement, wedding, and off on the honeymoon. There were hundreds of cakewalk contests throughout the country. Johnson & Dean, a Negro team, were the first to really do the professional stage cakewalk. Some years later Genaro & Bailey were its foremost white exponents. The craze lasted for many years and even today we are often reminded of it in pictures and TV.

In the early 1900s the old shuffle dance entirely disappeared; soft-shoe, too. People thought wooden-shoe dancing was harder (it isn't). There were very few makers of wooden shoes in 1900, and by 1907 there were dozens of firms specializing in them, so you can imagine what a hold wooden-shoe dancing had on the public. Buck dancing was also popular; contests were held and championship medals were. given out by owners of the *Police Gazette;* they were known as Fox Medals after the owner of the *Gazette.*

Some of the best hoofers within the memory of the boys and girls who played hookey years ago and brought their schoolbooks to their home-town vaude houses were Ben Ryan & George White. Ryan teamed with Harriet Lee and became one of the great mixed comedy teams, and White became the producer of the White *Scandals.* Milt Wood danced while seated on a chair. One of the best acrobatic wooden-shoe dancing acts was Emma Francis and her Arabs. Bissett & "Hello George" Scott carried a little fox terrier around with him that had a diamond tooth. He claimed it was better bait to get gals than etchings. He later had a diamond tooth in his own set (in case he didn't have the dog with him). The Brittons, a Negro dancing act, would shout to the audience after each step, "How's that?" Rose & Moon would dance back to back; Dick Henry & Carrie Adelaide would change clothes on stage while dancing. Purcella Bros. dressed like convicts with their legs fastened together with a ball and chain. Clara Morton danced while playing piano; Robert Stickney danced on stilts. When Sammy White & Lou Clayton split, Sammy teamed up with Eva Puck and Lou joined Jackson and Durante. There were the Three Du For Bros., the Three Hickey Bros., and Cook & Sylvia (Phil Cook was the holder of a Fox Medal and was one of the greatest of the wooden-shoe dancers). Others that held Fox Medals were Ida May Chadwick, Maude Kramer, and Lulu Beeson, all champ clog dancers.

The Four Fords were the greatest dancing family. Dotson, a Negro, was a fine dancer. Pat Rooney & Marion Bent were the king and queen of waltz clog. Sammy Lee (now a Hollywood dance producer) and Harry Evans had an act called "Trip Around the World" and did the dances of the different countries. Lou Lockett & Jack Waldron, Boyle & Brazil (Boyle was one of the best all-round dancers), the Six American Dancers, with the Lovenberg Sisters, Charles O'Connor, Pearl Davenport, and Purcella & Orbin, were all great hoofers. Among the brother dancing teams there were the Field Bros., Caits Bros., Foley Bros., Ward Bros. (hold-ers of the Fox Medal), King, King & King, Three Slate Bros., Four Small Bros., Ritz Bros., Condos Bros., all great.

When you think of stair dancing, you naturally think of the late and great Bill "Bojangles" Robinson. But there were a number of stair dancers before Bill. There were Al Leach (& His Rosebuds) who did the first stair dance, the Whitney Bros., who did a musical stair dance at Hyde and Behman's in 1899, and Mack & Williams, who did a single, double, and triple stair dance in 1915; Paul Morton and his lovely wife Naomi Glass also did a stair dance. But it took Bill Robinson's great showmanship and personality to make the stair dance his trade-mark and to make him one of the most popular dance artists on the American stage. It all came about by accident, like most successes. Bill started with his partner in vaude (Cooper & Robinson), then did a single, and was established as a single singer and dancer with a few gags thrown in when he played the Palace. At the Palace there are four steps on each side of the stage for the use of an actor when he has to go down to the audience or for a committee who are asked to come up on the stage. One matinee Bill came down to the audience to greet some friends (ad lib), and when he came back to the stage he ad-libbed a dance up the steps, which got a big laugh and plenty applause. Need I tell you more? A great showman like Bill "kept it in" the rest of the week. But all the theaters didn't have those steps, so Bill had his famous staircase built and made dancing history with something that had been done many years before him, but it was his great dancing and his great showmanship that put it over and made him a headliner!

The ballroom dancers started clogging up the vaude stages about 1915, and it brought hundreds of hicks in evening clothes to vaude. Maurice & Florence Walton were not only one of the pioneer acts but also one of the great teams of ballroom dancers. Irene and Vernon Castle (the Castles) were the darlings of dance-mad America. They set the style in ballroom dancing, women copied Irene's hair cut (she was the first to wear a bob), they copied her clothes, and they tried very hard to dance like her. In 1914 they were at the top of their career. On a week of one-night stands they brought in $31,000 (a lot of loot those days, especially for a dance team). The war, not a decline in their popularity, brought to a close the Castle legend. Vernon went to England to join the Royal Flying Corps as a second lieutenant, won a captaincy by shooting down two German planes, was sent back to Canada to train pilots, and when we got in the war he went to Texas to teach our boys. He was killed in a flying accident while there. Some years later Irene tried to do an act with other partners, but it just wasn't *the Castles*!

It would be impossible to mention all the ballroom dancers, because everybody who had or could borrow a full-dress suit became one! But there were a number that were real tops and remained in vaude long after the craze. Evelyn Nesbit and Jack Clifford, who really started out as a "freak act" via the great publicity Evelyn received in the Thaw case, became not only a good box-office attraction but a very good dancing act. Others were Martin Brown and Rozicka Dolly, Hale & Patterson, Joan Sawyer & John Jarrott, Carl Hyson & Dorothy Dickson, Carlos Sebastian & Dorothy Bentley, Mae Murray & Clifton Webb, Fanchon & Marco (who later became the producers of the famous Fanchon & Marco Units), Guiran & Marguerite, Jose & Burns (yep, that was George Burns of the now famous comedy team of Burns & Allen), Addison Fowler & Florence Tamara (first dancing act to have their names in lights at the Palace), the Gigatanos, the Merediths, Ramon & Rosita, Harrison & Fisher, the Dancing Kennedys, the Gliding O'Mearas, the Marvelous Millers, the De Forests, Cortez & Peggy, Moss & Fontana, Veloz & Yolanda, and of course the champs, Tony & Renee De Marco.

There were real great regular dancing acts that did all types of dancing, like Adelaide & Hughes (played twelve consecutive weeks at the Palace, the record), and Fred & Adele Astaire, who were stars on Broadway after a long and honest apprenticeship in vaude and broke up when Adele decided to become Lady Cavendish; Fred became tops of all-round dancers. I remember the ad the Astaires ran in *Variety* in June 1917, a full page that read, "Doing big in the West, what will the East say?" Well, as you know, it said they were great! Then there were Bradley & Ardine, Riggs and Witchie, Burns & Fulton, Hal Le Roy, and Ed Ernie & Emil Honegger, monopede dancers. One had the right leg off and the other the left, and they each wore the same size shoe, so they would buy one pair of shoes. Of course Peg Leg Bates, the Negro monopede dancer, is the greatest of them all. Ivan (Bankoff & Girlie) introduced the Russian hock step into regular dancing. Others were Dorothy Stone and Charles Collins, Martin & Fabrini (who now draws the cartoon "Winnie Winkle"), Vilma & Buddy

Ebsen, the Lockfords, Joe Frisco, the originator of the jazz dance, who with his cigar and derby hat created a sensation and had many imitators, and Pilcer & Douglas, assisted by George Raft (who did a hot Charleston).

Among the toe dancers of vaude we had Adele Genee, Bessie Clayton, Harriet Hoctor, Adelaide, Mazie King, and a local gal that Mark Leucher brought back from Paris where he took her to plant the rep. He called her Le Domino Rouge (her right name was La Belle Daizie); she wore a red mask on and off the stage and got plenty of publicity. She finally got tired of the continual masking and gave it up and was known on the stage as Mlle. Dazie (in private life she was Mrs. Leucher). Menzeli, known as Girlie (Bankoff & Girlie), was once picked by Adele Genee as one of the best dancers in the world. (She and Bankoff had to split because the booking office couldn't pay the act enough dough.) Sally Rand once did a toe dance at the Palace.

Of course we also had the adagio craze and it seemed that every acrobat became an adagio dancer. Myrio originated the Adagio Trios, and Ted Adolphus pioneered especially in comedy routines. The apache was done by William Rock & Maude Fulton at Hammerstein's, beating G. Molasso & Mlle. Corio to it by a few weeks. Molasso was the originator and really the starter of the tidal wave of apache acts.

Then there were the boys and gals with the "laughing feet," the Edisons of hoofology, the great eccentric dancers. In the early '90s the Majiltons were one of the first great teams of eccentric dancers, but to come down to near now, there was a guy named Tom Dingle who danced one night as an unknown at the Friars' Frolic and became the sensation of Broadway. There were "Bunny" Granville with his drunk dance and Jack Donahue with his famous shadow dance. Renee Riano, Daphne Pollard, Violet Carlson, Martha Raye, Nellie Breen, Charlotte Greenwood, Fanny Brice (with her dying swan burlesque) were all very funny gals. Richards (of Bennett & Richards) was acknowledged as one of the greatest eccentric dancers and would have been a star, but because of alimony trouble couldn't play New York. Harland Dixon (Doyle & Dixon, the classiest two-man hoofing act in show biz) was one of the great eccentric dancers, originating many steps now used by eccentric dancers. Fred Stone had a style all his own. Louis Mosconi did an acrobatic eccentric dance that was great. Others were Jim

Barton, one of the greats, Leon Errol, the original rubber-legged drunk, Al Leach, Al Lydell, Ray Bolger, one of the tops, Will Mahoney with his "falling-down" dance and his great novelty of dancing on a xylophone, Carl Francis, Ben Blue, a very funny dancer, Eddie Foy, Jr., Dick Carle, Gil Lamb, Rags Leighton, Bert Williams, Buster West, Willie Solar, Hal Skelly, Tom Smith, and Johnny Boyle.

Some are gone, some have switched from Sloan's Liniment to a throat gargle, and some are still hoofing.

With a deep bow of appreciation from me and Aggie to the real greats of years ago like George Primrose, Barney Fagan, Eddie Leonard, Patsy Doyle, Barney Ferguson, Eddie Foy, Sr., Bobby Gaylor, Bobby Newcomb (who originated song and dance), Blanche LaMont, the McNulty Sisters, Sam & Kitty Morton, Needham & Kelly, Mike Scott, and Pat Rooney, Sr., I am sorry to say that the dancers of today are miles ahead of the old ones. The steady development in the art in conception and execution of dance steps would amaze you. Any gal in the Radio City line can outdance any old-time gal you could mention—I did not say "outpersonality" her—but dancing—the old-timers couldn't even touch these kids. There are only two branches of vaude that are better today than years ago—dancing and acrobatics!

Okay, perfessor, play the last eight bars *forte* . . . and get us off. . . . SEZ

Your pal,
LEFTY

The Sketch

Dear Joe,

The "sketch" was the backbone of vaudeville! It shared honors with the great comedy acts and put "class" into vaudeville!

In the old variety days, the afterpiece was the sketch of the bill.

Later it was followed by Irish, Dutch, and blackface skits that used a thin plot to introduce a song and dance or the playing of an instrument. Many of us can still remember the skits of the early days that opened up with the lady of the act walking to the foot-lights with a letter in her hand, saying, "I wonder what I will do? I just received a letter from my partner saying that he is unavoidably detained and can not make the show tonight."

Just then a man enters with a trunk saying, "Say, lady, where do you want this trunk?"

"Put it in the next room. Say, you look like a bright young man. How would you like to be an actor?"

"You mean an actor on the *stage*?"

"Yes," sez the lady. "You will find my partner's clothes in the trunk. They should fit you; here's your part. Go in that room and change, and I will put you on the stage with me." He exits and she turns to the audience saying, "While he is getting ready, I will rehearse my song."

Then she would sing a song and after the song he would come out dressed in maybe a misfit Roman gladiator's outfit, and—yeh, you guessed it—he would replace her partner.

Crude? Maybe, but it served the purpose, which was to get away from a "specialty in one." In the early days of vaude a full-stage act was valuable because there were so many acts "in one" and a full stage would break up the monotony. In later years it was just the reverse.

To J. Austin Fynes, the manager of Keith's Union Square Thea-tre (New York), goes the credit for bringing the great stars of the legitimate stage to vaude. He paid fabulous salaries (for those days) to lure them to the field that was looked down on by the legits. They couldn't do specialties, so naturally Mr. Fynes had to supply them with a vehicle, usually a dramatic sketch, for which he had to hire a good author. There is no argument that these stars added class to vaude, and also brought patrons who had never before entered a vaudeville theater; they came, they saw, and be-came steady customers.

There were two types of authors for vaude. Some of them could write sketches, while others wrote comedy talk for specialty acts. Only a few were versatile enough to write for both. Some of the acts wrote their own stuff, but they were in the minority. Among the good dramatic writers were Dave Belasco, Paul Armstrong, Sir

W. S. Gilbert, Arthur Hopkins, John Golden, Willard Mack, J. M.
Barrie, Roy Fairchild, Jack London, Roland West, Robert Garland,
Ella Wheeler Wilcox, Sam Shipman, Sir Conan Doyle. Some of
the comedy-sketch writers were Paul G. Smith, Will Cressy, George
Totten Smith, Billy K. Wells, George M. Cohan, Junie McCree,
James Madison, Matt Woodward, George Ade, Tommy Gray,
Bozeman Bulger, George Kelly, Clay M. Green, Al Boasberg, Ed-
win Burke, Ren Shields, Len Hollister, Gene Conrad, S. Jay Kauf-
man, Ralph T. Kettering, Bert Leslie, Edgar Allan Woolf, Roy
Atwell, and of course one of the greatest of all vaude writers, Aaron
Hoffman. There were a few that could do almost any kind of
writing, "gag stuff," songs, comedy, and dramatic acts—but these
were very few. I believe that Edgar Allan Woolf, Will Cressy, Paul
G. Smith, and Tommy Gray wrote more acts than most of them.
Woolf and Cressy were practically booking-office writers; whenever
a legit needed an act for the Big Time, the office would recommend
a writer. Woolf and Cressy were great friends of Eddie Darling,
the head booker of the Keith Circuit, and his recommend was
practically an order.

Cressy & Dayne had a new sketch almost every season, sometimes
two. Ryan & Ritchfield were the first to introduce sequels to their
sketches: "Mag Haggerty's Reception," "Mag Haggerty in Society,"
etc. Ryan was one of the funniest Irish comics in all of show biz.
The way he said, "Is it?" was unforgettable! Bert Leslie also ran
sequels to his acts. He was the originator of slang in his skits, expressions like "Under the sink with the rest of the pipes," "Make
a noise like a hoop and roll away," etc. Junie McCree also used
slang in his character as a dope fiend; his was a natural slang while
Leslie's was sort of manufactured. J. C. Nugent was one of the first
sketch artists to open his act "in one," go to "full stage," and close
"in one." This enabled him to follow a full-stage act and also give
the stagehands a chance to set a full-stage act to follow him, which
made it an easy sketch to book. He would write his own acts, and
had a new one almost every season.

In the early days of variety and vaude, the sketch played in house
sets consisting of a "center-door fancy" or a "kitchen set," which
was a center-door fancy turned around. A kitchen in those days
was a miserable-looking place (according to vaude scenery). A
"rich man's home" usually contained odd furniture, a few rubber
or palm plants, and a few pieces of statuary. The property man was

given a few passes to hand out to people he borrowed the furniture from, but sometimes the stores insisted on program credits too. As the sketches grew better and more plentiful, the sets improved too, with better furniture, maybe a gold chair or two (that showed it was a rich man's hut), a settee, a practical door or window, drapes, and even a light switch. When vaude was firmly established, many sketch artists carried their own scenery and furniture, light effects, and even a stage carpenter and electrician.

The first record of a comedy sketch in variety shows was in 1873; the team was John & Maggie Fielding. Then in 1877 Charles Rogers & Mattie Vickers did a sketch. Later came Tom & Hattie Nawn in "One Touch of Nature." One of the first dramatic sketches (if not the first) was put on by Francesca Redding with her former stock leading man, Hugh Stanton. The act was called, "A Happy Pair," and that was in 1890. It was not until 1896 that dramatic acts really took hold in vaude, when J. Austin Fynes got Charles Dickson and Lillian Burkhart, Sidney Drew (the Barrymores' uncle) and Gladys Rankin Drew and John Mason and Marion Manola to enter the ranks of vaudeville.

Since then, I don't believe there has been a real great star of the legit and musical-comedy stage who didn't play at least a week or two in vaude. While some of them used vaude as a fill-in when their shows would close for the season or flop, many of the top stars found vaude very profitable and much steadier work than their regular shows, and played routes season after season. Someone once said, "When a legit loses his voice, he goes into vaudeville." But that wasn't really so, because many of them were very successful in the vaude field and would take a show every once in a while to sort of bolster up their reps as legit stars for vaude. Most of them would play dramatic sketches, as it upheld their dignity and they didn't have to combat the terrific opposition of the many great comedy acts. There were a number of "light comedy" stars who had comedy sketches that became standard acts.

To mention all the dramatic sketches would read like the Who's Who of the legitimate stage. I will try to recall just a few that impressed me and Aggie—sketches like Margaret Anglin in "The Wager"; Edward Abeles, "Self Defence"; Jean Adair, "Maggie Taylor, Waitress"; Julia Arthur, "Liberty Aflame"; Hobart Bosworth, "Sea Wolf"; Amelia Bingham, "Big Moments from Great Plays"; Sarah Bernhardt in a series of sketches; Harry Beresford,

"Old New York"; Valerie Bergere, "Judgment"; Richard Bennett, "The Common Man"; George Beban, "Sign of the Rose." Ethel Barrymore is supposed to have played only Barrie's *Twelve Pound Look* in vaude, but in 1913 she played the Palace with a skit called "Miss Civilization." After that she used Barrie's sketch for all her appearances in vaude, except once when she played "Drifted Apart," first done in 1882.

Lionel Barrymore, McKee Rankin, and Doris Rankin did "The White Slave." John Barrymore was a big hit in a comedy sketch, "The Honeymoon." Others were Mrs. Leslie Carter in "Zaza"; George Nash, "Unexpected"; Nance O'Neill, "Second Ash Tray"; Florence Reed, "Jealousy"; Julius Steger, "Tenth Commandment" (a great act, and a great artist, who demanded absolute quiet when he was on stage; he was nicknamed "Shhhhh" Steger); Lou Tellegen, "Blind Youth"; Henry B. Walthall, "The Unknown"; Robert Mantell and Genevieve Hamper, scene from *Macbeth* (Julia Arthur was first to do a scene from *Hamlet* in vaude); Henri Du Vries, "Case of Arson"; Allan Dinehart, "The Meanest Man in the World" (George M. Cohan made a play out of this); Walter Hampden, "Blackmail"; Frank Keenan, "Man to Man"; Mrs. Lillian Langtry, "The Test"; Willard Mack and Marjorie Rambeau, "Kick In" (this too was made into a show). Of course Nazimova in "War Brides," which she played during World War I, was one of the most dramatic acts, because it dealt with a war at the time a war was on, and it hit almost everybody in the audience. Comedy acts feared to follow this one (she was much tougher to follow than Bernhardt); the best comedy acts worked at least ten minutes before the audience dried their eyes.

Among the great comedy sketches (and me and Aggie are just trying to recall the belly-laugh sketches; others got plenty of laughs too, but the belly-laughers really counted), of course my list always starts with Imhof, Conn & Corinne in "The Pest House" as one of the most consistent belly-laugh getters. Running neck and neck with Imhof was Willard Simms in "Flinder's Flats," a guy trying to do his own paper hanging. John B. Hymer in "Come On, Red!"; Ryan & Ritchfield, "Mag Haggerty's Reception"; Harry Watson, Jr., "Tell Him What I Did to Philadelphia Jack O'Brien" or "Battling Dugan"; Leon Errol, "The Guest"; Bert Baker, "Prevarication"; Gordon Eldrid, "Won by a Leg"; Harry Green, "George Washington Cohen"; Mr. and Mrs. Sidney Drew, "Billy's Tombstones"; and Tommy Dugan and Babe Raymond, "The Apple Tree" are about all I have room for.

Of course there were standard comedy sketch artists of vaude that were sure-fire: Mason & Keeler, John C. Rice & Sally Cohen, Harry "Zoop" Welsh, Macart & Bradford, Barnes & Crawford, Halligan & Sykes, Dave Ferguson, Fred Ardath, Franklyn Ardell, Dolan & Lenhar, Mr. and Mrs. Mark Murphy, Cressy & Dayne, Tom Nawn, Claude and Fannie Usher, Emmett Devoy, Lulu McConell & Grant Simpson, O'Brien Havel, Stevens & Hollister, Harry Holman in "Adam Killjoy," and Alexander Carr, who with "The End of the World" (or "Toblitsky Says"), a kind of "Abie's Irish Rose," written by Aaron Hoffman, was one of the longest-playing sketches in vaude. Mrs. Gracie Emmett played in "Mrs. Murphy's Second Husband" for over twenty-five years, as did Ward & Curran in their courtroom act.

The property man was, I believe, the first "stooge"! In the young days of vaude it was too expensive to carry an actor for a bit part, so the property man was used. He would play such bits as a letter carrier, maybe with just a line like, "Here's a letter for you, madame," or the part of a cop who would say, "Move on," or, "And sure it's a lovely day, Mrs. Callahan," or an iceman, messenger boy, or even a dead body. For this he would receive 50 cents a show. Some of the old-time property men became very good actors and ad-libbers, sometimes forgetting their regular lines and ad-libbing lines that were so funny that they were kept in. George Williams, the property man at Keith's, Boston, was for many years the best of the ad-libbers and it was because of his popularity that many an act got over. When Mr. Albee opened the beautiful Memorial Theatre in Boston, it was Williams who received the biggest hand of all the celebrities that were introduced.

One trouble nearly all the comedy sketches had was a lack of good curtain lines. There were acts that had the audience screaming with laughter all the way through, but fell flat at the finish and just managed to get a couple of forced fast curtain calls. They were always offering big money for a "wow" curtain line, but, as I said, very few ever got it. The dramatic acts had some dramatic line for a finish, or a surprise twist, and didn't expect too much applause. They would get their applause for good acting or for the act's dramatic value. But bookers (who should have known better) judged most acts by applause at the finish. That is why so many acts "stole" bows or "milked" audiences.

Continuous vaudeville, with the noise made by people coming in and going out and changing seats, didn't help the sketch any. And when they started building the large vaude houses, the sketch was doomed. The dramatic people, instead of going to vaude "between shows," now were going into pics. Many of the standard comedy sketches went back to acts "in one" where they could be heard; many of them went to radio. The writers went to radio and pictures where the returns were twice and three times as much as they ever made in vaudeville . . . but there wasn't any fun making it! SEZ

Your pal,

LEFTY

The Single Woman

Dear Joe,

A vaudeville show without the "single woman" was like a jet plane that doesn't jet!

I mean the gals who used to belt over any kind of a song—comedy, ballad, or novelty; and I mean belt them over on their own power without the aid of an engineer, P.A. system, microphone, fancy arrangements, and all the do-dads that ruined vaude but started a bigger business. I'm not taking anything away from the modern single gals who whisper into mikes or become stars overnight by making a hit record (and become unknowns just as fast). They certainly have their place in today's show biz and a lot of them are real good and have talent and would have made good in the old days of vaude. But those gals of the two-a-day and its kindergarten, the "family time," were a different breed!

The Golden Dozen—Maggie Cline, Bonnie Thornton, Lillian Russell, Eva Tanguay, Nora Bayes, Vesta Victoria, Alice Lloyd,

Irene Franklin, Florence Moore, Helen Morgan, Fanny Brice, and Irene Bordoni—have all gone "upstairs." Sophie Tucker, "the Last of the Red-Hot Mamas," hasn't cooled off in nearly fifty years of trouping and today is the Deaness of all the single gals. Belle Baker is the runner-up among the still-working daughters of Mother Vaudeville and 'still is a drawing card and a show-stopper! Kate Smith is doing just as big and even bigger on radio and TV than she did in vaude, and that's *big*, brother! Mae West has 'em coming up to see her anytime she feels like playing. Helen Kane "boop-a-boops" her hit way in theaters and night clubs. Molly Picon is still a great international star headliner. Beatrice Lillie is jamming 'em in with her one-woman show, Fritzi Scheff takes a flyer now and then on TV and radio to sing "Kiss Me Again," as does Blanche Ring to keep the "Rings on My Fingers and Bells on My Toes" from rusting. Ethel Merman has added the scalp of pictures to her talented belt, while Ethel Waters is going strong in all mediums of show biz!

What a bunch of swell gals!

Many of the headliners have retired to become mothers and grandmothers, some are housewives, while others, like Gertrude Vanderbilt, are big business executives. May Usher is in the dress business, Marguerite Young is in the real estate biz, Gertrude Hoffman runs a dancing school, Grace Hayes had her own café, as did Janet of France; both entertained their customers until the registers overflowed and they retired. Blossom Seeley makes a few personal appearances with the picture about her life. Juliet takes out her one-woman show when she feels stage-struck, Aileen Stanley has a school where she teaches talented youngsters how to sock over numbers like she used to do. Ethel Levy shuttles back and forth between New York and London and still sings a great song. Elsie Janis writes for pictures, Trixie Friganza still does shows for the GI's, Pert Kelton does plenty of work on TV and radio, and Norma Terris is ready to come back to us. And the ones who are very happy in retirement or marriage are Rae Samuels, Nan Halperin, Louise Dresser, Grace LaRue, Frances Arms, Bobby Folsom, Yvette Rugel, Ruth Etting, Ruby Norton, Lillian Shaw, and many many more who are living on the dough they sent home every week when they were the queens of the two-a-day! And many more, I am sorry to say, are not playing the route any more, but their memories grow greener with the passing years!

She was a great gal, the single woman—she had to be! When she made her entrance, it was the signal for bookers, agents, managers, musicians, stagehands, actors, and "town guys" to go on the make. But you didn't have to worry about those gals; they had "routines" that were better than chastity belts. Some of them carried their mothers (or a facsimile) or "sisters" to dress 'em and to act as alibis. You know, "I got to take my sister along. . . ." Most of 'em were wise, smart-cracking gals who knew their stuff on and off. Many of them would put on the helpless act, moaning, "I don't know how to get my Pullman reservations," "I don't know how to check my baggage." (And the man dope would check it for her and pay the excess, saying, "Oh, forget it, it wasn't much.") They had a way of getting guys to do things for them. But it wasn't all fun, because they had to put in hours of rehearsal on their songs, hours with their dressmakers, hairdressers, writers, and, sez Aggie, "especially with their piano players." (A wisecrack.)

The single woman, more than any other act, was just as good as her material and dressmaker. No matter how pretty she was, she couldn't overcome a bad routine of songs. So the smart ones were on the lookout for writers of special material and especially comedy songs. Laughs always paid off in vaude, as they do today in radio and TV. Many a gal was made by a comedy song or a great ballad! A pop song they could get from the publishers, who even paid them for using it. But with competition it became tougher and tougher to depend just on pop songs. Using them meant getting to the theater first to grab the first check for rehearsal and so protect themselves from anybody else on the bill using the numbers they depended on. Many a single woman would rehearse ten songs (some of which she knew she wouldn't use) to keep some other gal or act from using them. The gals who didn't have a piano player to attend rehearsals had to appear themselves, sometimes at 7 A.M. for an 11 o'clock rehearsal. Orchestra leaders were bribed, stage managers overtipped, doormen perjured themselves swearing who appeared first, wires were pulled to keep other acts from using a new published number that maybe the single woman depended on to put over her act.

Publishers paid the headliners and features, because having a song introduced by Nora Bayes, Belle Baker, Sophie Tucker, Rae Samuels, and many more of that type entertainer meant a hit song. There were no radios and TV and it was mostly through vaude that pop songs were made. Some of the publishers even furnished clothes, special versions, orchestrations and arrangements, and even scenery and a "plugger" in the box, besides paying the salary of the piano player. The professional managers for the song publishers in the big cities would entertain the gals, paying for their meals, hotels, etc., so the gals were able to send most of their salary to the receiving tellers of their favorite banks.

Many of the headliners paid outright for their special material, but some paid 10 per cent of their salaries. It was worth it, because it helped their acts and, most important, raised their salaries and kept them "up there." Clothes were a very important part of the single woman's act, except the ones that did character comedy like Vesta Victoria, Lillian Shaw, etc. As soon as a gal appeared in what they call a "stunning creation," all the other gals would hunt up the same dressmaker, who overnight became a "modiste," and who would then enjoy a season or two of much moolah! It was the same with writers; when one turned out a good hunk of material, all the gals would try to get him to write for their acts. I believe Blanche Merrill was what the professors call a "much-sought-after writer," because she wrote many great songs for Tanguay. Irene Franklin and Elsie Janis wrote their own stuff.

In the 1900s many of the so-called single women carried "insurance" in the form of pickaninnies, or "picks," as they were called. After singing a few songs on their own, they would bring out the picks (a group of Negro kids that really could sing and dance) for a "sock" finish. It really wasn't a single act, but nevertheless they were so classified. There are a few come to mind that were tops, like Grace LaRue with her Inky-Dinks, Phina & Her Picks (she changed her name later to Josephine Gassman), and Ethel Whiteside and Her Picks. Laura Comstock's picks were three white boys blackened up: Henry Bergman (Clark & Bergman), Charlie O'Connor (later with Six American Dancers), and Nelson Davis. Then there were Mayme Remington & Her Black Buster Brownie Ethiopian Prodigés (shows you they weren't satisfied to bill 'em as picks), Josephine Saxton and Her Four Picks, Emma Kraus & Her Dutch Picks (they sang in German and made up like Dutch kids), and Louise Dresser & Her Picks (she was married then to Jack Norworth). Canta Day pulled a switch by billing her act, "Canta Day and Her *White* Picks"! Carrie Scott, "the Bowery Girl," was the first to use picks; that was in the early '90s.

There was great competition among the single women. Tanguay was the first to carry a "leader" instead of a piano player; she later added a cornetist. Many had fine pianists, then some had *two* pianists, some put in bands, others colored bands, jazz bands, special drummers, etc. When one would have a beautiful lamp at the piano, someone would top her by having three or four lamps; one would have a Spanish shawl draped on the piano, so someone else would outdo her by draping a mink, etc., etc., until the single woman, who used to just come out in front of a street drop and sing, practically became a "production." The terrific competition and jealousies paid off at the box office!

The headline single women were a temperamental lot. They would walk off a show because of a bad dressing room, billing, or spot on the program. Fritzi Scheff once walked out of the Palace and Mr. Albee had a sign put in the lobby saying that because she walked out she would never play the Palace again. She was back in a few weeks. The big moguls forgave anybody who could bring money to the till, but they could stay mad for a long time if it was just another act. Nora Bayes "walked" many a time, as did Tanguay (who was the most temperamental of them all). Fanny Brice was the least temperamental.

Nora Bayes was the "class" of all the single women—a truly great artist who did everything with class gestures. When she was married to Jack Norworth, they would travel in a private car (no actors did that before, and I can't remember anybody that did it since). She would sweep into a hotel, taking half a floor for her company. She would pay the expenses of her piano player and wife, her two adopted children and governess, her maid, and maybe of a few friends that were just traveling along. She allowed no interviews (and got more publicity that way, as the papers thought they were putting something over on her). She would always work with a fine lace handkerchief in one hand, or a fan. She was in the first *Ziegfeld Follies*. She was also the first to sing George M. Cohan's immortal song, "Over There"; Cohan came backstage at the Thirty-ninth Street Theatre, where she was giving her own show with a few acts, and told her he had just written a song and would she sing it, which she did with Irving Fisher a few nights later. Her first husband was an undertaker by the name of Cressing, Jack Norworth was next, then came Harry Clark, Arthur Gordoni, and Ben Friedland. She was one of the few gals who had a theater named after her, the Nora Bayes Roof atop the Forty-fourth Street Theatre. She died at the age of fifty; her last professional appearance was at the Fox Academy of Music for three days, and the last thing she did was to sing for the Doyer's Mission on March 19, 1928. She was put in a receiving vault in Woodlawn and wasn't buried until eighteen years later (1946, when her fifth husband died). Nora Bayes was not only a great artist but a great big-hearted gal.

Eva Tanguay, who to me and Aggie represented the true spirit of vaudeville, was everything a vaude headliner should be, a gal who came up the hard way, temperamental, good newspaper copy, always doing something to pump blood into the box office. Here are some of the billings of Tanguay, which I believe give you the story of the gal: "The Girl Who Made Vaudeville Famous," "Cyclonic Eva Tanguay," "Mother Eve's Merriest Daughter," "The Genius of Mirth and Song," "America's Champion Comedienne," "Our Own Eva," "America's Idol," "The Girl the Whole World Loves," "Vaudeville's Greatest Drawing Card," "The One Best Bet," "The Evangelist of Joy," etc., etc.

Eva Tanguay played first in Chamberlain's "My Lady Co." at Hammerstein's, when they played shows. She started in the chorus, then sang two numbers. The girls in the chorus crabbed her numbers by throwing buns, talking, etc. One night she stopped in the middle of a number and started a terrific fight with the girls, pulling hair, etc. Her name got in the papers the next day and she saw that it stayed there until her death. Starting with $25 a week and going to $3,500, she replaced Norworth & Bayes in the *Ziegfeld Follies* in 1909 and had her name as big as the show, the only one who ever had that kind of billing in the *Follies*! The next year P. G. Williams had a contest offering a prize for breaking the records at the Colonial; Tanguay, Hoffman, Suratt, and Nat Goodwin were the competitors. Tanguay won!

She once went on Amateur Night for her friend Joe Schenck (who, by the way, gave her a weekly check when things were tough with her) at Loew's National Theater in the Bronx; she was billed as Lillian Doom, and was a terrific hit! She fought with stagehands, musicians, bookers, managers, and even acts, but when she liked you she was a great gal, and she packed 'em in for years. Me and Aggie won't say she had a great talent, but she did have a beautiful form and a terrific personality that got her the kind of money that

meant Fort Knox! You could write a big fat book about Eva, and
it was too bad she had to end her days on charity, but she only got
back a small part of what she gave out. She was the greatest adver-
tiser of any vaude act in America . . . but besides advertising you
must have something to deliver. Tanguay had it!

Tanguay and Sophie Tucker spent more money on costumes and
material than any other single women in show biz. Sophie would
come back season after season with new ideas, material, scenery,
and clothes. For many years she had (and still has) on her payroll
as special-material writer the very talented Jack Yellen, who with
Lew Pollack wrote her famous "Yiddisher Mama." Ted Shapiro
has been her accompanist for nearly thirty years, and in all those
years Ted has never called Sophie anything but Miss Tucker (on
or off stage). I am not going to tell you much about Sophie, because she wrote a book about herself, so why should I crab sales,
but I do want to say that she is a gal whom everybody in show biz
is proud of, not only because she brought great talent to vaude—
but because she also brought a great heart!

To write biogs of all the great single gals in vaude would take
a book by itself, so I will mention just a few of the greats and see
if you can put them together in your jigsaw memories of vaudeville.
Not in the order of their importance, because they were all important. I have already mentioned many of them, so will kinda add to
the list as they come back to memory: Mabel McCane, Mabel
Hite, Lottie Gilson, Marion Harris, Frances White, Gracie Fields,
Clarice Vance, Edna Aug, Marie Cahill, Fay Templeton, Marie
Dressler, Lilly Lena.

There were a lot of single women that were headliners but not
box-office, gals that had terrific talent, big billing as attractions and
features, and were terribly important to vaude, gals like Sadie Burt,
Gertrude Barnes, Amy Butler, Olive Briscoe, Edith Clifford, Anna
Chandler, Ruth Roye, Reine Davis, Grace DeMarr, Aunt Jemima,
Maude Lambert, Ann Laughlin, Ray Cox, Marie Nordstrom, Ma-
rie Russell, Lucy Weston, Marguerite Young, Elizabeth Murray,
Daisy Harcourt, Bessie Wynn, Daphne Pollard, Adele Rowland,
Miss Patricola, Lydia Barry, Truly Shattuck, Frances Arms, Lillian
Fitzgerald, Edna Leedom, Bobby Folsom, Ann Greenway, Violet
Carlson, Sylvia Clark, Grace Hazard, Winnie Lightner, and a raft
of others.

Then there were the special attractions and middle and bottom attractions like Dixie Hamilton, May Usher, Emily Darrell, Ethel Davis, Grace Hayes, Frankie Heath, Dolly Kay, Annie Kent, Elida Morris, Sally Fields, Grace Cameron, Ray Dooley, Josie Heather, Irene Ricardo, Clara Morton, Flo Lewis, Marie Stoddard, Bessie Browning, Dorothy Brenner, and more and more and more.

Just a lot of names, you say? But when you think of them you have golden memories of great songs like, "I Don't Care," "Red Head," "Who You Gettin' At, Eh?" "Waiting at the Church," "Eli, Eli," "Some of These Days," "Military Wedding," "I'm an Indian," "Giddap Napoleon," "Toodle-oo," "My Little Bag of Tricks," "Push, Push, Push," "Down on the Erie," "Shine On, Harvest Moon," "St. Louis Blues," "Mississippi," "Strange Faces," "The Biggest Aspidistra in the World," "Rings on My Fingers," "When the Moon Comes over the Mountain," "Evening Star," "Forty-five Minutes from Broadway," "Kiss Me Good-Bye, Flo," "Bill," "My Man," "By Jingo," "Robert E. Lee"; try and place 'em with the artists to whom they belong.

All these songs and the ladies who sang them contributed a lot to the success of vaudeville, and there were many more who haven't been mentioned because of space, but it was swell knowing, seeing, and hearing you gals, and me and Aggie salute your standard-bearer, the hottest mama of 'em all, who is still carrying on the great tradition of the vaudeville single woman—*Sophie Tucker*! SEZ

Your *pal*,

LEFTY

Vaudeville Music

Dear Joe,

From the first days of the honky-tonks to the time when the last "exit march" was heard at the Palace, music played a very important part in vaudeville!

A show without music is like the sound going dead on your TV set! You just couldn't have a guy play your music on a comb covered with tissue paper. For many years the variety shows had the old "three-piece orchestra," piano, stool, and cover! There were many great ivory-beaters, most of them nonreaders but great fakers. I would say about 80 per cent of all the old-time piano players could fake anything you could sing, hum, or whistle!

I can give you a good picture of the early variety-house orchestras by telling you about Tony Pastor's famous pit boys, Mike Bernard, Burt Green, Tom Kelly, Ben Harney, and William Brode: they all played there at one time or another. Tom Kelly and William Brode played the supper shows, while the others played the two-a-day acts.

You never heard such a reception as Mike Bernard got when he walked down the aisle daily at 2:15 and at 8:15 P.M. Ragtime was just starting and Mike was tops. He won a flock of medals at Tammany Hall, where they would hold yearly ragtime piano-playing contests. Years later many a jazz combo copied Mike's stuff. He manipulated the ivories so that the average pop song sounded like grand opera. He kept interest in the show from the minute he seated himself at the pit piano to the final exit march. He did what the professors would call "extemporizing," but what me and Aggie would call "ad-libbing on the keys." Mike would take an ordinary melody and would stick in a lot of musical stuff that the professors would say "brought forth a technique and understanding of expression that were limitless." (I copied that part.)

Some of the acts when they first opened at Pastor's got kinda sore at Mike (and the others) for putting in variations on their piano-copy score. Many of 'em beefed to Tony Pastor that Mike was crabbing their act by playing so good that the audience was looking at and listening to Mike instead of their act. But me and Aggie will bet he saved more acts than he killed by his ad-libbing from the act's lead sheets. After the Monday matinee "beef," the acts realized Mike was helping them, and by the middle of the week they were ad-libbing with Mike, and getting over, because the audience was for *Mike* against *anybody*!

When Mike left Pastor's, Burt Green took his place and became a great favorite, which proved what a great guy he must have been to be able to follow the piano-playing idol of Fourteenth Street! Like Mike, he played the show alone as few orchestras could, and he ad-libbed operatic variations on the pop themes of that period. He had an original trick of playing the overture and changing the key and tempo while the house was singing and whistling what he originally started. He used this comedy bit when he was later headlined with his wife, Irene Franklin, for many years in vaude. It was always a hit!

Ben Harney was the pioneer of ragtime music. Modern jazz and swing stemmed from the same syncopation. His playing led to the ragtime craze and the cakewalk craze using the same tempo. They say that Charles Trevanthan, who wrote "Bully Boy" for May Irwin, was the originator. But Ben learned it when he was in Louisville, mastered the syncopated rhythm, and came to Pastor's about 1895. He later went into vaude and did a swell act and certainly popularized ragtime playing.

Tom Kelly and Bill Brode came after Burt Green and were fine ivory-ticklers and knew a lot of trick stuff with the eighty-eight notes, the same as Mike and Burt, but never got their rep. Anyway, these guys will give you an idea of the early variety pit music. They had local Mike Bernards (in popularity, not in talent) all over the country. There were even two guys on the same street that were pretty well known to the customers of Keith's Union Square Theatre, Emil Katzenstein and Nobel McDonald, and Harrington at Henderson's Coney Island, and Jack Connelly at Keith's, Boston, were favorites, too. Then there was Roesner in San Francisco's Orpheum; they had a full orchestra, but the old man would play on a small organ during intermission, and to make it harder he would place a silk scarf over the keyboard and play a tune (a gimmick). He was a swell musician and a good showman. But I saw many a piano player in a joint play in the dark when the cops were raiding it. (Don't say nothing to Aggie.)

The orchestras in vaude were built up gradually. First a drummer was added. Then some guy who liked music added a catgut scraper (violinist); we called them "Yeh, yeh men" because they usually led the orchestras and while playing the fiddle they had to beat out time for the other guys, which they did with their heads, making it look like they were saying "yes" all the time. Little by little they added cornet, trombone, and when they got real swell they added the "one-in-a-bar" or "live-forever" guy (which is the nice bass player). We never did meet an angry bass player! The drummer was a very important guy for acts. He was made the butt of all the jokes; the single woman would make love to him, stroke his bald head, and leave lipstick on it after kissing him. He would have to have a lot of accessories like cowbells, ratchets, horns, etc., to make noises with when someone would take a fall. When he would shake the cowbell, the comic would usually say "Milk it." (What a wow!)

It was William Morris, Sr., when he was booking the old Music Hall in Boston in opposition to Keith, who made the manager put in a small orchestra instead of just a piano player. Keith didn't like it, but had to follow suit and do likewise at his house. It was Martin Beck (who really was a music lover) that put in fifteen-piece orchestras on the Orpheum Circuit. They played classical overtures and Mr. Beck gave orders that they must play the last person out of the theater with the exit march. This was really a big idea of Beck's, because nearly all musicians would stop playing a few minutes after the stereopticon slide, picturing a little child dressed in a nightgown with a candle in her hand saying "Good Night," was thrown on the curtain. It left a void and was a letdown for the audience walking out of a silent theater. With the orchestra "playing 'em out," the customers carried out the joy of the show with them and maybe even hummed a hit tune heard during the performance.

Leaders and men in the pit of vaude orchestras were specialized musicians, because it's a lot different playing for vaudeville acts (that had dozens of cues, bits of business, etc.) than playing for musical comedy, opera, or symphony. To mention all the fine leaders is impossible, but there were a few greats at the New York theaters that you just have to give a nod to, like Jules Lensberg at the Colonial, George May at Hammerstein's, Louis Rheinhart at the Orpheum, Brooklyn, Benny Roberts at the Alhambra, Andy Byrnes at the Bushwick, J. Leibman at the American Roof, Paul Schindler, the first leader at the Palace, followed by Lou Foreman, Dan Russo, and Charlie Dabb, and Joe Jordan and Ruby Swerling at Loew's State. They were very important in helping to put over a show. A good leader could cut down rehearsal time, and could put over an act or louse 'em up. Many of them did both!

What I want to tell you about are the musical acts that played on "the shelf." One of the earliest of all novelty musical acts was way back in 1876 when a German magician by the name of Herr Schlam was the first person to play musical glasses in America. He billed himself a "cocophonist" (which is certainly high-class billing for a guy that plays glasses). There were hundreds that did this type musical act for many years (saw a couple on TV who did it better than we've ever heard).

Early variety performers learned how to plunk a banjo for self-protection from some of the piano players; they could at least give them the tempo and an idea of the tunes of their songs and dance numbers. (By the way, in 1874 they called a banjo a banjar.) There were more banjo players among the musical acts in the early days than there were uke players when that musical plague hit vaude many years later. Some of the real good banjoists were Bill Bailey, the Burt Earl Trio, Claudius & Scarlet (who accompanied themselves while old-time illustrated songs were shown on the screen—they did this in all the big-time houses and in the *Follies*—it was so old that it was new again), E. M. Hall (who would tell about the banjo's origin, etc.), Brent Hayes, Kimball & Donovan, Lee & Cowan, Polk & Collins, Perry & Bolger, Blackface Eddie Ross (he called it an African harp), and the Howard Bros. (with their flying banjos they were real great).

Variety bills had musical acts (mostly blackface) that did some singing and dancing and even acrobatics with their music. And when they became better musicians (they had lots of chances to practice while doing ten to fifteen shows a day), they naturally learned how to play many more instruments and those that couldn't do singing, dancing, or comedy started to do straight musical acts in white face and passed themselves off as musicians. Johnny Thompson, called "the Lively Moke" (blackface) was one of the first musical mokes (which meant he played many kinds of instruments).

The first straight musical acts played musical glasses, bells, banjo, cornet, violin, piano, Irish bagpipe, sweet potato, harmonica, xylophone, and harp. The ones who couldn't play well enough did novelty acts, which meant they went in for "gimmicks," playing musical rattles, gobletphones, and bells (Swiss, hand, and sleigh). Musical clowns played odd instruments (much like the guys years later who played balloons, tires, saws, and washboards). There were trick violinists, concertina players, drummers, one-armed cornetists, whistlers, bones and tambourine soloists, musical bottles, etc. Most of the guys who played the gimmick instruments couldn't read a note if it was endorsed by B. F. Keith! A few were good musicians, but figured a novelty would get more dough.

I'll never forget the time me and Aggie worked on a bill with a guy who did a musical act. He dressed as a waiter and had a table on stage all dressed up like a banquet table (a cheap banquet), with bowls of rubber oranges and apples, dishes, silverware, and napkins. He would come on after a musical introduction by the professor in the pit and start squeezing tunes out of the oranges and apples, and blowing the knives, forks, and spoons, which sounded like whistles—simple tunes like "Turkey in the Straw" and some German folk tunes. For the finish of his act (which was set in what was supposed to be a dining room), he would come to center stage and say to the audience, in a thick German accent, "Vile vaitin' for the beoples to come, I vill vater my roses." That was the cue for the lights to dim down, and the professor would play an introduction to "The Last Rose of Summer" (a very popular ditty those days). The guy would pick up a small sprinkling can and as it made contact with a rose, the rose would light up and he would play the song via bells, and the funny part of it was that it was a great finish for his act!

Me and Aggie were young those days and kinda full of fun, so we got all the acts on the bill (three) together and we switched his oranges and apples and knives and forks and even misplaced a few of the roses for good measure. Well sir, you have never seen such a look of surprise on a guy's face as when he squeezed the first orange. He looked as surprised as a guy being caught by a house dick. When he squeezed a few more and it was "nodding," he figured he'd switch to his rose finish and get out of it. When he made the first contact, he was exactly eighty-eight notes off key. He said, "Gottdammit," then turned to the audience and said, "Scuse, blease," and walked off.

It really was a dirty trick on our part, but we justified ourselves when we found out that the guy had learned his act via numbers. Each piece of fruit, knife, and fork, and rose were numbered, so we figured he was a lousy musician and maybe he would learn a lesson and also some music. Anyway, we did save him from being canceled for saying "Gottdammit"—said in a little town in Maine where they never heard that word except at home! There were many like this guy in early variety, but out of these beginnings came some really great musical acts that wouldn't be ashamed to hit the Carnegie Hall acoustics!

I'd like to tell you about some of the novelty musical acts in vaude. You may recall many of them. There was Fields & Hanson, one of the oldest comedy musical acts (there was one Fields, but dozens of Hansons, as he would get a new partner every few weeks). One of them would play the "Anvil Chorus" on a cornet while the other would beat him on the fanny with a slapstick in time to the music, and the player would pay no attention to him. At the finish of the selection he would keel over exhausted. It was a big laugh (then). Snyder & Buckley, another couple of old-timers, did funny bits between playing their instruments. There was a billy goat head on the wall with a sign on it, "Bock Beer." The straight man would go over after finishing a number, pull the horns, and get a glass of beer. The comic would follow him, pull the horns, and get milk! This was carried on all through the act to a real big laugh.

Adams & White played on farm implements, Josh Adelman & Co. played on tiny instruments, Beltrah & Beltrah, "The Musical Dairy," milked a prop cow and made music. Carmenelli & Lucille did "Music and Fun in a Butcher Shop" (you can imagine that one). Fitch Cooper was the originator of the musical saw (lots of acts claimed it). Mlle. Carie was a lady champ sleigh-bells player. Ferry Corway, a talented musical clown, was one of the best prop-makers in the country. George Dixon (not the humorous Washington correspondent) played xylophone on a skeleton. (At that, the modern George plays xylophone on politicians.) Luigi Del 'Oro played two instruments at one time. This was done by many others years later. Solly Violinsky was the first I ever saw to play violin and piano at the same time. Dave Apollon played a mandolin and piano (great). The Easterbrooks back in 1908 (long before the New York World's Fair buses had musical horns) had the first auto horn that played a melody. Phil Glissando, on a battleship, played the guns, life preservers, etc. Zelland Hunt, a deaf mute, played a great piano. Tommy Hayes played a bone solo, glasses, and dog biscuits. He would say, while picking up a biscuit, "I wonder are these dog biscuits good enough for my dog Prince," and proceed to "taste 'em," and they would turn out to be whistles, on which he would play a tune. Billy "Musical" Huehn was an expert on the "pepperina" (which was an ocarina or sweet potato); he also played a dozen other instruments, whistled, and danced (great). Lazar & Lazar played the "hypnotic glasses" (regular glass playing) and had a mechanical orchestra on the back drop.

Staley & Birbeck were one of the great novelty acts and played all over the world. Their act opened on a scene in a blacksmith shop; they were all dressed as blacksmiths and played the "Anvil Chorus," hitting horseshoes on large anvils, which sent out sparks of electricity and made a beautiful effect. Then in exactly *three seconds* the scene changed to a nice parlor set and all the members of the cast were in evening clothes and played many more instruments. Wilbur Swetman played two clarinets at one time. The Tom-Jack Trio threw snowballs at tambourines in frames, which made good music. They also fenced and made music by striking shields with swords. Toy & Toy played kid toys that were hanging on a Christmas tree. Tipple & Kilmet played on wheelbarrows, the Transfield Sisters got fine music out of playing on all kinds of bottles, and Will Van Allen played on knives and forks while seated at a table eating. Willard's Temple of Music had a large sawmill, and was the biggest musical act ever produced in vaudeville!

There were many musical acts with fine music and scenery. Most of them were produced by Jesse Lasky and B. A. Rolfe. Mr. Lasky, who is one of the great motion-picture producers, started in vaude years ago as a musical act with his sister; he played a cornet. B. A. Rolfe was one of the great cornetists of his day and had his own bands for many years and was a pioneer on the radio. Both men produced such fine musical acts as Lasky & Rolfe's Quintette, Ye Colonial Septette, Military Octette, fourteen Black Hussars (a swell Negro act), Pianophiends, Clownland, the Rolphonians, and many more. There were other big musical acts, like American Trumpeters, the Boston Fadettes, with Caroline Nichols as director (they had a bit where the all-girl group got mad and walked out and Caroline replaced them, playing ten different instruments), and the Banjofiends. The Bell Family (Mexicans) were really one of the great musical acts; they played xylophone, mandolins, and finished with mixed bells, sleigh, hand, and pipe. There were of course the Six Brown Bros. (nearly all related) with their saxophones, one of the best acts of its kind, Six Musical Cuttys (a great family musical organization), Four Emperors of Music, the Exposition Four, the Old Soldier Fiddlers (sons of Dixie and sons in blue), sure-fire applause getters (after about twenty minutes of bad fiddlin' on both sides of the Mason-Dixon line, they shook hands and all was forgiven), Gordon Highlanders, Musical Hodges, Six Kirksmith Sisters, Specht's Lady Serenaders, Wyatt's Scotch Lads & Lassies, and many more.

Among the great comedy musical acts were Bickle & Watson (originally the famous Bickle, Watson & Wrothe), Binns, Binns & Binns (they all made up like King Edward), Eckhoff & Gordon, Farrell & Taylor (he would light his cigar with a gas jet from his vest pocket), Goldsmith & Hoppe (a very funny act). Oscar Lorraine and his fiddle was another great comedy act. Grant Gardner did a blackface monologue and besides playing a cornet was the best large hand-bell player in the world. Turelly, a one-man band, also did paper tearing. Dave Harris was one of the most versatile of the musical acts; he not only could play almost any kind of an instrument, sing very well, but also was a fine song writer. Volant played a swinging piano, and Onaip (piano spelled backwards—and you thought Serutan originated it?) played a piano that went around like a wheel (very fast); the audience couldn't tell how it was done as there were no wires, etc. Wood & Shepherd were real old-timers and were the funniest of all the old comedy blackface musical acts!

We had fine pianists in vaude, like Alaphonese, Zalaya, Eric Zardo, Vilmos Westony (a talented Hungarian), Leon Varvara (a talented American), Dave Schooler (he was great even as a kid), and Arthur Stone, a blind artist and real good. Andre Renaud played two pianos at the same time. There were Erno Rapee, Daisy Nellis, Alexander MacFayden, Tina Lerner, Jack Little (who was real great), Kharum (he said he was Persian), Ismed (he said he was Turkish), and Hershel Hendler, who played for Texas Guinan when she first started and who became a great entertainer in his own right. Now me and Aggie knew the score and didn't let "billing" throw us, but many of the long-hairs that we thought were phonies turned out real important.

When I recall those Turkish and Persian guys, I must tell you about the time we played at the Colonial, New York. There was an Indian, not with feathers or war paint—but just an Indian from over there someplace. Anyway, he was billed like a circus and at rehearsal he was wrapped in cotton like a large sore finger and had an interpreter with him who told the orchestra leader what he wanted, etc. I looked at his act and thought the guy was real great, so when he came off I went to his dressing room to tell him. (You know, actors would rather get a compliment from their brother and sister performers, even if they know it's insincere, than from the public). Well, the interpreter makes a big federal case out of it, tells the guy what I said, he bows to me, shakes hands, but no speaka. Anyway, I goes out the stage door and there's a nice little lady out there who looks at me and sez, with a delightful dialect, "You're han hector?" and I sez, "Yes." Then she sez, "You voiking here?" I again yessed her. "Do you know Hagen Ben Alid?" she sez. (I'm faking the name, so Aggie don't get her sunburst taken away from her.) I again gave her a pleasant yes. "Den pleese tell him dot his sister Sara from the Bronx is vaiting for him." After that I even suspected Mahatma Gandhi!

It wasn't all hokey-pokey in musical vaude; we had top-notch artists on any kind of an instrument you can name except the cymbals and triangle.

We had one of the greatest cornetists in the world, Jules Levi. There were some fine violinists, like Otto Gygi (who was the hit of the Palace opening bill), Manuel Quiroga, Fred Fradkin, Susan Tompkins, Rinaldo, Nonette, Isabella Patricola, the Hegedus Sisters, Jules Saranoff, Countess Le Leonardi, Ross Roma, and don't laugh when I mention Ben Bernie and Jack Benny; those guys could play when they had to, but comedy paid off much better than fiddlin' unless you were a Heifetz, which those two guys certainly weren't!

There were some real good xylophone players like the Four Avalos, Friscoe (Lou Chiha), El Celeve, the Johnsons, El Cota, the Five Musical Spillers (Negroes and great), Lebonati (comedy but real good musician), and of course to me the funniest of 'em all, the Great Lamberti, whose special bit was that while he was playing a strip teaser appeared behind him (unbeknownst to him, of course) and when the audience applauded he thought it was for him (real funny).

Among the fine accordionists was Frosini (one of the first), Diero (Mae West's ex-hubby), his brother Pietro (they both sold thousands of records), Peppino, Marconi Bros., Countess Nardini, Charlie Klass, Santucci, Cervo, and my old pal Phil Baker, the only guy with a left-handed keyboard!

In the high-class field like cellists there were Van Biene (one of the best), Hans Kronold, Elsa Ruegger, Helen Scholder, Alfred Wallenstein, and David Sapperstein. Now don't get me wrong,

Joe, me and Aggie don't know if these guys were good or bad, we didn't go in for that kinda music, neither did most of the audience, because most of us didn't know what this high-brow soft music was about. But they brought in a lot of new customers that would yell "Bravo"—we didn't like 'em because that type guy doesn't go for belly laughs. But we made many a tour with these long-hairs over the Orpheum Circuit (Beck was a pushover for this kind of talent), where sometimes they were a terrific hit and sometimes they flopped good, but at the end of the tour even we liked their music and realized that it was harder to learn than a time step!

There were so many musical acts that they started fighting among themselves about originality for publicity purposes. There were two acts, the Four Musical Cates and Gray & Graham, who spent a lot of dough advertising in the trade papers that they had the largest saxophone in the world and proved it with pictures. Then another act would answer them and say that *they* not only *had* the largest saxophone in the world, but they also *played it!* (The trade papers reaped a harvest with them.) Then via the Actor's Forum, which was a column run by V*ariety* where the actors wrote in their beefs, one act claimed they were the *first* to use a piano *bench* instead of the regulation stool. They were always arguing via the Forum who was the originator of this or that. It made a lot of fun, because other actors would steam 'em up to keep the argument going.

The Hawaiian Trio (Toots Papka) were the first to bring the steel guitar around, and they were a sensation. Everybody on the bill and in the pit tried to find out how the guy got that wonderful tone on a guitar, but he would never tell, until one night an actor got the guy plenty drunkee and out came the secret. He showed him the small piece of steel he held in his hand when playing. That's all, brother! In a few months vaude was lousy with lousy steel-guitar players!

Brass bands were the first real big music in vaude—bands like John S. Eagan's and Arthur Pryor's. Maurice Levi and His Invisible Band played in front of a black drop with side lights (black-magic stuff), and you could hear 'em but not see 'em until the finish; anyway, it was mostly Levi playing his wonderful cornet solos. Creatore & Band of fifty went from vaude to the Hippodrome (formerly National) in Boston with pics and free parking space for customers (that was in 1915 and the first record of a theater giving

parking space). In 1916 the Vaterland Band from the interned ship
of that name played at Loew's. The Germans in the audience
cheered! (We weren't in the war yet.) It was three years later when
Lieut. Jimmy Europe's Band, which made history during the war,
toured all over the country and packed 'em in. He established jazz
on Broadway. He was the leader of the 369th Infantry Band. (He
was fatally stabbed in the neck by a member of the band, Herbert
Wright.)

And of course the tops in bands was John Philip Sousa. Here is
an interesting item about Sousa that you may not know. He had
a rug-covered podium, and when he first used it it was two feet
high, but as the years passed, its height was cut down to make it
easier for him to mount it. It was only five inches high when it was
presented to the University of Illinois Library, at Champaign,
Illinois. He also left the University forty-five trunks of music, and
three thousand band arrangements, many in manuscript form.

Bert Kelly & His Jazz Band started a new craze that was to last
a long time. Kelly is without a doubt the originator of that brand
of entertainment. There were thousands that followed him. Jazz
became so bad that the Pittsburgh Musicians demanded death to
jazz musicians and jazz music. There were amateur jazz-band contests held at Proctor's Fifth Avenue Theatre. There were about
two dozen acts in vaude using their own bands for accompaniment
instead of just having a piano player. It gave prestige to the act and
also got headline billing for some gals that never passed the deuce
spot on a bill before or since!

Henry Santrey & His Band came into the Palace and started a
new trend in band acts. He was the first to put in specialties (Harry
& Ann Seymour) between the orchestra numbers. You just shudder
when you think what he started! Vincent Lopez came along and
started the fine scenery and novelty electrical effects with his music.
Ben Bernie started the comedy idea.

Then along came Paul Whiteman and became tops. He received
$7,500 at the Hippodrome, which was the highest salary ever paid
up to then in vaude; remember, that was in 1925. He turned down
a million-buck guarantee for three years to play pic houses. He
said it would kill his concert tours and maybe somebody else would
step in. He was getting $9,000 a week in pic houses. He was
featured in ads at the Hippodrome with a cartoon of his face (this
cartoon became famous and he is still using it). It was the first

time a solo featuring for a single attraction was done at the Keith-Albee stand. There was even a list of his numbers in the ad. Whiteman made a great recording of "Three O'Clock in the Morning" which sold three million copies and he only got $75 for recording it. Why? Because he didn't get royalties. His "Wonderful One" recording got Mickey Neiland about eighteen grand and Paul nothing (same biz deal). Paul has learned a hell of a lot since then.

There were a number of really great orchestras (or bands, as we called them) that did swell in big-time vaude. Check your memory for these: A & P Gypsies (a string orchestra), Ben Bernie's bunch (with Oscar Levant at the piano), Don Bestor, Jimmy Carr, Joe Fejer & His Hungarian Orchestra, Eddie Elkins, Mal Hallett, Isham Jones, Ted Lewis, Abe Lyman, Art Landry, Harry Stoddard, Will Vodery, J. Rosamond Johnson, Ted Weems, Aaronson's Commanders, Dixieland Jazz Band, House of David, Kay Kyser, Guy Lombardo, George Olsen, Original Memphis Five, Will Osborn, Don Vorhees, and so many many more that made beautiful music. Otto Kahn's son Roger was first billed as Roger Wolfe's Orchestra, later billed under his full name, Roger Wolfe Kahn. He made his debut at the Knickerbocker Hotel. Paul Specht was the first modern dance band to make an appearance in vaude circuit as an attraction by itself. He was also the first to advertise catch phrases like "Rhythmic Symphonic Syncopation"—also first to send a modern dance orchestra (the Criterions) to Europe. Bob Bennett's Frisco Syncopators was the first singing band and first to use airplanes for transportation from London to Paris.

The guy who started all the dance bands, Art Hickman, only played a few vaude dates. He was the first to hit the East with modern dance music in jazz tempo, and the first to do the pull-out whistle. (Later he became VP of the St. Francis Hotel in Frisco.) Fred Waring's Pennsylvanians appeared for the first time in New York at the Strand about 1924. They practically started the autograph craze, when full-socked dames waited at the stage door for the collegians. Here is one of the real great band organizations in the country. They proved it by becoming tops in TV, which proves my old man's saying, "Quality is always in style."

There were over sixty well-known bands in vaude. That was 1925, the same year that the Marlboro, Massachusetts, public schools had fifty harmonica orchestras and there were twenty million harmonicas sold, and the uke was making a terrific comeback (like Arthur Godfrey made it come back now, after almost a quarter of a century). Bob Williams, a Negro, was the pioneer of the uke players; he taught the great Ukulele Ike. Borrah Minevitch with thirty-two kids playing harmonicas asked $3,000 to play pic houses. (He got that much and more later with just half a dozen kids.) He had the first professionally organized harmonica troupe. He got the kids through contests in theaters he played. Larry Adler without a doubt is the greatest of all harmonica artists!

Telling you about the regular bands, I almost forgot to tell you about the real comedy bands. (There has never been a "craze" in vaude that wasn't cashed in on by the comedians.) Frank & Milt Britton were one of the first and were the forerunners of Spike Jones (very clever) by many years. There were Charles Ahearn's Millionaire Band (all tramps) and Wynducjer, who did impersonations of great leaders and shaved a guy while leading his band. Al Tucker had a swell comedy band, and Dave Apollon with his Filipinos were real funny, but to me and Aggie, Jimmy Duffy's satire on class bands was the greatest; he called it "Jimmy Duffy's Mills Hotel Society Band"! (Mills Hotel, in case you don't know, is a flophouse for guys who have no peck-and-pad dough.)

Another thing I want to tell you about bands is that the "band craze" hit vaudeville a terrible wallop when they kept pouring bands into every bill. It got so that they put the pit orchestras on the stage to play the show (à la presentation houses—which to old vaudegoers was like operating on a guy and then giving him the ether). They dressed the pit orchestras in monkey suits, the nice flute and bass players became comics (they thought), everybody was trying to get laughs, but it just didn't work. The public got sick of the bands and about 1945 there were a lot of bands, but no dates for them. Many of the would-be comics went back to the pit and played for scale. It did develop a few, a very few, fair comics and singers, but it disappointed hundreds of others (who got neighborhood laughs and thought they were real).

I forgot to tell you about the great comedy piano players in vaude. Will H. Fox was the first. He did a take-off of Ignace Paderewski, the famous Polish pianist, and billed himself as "The Padawhiskey of the Piano"—a real funny man. Tom Waters and George Sweet started around this time too and were funny men at the keyboard. The comedy piano players all had about the same routines. They would play "Dixie" with the left hand and "Yankee

Doodle" with the right hand, or show how popular songs would sound if written by different composers. An imitation of a fife and drum corps always was good for a hand. One-hand playing was also a sure hit. Jimmy Conlin started playing while standing on his head. Chico Marx (Four Marx Bros.) had an original style of shooting into the keys with his finger. Herb Williams was the funniest of them all with his trick piano that served beer, housed chickens, etc.

I purposely didn't mention the dancing violinists. They had the orchestras play double forte so it would drown out their lousy playing. Did you ever hear one of those dancing fiddlers with just a piano in the pit? *Wow!*

But to come back to the bands, me and Aggie still claim that it was the bands that helped play vaudeville out. SEZ

Your pal,
LEFTY

Assorted Chirpers

Dear Joe,

Singing, like dancing, was the foundation of honky-tonks, variety, and vaudeville, and, when you come right down to it, of almost all entertainment! We had thousands of singing acts in vaude. Single men, single women, doubles, trios, quartettes, double quartettes, sextettes, and big glee clubs like the Meistersingers. I wrote you about the pop singers and serio-comic singers, so I'll tell you now about the straight singers, guys and gals who depended on their throats for a living, who when they couldn't hit a high note couldn't take a prat fall to cover it up.

One of the sure-fire singing acts was the old-fashioned quartette! I mean the close-harmony singers, the barbershop chorders, who used no microphones. There were two kinds of quartettes. The straight singing quartette would come out in regular street clothes (or tuxes), usually all dressed alike, and belch out ballads and pop songs and sometimes even a hunk of opera. The tenor would usually sing "When Irish Eyes Are Smiling," the bass would contribute "Down in the Coal Mine" or "Asleep in the Deep," the lead would usually sing a pop song, the baritone would render a mother song, and they all would finish with a yodel to imitation banjo and calliope accompaniment.

But it was the comedy quartettes that really wowed 'em. They all had about the same pattern. The straight man wore a straw hat or derby, stock tie, street suit, and of course carried gloves. Then there was the "sissy boy," with a large red bow tie (red was the sissy color) and a felt hat with the brim turned up in front. Of course the number one comic was a Hebrew or a Dutchman, and the fourth man (usually the bass) was a tramp or a "bum legit," with busted high hat and coat trimmed with near fur; sometimes this was switched to a "tough guy" wearing a cap, a turtle-necked sweater, and a black eye. These comedy quartettes sold rough comedy, hoke, hitting each other with newspapers and bladders and salving the wounds with close harmony.

There were some great real old-time quartettes, but I want to mention the ones of our time, because the standard chirpers were plenty good in their own right. The Bison City Quartette lasted the longest, remaining together from 1891 to 1931 with just a few changes in the personnel. The original four were Gerard, Pike, Hughes, and Cook. Milo joined in the early days and remained until the finish, as did Roscoe. They were a lot of fun. The famous Avon Comedy Four started around 1900, with Joe Smith, Charlie Dale, John Coleman, and Will Lester. When they first started, Dale did the Hebe and Smith did the tough guy; later Joe did the Hebe (and a great characterization) and Charlie did Dutch (nobody better). The other half of the four changed many times. Jack Godwin was an early replacement and stayed with the quartette many years; then great singers like Eddie Miller, Irving Kaufman, Frank Corbett, Mario, and Lazar all joined the company at different times. Smith and Dale split the quartette about ten years ago and did a two act (as they did when they first started) and today are the oldest team in show biz, together fifty-three years (but only ten years as a team). The Avon Comedy Four's "School Act," "The Hungarian Rhapsody," and especially their "Dr.

Kronkheit" will long be remembered. (More about them in the two-man acts.)

Who will ever forget the great Empire City Quartette (Harry Cooper, his brother Irving, Tally, and Harry Mayo)? Harry did a Hebe comic, no make-up except for an oversized derby which he kept tipping through the act to imaginary women in the audience, saying, "How's the Mommeh?" which became one of the first catch lines in vaude (years before "Do you wanna buy a duck?" and "Vass you dare, Sharlie?"). The boys had grand voices besides making 'em laugh.

The Empire Comedy Four (Cunningham, Leonard, Jenny, and Roland) were a standard comedy quartette, as were the Arlington Comedy Four (Lee, Roberts, Lane, and Manny). Roberts was a Negro, and I believe this is the first time a Negro was in a white vaude act (outside of pickaninnies). The Manhattan Comedy Four had Sam Curtis, and Al Shean (later Gallagher & Shean, and the uncle of the Four Marx Bros.). The Bootblack Comedy Four (Weber, Hayes, Elliot, and Adams), the Orpheus Four (Figg, Huffer, Hannand, and Ford), the New York Newsboys' Quartette (who were all Philadelphians, Roland, Killion, McLosker, and Dugan)—these were just a few of the many that were tops.

Of the straight and great singing quartettes there were THAT Quartette (Sylvester, Pringle, Jones and Morrell), one of the best, fine soloists and terrific harmony, and THE Quartette (Webb, Corbett, Campbell, and Scanlon; later Geoffrey O'Hara and Roberts were part of this outfit). The Big City Four did opera and ragtime. The Primrose Four were billed as "1,000 Pounds of Harmony"; each man weighed over 250 pounds and could do away with half a keg of beer at a sitting (and did). These were all tops. There were many more. Me and Aggie made a list of over three hundred quartettes. Many of them billed themselves as "the So and So Four" (like Quaker City Four), and there was one act called "Worth While Waiting Four!"

There were more male groups, but there were a few female quartettes that are worth mentioning. The Four Haley Sisters, one of the first (Grace, Bernice, Mabel, and Lucille), the Four Cook Sisters. THIS Quartette (a name copy of THAT male quartette), then another gal outfit called themselves THAT OTHER Quartette (get the angle?), A-B-C-D Quartette (later changed to the Connoly Sisters), the Swedish American Quartette, the Military

Girls' Quartette, the Four Rubini Sisters (also played instruments), and a few more.

Me and Aggie made another list of quartettes amounting to over a hundred that billed themselves as "Fours," like the Big City Four, and a hundred or more that billed themselves as "Quartettes," like the Clipper Quartette. But it's too tough to type out all those names; it would read like a directory. There were quartettes that tried to get away from that kind of billing, like "Nights with the Poets," Four Messenger Boys, "Night at the Club," Four Buttercups (all did tramps), Four Entertainers, Yacht Club Boys, who introduced special lyrics into quartettes . . . and "Memories," a quartette consisting of a doctor, banker, artist, and minister.

There were "double quartettes," like the Old Homestead Double Quartette, which included Fred Wykoff, Chauncey Olcott, and Dick Jose, who later became stars. Spook Minstrels were also a double quartette. You just can't stop four guys from singing harmony and near harmony. There is a national organization of amateur quartettes that runs into a membership of many thousands, the Society for the Preservation and Encouragement of Barbershop Singing.

Now I come to the single chirpers, whose field was as crowded as the Singer Midgets in a tiny elevator. Not the great single women that sang pop songs or were serio-comics, but the straight singers who depended more on their voices than their "catch lines" —guys and gals who stepped out with good voices, maybe with a piano accompanist. It was pretty tough for singers, who depended on proper musical accompaniment, to go from town to town trying to sing with an orchestra composed of guys who couldn't read anything but scales (and there were plenty of them). I'll never forget the gal who said to the small-town violinist at rehearsal, "You are not a musician. What is your regular job?" And the guy with the well-rosined bow looked up and said, "No. I'm the town undertaker, but I play to have fun!"

But Big Time can boast of many great singers in whose throats nightingales built their nests. When they got a bit rusty they went to the small time, where the audience wrapped 'em in their hearts, because they came to them with big reps, and they figured they were tops at pop prices. They never heard the "rust" in their voices; all they knew was that it was loud and at cheap prices. The small time used "tired voices" like the Smiling Irishman sold tired cars!

There were many great operatic voices on big and small time, sopranos, contraltos, tenors, baritones, basses, and intermediates. The regular vaude fans didn't go much for the high C's! But these acts made many a vaude fan out of opera lovers who started out as slummers and ended up as steady customers.

Me and Aggie liked pop singers much better, but figured these guys and gals with studied throats gave vaude a sort of high-toned touch. When we first met them, we figured they'd pull an "aria" on us, but when you got under their scales, they were regs. You know, that's why me and Aggie liked vaudeville, for we met all kinds of people from all lines of show biz and we didn't resent 'em if they had talent. They were just as jealous of our getting laughs as we were of their great voices. We each wondered "how they do it?" That was the swell part of vaudeville. Anybody could get in it from a guy who could do a time step to a gal who could reach high C!

There were a lot of Metropolitan Opera stars who exercised their tonsils in vaudeville! Grace Cameron was the first to leave opera for vaude. Aldrich, Cicolini, Calvé, and Gasparrio were others. There were also Jenny DuFau, Vinie Daly, Suzanne Adams, Fritzi Scheff (who was a vaude headliner and favorite for many years), Seli De Lussan, Josephine Dunfe (prima donna of Gilbert & Sullivan shows), Henry Scotti (one of the greatest), Herman Bisphan (who explained every song), Anna Fitzu, Nanette Guilford, Adelaide Norwood, and Madame Schumann-Heink. Vaude in return gave opera Mme. Marguerite Sylvia, who worked in vaude in 1894 for $100 a week and in 1910 was at the Met! There were Dorothy Jardon, Rosa Ponselle (one of the greatest Carmens) who did a vaude act with her talented sister Carmella, also later with the Met (both discovered by our mutual agent Gene Hughes), John Charles Thomas, Orville Harold, and Chief Capolican (an East Side Indian), who all went to opera from vaude.

An odd engagement for an opera singer occurred in 1893 when F. F. Proctor engaged Campanini, a great star in those days, to sing in the lobby of his Twenty-third Street Theater. Proctor's idea was, "When they hear such singing in the lobby for free, you can imagine what they must think is on the inside!"

We had a lot of fine singers in vaude from musical comedy and operetta, like Vera Michelina, Lina Arbarbenell, Craig Campbell, Robert Chisolm, Juliet Dika, David Dugan (a Scotch tenor), Jue

Fong (a Chinese tenor), Mlle. Fregoleska (a Rumanian nightin-
gale), Harnko Onkui (a Jap prima donna), Princess Lei Lani
(billed as the McCormack of Hawaii), Sirota (the Jewish cantor
of Warsaw), Cantor Rosenblatt (a small man with a large red
beard who sang "When Irish Eyes Are Smiling" for a finish),
George Dufranne (a French tenor), George Dewey Washington
(a great Negro singer), and Sissieretta Jones (better known as the
Black Patti). They didn't look down your throat for your color,
race, or creed in vaude.

Names come pouring from my memory of our fine singers—
Grace Fisher, Alice Gentle, Lora Hoffman, Eddie Miller, Grace
Nelson, Yvette Rugel, Lillian Russell, Olga Steck, John Steel,
Irving Fisher, Belle Story, Sybil Vane (billed as the Galli-Curci of
vaude), Estelle Wentworth, Marion Weeks, Manuel Romaine,
Lee Tung Foo (who sang in Chinese, Irish, and German), Harry
Mayo (of the famous Empire City Quartette), Muriel Window,
Madame Flowers (who was known way back in 1898 as the Bronze
Melba), Jack Allman, Charles Purcell, Allan Rogers, Ruby Norton,
Charlie Hart, and Olga Cook.

Irish tenors were sure-fire hits. There were Andrew Mack,
Thomas Eagan, John McCloskey, Joe Regan, Stephen O'Rourke,
Tom Burke, Gerald Griffin, Walter McNally, James Dougherty,
Joseph Griffin, John Fogarty, and the one and only Chauncey
Olcott! John McCormack was offered a vaude route, but he asked
for $25,000 a week, figuring on the basis of fourteen concert dates.
He didn't get it. Irish tenors had three musts on their program,
"When Irish Eyes Are Smiling," "They Called It Ireland," and
"Irish Mother O' Mine."

We had many singing doubles and trios, some who accompanied
themselves with instruments (mostly piano): the Three Brox
Sisters, the Three Dolce Sisters, Hahn, Wells & O'Donell (three
big voices), the Imperial Chinese Trio (a baritone accompanied
by string instruments), Keller Sisters & Lynch (one of the very first
to do modern harmony singing), Alexander & Lightner Sisters
(Winnie Lightner later was a big hit in pics), Sylvester, Jones &
Pringle (terrific voices). There were dozens of Italian operatic singing acts; nearly all of them would sing "Chirabeerabee"; in fact,
the bookers would describe them as "a bunch of Chirabeerabees."

The 1900s brought in a new craze in vaude, "The Rathskeller
Act," usually consisting of three men, a hot piano player and two

hot singers. They came from night clubs and cafés. They were full of pep, singing fast songs, with maybe a little clowning between numbers. They seldom used ballads, as they were too slow. The fast tempo of these acts would wake up any kind of an audience and get plenty of applause. Even the poor ones were hits. They pepped up vaude bills for about ten years and then gradually died out. Some trios broke up and became teams or singles. Some of the best of that type act were Sherman, Van & Hyman (later Tierney); Stepp, Mehlinger & King; Vardon, Perry & Wilbur; Stepp, Allman & King; Corbett, Shepherd & Donovan; Adler, Weill & Herman; Biglow, Campbell & Hayden; Dunham, Edwards & Farrell; Green, McHenry & Dean; Hurst, Watts & Hurst; Hedges Bros. & Jacobson; Hayden, Borden & Hayden; Medlin, Watts & Towns; Miller, Moore & Gardner; Sharkey, Geisler & Lewis (that was Ted Lewis); Taylor, Kranzman & White; Three White Kuhns; Weber, Beck & Frazer; Weston, Carrol & Fields; Yacht Club Boys (Billy Mann, Jimmy Kern, George Kelly, and Charlie Adler) and the one and only and greatest of them all, Clayton, Jackson & Durante! What a trio!

Among the great two-men singing acts were Rome & Dunn, Healey & Cross, Freeman & Dunham, Cross & Dunn, and the best of all two-men singing acts in show biz, Gus Van & Joe Schenck (Gus today is still one of our greatest dialect singers).

There were a few straight singing mixed acts, but many of them became better known when they put in talk and dancing, so I will write about them some other time. Among the greatest chirp teams were Whiting & Burt; and Joe E. Howard with his many wife-partners, Howard & Ida Emerson, Mabel Barrison, Mabel McCane, and Ethelyn Clark. But I'm sure nobody's gonna get mad at me and Aggie when we say the greatest man and woman singing act was Nora Bayes and Jack Norworth. Nobody has ever touched them as to class, diction, looks, harmony, and showmanship!

These were all honest singers, no microphones. It's a shame that the recordings of many of these fine voices don't do them justice, because the recording business in those days wasn't what it is today, and most of the records sound tinny.

But we that heard them in person have wonderful ear memories. SEZ

Your pal,

LEFTY

The Two-man Act

Dear Joe,

Out of the hundreds of two-man acts that paraded from the honky-tonks to the Palace, there are less than a half a dozen who are still active! Olsen & Johnson, Shaw & Lee, Arthur & Puggy Havel, Glenn & Jenkins, and Smith & Dale.

From the beginning of old variety up to the near peak of vaude, the two-man "talking" act was usually the comedy standout of the bill before the mixed comedy teams took over. I'm talking about the two-man acts that depended on talking routines and maybe used song, dance, or parody for insurance. There were many that did some talking, but really depended on their singing, dancing, and even acrobatics for results.

The original two-man acts were in blackface, and really tried to portray the Negro in looks and dialect. They later worked as blackface comic and white straight man. The next teams to win favor were double Irish, with exaggerated make-ups; later they too began working as straight man and Irish comic. Then came the double Dutch acts (they called the German acts Dutch); they too followed the trend. There were very few double Hebrew two-man acts; usually it was a straight man with a Hebrew comic.

You will notice that the comic characters followed the pattern of our immigration. The last character two-man acts were Italian (Clark & Verdi were the first to do this, with Clark doing the straight, but in Italian dialect). And let me tell you right now that in early variety and vaude nobody took exception to the billings of the different character acts, like "The Sport and the Jew," "Irish by Name but Coons by Birth," "The Mick and the Policeman," "The Merry Wop," "Two Funny Sauerkrauts." It was taken in good humor by the audience, because that is what everyone called each other in everyday life. There were no pressure groups and no third generation to feel ashamed of immigrant origins. So when I use the original billings, don't blame me; blame your fathers and grandfathers.

But the two-man act took on a different pattern as immigration died down, and the old-time comic stage characters "cleaned up" (as did the characters in real life). The comic became an "eccentric character," which meant anything, a guy with a funny make-up, baggy pants, big shoes, etc., anything to make sure the audience knew he was the comedian. Toward the last days of vaude, the comic would just use a funny hat to make him look different than the straight man.

Most of the old-time two-man acts had belly-laugh material. Their comedy was broad, physical, and rowdy. They could use gags that the mixed act couldn't use. They could get bigger laughs than the average single act, because they could feed each other and so build up the gags. In early acts the material consisted of what me and Aggie call "knick-knacks"—song and dance, cross-fire talk of unconnected gags, playing musical instruments, and acrobatics. They put everything they knew into their acts. Ninety-five per cent of them were Irish; later the Germans, Hebrews, and Italians came along; and still later the children of all of them, Americans, took over.

In the early 1900s the style of the two-man act changed from the kick-in-the-belly and spit-out-the-beans type to more rational stuff. Instead of both members of the team dressing funny, a distinct line was drawn between the comic and straight man. I always liked the old gag that's been circulating among show folk for many years. It's about the vaude actor waiting in the wings watching the first show, and he sees a fellow "artist" made up with a red nose, blue wig, green make-up, teeth blacked out, baggy pants, funny hat, loud vest, slap shoes, large checkered coat, and a big heavy watch chain. Turning to the stage manager the actor sez, "By the looks of that guy, he must be a very funny comedian." And the stage manager, very surprised, whispers, "Why, that's the *straight man!*"

But as I said, in the early 1900s they kinda changed. The straight man began to dress in street clothes, if you can call a flashy suit, gray derby, two-toned button shoes, and stock tie "street clothes!" The comic would wear "funny" misfit suits, etc., so you couldn't mistake him being the comic. And, most important, instead of catch-as-catch-can gags, which the straight man would lead into with "By the by, what happened to you at ———?" they now started to use regular routines and stick to one subject; a few of them even had thin plots, like Howard & North in "Those Were the Happy Days" and "Back to Wellington" (they were the first team to do this type act). They began to depend more on good routines than on funny clothes and mugging. Some even started to cut out parodies (which were the insurance of most of the two-man acts), and some were even brave enough to walk off on a gag. These were very few, because a "big finish" still meant a lot to the bookers. A parody was sure-fire, especially one that had double entendre.

The straight man or "feeder" was never really given enough credit by audiences, although actors recognized his great contribution to the comic. He was as important as the comic to the success of the act. A good straight man could make a fair comic look good and a great comic look better! A good straight man had to make a good appearance, dress well, have sex appeal, and have a good speaking and singing voice. They were usually fairly well-educated guys who had a good vocabulary (for an actor) and handled the business for the act. The comic just had to be funny and was the mixer of the team.

The best straight men in vaude were Ed Gallagher (Gallagher & Shean), George LeMaire (Conroy & LeMaire), Jay Brennan (Savoy & Brennan), George Walker (Williams & Walker), Frank Batie (with Jack Wilson), Dan Quinland (Quinland & Mack), Harry Klien (Klien Bros.), Joe Brady (Brady & Mahoney), Ed Smith (Smith & Campbell), Val Stanton (Val & Ernie Stanton), Paul McCullough (Clark & McCullough), Jack Lewis (Wynn & Lewis), Al Lee (Cantor & Lee), Al Lloyd (Aveling & Lloyd), Joe Wilton (Wilton & Weber), and more too numerous to mention.

The two-man acts were a temperamental lot and would often change partners. Of course, like in theatrical marriages, there were a number of them that stayed together for many years. Teams like Fox & Ward (together sixty years), McIntyre & Heath (sixty-three years together), and Smith & Dale (together for fifty-three years but only ten years as a two-man act). Others who stuck together for many years and were rated as solid two-man acts were Kenny & Hollis, Weber & Fields, Hoey & Lee, Kennedy & Platt, Klien Bros., Roger Bros., Willie & Eugene Howard, Lewis & Dody, Miller & Lyles, Cole & Johnson, Moss & Frye, Hawthorne & Cook, Raymond & Cavalry, Otto Bros., Howard & North, Wilson Bros., Friend & Downing, Brady & Mahoney, and many more. Many of them, on the death of one partner, never repartnered, like Bobby Clark, Bert Williams, Al Klien, etc.

Among the many that changed partners for one reason or another were Mr. Gallagher & Mr. Shean, originally in burly together; then it was Shean & Warren, Shean & James Carson, and Gallagher & Barrett. Ed Wynn had a lot of straight men; in 1907 it was Wynn & Jack Lewis, 1909—Wynn & Al Lee, 1910—Wynn & Pat O'Malley Jennings, 1911—Wynn & Russen (who played an English fop); then Wynn went into musical comedy and didn't need any more straight men. Jack Lewis later did straight for Bill Halligan. James J. Corbett was one of the best straight men in the business; he had authority, background, and personality. He "scolded" many a comic. He was teamed for a few seasons each with Billy B. Van, Frank Tinney, Jack Norton (who has made such a big hit on TV as a drunk), Neil O'Brien (the great minstrel), and Bobby Barry (of the famous Barry family). George LeMaire (Conroy & LeMaire) started with his brother Mooney, and also worked with Joe Phillips and Eddie Cantor. In the team of Russ Brown and Jim Fallon, Russ was a great straight man, but he turned comic in some acts, and worked with straight man Harold Whalen. There was a guy called Tony Pearl (a swell performer) who had a new partner nearly every week—Pearl & Tommy Meade (the jockey), Pearl & Dan Hyatt, Pearl & Charlie Diamond, Pearl & Yosco, Pearl & Matt Keefe, and many, many more. Charlie Mack, who originally started with Bert Swor as Swor and Mack, changed to Moran & Mack, and then had so many partners that he patented the name of Moran & Mack (the Two Black Crows) and used different partners under the same trade name; even Bert Swor, his original partner, worked in pictures with Mack under the name of "Moran."

There were many things that contributed to the breaking up of a two-man partnership. Two of the main reasons were woman trouble and the bottle. If one of the partners was married or courting or on the make, the other partner might feel it was only a matter of time before he would split the combination and put in the wife or sweetheart and have the dough all going in one pocket. The bottle broke up many an act, when one or sometimes both partners would start using the "nose paint" too often and too heavily. It was a case of getting a rep of being unreliable, one of the worst raps in show biz, because now vaude was out of the honky-tonk and variety era and was in the big-money class. Many a performer in the old days had a rep with stag audiences as a drinking man, who seemed to be funnier on the stage when half-lit, and the audience would be disappointed when he came on sober. You must remember that before the shows became "family style" the audience drank, the stagehands, musicians, and managers all drank, so everybody met each other on an even basis, and the drunk on the stage wasn't noticed very much. I'll tell you about the terrific "staggering talent" some other time.

Many successful two-man acts stuck together for many years by not chumming with each other. Some carried on a "yes-and-no" partnership off stage; they just spoke when they had to discuss business. They wouldn't live in the same hotel or eat in the same restaurants if they could help it. McIntyre & Heath didn't speak to each other off stage for years, Montgomery & Stone carried on a "yes-and-no" friendship and weren't mad at each other, but Fred Stone was a family man while Dave was a great mixer with the gang. The Russell Brothers (the famous Irish Servant Girls) never spoke to each other unless it was absolutely necessary (and they were actually brothers). These are only a few of a long list.

To offset the no-mix teams, there were many that were inseparable on and off stage. Aveling & Lloyd, Tom & Fred McNaughton, Arthur & Puggy Havel, Wilson Bros., Olsen & Johnson, Kaufman Bros., Raymond & Cavalry, Friend & Downing, Kenny & Hollis, Shaw & Lee, Savoy & Brennan, Fox & Ward, Gene & Willie Howard, Buck & Bubbles, Bill & Gordon Dooley, Otto Bros., Kane & Herman, Duffy & Sweeney, Roger Bros., Mack & Orth, Rockwell & Wood, Claude & Clarence Stroud, Glenn & Jenkins, Miller & Lyles, Weaver Bros., Burns & Kissen, Smith & Dale, Gitz Rice and Hal Ford, and the Klien Bros. are just a few examples of the ones you would always see together.

Sometimes one of the partners (usually the comic) would be offered a part in a musical comedy if he would split up with his partner, but because of loyalty would refuse a great opportunity. Jack Kenny (Kenny & Hollis) is a case in point. I personally know the many chances he had to become a name in musical comedy, but stuck with his partner to the finish. They started in Boston when they were very young; Kenny was a barber while Hollis was a box-office man. They stayed together until they became managers of a New England picture house, and then Hollis passed on. They were together for fifty years.

Other teams split to better themselves, and one or both became
stars. Eddie Cantor split with Al Lee (Cantor & Lee) to go into his
first show, *Canary Cottage*, and later became a star; Al Lee became
the manager of George White's *Scandals* and other big shows.
Willie Howard, after a long partnership with his brother Gene,
went into a show and starred; Gene became Willie's manager. Will
Mahoney of Mahoney Bros. & Daisy (Daisy was a dog) split and
became a headliner. Doc Rockwell, when he split with Al Wood,
took another partner, Al Fox, then went on his own as a headliner.
Jack Pearl split with Ben Bard and became a musical-comedy star.
Phil Baker and Ben Bernie split and both became tops in their own
fields.

The two-man acts were usually a good box-office draw because
the guys were spenders and joiners who belonged to clubs and fraternal organizations, mixed with sporting crowds and the town
businessmen and so built up a following; this usually paid off at the
box office, which naturally fattened up their pay envelopes and
billing!

In the later years of vaude, when the two-man act was dying
down, they looked around for gimmicks to pep up their acts. Many
of them put a wife or sweetheart in the act for just a "bit"—maybe
a flirtation bit; the gal might do a short specialty like a rumba and
maybe add a few bumps for good measure, or even do a song or
dance (if she was talented). This was called putting "class" or
"sex" in the act; audiences were getting tired of just looking at two
men. The booking office, who figured they were getting a bargain,
would add railroad fare for the "extra attraction" to the act's salary
—it made the show look "big"! It got so that when vaude was
suffering with arthritis there were so many stooges in the act that
they should have been billed as "assisted" by the two-man team!

It is unfair not to mention the really great two-man acts that
handed out so many laughs, but if I did, it would take more pages
than are in Congress. But you certainly must find room for guys
like Lydell & Higgins, Morris & Allen, Dave Ross & Nat Bernard,
Orth & Fern, Smith & Campbell, Cole & Snyder, Kolb & Dill, Kane
& Herman, Seed & Austin, Rome & Gault, York & Adams, Adams &
Ghul, Anthony & Rogers, Bixley & Lerner, Carson & Willard, Crane
Bros., Flanagan & Edwards, Kramer & Morton, Burns & Fabrito (remember them? "I think you touch," when the straight man busted
the balloons), Hawthorne & Burt, Bailey & Austin, Al Fields & Dave

Lewis, Hussey & Boyle, Collins & Peterson, Stuart & Lash, Burns & Kissen, Swor & Avery, Waldron Bros., Webb & Burns, Weaver Bros., the original Brutal Bros. (Geo. Cunningham & Fred Bula Grant), who would commit mayhem on each other, and Howard & Shelton, who walked right into radio and TV.

And so the old-time two-man talking act is gone, but the memory lingers on of the comics with baggy pants and big shoes. But what me and Aggie remember most is the straight man, who figured he was a lady killer, the "scolder," as we called 'em, because he scolded the comics with such lines as "I'm ashamed of you—what you did when I introduced you to that lovely lady. . . ." He was a "cuff shooter" (he would pull down his near-clean cuff after each gag). We remember how he would straighten his stock tie, and hit the comic with his gloves (which was more refined than hitting him with a newspaper). And while he was singing his ballad (usually in the middle of the act), he would look around the audience to see what "town gal" he could flirt with or date up. And how he would glance toward the entrance during the act to see how the "single woman" on the bill was taking it! Actors would call the matinee-idol-type straight man "brassiere busters"—because one time a straight man came off and remarked, "Did you hear that noise when I came on? That was brassieres busting." I've met some of these old-time straight men lately, and believe me, they couldn't bust a penny balloon with a hatpin.

No longer do we hear them pan each other to the actors on the bill, saying, "My partner is holding me back." . . . Yep, the old-time two-man act is gone—and so is their hangout—vaudeville! SEZ

Your pal,

LEFTY

She-He's and He-She's

Dear Joe,

Female impersonators started way back in what the professors call the "Greek drama," when women were not allowed to play in public. The same rule was in force during Bill Shakespeare's time, and many actors became famous in those days playing "dame parts."

In America we date the female impersonators from our minstrel shows, which, as you know, had all-male casts (except, of course, the female minstrels which came later). In the blackface after-pieces, the head comic would usually do a "wench." There was always a great wench part in every minstrel show, and nearly all great minstrel comics played a wench at some time in their careers.

The late Francis Wilson (first president of Equity) was one of the first to do a wench in variety as a member of the team of Mackin & Wilson. He was followed by such greats as McIntyre & Heath, Neil O'Brien, Bert Swor, and George "Honey Boy" Evans. George M. Cohan's dad (Jerry) did a wench in one of their early acts.

In the late '80s the top female imps around were Leon (Kelly & Leon), William Henry Rice, Charles Heywood, Lind?, and Harry Le Clair (the latter was the top female imp of that time and was billed as the "Sarah Bernhardt of vaudeville." The old-time imps were built kinda heavy for that line of work; Richard Harlow, George Richards (a fine toe dancer), and Harry Le Clair all weighed over 150 pounds.

There were many female imps in the honky-tonks and wine rooms working the boxes as hostesses and entertainers—never removing their wigs. Many years later during the tab show era in vaude there was a shortage of chorus girls, and a number of male chorus gals were recruited; there were a lot of surprised guys waiting at the stage door for the gal they saw in the show, because "she" would never show up. In 1840 there was a "Miss Smith" who was a top ballerina and was really a man! Not so many years ago Arico Wild, one of the few famous fem imps who is still working, did a dance in the Fokin Ballet.

When Tony Pastor made variety shows an entertainment for women and children, the "bitchy types" toned their routines and make-ups away down to respectability and some became very fine comedians, or should I say comediennes? Many of the early female imps went in for comedy and naturally didn't bother about clothes, make-up, or class. The famous Russell Bros. (John & James) did two Irish biddies; their act was billed "Our Irish Servant Girls" and was the greatest comedy act of all the fem imps of their time. Johnny Russell died in 1925. His son James was an undertaker in

Elmhurst, Long Island. James wrote "Where the River Shannon
Flows" (some others have also claimed to have written it). After
the death of Johnny, Jimmy took Bert Savoy and taught him the
tricks of the craft, and when he retired Bert went with Jay Brennan
and they did an act on the lines of the Russell Bros., but not a
copy; it was modernized. Bert Savoy did a character somewhat like
Russell, only, instead of a biddy, he did an overdressed trollop.
Savoy & Brennan were the tops of all fem imp comedy acts.

George Munroe did a great "Bridget" monologue, telling all
about his "Aunt Bridget." Dave Warfield did a biddy with Weber
& Fields (but never in vaude). Harry Bulger did a blond soubrette
number, Wilkie Bard did a swell old dame (many English comics
did dames in the pantomimes at Christmas—and very funny too),
Charlie Harris did an eccentric woman, Harry Leybourne (Englishman) did a pianologue and changed dresses very fast. J. C. Mack
did one of the funniest German housewives I have ever seen. A few
tried to copy him, but they couldn't even touch the hem of his
apron!

When Keith jacked up vaude standards, the old-time biddies
and wenches gave way to the "classy" female impersonators. Lind?,
"The Male Melba," and Stuart, "The Male Patti," had real fine
voices. The Great Richards was a fine toe dancer and soubrette.
Alvora was another fine toe dancer, as were George East, Allyn
Mann, and Bayes. The female imps did other things than just sing.
Thora and Lydia Dreams were fine ventriloquists, Marnello did a
pianologue, Havania did quick changes and balanced on tables and
chairs. There were a few that went in for big productions, singing
and dancing acts, like Bothwell Brown, who did "Cleopatra" and
"The Plantation Gal," and Cleveland Bonner, who also went in for
big dancing-act productions. They were all fine headliners for years.

Another great headliner in the heydey of vaude was the late
Karyl Norman, who as "The Creole Fashion Plate" made up as a
"high-yaller" gal and was great. In 1925 he received a sixty-week
route from the Orpheum Circuit, the longest route ever issued on
that circuit. He played at least two weeks in each house, four in
Frisco, five in Chicago, three in St. Louis, and full weeks in
Orpheum Juniors, changing his act when playing two or more
weeks in a house. He was the only one that ever did this, not only
among the female imps, but of any kind of act.

There were many more fine artists, like McGarvey, Vardman,

Taciano, Max Waldron, Eugene Pippin, Archie Guerine (a Chicago lawyer), Saona, Russell Bingham, Herbert Charles, Bisceaux, Divine Dodson, Love & Haight, Yarick & Yolanda, and Jackie May.

Those who went in for comedy were Malcolm Scott (an Englishman), Francis, who did an eccentric woman, as did Olin Landick, who talked about his "Cousin Cassey" and made a big hit on radio. Alfred Letine was swell, but the tops of all the single comedy fem imps were James Watts, Bert Errol, and Herbert Clifton!

The comedy teams where one did straight while the other did a comedy dame were of course headed by the incomparable Bert Savoy & Jay Brennan (later Brennan & Rogers—and even Lou Holtz did straight for Jay when he took over the comedy end of the act). Bert Savoy was killed by lightning while walking with Jack Haley at Long Beach. (When the great wit William Collier heard about this, he said, "I hear that all the female impersonators are now carrying lightning rods.") McIntyre & Heath in their skit, "Waiting at the Church," did a real funny wench bride. Yates & Wheeler were also a good comedy team. Many two-man acts would use a comedy burlesque dame for a "yok" finish, but were not fem imps in the true sense of the word. Among these were Bedini & Arthur, Jack Wilson, Bixley & Lerner, George Lyons & Eddie Parks, Miller & Mack, Dale & Boyle, Bowman Bros., Alexander & Scott (Scott really did a beautiful high yaller), and even George Jessel put on a skirt for a finish once! It was all sure-fire stuff.

There were a number of "trick" female impersonators in vaude. Ray Monde came on as a woman, at the finish of the act he removed his wig and showed that he was a man, then for an encore he removed another wig and showed long beautiful hair like a woman's. The audience was left guessing. Fagg & White, a man and woman act, with the man doing the "woman," did a switch on Ray Monde—he would take off one wig to show he was a woman, then take off another one to show he was a man . . . Some switch, eh? Did you know that the wonderful dancing act, the Mosconi Bros., started their dancing careers with Charlie doing a "dame" partner in a waltz number with his brother Louis? (If you want a punch in the nose, mention this to Charlie.) The late Lew Lehr (of "Monkeys are the cwaziest people" fame) did a burlesque gal in his vaude act. The straight act of the Musical Berrens had one of the boys doing a gal for no reason at all. In many acrobatic troupes there were one or two of the boys made up as gals, to make the tricks look harder or to remove the "too many men" curse for booking purposes. These people never took off their wigs.

The majority of the fem imps went in for real impersonation, fooling (or trying to fool) the audience with their wonderful make-up, clothes, demeanor, voice, and mannerisms. In the majority of cases the audience would never know or even guess it wasn't a woman until at the end of the act "she" would remove her wig to a big Ahh! from the audience (those who had never seen it before). He would thank the audience in a deep bass voice, stick out his chest, and walk off stage real mannish. These fem imps had a great draw at the box office. Women would come in to see them not so much for their talent as for the clothes and millinery they wore, to copy their really "advanced" styles.

Many of these guys had wives and families. Those who carried dressers to help them with their many changes would have women dressers. Funny? It was necessary in order to have the "woman touch" in their dressing, and also for the mending and sewing of new costumes. Some carried their wives for this job and a few even had their mothers dress them. The real good female imps were certainly not to be classed with "freak acts," because they had talent, fine voices, a sense of humor, and were good dancers and experts in the art of make-up. Many of them started via "college shows" where they played the parts of dames. After World War I there were plenty of fem imps in vaude. Service acts were partly responsible. At a Middle Western naval station during the war, a call was issued for volunteers for "chorus girls" for the show they were putting on . . . 125 responded.

Even if you're a kid, you must have heard your dad or mom talk about the late and great Julian Eltinge, the greatest of all female impersonators past, present—and even future! His make-up, wardrobe, dancing, artistic ability, and songs were never offensive. It was true art. He was one of the very few, in fact the only one me and Aggie ever knew, who made (and lost) fortunes as a female impersonator. He headlined for years in vaude, became a star on Broadway and in pictures, and traveled with his own show all over the world. Eltinge was the only female imp (or any other kind of an imp) that had a theater named after him. Al Woods renamed the old Chandler on West Forty-second Street the Eltinge Theatre (now an office building).

One of the reasons for Eltinge's great success (besides his talent) was a press stunt that was pulled when he first went into vaude after leaving college. It set him right with the public, who were a bit suspicious of female impersonators (especially the men in the audience). He was presold as a real honest he-man by a staged rough-and-tumble fight in a Forty-second Street and Ninth Avenue saloon, where he cleaned out the joint of tough characters because someone made a remark about female impersonators being "nances." The papers gave it plenty of front-paging. It was the first time that a fem imp had hit anyone instead of scratching 'em. The papers told what a great boxer Eltinge was in college, and that meant that he was a real man (anyone who could box or fight in those days was a real man). This publicity followed him wherever he went and kept him from being heckled throughout his career, because the average heckler is afraid of a punch in the nose! Eltinge was a well-educated gentleman and fine company, and actors liked him a lot. To have seen Eltinge (who was a pretty heavy guy) in a woman's bathing suit, evening gown, as the "Brinkley Girl," doing his "Incense Dance," or hearing him sing in his low sweet voice was something to remember as long as you lived. He was real talent, which he proved when he broke box-office records in vaude and pic houses.

Me and Aggie were thinking that since Etienne Giradot put on skirts in *Charley's Aunt* (over fifty years ago), many guys have followed suit, like Syd Chaplin in silent pics, Jack Benny in talkies, Jose Ferrer on the stage, and Ray Bolger in the musical comedy version. It must be fun putting on "drag" for that kind of dough!

When vaude died, the female imps went back to the equivalent of the honky-tonks where they started. They worked in New York's Greenwich Village joints, and a few "odd spots" around the country where the law winked. Of all the great female impersonators of two-a-day vaude, there is only one left, Frances Renault. Although he is now in another business and doing very well, he stages an annual recital at Carnegie Hall, where many of his old-time vaude friends appear with him as a sort of get-together. It gives Frances a chance to get the moth-ball smell out of his famous feathered wardrobe (he was known in vaude for his fine aigrettes, ostrich plumes, etc.). He had a pic in *Variety* showing him with Harry Bright (a fighter, who was a featherweight contender); the pic showed Bright on the canvas taking the count, and underneath it said, "Nothing ladylike about this." A page out of Eltinge's book, but it didn't work as well. Some of the many fem imps of vaude became famous designers, milliners, dressmakers, hairdressers, and some went to Hollywood where they are doing very well. Me and Aggie never heard of 'em going back to blacksmithing, but after all we are living in an automobile age!

They were nice guys, those "dames"!

And now for the He-She's!

The male impersonators didn't have any reason to "break out," like the fem imps did! With them it was just a case of trying to be a little different and add novelty to their performances. In England they had gals play "boy" parts long before us, in their Christmas pantomimes. We had sort of male impersonators in burlesque, if you can call a gal that appeared in a man's jacket and tights a male imp. These parts were usually played by the leading ladies as an excuse to show off their gams, and the majority of them had good excuses!

It was in the early '90s that the male imps really started to give an honest impersonation. The gals with the fine shapes naturally showed off men's clothes in a way that no man ever could. They looked like men would have loved to look, as to the fit of their clothes—but in spite of it, most of the male imps looked like women. There was a gal by the name of Lillie Western who did a musical act in the '90s dressed as a man. It was a kind of novelty. She played all kinds of instruments, and played 'em like a woman dressed in men's clothes. So what? Ella Wesner sang English music-hall ditties and did monologues, and was headlined on Tony Pastor's first show. She did one routine about falling asleep in a barbershop, another of a drunk—and very clever. Kitty Bingham, who dressed in evening clothes, also did music-hall songs copied from the English. In the '90s there were also Georgia Marsh, Louise Elliott, and Vivian Wood, who were all very good.

But it took a little English gal by the name of Vesta Tilley to really get the American audiences off their nut about male impersonators. When she sang "Dear Boy, Ta Ta," "Only a Chappie," and "The Eton Boy," you just felt like going up on the stage and kissing her (of course knowing all the time she was a gal). She was the Julian Eltinge of the male impersonators! Her hit in America opened up the gates to all the other male imps. The men's tailor shops were jammed with "wanna-be Tilleys." Men ordered the exact copies of Vesta Tilley's clothes, and wondered why they didn't fit them like they fit Tilley. There was another gal, Claire Romaine, billed as "London's Pet Boy," who was very good; she was sort of an American relation, because she was the stepsister of Dorothy Russell, her father, Ted Solomon, being Lillian Russell's first hubby!

To pay back England for Vesta Tilley, we sent a little Baltimore gal to London. Her name was Ella Shields! She went to England in 1904 and sang "coon" songs in skirts and was a big hit. It was in 1910 that she first did her male impersonation, at the Palladium, where she became one of the greatest hits of that famous theater. Her ex-husband wrote a song for her called "Burlington Bertie from Bow," which remained her insurance until her death. She came back to America and played all the Big Time as an English artist. She later played the small time and when things got rough in vaude played some night clubs (where they gave her perfect attention—which was a great compliment, if you know New York night clubs). At a get-together at the Palace in New York (to boost a pic), I called on Ella, and she walked down the aisle and sang "Burlington Bertie" (with Benny Roberts and his gang faking it in the pit), and she received a tremendous ovation. She went back to London in 1951 and that loyal audience received her as always, as a great artist and headliner. (Me and Aggie love those English for their loyalty.) On August 3, 1952, while appearing at a Sunday variety concert at a Lancashire seacoast resort, she had just finished her favorite song when she collapsed with a heart attack. Her last words were, "Thank God, I didn't let 'em down. I got through with 'Burlington Bertie.'" She went "upstairs" August 5, 1952. A fine artist and a great gal.

We had other fine artists besides Ella. Kathleen Clifford, Agnes Mahr, the "American Tommy Atkins," Eva Mudge, the famous "Military Maid," who did a soldier, Jean Southern, Hetty Urma, Toma Hanlon (both really great), Winnie Crawford, Tillie Santoy, Truly Shattuck, and one of the pioneers and the best of the old-timers, Della Fox. Eva Prout, Lucille Tilton, Ann Clifford, who had a double voice, Celia Galley, who sang her songs in French, Emma Don, and Nellie Coleman were all fine English artists.

We also had some mixed teams where the female member did a male imp, like Roy Cummings & Helen Gladying and Donahue &

Stewart (the great Jack Donahue); his wife did the comedy dressed as an eccentric male in their first act.

Ed Fennel & Lena Tyson (she did the boy), Inge & Farrel, and Farrel & Bartlett were some of the acts where the females did the male imps.

Sister acts like Tempest & Sunshine (Tempest did a swell boy), Mollie & Nellie King (Mollie did the boy), Adele Ferguson & Edna Northlane, and the Armstrong Sisters were some of the others, and in the Moore & Young act they both changed to male clothes for a finish.

Hetty King was in the same class as Vesta Tilley; she did a sailor, and when she sang "I'm Going Away," you just didn't want to let her. In the last twenty years of the Big Time, there was a little gal who without a doubt was the real American Vesta Tilley—Kitty Doner, who retired when the Big Time stopped, because she was Big Time! There were a couple of gals by the name of Grace Leonard and Lillian Schriber who took the billing of the "pocket edition of Vesta Tilley," but, although they were good, none of them deserved that billing but Kitty Doner! By the way, did you know that Fanny Brice did a male imp number in white tie and tails and finished with a good buck dance? Mae West at one time did a boy in her act. Can you imagine Mae doing a boy? I mean as an impersonation? She found out that doing a gal paid off much better.

The only male impersonator left today is the very clever Florrie LaVere, who played all the Big Time and who is still playing what is left of vaude, TV and club dates, with her composer-pianist husband, Lou Handman.

There is a reason for the passing of the male impersonator. It ceased to be a novelty to see a swell-shaped gal wearing men's clothes, when all kinds and shapes of gals started walking around the streets in slacks; the way some of them looked in pants, they looked like neither men nor women!

But they were nice dames, those "guys"! SEZ

Your pal,

LEFTY

Transfigurators!

Dear Joe,

Did that "Transfigurator" billing get you? Well, it sent me and Aggie to a guy by the name of Webster who knows more about words than Henry Mencken, and that's knowing words. Webster in his book sez that transfigurator means: "The act of transfiguring, or the state of being transfigured, a change of appearance or form; especially to give an exalted meaning or glorified appearance, to make glorious, idealize, etc." Well, this guy Webster was a smart cookie; he must have been, to just put a lot of words down without trying to make a story out of them. Anyway, regardless of what he sez, a transfigurator to me and Aggie meant a "protean" or "quick-change" artist.

In 1878 the *Family Story Paper* published a novelette called "Mansfield the Metamorfosis." And thirty-five years later Charles T. Aldrich and a few more added a *t* at the end and used it as billing instead of protean or transfigurator, because it sounded more mysterious. Anyway, there were very few of them in vaude, maybe it was because it was a tough act to copy. Besides requiring a good actor, it took a lot of time and patience to figure out the quick changes. My old friend Owen McGivney once told me that it took him sometimes a year to just "break in" a coat; he would put it on and take it off maybe 100 times a day before he ever used it in his act. The clothes had to be kept in perfect repair, linings, etc., had to be perfect, because a tear or a loose sleeve could spoil the whole timing of an act!

There is a difference between protean acts and quick-change acts. The latter just make quick changes with maybe a few words of talk, no plot, while the protean acts did a regular sketch with plot, and one man or woman would play all the characters. Sometimes they had an assistant to say a few words, not only to cover up the quick change but to further the plot, but there were very few of these. Of course a few covered up bad acting with quick changes. The sketches protean actors used were just fair, as the main interest was how fast they made the different changes.

The protean act was the first of the one-man (or woman) shows. In 1873 G. Swayne Buckley retired from minstrels and gave a protean show, "On the Track," in which he played eight different characters, ten musical instruments, sang twelve songs, and danced six dances. Robert Fulgora was one of the first of the American protean artists and was the first to use the billing, "Transfigurator." He also did a quick-change act, opening in street clothes and in full view of the audience making ten changes in costume, leaving the stage dressed in women's clothes; in less than five seconds he reappeared in full evening clothes. About 1895 there was in France one of the greatest protean actors, Leopold Fregoli, who gave the entire opera, *Faust*, running one hour and a half. He came to America in 1906 and when he died his wife, Mme. Fregoli, did her husband's act.

Some more early protean acts were Harry Le Clair & Edward Leslie, who were protean and burlesque artists in an act called "Cleopatra up to Now." Miss Johnstone Bennett & S. Miller Kent did a sketch, "A Quiet Evening at Home" (this act was formerly done by Mrs. Barney Williams), in which Miss Bennett played five different characters. In 1904 Charles T. Aldrich, who could and did do most everything from fine juggling to fine acting, was billed as the "American Fregoli." Roland West did a protean act called "The Criminal" (he later became a Hollywood producer). In 1909 Charlotte Parry did "Into the Light," in which she played the part of an Italian woman in a courtroom. She was accused of murder and she played the parts of all the witnesses—she finally got the chair (not for her acting). Her next act was "The Comstock Mystery," in which she played seven characters. She played this act both here and abroad and finally retired when she married "Jolo," the *Variety* rep in London for many years.

One of the real pioneers and great protean acts in vaude were two fine Belasco actors, Nick Long & Idaleen Cotton. They did many acts, but "My Wife's Diamonds" and "The Banker and the Thief" were the best. Idaleen would do ten or more characters. Margaret Wycherly, a fine actress, did an act called "In Self Defence," with which she headlined the Big Time for many years.

R. A. Roberts, the noted English protean artist, was a sensation here with his act, "Dick Turpin." He later did an act, "Cruel Coppinger," which was good, too, but never as much of a hit. Another big hit was Henri Du Vries in an act, "Who Is Guilty?"

(This was first done by a Dutch actor, Theodore Boumustin, in Holland.) There was an Italian, who billed himself as "Ugo Beondi," who made his changes so fast that the audience claimed he had a twin brother, and it crabbed his act. He was really great. Arthur Bernardi was one of the first to use a transparent set, so you could see how he made his changes. They all used this idea after going around the circuit a few times; it sort of created new interest.

H. V. Fitzgerald, Hal Stevens in "Reveries," Robert Hildreth in "A Four Leaf Clover," Errol in "Self-Judged," Richard Keane, and Mark Linder all did protean acts. Norton & Russell did a quick-change act, and in 1908 there was an eighteen-year-old Italian gal by the name of Fatima Niris who was a quick-change artist doing about fifteen characters. And about that time there was a Herr Jansen who did his act in German.

There were many acts around who were doing impersonations of famous musicians by putting on wigs, etc. These were not classed as protean or quick-change acts. Hymack was really one of the greats of quick-change artists. While he delivered a funny monologue, the color of his gloves, tie, and boutonniere would change right in front of the audience. Nobody ever did this act after Hymack died. "Doc" Baker in a flash act called "Flashes" did very quick changes.

Caesar Rivoli, a Frenchman, was in Fregoli's class and headlined for many years. Laura Buckley did a monologue-type protean act. It was in 1922 that Owen McGivney came to America with his protean act, "Bill Sykes." He was a terrific hit. He also would do a burlesque with other members of the bill called "The Wager," which was very funny. He too later used a transparent scene. He headlined the big and small time for many years, even into TV, where he appeared recently.

It was nice of England sending Owen McGivney to us. He has not only outlasted all the other protean acts in America, but also has outlasted vaudeville! SEZ

Your pal,

LEFTY

Mimics

Dear Joe,

Mimicry was started by monkeys and parrots and then taken up by humans making faces or using somebody else's voice or mannerisms. When a kid went to the theater and came back doing an imitation of an actor, as long as he had one or two of the characteristics of the original—a gesture, a voice, a look—it would pass with his parents and relatives for genius, and he was on his way to open the stage door—mimicry was the skeleton key!

I don't believe there ever was an actor who when starting on his career didn't copy some other actor whom he set up as his idol and model. This was especially true of vaude. Beginners would first copy their idol's voice and mannerisms and in the majority of cases even take his material! It was the simplest way to get into show biz with a ready-made act! Many of them, as they became better, dropped more and more of the things they had copied and replaced them with their own material and personality. Soon they were on the road to a silk-lined living, being imitated by others! Some just stuck to the regular "impressions" and went through show biz getting by. Those two words, "getting by," are chloroform to the mediocre actor. One who is willing just to get by is a "static" performer.

It was harder for the old-time impressionists to mimic anyone, because they didn't have the help of that magic hunk of invention, the microphone. The "impression" as to voice had to be pretty true. A mike can make a mimic out of almost anyone (and has); it gives a certain quality to a voice that doesn't sound anything like the original if done without a microphone.

There never was a shortage of mimics in vaude. Among the tops were Cecilia Loftus (who got $2,000 a week way back in 1907), Elsie Janis, Gertrude Hoffman, Ina Claire, Juliet, La Petite Mignon, Eugene Fougere, Jeanne Eagles, Edna Luby, Edna Aug, La Belle Blanche, Clarice Mayne (English), Chagnon, Venita Gould, and Sibylla Bowhan (who I believe has played to more GIs than any other gal, remaining with the USO since its beginning; she has played in all countries and on every front). Most of these acts used their own material, but in the style of the person they were imitating.

The men mimics were Julius Tannen, who did a great Cohan and Hitchcock, Taylor Holmes, who did Richard Mansfield, and Georgie Price, who did Jolson and Jessel. Willie Howard did a swell Jack Norworth singing "Smarty." Nat Goodwin started as a mimic, as did Willie Weston, Sydney Grant, and others. Some of the boys and gals graduated to stardom in legit and musical comedy, but only when they replaced mimicry with originality.

One formula (mostly with the woman mimics) was to sing a popular song straight and then sing it like different stars would. Of course the easiest approach is the one still being used: "I was at a party last night and all the stars were there. When they asked Ethel Barrymore to do something she sounded something like this . . ." and into the imitation. The mimic of today has a wider field to choose from among the personalities of stage, screen, radio, and politics.

One of the most imitated performers years ago was George M. Cohan, who was the rage in America for many years. Anyone who could remember the words of "I'm a Yankee Doodle Dandy," sing through his nose, and drop one side of his mouth did a Cohan imitation. Bobby Barry (who was practically his understudy), Johnny Stanley, Julius Tannen, Sydney Grant, Charlie King, and Seymour Felix among the men, and Elsie Janis, Gertrude Hoffman, Juliet, and La Belle Blanche among the women, all did fine imitations of George M. But Dave Mallen was the greatest of them all. He started in show biz with an imitation of Cohan and for forty years practically lived "George M." in talk and mannerisms; he knew all his songs, played his parts in revivals, etc. George M., after seeing him at a Friars shindig, turned to me and said, "I never was that good." A great compliment from a great guy.

It was only last year that Mallen met George M. Cohan, Jr., for the first time. They had a long chat at the bar of the Lambs about the "old man," and when Mallen left young Cohan turned to Mike the bartender and said (in a typical Cohan manner), "He's a great little guy, that Davey Mallen, a great little guy, but he does my old man from the wrong side of his mouth." Most everyone believed that George M. sang from the side of his mouth with the corner dropped down a bit as an affectation, but the truth was that as a kid he was hit with a baseball on the mouth and a few stitches had to be taken—and it left a bit of a droop to it.

A close runner-up to Cohan among the imitators was David Warfield. When he made his great hit in *The Music Master*, anybody who could beat his breast with his hands and say, "If you dun't vant her, I vant her," did an imitation of Warfield. Alexander Carr was the greatest in this field. Then Al Jolson started a couple of generations imitating him. All you had to do was to get down on one knee and yell "Mammy!" At one time when the Shuberts were having contract trouble with him they had five actors rehearsing to replace him: George Jessel, Harry Wardell, Lou Holtz, Georgie Price, and Buddy Doyle. (They found out you just couldn't replace Jolson by rehearsing people.) All of them made good on their own.

Eddie Foy, Sr., had thousands of imitators, but best of them all are Charlie Foy and Eddie, Jr. Ethel Barrymore, with her famous line, "That's all there is, there isn't any more," was a cinch for nearly everybody to mimic. Vesta Victoria was copied singing "Waiting at the Church"; just a bum bridal veil and a faded bunch of flowers were an excuse to use that great song in the guise of an imitation. Bert Williams' pantomime poker game and his song, "Nobody," were attempted by everybody. Anna Held singing "I Just Can't Make My Eyes Behave" was done by every female mimic that had eyes! Another favorite was George Beban reciting his poem, "In the Sign of the Rose," yelling "Rosa, Rosa!" Eddie Leonard, the great minstrel, had all of them (including Al Schacht, the "Clown Prince of Baseball") singing his famous songs, "Ida" and "Roley Boley Eyes." Florence Moore did an excellent imitation of him. Irene Franklin had to stop the mimics from doing her famous song, "Red Head," by law, as they were not even announcing that they were doing Irene Franklin.

Eva Tanguay was imitated by many gals who couldn't even say, "I Don't Care." At one time there was an epidemic of Teddy Roosevelt imitations which consisted of showing the teeth in a broad smile and saying, "Deelighted!" Anyone who could wave a large picture hat while singing announced it as an imitation of Grace La Rue. Other stock imitations were of Fritzi Scheff singing "Kiss Me Again," Blanche Ring singing "Rings on My Fingers," Bessie McCoy singing "Yama Yama Man," and Jack Norworth singing "Smarty" (Willie Howard did this almost as well as Jack).

As for dance imitations, I must bunch Joe Frisco's jazz dance with cigar and derby and Pat Rooney's waltz clog while singing "Daughter of Rosie O'Grady" as the most imitated. (Pat, Jr., was weaned on that dance and does it the best.) Many tried to imitate Bill "Bojangles" Robinson's stair dance, but it was a bit too tough. Many copied Harland Dixon's original trick of raising the shoulders while doing a step, Bunny Granville's "drunk" dance, Will Mahoney's "falling down" dance, and there were thousands of imitations of Moran & Mack (the Two Black Crows). And anybody who had a battered high hat at home tried to imitate Ted Lewis saying, "Is everybody happy?" Jim Barton's "mad dog story" and Ben Bernie's famous "Yowza, yowza" were favorites, and no act was an act unless you did Cantor singing "If You Knew Susie." Buddy Doyle and Milton Berle did very good imitations of Eddie. Imitations of Frank Tinney telling gags to the leader, Bert Fitzgibbons "breaking" the footlights, Vesta Tilley singing "Following in My Father's Footsteps," Laddie Cliff's style of dancing, Bee Palmer and Gilda Gray's shimmy dance, Clifton Crawford reciting "Gunga Din," and the Duncan Sisters' harmony singing were plentiful.

All you needed for doing Fanny Brice (so they thought) was to wear a short black dress, lean against a lamppost smoking a cigarette with a baby spot on you, and sing "My Man." Montgomery & Stone's famous scarecrow dance and Weber & Fields' choking scene were done a lot. Then came the hordes of "Boop-a-doopers" imitating the great little Helen Kane. Maurice Chevalier had every kid putting on a straw hat, sticking out his lower lip, and singing "Mimi." George Givot was one of the best on this one. Helen Morgan had a host of imitators singing "Bill"; Joe Frisco did the funniest satire on this that was ever done. Georgie Price and Willie Howard were really great mimicking George Jessel singing "My Mother's Eyes" (*off key*). Will Rogers was a cinch for anyone who could put on a Western hat, chew gum, and say, "All I know is what I read in the papers" (from then on they were lost).

I believe that the most imitated men in the world were Harry Lauder, Charlie Chaplin, Gallagher & Shean, and Jimmy Durante! Just try and find me a guy who hasn't tried to sing "She Is My Daisy" with a burr; they ran Charlie Chaplin contests all over the world; and there were so many imitations of Gallagher & Shean that the Keith office had to issue a rule that there would be only one on a bill! And of course as for the great Schnozzola, Jimmy Durante—there's *millions of 'em*! (Eddie Garr was the first mimic to do Durante and was great.) The most imitated women were Eva Tanguay and Mae West. Just think back and try to remember any kid just learning to talk who didn't say, "Why don't you come up and see me sometime?" and their doting mothers would say, "Another Mae West!"

From 1897 to 1910 there was an epidemic of mimics in vaude. It died down for about five years and then broke out again and lasted until about 1925, when the mimics took a powder for awhile. Creators, not imitators, became the order of things. Then radio came in and with it a plague of mimics got aboard the gravy train—many very good ones who have since given up mimicry—but as I said before, I'm only telling you about the guy and dolls in vaude up through the Palace days.

The reason mimics get over so well is that no one in the audience wants to be embarrassed by having the people around him think that he hasn't seen the artist being imitated, so he applauds. Nat Goodwin, while playing Boston, announced an imitation of Edwin Booth. He did a few lines and some man applauded. Goodwin walked to the foots and said, "I'll bet you never saw him in your life!" And the old one comes to mind of when Dave Warfield saw a certain mimic give an imitation of him, turned to a friend, and said, "One of us is lousy!"

There were acts in variety and vaude that called themselves mimics and imitators that were not. What they did was much easier than mimicry, because they used wigs, beards, mustaches, or complete false faces. They would announce imitations of great men, past and present, and would make up quickly in full view of the audience as a well-known president, general, or king (mostly King Edward and the Kaiser). Some of them would make up like a famous composer and lead the orchestra in one of his popular compositions. Among these "mimics" the best were Willie Zimmerman, who would also show how President Taft and William Jennings Bryan would lead an orchestra, Harry Allister, Joseph Callahan, Saona, and the Great Lafayette, who modestly billed himself as "Europe's Greatest Mimic." The greatest of all these so-called imitators was Henry Lee. To give you an idea, here is his opening speech.

"Ladies and gentlemen, introductions are always difficult things to effect. It is easy to say too much or too little. Then again we may introduce the wrong people. Today I propose to introduce to you several noted personages, Pope Leo, Prince Bismarck, General Grant, General Lee, Rudyard Kipling, and others. If you do not like them, the *fault* is either *theirs* or *yours*. They will do their best to please you. Of this I give you my personal assurance. But assurance was always a less marked feature of my character than modesty. Being modest, I am naturally retiring, and as I am retiring, I beg leave to withdraw. Strike up, oh music of the starry spheres, and captive lead our willing, listening ears."

Brother, that's what me and Aggie call "telling 'em!" Eh?

For young talent with spotlight fever, mimicry is good insurance. Youngsters may come along who will dare to break tradition and bring us something *new* in mimicry that so far nobody has done. Mimics will always be part of the entertainment personnel, because America loves to have its greats and near greats satirized, ridiculed, burlesqued, and parodied, and we'll always have guys and gals do it—for a price! And we don't blame 'em! SEZ

Your pal,
LEFTY

Abracadabra

Dear Joe,

I don't know about you, but the first goose pimples I got while watching a vaude show was as a kid when a mysterious-looking guy with a thin mustache and a little goatee, dressed in full evening clothes with a red ribbon across his white shirt front and a couple of medals dangling from his chest, walked on stage with a wand in one hand and made a pitch in a soft mysterious voice. I slunk down in my seat. I knew singing and dancing and acrobatics and even musical-glass players, but here was a guy that to me was like the genie in Aladdin's Lamp. He had me a bit frightened and a bit curious when he took a live rabbit out of a hat! From that day on I was interested in magic, and during our first season in show biz we had the good fortune to work on a bill with Roland Travers, a fine magician who produced not only rabbits, but geese and ducks and pigeons. I wasn't frightened any more, but I still was plenty curious. So between shows I'd fool around Travers' paraphernalia, and in no time I released the gimmick and had pigeons and ducks flying all over the place. And all Travers did was laugh. I've always liked magic and magicians since that day, especially Roland Travers!

I don't believe there is any branch of show biz that has so many outsiders interested in it as magic! When I say magic, I cover everything from producing a live rabbit to tricks with coins, cards, illusions, escape artists, mind readers, shadowgraphists, hypnotists, and even marionettes and ventriloquists.

There have been more books written on magic than on any other subject in the theater. There are seven magic magazines with a large circulation (for professional and working amateurs), and thousands of magic books are sold every year. There are six big magicians' societies with many branches. There are also thirty dealers in magic supplies in the country and about twenty-five builders of paraphernalia for professional magicians. I believe that right now there are less than 200 real professional, full-time magicians in all of America. But there are thousands of amateurs and semipros who work clubs and local entertainments after they finish with their bread-and-butter work. They seldom travel very far, as they have to get home in time to go on their regular jobs. Amateur magicians spend over half a million bucks a year on tricks for their own amusement. They are what me and Aggie call "life-of-the-party" guys. And many of them are really good. The late Fulton Oursler was a great amateur magician, as is Drake V. Smith, the advertising man, and Julius Proscauer, the attorney, Meyer Silverstein, the textile king, and J. Robert Rubin, the MGM attorney.

There is very little work on the stage for magicians today. The coin, card, and close-up workers can't play large stages and auditoriums, and the illusionists, who carry big loads of paraphernalia, can't afford present transportation costs, charges for extra stagehands, etc. So club work is very welcome and now provides the greater part of the magician's income. A few work night clubs and do very well. Some bars have magicians to keep the customers interested; they get parties together and boost the bar bills. These are mostly table workers who usually depend on tips.

Magicians will tell you that drunks and morons are hard to entertain, and kids must have special tricks because they don't go for misdirection! If you speak to the dean of magicians, Carl Rosini, who has played every vaude theater in the world, he will tell you that there is nothing new in magic, but just like gags, the old tricks get new switches. Fred Keating, an old vaudevillian known for his "disappearing canary" trick (not the first to do it but certainly the best), once said there are three kinds of magicians, "Those who *do* tricks, those who *shoot* at 'em, and those who *talk* about 'em!"

The oldest trick is the ball and cups. Tricks most used in vaude were those with cards, coins, rope, Chinese rings, silks, bowls of rice, and bowls of water; taking the rabbit out of a hat was like a time step to a hoofer.

There were about a half a dozen female magicians who were really good. Mrs. Adele Herrmann (wife of the famous magician) was one of the few that played big-time vaude. The Great Lala Selbini bought the magic paraphernalia and illusions of the Great Lafayette, but wasn't very successful with it. Mlle. Talma (of Le Roy, Talma & Bosco) was really great doing six coin manipulations at one time. Way back in 1898 Kamochi was a good lady magician. (Even today there are only two really top lady magicians, Del O'Dell and Lady Frances. But I'm not supposed to tell you about today.)

There were only a few magic sensations that got the audiences talking to themselves. The first was "esra," the levitation trick, brought to this country by Sam Du Vries and shown at Hammerstein's. (Sam later became a big agent in Chicago.) Another sensation was Cardini and his cigarettes (copied by hundreds of acts), and the biggest sensation in magic in our time was "sawing a woman in half," first shown here by Horace Golden (the trick dates way back, but Golden, who sued everybody (never figuring he would win), claimed that he was the originator and received tremendous publicity—which was all he wanted. Remember all the gags the comics pulled about it? "I sawed a woman in half; I got the part that eats!" "Who was that lady I *sawed* you with last night?" One guy advertised a brand-new novelty of the trick, "sawing a *Negro* lady in half!" (Some switch, eh?) He called it Black Magic.

The illusionists were looked up to by other magicians because they carried lots of paraphernalia, scenery, and assistants. The undisputed champ of magicians for many years was Kellar. He worked at Hammerstein's in 1902 with an ordinary magic act, but he soon left vaude to put on a full magic show playing the combination ($1.50 top) houses in America and all over the world. He retired after forty-seven years and handed the show over to Howard Thurston, who was his assistant. I will never forget the great ovation all the magicians gave him at the Hippodrome, New York, when they brought Kellar on stage and threw roses all over the stage. Howard Thurston carried on for many years in the tradition of Kellar and was the leading magic show in America. Alexander Herrmann also had a great show. Horace Golden was a top illusionist for many years before he brought out his "sawing a woman in half." Dante didn't play much vaude, but made a great name for himself as a road attraction. Blackstone, a fine all-round magician, played vaude for many years, and then took out his own full show and became tops. After retiring for a few years, he is again on the road with his big magic show, and I would rate him the greatest of the moderns!

The Great Lafayette did a terrific one-man show and played all over the world. While playing the Palace, Edinburgh, Scotland, the theater caught fire and Joe Coates (a midget), whom he used in the show dressed as a teddy bear, and two other assistants were burned to death. The firemen, thinking Coates was a real teddy bear, didn't bother saving him as they wanted to save humans first.

Carl Rosini is a vet of vaude that played all over the world, with a command performance in England to his credit, and a command performance for Joe Stalin in Russia to his discredit! Can you imagine what would have happened to him if, while playing in Russia, he had said *no?* He said *yes* and is now dean of the magicians in America.

Rush Ling Toy, Fredrick Stevaro, and the Great Fredricks were all fine illusionists in the 1900s. Carter did "The Lion's Bride," an illusion which the Great Lafayette did originally. The Du Boises, De Biere, Reuschling, the Tomasons, and Roland Travers were all great vaude illusionists.

Bunth & Rudd way back in 1879 were one of the original double comedy magic acts, and in 1880 Imro Fox was the first single comedy magician; he was real funny and good and lasted as tops way into the real Big Time. In 1899 there was only one Negro magician, "The Great Gowongo." Me and Aggie can't remember of ever working with or even seeing a Negro magician. Other great comedy magic acts were Jarrow, famous for his lemon trick and his very funny talk—he was the magician favorite at Hammerstein's; Judson Cole, who did comedy talk and cards; Martini & Maxmillian (burly illusionists); Ziska & King; and Chinese Johnny Williams, and, of course, Long Tack Sam.

But the greatest comedy magic act in vaude, that really had very little magic, was Frank Van Hoven, the "Mad Magician" (and this guy was really mad). If you ever saw him getting his two stooges to hold large cakes of real ice and trying to introduce them to each other, you would have seen one of the greatest comedy scenes of our times. Off stage he was just as crazy, and his practical jokes got him in many a jam. When he first started to work for Gus Sun, he was canceled regularly and he very seldom finished out an engagement. He didn't do his ice act then; just regular magic (he didn't have enough dough to buy ice). When he finally came to New York and was a big hit, he would always talk about his Gus Sun days in his ads in the trade papers. He would play one free week in America; that was for a manager who didn't cancel him when he played in his house in East St. Louis. He gave him encouragement and even staked him to a few bucks to get out of town. Two swell guys, Joe Erber and Van Hoven!

Among the great card men were Merlin, Si & Mary Stebbins, who worked as rubes and did fine card tricks. The Great Albini started out doing card stuff but later did practically nothing but the very old "egg and bag" trick, which he became identified with; I believe he did it the best. Cardini, a fine manipulator of cards and a good all-round magician, became famous for his cigarette trick; he was tops. Wallace Galvin did cards, and also balls and rings; Salval was a comedy card shark; Claude Golden was a master with cards; but I believe the tops of all the card workers was the one and only Nate Leipsig!

The great artists among the coin men were Allan Shaw, Mlle. Talma, Floenzi, who did great palming, and who did the cigarette stuff before Cardini, but never could do much with it. It was

Cardini who developed it with his showmanship into the hit it became. Welsh Miller and Manuel were both great coin men, but the greatest of them all was Nelson Downs!

There were a number of very fine all-round magicians in vaude, like the Great Leon, a vet who played everything in vaude. His assistant was Jay Palmer, who later, as Palmer & Doreen, played all over the world—a great comedy act, "The Magic Kettle." Gus Fowler struck a new note by making hundreds of watches appear; Johnnie & Nellie Olms also did this type act. There were Ten Ichi, the originator of the water trick, the Great Asehi Troupe, who made water come out of their finger tips, Ching Lee Foo, who created a sensation on his first trip to the United States and also on his return date in 1912, Henry Clive, a fine actor and one of our great portrait painters, who as a magician in vaude presented spirit paintings and the "wrestling cheese" (people tried to lift the cheese but couldn't), and the Valdos, who did spirit stuff in cabinets. Hong Ping Chien & Co. put sticks through their noses (sensational). Fakir Raaon Bey did a magical act, but for exploitation did the "buried alive" stunt. Atra defied a bullet fired from a rifle right at his stomach. Sparrow featured eating dozens of eggs. Maskelyn, an English magician, was very good, as was the Frenchman, Les Marco Belli. Crane, the Irish magician, was a vaude favorite for many years. Paul Valadon, an Englishman from the Egyptian Hall, in London, did sleight-of-hand stuff and later brought over the levitation trick and worked with Kellar. Mohammed Kahn, a Hindu magician, and Carl Hertz, an old-timer from Frisco, were both very good. Clement De Lion, a Dane, was excellent doing billiard-ball stuff. The Okito Family were wonderful (they came from five generations of magicians). Henri French was very good. Zemlock & Co. did spirit stuff, like tipping the disk, playing drums, moving tables, etc. J. Jerome Mora kept taking birds and animals from his magic casket. Jupiter Bros. did what is called "cabinet work," à la spiritualists, like producing flying tambourines and fresh flowers. Rameses, an Englishman, did a remarkable act with fresh flowers (changing them, etc.). Gilly-Gilly, a table worker, made noises like a chicken and a small chick would appear in his mouth—he used no hands. Henry E. Dixie, who was one of our great legit stars, did many acts in vaude—sketches, monologues, and also an expert magic act. Nora Bayes and Jack Norworth did a magic number in their act that was a novelty,

Norworth doing swell tricks while they were singing. (Jack is a very fine amateur magician.)

Mind reading, or mental telepathy, is certainly a part of magic. One of the greatest sensations to hit New York in the early 1900s were the mind readers; Anna Eva Fay was the greatest box-office attraction, helped a great deal by the wonderful publicity and showmanship of Willie Hammerstein. There was a family feud and the wife of John T. Fay (who worked with the Fays) left the act and did one called "The Fays Fazing the Fays," which was an exposé. It got over for a short time, but they went back to the regular mindreading act. It seemed that audiences didn't like to be disillusioned; they would rather be fooled!

Great showmen among the mind readers in vaude were Dunninger (who is still going strong on TV), Norman Frescott and Babe Stanton (one of the best), Jovedah, and the Sharrocks, who did a very good comedy act called "Behind the Grandstand." Mercedes with Mlle. Stanton was a sensation in vaude for many years; they even had the actors on the bills with them guessing how they did it. Anyone in the audience would just whisper to Mercedes the tune he wished Mlle. Stanton to play on the stage and without a word from him she would play it. Mercedes at times would ask someone to just *think* of the tune he wished played—yop—she would play it. (In the early '80s the "Modern Svengali" hypnotized a woman who sat at the piano and played selections whispered to him.) The Zancigs were popular in vaude, as were Harry & Frances Usher. "The Girl with the 1000 Eyes" really cleaned up. There were many more mental telepathists, mind readers, etc., who played all the small time and cleaned up with their "love advice," telling where you could find your lost articles, what business you should enter, etc., and also did private readings off stage. These were strictly "mitt readers" or fortune tellers. It was a sweet racket while it lasted, but only the real small-time manager would go for it. The Big-Timers didn't have to resort to side dough, as they received good salaries.

Another phase of magic is hypnotism! At one time vaude, especially small-time vaude, was just lousy with lousy hypnotists. The act was presented as educational (?), but really was amusing. The hypnotist would make a high-grade pitch, using words and medical terms he didn't even understand himself, explaining what hypnotism was and what he was going to prove. They never referred to

it as an "act," but always billed it as a "scientific demonstration."
They would request a "committee" to assist with the experiments.
(By the way, these were among the first audience-participation
acts.) The committee had to be loaded with confederates, which
was tough on the small-time hyps who had to do four shows a day;
they couldn't use the same stooges because many of the audience
would stay for two shows and naturally would get wise if they saw
the same committee every show.

Out of the hundreds of hypnotists, most of them were real bad.
Pauline was the tops; he had a fine personality, spoke like an actor-
doctor, always referred to "this experiment, which I performed before the world's greatest scientists," and proceeded to draw blood
from the arm of a "subject" selected from the audience while the
"subject" was under the influence of hypnotism. "This I insist will
be a great boon to medicine, surgery, and mankind!" Then he
would make members of the committee go through various crazy
stunts, such as barking like a dog, acting like a strong man trying
to lift a 1,000-pound weight (with nothing in his hands), making
like a rooster, etc. The *pièce de résistance* was hypnotizing a subject by putting hands in front of his eyes and saying the magic
word, "Rigid!" (which became a byword in vaude). The subject
would stiffen, then be laid across the tops of two chairs, and half-
a-dozen men would stand on the rigid body. In 1922 a hyp named
Vishnu, playing at the Empire Theatre in Kansas City, put a girl
to sleep on the stage by broadcasting from the local station a few
blocks away. She was placed in a local store window for twenty-four
hours, then taken back to the theater and brought out of the
hypnotic spell. This was also done many times without radio. A lot
of fun—for a while, and it died out just as quickly as it came in.

There were Polgar, Pelham (next best to Pauline), Prof. Theo
Pull, Harry Hyman, Powers, Ralph Slater, Ahrenmeyer, Banyan,
the Great Priscilla, Svengali, and a few others that were very good.

All these abracadabra guys were really great, because they were
always interesting. You went home wondering, "How did they
do it?"

And now to another phase of magic—"shadographists." There
were very few of these artists and it was a good novelty. Mr. and
Mrs. Gordon Wilde were among the pioneer shadowgraph acts in
big-time vaude. Others were Mr. and Mrs. Darrow, Maxwell
Holden, Frevoli (who also did magic), Massian O'Connor, Marcou

(one of the greatest), Stanley Gallini, and Chassino. The Halkings did electrical shadowgraphs. Lola and Fay Durbyelle were the only two women doing shadowgraphing.

Escape artists were also a part of magic. There were a number of these with carnivals, circuses, and in small-time vaude, but only a few stood out in the Big Time: Brindamour, the Vancos (who did handcuff and trunk escapes), Haslam, a strait-jacket escape artist, the Great Raymond, Hardeen (who was Houdini's brother), and Hilda, the "Handcuff Queen" and strait-jacket escapist. But when you add them all up, they couldn't even touch the handcuffs of one of the greatest showmen of our times, Houdini!

A kid who started out as a trapeze artist, Houdini (nee Ernie Weiss) became the world's best-known escape artist. Houdini once told me and Aggie a story about the time he played Glasgow, Scotland. They advertised that he would do his famous escape from a packing case, in which he was placed handcuffed and with feet tied, the cover nailed down, and the box lowered into the river. This was what Houdini used as a terrific publicity stunt for years; he not only got big newspaper coverage with pics, but thousands of people gathered to watch him do this trick (it was for free). So you can imagine his surprise when he showed up on the bridge in Glasgow to do this stunt and found that there were just a handful of people there. He asked the manager if he was sure he had the right date advertised. And the manager told him yes and showed him copies of the papers and handbills. Houdini went through with his escape (as a good showman would), and when he got back to the theater he found out the reason why nobody showed up. It was a *toll bridge!*

Houdini was the first dumb act that got a spot in the middle of the bill (they usually opened or closed a show), and was the first act of his type to be headlined. It wasn't what he did as much as the way he did it. He would make the simplest trick look difficult. He was a great student of the art of magic and when he died left a very valuable collection of books covering every phase of the field. He devoted the latter years of his life to exposing fake "mediums" and "spiritualists," offering $10,000 if they could show him anything he couldn't duplicate. He died from a burst appendix, brought on by a punch in the stomach. He would allow anybody to take a good punch at his stomach, claiming to have muscles that could resist any blow. The name "Houdini" was so well known that "to do a Houdini" means to escape!

Ventriloquism is definitely a part of abracadabra. Many years ago me and Aggie were on the bill with Arthur Prince, who was really one of the great ventriloquists of vaude. He kinda took a liking to us and after the show we'd "beer it up" and he would tell us a lot about ventriloquism or, as we used to call 'em, "belly-talkers." He was a classy guy and spoke good English (maybe it was because he was an Englishman), so naturally he had us at a disadvantage.

Prince told us that years ago ventriloquism was used in connection with religious ceremonies instead of stage entertainment. The priests of pagan tribes made noises come out of the idols and so made plenty of wampum (or whatever they used for dough) out of the savages. There is no such thing as voice throwing or what they call "distant ventriloquism." It's done by taking a deep breath and then letting it escape slowly, the voice sounds being modified by means of the upper part of the throat and the palate; the tighter the throat is closed, the further away the sound seems to be. It is then up to the vent to mislead the audience (like magicians do with misdirection) as to the man "on the roof," "under the ground," or "in the box." Remember how the old-time vents would say to the dummy when he got too fresh, "I'll put you back in the trunk," or, "Jerry, keep saying hello as you come up from the cellar"?

Baron Mengen of Vienna was about the first to build a wooden doll with movable lips; that was around 1750. But from the first, the thing that interested people most was the "distant" voice. The owner of the "second voice" was regarded with superstitious amazement. Many of 'em were burned for witchcraft.

Ed Reynard and A. O. Duncan were pioneers in American ventriloquism. All the vents tried at first to put novelty in their acts. Sam Watson had a "Barnyard Circus," Paul Sandor's "Miniature Cirque" used a circus for a background; Coram, with his Jerry, a crying doll, was one of the best. Cole Travis had walking figures, barking dogs, chickens, etc.—a very good act. Fred Russell was the first to work the whole act with one figure, which he called "Coster Joe"; they all copied working the figure on the knee from him and also took many of his gags. Arthur Prince was not a good voice thrower, but was marvelous when changing from one voice to another; he was the highest-priced vent in vaude. Prince was also the first to give his whole act in the form of a sketch with one figure placed away from the body. Then there was W. E. Whittle, who impersonated Teddy Roosevelt and talked with his dummy about topics of the day. George W. Hussey did dialects, Jay W. Winton had a laughing dummy, Walter & Emily Walters specialized in baby crying. John W. Cooper was the first Negro vent; Frank Rogers, also a Negro, came later. Harry Kennedy, a good vent, was also a song writer. Tom Edwards, from England, with his "Father and Baby" act was very good. Johnson Clare with his "tough kid" that he called Squire, Fred Howard, A. C. Astor, and Carl Nobel were all good.

We had vents from all over the world in vaude. Richard Nadradge was Germany's best, George S. Lauder (Australia), worked with five dummies, Alf Ripon and the Great Howard were from Scotland, Les Freres Nad were a couple of French vents, and Carl Nobel was Scandinavian.

Professor Davis and Trovollo were the creators of the mechanical walking and talking figures. Trovollo in 1910 had an act, "Reincarnation," using a lion and chimp for dummies.

All the vents were trying hard to get away from the old-fashioned way of just working with the dummy on the knee. Lieut. Walter Cole worked with a group of figures called "Merry Folks." Ed Reynard, with his "Morning in Hicksville," was ranked as the biggest and best vent production. W. H. Clement had the biggest walking figure act; he had a soldier and nurse outfit with a baby in a carriage. Lieutenant Noble was one of the first to bring out a walking figure.

The Great Lester was first to do the distant voice clearly before the mike was invented. He claimed to be the originator of drinking while making a humming noise, but a playbill dated 1821 shows that Mons. Alexandre, the French vent, drank while talking (and by the way, Alexandre was the founder of the Boston Public Library and his name is in the library entrance). The Great Lester's phone bit when he called up "Heaven" and "Hell" in search of his sister was outstanding and long remembered; you could hear when he lifted the phone off the hook, the busy signal, etc. His dummy was named Frank Byron. He was also first to walk among the audience with his lips tightly closed and his dummy whistling a tune. A real great vent was the Great Lester!

John W. Cooper's act was called "Fun in a Barber Shop." There was a manicurist, a Negro head in the towel box and when a towel was thrown in the head would pop out, man in chair getting shaved, newsboy standing with papers in hand, customer reading newspaper while waiting to be shaved, and a parrot on a perch. Real novel and real good.

Lydia Dreams (whose real name was Walter Lambert, and who came from England) was a female impersonator vent—but never removed his wig and the audience believed it was a lady. He was also a great portrait painter and made all of his figures and props. Jay W. Winton had a dummy named McGinty and at the finish of his act McGinty would climb up a rope. Jules Vernon, assisted by his wife, was stricken with blindness while playing the Orpheum in Spokane, Washington, in 1920. He kept on in the act with his six figures and kept it a secret that he was blind. When the stand on which the figures were mounted was moved onto the stage, there was a black thread tied to the stand and to the wings, and when Vernon entered he followed the black thread until he got to his stand. Some of the figures were worked from the back of the head, others with a pneumatic hose and foot treadle.

Frederick MacCabe was a famous English vent who played American Big Time; he did not use figures but was a distant voice exponent and a good one. George W. Harvel worked with two Civil War soldiers, life-size, both one-legged and using crutches. O. M. Mitchell (Orm McKnight) was said by nearly all vents to be the best of the distant-voice vents. Johnny Woods, a Negro, had a dummy do a restaurant eating act sitting at a table. Colby & Moy were the first to introduce the dancing doll in a vent act.

Leo Bill, a Frenchman, did a very novel act. There was a statue on the table and his wife entered with a feather duster and accidentally struck the statue and its head fell apart. Bill entered, found his wife all excited over the accident, and told her it was O.K. and he would put on a new head. He built the head on his fist and placed it on the broken statue and did his vent stuff à la Senor Wences (many years before Wences, who I believe is today's greatest).

Another novel act was "Prelle's Ventriloquial Dogs." Charlie Prelle, a German, had a bunch of dogs fitted with human masks with movable mouths. The dogs were trained so that when he spoke for a certain character, the mouth of that dog would move as if talking. (So Francis, the talking mule, is new, eh?)

William Ebbs did a travesty on vents. In his first act he was seated near a wicker lamp that had a large shade, with his midget brother concealed in the lamp. The supposed dummy, Ebbs, ate an apple and drank water while doing rapid-fire talk. Finally the light was put out and the midget fell down from the lamp, showing up the fake. In a later act he brought out the "dummy" in a suit case, took him out in front of the audience, worked as a regular vent act (of course with remarkable tricks because the midget did the talking), and put the dummy back in the valise for an exit. They gave it away when taking bows. Felix Alder, Mike Donlin & Tom Lewis, Dody & Lewis, Fred Allen, and many more, all did a burly vent bit using a live dummy.

Carl Nobel of Copenhagen had a remarkable act. A woman hobbled out with Carl on her back and a Frenchman on his, and beneath her heavy burden sang in a harsh voice, while Nobel also sang and the Frenchman on his back nodded and leered approvingly. The act looked like there were three living persons one on top of another, while it really was only one living person and two dummies. He made the figures and mechanism himself.

There were some clever female vents. Ella Morris was the first. Grace De Winters was a very clever vent and impersonator. Miss De Bussey had an act with soldier and boy figures. Winona Winter (daughter of the famous Banks Winter, the song writer) worked with one figure, telling funny stories and giving a good impersonation of Trovollo (another great vent). There was also Maude Edwards (sister of Tom), Hilda Hawthorne (one of the best), Mabel Johnson, who use a "highly cultured" Boston dummy, Kaye Varroll, Mabel Hudson, Emily Walters, Bessie Gaby, and Grace Wallace. Some used to work with male partners; others joined partners after doing a single.

Marshall Montgomery started as a musical act, gave an imitation of George M. Cohan, played comedy piano and some freak instruments, and was champ harmonica player, defeating the European champ, Jim Gouge (all this before he became a vent). He presented his vent act in sketch form (as did Arthur Prince), but it was absolutely no copy. Montgomery was one of the top headline vent acts on the Big Time for many years and was considered to be in a class by himself. Frank Gaby came a lot later, but was a very big hit and just beginning to click when he died, a young man who would have had a great future.

Edgar Bergen was the first vent to appear on radio and TV and in pictures. When he was in vaude he got away from the usual slapstick old-fashioned material that other vents were using. Although Edgar has often said that when working his "mouth swings like a gate," his manipulation of Charlie McCarthy is really expert stuff and he has the superb timing of a Jack Benny (which is good enough for anybody). Edgar Bergen has made more money in the art of ventriloquism than any other vent past or present.

There is an International Brotherhood of Ventriloquists, of which W. S. Berger is the president. If you are ever around Fort Mitchell, Kentucky, be sure and drop in and let him show you a large room in his home filled with the dummies used by famous vents. He calls it the "Vent Home," a very odd and interesting hobby.

Marionettes are one of the oldest forms of entertainment and belong also in the field of magic. They were used in the Holy Plays hundreds of years ago, long before stage plays. Of course Punch and Judy (hand puppets), with Punch slapsticking Judy and the Devil, goes way back. We had some real swell marionette acts in vaude. There were the Don Carlos Marionettes, John & Louisa Till, D'Arc's Marionettes (who gave imitations of famous stars), Rhoade's Marionettes, who had a "drunk" that was bounced by a cop between acts, LeRoy Marionetttes, Holden's Manikins, the Wallace Puppets, Petty's Puppets, Mantell's Mechanical Marionettes, Salaci Marionettes (great), La Petite Cabarette, which did an entire night-club show, Manikin Music Hall, and the greatest of 'em all, Mme. Jewel's Marionettes, a stage on a stage, with the marionettes giving a complete vaude show.

These were all a part of the Magic Family and they all contributed their share for the upkeep of Lady Vaudeville! SEZ

Your pal,

LEFTY

Special Attraction!

Dear Joe,

I believe that almost all the champs and near champs in every branch of sports appeared at one time or another in vaude or burly! In a way these were "freak acts"; very few delivered entertainment and they were just used while they were making newspaper headlines to sort of goose up the box office. Some were good for a twirl around the circuit, some good only in large cities, and many were played locally.

The old melodramas used fighters and wrestlers as stars, not because of their acting ability but for their box-office draw. John L. Sullivan, Bob Fitzsimmons, Jim Corbett, Terry McGovern, Jack Dempsey, Sandow, and even Ty Cobb (who played the lead in the road show of *The College Widow*) are a few who starred in shows. Jim Corbett was about the only one who could really act. He proved that in *Cashel Byron's Profession* at Daly's Theatre on Broadway in 1906. Burly shows used athletes as special attractions long before vaude did; there were very few burly shows that didn't have some sports celebrity as box-office bait!

Of all the kinds of athletes in vaude, there were more fighters than anything else; baseball players ran second. Willie Hammerstein played more champ athletes than any other theater manager. The clientele at Hammerstein's was 75 per cent from the sporting element of New York and naturally jammed the place to see a winner. The old gag around Broadway was that when someone won an athletic event, his manager would say to him, "Hurry up and take a shower and put on your clothes. You are booked at Hammerstein's!"

Mike Donlin, the great outfielder of the New York Giants, was kinda led into vaude through his marriage to Mabel Hite (a great soubrette), and they continued doing an act together when Mike left baseball until Mabel Hite was "booked out of town." Here is a story about them that had Broadway talking for many a day. When Mabel died, she was cremated, and her ashes were placed in an urn at a certain well-known undertaking establishment in

New York. After a few years a package was sent to Murray's Restaurant on West Forty-second Street by mistake. At that time there was a bomb scare, and when the package was delivered someone got suspicious and called the police, who promptly soaked the "bomb" in water. When they opened it they found the urn containing the ashes. (Mike sued for plenty.)

Although many used vaude and burly to grab off some easy dough once in a while, there was one champ who made show biz his profession when he hung up his gloves: that was James J. Corbett. (Slapsie Maxie, Max Baer, and the others came much later.) Gentleman Jim became a fine monologist, a great straight man, and a good actor, and remained in show biz until he had to quit because of ill health.

In the Warner Bros. picture of *Gentleman Jim*, they had him as a member of the famous Olympic Club in San Francisco. The truth was that he was Walter Watson's assistant. Watson taught him all he knew about boxing. Jim became amateur champ of Frisco and later was made an honorary member of the Olympic Club. At a benefit given for Jim at the Grand Opera House in Frisco, he boxed John L. Sullivan (world's heavyweight champ) three exhibition rounds. They stripped to the waist and boxed with their "dress" pants and shoes on. It was after this exhibition that Corbett turned to a friend and said, "I can lick John L. anytime I want to." He wasn't bragging; he just knew he could do it. A few years later he did do it and became the World Heavyweight Champion. (He knocked out John L. in the twenty-first round.)

Jim Corbett's monologue was a classic. He had an easy delivery, a fine appearance, and a delightful sense of humor, which is a pretty nice parlay in show biz. He had a poor memory on names, forgetting even those of his best friends. To cover this failing he would call everybody "kid," even if the guy had a long beard. One day at breakfast at the Friars Club, he greeted those around him by their first names. I turned to Bert Hanlon in surprise and said, "Hey, what happened to Jim? He's remembering all our names." And Bert said, "He is just getting over the Fitzsimmons fight" (which happened in 1895). After giving his regular "Hello, kid" to a stranger, he would follow it up with "How's the folks?" I once asked him why he said that when he didn't know the guy, much less his folks? Jim said, "Listen, kid, *everybody* has folks!" He was an ice-cream fiend, as was his friend and neighbor Fred

Hillebrand (the song writer and comedian), and during his illness Fred would drive him from Bayside to the Biltmore Hotel in New York for a dish of his favorite pistachio ice cream.

There is just one more story I'd like to tell you about my old friend Jim. When the late Flo Ziegfeld managed Sandow (the famous strong man), they issued a challenge to Jim, with a big side bet, if Jim would meet Sandow, Jim to box and Sandow to wrestle and winner take all. (The first challenge of its kind, but it has been used plenty of times since then.) It caused a lot of controversy at the time and of course got plenty of newspaper space. "Could a great fighter lick a great wrestler and strong man?" One night Jim was sitting in a restaurant in Frisco with some of his friends, including Frank Belcher, the great basso (who was in Jim's show at the time and who told me this story), Professor Bill Clark, "Bud" Woodthrope (Jim's secretary), manager Ollie Hagan, and the sporting editor of the Frisco *Chronicle* (whose name escapes me), when in walked Sandow and Ziegfeld. There was a tense moment, as the papers were playing up the "angry" angles between the two. But Jim invited them to his table for a drink. Corbett and Sandow got to talking about their respective rackets, Sandow of course speaking about wrestling and feats of strength and Jim about fighting and boxing. "I can't hold horses on my chest like you do, Sandow; mine is a different game," said Jim. And Sandow replied, "With all my strength I don't think I can punch as hard as you, Jim." Sandow was pleased with Jim's gentlemanly manners and they finished up friends. I personally think the "bad feeling" was all press stuff dreamed up by Ziggy; in fact I believe that he even rigged up the meeting in the restaurant. Maybe me and Aggie are wrong about it, but we've been in show biz a long time and even stopped believing our own press notices! Anyway there was no match.

Among the great fighters to play vaude was John L. Sullivan (we played on the Loew Circuit with him). He did a prohibition talk. (When their livers can't take it any more, they turn prohibitionist.) He was a kindly old gentleman, good company, but I certainly would love to have met him in his prime when he would clean out a barroom of its beer and customers at the drop of a remark. We also played with Bob Fitzsimmons when he did an act with his beautiful wife, Julia May Gifford, and later when he played the Pantages Time and we were playing the Orpheum

Circuit (bragging); we both played the same towns. In his act he introduced his son as the future "white-hope champ" (always got big applause on that announcement), but it was wasted because the son didn't inherit his father's punch; all he had was his father's gloves!

We also worked in the same towns with Jim Jeffries and Tom Sharkey when they made their tour for Loew. All show folks would meet after the show at night. Big Jim Jeffries told us about the time back in 1899 when he, Tom Sharkey, and Jim Corbett played in a burlesque skit called "Round New York in Eighty Minutes," at Koster and Bial's. When I told Tom Sharkey that I sold papers outside of his saloon (it was a joint) on East Fourteenth Street when I was a kid, he checked me about the rest of the street and was surprised that I knew every spot on the block, from the Unique Theatre (a penny arcade with two acts, that was east of his place) to the Dewey and Luchow's. (The Dewey is where William Fox really started—so did we. Luchow's was and is one of the most famous of New York restaurants.) By the way, the sailors that came out of Sharkey's gave us kids a nickel for a paper and the rich guys that came out of Luchow's only gave us the regular price, one cent! Maybe the sailors were drunk; anyway, we kids figured that sailors had more dough than millionaires!

The easiest way to name all the fighters that were in vaude is to take my friend Nate Fleisher's *Ring Record* or my friend Spink's *Sporting News* and say that 95 per cent of the guys they have mentioned played vaude. Not even excluding my friends Jack Dempsey and Jim Corbett, I don't think any fighter was better liked on Broadway than Johnny Dundee, who worked in vaude with his old pal Jimmy Hussey. I believe that he knows more vaude actors than anybody on Broadway. Jack Johnson, who headlined at Hammerstein's when he was a champ, ended his career just about 50 feet across the street at Hubert's Museum, doing twenty shows a day with a five-cent admission! Jack Dempsey & Co., in "Roadside Razz," written by his old friend Willard Mack, broke records in vaude. He did $41,000 at Loew's State (beating the best previous record by $12,000). Gene Tunney, who, by the way, broke in his act on the Gus Sun Time (as did Dempsey), was billed as "A Chap America Is Proud Of." Young Stribling came from a vaude family who did an acrobatic act, "The Four Novelty Grahams," which consisted of mother, dad, George, and another kid. Kid

McCoy, a terrific character in and out of the ring, started the no-hat craze, claiming it helped grow hair, and almost ruined the hat biz and the hat-check rooms. Philadelphia Jack O'Brien, another Broadway character, ran a gym 'for chorus gals. Harry Greb showed me the night life of Pittsburgh, the night before he fought Jimmy Delaney. We got to bed at 10 A.M., and that night he licked Delaney. (What a man!) Mickey Walker, who was a great artist in the ring and has now become a real fine artist on canvas (without taking the count), was a great idol of show biz. Mike "Twin" Sullivan, a great Boston favorite, would play the old Howard whenever they had a disappointment. Joe Gans, one of the greatest, met and was admired by many show folks when he was working at Kernan's Hotel, in Baltimore, at the oyster bar. Tony Canzoneri, one of our great champs, did his first act at Proctor's Fifth Avenue, and later became a great attraction with Joey Adams and Phil Plant in a night-club act. Jimmy Britt, who was known among actors as the handsomest fighter in tights (he had a swell pair of gams) became a pretty good monologist at the Empress Theatre, Frisco, way back in 1911.

Abe Attell, who was one of the first fighters to do a monologue, and a good one, talked about Kid Broad. He later did a double with Goff Phillips (a fine blackface comic). He also did an act with Leach Cross called "A Business Proposition." Speaking about Leach Cross (a dentist who put in the teeth he knocked out), he did an act in vaude where his brother, Sam Wallach, announced while he showed how he exercised. When asked what he thought about vaude he said, "In the theaters it's the same as when I fight: I pack the house with people who come to see me lose." Johnny Coulon, the bantam champ, did an act in vaude for many years (à la Annie Abbott) where he would defy anyone to lift him off the stage. Phil Bernstein and Kid Griffo (two well-known local fighters) did a real big fight act for one week at Proctor's 125th Street. I did the candy butcher for no dough, just to be able to see the act. They really had a great "fake" boxing act for vaude—but weren't known outside of New York. Benny Leonard was the most stage-struck fighter in show biz. He could tell very good stories and worked in vaude many times, once with Benny Rubin (a fine comic), another time with Herman Timberg (who was a top Hebe comic in "School Days") and also lost some money in a show he went out in. I know of no nicer guy, greater fighter, or better referee and friend—one of the great favorites of vaudevillians.

Jim Jeffries in 1909 was getting $3,000 a week at the Wigwam in Frisco. When he was training for the Johnson fight, he had a lot of vaude actors in his camp to keep him in good humor. Eddie Leonard and Walter C. Kelly (The Virginia Judge) stuck until he was counted out. He had a lot of show biz friends.

I just must mention a few more of the tops who played vaude. Jess Willard got $4,000 a week at Hammerstein's in 1915. Funny, he was a big disappointment as a drawing power, while at the Palace a style show was packing 'em in! Primo Carnera had shoes displayed in store windows with signs saying, "These are Primo Carnera's shoes." They were about size 50 and would fit Jack the Giant Killer—a phoney, but good showmanship (wish I knew the name of the guy that thought it up). There were Max Baer, Georges Carpentier, Stanley Ketchell, Jack Britton, Barney Ross (a great Broadway favorite), Midget Wolgast, Honey Melody, and not forgetting Slapsie Maxie Rosenbloom, who is sticking in all branches of show biz and is called "Erudite Maxie," a character who will be written up in years to come.

Show biz had some pretty good fighters who were smart enough to quit before their profiles were mashed up. Maurice Barrymore, the father of the talented trio, was originally a fighter; George Fuller Golden, the father of the White Rats and a great monologist, started out as a fighter; so did Bobby Gaylor, who was light-weight champ of Montana and Colorado; Pat Rooney, Sr., wanted to fight, but ended up as one of our great Irish comic song-and-dance men!

To go back a little bit, I want to tell you about Jack Burke, who with William McVoy did an act in 1897 called "Fun in a Gymnasium." Burke fought the longest battle on record with Andy Nowman, a mulatto, down in New Orleans. They fought 110 rounds lasting seven hours and twenty minutes; they could not continue and the referee called it no contest! Any one of the rounds would have made a modern fight. In 1908 Hammerstein's featured the Gans-Nelson fight pics. The fight ran twenty-one rounds, but Willie cut it to twelve for running time (first time anybody cut a fight pic). Jim Jeffries was the referee. Hammerstein had John P. Dunn, the referee and matchmaker of the Coney Island Club, explain the fight to the audience.

Another odd fight act was about 1906 when B. H. Benton

(known as Rob Roy) did a monologue on his thirty-five years of experience with champs of the ring. He worked in the vaude section of the old Howard shows in Boston. He reproduced scenes of the gym in the old Cribb Club, and had favorite Boston fighters like Matty Baldwin, Jimmy Briggs, Joe Lannon, etc., appear with him.

France sent over an odd fighting act, Louis Ducasse and George Jeannot, who did an act at Hammerstein's called "La Savette"; it was French-style boxing with feet—hit and step away. Joe Humphries did the announcing.

In 1926 there was Joop Leit, a Dutch boxer, who when he knocked out an opponent sang a hunk of grand opera. He went into vaude and was met by laughter at the Alhambra, but he didn't care, he kept on singing "Pagliacci." He played a week in London.

This I guess will give you an idea of the many boxers that played let's say a box-office part in vaude, and some even entertained. They were great guys to work with, because they thought they were great on the stage and we thought they were great off the stage. I'm not afraid of the many champs' and near champs' names that I left out, because by now they've lost their punch.

Many fighters took a few socks at vaude and usually were knocked back into the ring. So now let me tell you about the next greatest off-seasonal athletic industry in vaude, baseball!

After the last game of the baseball season, all the topnotchers in the baseball world would take a crack at batting out a few vaudeville fongos, and would stay just long enough to be struck out!

Hammerstein's was the baseball players' home plate! Most of them had to have acts built around them, full of regular vaude talent, to get 'em over. There were only a few who had talent. Some did monologues, some told about great plays and "inside stuff" of the big games they had been in, some danced, some did imitations, but most of them sang!

It was a natural for ball players to sing, because during training periods and before and after games they would get together and do a bit of "Sweet Adelining" in the clubhouse or on the hotel porch. They did this not only for their own amusement but with vaude dates in mind. There was big dough in show biz for pennant winners or those who stood out in a series or a season.

Mike Donlin and Mabel Hite were one of the first real baseball acts (Mabel Hite had a standard act as a great singing comedienne long before she married Mike). They had a number of acts in vaude. "Stealing Home" (in 1908, I think) was really a great act besides being a drawing card. In 1912 Mike did an act with the great comedian, Tom Lewis, who was the originator of the famous expression, "Twenty-three" (to which they later added "Skiddoo"; it was not in the original George M. Cohan show, *Little Johnny Jones*). They finished with Tom Lewis on Mike's lap acting as a vent dummy and Mike doing the ventriloquist. He also did an act with Marty McHale, which proves that the guy made vaude his biz after his baseball career was over. Mike finally went to Hollywood and did bits in pics until he couldn't make home plate any more.

Charles Dooin (Philly National catcher) did songs and in 1910 did a singing and talking act in Dumont's Minstrels in Philly. Joe Tinker, the famous short-stop, started doing a monologue, and then did a skit, "A Great Catch," in an act with Sadie Sherman. Johnny Kling (catcher) did a monologue and a champ billiard exhibition act. The great Christy Mathewson and Chief Meyers (pitcher and catcher of the famous New York Giants) did a skit with May Tulley written for them by the famous sports writer, Bozeman Bulger, called "Curves."

In 1911 Rube Marquard made his vaude debut at Hammerstein's, with Annie Kent. In 1912 he did an act with Blossom Seeley (then a headliner in her own right) in a skit, "Breaking the Record." They did the Marquard glide. I remember in this act he said to the audience, "You wished it on yourselves, so I got nerve enough to sing it alone" (and did it very well). Another act of theirs was "Nineteen Straight." In 1913 they did an act called "The Suffragette Pitcher," in which Blossom made Rube change into a dame's dress to pitch for her all-woman team. In 1917 Rube did a singing and talking act with Billy Dooley of the famous Dooley family.

John J. McGraw did a monologue on "Inside Baseball," and did very well, but didn't go for a vaude route, figuring he would have more fun at the Lambs. That same year (1912) there was the Boston Red Sox Quartette, with Marty Hale, Tom "Buck" O'Brien, Hugh Bradley, and Bill Lyons. Another quartette that year was Bill Gleason, George Crable, Tom Dillon, and Frank Browning in "Twenty Minutes in the Club House." Hugh Jennings did an act with Ben Smith (a vet blackface comic).

Capt. Adrian C. "Pop" Anson, the dean of baseball, went into
vaude about 1913 and did a monologue, finishing up with a short
dance. He liked vaude, because he came back in 1921 with his two
beautiful daughters in a skit written for them by Ring Lardner
with songs by Herman Timberg. George Stallings, the "miracle
man of baseball," also did a monologue. Hank Gowdy and Dick
Rudolph did a singing and talking act. I was at the party they gave
Hank Gowdy up in Boston when he went into service in World
War I. He was the first baseball player to enlist—a great guy.

There was a fellow by the name of George L. Moreland who
billed his act "Baseballology"; he answered all questions about
baseball from as far back as 1846. He showed stills of early baseball players, etc. He knew all the answers.

Wait Hoyt was practically raised in show biz, as his dad was
an old-time minstrel man. In 1921 Wait went on the stage with a
singing act; he had a very nice voice. About seven years later he
took another vaude plunge (after his season), and had a gal playing the piano for him who didn't do so bad for herself in show
biz since then; her name is Hildegarde! She also played for Mickey
Cochrane, and when she left him the noted composer Freddy Coots
played for Mickey (they did a swell act). In 1921 Babe Ruth did
an act with Wellington Cross (Cross & Josephine), a fine artist:
they had Cliff Dean at the piano. It's a funny thing about the
Babe in vaude. When he was at his height in baseball and was
getting a big salary in vaude, he didn't prove to be a drawing card,
while Jack Dempsey was breaking all records. Showmen explained
this by saying that people could see Babe Ruth any time for a
quarter or 50 cents, while it took at least three bucks to see
Dempsey when he was fighting! They sold Irving Berlin's song,
"Along Came Ruth," in the lobby of the Pantages houses when
the Babe played them.

Vernon "Lefty" Gomez did a very funny monologue. In 1932
Al Mamiux (the Newark team manager) did a very good singing
and talking act. A few years later, in his next time at bat in vaude,
he had Jimmy Rule at the piano. There was an interclub quartette
about 1925: George Crable (Brooklyn), Tom Dillon (Macon),
Frank Browning (Detroit), and Billy Gleason (Galveston). My
old friend Rabbit Maranville did an act with Eddy McHugh and
he was as good on the stage as he was on the diamond. Coombs,
Morgan, and Bender, world series pitching heroes of the champ

Athletics, did a skit assisted by Kathryn & Violet Pearl. Later
Kathryn Pearl did an act with Chief Bender called "Learning the
Game," by George Totten Smith with music by Arthur Behim.

Ty Cobb, Germany Schaffer, and Joe Tinker were all in vaude
about 1911. Mike "King" Kelly did a monologue; he also was with
Mark Murphy in "O'Dowd's Neighbors." Me and Aggie will never
forget the time we played in Jersey City with Ford Frick; he was
then a local radio sportscaster and sports writer and was very popular locally. He did something like his broadcast for his act, but
wanted some laughs to kinda lighten it up a bit. I gave him some
gags (the wrong ones, because he got laughs with them; we should
have kept them for ourselves in Jersey). Anyway, Ford didn't do
bad, leaving vaude to become the czar of organized baseball. He
is a swell guy in or out of vaude. We say he was a smart guy even
back in those days; he knew vaude wouldn't last!

Many of the ball players who played vaude became sportscasters when radio got going, players like Bump Hadley (Yankee
pitcher), Elbie Fletcher (Braves first baseman), Wait Hoyt,
Frankie Frisch, Harry Heilman (great hitter), Gabby Street,
Charles Gehringer (Hall of Fame guy), Fred Haney, and of course
one of the greats, Dizzy Dean (who played the Roxy with his
brother). And talking about sportscasters, we had Harry Howell,
the curve-ball pitcher of the St. Louis Browns, explaining the movie
of the Chicago-Detroit series in 1908.

And did you know that B. S. Muckenfuss, who is the owner of
the great Inter-State Circuit with vaude theaters all through Texas
and who played all the greats in vaude, was once the secretary of
the St. Louis Cardinals? He followed E. F. Carruthers as general
manager of Inter-State, and now owns it.

But I think the most remarkable man in baseball, as far as showmanship goes, is my pal Al Schacht, the "Clown Prince of Baseball." The guy belongs here because he played in vaude with his
partner Nick Altrock (they were the originators of baseball clowning). In their act they did a lot of comedy bits and Al did what
he calls the *pièce de résistance*, his imitation of Eddie Leonard
singing "Roley Boley Eyes," which started the decline of vaude. The
reason I say he belongs in a show biz story is that he has played
to more people *personally* than *anybody* in or out of show biz!
Sounds fantastic, but it's true. I am not counting the guys who
appear on radio or TV, but *personal* appearances. Here is his

record; figure it out for yourself. Al Schacht worked in baseball
from 1910 to 1936 as a pitcher and coach and did clowning for
the crowds on the side. He also appeared in twenty-seven world
series and in twelve All-Star games. He has done his clown act all
over the country every summer from 1937 to now. He did over
300,000 miles playing for our troops in Korea, New Guinea, East
Indies, Philippines, Japan, Germany, Austria, Alaska, France, Iceland, etc., doing 790 shows and playing in 310 hospitals. Figure it
out and tell me anyone that ever played to more people! And now
as a restaurateur he even plays to crowds in his restaurant. A great
clown and a great guy!

There were a lot of vaude actors who were great baseball fans.
It was the favorite sport of the actors, and many vaude road units
had baseball teams which would play the stagehands of the towns
(and get beat). Nearly all the big Broadway shows had teams rep-
resenting them, and would sneak in a ringer pitcher, usually Sammy
Smith, a song publisher who pitched in the big leagues, or Jack
Conway, critic on *Variety*. I remember when the National Variety
Artists were trying to get a team together to try and beat the Cohan
& Harris team. The manager asked an acrobat, "Will you play
third base?" and the acrobat said, "How big a jump is it?"

Yep, there were a lot of ball players in vaude; some hit home
runs, and others went to the showers—followed by vaudeville!

There were a lot of professional athletes in vaude besides fighters
and ball players. There were wrestlers who played many a catch-as-
catch-can date in vaude. Again Hammerstein's was the main mat
for the grunt artists. Wrestling in those days was a lot different
than it is today. Nobody sang about it being a fake. Everybody
took the championship bouts as seriously as championship fights.
It received big newspaper coverage, and so was duck soup for certain theaters, like Hammerstein's (and of course burly houses). A
wrestling champ was a national figure. I'm talking about the days
of George Bothner, Hackenschmidt, Frank Gotch, Strangler Lewis,
and a few others. In 1908 Frank Gotch did a skit with Emil Klank
called "All About a Bout"; they didn't have to talk much (thank
God)! Hitachuyma did Jap wrestling, and there was the Royal
Jiujitsu Troupe and the Tomita Jiujitsu Troupe and Miyakee, who
demonstrated jiujitsu, that started the craze in America. To prove
that all Japs weren't tiny, they sent Sumo, giant Jap wrestler who
was over six and a half feet and weighed about 300 pounds. There

was Joh Josefsson's Icelandic Troupe, who showed the secret sports of Iceland (why they were secret I don't know), gilma, self-defense fighting, and wrestling with the feet. These attractions were bally-hooed and were box-office, especially at Hammerstein's. They were novel and interesting, but they usually ended up in a burly show, because there wasn't enough interest in vaude except for "spot" bookings.

There were novelty wrestling attractions that became standard vaude acts, like the Bennett Sisters (not *the* Hollywood Bennetts). In 1908 May Harris, a female wrestler, appeared at Hammerstein's, and a few years before that a Female International Wrestling Troupe disbanded because of the death of one of the members; eleven went back to Europe. As a showwoman Cora Livingston was the greatest of 'em all. (So you thought those woman wrestlers on TV were new, eh?) I believe that Hackenschmidt and Strangler Lewis were the best wrestling box-office attractions.

Golfers didn't overlook hitting the vaudeville green. It was a hard act to put over, because the average audience didn't know much about the game, no more than they knew about polo. They admired the skill of the artist, realizing it must be hard to do, but didn't go applause-crazy about it. The only way vaude could enjoy this type act was with comedy. So nearly all of the golfers (trick-shot experts) used a stooge, usually the comic on the bill (who got paid off in golf lessons). Alec Morrison was the first golf act. His comedy partner was Flanagan (of Flanagan & Edwards). Jack Redmond, Jack Kirkwood, Paul Jacobson, Gene Sarazen, and John Farrell stuck on the fairway of vaude pretty well. They all used the trick shots, shooting balls from a watch, etc., and the comedy was shooting the ball from the mouth of a very frightened comedian. Most of these champs were booked because someone in the booking office wanted to learn how to improve his game. We had some pretty good golfers in vaude; Charles Leonard Fletcher was the first actor to take up the game seriously, and Fred Astaire played it when he was a kid. The golf acts became more popular in the later days of vaude—but then it was too late!

Because of the tremendous publicity which reacted favorably at the till, the marathon winners drew big audiences. Again Hammerstein's was the finishing line. John J. Hayes, winner of the marathon, played a few weeks later at Hammerstein's. He opened his act showing pictures of himself winning the race, and then came on for a bow. Dorando, who beat Hayes in 1908, was a sensational draw through great publicity and a tremendous Italian following; they even wrote a song about him. He appeared with his brother (who was his trainer) at Hammerstein's, and Loney Haskell, acting as M.C., introduced them to the audience. They both came out dressed in old-style European street clothes that needed pressing; the tight pants had "apples" in the knees and they really looked very funny by Broadway standards. Loney told the audience how Dorando won, how he trained, what he ate, etc., while Dorando and his brother just stood there. Finally at the finish of the spiel he asked the audience were there any questions? Ren Shields, a wit and a Hammerstein habitué, yelled out, "Yes, ask him who made his brother's clothes?" It broke up the opening matinee.

Every six-day bicycle-race winner played Hammerstein's. Elkes & McFarland, Walthour & McEachern, Leaner & Krebs, Root & Dorlon, Root & Fogler, Rutt & Stoll, Rutt & Clark, Goulette & Fogler, McNamarra, and many more runners-up. They all did about the same act, riding treadmills on either side of the stage for a mile race with clocks showing how they were doing, and of course in the last quarter they'd make it real exciting, like a sprint, dividing the "wins" for the week between them. Good thrill and good showmanship. These acts were only a draw the week following their win at Madison Square Garden.

Even tennis was represented in vaude, by Big Bill Tilden with a monologue. It was a good thing that after his act he didn't have to jump over a net and congratulate the audience for winning, if you know what I mean. Tennis those days was as strange to vaude audiences as was football. Someone once asked why football players didn't go into vaude? And Tommy Gray, a writer and wit, said, "By the time their injuries are healed, the vaude season is over." Those were the days when the starting team members stayed in the game until they were carried off. I am not sure, but the only real great football player I recall playing in vaude was Red Grange, who played a sketch called "Number 77" (which was his number). He was a big box-office attraction. He played in one game in California on percentage, and received $67,000 as his share.

There were also a few jockeys who played vaude; yop, the starting gate was at Hammerstein's. Tod Sloan, one of the greatest jockeys of his time, did a monologue written for him by George M. Cohan (who later wrote *Little Johnny Jones*, which was practically the story of Tod Sloan.) Tod had a sister, Blanche Sloan, who did an aerial act and received a lot of publicity because of her brother, but made good on her own and became a standard act for many years after Tod was gone. Garrison, who used to finish races with a fast finish (from which we got the expression, "a Garrison finish") did an act for a short time. Tommy Meade, a good boy on or off a horse, had a fine voice and was in vaude for a long time, working with different partners. There was a good jockey by the name of Tony Francisco who was a hound for the Charleston and played a few weeks doing it in front of a jazz band, which played him right back to the starting gate at the track.

It was 1926 when the Channel swimmers started their free-style crawl into vaude! The first of the women channel swimmers was Gertrude Ederle, and she cleaned up as to money and playing time, receiving $100,000 for twenty weeks. The second woman to do it was Mrs. Mille Gade Corson; she did pretty good, but being second cut her earnings in half; then Ernest Vierkotte and many others did it, and flooded the market. There was also a whole "school" of 'em who tried to swim the channel and failed, or who were going to swim it, or something. The small time picked these up here and there. They certainly made a big splash in vaude for a while. But it was a gal like Annette Kellerman, who wore a skin-fitting suit instead of grease, who outlasted all of 'em in vaude.

Billiard and pool champs chalked up their cues for vaudeville routes. They too, like golfers, had a limited audience, although their trick shots were interesting to laymen. They were no box-office draw, but they did empty the pool rooms and fill the balconies with the brethren. There were a few outstanding exhibition players and champs who played vaude for many seasons. Charles C. Peterson was the greatest trick-shot billiardist. Willie Hoppe went into vaude when he was the eighteen-year-old champ. Eric Hagen-lacher, the German 18.2 billiard champ, played six weeks on the Orpheum Circuit. George Sutton played without arms. Bob Conne-fax (billiards and pool) worked with Benny Rubin, the comedian, as a foil. Then there were Fred Tallman (pool), Walter Cocharane, Frank Taberski (pool), and of course Hammerstein would always play the champ of the year.

In the early days of variety the audience really went for athletic acts—club swingers, bag punchers, boxers, wrestlers. They all brought big crowds because of the audience-participation angle.

The so-called champs would challenge anybody in the theater to get up to fight, swing clubs, wrestle, punch bags, etc., for a reward they would announce as $1,000 (they didn't take in that much in a week). So you can imagine what chance you had to win. They had more gimmicks than a carnival at a county fair. Walking contests were very popular. "The heel and toe," sez my friend Frank C. Menke, "means you put weight quickly on the toe, which acts as the take-off spot for the next stride. The regular walker would do a mile in twelve to fifteen minutes, while the heel-and-toe speedster would do it in about six minutes and thirty seconds." Edward Payson Weston finished his walk from Los Angeles to New York and walked right into a route in vaudeville. George N. Brown, who was billed as a champ heel-and-toe walker, did a great act in vaude for many years with his regular partner, Pete Goldman, but he would take the comic on the bill and get a lot of laughs with him. Pat Rooney would be booked on the same shows with him so he would be able to work in Brown's act. They would work on a treadmill (à la the bicycle riders) and make it pretty close, besides getting a lot of laughs.

There was a fellow called Young Miles at Pastor's who was a champ walker. He'd get a timekeeper from the audience and the stage manager would call the laps as Young Miles would walk around the stage. If you remember how tiny the stage was at Pastor's, you can just imagine how dizzy he (and the audience) got. He did a mile in eight minutes!

The best all-round athlete in and of show biz was Fred Stone. I wrote you about the acrobats, etc., but these I mentioned here were the pros and special attractions! SEZ

Your pal,

LEFTY

A Fair Exchange

Dear Joe,

England had variety shows fifty years before we did over here and they have outlasted our vaudeville already by a quarter of a century! Vaude over there today is going bigger than ever, not only doing big biz but upholding the traditions. The English have been loyal to their artists and to vaudeville while we haven't. Over there when you become a favorite, you stay that way in their hearts, regardless of age and failing talents. In America you remained a favorite as long as you remained a hit; when you flopped you were soon forgotten by both the bookers and the public. Of course when you were a hit in America, it paid off a hundred times more than in England, but all the artists in America had, after years of giving pleasure to thousands, was money, while the artist in England has the love and affection of the people they have made gay and happy and are sure of a warm welcome whenever or wherever they appear! (And they also have dough.) Take your "cherce."

England sent us most of their great artists and they were welcomed here with open arms and purses. Harry Lauder, Wilkie Bard, Albert Chevalier, George Lashwood, Clifton Crawford, Beatrice Lillie, Gertrude Lawrence, Alice Lloyd, Vesta Victoria, Arthur Prince, Vesta Tilley, Gracie Fields, Will Fyfe, Cinquevalli, R. A. Roberts, Bransby Williams, and so many more that I will write you about later.

Much of Lauder's success in America (besides his great talent) was due to the great showmanship and management of William Morris, Sr., who managed him from 1905, when Lauder first came over for Klaw & Erlanger Advanced Vaudeville (brought over by H. B. Marinelli). When Morris took him on his first tour, he put on a big publicity campaign that showed how stingy Lauder was (it was started by Jack Lait) and which wasn't true, but Lauder as a good showman went along with the gag, realizing it was great publicity. Lauder gave thousands of dollars to wartime causes and other charities, gave the receipts of two shows a week to the Red Cross, and did hundreds of benefits during and after World War I. Me and Aggie will never forget the Christmas Eve we spent with Sir Harry and William Morris, Sr., in Parkerburg, West Virginia. Toward the end of the evening he said, "Lefty, would you like a wee doch an' dorris?" And I, being a drinking man, especially on Christmas in a small town, said, "I'd love it, Sir Harry,"—and he *sang it!* I thought he meant—oh well, I finally bought my own drink! He was a grand gentleman and artist and every theater he played in America still echoes with the strains of "She Is My Daisy" and "Roamin' in the Gloamin'."

Wilkie Bard, another great artist, first came over here in the early 1900s and played at Hammerstein's and was a terrific hit. He got $3,250 a week (a mighty sum those days). His friends told him not to come to America because he would be a flop, as there were many imitations of him and many acts who had stolen his material over here. He took four weeks to prove to himself that he could get over. He sang his famous "Nightwatchman," "Hail, Smilin' Morn," and his wonderful "Chrysanthemums." He was the talk of the town. He came back to play the Palace in 1919, and flopped; he quit in the middle of the week, but went back when Sime, the publisher of *Variety*, told him to rearrange his routine. He did and got over big and finished his route in America a hit!

Albert Chevalier came to America long before Lauder and Bard. He first played at Koster and Bial's and was a great hit. He came back a half a dozen times and headlined all over America. He sang many songs, but the song that will be ever green in the hearts and memories of all American vaude fans was "My Old Dutch."

There were many aristocrats of the two-a-day that our cousins sent over to us, and me and Aggie knew many of 'em personally and loved 'em. Great artists like Will Fyfe, who many claim was even greater than Lauder (but I claim you can't be greater than great—and Lauder was great)! Albert Whelan, a great entertainer, had the sole rights from Mark Sheridan, the original owner of "Three Trees," but Tom McNaughton and many more over here used it. I can rattle off dozens of great English acts that did big over here. Was there ever a funnier man than Bert Clark (Clark & Hamilton)? Griff (the juggler), Charles Irwin, Chris Richards, Handis & Millis, Lillian Ashley, Marie Lloyd, Lillian Morris, Daisy Harcourt, the Lupinos, Ada Reeve, Lottie Collins, Loie Fuller, J. P. Huntley (I can see him now buying the gun in that gun shop), Wee Georgie Wood, Gracie Fields, Laddie Cliff, Vesta Victoria, Cissie Loftus, Charlie Chaplin, and the McNaughtons are some of the blue bloods of the " 'alls" they gave to America, who not only brought artistry to us and taught the American single women to use restricted songs, but were great ambassadors of friendship.

But me and Aggie also remember the flopperoos we exchanged. In 1913 at Hammerstein's we saw Lord Kenneth Douglas Lorne MacLaine, who claimed he took the date to help pay off a $190,000 mortgage on his large estate in Scotland. He sang (his singing couldn't pay off a mortgage on a bird bath). After a few weeks he quit and took a job as keeper of the hounds at Meadow Brook

Hunt Club. He said, "It is steadier." That same year Lady Constance Stewart Richardson danced at Hammerstein's. Seems all the titled people were playing Hammerstein's. They had a certain draw; society went to fawn on 'em and the common people went to take a peek.

Cruickshank, an English musical clown, did one show at the Palace, and went back to England after the matinee. A few years later Wish Wynne, a fine artist, played the Riverside with tiny billing and her name left out of the ads. Never before was a great performer like her given this treatment (I don't know the reason, if there was any). But she more than made good later on all the big-time bills.

Maude Allen's first appearance was fair; then she came over in 1916 with a large company of "classical" dancers and did a terrible flopperoo. There were many more that flopped or just got by, but I'd rather talk about the hits. You will find a lot about them in my other letters under the different type acts.

We sent many an act from America that made good in England, and also many that "took the boat Wednesday." McIntyre & Heath, who were our greatest blackface act, got "the bird" at the Hippodrome in London. They did their "Georgia Minstrels," which was too slow, then changed to "Waiting at the Church," doing a bit better, but still no good. They did real darky characters that the English weren't familiar with. They got paid off for four weeks and only played one. Bert Fitzgibbons only worked four days and went home. He was too much like Frank Tinney (who was a big hit before him). Other "nut acts," like Fitzgibbons, also flopped. Acts like James J. Morton, Neil McKinley, and Jack Wilson (he played only one show) all came too early. Acts like Happy Jack Gardner, Nora Bayes, Elizabeth Murray, Edmund Hayes (he had too much American slang), Rock & Fulton, Trovato, Pauline, the hypnotist (they thought he was trying to put something over on 'em), the Big City Four (1908 was too soon for a straight singing quartette), Evelyn Nesbit (whom they sat through quietly) and many many more didn't get over. In most cases it was bad judgment in the selection of material, which the English just didn't understand, like we in America couldn't understand many of their artists. (Some of their single women couldn't use their best songs over here because they were very blue for America, but were a big hit in England.) In 1919 they didn't like the shimmy and sat through it quietly. (They were right.)

But we also sent them R. G. Knowles and Joe Coyne. Knowles went over for a few weeks and I believe stayed fifteen years; Joe Coyne went over for a few weeks and stayed forty years. Jordan & Harvey, one of the first Jewish comic acts, and York & Adams, another great team, were terrific, and Julian Rose, who went to England when his act was practically finished over here, became a big hit and started a new career over there. Bonita & Lew Hearn were a big hit over there both in vaude and revues. Will Mahoney and Frank Tinney were sensations. Jack Norworth stayed there during World War I in shows and vaude and was a big hit. Grant Gardner & Marie Stoddard, one of the early American comedy piano acts, were a big hit. Frank Orth & Ann Codee, the Duncan Sisters, Williams & Walker, and Avery & Hart all were sensational. J. Rosamond Johnson (Cole & Johnson) and Alf Grant did fine.

Herb Williams, when he saw his billing in London as the "funniest man in the world," demanded they take it down before he opened; with that kind of billing you have two strikes on you before you even say a word. He was a tremendous hit when he opened. (When Williams & Wolfus played there years earlier, they weren't received very well.) Arthur Tracy, the Street Singer, was a big favorite and could have stayed there for years. Riggs & Witchie, the famous dance team, went over big. Al Trahan, who appeared in a command performance (a great honor for an American act), was a riot, and billed himself over here as the "man who made the king laugh." George Fuller Golden was one of the first monologists and ambassadors of laughter we sent over—I'll bet he is still remembered over there (but not here). Fred Niblo did very big. Smith & Dale (the Avon Comedy Four) were tops on the first all-American bill over there. York & King went over big. Friend & Downing, who played all the Big Time over here, became terrific favorites over there and remained for most of their vaude career.

Harry Green went over on spec and remained to become one of the real big favorites both in vaude and shows. Kimberly & Page went over on spec many years ago and have only come back to America to visit. Fred Duprez also became established in England. Doyle & Dixon were a bit hit with their classy dancing act. The Mosconis danced into the English hearts, and Collins & Hart, with their burly strong act, were just perfect for the English. Clark &

McCullough could have stayed there forever. Jarrow and his lemon
trick, Moran & Weiser with their hats, the Three Swifts with their
clubs, and of course Van Hoven with his "ice" were just sensational!

The real old-time American acts that went over in the early
1900s really did the pioneering; they set the scene for the many
that followed. Some of them had it pretty tough and many of them
found booking easier to get than in America. Conditions there
were entirely different than here. They had play-or-pay contracts
that you just couldn't break. Performers carried little date books
that showed them where they would play two and three years
ahead. There was a case in England where a Charles Stevens was
booked fifty-two weeks a year for eight years with no open dates.
That was in 1912, when an act in America was lucky to get ten
solid weeks.

Some of the first American acts were Barton & Ashley, Mike S.
Whalen, Fanny Fields, Terry & Lambert, Maude Courtney, O. K.
Sato, Belle Davis & Picks, Margaret Ashton, and Dan & Jessie
Hyatt.

We sent over many acts that made good but couldn't accept
bookings because of salary differences. Irene Franklin did big, but
demanded too much money, as did Taylor Granville, George
Beban, and the Four Bards. THAT Quartette had to split the
act because they couldn't get their dough.

The Two Bobs and the American Ragtime Octette started ragtime in England about 1913. The Two Bobs are still over there, a
big hit on and off the stage. Rinaldo was the first American violinist to attract attention; ragtime made him a hit! Maude Tiffany
also bowled 'em over with ragtime. "Coon" songs made a terrific
hit in London about 1907, so much so that the English writers
started writing their own coon songs! One gal, I believe Clara
Alexander, sang a song, "Way Down in North Dakota." Another
sang an American song and, instead of singing "Down in Atlanta,
G a," sang it "Down in Atlanta, Gaaa." But don't forget they have
names of towns that it would take three Americans to pronounce
(and then couldn't do it).

When war was declared over there in 1914, many acts couldn't
leave London. Salaries were paid in paper money, which was hard
to exchange. Managers canceled all German acts, so one of them
opened under Jap names and make-up. There were over 150 Ameri-

can acts in London and managers were cutting salaries 30 to 50 per cent. They were cutting salaries in America too, because over two hundred American and three hundred European acts arrived and flooded the market. Some of them came via steerage. In spite of its being wartime, the English managers made more dough than they ever had and declared big dividends (as did the American managers).

English managers and agents began advertising in American trade papers for American acts, telling them not to be afraid of submarines or mines, there was plenty of work for good acts, etc. Many took a chance and went over because of salary cuts here. Actors had a tough time getting passports. In 1916 they were still advertising for acts. One ad read, "Safe in England for Americans. Air and sea cleared of danger. Zeps stopped during winter by new guns and cold high altitude. Eight Germans frozen in Zep during last air raid. Sea freed from subs by English control." But many American acts weren't interested because of the big English tax bite, which cut salaries in half. George Robey, one of England's greatest comics and top taxpayer in 1918, paid $60,000 (our Mary Pickford paid $300,000 that year over here).

In 1919 the talk about international exchange of acts died out because of the high income tax and the low exchange on the pound. In 1935 William Morris held a special showing of twenty vaude acts for English bookers at the Biltmore Hotel, with orchestra, etc., because there were no vaude theaters over here for showing acts!

The biggest hits we sent over there, besides the ones I've mentioned, were Charles T. Aldrich, Jim Corbett, Houdini, Bellclaire Bros., Joe Jackson, the Four Fords, Elsie Janis, W. C. Fields, Al Trahan, Hildegarde, Van & Schenck, Will Rogers, and of course the one and only Sophie Tucker!

Yop, me and Aggie think it was a fair exchange, SEZ

Your pal,

LEFTY

The Blackface Acts

Dear Joe,

I have written you before that the blackface performers were the first acts in variety. The Negro as a comic figure was popular after the Civil War, and besides it was an easy thing to put on "black," a pair of big shoes, and old misfit clothes—no outlay for wardrobe, and when you were in blackface you at least felt like and looked like a professional actor!

After a while many performers "washed up," or took off the cork, and went into other characterizations—Irish, Jewish, Italian—but the minstrels who went into vaude and had a rep as blackface comics stuck to their make-ups and identification. In the early days of variety everybody was trying to get away from the cork because there were so many of them, and naturally the smart ones tried to break away so they would be "different" and so get better dough and billing.

When vaude was in its Golden Age, blackface again became popular. Nearly all the singles started to do blackface, but it wasn't like the old-time minstrels who tried to portray a character; these new minstrels just put on "black" and talked "white." No dialect, didn't even try, in fact some of them told Hebe stories in blackface! For what reason they blacked up will never be known, except to hide some awful-looking pans! Just like many Jewish boys did Irish and Dutch in early days of variety, all the boys, Jewish, Irish, German, and Italian, took up blackface comedy. It became a craze. Maybe it was because a guy in blackface could get away with many things he couldn't in white face. People figured you were an "actor" when you had black on. And besides, working in white face demanded a personality, which many of the guys didn't have, but when blackened up with a big white mouth they looked funny and got over easier. They dressed in regular street clothes and didn't even try to do characterizations! The old minstrels went!

There were still a few old-time minstrels who did the Negro dialect and mannerisms and portrayed the Negro as he was. The tops in our memory were Jim McIntyre and Tom Heath, who did many acts in vaude, trying to keep up to date, but "The Georgia Minstrels" was the classic of them all, and as far as me and Aggie are concerned the greatest of all the blackface acts! No slapstick, just fine characterizations and belly laughs. They were the oldest two-man act in vaude—teamed in 1874. They very seldom spoke to each other, except for business reasons. They lived in d'fferent hotels when possible. One was a bottle man and the other liked champagne.

They were without a doubt the deans of all blackface acts. They were in variety and vaude most of their professional careers—took a few detours in minstrel and one Broadway show (*The Ham Tree*), but always came back to their first love, vaudeville. Tom was the straight man while Jim played the com'c. A guy by the name of Butler was McIntyre's first partner. While playing a honky-tonk, Butler had to leave town suddenly. There are a lot of stories why; some say he was shot at by the natives of San Antonio because he wore a high hat; others say he was shot at because he had his pants off—woman trouble. Anyway, Tom Heath, who was on the same show, joined Jim McIntyre and they stuck together all through the years, unto their deaths. Jim McIntyre went first on August 18, 1937, and Tom Heath followed him August 19, 1938.

I'll never forget the time Tom Heath and I were sitting in the lobby of the Hollis Chambers in Boston, looking out the big front window (hotels those days had big store windows and the sales-men and actors would sit there and give the local gals the eye). Tom was a tobacco chewer, and my foot was near the big brass cuspidor. I was afraid to pull my foot away for fear he would think I was underestimating his aim. (Remember, I was a kid and he was a big star.) He certainly had me nervous for an hour, but he proved just as big a star at spittin' tobacco juice as he was on the stage; he never missed the cuspidor once!

Fox & Ward were together even longer than McIntyre & Heath, but were not as well known. They did an ordinary blackface act and became popular because of their long partnership. When they were together fifty years, E. F. Albee gave them a route (and plenty of publicity for the Keith Circuit) for $350 a week. They were very fine gentlemen, never argued, and played out the string together.

The big-hit blackface act to follow McIntyre & Heath were Conroy & LeMaire—Conroy, a fine comic with a high squeaky voice (à la Tom Heath, but no copy), and George LeMaire, one of the greatest straight men in show biz. They changed their act every few years, but "The Pinochle Fiends" was one of their best.

Kaufman Bros. (Jack and Phil) were an old team who depended more on their fine singing voices than on their comedy. Irving joined his brother when Jack died. Irving Kaufman, I believe, has made more recordings than anybody in show biz—thousands of them under all kinds of names. You know him best as the man who sang the French commercial on radio about Martin wine.

Dan Quinland & Kellar Mack (later Quinland & Richards) were two old minstrel men who did a very funny act called "The Traveling Dentist." Dan was one of the greatest of all interlocutors, stood over six feet, had a booming voice, a fine vocabulary, and was a handsome guy (even when he was in the seventies). Haynes & Vidoq did a swell blackface act. Wood & Shepherd were one of the greatest blackface musical acts.

As for the single men in blackface, there were hundreds of 'em. Jack Norworth (later Bayes & Norworth) started in show biz as a blackface monologist and singer; he called his act "The Jailhouse Coon."

Al Jolson (Jolson, Palmer & Jolson) did the part of a bellboy in the act in white face and didn't get over until J. Francis Dooley (Dooley & Sales), on the bill with them, suggested that Al blacken up. He did, and from then on Al did black; no dialect—just did a Northerner's idea of a Negro dialect. He didn't do bad with it. His brother Harry did blackface later.

One of the greats was George "Honey Boy" Evans (got his nickname through singing Norworth's song, "Honey Boy"). He did a corking monologue and was a headliner for years, and also starred in shows.

Lew Dockstader, the famous minstrel in whose shows many of the great entertainers served their apprenticeships, was one of the tops of the blackface singles. He later took off the cork and worked in white face.

Eddie Cantor, who worked in blackface all through vaude and in the Ziegfeld *Frolics*, worked in white face in the *Ziegfeld Follies* and shows, but by some trick of the plot always finished the show ters and a great wife called Ida! There are a lot of blackface acts I wrote you about and will tell in blackface. He didn't do bad, for a guy with five beautiful daugh- you about under different headings—two-man acts, entertainers, monologists, etc. But here are a few names that come to mind that were real good: Bert Swor, Rawls & Von Kaufman, Ben Smith, Emil Subers, Swor & Mack (the original of Moran & Mack), John Swor & West Avery, Spiegel & Dunn, George Thatcher, Bill Van, Neil O'Brien (who did singles, doubles, and sketches and who at this writing is the only top minstrel still alive—a real great trouper), Pistel & Cushing, Jay C. Flippen, Jack George Duo, Lew Hawkins, Lou Holtz, Al Herman, Hufford & Chain, John Hazzard (who later wrote "Turn to the Right"), Mel Klee, Kramer & Morton, Mackin & Wilson (Francis Wilson years later became a Broadway star and the first president of Actors' Equity), Amos 'n' Andy (who went under the name of Sam 'n' Henry), Coakley & McBride, Hugh Dougherty (who did one of the first stump speeches), and many many more I will tell you about later.

While on this subject, when Frank Tinney (one of our greatest blackface comics) played London, he was a terrific hit. He had to make out an income-tax return over there and when the authorities saw an item of $750 for burnt cork (used for make-up), an English gentleman of the income-tax bureau came to visit our Frank. "My dear Mr. Tinney, we just cawn't understand your item of $750 for burnt cork; surely it doesn't cost that much for plain burnt cork?" Tinney looked at him with a typical Tinney look (like a kid that's been caught stealing jam) and said, "But my dear man, I use *champagne corks!*"

This same gag was later used (with a twist) by a certain burlesque comic who charged $500 for nose putty. When asked why such an absurd amount, he said, "Ah, but I put a spangle on my nose!" (I still claim Tinney's answer was funnier—and earlier.)

The old-time blackface acts are now washed up; there isn't a blackface act today in show biz (except when the Elks put on a minstrel show), but they are not washed up in our memories, SEZ

Your pal,

LEFTY

Meet the Family

Dear Joe,

Me and Aggie are kinda proud of show biz and its people, and especially proud of the many show folks who raised a family under tougher conditions than average people do. They had to keep working and that meant plenty traveling, and that's tough on grown folks, so you can imagine what it does to kids! Some left the kid with the in-laws, or a good aunt, or even a cousin, or many times had to board the kid with strangers. Those who weren't lucky enough to have relations (if you can call having relations lucky) or couldn't afford to pay for boarding the kids just had to take 'em on the road. Many of the kids were left with the boardinghouse lady, or the chambermaid, or even the bellboy at the hotel (the first baby sitters) while the parents went on at the local theater. In those days they didn't have any formulas, or if they did, actors didn't know about it; all they knew were routines.

The kid was gotten up at all hours of the night to make trains, and after making the trains, the family had to sit up in a day coach to save dough. The theatrical baby was raised on a formula of candy, popcorn, sips of coffee, and smoke rings. Anything to keep the kid quiet so he wouldn't wake up the people who were trying to get some shut-eye. In the company cars on which the actors on circuits would ride (the whole show in one car), the kids of course had the run of the car (and the train). All the actors would cater to the kids, if you can call stuffing them with candy and fruit catering. The old guys would figure they should of had a kid and maybe wouldn't have had to work any more. The older gals just showered unused motherly love on 'em. And the younger guys told 'em gags and taught them a time step, figuring these kids were different than regular kids and had to be "smarted up." The dirty stories and bad words picked up on the tour were from outsiders, not from actors, who were always careful with their talk and conduct when "the kid" was around.

Naturally, the parents were proud when the kid imitated some act; they felt the youngster might become a great "somebody" in show biz some day, something they'd been struggling for years to be—and never made it. Me and Aggie have heard hundreds of actor parents say, "If this kid grows up to be an actor, I'll kill him." But if the kid showed no signs of talent, they would grieve. A lawyer would like to see his son become a good lawyer, the same with a doctor, baseball player, etc., and if they don't the father is especially disappointed. With show folks, if the kid turns out to be a lawyer, doctor, engineer, or a banker, they are proud—but very disappointed!

Many a show biz kid have we "baby-sitted" while their parents were out "making a buck," playing a club or date. Many a kid we and the other acts on the bill "rocked" to sleep singing "St. Louis Blues" while their parents were on stage. (Now you know regular kids don't get that kind of lullaby!) Many an act's kid we gave a bath to, because we had a bathroom with hot water, and their parents at the boardinghouse didn't. (We went back to those public baths later.) One of the greatest kicks is to bathe a youngster about three years old; you play "seal" with him, throw him the sponge, and tell him it's a fish. They were show kids and belonged to all of us. Around Christmas time everybody on the bill would go all out for the kid on the bill! They would get the most useless presents anybody ever got, because everybody bought what he wanted when he was a kid!

Some of the kids grew up smart, some too smart, and there's nothing worse in the world than a show kid that's smart and fresh! A show kid seemed to grow older faster than regular kids. The kids got tired waiting in the wings, and eventually Pop and Mom would take them out for a bow, not that they wanted to commercialize the kid (although I know many times the baby taking a bow saved the act—many's the time me and Aggie could have used a kid). But the parents wanted to show off to the town people that they too were "family" people and had a kid. Of course a "traveling kid" sort of itched to get on the stage. So it was a short step from just taking a bow to letting the kid do a bit. They usually knew everybody's act word for word and could imitate anybody (fresh memories), so when they did something real good, the parents were kinda proud, and instead of standing 'em up in a parlor to recite to the company, they would stick 'em on the stage to do it in front of an audience, and if it was good, they'd keep it in the act (where there were no laws against it). Many of the kids when they

grew up lost their talent and voices at the time when it really
counted. Those who had talent were sometimes used by parents
to keep their "old act" alive. They naturally "pushed" the kid,
who made it possible for them to stay on the stage; most of these
acts were booked because the kid would put the act over in spite of
the parents being passé.

Other acts kept their kids off the stage and put them in boarding
schools and military academies, figuring the kid would be a big guy
in some other line, and praying all the time he wouldn't! I'm telling you about kids that were weaned on applause and educated
on the show biz Three Rs, gags, singing, and a time step! Some of
'em made more dough at the age of eight than most bank presi-
dents. Jackie Coogan, Jane and Kathryn Lee, Jackie Cooper, Mickey
Rooney, Mary Pickford, etc. etc.

A stage mother starts out like regular mothers but soon becomes
a combination manager, house detective, tigress fighting for her
young, banker, and live chastity belt! She fights with everybody for
the rights of or fancied wrongs to her offspring, running to get
the proper billing, good spot on the bill, best dressing room, and
an easy future for the kid . . . *and Mom!* Mothers of vaude kids
are seven degrees worse than nonworking husbands of celebs. An
agent can kick a husband out if he gets too tough, but he can't do
that with a vaude mother (she's liable to throw *him* out). The only
escape for the agent is to book the kid out of town and get rid of
'em both! There are three kinds of stage mothers, the non-pro,
the ex-pro, and the "working mom." Years ago Ned Wayburn
offered a prize to anyone who could make a "mother powder"—
something to sprinkle on the stage mother and she would drop
dead, or at least disappear. Nobody ever got the prize. We had a
lot of S.M.s years ago in vaude. Some were swell, some good, and
some very bad!

The non-pro mom was the gal who didn't know anything about
show biz and its traditions; all she knew was her kid was a genius.
The ex-pro, who was now just traveling as a guardian for her kid,
sort of resented not being able to still "go on" . . . and of course
the working mom's main job was to keep the kid from falling in
love with some actor (or actress), and so break up the "family"
act. One thing I will say about the latter, when a real clever guy or
gal came along that looked like he had star-dust in his eyes, they'd

O.K. the match. Stage kids followed their parents' wishes more than other kids.

There were quite a number of stage families in vaude—maybe it was because there were many small towns the acts played where there was nothing else to do besides the act.

In vaude where mother and father were doing an act, motherhood was a big problem. The lady had to stop working at least four months before the happy event. She wanted to work longer (many of 'em did), but the costumes didn't fit, and the folks out front always looked at a pretty gal where they shouldn't. After it was all over they would have to lay off at least a month, so it was a great drain on the team financially, and sometimes maybe they'd even lose a whole route. So it was pretty brave couples that went in for raising families while working in show biz. It showed a great "family spirit" to make all the sacrifices. Of course there were acts of God, but on a smaller percentage; the professional couple had to figure it out, because it meant a lot to them financially and careerwise.

We know some kids in show biz that were born backstage and the mothers went back to work in a couple of days. You expect this from Indian women, but not from glamorous gals! The greatest family acts were in the circus. That is easily understood, because circus kids were added to the act as soon as they were able to do a handspring, and immediately earned their keep. They never figured the kid would want to do anything else, and I don't think the majority of circus kids did. What a break for a kid to be born in a circus; he didn't have to pay to get in!

There were many great families in vaude. Me and Aggie feel that the Four Cohans were the royal family of vaudeville, as the Barrymores were of the legit! The Cohans stuck together as a family for many years, in and out of vaude—Jerry, Helen, Josephine, and George M. George started out playing a fiddle and ended up with a flag and a Congressional Medal! The Barrymores all appeared in vaude, but not together. Maurice Barrymore appeared as a headliner in many sketches, Ethel played vaude with a few sketches (between shows), as did Lionel, with "The White Slave," and Jack did a sketch, "His Wedding Morn." Their uncle and aunt, Mr. and Mrs. Sidney Drew, were famous vaude headliners for years in comedy sketches like "Billy's Tombstones." You just have to mention the Barrymores whenever you talk about any branch of show biz.

The heirs apparent to the Cohans were the Mortons, Sam, Kitty, Clara, Paul, Martha, and Joe. In fact, they were in vaudeville much longer than the Cohans. They stuck in vaude until the finish —a great act! Then 'there were Eddie Foy and the Seven Little Foys, Bryan, Charlie, Mary, Madeline, Dick, Eddie, Jr., and Irving; the boys looked like their dad and the girls looked like their brothers. Their mother was a fine ballerina. What a family! They all were talented, crazy, and lovable! (Eddie, Sr., would say, "If I lived in Flatbush, it would be a city.") The Marx Brothers, with always an extra Marx for a spare, were great—Groucho, Harpo, Chico, Gummo, and Zeppo, and their wonderful mother, who was a great showman, Minnie Palmer! The Five Columbians were a musical act consisting of Pop and Mom Miller, Claire, the doll pianist, Ruth, the singer, and little Marilyn, who played the drums and danced, and who later became the famous Ziegfeld star, Marilyn Miller! There were the Four Diamonds, Mom, Pop, and two sons; the kids later did swell for themselves in their own act. The Sully Family, who did an act in vaude for over fifteen years, consisted of John Sully, Sr., Grace (mother), Bill Sully (later of Sully & Houghton, great act), John, Jr. (of Sully & Thomas, still going big), and Estelle (now retired). They all packed a lot of talent.

James C. Morton & Family, Pop (from Morton & Moore), Mom (Mamie Diamond), and their two kids were a grand bunch. There were the Keatons, Joe, Myra, Buster, Jingles, and Louise. Buster Keaton is still one of our greatest pantomimists. The Dooley family, Johnny, Billy, Gordon, and Ray, didn't all play together, only as brother and sister, two brothers, singles, etc., but they certainly belong with the vaude families. Ray is the only survivor. The Mosconi Family appeared as a family dancing act, Pop Mosconi (who could outdance all of his kids), Charlie, Louis, Verna, and Willie (tops in this type act). May Wirth & Family, the great equestrian act, is an old and honored one not only in the circus but in vaude. The Breen Family, Nellie, her dad, and her brother, Charles B. Lawlor and Daughters (he wrote "Sidewalks of New York"), Keno & Green and their daughter Mitzi (the very talented Mitzi Green) are others. The Musical Hodges and the Musical Cuttys were two large and very well-known vaude families.

The Bell Family (there were about ten of them) were the famous Mexican bell ringers. Other families were Carter De Haven & Flora Parker with their talented offspring, Gloria and Carter, Jr. (class); Ross Wyse, Jr., and his Pop and Mom; West, Virginia & West (that's Buster West); the Rianos (Renee became a very funny gal); the Three Graces (Dad, Mother, and Frankie); Crawford & Broderick, and their talented son, Broderick Crawford; Lulu McConell & Grant Simpson and son; and Chic York & Rose King and daughter—when she got married, they ran a full-page ad in *Variety* about the marriage; on the bottom it gave their route and said "Booked Solid"—the first time this was ever done in a trade paper. I also remember the time when the Happy McNulty's (a family act) put an in memoriam notice in *Variety* saying, "In memory of our dear departed Father—The Happy McNultys."

A double family act was Herman Timberg and his son (now a swell comic known as Tim Mack) and Pat Rooney and his son, Pat, Jr. (a swell dancer). They all worked together for a number of seasons and were a great act. There was the Kelton Family; later Sue (the mother) and Pert did a "sister" act and Pop was the leader in the orchestra (faked it). Pert did a Chaplin imitation when she was a kid in the act and later became a swell single in the *Follies*. More of the families were Grace Hayes and her very talented son, Peter Lind Hayes; Montrose & Allen and their funny son Steve; Arthur Byron, wife, and daughter Eileen; Johnny Hyams & Leilia McIntyre and their pic-star daughter, Leilia Hyams; George Whiting & Sadie Burt and their daughter Virginia May; the Chadwick Trio, Mom, Pop, and Ida May; Ed Blondell with his beautiful daughter Joan; J. C. Nugent with his wife, son Elliot, and daughter Ruth; O'Brien Havel and two sons Arthur and Puggy (they didn't work together); Mr. and Mrs. Norman Phillips and Jr.; Wells, McGinty & West (father and two sons—wonderful pantomime comedy act): Annie Yeamans and daughter; and so many many more that it would be impossible to mention because of space. But they were all nice folks.

Me and Aggie get a big laugh when we recall the sister acts we played with. How each wife would watch her husband, and every gal partner would watch her boy partner, because the sister acts were supposed to be always on the prowl for a husband or loose partner to kind of better themselves, figuring one or the other was gonna get married sooner or later and quit the other sister or even the stage, so it was open season all the time. This wasn't really true, because the majority of 'em were swell, decent gals.

In small towns, especially where the manager was a wolf, the sister act would get the best dressing room, regardless of their billing. The stagehands and musicians would cater to them, they'd get away with excess baggage charges at the railroad station, and the clerk in the hotel would give them a good rate. Most of the gals were a lot of laughs, giving the town yokels a play while sidewinking at their fellow artists. You see, the poor gals couldn't go with anybody on the bill, because the wives and partners were jealous. The sister act knew what it was all about, and after all the gals had to live, and that's how the agents and bookers figured too. Audiences would rather see a mediocre sister act than a good brother act (they were better to look at). The women out front could either pan the girls' hair-dos or their clothes, and maybe copy them. They could also argue about, "Which is the youngest?" and "I wonder are they real sisters?" (and many of them weren't—some were even mother and daughter).

There weren't very many top-notch comedy sister acts; you could almost count them on one hand. The Nicholl Sisters (the first great two-woman blackface act) were swell. You had to give them credit for blackening up, because a swell-looking gal (which each one was) doesn't like to smear that cork over her face, but those two gals figured it would be a novelty, and they were right; they outlasted many a sister act in vaude. The Elinore Sisters did a comedy act, worked like the Russell Bros., and split when Kate married Sam Williams (they worked together for years). Mary & Ann Clark were a standard comedy act for many years and remained together until Ann died. The Watson Sisters (Kitty and Fanny) are the Smith & Dale of the sister acts; they are still together and those two gals still pack plenty of comedy. The runners-up are the Duncan Sisters, who started out as a harmony act and ended up as a great comedy act.

Most of the regular sister acts did singing and dancing and featured clothes—and looks! When me and Aggie say anybody was tops, it is our own opinion, but we are sure the record will bear us out. You know the old story about Montgomery Epstein, who said, "It's a good thing we all don't like the same things, or else we would all be eating *herring!*"

The biggest drawing card among the sister acts were Rose

(Rozicka) and Jenny (Yanci) Dolly. They had plenty of class. First billed as the Dolly Twin Sisters, they ran an ad in *Variety* when they first came to New York saying, "Rose gives imitations of Isadora Duncan, English fantastic dancer" (and gave their Bronx address, 669 Caldwell Ave.). They later became the talk of two continents! There were many classy dancing and singing sister acts: the Cameron Sisters (beautiful Madeline is now the wife of Billy Gaxton), the Barr Twins, the Millership Sisters, the Fairbanks Twins, Mabel & Dora Ford, the De Long Sisters, the White Sisters, the Oakland Sisters, the Stewart Sisters, the Lorraine Sisters, the De Wolfe Sisters (Georgette & Capitola), Julia & Josie Rooney, and the Crisp Sisters.

Some of them even threw in a piano for good measure and did real good singing; tops among the sister singing acts were Rosa and Carmela Ponselle. It was Carmela who brought Gene Hughes, the agent, to her home to hear her sing and had her sister Rosa accompany her on the piano. Gene asked if Rosa could sing. She sang for him, and he made them do a double act. They were a tremendous hit on the small time, held over for full weeks (where they only played acts split weeks). They got the Big Time and again were a big hit for very little dough. They should have received at least $2,000 a week according to the hit they made, but all they asked for was a $50 raise—$400—and the booking office said *no*. So they split the act and Rosa went to the Metropolitan and did one of the greatest Carmens that ever was in the place.

The Courtney Sisters, Fay and Florence (the latter was married to George Jessel twice), were one of the first great harmony sister acts. There were the McCarthy Sisters (Marguerite and Dorothy), the Four Haley Sisters (one of the first girl quartettes), the Misses Campbell, Mae & Rose Wilton, the Trix Sisters, Tempest & Sunshine, the Boswell Sisters, the Meredith Sisters (first to sing "Hiawatha"; they were mulattos and passed as Indians in England), the Three Dolce Sisters, the Chesleigh Sisters, Thelma & Margie White, the Williams Sisters (Hannah married Jack Dempsey), Lillian & Ann Roth (did a kid-sister act), the Aber Twins (beautiful gals), the O'Connor Twins, June and Cherry Preisser (Cherry married the son of Harry Hopkins), the Three Allen Sisters (with Larry Reilly; one of them was Gracie Allen), and Clara & Emily Barry (of the famous Barry Family, Lydia, Bobby, and their dad, who was the famous Irish star Billy Barry of Barry and Faye).

There were no dumb sister acts, but many of 'em did dumb acts. One was the great aerial act of the Leitzel Sisters (Lillian became the greatest aerialist in the world before she died from a fall during her performance). Other great sister acts doing aerial acts were the Austin Sisters and the Alfretti Sisters. Remember the Lunettes, and the Curzon Sisters (they had all kinds of colored spotlights on them while they swung in the air, hanging by their teeth). The Bennett Sisters did boxing, fencing, and wrestling; the Weston Sisters sang German songs and boxed; the El Rey Sisters did a skating act; the Similete Sisters were contortionists; the Three Athletas did a strong act (Ann Codee was one of the sisters and became a great comedienne); Maude and Gladys Finney were billed as "mermaids" and did a diving act; the Ioleen Sisters did a wire act, as did the O'Meer Sisters. Another swell sister act was Jane and Kathryn Lee, who started as tiny kids in pics and then became headliners in vaude.

Among the sisters who played sketches were Bessie & Harriet Rempel, Vivian & Genevieve Tobin, Crisp Sisters, Josephine Harmon & Sands, and Edith & Mabel Taliaferro.

The legit had plenty of sister acts (if you can call 'em that). Many of them played vaude; that's why I am mentioning them. Usually the one who hit the top would get the other one a bit part or a chance at a small part so they would be together. Sometimes the youngster would beat out the veteran. Maxine Elliot was already established when her sister Gertie made her start. Kate Terry was the toast of London when Ellen, her sister, came over here and topped her popularity. Lillian Russell's sister, Suzanne Westford, wasn't as pretty as Lillian and didn't get very far in show biz. Blanche Ring and her sister Julia both did well. Bessie & Nellie McCoy did a sister act in vaude and when they split Bessie became a star. (Remember her singing "Yama Yama Man"?) The Irwin Sisters worked for Tony Pastor; May became one of the great comic stars of her time and Flo took out the road companies. Rose & Nellie Beaumont were with Weber & Fields, split, and then went in vaude with Nellie's husband, Billy B. Van. You've heard of Tetrazzini? But few ever heard of her sister Eva, Signora Campanini, who was also a fine singer but couldn't overcome her sister's lead.

Ray Cox & Hazel were sisters, but never worked together. Lottie Gilson (the Little Magnet) had a sister Gertie, but Lottie was the star. There was a very novel sister act in vaude called the Bergere Twins; one sang and the other took encores, and the audience couldn't tell which was which.

There were a few mother and daughter acts that were billed as "sisters," like the Flood Sisters (they did walking on a globe), Pert & Sue Kelton, and Pauline & Marie Saxton. Pauline was the mother, and did a "rube" single for years after splitting the act; Marie became a Broadway singing and dancing star of musical comedy, until she retired after marrying Sid Silverman, the publisher of *Variety*. All three have passed on and Sid, Jr., is now the owner and publisher of *Variety*.

Many acts billed as sister acts were really two-woman acts, which I'll write you about some other time. I just wrote you about the on-the-level sister acts this time.

As you see, many of the sister acts changed partners or got married, and didn't stay together very long. But there were *two* sister acts in vaude that stuck together through thick and thin and never even dreamed of splitting. They were Mary and Marguerite Gibb (who were the Siamese twins) and Daisy and Violet Hilton, "The American Siamese Twins"!

The story about the brother acts is the same as the sister acts. There were many acts billed as brothers that weren't. It was an easy way to stop arguments about who should be billed first. The early brother acts were mostly hoofers; they would dress alike, and so it was natural for them to be billed as "brothers." In real life I never saw real brothers dress alike unless they were twins. Where I was raised, the younger brother wore the older brother's clothes, and when he got some of his own he'd get a different color so people would know it was a new suit. But the stage "brothers" dressed alike because they got a price on two-suit orders. It was very funny to see a typical Italian boy and a typical Jewish boy billed as "brothers" (or any combination you can think of). Audiences would look at the billing, then look at the act, and say, "I guess they're stepbrothers."

Me and Aggie are just gonna mention a few of the real brother acts in vaude; those we leave out no doubt will be mentioned in my other letters to you under some other kind of a heading. The Musical Johnstons were together over forty years, and only the great Stage Manager parted them. There were the Patti Bros. (one of them went downstairs on his head), the Otto Bros., Al &

Harry Klien, the Roger Bros. (successors to Weber & Fields), the Siddons Brothers (dancing policemen), Joe Cook & Bro. (Joe was the guy who made the Four Hawaiians famous), the Rice Bros. (there were two teams by that name, one a great comedy bar act and the other a double Dutch act), the Six Byrne Bros. (a terrific act), and the Rigoletto Bros., who have been together for thirty-five years to my knowledge and are still going big, even unto TV. I believe they are the oldest real brother act still working, outside of the Gaudschmidts and the Arnaut Brothers.

Then there were the Bush Bros., Fields Bros., Teddy & Blackie Evans, the Sharp Bros., Van Bros. (another long-time team), Bowman Bros., Terry Twins, Mahoney Bros. (Will Mahoney became a headliner), Six Brown Bros., Harry & Bert Gordon (Bert became the famous Mad Russian of the Cantor program), the Arnaut Bros. (Two Loving Birds), another old-time act now on TV, the Schwartz Bros. (the double mirror act), who were together over forty years, Arthur & Puggy Havel, who started together and are still together (great kids), the Bernevici Brothers, who started as two violinists and when they split the "Count" went on his own as a successful band leader, Bert Fitzgibbons and his brother Lew (later Bert became king of the "nut" comics), the Musical Berrens, Three Leightons (Joe, Bert, and Frank), who rewrote and sang the pop version of "Frankie and Johnny," Val & Ernie Stanton, and the Girard Brothers (who were with Mae West for awhile).

One of the greatest brother acts was the Four Marx Bros.; another great brother act was William & Gordon Dooley; the Three Du For Bros. (Harry, Denis & Cyril, fine dancers); the Wilson Bros. (Frank & Joe) were a popular team in vaude and were together for many years (when anybody in the audience would laugh, Joe would blow a whistle and say "Ged oud"). The Purcella Bros. were part of the great Six American Dancers; the Callahan Bros. were great comics who acted as stooges with many acts, besides being good hoofers as were the Pearson Brothers; the Rath Bros. the classiest of all acrobats; Ed & Lou Miller were great singers; the Swor Brothers did acts with each other at various times; the Hickey Bros. did a great comedy act for years.

The Gaudschmidts are the oldest acrobatic act of its kind in the business; they must have been together over fifty years. There were Claude & Clarence Stroud, the Kelso Bros., Reis Bros., Weaver Bros., Ritz Bros. (still together and doing a swell job on

TV), Jim and Mercer Templeton, who worked together for many years, the Three Small Brothers, Joe & Pete Michon, the Caits Bros., Four Slate Bros., Frey Twins, Russell Bros., and the greatest of 'em all, Willie & Eugene Howard, who were together for many years until Willie was starred in a show (Gene was his manager). They had a brother Sam who was a very good comic in his own right, but couldn't get anywhere because Willie was so wonderful (the comparison just kept him out). Another case of that kind was Al Jolson and his brother Harry. Of course no brother or even a distant relation or even a stranger could touch Al Jolson!

There were a number of brother and sister acts in vaude, but for business reasons many of them didn't bill themselves that way. Somehow or other a gal lost her glamor for the gents out front when she was a "sister." I believe it cooled them off to know that her brother was looking out for her. It was the same as the Mr. and Mrs. billing. It sounds screwy, but maybe this new kind of mind docs that lays you on a couch instead of an operating table can explain it. All me and Aggie know is what we saw through our many years in vaude. We can mention many brother and sister acts that did very well in spite of the billing, but many felt it was best to "let 'em guess out front."

The ones who were unafraid were Victor Hyde & Sister, Harry & Eva Puck, Bud & Nellie Heim, Bernard & Dorothy Granville, Harry Fink & Sister, Al & Fanny Stedman (a great comedy piano act), the Aerial Budds, Hattie & Herman Timberg, the Cansinos (Elisa, Eduardo, Angel, and Jose), Kitty, Ted & Rose Doner (a great family), Billy Wayne & Ruth Warren (brother and sister—a swell comedy act), Rae Ball & Brother, Mollie & Charles King, Elsie & Harry Pilcer, Keller Sisters & Lynch (brother and sisters), Alice & Sonny LaMont, Jack & Kay Spangler, the Three Reillys, Vilma & Buddy Ebsen; Annie, Judy & Zeke (Judy Canova), Florence Moore & Brother. Some, as you may notice, weren't billed as brother and sister, but the advance notices for all these said that they were brothers and sisters. (Did I forget Fred & Adele Astaire?)

What I am trying to tell you, Joe, is that vaude people were no different than anybody else. They had pops, moms, brothers, and sisters, and most of all, they had *talent!* They were for real! SEZ

Your pal,

LEFTY

Animal Acts

Dear Joe,

Me and Aggie really shouldn't like animal acts, because when we first went out West on a vaude tour, we rode in a "tourist car" which was practically third class. Now, don't tell me there never was third class in America on railroads. They gave you a cheaper rate than a day coach in a car with cane seats and a stove at one end where the passengers could cook their food. (In summer the cane seats were much cooler than the plush ones in the pullmans.) These tourist cars were mostly for emigrants, but our show had one all to ourselves—we all wanted to save dough (but me and Aggie didn't have any dough to save; in those days Aggie's grouch bag was flatter than a record). Anyway, what I want to tell you is that we had a dog act on the show; the dogs were in the baggage car, but the owner cooked all the dog food in our car. Brother, did you ever smell dog food cooking—in a train? I'll tell you what it did for me and Aggie: the railroads lost two tourist-rate customers. After that trip we traveled first class, if you can call a day coach first class!

The circuses furnished the variety theaters with the "small stuff" animal acts, like dogs, monkeys, ponies, pigeons, etc., that could play on small stages and get into the small stage doors. When the circus would close, those acts would fill in the winter with vaude dates. The variety houses had no room to keep the animal acts, so the owners would keep their animals in the dressing room during the show, and sleep 'em in a local stable or barn.

European managers always played animal acts and headlined many of them. They had special entrances and quarters for animals right in the theater.

There weren't very many wild-animal acts in American vaude. There were some elephant acts, but few "cat" acts, like lions, tigers, panthers, and leopards. Even in later years, when there were big stages and large stage doors, the managers were a bit afraid to play the wild animals for fear of frightening the women and children.

Me and Aggie will never forget the time we played the Moss

and Brill house on East Eighty-sixth Street, New York, about thirty-five years ago. There was a lion act on the bill. Some drunken assistant forgot to close the door of the cage while they were on stage and the lions got wise and started to scram through it like they had a vacation. They went over the foots and through the side boxes, and you can imagine the panic. The remarkable part of it was that nobody got hurt by the animals, who went for the exits, and believe me nobody was in their way, but a few of the audience were hurt by the panic among themselves. Maybe the lions thought they were a lousy audience and didn't want anything to do with them. At the time we were all panicky backstage, but it all ended up in a laugh. One lion got on the fire escape and jumped into the skylight of a photographer's next door. The lion was scared worse than the photographer, and they captured him easily.

By now the cops were out holding back the crowds on Third Avenue, where a few of the lions were roaming around. They shot two of them and then spotted one standing outside a saloon on the West Side of Third Avenue, between Eighty-fourth and Eighty-fifth streets. There were hundreds of people watching as the lion scratched himself and then lay down; he didn't seem a bit worried except when the elevated train went by. The crowd and cops were tense—and then a drunk who was rushing the growler staggered through the saloon's swinging doors with a tin pail of beer in his hand, saw the lion sitting there, and, mistaking him for a dog, walked over and patted his head and walked on. The lion never even looked up. He was brought home alive. After this incident there were *no* wild-animal acts in vaude for years!

While I'm on a lion kick, I must tell you a couple more experiences me and Aggie had, and to which we have witnesses. While we were playing a theater in Germantown, Pennsylvania, there was a certain lion act on the bill (I said certain lion act, because I don't want the owner or her heirs to be embarrassed and get notions of suing). There were three shows a day, one in the afternoon, house cleared, and two at night. After the matinee we put the feed bag on and I came back to the theater where everything was dark except a tiny pilot light upstage. I made for the stagehands' room, which was one short flight up from the stage, where a poker game was going on. The tiny room could hold about five people comfortably, but there must have been a dozen guys, stagehands and actors. To get your cards you had to pass your money via somebody and they in turn had to pass you your cards. One guy was sitting in the wash basin and most of us were against the wall. There was one tiny window in the room about a foot by fifteen inches big.

We were all playing penny ante when there was a noise at the door. Nobody paid any attention to it, but after a half a dozen of these sounds, someone said, "See who that funny man is at the door." Someone did—and there was a lion standing there! We all knew he didn't come to play poker! I don't know exactly what happened, but I *do* know that in two seconds there were four guys on top of me under the table (I wanted to be eaten last), and a guy weighing 250 pounds had his body halfway through that tiny window—and don't say it can't be done! Did you ever have a loose lion facing you? And all through this excitement the lion didn't even move! In a few minutes (which seemed a whole season to me) the guy who cleaned the cages and fed the lions between shows, and who had forgotten to close the door (the drunken bastard), got hold of the lion's mane and took him peacefully back to the cage. We found out later the lion had no teeth, but you know the old gag, "A lion can *gum* you to death!"

To finish this story, and it's God's truth, on Saturday night when the show closed the lions were put in crates and put on the transfer wagon (which was horse-drawn in those days) and on the way to the railroad station, over cobblestones, the pins on the crates jiggled out and opened the crates. Two lions got out (or fell out), but they made no fuss, no bother—they just followed the wagon to the station, where the same drunken attendant put them back in the crates as if things like that happened every day. Could you blame the managers for not booking that kind of act?

But there were really some swell cat acts, like Adgie & Her Lions. She once put mirrors around the big cage to make the setting prettier, and it did, but she didn't rehearse the lions with the mirrors, so when they got into the cage and got a gander at themselves in the glass, they went wild. They had to remove the mirrors before the act could go on. There were Marck's Lions, Bert Nelson and His Lioness, Princess Pat, a very fierce animal (if she had been at that door in Germantown instead of the other one, I wouldn't be writing you now), Arnaldo's Leopard and Panthers, Furtell's Jungle Lions, Richard Herman's Jungle Kings, Dolores Vallecita's Leopards, and Captain Proske's Tigers. When me and

Aggie worked on a bill with anything bigger than white mice, we called it "nervous weeks."

The big elephant acts were Lockhart's, Gruber's, and Powers' Elephants (Powers' Elephants were for many years at the New York Hippodrome), Roxie and Baby Rose. And speaking about Powers' Elephants, here's a story that never was told before except among a few newspapermen and actors. When my very dear pal Gene Fowler, the famous author and newspaperman, was made president of the New York Press Club, he decided to do something for the newspapermen's kids on Christmas. In those days the guys had to work on the one day they would have loved to spend at home. So Gene staged a big party for the children of the working newspapermen at the clubrooms, which were on the twenty-first floor of a West Forty-second Street office building. Besides the Christmas tree, there were many gifts and a big feed, and Gene had arranged a big surprise: Powers' Baby Rose, a tiny elephant (if you can call any elephant tiny), who was playing at the New York Hippodrome at the time, was coming to amuse the kids. If you remember, Baby Rose was made up with a large white circle around one eye and wore a clown hat on her head.

Everything was set. The kids were all upstairs and Baby Rose was delivered at the building, but Gene forgot that she couldn't go through the elevator door. He asked the starter to open the other door on the elevator. The starter told him it was screwed closed and couldn't be opened. Gene couldn't budge him. So he asked, "Who is your boss?" The guy told him, Gene called the owner of the building, and he also said *no!* Then Gene whispered in the phone a certain story he knew about the gentleman, that wouldn't look good in the papers (anything to make the kids happy, even blackmail), and the boss immediately gave orders to open both doors of the elevator. The elephant got in, the door was screwed back in place again, on the twenty-first floor they had to take the door off again, and Rose finally got out. Gene told the elevator man that it would be at least a couple of hours before he would need the elevator again. Beaming over what a hit Rosie would be with the kids, he brought her into the room where the party was going on—and one kid promptly became hysterical! It was Gene's own little daughter Jane (now a newspaper exec). Gene got panicky and yelled, "Help me get this gawdam elephant out of here!" The elevator didn't answer the ring, since Gene had told the man to take a breather, so the only place to put Rosie was in the men's room (regardless of her sex). They had a tough time getting her through the door (she was bashful), but finally made it.

There happened to be in the men's room at the time a very well-known newspaperman who had just been discharged from Bellevue's Alcoholic Ward after a three-week siege of the D.T.s. When he saw the elephant and Gene, he blinked, rubbed his eyes, and in a low shaky voice said, "Gene, I'm seein' 'em again. I see an *elephant!*" Gene, who was in a panic because of his daughter yelling and screaming in the next room, explained hurriedly that the guy wasn't seeing things; it was a real live elephant. The man against insisted he saw an *elephant*, and again Gene told him that it was really a *live* elephant he was seeing. The guy kept getting louder and louder, and so did Gene, who kept telling him it was a *real elephant!* Finally the man yelled, "Yeh, Gene, but this one has *a hat on!*" They took him back to Bellevue!

Another elephant story that really belongs to vaude is also about Powers' Elephants. Me and Aggie played Derby, Connecticut, at the old Sterling Opera House in 1910. It was an "upstairs" house with a small stage door that not even a mouse could come through. So Powers and his beautiful wife Jeanne (who worked the elephant) brought Roxie up the outside steps and onto the stage from the front of the house. Roxie walked up the stairs like a baby and came down the center aisle. They had a heavy plank leading to the stage, and all the actors (three acts), on stage for rehearsal, were watching Mr. Powers lead Roxie up the plank. Now I've heard a lot of stories about elephants and horses not going over anything that wasn't safe, but I guess Roxie had never heard those stories, because the plank didn't have a board to keep it from slipping and when Roxie was halfway up the plank started to slip back. Roxie got panicky, jumped down, broke the piano (which was the orchestra) and three rows of seats, and started to yell (or whatever an elephant does when he is as scared as we actors were. (We didn't yell; we just sent out our laundry.) But Mr. Powers got the hook they guide the elephant with and tried to calm Roxie down, which was a very brave thing to do with a scared elephant (I wouldn't do it with a scared butterfly), and finally he got Roxie under control. It was an old opry house with a lot of skinny iron columns holding up the balcony. If Roxie had gotten mad at one of those columns, the whole place would have come down. The most wonderful part of the story is that when they finally cleaned everything up and nailed down a board to keep the plank from slipping, Roxie went over it like a baby, which is contrary to all elephant stories. Of course, after the excitement there is always a laugh. The manager was laid up for the week from the rehearsal incident, but showed up to pay us off, and me and Aggie congratulated him on the big business Roxie did for him. He said, "Yes, but from now on I'll never book anything in this house bigger than a canary!"

There were not very many equestrian acts in vaude. Transportation costs were big; special cars were very expensive and it took twenty-five railroad tickets to get a baggage car, so there were not over a dozen of these acts that played Big Time. (Few small-time houses could afford them or had stages big enough for them.)

May Wirth & Family and the Poodles Hanneford Family were both without a doubt the tops of 'em all, May Wirth as the greatest straight rider and Poodles Hanneford as a clown rider. They were both members of old and respected circus families that date back many many years. There were other swell acts of this type, like Professor Buckley's Curriculum, Mme. Etoile's Society Horses (also her boxing stallions), the Davenports (who were bareback riders, better known as rosin-backs because they put a lot of rosin on the animal's backs to keep from slipping off), Ella Bradna (wife of the famous ring director of Barnum & Bailey's Circus for almost fifty years) and Fred Derrick, the Duttons (swell act), the Five Lloyds (who were dressed like Indians), the George St. Leon Troupe (with Ida, Elsie, Vera, and George—a solid standard act), and Bostock's Riding School with Lillian St. Leon. Ida St. Leon played the lead in *Polly of the Circus*. They all were headliners with great show biz backgrounds. It's funny (or is it?), but there was only one Negro who had an equestrian act, and he never played in America. He was an Australian aborigine by the name of Harry Cardello, and they tell me he did a very good act.

There are two kinds of horse acts: Liberty and High School. Liberty work is jumping tricks at liberty—no rider, obeying sign or command of trainer. A talking, counting, posing, or drill horse is called Liberty. High School work means with a saddle and riders. I threw that in for free; thought maybe you'd like to know.

Most of the animal acts in vaude were dogs, ponies, monkeys, cats, birds, and "odds and ends." They were good attractions for the kids at matinees and even some of the grown-ups let out an "Ah" once in a while. Frank Stafford had a beautiful posing act with his dogs; he also was a fine whistler and was assisted by a beautiful gal, Marie Stone. Wormwood's Dogs and Monkeys were pioneers. Then there were Meehan's Leaping Dogs, Fred Gerner & Co., who also had leaping dogs, Stella Morrissini's Leaping Wolfhounds, and Prof. Harry Parker and Fred. H. Leslie, who both had leaping-dog acts in 1893. Rin-Tin-Tin, the famous movie dog, did well in vaude. Ed Vinton & Buster were good; the dog imitated everything the trainer did. Big Bill Bloomberg's trained Alaskan dogs did the only act of its kind. Svengali was a mind-reading dog. Sandow made personal appearance after his hit in pics. Alice Loretta had statue-posing dogs. Other acts were Alf Royal & His Dog, Wm. A. McCormick (whose collie barked out arithmetic lessons), and Professor Duncan's Scotch Collies. Roser's Aerial Dogs walked the tight rope. Meredith & Snoozer (white bull dog) was a standard act. M. S. Ferrero's Dog Musicians played toy instruments. There were Hector & His Pals (his pals were dogs), Max & His Gang (his gang were dogs), the Rex Comedy Circus, and Howard's Dogs and Ponies. Again a story comes to mind about my favorite clown, Eddie Carr, at Bedford, Massachusetts. Howard's ponies were on the bill; they were tiny things, and on rehearsal morning Eddie took one of them and brought him downstairs to his dressing room. An Englishman who had just come in from Canada to play his first date in this country was dressing with Eddie. Coming to America and doing his first show here made the guy a bit nervous. He went to the dressing room and introduced himself to Eddie. He kept looking at the pony tied to the sink. Finally he said to Eddie, "Yours?" Eddie looked around at the pony and said, "No. Yours?" The Englishman shook his head and said, "Good God, no!" "Well," said Eddie, "I guess he's dressing with us." "Why, I never heard of such a thing. I'll tell the stage manager. I won't stand for it. Why, look what he's done!" said the Englishman. Eddie looked and said, "I wouldn't kick if I were you. Last week I dressed with a camel!" By that time, Howard, half-crazy, came in and grabbed his pony.

I must tell you about a certain dog act (again I don't mention the name, because the dog is liable to sue or at least bite me). The man had an act with a lot of dogs performing on a large table.

At the opening of the act there was a dog standing on a pedestal who never moved throughout the act; he was like the Washington Monument. At the finish of the act the curtain came down, and when it went up again, the trainer turned to the posing dog and said, "Come on, the act is over," and the dog shook himself and walked off. This of course got a terrific hand because he was in one position for about fifteen minutes. Well, the gimmick was, the original dog on the stand was a dummy, and when the curtain went down the trainer switched the live dog for the dummy. They looked exactly alike and the live one took the identical pose, but only had to hold it for a minute. A smart gimmick, eh?

Of all the different animal acts we played with, we liked the novelty acts best. I'm not taking anything away from the straight animal acts. We certainly know how much patience and hard work it takes to train lions, elephants, tigers, horses, monkeys, and dogs. And it was the trainers that led a dog's life. They were up at all hours to feed, nurse, and train the animals, and they were never sure if the animals would come through, because animals couldn't tell you when they were sick. We especially loved the dog acts. You won't believe this, but we saw dogs that knew when they went over big, and when they didn't get a lot of applause for their tricks they would actually slink back to their positions. We worked with clown dogs that when they'd get a big laugh would add something else (not part of the trick) to get another laugh. We saw dogs that when the act's music started acted as nervous as fighters; they knew their "traveling days" and when they got in a new theater. Honest, they would act different on opening shows. They remembered return dates and seemed to remember the alleys they were exercised in.

And don't let anyone tell you that any of the animals are mistreated (maybe, when they were being trained—maybe, like a bad kid, they got spanked). But once they were "performers," the trainer treated 'em like babies, because after all they were his bread and butter (and sometimes jam). When you went on the stage with an animal act you never knew what would happen. I worked with a dog act that on one show refused to do a trick; none of the dogs would work; they had to ring the curtain down. I don't know why they refused, neither did the trainer. They just didn't work. The next show they were great!

Once a guy down in Dallas, Texas, told the local manager that he had a great cat act that he had trained in his barn for over a year and they were very good. The manager told him to bring them down and show him the act and if it was good he would use it the first time he had a disappointment. The farmer came down with a station wagon full of cats. It was early in the morning, the theater was empty, and there was only a pilot light on the stage. The cats went through their act, which really was very good and showed fine training. The manager said he certainly would use them the first chance he got. During the winter an opening act was held up by a snowstorm and couldn't make it, so the manager called in the cat man. He got all set to open the show. The cats were on their stands, everything was fine, the cue was given for the lights and music, the curtain went up—and all the cats scrammed off the stage. It seems the guy forgot to rehearse his cats with lights and music. I think the cats were later found on a Major Bowes Unit.

There were a number of bird acts (that's one act that gives the audience "the bird"). There were a lot of cockatoo acts (they were easy to train): Swain's Cockatoos, Merle's Cockatoos, Marzella's, Lamont's, and Wallace's. They walked the wire, rang bells, put out a fire in a toy house, etc. Very entertaining. There were Marcelle's Birds, Camilla's Pigeons, Conrad's Pigeons, and of course Olympia DesVall's was the best bird act of them all. There was also Torcat's & Flora D'Aliza's Educated Roosters, followed by Kurtis's Educated Roosters. (All through vaudeville history, when a certain type act made good, there were many copies.)

Among the best bear acts were Pallenburg's Bears, Alber's Ten Polar Bears, Batty's Bears, and Spessardy's Bears. All well trained.

Monkeys, especially apes and chimps, were good drawing cards, and even the trainers never knew what they were liable to ad-lib. Wormwood's Monkeys were among the first trained monkey acts, and Belle Hathaway's acts also go way back. She had one act where a baboon would catch plates thrown at him. A great act. There were Gillette's Baboons and Monkeys in "A Day at the Races" (the monkeys acted as jockeys), Norris' Baboons in "A Monkey Romance" (opened with a pantomime romantic scene between two monkeys—very funny), and Jean Clairemont's Circus Monkeys (monks on the dogs' backs and also dummy figures on ponies' backs). MaCart's Monkeys had 'em riding autos and bicycles. La

Bella Pola was a chimp that danced the Charleston, varsity drag, etc.

It was "Consul the Great" that put the chimp acts on the vaude map. (Alfred the Great, another chimp, also claimed to be the first.) Consul received tremendous publicity. He had many copies; one ape was called Consuline. (How close can you get?) There was another good chimp, Peter the Great, who was billed as "Born a monkey, made himself a man!" He later was called Consul Peter the Great (after Consul became a hit). And there were Alfred the First (get the angle of making people believe he was the first) and Mende, a very clever but a very mean chimp, who when he died was replaced by Buster, a great chimp owned by Jane and Kathryn Lee. They all practically did the same routines, like riding a bicycle, smoking, eating with a knife and fork, saying their prayers, doing acrobatics, writing on a typewriter, etc. Still Consul stood out and was without a doubt the greatest drawing card of all the animal acts!

Talking about Consul, when he first showed at Hammerstein's, an actor saw his opening show. He came back to the White Rats Club and raved to a brother actor about what a wonderful act Consul was. "Why, he eats with a knife and fork, smokes a cigar, writes on a typewriter, etc. etc." The other guy doubted it; he had never heard of a chimp doing those things. "O.K.," said the first actor, "I'll get a couple of Oakley's from Willie and you can see for yourself, and if Consul is all I said he was, the drinks are on you." What he didn't know was that Consul was taken ill after the matinee and was replaced by another headliner, who happened to be the international storyteller, Marshall P. Wilder. As everybody knows, Mr. Wilder was sort of a dwarf; he was about four feet high and was hunchbacked. The two actors, seated in the orchestra and not knowing about the change in headliners, saw Marshall P. Wilder walk out and say, "Ladies and gentlemen . . ." The actor turned to his doubting friend and said, "Geezus, they got him *talking*!"

We especially liked the "goofy acts," as me and Aggie called 'em, like Gordon Bros., Jeff, who was a boxing kangaroo, Swain's Alligators, bears like Moxey, the wrestling bear, Big Jim, the skating and dancing bear, Alice and Lolette, who also did dancing—they all claimed to be the first. A novelty animal act, like any other novelty act, could get more dough, so all trainers tried to get something new and many of 'em succeeded. Way back in 1893 Guy Leon had two donkeys called Jack and Jill that sang(?). The orchestra played loud music and the mules brayed, which passed for singing (as it does today with some humans). This was followed by singing dogs, singing wolves, and Rossi's Musical Horse, who also laughed! They all had the same technique; the "dancing" animals did the same movements to every dance; the only thing that was changed was the music, and it always appeared like the animal was doing the particular dance the music was playing. (Lots of human dancing acts do the same routines to different music and that makes them look like different dances.)

In 1897 there was an educated horse called Beautiful Jim Key, who would spell names, pick out any letter in the alphabet, playing card, or number asked for, use the telephone, make change, file letters, and play the organ. He was the main attraction with the John Philip Sousa road show.

We liked Guy Weadick's "Stampede," which was the first rodeo in vaudeville, and Muldoon with his champion wrestling pony. We liked E. Merian's Pantomimic Dogs, who presented a one-act drama, "A Faithless Woman," and Hughling's Seals, especially Sharkey, who was almost human; he juggled and played chimes and was one of the first to applaud himself. Rosina Coseli's Midget Wonders were a gang of Chihuahua dogs; they'd go off the stage in a toy auto and after they were off there would be a big explosion and the tiny dogs would come back pushing the tiny auto. Then there was Don, the "Talking Dog." (John Coleman claimed that his dog Roj was the first talking dog; he was playing the Orpheum Circuit while Don was in Europe. He didn't stand a chance, because Don beat him to New York and received his publicity via the great Willie Hammerstein.) Don was a hit only because of Loney Haskell, the assistant manager and M.C. of Hammerstein's. I heard Don struggle with words, and all I could understand, using my imagination, was "Hunger" and "Küchen" (Hunger and Cake); that's the only German I knew, and I'm still not sure if he said it or not, but I am sure of the laughs Loney Haskell got talking about Don. He had to travel all over the circuit with Don to put him over.

Another great novelty act was Barnold's Drunken Dog, who did a drunk almost as good as Jim Barton. He was signed by Klaw & Erlanger during their Advanced Vaudeville trip for $1,000 a week.

He played at Hammerstein's for $300 before that. Barnold was the highest-priced animal act at that time, the previous one being Lockhart's Elephants. There were many copies of this act. Officer Vokes had a great drunken dog too. Jenny Conchas had a fine posing-dog act; the dog smoked, changed costumes, and his face went great with the different costumes for plenty of laughs.

Maude Rochez's "Night in a Monkey Music Hall" was really a great novelty act. There was no trainer on stage. There was an orchestra pit, where the monkey "leader" kept turning over the music, and the monkeys played a "sketch," did a trapeze act, danced, etc.—really funny and great! There were La Valliere's Football Dogs; they had a wire strung across stage with a ball on it and when the trainer blew the whistle the dogs would jump in the air and butt the ball and the ones who butted the ball to their goal won! Another novel dog act was Dick, a dog who drew with pen and ink. He had a fountain pen tied to his paw and really drew pictures.

May Barkley's "Bulldog Music Hall" was a lot like the "Monkey Music Hall," only done by dogs. She had a mechanical orchestra on a small stage, three dogs appeared in tabloids and posing, and she also used a lot of dummy dogs and it was hard to tell the real ones from the dummies. John Agee had a trained bull and horse. "Gautier's Bricklayers" made a terrific hit lately in TV. It is one of the greatest trained dog acts that ever was in vaude. Dogs work without a trainer on stage. It's a funny thing about this act. Mr. Gautier's father, a great dog trainer, did this act many years ago and just about got by with it, so when he retired he stored the scenery and props away in his barn. Years after, his son, who was doing "Gautier's Toy Shop" (a swell act for years), figured he would revive the father's act, so dug up the props etc. and put it on. It became a sensation, not only on the stage but in TV, and was rated as one of the greatest novelty animal acts.

There was Swain's Cats and Rats, a very interesting act (they must have fed the cats before the show). Haveman's Animals was the first act I ever saw where the tiger licked the trainer's face and the trainer wrestled with a full-grown lion. After seeing that one, me and Aggie decided we'd never earn our living kissing tigers (kissing agents was bad enough). Apdale's Animals had a chariot race, with dogs made up like horses and monkeys as the drivers. Torcat's Roosters boxed and rode a dummy horse. Wormwood's dogs rode a bicycle race for a finish. Al Mardo had a "lazy" dog who would take his time doing his tricks—a very funny act. Nelson had boxing cats, while Coleman had one of his cats jump from a basket way up in the flies into his arms.

In 1911 we worked with a very funny monkey act, Gillette's Dogs and Monkeys; in this act Adam and Eve were bowling monkeys. Adam would make a strike or spare and a monkey pin boy would set up the pins and return the ball. After each play Adam would order a drink, and he got drunker and drunker as the game went along and finally tore up the joint (a very funny act)! In Charles Baron's Burlesque Menagerie the dogs were disguised as wild animals; the big laugh was when the dachshund, made up as an alligator, was brought on with a rope.

Rhinelander's Pigs had a trainer dressed as a butcher; he had the pigs go through simple tricks like walking up and down stairs on their hind legs, sitting down, forming pyramids, playing see-saw, etc. But the funniest part of the act was when the pigs would "balk" at doing a trick. He would take out a big butcher knife and start sharpening it on a whetstone, and the pigs, seeing this, immediately did the trick! The Butting Ram act had five goats and two pigs; they too would go through simple tricks and the goats at the finish would butt the trainer all over the stage. He did do a very funny bit. He came out dressed in a Prince Albert coat, and so as not to get it dirty took it off, rolled it up, and stuck it in his pants pocket. It didn't make the big bulge it should have, and had the audience guessing all through the act as to what happened to the coat and why it didn't show in his pocket! There's a story that goes with this act that I just must tell you. One show a "clown" on the bill (no, it was not Eddie Carr this time) had an idea and he painted a very prominent part of the goat with gold paint; when the goat went on and turned its back to the audience, the laughs were so big that the trainer got panicky—he never did get wise until later. When he came off stage, he said, "That's the best owdience I hef hever blayed tu. They know someding's good." I wonder what he said when he discovered the gold paint?

White, Black & Useless, the latter a mule, had a great comedy act where the men were trying to "shoe" the mule. Cliff Berzac's Circus was very funny, with a bucking mule; people from the audience were invited to ride him for a reward and of course the stooges came up and were very funny. This had been done for years in vaude and in circuses, but Berzac was the first to have a turntable to try to ride and it really had the customers in hysterics!

One of the really fine and oldest animal acts is Karl Emmy & His Pets; he is now working night clubs and TV. But the greatest animal novelty act I ever saw, that never played theaters but was a big attraction in museums for years, was "The Happy Family." There was a large cage on the platform which was covered with a big cloth between shows. In this large cage were a lion, lamb, owl, sparrows, cat, dog, mice, tiger, panther, snakes, pony, monkey —in fact, almost any animal you could mention, and in the center sat a beautiful woman on a large throne. There were no fights or arguments between all these animals that were supposed to hate each other. What an act that would be as a lesson to the world today!

As I said before, it took a lot of time and patience on the part of the trainers to produce these great animal acts. And there was plenty of danger when you trained wild animals. I used to sit in the company car on our travel days over the Orpheum Circuit and talk to a "cage boy" by the name of Slanty. He was a little guy who wouldn't weigh 115 pounds with anchors in each hand, all wrinkled up like an accordion, and the last man you would figure had anything to do with wild animals. He was an old circus and carny guy and had been with animals all his life; he knew every gimmick you ever heard of. Slanty and me and Aggie would "beer it up" some nights after he took care of the "brood," as he called them. I learned a lot about animal acts from him; I was a guy who always wanted to know about any angle of show biz, and believe me, this guy Slanty knew plenty. He told me that lions are trained to roar and make passes at the trainer to make it look more sensational. That tigers are the most dangerous and unreliable of the cats—the Royal Bengal tiger is very dangerous and the Indian tiger you can trust just a little more; they are both vicious, but easy to train because they have a high I.Q. Leopards are tough to train. Black panthers are the toughest and most vicious to work with. The only reason trainers get hurt is that, like airplane pilots, they get too confident and forget the animals they are working with are killers!

Elephants are very smart; the same as chimps, but elephants can't be trusted. Cutting the tusks from an elephant doesn't hurt them. Vaude acts use female elephants. There are a few guys that get "raw" animals and train 'em, then turn 'em over to other trainers to work in circus and vaude. To me, those original guys who take a wild beast and train it are the real top guys (not taking anything away from the other trainers who work with them for years); a wild animal is never tamed. Another thing Slanty told me was that the guy outside the cage, when a trainer is working with wild animals, doesn't have real bullets in his gun, just blanks. The reason is that in a circus, if the guy would shoot real bullets to save the trainer, it might hit somebody in the audience, and they'd rather lose the life of the trainer than some guy out front who would sue. But I'm just kidding. It seems that a blank cartridge is as good as a real bullet, because it frightens the beast for a minute—and that's the time the trainer can get out of the jam.

It's funny that me and Aggie knew Slanty for about twenty-five years, but don't know his right name. (I've nodded hello to guys on Broadway for over forty years and not only don't know their names, but don't know what they do.) He never registered at a hotel because he would "bed" with the animals in the barn. I tried to draw him out as to who he was or where he came from—you know, after a few beers you get curious—but he never told me. I am sure he was no count or baron or lost heir of a big estate; the guy's English was worse than mine—but he was a real nice guy. When he got liquored up, his first thought was for his animals. He'd call 'em by name like they were his kids. He'd make excuses for the "tough" ones like a mother would for her black sheep. The only thing I was sure of was that he was Irish; he would drop us a line once a year on St. Patrick's Day, and would recall when we were together on that day.

I could listen to his "circus slang" for hours. I once asked him why he left a certain circus and he said, "No pay-off. I was tired of working just to hear the band." I asked him what he did in the winter? "I wear an overcoat," was his answer. He called elephants "rubber cows." Putting the tent up was "getting the rag in the air." He told me that all the circus and carny guys would wear white handkerchiefs around their necks so that on a "Hey, Rube" call they would know each other when they started swinging with stake pins or blackjacks. "Hey, Rube" was the call for help among circus guys when a "towner" would start to make trouble. I asked Slanty how did the call start? I've asked many a circus guy that question and they all give you a hunky-dory answer, but Slanty gave me an answer that I think sounds pretty true. He claims that it started when a rube (a farmer or rural guy) was caught peeking into a gal's dressing room on the lot, and someone yelled, "Hey, Rube, what you doing there?" and started beating him up. That was Slanty's explanation of the expression and it's the best I've heard.

Here is what he told me about looking for a job with a circus, in his own real circus slang. "Things are rough and I could use some scratch—so I asked, 'Do I wear a monkey suit or my own front? I'll gladly come in on the thumb route. Grind or Bally?'" Meaning, does he have to talk all the time or only before each show? "What's the line," meaning how much salary? "How much time off to scoff?" or does a guy get a chance to eat in peace? "Do we work with the 'first-of-the-May' boys?" meaning, will he be associated with inexperienced helpers? "I'm great with lame-brain shows," which meant he worked with freaks. A "life show" (incubator baby show) spieler would say, "I worked for 'pickle punks' at Cooney Ireland."

A broad was known as a "bree," a guy, "a gee," a shill, "a stick," and a sucker was always."a monkey."

Me and Aggie liked Slanty a lot and we liked the animals he took care of—as he did. With a bow to the trainers, me and Aggie still say all the Slanty guys made it possible to carry on these great animal acts. Lots of people don't remember Slanty but I'll bet the elephants do, even if they can't remember vaudeville. SEZ

Your pal,

LEFTY

Monologists and Entertainers

Dear Joe,

The other day me and Aggie were talking about vaude in general and monologists in particular. Practically a lost art today! Why? Because it was the toughest act to do in the vaude biz. This will

probably bring smiles to the faces of the guys and gals that have
watched a guy with no make-up and wearing street clothes stroll
out on the stage and just gab—get big laughs and stroll off—and
not a bit of sweat on his brow. It burned up acrobats, dancers,
sweaty comedians, and guys that had to work physically to get by.
But no other effort in the field of entertainment demanded such
originality or made such heavy demands on the nervous system.
There were maybe fifty thousand acts in show biz (counting the
lay-offs), and there were only *five* real monologists among them.
Which proves it wasn't an easy racket, or else there would have
been thousands of monologists, because actors like "easy" work!

That's why in the hey-hey days of vaude the monologist was
king! He was envied by all the other performers because he didn't
have to carry any scenery, orchestrations, or wardrobe, and didn't
have to put in hours of practice like acrobats, jugglers, and dancers
had to do. All the monologist needed was a stage (a platform
would do) and an audience. The only music he would use was
something "faked" to bring him on and a few bars (played forte,
to cover up no applause) to take him off. The pit musicians loved
monologists and sketches because it gave them at least twenty
minutes to play pinochle while the act was on. Many of the
monologists never had a regular finish; when they thought they had
done enough time, they'd walk off on the next *big laugh*! To the
audience and to many of the actors it looked so easy, but to do a
straight monologue (just gab) was the hardest of all specialties!

The real monologist had to depend on himself. There was nobody to feed him, no songs or gimmicks to help him, and nobody
to share his "flop sweat." He had to know how to switch routines
when the one he was doing wasn't getting over. He was on his own;
he had nothing to help him but his wit and humor and personality!

In the early '70s and '80s, in the days of the honky-tonks and
free and easies, there were hardly any monologists. It was very
noisy in those places and hard for any one man to get attention
from the rowdy audience. They usually did short gags, danced, or
plunked a banjo for insurance. It was later-day variety that developed the straight monologists. And they really came into their own
when the reserved seat policy came in.

Early monologists worked in blackface, then they did tramp,
Irish, Dutch, Hebe, and Italian characters, and finally did "straight"

stuff. A true monologist didn't use songs, parodies, dancing, musical instruments, or acrobatics to put him over. His job was to get laughs through just "gabbing." A storyteller is different from a real monologist in as much as his stories are disconnected. Same goes for "topical talkers," who are not really monologists, although they are according to Noah Webster. But I'm talking show biz, kid!

The "entertainers" had a half a dozen gimmicks and so were able to get laughs and applause much easier. You've seen many a single guy, who would try to be funny for twenty minutes and not even get a chuckle, finish with a dynamite song or dance or other gimmick which was bound to put him over as a hit!

When I tell you these monologists were great, I may tell you what they did, but you can never write down *how* they did it! After all, it was personality that put over 65 per cent of all monologists, plus good material.

As I said before, a real monologist just did "gab," but there were a number of guys who, if you don't get too technical, really were monologists, with 95 per cent of their act consisting of gab, who finished with a song or dance or other insurance. I am putting them here because many of them really didn't need anything but their gab to put them over for laughs, but still they also liked applause—and the only way to get a lot of it was with insurance!

It's funny that I should start our list (and not in the order of their importance) with a guy me and Aggie never saw, but after talking for hours with guys who did know and work with him, or saw him perform, I respect their judgment enough to believe he must have been the greatest! So we nominate as the king of all monologists, J. W. Kelly, "The Rolling Mill Man."

Kelly, who had been a steel-mill worker, would go on the stage, sometimes take a chair to sit on when he couldn't stand, excuse himself for sitting down, and ask the audience what they would like to hear. Any subject called out by the audience provided him with a monologue that had them howling for a half an hour or more. At one time he had a continuous run of twenty-five weeks at Tony Pastor's. (Pastor's was surrounded by saloons; Kelly loved that.)

Stories about him told to me by Junie McCree, Steve Maley, J. C. Nugent, and George M. Cohan (they all worked on bills with him) are fantastic. I realize as we grow older we put on rose-colored glasses when we talk about the past, but I'll take the word of these guys that Kelly was the greatest ad-libber they ever heard. Today "fast boys" use stock "ad libs" and parts of routines they have heard and remember. Not J. W. Kelly! So me and Aggie salute J. W. Kelly, "The Rolling Mill Man," a guy who was voted by all who were fortunate enough to see and hear him as the *tops!*

George Fuller Golden started as a pug in Michigan, where he was born, a funny start for a guy who was to become our first intellectual monologist. He used to dance a bit too, and when he got tired of punching and being punched, he teamed up with big Jim Dolan (later Dolan & Lenhar) and did a dancing act. When they split, Golden did a monologue. He was a handsome guy with curly hair and a face like a poet (which he was). He read all the classics and was a great fighter for the rights of others. He founded the White Rats and fought for the actor all his life. He could rattle off poetry and chapters of the Bible by the yard.

He was the first American to appear in a command performance before the King and Queen of England! His monologue consisted of talking about his friend "Casey." He had Casey one season in Paris, the next at a wedding, etc. He spoke perfect English (a novelty for a monologist or any actor in those days). One of his stories which I remember, and which no doubt you've heard (if you listen to radio and watch TV), but of which he was the originator was this one:

"One day I was riding on top of a bus in London with my friend Casey. I was nearly worn out with several hours of sightseeing, and the bustle and excitement of the London streets, the hoi polloi, the Billingsgate, and the rattle were becoming almost unbearable, when we came in sight of Westminister Abbey. Just as we did so the chimes burst forth in joyous melody and I said to Casey, 'Isn't that sublime? Isn't it glorious to hear those chimes pealing and doesn't it inspire one with renewed vigor?' Casey leaned over, with one hand to his ear, and said, 'You'll have to speak a little louder, George, I can't hear you.' I said, 'Those magnificent chimes. Do you not hear them pealing? Do they not imbue you with a feeling of reverence? Do they not awaken tender memories of the past?' Casey again leaned forward, and said, 'I can't hear you. You'll have to talk louder.' I got as close to him as possible and said, 'Do you not hear the melodious pealing of the chimes? Do they not recall the salutation of old Trinity on the Sabbath morning? Do they not take you back to the dim vistas of the past when the world was young and touch your heart with a feeling of pathos?' Casey put his mouth close to my ear and said, 'Those damn bells are making such a hell of a racket, George, I can't hear you!' "

He was blacklisted by the managers for organizing the White Rats. He later contracted TB and was taken care of by his fellow actors, who loved him and what he stood for. Years later, when he was finally allowed to come back to vaudeville, it was too late. It wasn't long before he died, and all of show biz "bent a knee" for him. He was cremated and his ashes were flown above the Statue of Liberty, where George M. Cohan sprinkled them. A gentle soul was George Fuller Golden.

Charlie Case was the most original in style and material of all the monologists I ever saw. He wrote his own material, which was all about his family: true American humor, exaggeration at its best. Charlie was partly colored. His mother was a Negro and his father of Irish stock. While doing his act he would play with a tiny piece of string. He wouldn't (or couldn't) go on the stage without it, and one day, when someone stole it, he didn't go on the stage.

Charlie Case suffered more from pirates than almost anyone in show biz. In fact, entertainers are still using his stuff on radio and TV, but it's not like Charlie Case. Arthur Hopkins, the noted producer, said that "Charlie Case was the greatest master of un- expected statement in the world!" Although light-colored, he blacked up (as did Bert Williams) and always wore black gloves and a black suit.

"I was born in Lockport, New York," he'd say. "But a number of other cities have claimed me. Take Yonkers and New Rochelle. They have been arguing about my birthplace for five years. The Yonkers people claim that I was born in New Rochelle and the New Rochelle people claim I was born in Yonkers."

Charlie Case started doing his act in white face in 1910, because, he said, there were "so many blackface comics around." He was working for the Loew Circuit at the time.

He died of what was called a self-inflicted wound while cleaning his revolver in his room at the Palace Hotel on West Forty-fifth Street, New York, in 1916. When his wife was notified in Lockport, she dropped dead!

I believe that Charlie Case and Bert Williams were two of the greatest artists the Negroes gave to vaudeville. Both were entirely different types, Charlie Case a pure monologist and Bert Williams a song-and-dance comedian and excellent pantomimist.

James J. Thornton walked out on the stage dressed in a black Prince Albert, wearing glasses and holding a newspaper in one hand, and with the other hand he would raise his forefinger over his head (à la Dr. Munyon) and in a deep rich voice would say, "One moment, please!" Yep, he was the one and only James Thornton (later James & Bonnie Thornton). He was known as a pretty good guy with a bottle and would get a terrific laugh when he would acknowledge his reception with, "Thank you. I'm glad to see you *sober!*" He worked dead-pan, and pronounced every word clearly and delivered his monologue more like a sermon. He would sing his own composition, "Sweet Sixteen" (when he was able), but didn't need any songs or gimmicks to put him over. He was 99 per cent monologist!

There have been many stories told about this great artist but I like the one about the time he went to Bethlehem, Pennsylvania, and didn't like his billing and spot on the bill, and told the manager he was quitting. The manager, all excited, said, "You can't walk out!" Thornton fixed him with one of his extra-special alcoholic stares and said, "Christ walked out of Bethlehem. So can James Thornton!" and left. And I like the time he played in Wilkes-Barre, Pennsylvania, for Johnny Galvin (one of the real great managers), and Jim wasn't doing very well, but there was a young comic on the bill who was knocking the audience for a goal at every show. He came to Jim's dressing room and said, "Mr. Thornton, you see what a riot I am here. Why can't I get a date in New York?" Jim looked at him over his glasses and said, "Because you are a *hit* in Wilkes-Barre!"

Jim was a well-educated gentleman and a fine artist when he wasn't under the influence of liquor, and even then could out-monologue many a sober guy. During prohibition he was playing the Palace and received a great ovation. In his curtain speech he said, "I surprised you, eh? I have been on the wagon for a year. (Great applause.) I see all around me what liquor is doing, and I am saving my money . . . (More big applause.) . . . and when I have enough I shall open a *speakeasy!*"

Joe Welch was another of the greats. It's strange but true that it was three gentiles around 1896 who started the "Jew comic" vogue. But it was Joe Welch, a Hebrew, who practically originated and started the Hebrew monologue. Where the others did bits and stories of the character, Joe did a complete monologue! Another funny thing was that the Hebrews in the early variety days did Irish, Dutch, and blackface.

Joe came on stage to what practically amounted to funeral music wearing misfit coat and pants, hands in his sleeves, derby hat over his ears, and beard brushed to a point. He stood center stage, faced the audience for a half a minute, and with the saddest look ever on a human pan, said, "Maybe you tink I'm heppy?" That's all, brother! From then on he took over with a terrific belly-laugh monologue about his troubles with his family, with hoodlums, in court, and in business. It was Joe's original story, which has been in about every joke book in the world, that went, "The other day I took mine son to a restaurant to get a bowl of zoop. Jakey commenced to eat and den grabt me by the arm and sed, 'Papeh, dere's a fly in my zoop.' I sed, 'Eat der zoop and vait till you come to the fly, den tell de vaiter and he'll bring you another bowl of zoop for nudding!'" I first saw Joe at Pastor's, then at the Thalia Theatre on the Bowery in a melodrama called *The Peddler*, in which he starred. Nearly all the Jew comics patterned after his style and delivery. But nobody touched him. He was in a class by himself—a great and original artist!

Julius Tannen was one of the real great monologists of our time. (Even Aggie agrees with me on that.) He started in show biz as a mimic imitating Raymond Hitchcock and especially George M. Cohan, then turned straight monologist! He had a fine command of English, but would like to switch in the middle of his monologue into "dese, dose, and dems"—maybe just to show he was the same kind of a guy that was sitting up in the gallery. I remember when a heckler at the old Colonial Theatre yelled something at him and he said, "Save your breath, you may want it to clean your glasses later." Some of his famous cracks were, "I was as welcome as a wet goat," "Those paper cups that give you a sensation of drinking out of a letter," "Pardon me for being late—I squeezed out too much toothpaste and couldn't get it back," "I sent my collars out to the laundry to be sharpened." (These were all topical at the time.) Hearing a loud noise backstage, he said, "Sneak thieves."

Tannen did a general monologue covering matrimony, politics, news of the day, etc., but all done in regular monologue form. He would walk off on a gag or a poem. A fine wit, a fine gentleman, and I'll lay you six, two, and even he can outmonologue anybody around today!

Fred Niblo was a cultured and original monologist. He was once the husband of Josephine Cohan, sister of George M. He doesn't need this identification any more than Josephine has to be identified as the sister of George M., because they were both great artists in their own right. Fred was a handsome-looking guy and a "class" monologist that made 'em laugh plenty.

It was Fred who originated a gag that's been used by many comics and "unquoted" in many a joke book. "I asked my girl to marry me. And she told me to go to Father. Now she knew that I knew her father was dead, and she knew that I knew the life he had led, and she knew what she meant when she said, 'Go to Father!' Well, we weren't married!" After leaving vaude, he became one of the great pic directors in Hollywood. A great monologist and a great guy.

James J. Corbett, the ex-heavyweight champ of the world, was the only pugilist who became a top straight monologist! He really told stories, but they were so cleverly dovetailed that he could honestly be called a monologist. He was a handsome-looking guy and was a natural actor. His story that became a classic and has been repeated in many ways since was about the man who came backstage to see the champ and insisted he knew him. "Where do I know you from?" asked Jim. The fan said, "Don't you remember when you beat John L. Sullivan at New Orleans, you stood on the back of the train passing through Chicago and there was a big gang to meet you; there must have been a couple of thousand people?" "Yeh, I remember that," said Gentleman Jim. "Well, don't you remember me? I was the guy with the *brown derby!*" That story became a classic! He loved show folks and vice versa.

Andy Rice did a Jewish character, but with a difference. After Joe Welch, there were a number of Jewish comics who stuck to the old make-up, crepe hair, misfit clothes, hat over the ears, etc., until a man by the name of Jess Dandy "cleaned up" the character. He didn't use any of these traditional things. He did what Barney Bernard and Alexander Carr did many years later in *Potash and Perlmutter*. He was a fine monologist, but didn't play vaude very much, as he made a hit in musical comedy. The next man to bring even a greater change in Hebrew monologues was Andy Rice. He was dressed immaculately, used just a slight dialect, and, with one of the greatest monologues ever written by Aaron Hoffman and delivered plenty good by Andy, added up to a big hit.

He spoke about a wedding. "There were two hundred in the grand march, we invited one hundred, expected eighty, so we ordered supper for fifty! The supper was a success, very little pushing. The hall was decorated with shamrocks from an Irish ball the night before. They must have had a great time, because every chair in the place was broken! We had three detectives watch the presents and my three brothers watched them! We had fine presents. Rosenbloom sent his card, the tailor his bill, Mrs. Bloom a fruit bowl, cut glass—cut from a dollar to ninety-eight cents! Stein the crockery man sent six little Steins—and *could they eat*! The wedding cake was made like a ship. The little Steins were left alone with it, and they *sunk the ship*!"

Andy retired as a monologist and became a great comedy writer. He wrote many reviews and vaude acts and pics. Many Hebe comics followed Andy's lead and threw away the crepe hair and generally cleaned up their make-ups.

Rube Dickinson was a different type "rube." In the early days of variety (and even on the legit stage) the farmer or rube was portrayed with a large straw hat, overalls tucked in his boots, a long chin piece, and a straw in the mouth. He was supposed to be a "sucker" for "city slickers." Then along came a little fellow dressed in a Palm Beach suit and a clean Panama hat, with a short neat white beard and carrying an umbrella. This was Rube Dickinson, who did a new type "rube" monologue, sort of a wisecracking farmer. His monologue started a new trend. Instead of the farmer being a stooge for the "wise city fellers," he turned the tables on the "slickers."

Rube told about going to a society party in New York. He said, "What interested me most was the necks of the women. Why, some of the necks I saw last night reached from the ears down almost to where the mermaids become fish!" And, "My folks asked me did I think there was enough going on in New York to amuse me? And I told 'em I wasn't taking any chances; I'm taking my checkerboard with me." And, "There's one thing I didn't do while in New York, I didn't buy a gold brick—but I'm saving up!"

He always had fresh material and was a big hit. He met an untimely death, while playing Kansas City, when the marquee of the newly built Muelbach Hotel caved in on him. A fine guy and a great artist!

Tom Lewis, the man who originated the catchword "Twenty-three" (they added skiddoo to it later) in George M. Cohan's *Little Johnny Jones* was an old-time trouper from Frisco with schooling in the honky-tonks and graduate work at the Palace! He did an original monologue (which has been copied since—naturally). He would start a thought, but when he got to the point he never would finish it and would go immediately into another subject. Of course you could guess the finish of the gag, but he never actually said it. It was not "pointless" stories but a very funny monologue, which Jack Donahue revived many years later. Tom Lewis was a great trouper (he was at one time the blackface comic of Sam Ryan & Tom Lewis—a hit team) and a real swell guy. He was the master of his type monologue!

Ben Welch, the very talented brother of Joe, took the other angle of a Jewish comic. He did a lively, cheerful, wisecracking Jew, in contrast to his brother Joe's sad Jew. He also made a change to an Italian character (a very quick ten-second change), and did both characters very well. He soon discarded the Italian characterization and just did the Jew. He went to burly and became a star, but came back to vaude and became a big card on all bills until he "blacked out." It was never announced to the audience that Ben was blind; he wanted no sympathy applause, but the audience was hep. He had to get away from his monologue and do a two-man act. Frank Murphy, an old burly pal, did straight for him and took care of him like a baby. Ben was a great comic (when he could see or when he was blacked out) and Frank Murphy was a great straight man, besides being a great guy and a loyal pal.

Me and Aggie can remember Ben's entrance; he ran out on stage shooting a couple of cap pistols.

"I vas to meet her here at halluf past six. It is now five o'clock. Vile I'm vaitin' for her, I'll go home! How do you like my suit? A fine piece of merchandise. I got it in a restaurant. The fellow is still eating!

"I bought a house in Malaria Junction. A large bingelow mit eleven rooms and two vindows. A bedroom so large I can change my shirt in it mitout going outdoors.

"Ve got two kinds of vater—clean and dirty. Steam in the pipes—in *July!*

"My oldest boy is seventeen years old. He smokes Oakum! He asks, 'Has anybody got change for a million dollars?' Last night he bought St. Louis. He has a little silver pencil he sticks into his wrist. Last time he stuck it in his arm, he was elected *governor*. He stuck it in my arm, and I *paid the rent!*"

Two great artists in one family, Joe and Ben. That only happens once in a great while.

Julian Rose was another great Hebrew monologist, with a famous monologue, "Levinsky's Wedding." He was a Philadelphia book-keeper who went into show biz and became a headliner almost overnight! He was a Jew comedian in the old-school tradition; make-up heavily exaggerated, baldhead wig, long beard, etc. But he had a great low-down monologue that got plenty of belly laughs. When he wouldn't change his make-up and methods, which became outdated in America (there were no Hebrews left here who looked or acted like his portrayal), he went to England on spec and became a favorite and one of their headliners.

He pulled the original line when talking about a Jewish wedding where Finnegan, the Irish janitor, oozed in and started a fight, "Ah, he was no fighter, me and my two brothers and a cousin nearly licked him!"

Once at the old Friars Club I asked him why he didn't change his act. He said, "Why should I change an act that gets big belly laughs everytime I do it?" I had no answer.

J. C. Nugent is a guy who's been "booked outta town" for some years now, but me and Aggie will never forget him, because I learned a lot about show biz listening to him. He knew plenty. He started in stock, rep, and medicine shows and went into variety, with his own written sketches in which he played with his wife, son, and daughter (Elliott and Ruth), and later with others (as I told you in the letter about sketches). He was a self-educated guy and a fine speaker. He had a terrific memory and could rattle off routines by the hour.

He spark-plugged the first White Rat strike and was blacklisted by E. F. Albee. It was the best thing that ever happened to him. He wrote a play, *Kempy*, with his son Elliott (now a star and great Hollywood director) and invited E. F. Albee (the man who black-listed him) to the opening night. Albee came. J.C. told me that that was one of the greatest thrills he ever had, to see E. F. Albee there—and of course the show was a hit!

Nugent in vaude played "neat" drunks (there's a new one); by that I mean he was always dressed immaculately and was not a staggering, blubbering drunk, but acted just a bit tipsy. As a monologist he walked on with white tie and tails, high hat (and of course pants), and started to rattle off a funny line of classy gab—sort of philosophical (See what you can do with a Thesaurus?) gab. He was a lot like Ezra Kendall, not in material or delivery, but because he kept the chuckles rolling until they became a wave.

He would come on and say, "I'm so glad to be here. I'm lonesome. I got lonesome in my hotel room this afternoon. I took all my Christmas presents and—drank half of them." "I'm glad I was good to my mother when I was a kid. I could never sit around and see her do all the work. I couldn't stand it—I used to go to bed!" He would finish up by asking the audience to call out any subject and he would talk about it for a minute (à la J. W. Kelly—but only for a minute instead of thirty). He had one of the finest one-minute talks about the late President Woodrow Wilson that I ever heard.

I loved the guy. He was a fine gentleman, a fine actor, a fine writer, and a fine monologist!

Charles "Chic" Sale was one of our great "character" monologists. His characters were from a country school; he did the teacher and some of the pupils and the caretaker, and other small-town characters. His old man playing the "tuby" was a classic. About 1906 Chic came into the Palace with a new act in which he introduced a new character, a small town "smarty" who was always called the "wise guy." He said, "I'll just tell you a couple of riddles and make a 'wise crack' before I have to beat it back to the poolroom." Then he'd take a pair of dice from his pocket and slyly toss 'em in the air, before spying someone in the audience he knew and giving a stiff wave (as only he could do it) with a huge hand and gangly arm. He'd yell, "Hi-yah, Roy. How did *you* get home that night? Huh? Oh, you laid right there!" It wasn't long before the whole country was using the expression, "wise crack" and yelling, "Hi-yah, Roy" to each other.

He had a routine about a Sunday School entertainment with new steam heat clanking through it, "entertainment with steam," as the teacher announced it. His little girl character spoke a piece thus, "Would I fly East? (flying to the right) Would I fly West? (flying to the left) No, I would fly back South for I love it best—back,

back, back, to the land of charm (fluttering back) back, back, back, where things are warm (bumping into the radiator and burning her fanny) *Ouch!* That thing's *hot!*" It is funny that such a fine artist, who did so many fine things in vaude, shows, and pictures, will be known by future generations by a thing he wrote kiddingly and which sold millions of copies, *The Specialist*, which in its own way was great. But me and Aggie think his act was greater!

James J. Morton, the "Boy Comic," was one of our favorite people. You just had to laugh at this big 250 pounds of man who worked with a dead pan and acted as an overgrown kid trying to make good. Way back in the '90s he did an act with his wife, Maude Revel. Then he became a monologist, a new type of monologist, because he sang songs without music and without rhyme. His poetry had no sense to it and his jokes were pointless, but he made an audience yell. He was what we in the profesh would call ? "semi-nut" act. He would come out after an encore and say, "I am sorry, folks, when I was on the acting shelf (he called the stage an acting shelf) I left out a couple of lines of the song I sang, so I will sing 'em now." And he would sing a couple of lines with absolutely no sense to them. He would talk about the acts on ahead of him, and in 1906 he did his first job as a professional M.C. It was at a Ted Marks' Sunday Concert at the American Theatre, on West Forty-second Street. Instead of music to bring him on and take him off, he would just use the drummer. He would tell you what the next act was going to do, which had nothing to do with what the act really did. He was a very comical man. I put him down as a monologist, although he sang a song. Sometimes he didn't even sing the song, but just explained what the song was going to be about. He did 98 per cent talk—and what talk!

To us, the most tragic story in the life of Big Jim was the one about him advertising in all the trade papers for many years that he was James J. (not James C.) Morton. The James C. Morton was of the team of Morton & Moore, who came from burly and played a lot of vaude, and when they split he did an act with his wife and kids. There was a great feud between James J. and James C. for many years. James J. was a big spender, always giving wine parties, and when vaude was gone and there were fewer and fewer places to play, he was pretty old and ill and finally decided to spend the rest of his years in the Actors' Home. It wasn't long before he died. Sometime later a headstone was placed on his grave. The headstone read JAMES C. MORTON! It doesn't matter, they were both swell guys, and I'll bet Big Jim looked down, smiled, and said, "Can you imagine, after all the advertising I did?"

Frank Fay was made to order for Broadway. He had wit, poise, a sense of humor, could give out with "asides" that the Palace audience loved, but which Oshkosh didn't understand and didn't care about. He certainly was not a "road" comic, unless it was in Chicago, Frisco, Los Angeles, Boston, and Philadelphia. It wasn't that Frank was too smart for the small towns; it was that they were too smart for him. They just didn't like a "city slicker," and Frank was a city slicker—he was strictly for what we called the "smarties," not that they were smart, but they just happened to know "the language" he spoke.

Frank had a certain something that was really great—but he just didn't hit the top level in vaude that he should have, I mean way up there with Jolson, Wynn, Cantor, Benny, Hope, etc. Me and Aggie never met an actor yet who didn't say Frank Fay was a very very clever artist. How can you go wrong saying that after you look at Fay's record!

Walter Brower was one of the smoothest, slickest, cleanest, and most talented monologists we ever worked with. He came from Louisville and spoke with a soft Southern accent. He brought freshness to the old courtship and wedding routines. "The wedding supper was the finest I ever sat down to—I sat down *three* times. There was only one chicken and the way everybody made a grab for the legs was positively disgraceful—although the *two* I got were delicious!" He would work in his street clothes, no make-up, but he always brought a new pair of shoes (wrapped up in a newspaper). He would put the new shoes on before making his entrance. I asked him once why he did this. And he said, "Lefty, when you got new shoes on, you're dressed up!"

He was a standard act for many years, but never got into the big money and billing class. It was partly his own fault, as he never took his work seriously. He certainly had a great talent. He would finish his act with a poem he had written called, "The Prodigal Girl"—a tear-jerker, but he did it "classy."

David D. Hall is unknown by that name to the vaude fan because he never used it. He spent thousands of dollars in advertising "D.D.H.?" and was known to vaude fans by just those initials.

He brought a new twist to the very old "stump speech," using the same props of a stand and book and the method of "yelling over his points." He was dressed in a professor's mortar and gown and was supposed to sell encyclopedias. Taking each subject that was on the page he turned to he talked about it in a highly comical way. He had great routines. He was going great guns when he was stricken with TB and had to retire; he never did come back to the stage. If he went on TV today his material would be as fresh as a new chorus girl. A fine monologist.

Johnny Burke built up a monologue that became a "cameo of humor" that outlasted two wars! After World War I he did a monologue about the troubles of a draftee; he was a riot with it. The smart guys in show biz began shaking their heads and saying, "Yeh, yeh, he's a riot now, but what's he gonna do when the war is over?" Well, he kept on doing the same monologue, with the same results. The war vets and their families and other people too were still laughing. Then along came World War II (which I don't think Johnny's agent started so he could get his commission) and Johnny got a shot in the arm again. The wise guys shook their heads again, saying, "Johnny can't do that old stuff. He will have to get an entirely new routine, all about this war." But Johnny kept the old routine, dressing the same as he always had in a 1917 outfit, and became a bigger hit than before. The new draftees laughed because they saw there was practically no change in the "beefs" from the other war!

I know there were minstrel men after the Civil War that talked about the war, and drafts, etc., and I also know there were some after the Spanish-American War (like Lou Anger) that talked about it, but up to the time Johnny first did his monologue there were just loose gags, no organized routine, and Johnny was the first to do a complete monologue about the troubles of a draftee. At first he used his comedy piano playing as insurance, but later cut it out because he didn't need it; he had a dozen belly-laugh exit lines!

Nobody did Johnny's routine after World War I, as they didn't think it would last, but after World War II there were dozens of GIs who entertained their fellow GIs in camps with gags about the war, draftees, tough sergeants, K.P., Big Brass, guard duty, cowardice, heroism, etc. They are sure-fire topics in any war. I don't believe any of these youngsters ever saw or heard Johnny, and when they were discharged they started in show biz (having had a taste of getting laughs) and naturally did the stuff they had heard in the camps. One of them came out with a terrific monologue and got into the big dough. He is really a top monologist today; his name is Harvey Stone. But I am only writing about the guys of the old Palace days. These newies will get plenty of credit years from now, but I had to put it in. Johnny and Harvey did the same type monologues, with entirely different material. I doubt if Harvey ever saw or heard Johnny, but just for the record, Johnny Burke was the first to do a complete monologue about a draftee.

Joe Laurie, Jr., did a straight monologue talking about his family and relatives. He'd come on in street clothes, wearing a cap and smoking a big cigar (his trade mark). He would say "Hello" and finish with "Good-by." His gimmick was to bring on his father and mother (?) who were standing in the entrance watching their son (?). This couple were a fine-looking pair, dressed in street clothes, no make-up, and they acted as much surprised at being brought out as the audience was. Joe would talk about them for fifteen minutes. They never sang, danced, or uttered a word, and at the finish would just walk off throwing a kiss to the audience. It was the first and only time stooges were used without doing anything! He later followed this with a sequel introducing his "sister Annie" who also stood there without doing anything while Joe spoke about her and her boy friend. He later added nephews and nieces who sang and danced (that was when vaude insisted on "sock finishes.") Joe even did a few steps at the finish (anything to keep up with the times). But even his dancing didn't help vaudeville; in fact, some say it helped kill it!

Doc Rockwell, "Quack, quack, quack!" belongs to the really great monologists. He, too, was in vaude when you needed (or felt you needed) insurance to get off big. So Doc used to play a tin whistle for a finish (and very well too) after gabbing for twenty straight minutes. But the score of belly laughs he scored proved he didn't need the tin whistle. I believe it was John Royal, then manager of Keith's in Cleveland, and a great showman, who had Doc break in his act at a Rotary Club luncheon in that city. Doc needed a "spinal column" to illustrate his "lecture." The best the property man could do was to get him a large banana stalk. Doc used it, and it was such a big laugh that he never used anything else. Doc is a fine student, a great reader, and a very intelligent guy, and his monologue about the human system, medicine, etc.

was not only intelligent but hilarious. Today he comes in for a TV or radio appearance with his pal Fred Allen to kinda get a little green stuff to bait his lobster pots with at his place in Boothbay Harbor, Maine, where he spends most of his time.

In my book, Doc Rockwell brought a new note to the monologists' art, and was (and is) one of the tops! They don't come any better.

Johnny Neff (formerly Neff & Starr) was another novelty monologist. As the proprietor of a music shop, he would start his talk, holding an instrument in his hand, as if he were going to play it, and during his gab he would lay the instrument down and pick up another one. He would go through a half a dozen instruments without playing any of them, and meanwhile putting over a swell line of laughs. He did it all so naturally that sometimes someone in the audience would yell out, "Hey, you forgot to play that trombone!" (or whatever instrument he happened to lay down). He certainly brought a new note to monologism. (That's Aggie's word, and she can't spell either.)

Harry Thompson, "The Mayor of the Bowery," was sort of a rough Walter C. Kelly. He did an act a lot like Kelly's, but instead of a Southern court as a background, Harry did a night court in New York City. His characters were rough and very unsubtle (if you know what I mean). He was stage-struck and would do an hour if you let him (and, by the way, keep 'em laughing all the time). It was a standing gag that when Thompson went on, the stage manager would say, "Here, Mayor, is the key; lock up the store when you're through." Thompson played very little two-a-day but was an excellent monologist and a big favorite, especially on the small time, and in some houses a drawing card.

Taylor Holmes started as a mimic and later became a fine monologist and also a star in legit. He did the regulation monologue, using matrimony, courtship, etc., that got plenty of laughs. He finished with a poem, "Gunga Din," which he used for some time and got great results with. Along came a young fellow by the name of Clifton Crawford (a great artist) whom Keith was pushing along as a headliner, who also put "Gunga Din" in his act. (He really did it great.) The Keith office asked Taylor Holmes as a favor to cut out the poem for a few weeks as Crawford was following him in and it was the top spot of his act and it would take the edge off, etc., etc. Taylor cut out the poem as a courtesy (and also not to get in wrong with the booking office). And Crawford became more and more important and "Gunga Din" was his insurance and the audience began calling for him to do it. A few months later Taylor Holmes thought it was about time to use the poem again. He did, and was accused of doing "Crawford's stuff" and had to take it out. You can't argue with the public. It got so that every act that needed an applause finish used "Gunga Din"! Some theaters had signs backstage saying, "If you use 'Gunga Din,' don't even unpack!" Taylor Holmes had a fine personality and plenty of class. (By the way, he was on the opening show of the Palace.)

"Senator" Ed Ford spoke on topics of the day. He worked with a dead pan and with a voice almost as deep as Jim Thornton's. He used perfect English and had his own material that was sure-fire. He would open his act saying "Although my name is Ford and I was assembled in Michigan, I am in no way related to that obscure Middle Western manufacturer who put a radiator on a roller skate and called it an auto—or manufacturer of knickknacks." He was sure-fire.

Joe Browning, in his "timely sermon," was another dead-pan monologist. He dressed in a black Prince Albert, white gloves, and white tie, and looked and acted like a preacher. Once in a while he would give out with a "sickly" smile (showing blacked-out teeth) which was always a yell. His monologue went something like this. "Brethern and Sistern! The text of my remarks will be sweet femininity and her relation to the masculine *jellyfish*! Woman—*woe man*! Man—meaning *nothing*! Definition of female—a wonderful invention. Definition of man—*a flop*! Woman—feminine. Man—*assinine*!

"Average age of female—Who knows? Male—Who cares? Average weight of female—about 115 pounds. Above that all scales *are wrong*! Nature of female—mostly kind. Nature of Man—mostly *dumb*! Woman stands at the altar and promises to love, honor, and obey—Man promises the same thing but reserves the out-of-town rights!"

Browning wrote all his own stuff (beside writing many acts for others). A sure-fire monologist.

Hugh Dougherty, the famous minstrel, was one of the first to do a "stump speech" (the oldest form of monologue). All you needed was a stand and a big book, and to black up and holler like an old

Baptist preacher—talk about any subject and to slam home the point—*yell* it and *hit the book!* It was sure-fire. There were a number of minstrels who did this type monologue. Then it kinda died down, until Jack George and Slim Timlin revived it and did very big with it. They were two very good comics.

Arthur Rigby was a great minstrel monologist who never hit the headline spots but was a good standard act on the Big Time for years, with his great monologue and his famous $10,000 challenge dance. At the finish of his monologue he announced that he would pay $10,000 to anyone that could beat him dancing. He would go through a lot of preparation with the orchestra, etc., and go into a time step, then start doing a "nerve roll" with his left foot, then try to do it with his right foot, get stuck and go back to the left foot and a time step, then try his "roll" with his right foot again, and muff the roll again. He would do this a few times, then finally turn his back to the audience and do the roll with his left foot, which was the right one to the audience. It doesn't sound funny in reading it, but it was a big yok; it must have been or else a half a dozen comics wouldn't have stolen it. When Rigby got to the end of his "life route," he was in his home town of Paterson, New Jersey. A local priest came to give him the last rites. He asked the priest to please call Father Leonard of St. Malachy's in New York (the actors' church) to give him the last rites. The local priest explained to him, "It's all the same, my son, no matter who gives it to you." Rigby smiled and said, "Yes, I know, but Father Leonard will fireproof me better!"

Loney Haskell was a fine monologist, and one of the best things he ever did was his "stuttering stuff." He was the first to do what is now an old gag, about the man who stuttered and asked a newsboy the way to the depot. The newsboy didn't answer him, and the man walked away in a rage. A man who was standing nearby, watching this, asked the boy why he didn't answer the stuttering man. The kid looked up and said, "Wh-wh-wh-what? And g-g-g-get my h-h-h-head kn-kn-kn-knocked off?" Loney became better known when he quit vaude and became an assistant to Willie Hammerstein. In that job he acted as M.C. for certain type "freak acts" and it was through his gab that he helped put many of them over. His monologue on "Don, the talking dog" was a classic.

Walter Weems did a blackface monologue using perfect English, and a slight Southern accent. He had great material, which he wrote himself. He knew how to get laughs. He also used insurance in the form of a French horn, which he played very well. Walter was one of vaudeville's best.

George Roesner, as the "Old Soldier," was also one of the outstanding vaude character actors. He did an old Civil War veteran who liked his liquor. It wasn't a new character, but he made it seem fresh the way he did it. I remember one of his lines, "I'm going to town to get drunk—and *how I dread it!*" He was a very well-educated man—wrote, edited, and published everything for his monthly magazine, *Pan*. He would take any side of an argument. Once he asked an actor, "Do you believe in God? Take either side." I remember that when we played on the bill together at Loew's Greeley Square Theatre in New York he pulled a line on a heckler that has been claimed by many, but it was Roesner's. When the heckler got real bad, George stepped to the footlights and, pointing to this guy in an upper box, said, "Ladies and Gentlemen, there you see the greatest argument for birth control!" A delightful and interesting companion and a swell artist.

Frank Tinney was the most natural comedian I ever saw. He got more out of a silly line than any comedian I have ever heard. To tell what he did sounds like nothing (I've heard many imitators—who failed). He had the quality of a mischievous kid when he was telling a joke. He was a great monologist, even though he used the leader of the orchestra as a foil in part of his act, and also played the bagpipes for insurance.

He would go to the leader and say, "I'm going to recite some poetry, I am. Now, you must ask me why I am going to recite serious poetry? Go ahead and ask me." And the leader would say, "All right, why are you going to recite serious poetry, Frank?" "Because I'm ambitious, I am." The leader would then say, "I don't think it's ambition, Frank, I think it's a hangover." Frank would look surprised and say, "No it isn't a hangover. Now you ask me why it isn't a hangover, and I'll answer you. (Turning to the audience he would whisper, "This is gonna be dirty.") Go ahead and ask me." "Well, why isn't it a hangover, Frank?" "Because I was out with you last night, and it was your turn to treat!" You wouldn't believe he had an audience laughing hysterically with this sort of stuff. You can't write down a delivery or a personality. He just was great!

Raymond Hitchcock was a lot like Frank Tinney, not as to material and delivery (entirely different), but as to personality. You just had to see and hear him to appreciate him. With him, especially, it wasn't what he said but the way he said it; in fact, he never did have "sock" material. He would speak about almost anything, topics of the day, and during prohibition he did a monologue on booze, and he always looked as if he was half stewed, without playing the part of a drunk. The most remarkable thing about Hitchy was that even some of his best friends believed he was a drinking man. The truth is, Hitchy never took a drink in his life. And you can bet on that!

Jack Benny we knew when it was Salisbury & Benny and later when it was Benny & Woods; he played the violin and his partner played the piano. When they split, he branched out as a monologist and became one of the real great ones, using his fiddle for insurance. He is suave, classy, witty, and can time a gag better than anyone I have ever seen. Can you say more about a guy, except that he is a nice guy, too?

Charles Kenna really brought a novelty character to vaude, the "pitchman." Willie Hammerstein got him right off the street, where he was doing a "low pitch" selling a potato peeler, and made him a standard act. He was plenty original and a natural funny man. His material was copped by many acts; it got so bad that he put ads in the trade papers reading, "Please let me know what stuff of mine you are using, so I won't have to follow you in with the same material. I'll change mine." It was a subtle way to get back at the "stealers" and prove to the managers that he was original. And don't let anybody tell you that the expressions, "It's an old army game," and "Go away, boy, you're bothering me," belonged to W. C. Fields. It was Charles Kenna who used both these expressions in his act many many years before Fields even talked on the stage. One season, after playing a few dates at Hammerstein's, he couldn't get any immediate bookings, so he booked himself at Huber's Museum on East Fourteenth Street, and advertised, "You've heard of acts coming from Huber's Museum to Hammerstein's; this is one guy who is going from Hammerstein's to Huber's." Huber paid him a very big salary (for Huber), but he had to do at least eight shows a day to get it. He had a funny song he'd finish with, but didn't need it. A natural funny man was this guy Kenna!

Bert Swor, an old and dear friend, was one of the vet comedians

of minstrelsy and worked in vaude when he wasn't starring in Al
Field's Minstrels—a great trouper who started in honky-tonks and
reached stardom. He was the original partner of Charlie Mack
(Swor & Mack); Charlie later became the owner of the "Two
Black Crows" (Moran & Mack). Bert had a very funny monologue.
In it he would take out an old piece of butcher's wrapping paper
and say, "Just got a letter from home." Then he would read the
letter, which was plenty funny and got plenty of belly laughs and
at the finish he would read, "God bless and keep you—*from* your
loving Maw and Paw." Yeh, I know you've heard the comics use
this on radio and TV, but it was Bert Swor who originated it. Bert,
like many others I have mentioned, did a 99 per cent monologue
and used a song or even a short dance for a finish. A very funny
man was Bert Swor.

Eddie Foyer was a peculiar type of monologist. He did straight
talk, no songs or dancing, but most of his act consisted of reciting
poems. He would open with a routine about how a tough waiter in
a tough restaurant would call out the orders to the cook. When a
customer ordered "two eggs on toast," he would shout, "Adam
and Eve on a raft—and keep their eyes open." (That meant, don't
turn 'em over.) If someone ordered hash, he'd yell, "Gentleman
wants to take a chance." Another customer would order hash too.
Waiter would yell, "Another sport!" "Waiter, where's my boiled
potato?" "Mrs. Murphy in a sealskin coat!" Etc. etc. After this
routine he would recite "Gunga Din" (always sure-fire), then he
would ask the audience what poem they wanted to hear? He would
do a half a dozen a show, and the audiences loved it, even the
tough audiences. He would recite very theatrically, plenty of gestures and with plenty of voice in the high spots. He once told me he
knew five hundred poems by heart. What a filibustering senator
he would have made!

Ed Wynn, now celebrating his fifty-second year in show biz,
used his crazy inventions as the gimmick for his monologues. He is
one of our greatest buffoons. His billing, "The Perfect Fool," tells
the story. He wrote his own stuff and prided himself on always
doing a clean act. There never was another Ed Wynn; though many
tried to copy him, they just couldn't do it. He started in vaude and
had many partners, but reached his height when he went on his
own, and became a great comedian and star in musical comedy.
A guy that can last fifty-two years in show biz, and remain up

there in lights and big-bracket dough in all the branches of show biz (with all the terrific competition), must be a very funny man—which Ed Wynn certainly is!

Beatrice Herford was one of the first real female monologists and had the field to herself for a long time. I also believe she was one of the first to do a one-woman show. On concert tours there were quite a number of women singles who did a lot of gab, mixed up with songs and dances. But Miss Herford did a straight series of monologues with no gimmicks! She was really great!

Tom Mahoney, a big heavy-set Irishman, was another one that gave the old stump speech a new twist. He acted as chairman at an Irish rally, and instead of a gavel he kept order with a *brick*! A fine monologist who got plenty of laughs.

Cliff Gordon represented the real *big belly-laugh* monologist in his act, "The German Senator," which really was another switch of the stump speech, using timely topics of the day. He did a dumb "Dutch" orator who tangled up the English language (as all German comics did), and it started a new style of "topics of the day" talkers. It had been done before Cliff Gordon, but never in his "excited" style. He would start off on a subject quietly, but by the time he got to the point he would be so excited that he'd get the whole thing balled up. He had great material, fresh as a baby's breath, written by the greatest comedy writer of his time, Aaron Hoffman. When the *Lusitania* was launched, Cliff said,

"This is surely a great country we live in, full of mountains, valleys, and *bluffs*! This is a great age. Look at the *Lusitania* with its modern improvements, elevators and everything. All you got to do when you feel her sinking is to take the elevator upstairs." (This was long before the tragic end of the *Lusitania*.)

When Cliff died, Aaron Hoffman authorized Milt Collins to carry on with the same monologue (freshened weekly by Mr. Hoffman), and also "Senator" Murphy (who is still doing it as an afterdinner speech). They were both great performers and got plenty of laughs, but it just wasn't Cliff! By the way, Cliff's right name was Saltpeter; his brother was at one time the head booker of the Orpheum Circuit, besides having a great background as a vaude agent and vaude-act producer (Lewis & Gordon), and a pretty swell guy in his own right, but Max will tell you that Cliff was not only tops in vaude but also tops of the family!

Harry Breen was born on the Lower East Side of New York City, and talked about the people that lived there; it was really very funny. His recollections of the East Side got just as many laughs out of town, because they were funny in a folksy way. Breen did a sort of semi-nut act. He was a writer of songs and acts, and was the best of the extemporaneous singers. He would pick out people in the audience and sing about them, which had been done before, but Harry did it just a little better. Like:

> "There's a lady sitting over there
> In the second row on the third chair.
> She has her hand up to her face,
> And the hat she has on is a disgrace."

He would make up verses about what the audience was doing. He was a fine artist, and what a guy in a gabfest!

James Richmond Glenroy originally did a double act with his wife (Richmond & Glenroy); on her death he took the name of James Richmond Glenroy and did a monologue. He was billed as the "Man with the Green Gloves." (Guess why? Yop, because he wore green gloves.) He introduced a new kind of monologue, using epitaphs that he read in cemeteries—for laughs (and got plenty)! Like:

> "Rum is a curse, and many it kills;
> But this unfortunate took some pills."

(Aside he would say, "A foolish move on his part, I'm sure."

> "Off a fast-moving car stepped Lizzie Russell;
> Too bad she didn't wear a bustle."

> "Here lies my husband, Harold Cain,
> Let him rest in peace till we meet again."

> "Here's where the body of Mary Nash is,
> She ran a boardinghouse;
> Peace to her 'hashes'."

> "A bulldog chased Eliza Fair,
> It bit her on her—never-mind-where."

Jim was a very funny man even off stage.

Walter C. Kelly, "The Virginia Judge," was the greatest dialectician of his time. He could do any dialect and do them all great. He would come on stage dressed in an alpaca coat, walk over to the table, pick up the gavel and imitate an Irishman as the court crier: "Hear ye, hear ye, the court of the Great Sovereign State of Virginia is now opened!" He then would act as judge of a small Southern town, and as the different cases came up he would speak in the different dialects of the defendants and plaintiffs.

"You here agin, Lem? What you do this time?"

"Ah din't do nothin', Jedge. The railroad run over my mule and killed him and they won't pay me. They won't even give me back my rope."

"What rope?"

"Why, Jedge, de rope ah done tied de mule on the track wif."

"Go on now, you're lucky I don't have you hung with it. Get out! Next case. . . . Well, Sam, I see where you are charged by Milligan, the arresting officer, with stealing a watch. What have you got to say for yourself?"

"Jedge, I jes' wanted to know the time."

"The time is *five years*! Take him away, Joe."

For a finish he would imitate a small Negro boy: "Say, Jedge, Colonel Stevens wants to know if you want to go fishin'; he sez they're bitin' pretty good."

"All right, tell him I'll be right along. Court adjourned!"

He was born in Philadelphia but spoke in a fine Southern drawl. He was a big hit in Europe and also played in legit shows.

Will Rogers, I believe, was the greatest of them all (as long as we put the "topics of the day" guys in the list and also the guys who used insurance). He used a rope; certainly didn't need it, but he never gave it up. I told you about J. W. Kelly, "The Rolling Mill Man," and I don't doubt that what my friends told me about him was true, but this guy Rogers we all saw and heard and knew. He was in our time. We know that in the *Ziegfeld Follies* he changed his act every show for a year. He wrote columns for the papers that are just as fresh today as they were twenty-five years ago. That proves something. In our time nobody that I know of touched him for a combination of humor, grass-root philosophy, and ready wit. He capsuled whole editorials into a few lines—and got laughs out of truths. He also knew his Broadwayites and how to talk to them—and best of all knew how to talk to the folks everyplace else.

There have been so many guys who claimed they got Bill "to talk." I was pretty close to the guy and, believe me, you didn't have to get him to talk. I'm a pretty good gabber myself, but the guy outfoxed me many a time. To settle all arguments, here is what Bill told me and Aggie and Al Ochs (a buddy of his, now a Hollywood agent) one night in our room at the Sylvania Hotel in Philadelphia.

He started out doing a straight roping act, then added a horse and rider, etc. Well, one day he missed a trick (as you know, he was really a great roper), and he made some remark (which he didn't remember); all he knew was that it got a laugh. Now, in those days when a "dumb act" (which he was) got a laugh, it meant a lot. The next show he kept in that "miss," and made a new crack, and little by little he kept adding laughs to his "misses." Getting a laugh for a dumb act is the worst thing that can happen to them; they begin to believe they are comedians. Well, Bill got better and better and added "side remarks" (not routines) and for fresh material looked in the papers and soon started remarking, "All I know is what I see in the papers," and started talking about topics of the day. With his natural wit and humor, he soon realized that his roping was just a side line or insurance. Now Joe, doesn't this sound truer than those other claims, like, "Ziggy made him talk," when he already had been talking for years and had appeared in a legit musical show, *The Wall Street Girl*? It was his talking that made Ziggy buy him.

His monument out in Oklahoma not only stands for a great American but a fine philosopher and the greatest stage "topics of the day" gabber of our time!

I know you are gonna tell me that I left out a lot of monologists —guys like Heywood Broun, who really did a great monologue at the Palace, and Bugs Baer, who could have been one of the best, but he liked printer's ink better. I am sure you'll find most of 'em in some of my other letters. I just wanted to give you an idea of the many great gabbers vaude had.

As for the "entertainers" in vaude, we had thousands of 'em! I mean the single-men entertainers who sang, talked, danced, played instruments, gabbed, used stooges and plants, and did acrobatics and even paper tearing. These I separate from the straight monologists, although many of these entertainers did swell talk routines, but they depended more on songs, dancing, etc. Most of them were what we call "socko" acts, and would hold down the next-to-closing spots, which is an honor spot. It didn't mean that you were a headliner or got the most money of the show, but it did mean that the booker figured you could follow a hit show and "hold 'em in" after a bad show. Both tough jobs for an act away down on the bill. The next-to-closing act got good dough and good billing (if it didn't happen to be the headliner). There were few men headliners, compared to the number of them in show biz. Many were split headliners, not strong enough at the box office to go it alone, so would split headline honors with another act. But most of the good ones were features or bottom, special, and added attractions.

The average single man was a crazy guy, traveling alone (some were married, of course, and even carried their "excess baggage" with them), but most of them were on the loose. They had no problems of scenery, costumes, or make-up. They had nobody to take half the blame when they flopped. Between you and me, many men singles (and that goes for many acts too) had a good opening and, what was more important, a smash finish, and in between used a lot of baloney or what we called "time-wasters." Many an act got over because of a great finish, with nothing real good ahead of it. But the bookers could never forget the big applause that may have earned the act a half a dozen bends at the finish, which means a *hit*!

Everybody introduced today is called a "headliner." The truth is that there were few headliners, especially single-men entertainers. There were many standard acts that played vaude season after season and were plenty good. There were single men who came from a hit show and naturally were headlined (or co-headlined) to take advantage of their box-office value at the moment. These are what we called "strays"; they would just play vaude between shows. Many regular standard acts would be headlined in the smaller towns, especially if you just came from the Palace. (I saw an acrobatic act headlined in a small town because they had played the Palace.) But when they got back to New York and the regular big-time circuit, they would go back to their regular billing. The average single man was free from sex appeal and had to depend on being funny or entertaining.

Al Jolson was the greatest of all American entertainers. Al started with an act, Jolson, Palmer & Jolson. (Palmer worked from a wheel chair.) Then Al went out and did a single blackface act on the Sullivan & Considine Circuit. He ran ads in the trade papers reading, "You never heard of me, but you will!" (He was a great hit on the Circuit.) Then he joined Dockstader's Minstrels, in which he was a riot. He went over so big that Dockstader gave up his own next-to-closing spot to Al. (And Lew was a great big favorite—but realized he couldn't follow this kid, who was just great.) When the show laid off, Al played Hammerstein's and was a riot, played a few more vaude weeks, then rejoined the Dockstader show. He then signed with the Shuberts, and a few years later played a week at Brighton Beach for $2,500. He never played the Palace (just got up one Sunday night, at the request of Dave Apollon, the M.C., and sang a few songs). It was many years later that he made a tour of the pic houses and broke records. Just a dynamite guy!

We figure that Sir Harry Lauder was the greatest of all international entertainers because he played as a headliner all over the world and always in vaude. Jolson and Lauder were two entirely different types. Lauder was deliberate and slow, while Jolson was nervous and fast. Lauder received four and five thousand dollars a week for many many years and broke BO records all over the world. They were two great artists. Al got the edge on Lauder for publicity when he was on radio and in pics (which went all over the world). But I am only telling you about vaude, and as for vaude, there is no argument that Lauder was the greatest (Jolson didn't play enough vaude to really compare). Harry Lauder never played the Palace, either!

Some of our great entertainers were Englishmen, like Wilkie Bard, Albert Chevalier, Clifton Crawford, George Lashwood, Will Fyfe, and Laddie Cliff.

But we had plenty of American artists who could match them as entertainers. I am not mentioning them in the order of their importance, no more than I did in my other letters to you; it wouldn't be fair and it would take an awful lot of hard work, and besides it would only be our own opinion! Me and Aggie figure that the top all-round artist of today is Jim Barton, who was a burly comic, a skater, a storyteller, a dancer, a singer, a dramatic actor, and a pic, radio, and TV star. He can also play an instrument and baseball! There were many single men that could do many more things, but Jim was tops in all the things he did! I know I won't have room to name all the great single-men entertainers, but here are a few that come to mind (see if you agree): Eddie Cantor, Joe Cook, Henry E. Dixie, Lew Dockstader, Honey Boy Evans, Joe Frisco,

Eddie Foy, Sr., Frank Fay, Bunny Granville, Ralph Hertz, Will Mahoney, George Price, Jack Norworth, Pat Rooney, Sr., Harry Richman, Ted Lewis, Bill Robinson, Nat Wills, Willie Weston, Ernest Hogan, Richard Carle, Fred Allen, Phil Baker, Milton Berle, Ben Bernie, Sam Bernard, Billy "Single" Clifford, Richie Craig, Jr., Thomas Potter Dunn, Jack Donahue, Eddie Dowling, Harry Delf, Billy Glason, Bob Hall, Bob Hope, Jimmy Hussey, Bert Hanlon, Al Herman, George Jessel, Henry "Squigilum" Lewis, Harry B. Lester, Hal Neiman, Oscar Lorraine, Will Morrisey, Ken Murray, Carl McCullough, George Munroe, Bobby North, Blackface Eddie Ross, Herman Timberg, Billy B. Van, Violinsky, Al B. White, Harry Fox, Dave Ferguson, George Beatty, and William Dillon, and of course the one and only Bert Williams. (Yeh, I know, there are at least 250 more that should be in this list. But the publisher yells about the cost of paper. The guy never saw real vaudeville.)

Storytelling was a specialty. I don't mean the single guys who threw in a story in their act, but the men that were specialists in the art (believe me, it is an art). They, too, were monologists in a way, depending only on gab—but as I told you before, they didn't have a plot, or continuity; they jumped from one story to another. Some put cement in between stories; by that I mean they hooked 'em together by saying, "Then there was another little Irishman . . ." or "That reminds me . . ." etc. But there were a few really great storytellers in vaude.

Leo Carrillo specialized in Chinese stories and did them the best; he was raised in California among them. (Billy Gaxton, his relative, also does swell Chinese stories—off stage.) Frank Fogarty was one of the fastest Irish storytellers; he was usually two stories ahead of the audience—a great teller of tales. Harry Hershfield, I believe, knows more stories than anyone in show biz, and is one of our experts in that line. Lou Holtz I certainly must put among the storytellers, and the great ones, too, although he used his song "*O Sole Mio*" for a finish, while the others just walked off. Walter C. Kelly, "The Virginia Judge," had no equal in his particular line; he could do any dialect, while many of the others were limited. Robert Emmett Keane was swell, as were Dick Knowles and George Austin Moore (Southern stories). Marshall P. Wilder was a really great storyteller, but his material was mostly taken from others.

And I am going to mention a guy very few of you know or have heard of, because he played very little vaude. He was a letter carrier and vaude interfered with his hours, so he mostly played clubs. But in my humble opinion he was one of the greatest storytellers I ever heard—Bob Willis. But when you talk about storytellers, you must mention the pioneer, who remained the greatest for many many years. He could hold the stage for over a half hour doing dialect stories and have the audience hysterical. He was one of the first to do a Hebe character (he was a German, and very eccentric) and a headliner in his day. He played a tin whistle at the finish of his act, and musicians wondered at his skill; they claimed nobody could play the notes he did—but he did it (between shows he would go around and sell tin whistles in the towns he was playing). He was the greatest of 'em all—Frank Bush!

There were entertainers, who were a bit different than the others, called "nut acts." They were a vaude craze at one time; every show had one. Most of 'em were goofy guys off stage as well as on. Audiences loved 'em because they did the things the audience would have loved to do, like yelling, screaming, breaking hats, breaking the bulbs in the footlights, tearing drops, saying anything that came into their heads (that was first well rehearsed), etc. Among this private circle of "crazy guys," the man crowned king was Bert Fitzgibbons, who started in show biz with his brother in a musical act (McCoy, Fitzgibbons Trio), later doing a single that included breaking footlight bulbs etc., singing, talking, sitting in women's laps, etc. etc.—you just can't explain it, but it had the audiences roaring and applauding. Many tried to follow his antics and even tried to top 'em, but a funny side light is that when the booking office started to charge them for broken foots, torn drops, and other damage, the "crazy guys" toned down and didn't break or damage so many things.

Other great nut acts were Ted Healey, Jack Inglis, Neil McKinley (who would bring out a ladder and sing to a girl in the box), Jack Rose (who started the breaking of hats), Joe Whitehead, Harry Rose, and of course the nonviolent nut act, James J. Morton. Charlie Wilson, "The Loose Nut," besides his crazy act could play a good fiddle. Sid Lewis, who worked on the same lines as Fitzgibbon, had some funny stuff of his own, Joe Towle, who billed himself as the "cleanest act in vaudeville," played a swell comedy piano and used a keg as a stool. Of course the wildest nut act in vaude was Frank Van Hoven, billed as "The Mad Magician," which he was. He only did a few tricks of magic, but he was a wild man who kept up a stream of gab with two kids who held cakes of ice in their hands and whom he tried to get to shake hands as he introduced them to each other.

No, I didn't forget Duffy & Sweeney. They were too crazy to mix with these normal crazy guys. They say you don't have to be crazy to be an actor, but it 'helps! Well, these nut acts sure proved it. They were swell company; you never knew what they were going to do next, which is pretty interesting, especially when you are young.

I realize there are hundreds of entertainers who played in vaude for years, real small time, some who never passed east of the Mississippi, some never west of it, and they were all a definite part of vaude (which didn't mean just the Big Time). Many of them had talent, but just didn't get the breaks, or didn't look for them. Maybe they were afraid of the big towns and cities and were satisfied playing small towns, working steady, saving a buck, having no worries, and being happy in knowing a lot of nice folks in the towns they played. They say actors are different than other people, to which I say *nuts*. There are lots of clerks, bookkeepers, auto workers, plumbers, etc., who have the ability to get ahead in their biz, but just don't care to move away from the things and people they feel comfortable with. They aren't built to "take a chance." They aren't gamblers or ambitious. They're satisfied. To kinda clinch my argument, Aggie just yelled from the kitchen, "How about country doctors, who have cured and taken care of more people and know more about medicine than some of the guys with their shingles up on Park Avenue, but wouldn't exchange places?" My Aggie is smart.

Love and Kisses SEZ

Your pal,

LEFTY

The Negro in Vaudeville

Dear Joe,

After the Civil War there were a few Negroes playing in the nonslave states. Most of them were in minstrel shows and buskin' in saloons or dancing on streets for throw money. About 1890 there were plenty colored shows (mostly minstrel). Some of the white minstrel shows, like Primrose & West, added about twenty-five Negroes to their white cast of fifty and were a terrific hit. But I want to tell you about vaude, not minstrelsy.

One of the things that got Negroes into variety was a dance then known as the "chalk line walk," which later became a hit as the cakewalk. It was not exactly originated by Charles Johnson and Dora Dean, because the dance was done in many different ways in minstrel shows and even on plantations, but it was this really great team of Johnson & Dean who put it on the vaude map, and for many years they were big features on vaude bills both here and all over Europe with their cakewalk! It became a craze and was taken up by many Negro acts (it was their dance) and sort of opened the door of variety to them.

Another door opener was the "coon" songs. The first to become a hit with this type song was Ernest Hogan (his right name was Reuben Crudus). At one time he had played an end with Bert Williams in a minstrel show before George Walker joined up with Williams. In 1897 Hogan did a skit, introducing the cakewalk, in Ed C. Rice's "Summer Nights" on the Casino Theatre Roof. His own song "All Coons Look Alike to Me," was one of the first of that type and really started the craze. In later years he got into a jam with his own race, who were trying to get him to stop singing the song because of the word "coon." He kept on using it until he died. By the way, Hogan was the first Negro to play Morrison's Rockaway; he played a one-day date there. Ernest Hogan, besides being a great artist, was also a fine song writer.

When Williams & Walker first showed at Koster and Bial's, they were the talk of the town and stayed there for a long run and later became the greats of all Negro performers in or out of vaude.

When they were billed at Hammerstein's as co-headliners with Walter C. Kelly, "The Virginia Judge" (he was born in Philadelphia), Kelly refused to be on the same bill with Negroes. He later played there to big biz, as did Williams & Walker. I personally believe it was one of Willie Hammerstein's press stunts, as it received a lot of publicity for both acts. I knew Walter C. Kelly very well and played with him on many bills on which there were Negro acts, and he never complained about them. The only other incident of this kind that I can recall happened years later (1933), when Mary Garden made her first pop-priced appearance, splitting top billing with the Mills Bros. (I believe it was at the Capitol). Grace Moore, because of this, demanded a no-colored clause in her contract and Loew called her booking off. The Chase Theatre (vaude) in Washington, D.C., caused a lot of talk when they barred Negroes from any part of the house, the only theater in America to do this. Outside of these few incidents, I have never known of a color line in vaude. Talent has no color.

With the doors now opened by the cakewalkers and coon shouters, there came to variety many talented Negroes, mostly singers and dancers. Don't know why, but audiences would applaud a Negro dancer with inferior talent more than they would a much better white dancer; maybe it was because the average Negro dancer showed he enjoyed his work so much and "worked his feet off," and that sold it to the audience.

There were many great Negro song writers who went into vaude. About 1890 there was a contest between song writer Gussie Davis, a fine Negro ballad writer, and Jim Thornton. A gal by the name of Helena Mora (a great white singer) sang Jim Thornton's "It Doesn't Seem Like the Same Old Smile" and Gussie Davis's "Send Back the Picture and the Old Wedding Ring." It came out as a tie. The funny thing to me was that the Negro was going in for ballads at the time, instead of the coon songs that they wrote so well and were such terrific hits. Among the Negro musicians who wrote for vaudeville and shows were Bob Cole, Bill Johnson, J. Rosamond Johnson, Irving Jones (remember his great song, "St. Patrick's Day Is No Day for a Coon?"), Shelton Brooks ("Some of These Days"), Will Marion Cook, and many others.

There were many colored acts on Broadway. Shows at the Casino Roof, Koster and Bial's, and the New York Roof were all practically made up of vaudeville specialties. One of the first Negro acts to play museums and variety houses was Sam Lucas and his wife. He was a very talented gentleman and the first Negro to play Uncle Tom in a white company; he was also a song writer; "Grandfather's Clock" (still being played) was one of his. In later years he played the Loew Circuit as a monologist, after starring in many colored shows. He ended up in pics, playing the part of Uncle Tom. He had to rescue Little Eva from a river, and he got pneumonia and died. He was the oldest and most respected of all the Negro performers of his time.

Another great Negro composer was Jim Bland, who wrote many songs that were sung and danced in (and out) of vaude for years: "Carry Me Back to Old Virginny," "Them Golden Slippers," and "In the Evening by the Moonlight." (All of these made many a bad quartette sound good!)

Billy Kersands started out in the early '80s; he weighed about 200 pounds and had a real big mouth (Joe E. Brown's mouth is just a cupid's bow against Kersands'). He did a buck and wing with two billiard balls in his mouth. He would say, "If they ever made my mouth bigger they would have to move my ears." He also was a great tumbler and dancer. His favorite song was "Mary's Gone," and besides doing a buck and wing he did a beautiful "essence" to Stephen Foster's "Sewanee River." In 1911 he made a comeback on the Loew Circuit; at that time he had five large soda crackers and a cup and saucer (regulation size) in his mouth while he danced.

According to the trade papers of 1907 there were 270 colored people rated as principals and about 1,400 colored performers altogether in show biz. Eph Thompson, Williams & Walker, Ernest Hogan, and Cole & Johnson were considered tops.

Many of the standard Negro acts first started in vaude as pickaninnies (Ernest Hogan and Jones Bros. started as picks). Single white singers would have from two to a half a dozen little picks in their act as insurance for a sock finish. I never saw any picks flop.

Negro performers did more than just singing and dancing; they contributed their many talents to all lines of vaude. Mr. and Mrs. Tom McIntosh did a skit in variety (about 1895) called "The King of Bivarid"; Tom also did knockabout comedy and played the drums. Although me and Aggie never did see a Negro do a sketch in vaude, there were a couple of fine sketch artists back in 1895— Al and Mamie Anderson and Charles Hume and May Botrell. I don't know what happened, but there is no record of any more after that date. (Years later they played many dramatic sketches at the Lafayette Theatre in Harlem.) Florence Hines was a male impersonator; the Great Gowongo, a magician; Allie Brown, a slack-wire walker (I don't know of another one who did this work); Wilbur Swetman, a great clarinetist, played vaude for years.

Williams & Walker started out with Walker doing the comedy. Avery & Hart were practically a copy of W. & W.; Hart was a bartender and doubled up with Dan Avery, who did Walker and looked like him too (he wore a big diamond ring outside his gloves). The Holiday Sisters (Grace Holiday and Ada Overton Walker) were a fine team. Ada, who married George Walker, was a great soubrette. She did "Salomé" in vaude—only Negro who did it on the Big Time. Cooper & Robinson once made up like Hebes and did a heavy burlesque dialect, doing an imitation of Howe and Scott, at Hyde and Behman's. (They split in 1910.) Bill "Bojangles" Robinson soon became a headliner and star (like I told you in my letter about dancers). Bojangles' first wife was Fanny Clay, who worked in a drugstore in Chicago. She would read him his scripts, as Bill couldn't read or write. He later divorced her and married Lamme Chase. Both very fine ladies.

Charles Gilpin played a little vaude with the Jubilee Singers before he became the number one and first Negro dramatic star in *Emperor Jones*. Florence Mills worked as a pick in the Bonita and Lew Hearn act when she was a kid, and later formed the Mills Sisters (Olivia, Maude, and herself). She was also at one time part of Cora Green, Ada Smith & Florence Mills, playing the Pantages Time. Later she went with the Tennessee Ten. U. S. Thompson was the comic with the act, and they got married and did a double. She replaced Gertrude Saunders in *Shuffle Along* and was a riot. She played the Palace and was a star with Lew Leslie's shows until her death. A wonderfully talented gal, besides being one of the finest ladies we ever met in or out of show biz.

Miller & Lyles, who were Fisk University students, were a real great comedy act and played all the Big Time as a feature, then went to London in a review, and came back here to star in their own show, *Shuffle Along*, the greatest Negro show we ever saw.

Tom Fletcher played a few vaude dates in the old variety days and also in regular vaude, but got away from it and became one of the greatest of the club entertainers. He was hired by millionaires and society folks for their big parties and yachting trips to keep them entertained. He could sing songs for hours and hours and never repeat. A fine artist. Fletcher Henderson & Eubie Blake once teamed for vaude. Blake later joined Nobel Sissle and they wrote the music for *Shuffle Along.* J. W. Cooper was the first Negro ventriloquist. Frank Rogers was another, as was Johnny Woods. The Kratons were the only Negro "hoop act," Janet Collins was the first ballerina of note; she was half French. James O'Brien was a fine violinist.

There were many real funny men among the Negro vaude acts. I've already mentioned some, but I've just got to name such greats as Anderson & Goines (Anderson was the father of Eddie, the famous "Rochester" of the Jack Benny show, who is not bad himself); Buck & Bubbles, who were great in "Weather Clear—Track Fast" (and Bubbles did swell in *Porgy and Bess*); Harry Brown, the first to yell to the audience, "Is everybody happy?" (that was in 1906); Butler and Sweetie May (better known as Butterbean and Susie); and Charlie Case, one of our greatest monologists. Cook & Stevens were a standard big-time act for many years. Canada Lee played a little vaude, doing songs and comedy. Fiddler & Shelton were the first Negroes to wear full dress in vaude and started a vogue (Fiddler was an understudy of Hogan's). There were Hamtree Harrington (a very funny man) & Cora Green, Jolly John Larkins (very good), and Arthur Moss & Edward Frye, who brought a new type of comedy for two-man acts (remember their "How high is up?")—two very original and funny boys, who could sing plenty good too. Murphy & Francis billed themselves, "Though Irish by Name We're Coons by Nature." Rucker & Winifred, Tabor & Green and Epps & Loretta were acts with some more of the real funny men.

Among the many great Negro singers who appeared in vaude were the Whitman Sisters, Louis Armstrong, Ralph Dunbar's Maryland Singers, the Ink Spots, Mamie Smith (first to do records), Mary Stafford, Josephine Stevens, the Tennessee Ten, Rolfe's Ten Dark Knights, the Norman Thomas Quintette, Sara Vaughn, Mattie Wilkes, Ethel Waters (who is not only one of the great song stylists but also the number one Negro dramatic actress), the Black Patti, Ma Rainey, Bessie Smith (tops of the blues singers), Abbie Mitchell, Florence Mills, Maude Mills (her sister), Alice Mackey, Duke Ellington, Kate Griffin, the Golden Gate Quartette, Adelaide Hall, Hodges Lunchmore (who did a feline opera), the Charioteers, Cab Calloway, George Dewey Washington, Carita Day, Desmond & Bailey (sister act), Old Time Darkies (big act), the Watermelon Trust (one of the real great big acts, and also one of the first), Mildred Bailey, Pearl Bailey, Josephine Baker, Ella Fitzgerald, and Cole & Johnson. I once asked Bob Cole why he tossed a large white silk handkerchief from one hand to another and up in the air while he was singing. He said, "Well, you see, the pipes ain't what they should be, and when I am supposed to hit a note that I can't, I toss the handkerchief in the air, and the audience pays more attention to it than to my voice and so don't notice that I didn't make it." (First time I ever heard of "misdirection" in singing.) He could sure sing a song, as could my old friend J. Rosamond Johnson—a real great team.

I think here is the spot for the story you told me about the time you had your "Memory Lane" act, which was a big act with sixteen of the great old-timers of vaude in it. They wanted you to play in Washington, D.C., but wanted you to bring the act without W. C. Handy, the daddy of the blues, and J. Rosamond Johnson, as they were afraid that it might cause trouble to have them working with you and a dozen white men and women. You refused to play it unless they were with you, as you had already played down South and had been met by governors, mayors, etc., and Handy and Johnson had been received better than you (which they rated). Anyway, the Washington, D.C., manager finally O.K.'d the date. He was a very nervous man before the act went on. It was a terrific hit. W. C. Handy took three encores (first time it ever happened in the act) and Rosamond went bigger than ever, too, singing his "Under the Bamboo Tree." The manager came back after the show and was tickled to death there had been no trouble, but asked you to please eliminate just one thing in the act, shaking hands with the two Negro performers. You refused and kept it in.

What I like most about your story was how you called the manager backstage every day and showed him the many fine Southern ladies and gentlemen who came backstage to see Bill Handy, and the ladies threw their arms around him while the men shook his hand heartily. They had known Bill when they were kids, because he had played at their weddings and birthdays for many years down in Tennessee, and how happy and gracious they were about his big-time reputation! I wonder what that manager thought when he saw that people don't start riots when they see two decent people shaking hands, even if one hand is black.

Me and Aggie never met two finer gentlemen in all of show biz than J. Rosamond Johnson and W. C. Handy, who not only gave us great music but great friendship.

The Negro contributed plenty of color to vaude in more ways than one. SEZ

Your pal,

LEFTY

Printer's Ink and Grease Paint

Dear Joe,

Printer's ink and grease paint haven't always mixed well.

Today feuds between actors and critics are practically things of the past. The critic seldom deals in personalities, and seems to prefer writing a good notice to a bad one; if he doesn't like the show or act, he picks on the producer and author, or even the scenery painter, rather than the actors. I've even seen notices where the critic was sorry for the actors!

Not so many years ago the critics were pretty cruel, and so were the actors; they didn't have any paper space to answer back, but would do it by word of mouth at their clubs, or anyplace someone would listen. They talked *loud*! I won't mention the names of the critics or the actors who said these things (many of them are gone, and anyway, why start it all over again?), but here are some of the things with which they steamed each other up. From the critics:

"So and So opened at the Orpheum last night. If they are not lynched this morning, there will be a matinee today."

"New York sent us one of their magicians last night. He was so good he made this critic disappear in ten minutes."

"He fell on the stage. The audience was sorry to see him get up and continue his act."

"More acting by the horse and less by the people would help."

A certain act missed a train and got into Frisco too late for the matinee. After the night show the local critic wrote, "So and So arrived late, but not late enough!"

About a juggling act, "All hands and no feat."

"The kid is growing. It is the only indication of progress in the act."

"The boys couldn't dance their way off a hot stove."

"The act had something old, nothing new, plenty borrowed, and laughs are few."

About a foreign dancer, "She left most of her youth abroad."

"So and so sings three songs and wears three suits; the songs are good ones and his suits are white, brown, and black."

Shortest review ever written for *Variety* (or any other paper) about a horse called Napoleon. "Giddap, Napoleon. Small time bound." (JOLO)

"When a legit loses his voice he goes into vaudeville."

"Vaudeville, a place where a great many bad actors go before they die."

The actors returned the compliments:

"Why, that paper won't even *pan* an act unless it advertises."

"That critic is an optimist; he signs his name at the bottom of his review."

An actor, getting on the train, to a rural critic who gave him a bad notice, "When that engine toots, I'll be outside of your circulation."

"It took me twenty years to perfect my act, and it only took you thirty seconds to become a critic."

"I didn't mind you panning my act, because today's newspaper is the toilet paper of tomorrow."

"A critic is a man who can take a clock apart, but doesn't know enough to put it together."

Oscar Hammerstein was asked about a certain critic, "What does he write for?" "Like all of them do, for *passes!*"

"Critic—he's just a *pan*-handler."

"A reviewer is a guy whose parents wanted a boy."

"A critic is a newspaperman whose sweetheart ran away with an actor."

These are just a few samples of the way it was. But they don't seem to do it anymore. Maybe it's because the critics figure there are no personalities like Maurice Barrymore, Richard Bennett, Arnold Daly, and many others, who, when baited, would answer them back in kind, which made another column. It is the trade papers that still criticize vaude acts, but it is constructive criticism.

Most of the playwrights, theatrical press agents, and skit writers were raised in the nursery of the newspaper world. The temptation to make more dough has made many newsmen into top-flight playwrights, producers, managers, press agents, and vaude writers. A few examples are Jack Lait, Arthur Hopkins, Roy K. Moulton, W. F. Kirk, Bugs Baer, Bide Dudley, George Ade, S. Jay Kaufman, Neal O'Hara, and H. I. Phillips, who among them wrote many a vaude act. There were hundreds of others who wrote for the legit and musical-comedy stage.

Critics William Winter, J. Austin Fynes, and Alan Dale represented the drama critics of their day. Acton Davies and Alan Dale were figured as "eccentrics" of their time. E. D. Price, as "The Man Behind the Scenes" on the *Morning Telegraph*, was Broadway's first theatrical columnist. S. Jay Kaufman was the first columnist of Broadway to cover everything.

Again space stops me from mentioning the many newspapermen who contributed their genius to scripting, from a few gags to sketches, plays, pics, radio, and TV. But to give you an idea of how important they were, I will mention just a few: Ed Locke (*The Climax*), Ben Hecht, Charles MacArthur, Jack Lait (who wrote many vaude acts and plays, besides being a top critic on *Variety*), Alexander Woollcott, Ring Lardner, Damon Runyon, Bozeman Bulger, Arthur Hopkins (who as a reporter scooped the country with the assassination of President McKinley, wrote many sketches, was press agent, manager, and booked animal acts at Luna Park, and also produced nearly all the shows starring Jack and Lionel Barrymore—I know of no man who liked the "theater" any more than Arthur Hopkins), Paul Armstrong, Anita Loos, Bartlett Cormack, Bayard Veiller (who was on the *Morning Telegraph* as Robert Spears, then went with Proctor as a press agent, later writing great Broadway hits), Maurine Watkins, Mark Hellinger, Wilson Mizner, Edna Ferber, Bide Dudley (did an act for four days at Yonkers), Claire Boothe, George S. Kaufman, Channing Pollock, Rennold Wolf, Maxwell Anderson, Marc Connelly, Lawrence Stallings, Morris Ryskind, Russel Crouse, Ward Morehouse, Don Marquis, J. P. McAvoy, Jo Swerling, Dorothy Parker, Montague Glass, Max Lief, Allison Smith, Fulton Oursler, Irving Cobb, Adolph Klauber, John Anderson, Gilbert Gabriel, Charles Emerson Cook, Eugene O'Neill, George Jean Nathan, Jimmy Montague, Claude Binyon, Bob Sisk, Joe Bigelow, Jack Conway, Robert Sherwood, Walt Whitman, Richard Lockridge, Augustus Thomas, the Spewacks, and Goodman Ace—and these are just a few of the many type-stained vets who wrote for show biz!

The *Dramatic Mirror* (an old trade paper) was an incubator for celebs. George Tyler, Frederick McKay, Porter Emerson Brown, Randolph Hartley, and Jules Eckert Goodman were former newsmen who made good in show biz.

Among the great press agents who were former newspapermen were Harry Reichenbach, the greatest of all stunt P.A.s, and Walter Kingsley, who covered the Manchurian battlefronts for the London *Mail*, before he did press work for the Palace and Ziegfeld. Bronson Howard, who wrote the great play *Shenandoah*, and Willis Brill, a fine P.A., were also war correspondents. Charles Dillingham left the New York *Sun* to become advance man for Charles Frohman, and later became one of the most successful musical-comedy producers. George Atkinson of the Columbia *Dispatch* is now the dean of the press agents. Bob Sisk (an old *Variety* mug) became P.A. for the Theatre Guild and now is one of the top Hollywood producers. Howard Dietz is not only a great P.A. but one of our finest lyric writers. N.T.G. (Nils T. Granlund) was Loew's great publicity man. Jesse Lasky, the noted Hollywood producer, once worked in the office of the San Francisco *Post*, Ruth Hale (Heywood Broun's wife) was P.A. for Arthur Hopkins, Frederick McKay, critic of the *Evening Mail*, was once husband and manager of Blanche Ring. Then there were Mark Leucher, John Pollack, Ann Marble, Lou Cline, Brock Pemberton, Wolf Kaufman (another ex-*Variety* mug), and Nellie Revell, who started in the circus, went into vaude with a monologue, and later became one of the greatest of the lady P.A.s. Ralph Kettering is not only a great P.A. but also a playwright and producer-manager. And Bonfils and Tammen, publisher of the famous Denver *Post*, owned the Sells-Floto Circus.

There were a few critics that also wrote plays: Jack Lait, Gene Fowler (yeh, he was a critic once), Bartlett Cormack, Bide Dudley, George S. Kaufman, Channing Pollock, Rennold Wolf, Ward Morehouse, Alan Dale, George Jean Nathan, and a few others.

Many newspapermen became stage-struck! The cartoonists, especially, flocked to vaude, because it was vaude patrons who read
the funnies. Harry Hershfield's gag fits perfectly here. When he
was once asked if a cartoonist is a newspaperman, he said, "Is a
barnacle a ship?" Cartoonists served long and well on the big and
small time. Many headlined because of the popularity of their
strip. They were, in a way, "freak acts." Many of them just played
locally where they had a reputation and small circulation. The
first of the top cartoonists to play vaude was Windsor McKay
(who invented animated cartoons).

Tom (Mack) McNamarra (of "Skinny Shaner" fame) did an
act with Meyer Marcus; they were the first to do a double cartoon
act. Later McNamarra appeared with Bud Fisher. Others were
Rube Goldberg, Richard F. Oucault (Buster Brown), George
McManus (Jiggs & Maggie), Sidney Smith (The Gumps), Ken
Kling (Joe & Asbestos), and H. B. Martin (illustrator and cartoonist). Even Milt Gross (Nize Baby) did an act that lasted a
couple of weeks, and the great Tad appeared on a Sunday concert
at the old Herald Square Theatre. Hy Mayer, the noted carica-
turist, was on the Palace's first bill. Martin Branner, now doing
the great "Winnie Winkle" comic strip, did a great dancing act
on Big Time, with his wife Edith, known as Martin & Fabrini.

Leo Carrillo and Bert Levy gave up their newspaper cartooning
to remain in vaude. Harry Hershfield, a cartoonist and columnist
for over a half a century, although still writing a weekly column,
devotes most of his time to after-dinner speaking, and radio, stage,
and TV storytelling, while Ham Fisher, Al Capp, and Bob Dunn
also keep their voices and faces going on radio and TV.

Some more ex-newspapermen who took up vaude as a regular biz
were Robert Dailey, Lee Harrison, Leo Donnelly, Russ Brown,
Ezra Kendall, Billy Gould, J. H. Murphy (Adam Sourguy), Russell
Mack, Robert Benchley, and Jack Barrymore (ex-cartoonist).

The great old humorists like Artemus Ward, Josh Billings, Eli
Perkins, James Montgomery Bailey, Bill Nye, Mark Twain, and
James Whitcomb Riley were newspapermen who made pretty good
side dough playing Chautauqua, which in those days was practically
vaudeville. Even the great Elbert Hubbard played a few weeks in
vaude—opened at the Majestic, Chicago, did very well, and wrote a
great article about how nice vaude was in his mag, The Philistine,

next week. He then played Cincinnati, where the gallery sort of heckled him, and he walked out and went home and vaudeville never saw him again.

While I was telling you about cartoonists, I should have told you about what the professors call "an allied art" that was very popular in vaude for many years. They were the rag-picture and sand artists and clay modelers. The rag-picture artists would usually come on with a pushcart full of rags, put up an easel and stretcher, and pinning the rags on it would really make beautiful pictures, usually ending up with the Statue of Liberty or the American flag. The best in this work were the Clintons, Marcello, and Ralph Ralfaely. The sand painters put all kinds of colored sand in a frame and made beautiful seascapes and also ended up with some patriotic picture. Many of them would work upside down, then turn over the frame. Outstanding acts were Eldridge the Great, Jules LaRue & Jean Dupre, and Lieut. R. Eldridge, who did sand painting while his partner, Sally Randall, sang. The clay modelers also had a regular pattern. Some of them were really fine sculptors, but did clay modeling because it was fast and had some element of comedy in it, and besides I guess it was a faster buck than in sculpting. They would first make a few busts of famous men, then for comedy relief would make a "mother-in-law" and throw wads of clay at it, (or a bust of an unpopular political figure and throw a big chunk of clay at him, which would always get a big hand and a laugh). Gallando, Bicknell, Zoubalkis, McNamarra, and George Wichman were some of the best.

Karlton & Klifford did water-color lightning drawings, Les Dodattis did copies of famous paintings, Vandioff & Louie did novelty oil paintings. Sartello, besides drawing pictures of landscapes and birds, also did magic. Froehlic did pics in crayons and oils, as did Karl Krees (very fast oil paintings). Gene Smith was a great painter of animals and did wonderful horses' heads, and for an encore did a fast drawing of a lion and tiger. Sylvester (the most versatile of all vaude actors) also did speedy oil paintings.

There were a number of cartoonists in vaude that I don't know if they were newspapermen; no doubt most of them had been at one time, but they certainly belonged in vaude—guys like Arthur Birchman, Walt McDougall, Rem Brandt, F. A. Clement, Rouble Sims (a good comedy act), Harry Brown, who sang while cartooning, as did Bowen & Cody. Florence Pierce was a quick-sketch artist, as was Lightning Hopper. Felix was a European cartoonist. Mr. Quick was a fast cartoonist, as you can guess from his name. Hubert DeVeau, George Paris, Jr., and the Great Weston were all good cartoonist acts. Then there were a couple of Frisco boys by the name of Billy Hon and Harry Price, who made a comedy entrance, one with an umbrella and the other sprinkling water on the umbrella; they did Tad and Rube Goldberg stuff. Harry Hirsh had a little Negro boy as an assistant. Lawrence Semon did four baseball figures and talked about them. R. C. Faulkner, who was the image of Woodrow Wilson (and cashed in on it plenty), did cartoons while he talked. Rudinoff did smoke pics and whistled (à la Bert Levy).

Columnists were booked in vaude and pic houses. Someone once said that they were "middle men" between celebs and the public, shrugged at by performers, and booked on the basis of their getting top talent to appear with them for free. It got so the actors carried their music around with them because they never knew when they'd get a call from a columnist to appear. Most of the columnists acted as M.C.s for the show. It was Mark Hellinger who started the stage-door parade of columnists! Many of them proved very good drawing cards, mostly because they could put on a show of great headliners that the management could never afford to play or pay, whereas the columnists paid them off with "column mentions." It worked all the way around. The columnist got publicity for his column and his paper (and of course plenty dough), the actors got publicity, the manager did good biz for small dough, and the audiences saw good shows!

And so the boys followed Mark Hellinger's lead: Walter Winchell, Ed Sullivan, Nick Kenny, Louis Sobol, Rian James, Hy Gardner, Danton Walker, Earl Wilson, Walter Kiernan, Paul Yawitz, Ted Friend, Jerry Wald (now a big Hollywood producer), Heywood Broun, Floyd Gibbons, and Alec Woollcott, who took a flyer in legit. There were a few more that later parlayed a by-line into big billing and dough in vaude, radio, and even pics, like Bob Considine, John Kieran, F. P. Adams, Clifton Fadiman, Goodman Ace, Mary Margaret McBride, Harriet Van Horn, Dorothy Kilgallen, H. V. Kaltenborn (who left the Brooklyn *Eagle* for radio), and H. I. Phillips, who was M.C. on the Robert Burns program before Burns & Allen took over.

We also have a few cases of actors turning columnists. Of course the top example is Walter Winchell, who exchanged his dancing shoes for a very talented typewriter, Hedda Hopper, and of course the immortal Will Rogers. (Some actors wrote columns, but most of them were ghostwritten by press agents.)

So you see, today grease paint and printer's ink mix pretty well. At the Lambs you can see the comradeship enjoyed by actors, critics, news columnists, press agents, newspapermen, and cartoonists, all Brother Lambs! And if you look real close, you may even see the actor pay for the drinks, but you'll have to look *real close!* SEZ

Your pal,

LEFTY

Freak and Odd Acts

Dear Joe,

The struggle for novelty brought out some very odd acts, and the manager's struggle to get box-office attractions brought out the "freak act"!

Willie Hammerstein was the daddy of the freak act. He would take anybody who was "news" and make 'em box-office through build-up and publicity. Freak acts were paid big dough, but lasted only a short time; a full season was an exception. Usually a few weeks were enough to blur the newspaper headlines that had made the act worth putting on the stage. But there certainly was a mess of 'em in vaude at one time.

The "odd acts" were different than freak acts, and some of them played in vaude for many seasons. The odd acts were unorthodox in style and presentation—for instance, there were the Australian Woodchoppers (who were champs of Canada too). They had big logs on the stage and would chop them up as fast as Max of the Stage Door Delicatessen could slice corned beef. When playing fairs, the boys would sell axes on the side and demonstrate how good the axes were, never tipping off that they were wood-chopping champs. The yokels bought the axes, but when they tried 'em on their trees at home they found they didn't chop as easy as the boys made it look.

Charles Kellog was a handsome man, over six feet, who opened in a wood scene and announced he would give imitations of bird calls, but unlike the regular acts that did this, he didn't whistle— he *sang* them! Without opening his mouth he would sing (?) bird calls. (The Great Lester, a vent, whistled with a handkerchief stuffed in his mouth as he walked down through the audience.) Anyway, Kellog got away with it for many years as a headline attraction. He also showed woodcraft, like how to build a fire by rubbing two pieces of wood together. Interesting act, done by a fine showman.

The Lutz Bros. were sort of a half-odd and half-freak act. They were both armless, but performed wonders with their feet! They put a motor together, did sharpshooting, writing, etc. Armless wonders had worked in museums for many years, but the Lutz Bros., with their good showmanship, put it over in vaude as a regular hunk of entertainment instead of looking "freaky." Working on a stage with proper lighting, etc. (instead of working on a bare platform), helped sell the act too.

Louis Ducasse & George Jeannoit, a couple of Frenchmen, had an act called "La Savette," which I guess means boxing. They gave an exhibition of fighting with their hands and *feet*. (New at the time for the U. S.) They got a lot of publicity with the old gag, "Can an American fighter using his fists beat a Frenchman using his feet?" By the time they found out, the boys were back in France with plenty francs!

Monzello was a minstrel show with dummies on the stage and the gags done via phonograph. Kinda crude but a novelty. There was another act something like this one called "The Automatic Minstrels," which played at Gane's Manhattan Theatre (where Macy's is now). This one had a live interlocutor; the rest were dummies, whose jokes and songs were done via phonographs. Didn't do so good.

Willard, "The Man Who Grows," would come on stage, get a committee from the audience, and stand next to them while asking a lot of questions. He looked about as tall as the men he was talking to. Then they would stand aside and he would show the folks how he grew almost a foot. (They didn't notice the drop coming down little by little maybe a half inch at a time, as he was growing up; it helped the illusion a lot, but the guy did make himself taller.) He did a lot of flash advertising and was a good freak headliner for a number of years. I guess he quit the business when Adler's elevator shoes came in.

Back in 1907 the National Theatre in Frisco played a man by the name of L. B. Hicks who got a lot of publicity because he had been entombed in a mine at Bakersfield, California. He was supposed to get $2,000 for the week. Some actor came out with him and told the story for him. Then people started to ask questions and the guy got stage fright and couldn't answer, and he kinda got mixed up with his chew tobacco—and went back to the mines!

Did you know that as late as 1908 there was a freak show showing a cow with human skin, a mule "that he-hawed on cue" and a hairless horse for a 10-cent admish—and it was right on Broadway and Forty-second Street, New York (supposed to be a pretty "wiseguy" spot in those days).

In a man and woman talking act, Fox & Fox, he did an Irish comic, and talked all through the act while standing *on his hands*! Marcel & Rene Philippart were the world's champs of the diabolo (a spinning bobbin) and tried to make it a craze (like the later yo-yo), but it didn't catch on. They really did remarkable tricks with it. Alier Norton did a sort of a chemical act, producing rubies and sapphires in full view of the audience (really a magic act disguised as a scientific experiment). Luigi Marabin, who was an ice sculptor, chopped away at a large cake of ice and made a bust of a prominent man. Very clever. (You now see a lot of those things in restaurant windows.)

Marcello was the first one I ever saw drape odds and ends of material and ribbons on a live gal and make beautiful dresses right before your eyes. The finish, of course, was a wedding gown. Very novel, then. Willie Hoppe, a champ at eighteen, gave a billiard exhibition on a table surrounded by mirrors so that the audience saw every shot. Howard & Heck, two midgets, did the "Kugelwalker Twins," one on the shoulders of the other with a long coat covering them, which made it look like one guy—a very funny act.

Burr McIntosh, who was a very well-known legit actor, did a lecture on the Merchant Marine in 1909, a sort of recruiting and publicity idea, which he illustrated with slides. At the finish he would say, "Will those in favor of the Merchant Marine get up and sing the 'Star Spangled Banner'?" Of course everybody stood up when it was played. He was a natural, and a good showman.

There were only a couple of fencing acts in show biz. Carstans & Brosins were one of them, and I can't recall the name of the other. Vaude had never seen this style act. It was a novelty, but the audience would rather see boxing. A very different sort of act was done by Mme. Ann Diss DeBar, who did a lecture on "Right Thinking Is Right Living." She didn't last long. I guess nobody wanted to live right if they had to think. Hap Handy & Co. manipulated soap bubbles, juggled 'em, bounced 'em around all over the place, and put colors in them which made beautiful designs. (This was long before the song "I'm Forever Blowing Bubbles.")

Dr. Carl L. Perip, who at Hammerstein's (where else?), read palms and told you your destiny at long distance, gave out a "lucky bean" which you held up and he read your palm right from the stage and also answered questions. (Good eyesight, eh?) A man billed "Thermos" did air experiments. He froze rubber, quicksilver, and raw steak, fried eggs on ice, and finally produced a concentrated snow. (That was in 1911.) Jack Irwin, who was the wireless operator on the *Wellman*, received the CBQ (then the SOS signal) from the steamship *Republic* and saved the ship. He told about it in a short monologue. Jack Binns, the Marconi operator on the *Republic*, also did a few weeks of vaude.

Dr. Cook, who claimed that he and not Admiral Peary discovered the North Pole and who received reams of publicity, decorations, etc., did a talk about it at Hammerstein's. The big laugh was when he complained to Mike Simon, the stage manager, that his dressing room was cold! The Spook Minstrels were a minstrel show on film with regular actors behind the screen doing the jokes and songs. At the finish, the curtain went up and the audience saw the live actors. (This was long before the talking pics.) Mrs. Dr. Munyon (the wife of the famous doctor who advertised that he cured everything that Lydia Pinkham didn't) was the attraction at Hammerstein's during Christmas week of 1910. She cured everybody that week including herself; she quit show biz when the week was over!

Rillow billed himself as a "menaphone novelty," but nobody knew what it meant until they saw that he made musical noises on his teeth, cheeks, head, etc. It was something like playing "the bones." Tarzan was a man dressed like an ape (I can't recall his name, but he was a great artist). He worked with a trainer, did the regular ape "tricks," and never took his make-up off. It left the audience puzzled, some saying it was a man and some believing it was an ape (that's how good he was). Later he went over the circuit, running through the aisles and over seats, scaring the audience (they liked to be scared), and at the finish took off the mask. There was an Englishman by the name of Nathal who was the best of all the animal imitators.

Harry Kahane wrote upside down, frontwards, or backwards anything you would call from the audience, while concentrating on a newspaper article. A remarkable performance. Sessukikima also did this act years before Harry, but in this type act it is so tough to do that they all deserve credit. Charlie Chase, who played everything from the Gus Sun to the Palace and *Ziegfeld Follies*, ate paper, electric bulbs, flowers, wood, matches, etc., and also did a very funny dance. A novel act.

George Schroeder was billed on Pantages Circuit as "Convict 6630, the man who sang himself out of the penitentiary." He was a former forger (this shows how hard up the managers were for headliners). That same year (1913) Pantages also played Ed Morrell, who was the youngest member of the famous Evans-Sontag gang of outlaws in California; he served sixteen years, was pardoned, and got a contract from Pantages. A few years later, McVicker's, Chicago (the Hammerstein's of the West), played Barney Bertsche, a swindler, who chirped about the cops that stood in with him in a fortune-swindling racket. He got $700 for the week. (Another swindle.) Even Bugs Baer, the great of the humorists, wrote a skit for James J. Curran, a confidence man with a long prison route.

But the tops of "prison talent" was a guy called Snodgrass, who was in on a rap for accomplice to murder, broadcasting from the penitentiary at Jefferson City, Missouri. He got carloads of gifts and letters. He couldn't read a note, but his rendition of "Three O'Clock in the Morning" was really a masterpiece. Through his popularity via the radio, he got a pardon and reinstated citizenship, and also got on the Orpheum Route (they never played freak acts) for $1,000 a week. He was assisted by an announcer from WOS, and he did very well. The booking of "behind the bars" talent got so bad that E. F. Albee issued a letter that "criminal proceedings, publicity headlines" were out for the future as vaude headliners. (But they played them just the same—if they figured to clink at the box office.)

McNaughton, "The Human Tank," did an act where he swallowed live frogs and other things and emitted them alive. He was stopped by the ASPCA, claiming cruelty to animals (and to audiences). Another smart (?) booking was a freak act that was playing at Coney Island and some booker thought it would be a novelty for vaude. The guy's name was Hadji Ali, and he swallowed hickory nuts, then drank water, then swallowed more hickory nuts, then more water, then more hickory nuts and water. Then in front of the audience he would eject the hickory nuts, followed by water, then—Oh, Nuts! (We saw him.) A fine act for family audiences! And yet he lasted four weeks before they got wise that he was killing their supper shows. He never played Big Time or Hammerstein's (Willie had too much good taste for that one). I only mentioned these two acts to show you how far a manager would go for an attraction.

Sidney Franklin is the only American who has become a topnotch bullfighter or what they call a toreador. Naturally the vaude audiences were proud to see a guy, especially from Brooklyn, who could go to Spain and beat 'em at their own racket. Of course the audience knew as much about bullfighting as about Einstein's Theory, but they applauded the guy loud and long (for his showmanship). The Five Gaffney Girls did an act with each girl dressed half boy and half girl; they looked like they were dancing with a guy. A very novel act. (This was long before those Danish renovating jobs.) Vasco, "The Mad Musician" (an Englishman), played twenty-eight instruments at every performance (a great act). Me and Aggie didn't know if he played 'em well, but we gave credit to the guy for even picking 'em up! We saw a gal by the name of Fuji-Ko, a Jap mimic who did an imitation of Harry Lauder "as seen through Jap eyes"; well sir, you know Jap eyes are slanted, but we never knew they slanted that much. A Jap trying to do a Scotchman, when even a Scotchman couldn't do a Scotchman! Swain's Cats and Rats had cats actually working with rats. (I guess they fed the cats *before* the act went on.)

A very odd act was the Hakoah, champ Jewish soccer team. They made a tour of the vaude theaters in the larger cities. Edna Wallace Hopper gave a special matinee for women at Pittsburgh,

Pennsylvania. She gave them a spiel on how to keep young etc. She took a bath in front of the lady audience. Four college boys got in dressed as dames and were spotted; they claimed it was a press stunt (which no doubt it was).

Jack Johnson, the world champion heavyweight, did an act at the Pekin, Chicago, but stopped showing pics of the funeral of his wife, Etta Duryea (white), who committed suicide. He thought the public would think he was cashing in on her publicity.

In 1912 Hammerstein's ran a Women's Suffragette Week. Speeches outside, no customers inside. Fola La Follette (daughter of the famous senator from Wisconsin) spoke fifteen minutes on women's rights, while one hundred women in white dresses stood on the stage. One carried a baby (to make it look harder, I guess). They sold buttons and flowers to the audience for "the cause." There was a big laugh when George May (the orchestra leader) played "Battle Cry of Freedom" for their entrance. The week, from a money standpoint, was a fliv, but it got plenty of publicity for Hammerstein's and the Suffs, and besides Willie got 'em for free.

Another freak act was Rev. Frank Gorman, pastor of the Congregational Church of Portland, Oregon, who sang a ballad, told stories, and finished with a baseball poem. Said he was out for money the same as Billy Sunday. (He certainly didn't get it in vaude.) In 1922 there was a Dr. W. B. Thompson, who claimed to cure deafness, baldness, bad eyesight, etc., by the patient's just putting his fingertips together, touching fingernails. He caused quite a stir for a while, like Dr. Coué did with his "Every day in every way I'm getting better and better"—but Dr. Coué was smart; he didn't go into vaude. Anyway, this Dr. Thompson must have talked to guys with no fingernails, because he wasn't booked for very long.

Here is a pip. In 1910 we saw Mrs. LaSalle Corbell Pickett, a charming Southern lady, the widow of the famous General Pickett of the Confederate Army, do an act consisting of a poem, "Pickett's Charge," and of all the places to book her, they picked the Colonial Theatre, New York. All the boys from South Ferry, South Brooklyn, and South Street applauded as she retreated south of the Mason-Dixon line after a week. I'll bet she said, "Vaudeville was damyankee propaganda!" How could an intelligent, charming

Southern lady figure a thing like that would go in vaude? I don't blame her; I blame the lousy agent who talked her into it!

In 1917 there was an act called "The Shrapnel Dodgers"; they told about their experiences in the war and sang. One had only one eye, the other had a leg and arm off. They were Canadians. They did a real good act, and certainly didn't depend on sympathy, but when they finished there wasn't a dry eye in the house.

There were many freak acts in vaude in spite of the trade papers claiming that 1917 saw the end of them. Bubbles Wilson, who got so much publicity with Frank Tinney, got a date at the Bowdoin Square Theatre, Boston, Massachusetts, to do a dance act for $600 a week. Patricia Salmon was discovered with a tent show at Shelby, Montana, by Heywood Broun and other sports writers who were there to cover the Dempsey-Gibbons fight, and they gave her more publicity than the fight got. The result was that she came East to go into vaude and the *Ziegfeld Follies* and finally went back to the tent show she was with when originally discovered. She was a swell gal who couldn't take New York, and vice versa. Then there was Peaches Browning, the Cinderella Girl who married the multi-millionaire eccentric real-estate man. She was the first to play a route for RKO on percentage (Keith Circuit never liked to play actors on percentage, and didn't. Peaches did it through her very able manager, Marvin Welt. She did very well as a drawing card. She sang a song in her act, "I'm All Alone in a Palace of Stone" (à la "Bird in a Gilded Cage").

Then came a flock of Atlantic flyers. Ruth Elder was the first woman to do it, and was immediately offered $6,500 for one week for Loew, but took twenty-five weeks at $5,000 instead. Then there was a rush of Atlantic flyers, replacing the Channel swimmers. Lindbergh turned down fabulous offers (see my letters on salaries). The Channel swimmers who cashed in were Gertrude Ederle and Mrs. Mille Gade Corson. (Eleanor Holm made more than both of 'em and hardly swam a stroke.)

Then there was Aimee Semple McPherson, the Hollywood evangelist, who laid a big egg at the Capitol Theatre, New York, at $5,000 for the week. Bob Landry, then on *Variety*, reviewing the act, said, "She wears a white satin creation, sexy but Episcopalian!" The house lost $20,000 on the week. When me and Aggie played with her mother, "Ma" Kennedy, and Ma's husband, "What a Man" Hudson, in Los Angeles, she laid an even bigger egg (but not at that price); she just quit after one week of vaude. But "What a Man" stuck it out for two more weeks to prove what a man he was!

A few years later Jafsie Condon (cashing in on his publicity as one of the important witnesses in the Lindbergh case) played at the Capitol Theatre at Lynn, Massachusetts. In between shows he appeared for one hour in Kane's Furniture Company store window to demonstrate the model of the ladder, nails, chisels, etc., used at the trial.

"Prince" Mike Romanoff (now a very reputable restaurateur in one of Hollywood's finest restaurants) appeared at the Palace, New York (when the Palace had stopped playing the blue bloods of vaude, and was playing freak acts, which they had never done before). It was a time when the motto was, "Anything to ring the cash register." The "Prince" was really a great character; too bad he came too late for Willie Hammerstein, because between them, with their great showmanship, the "Prince" would have mounted the throne!

In 1924 there appeared at Proctor's Twenty-third Street Theatre a really swell freak act by the name of Miss Bird Reeves. She was sixteen years old, and a champ typist. She did twenty strokes a second and 300 words a minute. Read a newspaper while typing other things being dictated to her. Had a terrific memory—she would ask for the name of a prominent man and would type and recite an excerpt from one of his speeches. She passed the copy to the audience, and it was neat and clean. She answered questions and exchanged wisecracks with the audience and was very good at it. She typed one speech while reciting an entirely different one. She put a piece of tin in the machine and gave imitations of a drum and a train. She didn't get very far in vaude, although everybody said she had a great act. We often wondered what happened to her. Too bad Willie Hammerstein was gone; he would have made her a headliner! This is one of the freak acts that really had it. Maybe she found out she was too smart for vaude and became a secretary!

Another odd act was Cantor Joseph Rosenblatt, a little man with a long red beard. He opened at the Fox Theatre, Philadelphia, as an experiment; he was the first cantor in vaude (outside of Eddie). William Morris didn't know if the Jews would resent it, or the gentiles wouldn't go for it; it was a "touchy" booking. He was not only a big hit but a terrific box-office draw. (There have been great applause hits that couldn't draw a dime to the till, and on the other hand there were acts that didn't get a hand, but would draw 'em in.) Anyway, for an encore Cantor Rosenblatt sang "Mother Machree," which made his applause "unanimous"! He lasted a few years in vaude.

Jack Connelly (who for years was the piano player at Keith's, Boston) and Marguerite Webb did an act called "The Stormy Finish" in which he played the piano with bananas and lemons, and at the finish he described a tornado while playing, and everything on the stage flew off!

We loved Scietler's Manikins; he had a juggler, three hobos, and an ostrich which laid an egg and a snake hatched out of it. One of the manikins made a quick change on the stage from a man into a woman. (At that time a thing like that was odd—but since then we have progressed.)

Right now, Joe, I feel I am repeating to you about many acts. Forgive me. You may find the same info in several letters because so many acts belong in so many categories, and the same memories come up each time.

Charlie Matthews, who was England's long-distance jumping champ, leaped from a table over an upright piano. (O. G. Seymour did the same trick many years before him. He jumped over an upright piano with a short start.)

Morris & Allen, dressed in Scotch kilts, with a Hebe make-up, sang an Irish song before making their entrance—a very big novelty. George Dixon did a musical act and used a skeleton for a xylophone. I've never seen it done since, but I bet I will.

Eddie Mack described a whole baseball game while he danced. Crane Bros., "The Mudtown Minstrels," were the first three-man minstrel act.

The Four Mignanis, "Musical Barbers," played all of the stuff in a barbershop: razors, strops, bottles, etc. Ben Meyer, billed as the "Human Elevator," lifted a man with his teeth and walked up a ladder with him. Contino & Lawrence were the original upside-down dancers; that was in 1906. A few acts copied them later. Toy & Toy played all the toys on the Christmas tree. "Dates" was the act of a memory wizard; when you'd call out any historical event, he would tell you the date it happened. I know the guy was on the level, because I hollered out, "When was Lincoln born?" and he told me the right answer. Zeno, Jordan & Zeno did thirty-five con-

secutive somersaults in a bounding net. I tried it once and couldn't
get out of the net, let alone turn over. (It looks so easy.) The
Mozarts were the first and only snowshoe dancers we have ever
seen. Canard was a contortionist who worked on the dial of a clock.
Annie May Abbott, "The Georgia Magnet," was one of the first to
do the act where nobody could lift her off the stage. Sam Rowley
(an Australian) was the first we ever heard who talked with a
whistle every time he came to the letter *s*. (Yop, it's been copped
many times since.)

Dr. Herrmann called himself the "Electrical Wizard." There
were many acts of this kind, with a lot of important looking paraphernalia on stage, and when they turned on the juice, it would
give out tremendous sparks, etc. The "professor" would tell you
how many thousand volts his machinery produced. Then he would
sit in an electric chair and they would send 100,000 volts (that's
what the man said) through him! I recall one incident at Keith's
in Philadelphia. The stagehands didn't like anyone to stand in the
first entrance, so they rigged up a comfortable-looking chair and
connected it with a five-volt battery; when you sat down you made
a contact, and you'd keep out of the entrance from then on. One
day after Dr. Herrmann finished his act, where he claimed 100,000
volts shot through his body with not even a twitch from him, he
sat down on the chair in the first entrance, and you never saw a
guy jump so high or yell so loud!

In 1909 we saw a troupe called Mlle. Toona's Indian Novelty
Co. They did an operatic act (I believe the first and only operatic
Indians that were ever in or out of vaude). Kennedy, Nobody &
Platt, had a novel idea in a two-man talking act. "Nobody" was
an imaginary person that Kennedy & Platt would talk to as if he
were part of the act. Later Kennedy did the act with just "Nobody."
In the late '20s there was Thelma De Onzo, world's greatest
candlestick jumper; she had lighted candles on tables of different
heights and put them out as she jumped over them. (Some actor,
seeing the act at Hammerstein's, remarked, "What a finish for a
Pontifical Mass!" Anything for a laugh.)

Robert Stickney danced on stilts. Will Mahoney did a dance on
a huge xylophone with the hammers strapped to his shoes (great).

In 1923 Freddie Thomson was acquitted of the Tessmer murder.
The "Man-Woman" appeared at Linnick and Schafer's Rialto
Theatre, Chicago, for $500 a week. It came out at his trial that he

led a double life as wife of a man and husband of a girl. Drew the jurors' sympathy through his helplessness. The act was stopped by police.

In 1811 the original Siamese Twins were born to Chinese parents in Siam; they were discovered by an English merchant and when in their teens were brought to Boston, where P. T. Barnum snapped 'em up for his side show. In 1925 the Big Time refused to play another pair of Siamese twins, Daisy and Violet Hilton. Loew booked them at $2,500 a week and they broke all house records for him throughout the Circuit! Loew also booked a freak head-liner in the person of Miss Elinor Glyn, the famous author of *Three Weeks*. She did very big.

Here is a pip! In 1927 an Egyptian showed his act to the bookers at the Palace. He called it "The Crucifixion." He put needle-point spikes through the palms of his hands and there was no blood. There also was *no booking*.

In 1913 Rev. Alexander Irvine & Co. played a sketch, "The Rector of St. Jude's." He was an excommunicated minister. There were two "hells" and one "damn," in the act. It was sort of socialistic propaganda. One wag said, "Hammerstein should book a priest next week just to show no favoritism."

The greatest of all the odd and interesting acts we have ever seen or worked with was Helen Keller, who was deaf and blind. We spoke to her like you would speak to anybody, and she touched our lips with her hand to "hear" us. Miss Sullivan, the great lady who taught her, was her constant companion. Miss Keller's act was a great lesson in courage, faith, and patience to everyone in the audience and to everybody backstage. She headlined in vaudeville for a number of years. A great lady.

There were a good many more freaks and odd acts, but I'll tell you about them when I tell you about the Hammersteins. SEZ

Your pal,

LEFTY

The Mixed Act

Dear Joe,
The comedy man and woman talking act that worked "in one" (the first drop behind the proscenium) was one of the important factors in starting vaude on its golden journey. It broke up the monotony of seeing mostly men on variety shows and also brought some class and cleaning up of material. The pioneer man and woman acts (or "mixed acts" as *Variety* named them) consisted of the man doing the comedy, tumbling, dancing, and maybe even a bit of juggling, while the woman (usually as a soubrette) did "straight" and contributed a song and dance and good looks.

The following billing in the program of May 7, 1893, of the Elite Theatre, 607 California Street, San Francisco, California, will give you an idea of the average type of man and woman act of that time.

JOHN F. BYRNES & MISS HELENE

Mr. Byrnes is America's greatest essence dancer while Miss Helene is the best wench dancer in existence. In their side-splitting plantation act entitled "Rescued," introducing essence dancing, double songs, and flashes of wit.

And here's another one from the London Theatre, New York, program dated October 28, 1889.

The performance begins with the eccentric character comedian

FRED H. HUBER

And the talented actress and vocalist

KITTY ALLYNE

In their own original act, entitled "Pleasant Dreams," introducing Violin and Banjo accompaniment, bone and whiskbroom solos, comedy and tragedy sandwiched into "One Night's Rest."

No matter what they say about the "old days" in variety, you can't say that the managers were stingy with their billing of an act! I don't want to dig way back to the early '70s and '80s, but I think it's the best way to give you examples of what the mixed acts used to do, so you may see what a change took place in this type of act.

Miss Beane of Fanny Beane & Charles Gilday was the greatest song-and-dance woman of the early '70s. She danced with a fan, not like Sally Rand, but a small fan held in one hand to accentuate style and grace. Charlie Gilday, her partner, did the comedy. Sam & Carrie Swain did a blackface song, dance, and comedy act. Carrie Swain was the only woman at that time to do back and forward somersaults while dancing. In the act of Dolph & Susie Lavino, Dolph did comedy and crayon drawings while Susie sang. John & Maggie Fielding did Irish acts "in one" with songs, and Maggie did "straight." Jap & Fanny Delano did acrobatic song and dance and comedy talk; they were one of the better known mixed acts of that day. In the Two Jacksons, he did comedy while she punched the bag and they finished the act with what the program billed as "a refined set-to" (boxing). Richmond & Glenroy, Hallen & Hart, Morton & Revell, Jim & Bonnie Thornton, and Dick & Alice McAvoy were all standard acts, and there wasn't one "funny" woman among them!

It was in the late '90s that the comics began replacing their straight man with a woman foil. Most of the ladies were picked for their beauty and their ability to wear clothes, the man figuring he could take care of the comedy. This added class to the act and contrast to the heavily made-up and baggy-pants comic. He gave her a few lines to speak and maybe let her do a song or dance, but the burden of carrying the act was on the man's shoulders. The majority of the mixed acts were married couples; they didn't have to split salaries like the two-man acts, and so could afford to take many dates at "a cut" that the other team acts couldn't take. It was almost as cheap to live double in the old days as it was single. And all the money went into one grouch bag (the wife's). (A grouch bag was a chamois bag, usually worn around the neck, where the family jewels and money, if any, were placed—called grouch bag because when empty, one, and even two, would get grouchy.) Nonworking wives who traveled with their husbands were called "excess baggage," so many men stuck the wife in the act to do a bit to sort of let her earn her keep. Sometimes it bettered the act; sometimes it didn't. They would only ask for a slight raise (to cover fares, etc.), so the price was right for the bookers and that had a great deal to do with the flood of man and woman acts in the early 1900s. Some of the gals became real great "straights" and fine performers.

"Funny women" were at a premium. Vaude was making big strides and there was keen competition. Man and woman acts "in one" (especially comedy) were in great demand. The male patrons came to get some laughs and look at the beautiful women and the lady patrons came to see the latest styles in clothes and hair-dos. The comics were trying to develop their female partners into comediennes; it meant getting away from the regular stereotype of mixed acts. At first they would let the partner get a few laughs in the act, then maybe next season the lady got 50 per cent of the laughs (alternating funny answers). In this way some of the women (very few) developed into excellent comediennes. In many cases, where they were real funny, the comic would turn straight man and let the woman get all the laughs. (It hurt his pride plenty, but it was good business.) Sometimes the comic would turn to a "light-comic" straight, getting some laughs, but giving the boffolas to the woman. Laurie & Bronson, Ryan & Lee, Donahue & Stewart, and Burns & Allen all started with the man doing the comedy and later turning to light-comedian straights.

The early funny women would wear funny make-ups and funny clothes. Some mixed acts would both dress funny. Melville & Higgins (a very funny team) was an example of that type act. Little by little they began to use regular clothes and soon there were very few women doing comedy in funny clothes or doing "low" comedy.

In the 1900s Wilbur Mack & Nella Walker started a new craze, called the "bench act," for man and woman acts. They would have a bench on the stage where they would sit and do "flirtation stuff," and finish up with a neat song and dance, during which they would exchange wisecracks. It was Mack & Walker who brought the "class," natural talk, and street make-up to vaude. Miss Walker possessed great beauty and talent, while Wilbur Mack was a fine light comedian with plenty of class. They were copied by many, but were never caught up with as to class and fine material. They started a trend that led to making "funny women" without using funny clothes.

Later Ryan & Lee and Laurie & Bronson brought a new type of mixed act to vaude—the "dumb girl" type comedienne and the smart-cracking straight man, depending on cross-fire "semi-nut"

comedy, using a song-and-dance finish. Burns & Allen, Block &
Sully, Allan & Canfield, and Dooley & Sales came later. (Dooley &
Sales were a team in show biz much longer than the others, but for
years Jim Dooley did the comedy. When the trend changed, he
turned all the laughs over to Corinne Sales, and she did plenty
good.)

There were many types of mixed acts working in one. Some did
singing or musical acts with a little comedy talk between selections.
Others depended on their dancing, but used a "flirtation" routine
as an opening, and went into their dance for the "sock finish."
But most of the mixed acts tried to put "talk" in the act and to
make the woman the "funny" one of the act. Some of 'em made it,
but most of 'em didn't!

There were a number of mixed acts that did "skits" in one. They
practically used a plot, also using a song or dance. These acts could
fit on more bills than the regular sketches that used full stage.
Among the best examples of this type skit were McMahon &
Chapple, Mr. & Mrs. Jimmy Barry, McLaughlin & Evans, Billy
Wayne & Ruth Warren, and Jim & Sadie Leonard.

But the "funny women" were still in demand, and it wasn't long
before they came along. All you needed in vaude was a demand,
and it was supplied (like in any other biz). Marie Stoddard
(Gardner & Stoddard), Florence Moore (Montgomery & Moore),
Fanny Stedman (Al & Fanny Stedman), Marie Hartman (Hibbit
& Hartman), Emily Darrell (Tower & Darrell), Harriett Lee (Ryan
& Lee), Aleen Bronson (Laurie & Bronson), Gracie Allen (Burns &
Allen), Marion Cleveland (Claude & Marion Cleveland), Irene
Ricardo (Cooper & Ricardo), Lulu McConell (McConell & Simp-
son—who really did a sketch but she was a real funny woman),
Gracie Deagon (Dickerson & Deagon), Alice Stewart (Donahue &
Stewart), Corinne Sales (Dooley & Sales), Eva Sully (Block &
Sully), May Usher (Ben Rubin & May Usher), Annie Kent (Kelly
& Kent), Rose King (York & King), Helen Broderick (Crawford &
Broderick), Charlotte Greenwood (Sydney Grant & Charlotte
Greenwood), Edna Leedom (Harry Tighe & Edna Leedom), Stella
Mayhew (Mayhew & Taylor), Elsie Canfield (Allan & Canfield),
Flo Lewis (Gould & Lewis), Blanche Leighton (Jim Kelso &
Leighton—really did a skit, but she was one of the best stage
"drunks" ever seen), Ann Codee (Frank Orth & Codee), Maude
Ryan (Innes & Ryan—she was the best ad-libber among all the

women comics), Irene Noblette (Ryan and Noblette), Patsy Kelly (Kelly & Wood), Ina Williams (Keene & Williams), and Sara Carson (McLellan & Carson), were just some of the real funny women.

The comedy mixed teams where the woman did the "straight" outnumbered the other type of mixed acts. The great comedy acts that come to mind are Brendel & Burt, Bonita & Lew Hearn, Lester Allen & Nellie Breen, Anger & Parker, Barry & Wolford, Brown & Whittaker, John & Mae Burke, Buzzell & Parker, Bevan & Flint, Conlin & Glass, Eddie & Bertie Conrad, Clifford & Marion, Clark & Hamilton, Billy Gaxton & Ann Laughlin (did a bench act way back in 1915), Sam Hearn & Helen Eil, Gladys Clark & Henry Bergman, Johnny Stanley & Stella Tracy, Raymond & O'Connor, Skeets Gallagher & Irene Martin, Jack Haley & Flo McFadden, Jim & Marion Harkins, Bert & Betty Wheeler, Bert Lahr & Mercedes, Toney & Norman, Harry Fox & Beatrice Curtis, Bill Frawley & Edna Louise, Harry Lang & Bernice Haley, Joe E. Brown & Marion Sunshine, Fred Leightner & Rosella McQueen, Queenie Williams & Jere Delaney, Jack Norton & Lucille Haley, Louise Groody & Hal Skelly, Russ Brown & Aileen Cook, Inglis & Reading, Si Wills & Joan Davis, Ken Murray & Charlotte. Fred Allen & Portland Hoffa and Jack Benny & Mary Livingston really didn't do a "mixed act," but just used the gals for foils in bits, and were plenty good. Then there were Montrose & Allen (talented parents of the talented Steve Allen), Ben & Hazel Mann, Davis & Darnell, Sid Marion & Marion Ford, Tom & Stacie Moore, Lola Merrill & Frank Otto, Newhoff & Phelps, Sully & Houghton, Johnny Neff & Carrie Starr, Bert Gordon & Gene Ford, Pisano & Bingham, Lou Handman & Florrie LaVere, Arthur Stone & Marion Hayes, Burke & Durkin, Sully & Thomas, Morris & Campbell, Whiting & Burt, Billy Gaston & Ethel Green, and one of the greatest, Williams & Wolfus!

There were many "kid acts" that were an important part of "mixed acts"; Harry & Eva Puck (one of the first real great ones), Bud & Nellie Heim, Laurie & Aleen, Felix & Claire, Eddie & Josie Evans, Guyer & Goodwin, and two teams that were grown-ups who did great kid acts, Rawson & Claire and Sager Midgley & Fanny Carlye; the latter were old people and did the greatest kid act in show biz.

Toward the last dying years of vaude, the mixed acts contributed a lot with their "blue" material or "shock laughs," "hells," and "damns," to help vaude die! Everybody began to steal each other's acts until it seemed that everybody was doing the same act. It did a lot to push vaude off the entertainment shelf.

The writers of vaude acts, who supplied the funny material that made a nation laugh, were a very important part of vaude. They supplied it for years with the plasma that kept it alive. When all the acts started stealing from each other, the writer was helpless. The booking office was a lot to blame for booking "copy acts" because they were cheaper. They didn't care about the future of vaude; it was a case of "get it while you can" with the managers. They didn't realize that without the writers vaude would die. Outside of a very few actors who could write their own stuff, talking acts depended on writers who could give them material that would make them a living. The writers became disgusted and luckily walked into other facets of show biz that needed them. They contributed their talents (for much bigger dough) to the new fields of radio and pics—great comedy writers like Paul Gerard Smith, Al Boasberg, Charles Horowitz, Felix Adler, Harry Conn, Tommy Gray, Hockey & Green, Jimmy Conlin, Harry Breen, Benny Ryan, Henry Bergman, William Cartmell, Jack Lait, Eddie Clark, Joe Browning, Frank Fay, Joe Laurie, Jr., Will Morrisey, Bert Hanlon, Gene Conrad, Junie McCree, Harry C. Green, Ren Shields, Billy Jerome, James Madison, Tommy Dugan, Fred Allen, Eddie Cantor, Billy K. Wells, Andy Rice, and the tops of 'em all, Aaron Hoffman, were disgusted with vaude and quit.

It is tragic to think that of all the great mixed acts of vaude, the only one that has survived through vaude, radio, pics, and TV is George Burns & Gracie Allen! They met the challenge and won!

Again there is a shortage of funny women. There are just a few around today, and they are mostly from the vaude school—Gracie Allen, Martha Raye, Lulu McConell, Pert Kelton, Patsy Kelly, Joan Davis, Bea Lillie, and of course Imogene Coca!

Maybe women need guys to make 'em funny. Aggie sez "that many a woman has made a guy into a clown" . . . but not in vaudeville, SEZ

Your pal,
LEFTY

Big Acts, Girl Acts, Flash Acts, and Tabs

Dear Joe,

To break up the monotony of watching singles, doubles, trios and quartettes, and maybe sometimes a large troupe of acrobats, vaudeville used what was called "big acts" or "girl acts" for a "flash" of bigness on the show. A fifteen-people act, with special costumes, scenery, book and lyrics, lighting, and "leader" in the pit with white gloves, made a big splash. These were not condensed musical comedies, and were produced by men who knew their business—men like Joe Hart, Ned Wayburn, Jesse Lasky & B. A. Rolfe, Gus Edwards, Charles Maddock, Fred V. Bowers, Harry Delmar & Jeannet Hackett, Bart McHugh, McMahon & Chapple, Minnie Palmer, William Friedlander, Velaska Suratt, Taylor Granville, Herman Timberg, George Choos, Benny Davis, and a few others.

Lasky's "Nurses," starring Gladys Clark & Henry Bergman, was one of the first and best. His "Redheads" starring James Carson, "Night on a Houseboat," starring O'Malley Jennings, "The Bride Shop," starring Andy Tombs, and many more big musical acts were done with B. A. Rolfe, who also produced on his own some very fine big acts.

One of the first big acts was Gus Edwards' "School Boys & Girls," starring Herman Timberg, and he followed this with some of the best big acts in vaude. His "song reviews" were packed with talent and were well done—"Kid Kabaret" (starring Eddie Cantor and George Jessel), "Band Box Revue" with "Cuddles" (Lila Lee) and Georgie Price as stars (and you can bet Georgie and Cuddles never appeared in the school act), "Blonde Typewriters," starring Johnny Stanley, and "Carlton Nights," starring Ray Bolger. Ned Wayburn, who produced for Ziegfeld, also produced some beautiful big acts—"Daisyland" with Dorothy Jardon (who later left vaude for opera) singing "Fedora," and "The Rain-Dears," which had a wonderful rain effect. Joe Hart was a prolific producer; his "Bathing Girls" was a swell act. Charlie Maddock produced in association with Lasky and Rolfe. McMahon & Chapple produced

"Pullman Porter Maids" and "Sunflower Girl." Minnie Palmer (the mother of the Marx Bros.) produced all their big acts. "Home Again" a seventeen-people act written by Al Shean (Gallagher & Shean), their uncle, was not only a great comedy act but a fine scenic and costumed production. Velaska Suratt in "Bouffe Variety" showed the one and only Velaska with gorgeous wardrobe. Herman Timberg did "Chicken Chow Mein" with Jay Gould & Flo Lewis (Sophie Tucker was in this one for a while too). Rooney & Bent's "Rings of Smoke" was a wonderful act (Vincent Lopez played the piano for them). George Choos was a lavish producer; his "Battling Butler" was later made into a show. Sam Bernard did an act at the Forty-fourth Street Theatre for Hammerstein and William Morris, when they tried to buck the Palace. It had sixty people in it (never traveled). Anatole Friedlander and Benny Davis always had fine acts of young talent. Eddie Clark was a pioneer in girl acts with his "Six Winning Widows," a great act. (When they played England it was billed as "Eddie Clark & His Merry Kiddos.") Others were "Ray Dooley & Her Metropolitan Minstrels," "Frank Dobson & the Sirens" (which played 150 consecutive weeks), and "Rubeville," a Maddock act, which played for six consecutive years, except one summer when the cast took a six weeks' vacation.

In 1910 William Morris produced "Chanticler" on his American Roof. It ran for two hours and a half, but was really a vaude act and featured Mitzi Hajos (later was known as Mitzi). She made her debut in this act and was immediately discovered and became a great star. Joe Hart's "Eternal Waltz," with thirty people, special music, etc., was on the opening bill of the Palace. Doc Baker's "flashes" and "song revues" were swell. Gertrude Hoffman had the biggest act in vaude way back in 1908; she had thirty musicians with her, did about fifteen imitations, ending up with a burlesque on Annette Kellerman diving into a tank. "The Love Shop" was a rhapsody in velvet, silk, and lace. Will Morrisey & Elizabeth Brice's "Overseas Revue" was a condensation of their show. Way back in 1904 Oscar Hammerstein wrote the book and lyrics and music for a big act, "Parsifala," with a cast featuring Eleanor Falk and a chorus and ballet of seventy!

Al Von Tilzer's "Honey Girls," with McBride & Cavanaugh, was produced by Arthur Hopkins. The Weaver Bros. & Elviry had their big "Hill-Billy Revue." There were Bart McHugh's "Housewarmers," with Johnny Dooley & Yvette Rugel, Jessel's "Troubles of 1920," produced by Al Lewis & Max Gordon, Annette Kellerman's "Revue" at the palace, with ten scenes; she talked, danced, sang, and walked the tight wire besides doing her diving act. "The Lawn Party," with Billy Dooley, was produced by Bart McHugh; he was the Philadelphia Gus Edwards, discovering neighborhood talent. Joe Laurie, Jr.'s "Memory Lane" had sixteen old-time favorites including W. C. Handy, Emma Francis, Al Campbell, Dave Genaro, Annie Hart, Rosamond Johnson, Tommy Harris, Eddie Horan, Lizzie Wilson, Bill Swan, Harry Brooks, Tom Phil-l'ps, and many more. Of course, Harry Carroll's big acts were always tons, with fine music, scenery, and book. Joe, it was in one of Carroll's acts that you met June (now Mrs. Joe Laurie, Jr.).

The small time couldn't afford these first-class attractions, so had to devise something that looked like a big flash for short dough. That brought a flock of "flash act" producers. The flash act consisted of a two-man act (with their own vaude material), a singing and dancing soubrette, a prima donna in the lead, and a line of six to eight girls. Scenery was carried in one trunk and costumes in another. "Reel Guys," produced by Harry C. Green, "Get Hot," with Milton Berle and nineteen people, "The Little Cottage," with Frank Sinclair, Maddock's "Not Yet, Marie," Clark & Bergman with "Seminary Mary," and "The Wedding Party" were a few of these.

The history of show biz tells us that public taste undergoes a change every few years, and it proved it with the quick growth of the tabloid musical comedies, which commenced about 1911. They were made up to save dough when vaude salaries went up. The "tabs," as they were called, stayed in towns (of single- and double-week splits) a full week, sometimes two weeks, changing their shows two and three times a week, which was great for the small-town managers and saved transportation for the producers (a big item). Many vaude acts joined these tabs. By 1912 there were over thirty theaters playing small-time vaude that had converted to tabs. They first came into their own in the Middle West at a 10-20-30-cent scale and ran up bigger grosses than the old road shows did at $1.50 scale. They averaged $2,500 to $3,000 a week for the show's end. The tabs soon consisted of four or five principals and eight chorus gals, with one set of scenery. Salaries were about $700, with transportation paid by the manager. Many of these tabs were just midget burly shows!

Fisher, in Los Angeles, Lewis & Lake, Dillon & King, and Charley Alpin were the pioneers. The first traveling tab musical comedy was organized by Adams & Ghul (an old double Dutch team) in the fall of 1911. It gave two bills, changing in the middle of the week. The W. S. Butterfield Circuit (with houses all over Mich-igan) played it and it was a big money-maker. The second tab was headed by Rube Welsh & Kitty Francis, who hung up many records on the Inter-State Circuit (all through Texas). The third show was Max Bloom's "Sunny Side of Broadway"; on its first showing, in Springfield, Illinois, it received contracts for twenty-five weeks. Tabloids were getting recognition.

Boyle Woolfolk became a leader and produced over a dozen tabs, then became ambitious and tried to play them in "combina-tion houses" instead of in vaude houses. It failed because they just weren't good enough to get the higher prices. The tabs were good for third- and fourth-grade houses that were a bit tired of playing tired vaude acts and were looking for a cheap novelty. The tabs started out to play the Pacific Coast for a season for John Cort (later John became a big Broadway producer and theater owner), but the tabs failed and the Chicago boys who thought they had show biz by the throat were left holding the bag. Minnie Palmer (mother of the Marx Bros.) put on different type tabs, better than the others, and did very well with them. Dwight Pebble put out small-scale tabs for the Gus Sun Circuit (fourth- and fifth-grade houses). He did this long before tabs were recognized by the larger circuits.

Robert Sherman put out a dramatic tab and it was such a big hit that he soon had a half a dozen out and became the leader in the field. He kept salaries down (only way you could keep a tab going). Charles E. Kohl and Mort Singer, under the name of the Western Extravaganza Company, sent out some very fine shows, figuring people were now ready for them, but they weren't—so they quit.

William B. Friedlander put out his first tab, "The Suffragettes," with Nan Halperin (then his wife) featured. It was a record breaker. Ned Alvord was the original tab booker and there was a time when he practically controlled the tab biz. He was a terrific publicity man. (It was Ned who turned Bill Rose's *Crazy Quilt* flop into a box-office smash.) Tabs were very popular in the South, where Winfrey B. Russell was the tops. John & Ella Galvin, in "Little Miss Mix-Up" introduced the tab in the Middle West, but it was Adams & Ghul who were the first to play the Western Vaudeville Association Time (better houses). The Galvins first started in Oklahoma City about 1907.

The tabs became a craze for the small time and a box-office lifesaver. By 1915 they began being censored, because they were getting a bit on the burly side and the comics catered to small town smart alecks who liked their jokes spicy.

When the tabs became bigger and better, with good performers, special music, book, scenery, lighting, wardrobe, etc., the managers in the East figured this might be the "new" form of entertainment people were looking for. The Big Time started booking the better type tabs (which cleaned up and put on their Sunday manners). But they didn't do so good back East on the Big Time because they took up too much running time, which cut out a couple of regular vaude acts, and the regular vaude audiences no liked. The producers had sunk a lot of dough in the tabs, making them too expensive for the poor results on the Big Time. When the managers didn't come through with the big salaries asked, the producers began to cheat on wardrobe, scenery, cast, etc., so they could make a little profit. They couldn't book these big productions on the small time, because it already had its own producers who knew its needs and budgets.

A few of the real good tabs that played the Big Time were "Court by Girls," "The Fair Co-Eds," "The Four Husbands," "Kiss Me," "Back to Earth" (with Frank Lawlor), "The Leading Lady," "Naughty Princess," "Oh, Doctor," "The Only Girl," "Reckless Eve," and "Suffragette Revue." We still say it was nothing "new"; it was just the old Lasky idea of big acts, and not as good.

In 1921 A. B. Marcus Shows were elaborate tabs playing the road on percentages. They were closed in many towns for naughtiness and sexy advertising. He later took his shows to the Orient and they made a lot of dough.

In 1922 there were tabs in the Midwest playing pirated musical-comedy versions of big hits. In 1926 there were 100 tabs—it was the top year for tabs!

While on the subject of tabs, I must tell you about a man who owned the Playhouse, at Frigonia, North Dakota. He got a tab to play for him by offering them the first $1,000 that came in. The tab took $800 and told the manager they were sorry he had played to a loss. (It was an 800-seater.) The manager said, "Me and my wife get lonesome up here in the winter and we wanted some nice company. It was worth it."

The tabs made a lot of dough while they lasted, but they didn't last long enough. The best that could be said about the tabs, flash acts, and girl acts was that it gave people work, which is O.K. with me. SEZ

Your pal,

LEFTY

The Small Time

Dear Joe,

When V*ariety* first started, someone on the paper (I believe it was Chicot) wrote up an act, saying, "Good for the small time." That was the first time the expression, "small time," was used in show biz. Before that, they used "act good for smaller houses" or "for cheaper houses," but calling the cheaper and smaller houses "small time" clearly divided the better time (Big Time—two-a-day) and the small time (the houses that did more than two-a-day or charged a cheaper admission).

Marcus Loew was the Keith of the small time. Sullivan & Considine, Pantages, and William Fox were runners-up, and Gus Sun was low man on the vaude totem pole!

There were always different levels of show biz, even in the days of the honky-tonks. Koster and Bial's was certainly "Big Time" against Big Bertha's Casino in Spokane. Eden Musee was higher-class than Huber's Museum; Loew's National, in the Bronx, certainly had more class than Gus Sun's World in Motion in Coatsville, Pa.; and the Keith and Morris circuits certainly topped all of them!

The small time really started with the museums, when variety acts were added to freak attractions and curiosities. Five or six acts played over and over again, and continuous vaude developed from this. The museum annex was dropped and a good bill was provided at small cost, and with prosperity came an increase in salaries. Managers then had to raise prices, and this was followed by reserved seats (for extra dough). Higher prices demanded better shows and forced out the acts that didn't belong; these found work at the ten-cent houses, just as their forerunners had turned to museums.

The Nickolat Company was organized to give five-cent shows in stores—moving pics with illustrated song slides and a piano player. They got the illustrated songs for free from the publishers; this was one of the few ways of plugging a song. Every half hour a Negro porter shouted out front that the show was over. Soon, because of competition, these houses provided piano playing to accompany the picture, then added a drummer and maybe a fiddler, and some even went as high as a five-piece orchestra. Then an act was added to the bill, then a couple more acts, and soon these houses were presenting regular small-time vaude. It was about 1908 that the "pic-vaude" combination really became hot!

The People's Vaudeville was a fair sample of the two hundred or more store shows in New York City giving moving pics and vaude for five cents in the afternoon and ten cents at night. Located just east of the southeast corner of 125th Street and Lenox Avenue, it had entrances from two sides, a narrow store space having been taken on Lenox Avenue and turned into a passageway leading into the theater proper. Tickets were sold at both entrances. Originally the arcade fronts were studded with incandescent lights, which stopped burning after the first few days; thereafter the front illumination was furnished by two flaming arcs, which made a bigger show for the money.

Shows ran for over an hour and included three 1,000-foot films, two vaude acts, and an illustrated song. When biz was light, they were even longer, with a fourth film and an extra song added. But around 10 P.M. when people started piling in and packing the hall, the entertainment went down to two and a half reels and one vaude turn not running over twenty minutes. This was on a slow week night; what the show was cut to during rush hours on big nights may be imagined. Capacity was about three hundred, with

one hundred standing in the back. They put a card out at the side
of the stage with the name of the vaude act, and when the pic
was on, they put out a card reading "moving picture," as if you
wouldn't know what it was. Sometimes when there were no titles
on the pics you just made up your own. There was no "dip" to
the house, which made it tough for the customers to see. (Marcus
Loew and Joe Schenck were part of the People's Circuit.)

Speaking about cutting shows when there were crowds, I must
tell you about the time Clark & Verdi (the first two-man Italian
act) played Proctor's Twenty-third Street. They had an amateur
night, and the crowds were waiting to get in. The manager ran
backstage and told everybody to cut their acts so they could get
the crowds in. "How much shall we cut?" asked Clark and Verdi.
"Cut, cut, cut," said the manager, "We have to get those people
in." Clark & Verdi, who usually did a 20-minute comedy act, that
night opened with "Hiya, do you wanna job?" "Shoes," said the
partner. "Then come witha me!" And they walked off the stage.
The shortest act on record. The manager came back roaring mad,
but all Clark and Verdi said was, "You told us to cut—we did!"
The manager had no argument. This is one of the classic stories
among vaude performers.

Just think, in 1904 there was not a single five-cent theater devoted to moving pics, and in 1907 there were 5,000 nickelodeons!
They were developing new theatergoers. Attendance was two million people a day, of which one third were kids. The average
expense of running one of these store shows was $175 to $200 a
week. Seating capacity was usually 199, because over 199 seats
meant a higher license fee. Some of the places did twelve to
eighteen shows a day.

This pic-vaude combination was essentially a poor man's amusement. It looked to the lower classes for support. Immigrants
learned to read English from watching the pics and having their
sons and daughters explain the titles to them. The combination
shows gathered in the rough and tough of both sexes who had
little to spend but a long time to spend it in. Where there was
competition, features had to be added to attract the opposition
business, and this increased the cost; then the admission had to be
raised, and with increased admissions the poor man, whose patronage built up these shows in the first place, was cut off.

William Fox was a pioneer in small-time vaude. He took over

the Dewey Theatre on East Fourteenth Street (an old burlesque house) for $50 a day rent. He gave Kraus (the owner) a check for $3,500, for a ten weeks' advance. He did great and took over the Gotham in Harlem, paying $40,000 a year, then took a lease on the Dewey for $60,000 a year. Fox became the owner of the Greater New York Film Exchange and developed more of an interest in pictures than he had in vaude. He became one of the biggest men in the pic business. And at one time he tried to buy up all the theaters in America. He failed (thank goodness).

The Bronx Theatre, which Arthur Jacobs owned, was the first in the Bronx to play vaude with any pretensions. It was only a 299-seater. The Bernheimer Bros. store in Baltimore played seven acts of vaude six shows a day, and seated only 300 people. There was even Yiddish vaude at the Mt. Morris Theatre on 116th Street and Fifth Avenue. At one time there were five theaters on Fourteenth Street playing vaude and pics, charging 10-20-30: Pastor's, the Unique, Union Square, the Fourteenth Street Theatre, and the Dewey.

There were many acts that had angles, even in those tiny theaters. One act bought $2.00 worth of tickets for the first show and packed the place to make sure the act would go over and maybe save itself a cancellation. Over on Avenue A (New York) there was a pic show that gave you soda water with a tiny dab of ice cream all for five cents!

The Imperial Theatre on 116th Street and Lenox Avenue, originally opened by Sam Taub (a great showman), then later owned by the McKibbon Bros. and booked by Joe Wood, was an incubator for future headliners. Mrs. Jessel (George's sainted mother, who loved show folks, and whom Georgie is keeping alive by his famous "telephone calls") was in the box office. Walter Winchell, Jack Weiner (who later became a great agent), Eddie Cantor, Bert Hanlon, Burns & Fulton, Laurie & Bronson, Leonard & Ward, and the Evans Bros. were just a few that hatched there. The McKibbon Bros. would cancel the real bad acts, and the Evans Bros. (hoofers), who lived next door, would come in to see the opening show with their wooden shoes in their hands, ready to go on any minute.

M. R. Sheedy left the United Booking Office and became independent opposition with a small-time circuit (Ben Piermont later was the booker of this circuit and a very good one), and Sheedy had many houses on his circuit. Walter Plimmer, an old-timer, also was a big inde in the early days of small time. His son, Walter, Jr., became a very good actor; he now is a priest and has been made an honorary Lamb, which is a great honor to the Lambs! W. Cleveland, an old minstrel manager, was another big inde agent. The Unique on East Fourteenth Street put in illuminated signs on the sides of the stage of the name of each act as it appeared, getting away from the card system. There were no programs.

The small-time theaters couldn't play a big act, so they had to take what they could get. Hokum (originally called "okum") and slapstick acts were fed to the small-time audiences, who loved them. It undid five years (1903-1908) of trying to promote cleaner and better bills, but it made dough, and that's all the managers were thinking of.

Illinois is credited with having introduced small time to the Middle West. The Bijou in Quincy was first to enter the field with a store show in 1908. Chicago booked 150 to 200 of these small theaters in a week!

The Dewey, in New York, advertised twenty-five fans, making it the coolest house in town. They had to turn off the fans when the acts went on, as you couldn't hear a thing with them going. People were standing in long lines to see pics and vaude at a time when only some world-wide star could get such response in legit. Gane's Manhattan (on the spot where Gimbel's is now) gave them two acts and three reels of pics, a one-hour show for ten cents. Gane barred sensational, crime, or suggestive films. Acts playing the real small-time theaters had to use the floodlights from the pic machine, because the small-time houses had no spotlight.

In 1909 Joe Leo was booking fifteen weeks of small time for William Fox. There were thirty-two small-time houses in the U.B.O. Then there was the Metropolitan Vaude Exchange, booked by Joe Wood, with fifty small-time theaters on his books.

It was in 1909 that New York's Mayor McClelland tried to revoke all moving-pic licenses, but the court stopped him. Dan Hennessy, an old-timer, took charge of the U.B.O. family-time (small-time) houses and was in that spot for many years. He could have made a fortune, but died a poor man—because he was honest. (A swell guy!) Pat Casey (at this writing the last of the greats of old vaude) took over the Metropolitan Exchange and booked fifty weeks of small time; his brother Dan was treasurer, and Joe Wood, to whom it had originally belonged, became just a part of the agency. Then he and it were both taken over by the U.B.O.! People's Vaude, with Joe Schenck as head man, booked twelve houses (including Loew's).

Pop Grauman (father of the famous Sid) was up for mayor of Frisco, in 1909, but didn't make it. He was a great showman for thirty-four years; he took out the first colored minstrels on the road after the Civil War. He was also the first to introduce high-class vaude at a ten-cent price on the Coast, at the Unique (afterwards named the National). A man always kind and considerate to the actor.

A sensation was caused on Broadway when Big Jim Morton was booked in two small-time houses (doing eight shows a day), the Circle and the Manhattan, for Gane, at $2,000 a week. He called himself the "human film." And it was the beginning of "small time" growing up!

In 1909 the small-time vaude houses were driving out the straight pic houses (as the talkies drove out the silent-pic houses). The small-time manager with from $400 to $1,500 a week to spend was a self-satisfied person. He was looking further ahead than the big-time manager.

Hurtig and Seamon's Metropolis Roof played vaude in summer —vaude, beer, and delicatessen. The orchestra, with Joe Ali and six musicians, played twenty-minute intermissions so the customers could beer up and visit the delicatessen. Neatly printed cards were given to the audience, saying that there was a lunch counter in the rear of the hall; pig's knuckles, cold jelly, and potato salad could be had for twenty-five cents! The orchestra played ten overtures during the evening to give the customers a chance to buy!

In 1907 there was an epidemic of "living pictures" (a revival of the old honky-tonks). Ladies posed in tights, which brought them under the head of theatrical performances and required a $500 license. Small-time acts (some Big Timers too) went in for pathos, singing mother songs with a recitation (in an amber spot) or doing a poem about a dog. The guy would stand dejectedly, gazing at the floor with a pained expression, wringing his cap, while the piano player rendered "Hearts and Flowers"; it was not pathos, it was pathetic! (But it got a big hand.)

As the small time progressed, the music publishers began charging the managers for the song slides (which up to now had been given for free). The slides, which started at $5.00 a set, brought in a quarter of a million dollars a year to the publishers.

Vaude was getting pretty dirty in 1908. (It cleaned up again later.) The following notice appeared in the local dailies in Seattle: "Clean Bills—The following houses at their performances yesterday presented programs free from vulgarity—Coliseum, Pantages, Star." The omission of the Orpheum, which was the standard vaude house, showed that the "blue material" was creeping into the Big Time. (It was the only time I ever knew the Orpheum Circuit to step away from the strict censorship of blue material.)

Chicago was a hotbed of "pop" vaude. The Western Vaudeville Association cared for a large string. William Morris looked after a long string of pop houses, as did Walter Keefe, Coney Holmes, Frank Q. Doyle, and Charles Doutrick, who all supplied acts to a number of small houses. In the South they had plenty of small houses and agencies. The Greenwood Agency, with headquarters in Atlanta, was the biggest one down there. It was rough going for an act playing the South around 1909. The managers there were new to show biz and were even smaller than their houses. Philadelphia had hundreds of houses playing "pop" vaude. Between Chicago and Frisco there weren't very many small-time bookings of importance. In later years there was the Ackerman & Harris Circuit booking that territory and it was called the "Death Trail." The jumps were terrific and the acts had to play three days and lose the rest of the week to make the next jump. They would owe themselves money when they finished the tour. I do want to say that Mr. Ackerman was a fine gentleman and showman, as was Mr. Harris, but their ideas didn't work out for the actor. George Webster in the Dakotas headed a small circuit of houses controlled by people of many occupations; it was rough. At Frisco there was a great independent by the name of Bert Levy (no relation to the vaude artist). Sullivan & Considine and Pantages were not classed as small time, but were medium time, as distinguished from Big Time, small time, big small time, and small time.

Pop vaude attracted small investors. Cases are known where the investment was less than $100 for a two-act and pic show. The arrangements in those cases were an agreement between the promoter and the prop of a failing straight pic house or the manager of an opry house who couldn't get enough combination or rep shows to keep his place open. These places were often booked by fly-by-night agents and many acts were paid less than their contracts called for, or sometimes not paid at all, the manager closing up or pleading poverty. The act was at a disadvantage in a small town, as far as taking their troubles to court, because many times the manager was the sheriff or even the judge, so you just packed up and tested the next bookings. In the early days of vaude, acts, when with a "shaky" outfit, would always draw in advance from the manager so they would be that much ahead if there was no pay-off and the habit hung on in the small time. When an act got into town they'd touch the box office with the excuse that they had run short of dough because of the big jump, or that they had sent their money to the bank and left themselves short, etc. Later, as the business grew solid, there were few box-office touches, although I do know of cases on the Big Time where the first thing an act did was to get an advance on some pretext or other. The big-time manager had nothing to lose because he was going to pay them anyway, and if anything happened to the act that they didn't play out the week, the booking office would collect (or the act would lose its bookings).

Jones, Linick & Schafer, in Chicago, started in the slot-machine business and later built up a big small-time circuit around Chicago. James L. Lederer was the pioneer "pop" vaude manager in Chicago. There was a theater there called Shindler's; when the manager canceled an act, he would walk down the aisle and yell, "You are *shut!*" (instead of closed). Actors hated him!

At the beginning of small time, the illustrated song played a big part, as the singers became local favorites (like M.C.s did many years later). Edward Roesch at the S. & C. in Seattle sang 110 consecutive weeks. Arthur Elwell at Pantages in the same city did 174 weeks. Jack Driscoll sang illustrated songs at the Fourteenth Street Theatre, New York, for five years.

There were some funny combinations on the small time. There was a family by the name of Hope (not Bob). The Six Hopes came from Brooklyn, and did twelve acts for $36. They all played a variety of instruments and supplied the accompaniments when the others sang or danced. They did a musical sketch, and all did single acts and acrobatics. Everybody filled in with a specialty. They could do anything from a two-hour show to a full night's entertainment.

Small time was originally called "family time"—the small store shows were usually run by the family, mother selling tickets, father at the door, daughter playing the piano, and son running the pic machine. In 1909 there were 2,000 small-time theaters, 1,000 east and 1,000 west. Grauman's National Theatre in Frisco never billed the house on billboards or advertised in the newspapers, and the place was always jammed. Sid Grauman (his son) later became the greatest showman on the Coast. Remember the stars' footprints in the cement outside Grauman's Chinese Theater in Hollywood? That stunt of Sid's received world-wide publicity.

By 1910 Loew was starting to book big-time headliners in some of his larger theaters, like Amelia Bingham (great legit star) at $1,500 a week. (This was a far cry from earlier salaries of $20 for singles, $40 for doubles, $60 for trios, and $80 for quartettes; if you had five people in the act you were out of luck, or maybe they would tag on ten bucks to the pay check.) At Loew's National Theatre in the Bronx he had thirty-three musicians and at his Seventh Avenue Theatre there were twenty-five musicians. He changed his prices from twenty-five cents to $1.00 top. William Fox opened his Nemo Theatre (originally Lion's Palace, built in 1908). Ushers wore tuxedos and there was a class audience for vaude-pics. Sigmund Lubin already was retiring from his vaude-pic houses in Philadelphia where he had introduced this form of entertainment.

To give you an idea of what strides the small time was making, at the Circle Theatre (New York) they offered a ten-act bill for a dime; it was the most costly line-up ever offered for the price, paying as high as $500 for an act (the opposition was Loew's Lincoln Square). There were over 500 theaters who were playing acts costing a maximum price of $300! Standard acts would play the small time under assumed names, to grab a few weeks' work in out of the way spots. (If they played under their right billing their value on the Big Time would be lowered.)

In 1910 they were opening "Hippodromes" all over the country and putting on open-air vaude shows in baseball parks, etc., with prices from ten cents to fifty cents. Some spots made plenty, but most of them were flops. They used "sight acts," bands, circus, dancers, and acrobats. (No microphone in those days and a talking act couldn't be heard.) In Los Angeles they had a theater called the Nine Cent Theatre that advertised eight acts and 6,000 feet of film for nine cents' admish! In New Orleans they had "premium vaudeville." At your favorite store you bought fifty cents' worth of merchandise and they gave you a coupon; two coupons admitted you to the theater. In 1911 the famous Brandenberg Museum in Philadelphia closed after trying burly, vaude, and pics. There was plenty small time; they played acts to take the monotony off the films. It was a case of quantity, not of quality. The price was the main consideration. Herman Robinson, the New York Commissioner of Licenses, approved 104,000 contracts, and said, "The average salary was $80 for singles, $115 for teams, $150 for trios, and for acts with four or more people $250."

By 1912 there were more than 1,000 theaters playing class and medium vaudeville acts and 4,000 playing small time. Stagehands demanded that acts with one or more stage sets must carry a special stagehand, property man, or carpenter. Stagehands got $35 a week, the carpenter $40. (Now stagehands make as much as two and three hundred a week with overtime, etc.) Acts naturally had to ask for more money to cover the stagehand's traveling expense and salary (and to make a little on it). The big-time was affected more than the small-time act, but there were many on the small time using "Diamond Dye drops" (could be folded and carried in a trunk). Producers of acts left the Big Time because of no consecutive bookings, slashed salaries, and grafting agents and bookers. They came to the small time where they could get a break, maybe at smaller salaries, but with consecutive bookings. The year 1912 gave small time a terrific boom, some houses making a net profit of $18,000 a week. They were getting a lot of acts from the Big Time because the acts were sure of a longer route and no cancellation clause in their contracts! On the Big Time an act wasn't sure of his dates, even if he held contracts for them; they could switch routes or cancel on two weeks' notice.

Jones, Linick & Schafer opened their Colonial Theatre in Chicago, with four shows a day, and on opening day 10,000 people showed up. Tickets were sold at the Boston Store (a department store) for *one cent* as an ad for the house. In California one place advertised "hot and cold" vaudeville; when it was hot they gave the show in the airdome and when it was cold they gave it in the theater. There were many airdomes throughout the country; they were small outdoor theaters, and anybody who had a back yard could (and did) open one. The gag among actors was, "We couldn't play today at the airdome; the manager's wife had her clothes on the line." Some small-time managers were a bit larcenous. They would pay off the acts, just before train time, in dimes, nickels, and quarters (making an excuse that they had to pay off from the day's receipts). The act had no time to count up until they were on the train, and would then find their salaries short at least $2.00. Too late to kick for such a small amount. But when you figure it up on a season, the thieving manager had a few easy but dirty bucks!

In 1913 Gordon & Lord opened the Scollay Square Olympia Theatre in Boston, a 3,200-seater with no posts, and did six shows a day at a twenty-five cent top. The United Booking Office raised salaries because of an act shortage, then later on, in the year 1914, cut them on account of the war bringing in lots of acts from Europe. Detroit had vaude represented in all different grades because U.B.O., Pantages, Loew, Western Vaude, Gus Sun, and Earl Cox were all booking theaters there. Loew opened Ebbets Field in Brooklyn as an open-air night resort with pic and vaude—and showed a profit. The open-air theaters had a tough time showing pictures in the pioneer days of films. When the full moon was out, the audience couldn't see the pic. It was "Roxy" who introduced the daylight screen on which you could show pics outdoors (or indoors), regardless of the light.

Commutation tickets were given by Moss & Brill at their McKinley Square Theatre, New York, for the first time anywhere. Six admissions for twenty-five cents at matinees and seven admissions for $1.00 at night shows. Loew started the personal appearances of prominent pic players with Sidney Bracy and Frank Farrington, stars of a serial, "Million Dollar Mystery," which was playing his houses. They did a piano act at two houses a night, but no matinees, as they were shooting future installments of the picture in the afternoons. They received $300 a week and did big at the box office. Some years later Nils T. Granlund (N.T.G.), who was Loew's press agent, had many stars from pics make personal appearances at Loew's theaters, just taking a bow, and making seven and eight houses a night (with motorcycle escorts). And still more years later the personal appearances were run into the ground when pic stars tried to do an act, which proved that they were pic stars only.

Small-time vaude opened at the Lexington Opera House (New York), built by Oscar Hammerstein for his operas, but according to his contract with the Metropolitan Opera Company (to whom he sold out), he could not play opera for ten years. In 1915 we saw the passing of the first Keith house in New York City, Keith's Union Square; after thirty years it was returned to the landlord, the Palmer Estate. It later became a small-time pop house and even tried tab shows and pics. It was finally rebuilt as a store. The Hippodrome, Boston (formerly Keith's National), played Creatore and his band of fifty pieces along with pics, and also gave free parking space to customers (first time any theater gave away parking space).

Lillian Russell, brought to Loew's National, by Zit (publisher of *Zit's Weekly*, a trade paper—he also handled some acts, business and advertising), was called to take a bow, and made a speech —and got hell from the U.B.O. Loew's New Orpheum, Boston, opened and had box offices on three streets. Vic Morris, the manager, was a great showman.

The opening of the State-Lake Theatre, Chicago, in 1919 marked a new era for small-time vaude and in entertainment. It seated 3,100 with grosses never less than $20,000 a week. It started a rush to build large theaters for pop vaude. Orpheum Circuit went in for it good and heavy and called their pop houses Junior Orpheums. It was that same year that the United Booking Office changed its name to Keith Vaudeville Exchange in memory of B. F. Keith. The Capitol Theatre, New York, opened as the largest theater in the world, with 5,300 seats; the plot alone cost three million bucks. There were fourteen dancers in the chorus, twelve show gals, nine men and nine gal dancers, and Arthur Pryor and seventy musicians; with twelve specialty acts. It played to $18,000 the first week and went into vaude and pics later.

William Fox was doing many unethical things with his booking of acts. Finally he couldn't stand the pounding the trade papers and the Vaudeville Managers Protective Association were giving him, so he finally issued a play-or-pay contract and even went further; he put in the contract what spot the act would have on the bill (first time this was done). Fox was having a tough time getting acts, because Keith, booking the Moss houses (which were opposition to Fox), barred all acts that played for Fox. In 1921 there were 156 weeks of three-a-day split weeks. There were 12,000 vaude acts idle, as 20 per cent of the houses changed to straight pics!

The small time was the breeding place of gag and act pirates.

Managers would play them because they were cheaper than the originals. Vaudeville was not variety any more, it was repetition. The great Eva Tanguay was playing the Pantages Time doing four or five a day. In 1923 the Orpheum Circuit put small-time vaude in three of their big-time houses, Majestic (Chicago), Majestic (Milwaukee), and Orpheum (St. Louis), all playing the State-Lake policy. The next year there was talk about eliminating the Big Time and small time—all to do vaude and pics. It was getting tough on the Big Time, because the "pop" houses were playing almost as good shows as they were, maybe with just a few less acts, but a much cheaper admish. The New York Hippodrome, taken over by Keith, did $50,000 weeks, and none less than $35,000, and with small-time shows.

In 1926 it was very tough for the independent agents and circuits; these were tiny places playing just a few acts. It got so bad the acts were getting $7.00 a day (they were getting less, but the N.R.A. put that price as the minimum). One strong man who tore a phone book in half at every show had to go out and steal the books from phone booths, as they cost forty cents apiece. He also would bend nails and spikes in his act and throw 'em away, but on that salary he would bend them back for the next show.

When small-time vaude got that low, it was breathing its last. It kept gasping for a few more years and finally gave up when the Palace went into four and five shows a day with vaude-pic policy, and a few more years saw Loew's State Theatre, the small-time banner house, give up vaude and just play pics! Now there is no Big Time or small time—in fact, there just isn't anything you can really call *vaudeville*! SEZ

Your pal,

LEFTY

Big Pay Checks

Dear Joe,

Years ago when we said a guy was "loaded," it meant just one thing: he was drunk! But today when you say a guy is "loaded" it means he has much moolah. Me and Aggie have also noticed that years ago we used to talk about a guy having talent, but today they speak about his heavy money belt, collection of banknotes, or junior Fort Knox vault. Stars of today have a half-a-dozen things going for them—oil wells, real estate, horses, breeding farms, radio and TV stations, baseball clubs, chain stores, etc. Most of yesterday's rich performers made their fortunes with pure show-biz money! With living expenses comparatively cheap and no taxes, they made net almost as much as the stars of today who receive much larger salaries, but they don't add up to so much "take to the bank" pay!

You could almost have given a party at Rector's, Churchill's, or Shanley's for what a tab for two at the Stork Club, Twenty-One, the Colony, or Chambord comes to! A $50,000 estate in those days was equal to one of $250,000 today. Servants and help were cheap. A star had a valet or maid who worked at the theater as well as at home and who also acted as secretary, etc. Today a star's payroll includes a private press agent, personal rep, secretary, valet, writers, musicians, and at least half-a-dozen hangers-on; office rent, transportation, and advertising are additional expenses. The old-timers paid no taxes (until 1913—and then only about 1 per cent, I believe), and the buck was worth a buck! They did eight shows a week in legit and two a day in vaude, and never heard of psychiatrists or ulcers. No worries about "capital-gains deals" or how much the other fellow was getting, and yet they made plenty of dough and got plenty of laughs.

At the Theater Comique (a honky-tonk) they paid the Boisettes and the Garnellas, two acrobatic acts, $300 each, and the cheapest act on the bill got $75. Expenses of the house were $3,200 a week, and they played to $4,500 a week for many months. This was in 1879!

In 1895 Oscar Hammerstein paid Yvette Guilbert $4,000 a week for a four-week run at his Olympia Theater. She played to $60,000 during her stay. In 1900 he paid Williams & Walker $1,750 a week and Proctor paid 'em $2,000. In 1906 Huber paid $9,000 to Libbera, "The Man with Two Bodies." He hired Madison Square Garden (the old one) for February and March, because his small museum on Fourteenth Street couldn't possibly get him his dough back for this high-salaried attraction. Remember, this was a museum act!

Eva Tanguay was getting $500 a week in 1907 and in a few years had jumped to $2,500; Cecilia Loftus was getting $2,000; Peter Dailey, $1,000; Marie Lloyd, $1,200; Vesta Victoria, $2,500 (then $3,000—highest-priced act in vaude); Elsie Janis, $2,500. Lauder came over for Klaw & Erlanger for $2,500 and later reached $5,000 for William Morris (with Morris paying the English managers $1,000 a week for Mr. Lauder's release). A couple of years later Blanche Ring received $1,500; Denman Thompson (*Old Homestead* fame) got $2,100; Gertrude Hoffman & Co., $3,000; Albert Chevalier, $1,600.

James J. Jeffries received $3,000 a week at the Wigwam in Frisco. Bayes & Norworth got $1,750 (later got much more). Marcus Loew offered George M. Cohan $10,000 to play a week for him, and George M. said no (that was practically like $50,000 today). Lina Cavalieri at the London Music Hall received $5,000, the highest salary ever paid over there for a single. Sarah Bernhardt, in her first vaude plunge, was paid $4,000 a week by Sir Alfred Butt. Buffalo Bill was signed by Frank Evans for $3,000 a week. Nat Goodwin signed his weekly pay check for $2,500, Amelia Bingham for $2,000, and Jacob Adler (the famous Jewish actor) got $1,300 a week!

In 1911 Leoncavallo (composer of *Pagliacci*) and orchestra received $5,000 a week in London. In 1912 Caruso received $3,000 a concert in the United States. He got $8,000 a night in Buenos Aires (eighty-four grand in all) with the proviso that he must sing at least two songs a night. Two years later Al Jolson got $2,500 at the Brighton Beach Theatre. Ten years later he broke away from Columbia Records, where he got $7,000 a side, and went to Brunswick, where he got $10,000 per release. In 1929 he broke Coast records in pic houses. At the Warfield Theatre in Frisco he played to $57,000 on percentage. The next year, at the Capitol,

New York, Jolson got $20,000 on a 50-50 percentage deal over
$100,000; he did about $80,000. Show folks were betting he would
do over $100,000 (and lost). He did five and six shows a day and
would have gone way over $100,000, but he changed his songs
every show, and the audience would stay to hear the new songs, and
so cut down the "turnover." The management went wild, but Al
was only interested in "getting over."

In 1913 Wilkie Bard got $3,250, John Bunny nabbed $1,000 for
a monologue, Mike Bernard signed with Columbia Records for
$10,000 a year to make a few records twice a year. The Singer
Midgets had a funny contract; they received $1,000 a week clear,
the Loew Circuit paying all expenses—hotel bills, food, and travel
—for the thirty-three people, animals, animal trainers, etc. (which
amounted to real big money). In 1915 Jess Willard got $4,000 a
week (and didn't draw). John McCormack, the famous Irish
tenor, asked for $25,000 a week, based on his concert-tour guarantee
of $1,500 a concert, fourteen shows a week, etc. Managers gasped
a loud *no*!

George Robey was in 1918 the highest taxpayer in England, paying $60,000. That same year Mary Pickford paid Uncle Sam $300,-
000. Shubert Vaude paid Nora Bayes $3,500 (she later received
$5,000 in pic houses). Will Rogers got $3,000 from Shubert
Vaude, but he made six and seven grand a week on his concert
tours, besides his after-dinner speeches and pics and newspaper
articles. The Dolly Sisters played two houses a week and got $5,000.
In 1924 Dempsey's income tax was $90,000; his manager, Doc
Kearns, paid $71,000. Kearns and Dempsey sometimes split their
earnings in vaude. Kearns introduced Jack at the State and did a
short bit "in one" with him and got $2,500 for his bit (the highest-
priced straight man in show biz in 1924). Dempsey got $8,000 a
week for four weeks at Luna Park, Berlin. It was 1924 that Gilda
Gray, at the Metropolitan Theatre in L.A., got $14,000 for her
share—and it was Holy Week! Paul Whiteman and his band received $7,500 at Keith's Hippodrome, New York—top vaude salary
at that time. A few years later the pic houses paid him $12,000 and
paid for the transportation of thirty-three men. He gave the full
show on the bills. It was the year the pic houses, with their large
capacities, were skyrocketing salaries. Regular big-time acts that
had been getting $500 to $750 were getting $1,500 to $3,000 a week
from the pic houses. Ina Claire was getting $3,000 a week in vaude.

Gertrude Lawrence, doing five shows a day at the Paramount (Charlot's Revue Unit), collected $3,500 a week for herself. Ruth Elder signed for twenty-five weeks at $5,000 a week. The Lee Kids (Jane & Kathryn), the first vaude and talking act to play the Metropolitan at Los Angeles, got $2,000 for the week. It was 1927 that the most exploited individual of the century, Lindbergh, was offered the most fantastic salaries ever heard of in show biz: $100,000 for a twenty-eight-day tour doing two shows a day; $25,000 a week at the Roxy; $500,000 a year in pics; $100,000 for one week to play a theater on the Coast. (This was the absolute top figure that anybody was ever offered anyplace! And they meant it—and no doubt would even have showed a profit.) Al Woods, after hearing all the offers, said, "I'll take his cat for $10,000 a week." He received 3,500,000 letters, 100,000 telegrams, seven million business offers. One pic company wanted to pay him a million bucks if he would marry any girl of his own choosing (nice of them) and let them photograph the wedding. He received thousands of marriage proposals, three invites to go to the moon via a rocket, 14,000 gifts, and 500 close(?) relations asked for dough. He got more letters from women than from men. Over $100,000 in stamps were enclosed for return postage. So you can see he could have been the highest salaried act in vaude—but he settled for $2,500 a week with the Guggenheim Foundation for five years.

Peaches Browning did big in vaude playing on percentage. Amos 'n' Andy received $5,000 a week for Keith-Albee dates, and $7,500 in pic houses. Fanny Brice got a $3,500-a-week guarantee and percentage from Keith. Maurice Chevalier turned down $5,000 to sing six songs at a Clarence Mackay party because he had to pay commission—he never paid commission, he said.

Eddie Cantor got $7,500 single at the Palace (tied Ed Wynn), and in 1931 with the Cantor-Jessel Unit his end was $8,000, which was tops for a single on the Big Time (not pic houses). Rudy Vallee started at $3,000 at the Paramount in Brooklyn and was raised to $4,500 (he stayed two and a half years). Ed Wynn (in 1931) received $7,500 as M.C. (tying Eddie Cantor) at the Palace eighteen years after he was on the opening Palace bill. The Marx Bros. got a sweet $10,000 a week at the Palace (a very big act), the highest-priced act in vaude.

In 1921 Vallee, Maurice Chevalier, and Amos 'n' Andy were the only new actor millionaires in three years!

Gene Tunney got $7,000 at Loew's State. Van & Schenck made $4,500 at the Chicago Theatre and sweetened it up by doubling in a café and getting $3,500 more. Lou Holtz "Sole-Mioed" for $4,250 and went to $6,000. Kate Smith in 1921 was playing full weeks for $3,500 and got $7,000 in pic houses. Maurice Chevalier got $12,000 at the Chicago Theatre (house lost $15,000). When Aimee Semple McPherson played at the Capitol, New York, for $5,000, the house lost $20,000. Ben Bernie & Band got $6,500, the same for Fred Waring, and Ted Lewis and his group got $7,500!

Guy Lombardo and his show toured for Standard Oil of New Jersey for ten grand a week (free admissions). Joe Penner went from $950 a week to $8,000 a week in three months. One week he got $13,250 (on percentage). It was all due to his terrific radio build-up. (Did seven shows a day in some houses.) Sally Rand started at the Chicago Fair in 1933 for $125 a week and ended up getting $5,000. Ethel Waters, playing pic houses, received $4,500, which up to then was tops for a Negro performer. Later Lena Horne and Josephine Baker topped this.

Eddie Cantor at the RKO, Boston, got $25,000 for a six-day week—he carried six people with his unit (whom of course he had to pay). Jimmy Durante got $5,000 a week in London, which was the top American single salary up to then. In 1929 Bea Lillie got $6,500, and Dempsey, for "Roadside Inn," received $6,500. Cantor got $7,500 for endorsement of Old Gold cigarettes (Jolson only got $2,500). In 1932 the most important draws were, one, pic personalities, two, musical comedy stars, and three, radio, followed by vaude headliners! It was this year that Loew paid big dough to acts for his de luxe pic houses to cover up a siege of bad pics. They did this to keep their patronage; once a customer switched to another theater, it was tough to get him back. Loew paid Belle Baker $4,000 (she got $2,500 from Keith), and Sophie Tucker $7,500 (she got $2,500 from Keith), etc. Loew played the tops and paid the top salaries for about eight weeks, until the pic drought was over!

Through his appearance on the Vallee radio show, Edgar Bergen's salary jumped from $300 to $2,800 (and got much bigger later). Helen Morgan, at Loew's State (her first time in vaude after two years), got $2,500. Rubinoff, who made his rep on the Eddie Cantor radio show, was getting $6,000 a week in pic houses. Kay Kyser & Band, on percentage deals, pulled down $26,000 at

Fox, Detroit. In 1931 East & Dumke ("Sisters of the Skillet") through their radio build-up jumped from $350 to $1,500.

Radio did a lot to boost vaude salaries. In 1926 Cantor got $1,500 for fifteen minutes, and the next year Amos 'n' Andy jumped from $250 a week to $2,000.

Of course when you start hitting 1943 and up you get into the real crazy era of salaries. Sinatra with $15,000 guarantee and 50 per cent of the gross gets himself around forty-one Gs at the Chicago Theatre. Danny Kaye packs a bundle of $79,000 for two weeks at the same place, with same guarantee, only Danny did it in *two* weeks! But Major Bowes was making $100,000 a week at one time with his Amateur Units, radio, and Capitol job! He paid his male amateurs $50 on the road and the gals got $60. (I guess he realized that gals needed more money to live.) When his units went down to $200,000-a-year income, he gave it up as not worth while bothering with. At one time he had gross units bringing in $900,000 a year! (And the guy paid the kids fifty and sixty bucks!—doing as many shows a day as called for, riding on buses, and sleeping in flea bags—that's what you get for being stage-struck! We did the same thing, but had laughs with it.) The Major left a lot of money to charity!

High salaries of the '40s included Jack Benny's $40,000 at the Roxy (paying for his own show), then $92,000 in Detroit and Cleveland; Bob Hope's $40,000 at the Paramount; Grace Moore, $20,000 at the Roxy; the De Marcos, $5,000, a new high for a dance team. However, years ago the Castles did a week of one-night stands to a sweet $31,000, Lillian Russell was paid $2,500 a week, and the Dolly Sisters were guaranteed $2,000 a week at the Hotel Knickerbocker.

How about Milton Berle with fifteen Gs for four days at the Copacabana in Florida, and his ten grand a week in cafés and TV shows? Jess Willard got $1,000 a day with the 101 Ranch, as did Tom Mix, and Gene Autry doubled that, I believe, with Barnum & Bailey, besides his pics, records, and royalties on clothes for the kiddies!

A guy by the name of Bing Crosby was not doing too badly. In 1948 his royalties from records were $650,000 and his radio brought in another $650,000, besides his pics, publishing house, and his interests in a hundred things from orange juice to gadgets.

The boy can match bankbooks with anyone. Did you know that Red Grange (who played vaude), got $47,000 as his share on a percentage deal for one game in Los Angeles? The gate was $130,-000 gross. Of course, if you wanna call fights entertainment, the highest-paid entertainers were pugilists. Dempsey and Tunney were tops, and Joe Louis didn't do so bad either.

Mae West, Hildegarde, Charlie Chaplin, Bill Hart, George M. Cohan, Joe E. Lewis, Jackie Gleason, Abbott & Costello, Judy Garland, Betty Hutton, and Olsen & Johnson were all top earners. And how about the $70,000 that Martin & Lewis dragged down at the Paramount for a week's wages? I could mention many more of today's stars like Billy Daniels, Johnny ("Cry") Ray, Frankie Laine, Billy Eckstein, etc. But these guys all did it the hard way. Today it all adds up to big grosses, really small "nets," and a lot of hard work.

The old-timers made money so much easier. They played to people who didn't yell and scream when you mentioned Brooklyn, or dance up and down the aisles, or tear you apart for an autograph. They were nice respectable audiences, who had reserved seats and feelings.

And when you talk about big dough, there's a kid from vaude you just can't leave out; that's Walter Winchell. His $1,352,000 Kaiser-Frazer pay-off for ninety broadcasts, his syndicated column, his TV show, and the two-dollar bets he makes on long shots makes him one of the top income guys in show biz. Another kid by the name of Arthur Godfrey, who is on TV and radio so many hours a day he has no chance to spend his dough, also has a very neat income.

But a very funny thing about show biz that me and Aggie have seen through the years is that some guy dies who you think never earned a dime and leaves a "bundle," and the guys who made a lot of dough may not end up with enough for their lawyers to even pay the inheritance tax.

We hope that none of the present-day stars will ever need a benefit, and by the looks of their bankbooks, they won't; they worked hard (much harder than the old stars) for every penny, without the laughs and the ease of the old-timers.

But me and Aggie say that the little frankfurters we bought at Coney Island for five cents tasted much better than the jumbo franks they peddle now for fifteen cents—and so no matter how much dough they have, against Rockefeller—they're still bums!—SEZ

Your pal,

LEFTY

Memories with Laughs

Dear Joe,

It's funny how certain things stand out in your mind after years have passed, and how you have forgotten other things until you start punching the bag about show biz and memories come trickling back. This is especially true about things that made you laugh. For instance, I remember the time when . . .

Johnny Stanley, one of Broadway's fine wits and wisecrackers, came to rehearsal one Monday morning at Hammerstein's, and had George May, the musical director, and his men rehearse his music for half an hour, making them play it over and over again. There were many acts waiting to rehearse and finally George said, "All right, Johnny, you know we always play your stuff O.K." Johnny thanked him and was about to walk away when George looked at his list of the show and said, "Say, Johnny, I haven't got you down on my list of acts that's on the bill. Are you replacing someone?" "No," said Johnny, "I ain't working here this week, George, but it's been so long since I've worked I just wanted to hear how my music sounds!"

The time when Wilton Lackaye was getting over a two-week bender. The boys from the Lambs came to visit him in his two-room suite. While some of them were talking to him in the bedroom, a couple of the boys sneaked in two dwarfs (not midgets—dwarfs are deformed), who stripped naked, got up on the large table in the sitting room, and held the large bowl of fruit. The other boys got the sign that everything was O.K., so said good-by to Wilton and left. When Lackaye got up a short time later to go to the bathroom and saw the naked dwarfs holding the dish of fruit, he blinked, let out a yell, and staggered back to the bedroom. The boys, who were waiting outside, rushed in and asked what was the matter? Lackaye told them that he was getting the D.T.s, that he saw naked dwarfs holding a fruit dish. By now, the dwarfs had dressed and sneaked out, and Lackaye was led out to the sitting room and shown that there was nothing there. He blinked again, took a couple of drinks, and went off on a fresh bender. When the boys told him later what they did, he thought they were kidding. He never believed them!

The time Luke Barnett, the king of ribbers, was introduced to Jack Lait, the noted editor and playwright, at the Friars Club. Jack was told that Luke was a Polish millionaire who owned coal mines and was looking for a play for his stage-struck son. "I hear you are a writer of plays, Mr. Lit," said Luke in his rich Polish dialect. "Yes, I write plays," said Jack modestly. "Well, I will give you a check for $25,000 in advance if you will write a play for my boy." Jack's eyes almost popped, and he started "selling" Luke an idea. Luke was very interested. Jack ordered drinks, Luke ordered drinks, Jack wove a beautiful plot right in front of Luke's eyes, he was entranced, took out his checkbook, made out a check, misspelled Jack's name, tore it up, and started on another one (some more drinks). Lait was pouring it on, but whenever Luke was about to sign the check, he raised some kind of an argument about the play's plot and in a drunken rage tore up the check. He was cooled down again and Lait again started "selling" him the show. Again the check business, again a fit of rage and he tore it up. This kept up all night. Jack was sweating plenty, and nobody laughed louder than Jack did when he was finally told that it was a rib.

The time when Jimmy Hussey (that lovable comic) was introduced to Louis Mann, by George M. Cohan, as Paul Keith, the owner of the Keith Circuit. Mann had just signed for a short route on the Keith Circuit and was delighted to meet the great Mr. Keith. During the drinking and talking Jimmy Hussey (as Paul Keith) asked Louis to show him his route. Louis did this and Jimmy started fixing it up. "Instead of one week in Boston, I want you there for *two* weeks, Louis. I'm up there a lot and we'll have a nice time." And looking at the route he switched a week here and there, because it was too big a jump, etc., and when he finished

Louis Mann had the sweetest route ever given to anybody; and to finish it off, Jimmy whispered to Louis that he would see that he got a better salary. Even Louis bought a round of drinks! He never knew until the next day when he went to the office (to get his new route) that it all was a rib. Hussey ducked Mann for months. It took Louis that long to cool off.

The time when some clown nailed a dead fish to the bottom of the table in the dining room of the old Comedy Club. For days everybody tried to find out where the terrible odor came from. They opened all the windows and even stopped sitting with certain members.

The time Charlie Judels, during World War I, dressed like a French sailor and, surrounded by high-ranking French officers who were here on a mission, and many of the Lambs, attended a ceremony on the steps of the New York Public Library at Fifth Avenue and Forty-second Street. Judels made a speech in "French," the officers applauded him, and many bonds were sold. When they all got back to the Lambs, someone asked the Frenchmen did they understand Judels? They said just partly because he came from a different part of France than they did, but they understood enough to know it was a fine speech. No one ever told them that Charlie was doing "double talk." He never spoke a word of French in his life!

The time when Will Rogers, at a dinner given by the Jewish Theatrical Guild to Eddie Cantor, made a speech in pure Yiddish for twenty minutes, then translated it. It was a riot. (Must have taken him a month to learn.)

The time when Bert Fitzgibbons' brand-new shoes hurt so much that he took them off while standing against Mark Aaron's bar next door to the Palace. Morris, the call boy, came in to tell him he would be on in a few minutes. Bert tried to put his shoes on, but his feet were swollen. So Bert took his shoes in hand, went on the stage in his stocking feet, and did a 10-minute monologue about swollen feet and new shoes. Big laughs!

Tommy Dugan (Dugan & Raymond), the greatest of all dead-pan comics, would go into a picture show and read the titles out loud, being shushed by everybody, and things would end up in almost a riot when he argued that he couldn't read to himself, he had to read out loud to understand what the picture meant, he was an American citizen, paid for his ticket, etc. etc. He always finished up by getting his money back from the management.

Sid Grauman was a great practical joker. He once filled a softly lighted room with wax figures and had a certain film exec speak to them about censorship, telling him they were representative censors of the different states. The man never got wise until one wax figure happened to fall over.

You would never believe me if I told you the names of the real big guys in show biz who fell for "the trainman's daughter"! It was usually worked from Wolpin's and Lindy's restaurants. The gag was to tell the "fall guy" about a beautiful gal on the West Side, who was the daughter of a trainman who worked nights. All you had to do was to bring her a strawberry pie (or any messy pie in season) and you'd have a date. It was all done in an offhand manner by expert ribbers. The victim would buy the pie, which was carried by his guide, and would be taken to a certain tenement on the West side that had small gas lights in the halls. As they got to the top floor, he would call "Anna. Anna." At this moment one of the boys planted on the top floor would look over the banister and yell, "So you are the So-and-Sos who are ruining my Anna! I'll kill you!" With that he would throw an old electric bulb, which would explode and sound like a shot from a gun. By now both guys were racing down the steps, and the guide would manage in the excitement to throw the gooey pie into the victim's face, and as they ran up the street, the fellows in on the gag, who were hidden in doorways, would keep throwing bulbs. Both guys would run back to Wolpin's or Lindy's with the victim scared to death and the victim's face covered with pie! When I tell you that a "smarty" like the late Wilson Mizner (the wisest of all wise guys) went for this, you can imagine how the other un-smarties went for it. It got so bad that the police of the West Forty-seventh Street station gave orders to quit it. (They were in on it for years and got many a laugh out of the gag.)

The time when Arthur Caeser (a Pulitzer Prize winner for his one-act play, "Napoleon's Barber") got the number of a phone in the hall of a tenement in the Bronx. He called and asked for Mr. Cohen (the building maybe had a half a dozen) and told him that the musicians he ordered for the party would be a little late, but not to worry. Mr. Cohen said angrily that he didn't order any musicians, he had no party, and anyway it was 9 P.M. and everybody was asleep, and he had to get up early, so please stop "boddering" him. Fifteen minutes later Arthur called again and apologized, saying he had made a mistake in the address but as long as the musicians were on their way the union rules demanded that they had to play where they were sent even if it was just for half an hour, so they could prove they worked. By now Mr. Cohen was raving, saying that this was a respectable house, they would wake everybody up, he wouldn't let them play, he'd call the police, etc. Now Arthur got a bit angry, and his argument was, "You're a union man? You won't let other union men make a living? It won't cost you a penny, I tell you. They should be there any minute. Please like a good fellow let them play." Some time later he called Mr. Cohen again and told him it was all a mistake, the musicians got to the right place, not to worry, etc., etc., way into the night. You just can't write those things, but me and Aggie sure laugh when we even think of that night!

Johnny Johnston was told not to let Little Billy (a midget) leave the Friars to join a party that was being given that night, because Billy needed his rest, as he was to open the next day. Johnny stationed himself outside the door of the Friars. One of the boys put Little Billy over his arm, threw an overcoat over him and walked past Johnston. He never could figure how Little Billy got out!

The time George M. Cohan and Willie Collier cut cards (strippers) for $1,000 a cut. (They did this to rib Louis Mann.) In a few hours Collier had won $100,000 in cash and also two of Cohan's theaters. Everybody was looking on, all hep that it was a rib, but Louis figured Cohan was drunk and didn't realize what he was doing. He pleaded with Cohan to stop and told Collier what he thought of him, taking advantage of Cohan's condition, etc. When Collier finally said to Cohan, "Listen, George, I'll give you a chance to get even. I will now play you one cut of the cards for Sam Harris" (Cohan's partner), it was then that Louis Mann tumbled it was a rib!

The time in Atlantic City when Jack Norworth and Nora Bayes were breaking in a young piano player, Dave Stamper (later a noted composer, who wrote the music for many *Ziegfeld Follies*). Norworth told Stamper he didn't look very good as a straight piano player, and it would be a novelty if he made up like a Jap, and proceeded to teach him how to make up for it. He bought a load of make-up and Stamper started to make up at 10 A.M. and every time he would put a make-up on, Jack would say, "Nope, try it again." By matinee time Dave's face was raw. During the week newspapermen would ask for an interview with the little Jap piano player (only one of his kind), and Jack would say, "He just left the theater." Dave was standing there all the time.

Another time when Jack and Dave would cut cards in the dressing room for ten cents a cut. Jack (a very good amateur magician) was using a strip deck, and before Dave knew it, he owed Jack $2,500. He became panicky, He was only getting about $100 a week and had a family to support. He would double the bets, figuring he had to win sometime and so would get even. Week after week this kept on, until finally Jack told him he would give him a chance to get even. They would cut for the high card for the money Dave owed against Dave taking out Nora Bayes' two dogs every morning, noon, and evening for the rest of the season (which Jack was doing). Dave grabbed at the chance, they cut the cards—and Dave took the dogs out for the rest of the season and never found out about the strip deck until the end of the season. Norworth would spend hundreds of dollars to put a gag over.

The time a gag didn't turn out so funny. I thought it was a cruel idea, and was done thoughtlessly. Ward & Vokes were starring in their own show, and there was a member of the company who was a pretty tight guy with a buck. After the show he would go and buy a drink for himself and never treat anybody. Hap Ward claimed he could get him to buy drinks for everybody in the company. The whole company bet him he couldn't (unbeknownst to the victim, of course). W. & V. spent almost $500 to have fake lottery tickets and a result sheet printed. Everybody bought a ticket, including the "sucker," who got a "certain" ticket. After a month Hap announced that he had received the result sheet, and everybody checked their tickets with him and nobody won. When the victim came in the saloon that night for his regular glass of beer, Hap told him that nobody in the company had hit the winning ticket. "By the way, you have a ticket. What's the number?" The man dug in his grouch bag and brought out his ticket. Hap checked it with the sheet and yelled, "You *won!* You won $25,000!" The guy almost fainted. He ordered champagne for everybody (he had to be talked into it, but finally came through), but they couldn't drink the grape when he said, "The first thing I got to do is to call up my brother in New York and tell him he doesn't have to worry

any more. He can have that operation that may save his life."
Ward & Vokes paid the tab! That's one time there was no laugh
finish.

The time an actor found a large bone near the stage door, and
for a gag brought it in the dressing room and with another actor
decided to play a joke on Sim Collins (Collins & Hart). On the
last night, they opened Sim's trunk (had a key made) and put the
bone at the bottom of it. When Sim came off the stage, he threw
his clothes in the trunk, locked it, and soon it was on its way to the
next stand. When he opened the trunk and got his stuff out, he
was surprised to see the large bone, and couldn't figure out how it
got there. He threw it in the wastebasket. The actors quickly
recovered it, hid it until pack-up night, and again put it in Sim's
trunk. Again Sim was surprised to find the bone. This time he
threw it out in the alley, where it was recovered by the boys, and
the same routine repeated. When Sim found it in the next town,
he wrapped it in paper, took a long walk into the country (followed
by the actors), and finally threw it away in a field. Again it was
recovered and stuck in his trunk. At the next stand, he was smiling
when he opened the trunk, by now figuring it was some kind of a
gag but he had outfoxed 'em—and let out a yell when he again
found the bone in the trunk! He had the janitor put it in the
furnace and stood there watching it burn to ashes! The next week
he found in his trunk a tiny chicken bone!

The time Bert Swor, the great minstrel, and his brother John
were practically stranded in Chicago and had just about enough
dough to get back to New York by buying cut-rate tickets. In those
days you could buy these cut-rate tickets in almost every big city.
People would buy a round trip for only a few more bucks than a
one-way fare and sell the return stub to "specs" who made a business of it, and so make a little profit on their trip. The railroad
people tried to stop this practice by making the purchaser sign his
name on the ticket and, when using the return stub, sign it again in
front of the conductor, who would compare the signatures, and if
it wasn't satisfactory, you were out of luck. The smart guys, when
buying the tickets originally, would sign a simple name like Joe
Smith and write their name very plainly (that was an easy ticket to
sell to specs). But some really signed their own names and these
of course sold for much less to the specs and to the final purchaser.
The Swor brothers bought two tickets, one signed Joe Jones, the

other Uli Soferkauefsky! John practiced writing Joe Jones and did swell, but Bert had a tough time trying to even read Soferkauefsky, let alone write it. He told John to get on the train and not to worry about him.

Bert got a quart of liquor, sprinkled some of it (very little) on his clothes, and took a couple of good internal swigs. He made himself very objectionable to the passengers, acting very drunk. When the conductor asked him for his ticket, he told him he had already given it to him. The conductor, realizing his condition, told him to look through his pockets and he was sure he'd find it, and he'd come back for it. Bert kept mumbling to the other passengers that he gave the conductor his ticket. Again the conductor came back and again got an argument from Bert, who had a real Southern accent, but was trying to talk like a Russian or Polack, figuring Soferkauefsky certainly wasn't a Southerner! The conductor insisted he look through his pockets, which he did, dropping a lot of stuff, which the conductor kept picking up. Finally, after a thorough search, he said, "Maybe you have it in your valise?" The valise was opened and dirty laundry etc. thrown all over the floor of the car, and the conductor finally spied the ticket. "See, there it is. You didn't give it to me." Then followed a crying apology by Bert, weeping all over the conductor, who by now was disgusted with the whole business. He took out his pen and asked Bert to sign his name on the ticket. Bert made a few stabs at it, shaking the pen and getting ink on the conductor's trousers. By now the conductor was fit to be tied, and, angrily grabbing the pen, said, "Never mind!"—and signed the ticket himself! That is how Bert got to New York! (Oh, by the way, he used up the rest of the quart when it was all over.)

The time when the great "nut" comic, Ted Healey, had a couple of his friends visit him in his hotel room to help him split a fifth in three parts. One of the boys dropped a lighted cigarette in a big armchair and set fire to it. They managed to put out the blaze, but the chair was ruined. Ted realized the hotel would charge him for the damage, and at that time he didn't even have enough to pay the rent, much less pay for the damage. He borrowed a saw from the hotel porter, cut up the chair in three parts, got paper and twine, made a bundle of each piece, and each of the boys carried out a bundle. The management never could figure out how a big chair could disappear from the room, when the housekeeper reported it missing. They couldn't charge him for it, because he claimed there never had been a chair in the room. What could they do about it? Nothing! That's just what they did!

There were lots of laughs in those days. They don't have 'em anymore. (Every old guy that thumbs his memory says that.) SEZ

Your pal,

LEFTY

Grapes of Laughter

Dear Joe,

Vaudeville had many "heisters," "nose-painters," and users of liquid groceries. They were not ordinary drunks, because these men were funny and witty even in their cups! They were admired for their ready wit even by "spigot-bigots!" Most of them are gone, but their escapades, stories, and wit have been preserved for us—in alcohol!

These lost week-enders had many excuses for drinking the "silly-milk" and "sentimental water." Some drank because they were a hit, or because they were a flop. Some because they were lonesome, or because they were with a lot of good company. Others because they were broke, or because they had plenty of money. Some because of family troubles, or because they had no family to make trouble. And many drank without an excuse!

Me and Aggie mention their names in reverence, because through the years they gave us more laughs drunk than many of the sober people we met. Many of them reformed, and became unfunny!

James Thornton, the great wit, monologist, and song writer, had more stories told about him than even the famous Duffy & Sweeney! In his vaude career he often capitalized on his alcoholic rep. His first wife, Bonnie, is nearly always coupled with stories told about him, because all through their long married life she tried to keep James away from the liquor and the liquor away from Jim. Kate, his widow, a great gal and a fine performer (originally introduced Jim to Bonnie), practically inherited a sober Jim. Bonnie once locked Jim in their hotel room while she went out shopping so he wouldn't be able to go out for any liquor. Jim got the bellboy on the phone and ordered a pint of liquor and two straws. He had the bellboy insert the straws through the old-fashioned large keyhole, and Jim sipped the pint through the straws while the bellboy held the bottle outside the locked door.

Another time, when Bonnie left orders with the clerk not to serve Jim any liquor, Jim called the bellboy and, keeping the door just a bit ajar, spoke to an imaginary guest in the room. "What will you have, Harry? Rye? Fine. I'm on the wagon I'll just take a lemonade." Turning to the bellboy, "My friend wants a rye and I'll have a lemonade." This order was repeated a dozen times during the afternoon, and when Bonnie came back she found Jim passed out and a dozen untouched lemonades on the dresser.

Someone once asked Jim why he was always stewed (which he wasn't). "I like the idea of being drunk continuously. It eliminates hangovers!"

One of the classic Thornton stories is the one about the time he and his drinking companion, George C. Davis (who was also a fine monologist), were on a two-week bender and ran out of funds. While Jim always remained immaculate during a spree, George was exactly the opposite; after a few drinks he looked as if he had rolled in the gutter (which he often had). So you can imagine how he looked after two weeks, unshaven, filthy clothes and linen, etc. They were walking along Broadway and Jim asked a friend to loan him two dollars. The friend, seeing Jim's condition, said no. "Make it *one* dollar," pleaded Jim. "No," said the friend once again. "Then how about a *quarter?*" insisted Jim. This time the friend practically shouted *no*. "Is that final?" asked Jim. "It certainly is," said the friend. Jim slowly turned to George and in his low-down solemn tones said, "George, *throw a louse on him!*"

Just a few years before he passed on he said, "I'm not drinking any more. I figure I have established a high average and I wouldn't advise anybody to try to tie it!"

Next to Jim Thornton, there have been the most stories told about James Terence Duffy and Fredrick Chase Sweeney. They were both good performers and had a wonderful sense of burlesque and satire. Duffy was a good writer and Sweeney was a good rider (he started as a bicycle rider). I remember the time Duffy got into an argument with a Chicago gangster. He was taken aside by a mutual friend, who told him, "Jimmy, be careful, he is a gangster and gets very nasty when he gets a few drinks under his belt." "Yeh, I know," mumbled Jimmy, "but I don't have to worry. He's wearing suspenders tonight!" Another time, when Jimmy (a devout Catholic) was just getting over a four-dayer, he said, "I'm so nervous I could throw pool balls at the Pope!"

Once when Jimmy and Sweeney had been up against the bar for about six straight hours, Sweeney suddenly fell flat on his face and laid there. Duffy turned to the bartender and said, "That's one thing about Sweeney, he knows when to stop!" They tell about the time Jimmy met E. F. Albee, the head of the Keith office (who liked Jimmy). Albee looked at Duffy and said, "Drunk again, Jimmy. After promising me you wouldn't drink any more and after you took the pledge too!" Jimmy looked at him with bloodshot eyes and said, "Are you sorry to see me in this condition, Mr. Albee?" "Yes, I am sorry," said Mr. Albee. "Are you sure you're *very* sorry, Mr. Albee?" "Yes, very sorry, Jimmy," said Mr. Albee. "Well, if you're very very *very* sorry—*I'll forgive you!*" said Jimmy, and slowly staggered away. Another story about Duffy and Sweeney was about the time they played in New Orleans and were a terrible flop. At the finish of the act, Duffy made the following speech, "Ladies and gentlemen, I wish to thank you all for the way you've received our act. And to show you our appreciation, I will now have Mr. Sweeney pass amongst you with a baseball bat and beat the begeezes out of you!"

Maurice Barrymore was another honorary member of the liquid fraternity. One day while standing at the bar at the Lambs, a certain member said, "Hello, Mr. Barrymore, don't you know me?" "I didn't at first," said Barrymore, "but when you didn't buy, I knew you right away!" He once said, "Staggering is a sign of strength. Weak men are carried home!" Coming back from a tour, he told the boys at the Lambs that he was arrested in Kentucky for violation of the liquor law. "I refused to take a drink!" And when he was getting over one of his periodicals, a friend asked him did he want a doctor? "No, I want a *snake charmer!*"

His son Jack also staggered in his father's footsteps. He once promised his manager he wouldn't take a drink on the whole tour. The next day he came to the theater with a cute bun on. "I thought you promised me you wouldn't drink," said the disappointed manager. "Well, I had to cash a check and had to go where they knew me." said Jack. Someone remarked to Jack one night, "You are too great an artist to be drinking all the time." "Are you a reformed drunkard?" asked Jack. "No, I'm not," said the gentleman. "Then why don't you *reform*?" asked Jack.

In the old days when alcoholics were sent to Bellevue Hospital to sober up, someone asked William Anthony McGuire, the famous playwright (who was quite a heister in his time) if he had ever met James Thornton? "Oh, yes," said Bill, "We were in *stock* together at Bellevue!"

Willard Mack, the famous actor-playwright, took his liquor where he found it and they usually found him where he took his liquor. One time at Billy LaHiff's Tavern he got a bad case of hiccoughs. LaHiff advised Mack to eat some bread crumbs to stop the hiccoughs. "Nope," said Bill, shaking his head, "I don't like to interrupt!"

Big James J. Morton was a great lover of the grape and he and Gene Hughes, the agent, were buddies. They both weighed over 250 pounds and could (and did) finish a couple of cases of champagne at a sitting. One day at the Comedy Club, Jim was telling us a session he and Gene Hughes had had the night before. "I got Gene so drunk that it took two bellboys to put *me* to bed!" He would speak about bartenders reverently. "They are fine gentlemen. They moisten the thirsty!" Big Jim was against Mark Aaron's bar (next to the Palace) with Tommy Gray, a good writer and a fine wit. After a few hours, when they were ready to leave, Tommy stepped away from the bar and fell. "Come over here, Jim, and pick me up," pleaded Tommy. Big Jim turned around, looked at Tommy on the floor, and said, "No flattery among friends, old boy!"

In all the years I knew William Collier I never saw him intoxicated! I've often seen him have a bit of an edge on, but that's all, and I've seen him outdrink many a veteran. As you know, he was the fastest guy on the ad lib in the business. During prohibition a member of the Lambs who had some family trouble was trying to drown it by drinking up in Bill's room. He soon got one of those crying jags on and said, "Nobody cares if I drink myself to death, Bill." And Bill quickly answered, "I do. You're drinking my liquor!"

Walter C. Kelly, "The Virginia Judge," after a big night with the boys at the Friars, went to his room and called the clerk, saying, "Wake me up at ten." "It is ten now, Mr. Kelly," said the clerk. *"Then wake me!"* muttered Kelly.

Bert Leslie, the king of slang, who could handle a bottle with the best of them, once was asked by a friend at the White Rat's Club to sit down and have some tea. "I never touch it," said Bert, "it makes me *weak!*"

Walter Catlett, one of our really great comedians, was talking with some friends about the Men's Bar at the Waldorf, and someone remarked that they were thinking of opening a Women's Bar. Catlett looked over his glasses and said, "What are they going to serve, Lydia Pinkham on draft?" I asked him once, "How about walking around the corner and having a drink, Walter?" He said, "I have a better idea. Let's *run!*"

Bert Fitzgibbons (one of the best of the "nut" comics) was at a bar pouring himself a drink into a water glass. "Say, Bert, that's whisky you're pouring, not water!" said the bartender. Bert squinted his eyes and said, "Do I look like a man that would drink that much water?"

Someone told Harry Hershfield, about a certain actor who had been a quart-a-day man, that the guy had quit drinking. Hershfield said, "Yeh, I know. You see, when he got drunk he started buying, so he quit drinking!"

Henry E. Dixie, one of America's great actors, liked his liquor straight and disliked mixed drinks. He once said, "The continual use of ice cubes in drinks will develop a race of people with black and blue upper lips!" When a busybody once asked Dixie why he drank, he answered, "When I drink, I think, and when I think, I drink!"

Old Sam Morton (The Four Mortons) was playing at Hammerstein's on the same bill with Rajah, the snake dancer. He was standing in the wings with Mike Simon, the stage manager, when Mike said, "Isn't she afraid the snake will bite her?" "No," said Sam, "She ain't afraid of the snake biting her, she's worried of it *hissing her!*" It was Sam who once said, "Too much of anything is not good, but too much whisky is just enough!" There was an old German by the name of Schmidt who owned a saloon next to Keith's Union Square, on East Fourteenth Street. One time he was trying to get Sam to stop drinking liquor and drink beer instead. Sam asked him, "What's the difference?" To which old Schmidt replied in his thick German dialect, "Visky makes you kill someboty else, but mitt beer you only kill yourself!"

At a Christmas party at the Lambs, they were serving some liquid refreshment from a large bowl. Benjamin Hapgood Burt (the brilliant lyricist of many Broadway shows) asked me what it was. I said, "Punch!" "Well," said Ben, *"let's punch it!"* He was a great Lamb, but when in his cups a few of the members tried to duck him (and his sharp wit). One night when Burt was feeling his oats (or I should say rye), he looked around an almost empty room for someone to talk to. He spied Wilton Lackaye, who had as his guest the famous sculptor, Gutzon Borglum. Burt staggered over to the table and hung around until Lackaye just had to introduce him to his guest. "Burt, I want you to meet the famous sculptor, Gutzon Borglum." "Who?" asked Burt. Lackaye had to repeat the name to make Burt understand. "It's Borglum, Borglum, Borglum." Finally Burt, shaking his head, said, "It sounds to me like the breaking of wind in a bathtub!"

Someone was boasting to Walter Catlett how much he could drink. "Why, I drink a quart a day!" Catlett gave him a look and said, "Why, I *spill* that much!"

Ring Lardner was on his famous three-day toot at the Lambs. He sat at one table all this time, just getting up once in a while to go to the men's room. A certain member who had wild-looking long hair kept passing his table looking at him. Ring blinked his large owl eyes, called the man over, and said, "Would you please tell me how you look when I am *sober?*"

Big Charlie Wagner, the bartender at the Friars for many years, served a member a drink with, "This is ten-year-old stuff, so don't be afraid of it." The man looked at the bottle, and said, "Why Charlie, that bottle is marked *two* years old and you said it was *ten* years old." "Well," shrugged Charlie, "it took me eight years to sell it!"

I remember the time George M. Cohan, after a pretty rough night with the boys, came in the next day and someone asked him how he felt. "Oh, I'm all right. I got up this morning and drank my bath!"

During the war, a very heavy drinker came to the bar at the

Lambs and announced that he had just come from the blood bank where he had contributed his blood. Charles O'Brien Kennedy, the actor-poet, remarked, "What are they going to use it for, sterilizing their instruments?"

But my favorite story is about my old friend Richard Carle, who was a famous star of musical comedy, vaude, and pictures, Wilton Lackaye, one of the great stars of legit and vaude, and Tom Terris, a fine actor who was a headliner with his sketch, "Scrooge," in vaude, and is the only survivor of the King Tut Tomb expedition, every one of whom met an untimely death. Tom lost an eye.

It was a dismal Sunday afternoon on a real hot summer day at the Lambs, which was deserted except for these three gentlemen. They had no air conditioning those days, only a rotating fan at the end of the bar. There were a few dim amber lights to make it look cool. Wilton Lackaye was at one end of the bar facing the rotating electric fan, Tom Terris at the other end of the bar, when Dick Carle, starting on a bender, came in and asked Mike the bartender for a scotch and soda. He was served, and after another one, started to look around. He saw Lackaye (who did not like to be disturbed when drinking) facing the fan. As everybody knows, Lackaye wore a heavy toupee, and, because of the heat, the glue on it had loosened up so that when the breeze from the rotating fan would hit it, it would raise about half an inch, and as the breeze passed the toupee would go back in place. Carle couldn't believe his eyes and watched the toupee with fascination. He kept ordering scotch and sodas and glancing sideways at Lackaye's hair still going up and down, feeling that he was getting a bit drunk and maybe was imagining this.

Finally, after a few more scotch and sodas, he turned his face away from Lackaye and looked at Tom Terris, who was standing next to him. Tom had a glass eye to replace the one he lost while on the King Tut Expedition. Dick looked at the eye, then looked closer, and saw a *fly walking around the eye*! By now Dick thought he was on the D.T. train, so gulped his drink and yelled, "Let me out of here." It so happened that at this time the Hippodrome (at Forty-fourth Street and Sixth Avenue) was just through with the matinee and the Singer Midgets, who were playing there, were going to Rosoff's Restaurant, which was a few doors past the Lambs. When Dick Carle came out of the door of the Lambs, he saw forty midgets. He took one look and yelled to a taxi driver, "Quick, driver, get me to *Bellevue!*"

A grand lot of Merry Andrews who drank their liquor "straight" and used "laughs" as chasers! SEZ

Your *pal,*

LEFTY

The Cherry Sisters

Dear Joe,

There has been so much written and said about the Cherry Sisters that I thought me and Aggie should add our bit.

They were like the sterling mark on silver, only different—in show biz the Cherry Sisters meant lousy!

Known as the "vegetable twins," Effie and Addie played Hammerstein's Olympia (where the Bond Clothing Company now stands) on Broadway in 1896. They played behind a net for eight weeks at $500 per and that "direct from Broadway" billing kept them going for years in smaller towns. The idea of playing behind a net to encourage the audience to throw vegeables at the actors wasn't new. In the 1870s Shakespearian actors (?) like James Owen O'Connor, Count Johannes, and Dr. Landis hammed it with *Hamlet* (all worked behind a screen) and got rich from the box office. Many came just to try out their pitching arms with eggs and vegetables. It was Oscar, not Willie Hammerstein, who got the idea of using a screen in front of these gals. The papers said they were "so bad they were good." Years later Billy Rose tried to bring back the idea at the Casino de Paree during the time we had Prohibition, and it died. His ads read, "Sunday Nite—Amateur Nite. Come and throw vegetables at actors!" A few drunks threw ice cubes and almost blinded the performers. (They were not amateurs but hired for the occasion and didn't know about the ads inviting the audience to throw things.) It was a terrific flop, not funny, but very sad!

One of the stories the Cherry Sisters told about why vegetables were heaved at 'em was that it was started by managers who tried to "make 'em." To get the angle of how funny that is, I must tell you what kind of an act they did. There were originally five Cherry Sisters, who appeared in their home town of Marion, Iowa, in a sketch with songs called "The Gypsy's Warning!" The girls wanted to visit the Chicago World's Fair of 1893, and to raise the coin, they hired Green's Opera House, Cedar Rapids, to stage their show. The audiences made funny noises (long before the official raspberry) but the performance went on.

When they saw the notice in the morning paper they sued for libel. The case was heard in the theater, and after the judge saw "The Gypsy's Warning" he gave the verdict to the newspaper. Eventually deaths cut down the act to a duo, Addie and Effie. But they worked as a trio for some time.

Addie and Effie did Salvation Army girls. They were tall and thin, while Jessie was short and plump. They wore drum major costumes and sang about themselves to the tune of "Ta-ra-ra-Boom-dee-ay." They had voices like the rattle of an empty coal scuttle. "For Fair Columbia" was sung by Jessie, the composer. A ballad, "My Daddy and Mama Were Irish," composed by Lizzie (the absent one), was sung by Addie and Effie in calico gowns, white aprons, and straw hats. Jessie then sang "The Bicycle Ride." Next Effie came on wearing a pair of gray trousers, Prince Albert coat, high hat, and small mustache and carrying a grip, and sang "The Traveling Man." Other numbers were "Corn Juice" by Jessie, and "Gypsy Warning" by Addie, Effie, and Jessie. And they finished with a tableaux, "Clinging to the Cross," and for an encore, "The Goddess of Liberty."

Now that just gives you an idea of the act. When the audience got noisy, it was nothing for Addie to walk to the footlights and say, "If you don't keep quiet we will ring down the curtain; we ain't desirous to sing here tonight, no how."

They changed their act at times; Effie also sang, "She Was My Sister and Oh, How I Missed Her." And she talked about everything from Prohibition to the Equity Strike. (This was on their "comeback.") They wanted to clean up the stage and to close theaters on Sundays. They didn't dance because they claimed it was immoral, so all they did on the stage were recitations and singing.

They went back to the farm in 1903 (with a boodle). In 1924, when the surviving sisters were becoming aged, they appeared at the Orpheum, Des Moines. *Variety* covered it as a new act; the notice stated in part:

"Effie and Addie Cherry are the famous Cherry Sisters who startled Broadway in the early '90s. 'Perfectly terrible' was never more applicable. As terribleness, their skit is perfection. . . . Effie got in the spotlight recently by being defeated for Mayor (Cedar Rapids). Effie sings a song, 'She Was My Sister and Oh, How I Missed Her.' If it were not for a reputation for being a bad act gained thirty years ago, the Cherry Sisters would not get a hearing. Effie explains they retired from the stage before on account of the war. The reporter took it for granted the recent affair with Germany was referred to, but the stagehands are at odds over the question. Some insist she meant the Civil War and others say it was the Spanish-American."

The late Chicot writing in his *Chicot's Weekly,* years before he joined *Variety,* and reviewing the Cherry Sisters' first showing on Broadway, said, "The Cherry Sisters do not care to be exploited as freaks and insist on being treated with due respect. By way of material for press notices, they wrote E. D. Price, manager of the Pleasure Palace, New York, whom they were soliciting for a booking, that the terrible pair had been given 'four golden horseshoes' in Chicago, and presented with a glass cane handsomely decorated with ribbons at St. Louis." (Shades of Lou Holtz.)

"If arrangements could be made," continued the vitriolic Chicot, "I should be glad to present them with a horseshoe attached to the business end of an able-bodied and hard-working jackass."

You remember, Joe, what you told me about when you had your "Memory Lane" act at the Chicago Theatre and Effie and Addie came to see you. Two old gals with baggy skirts introduced themselves as the Great Cherry Sisters and said they would join your "Memory Lane" act (which featured some real great names) if they were billed "in lights" as the headliners of the act. I think that you stated, "Let me think it over; I'll call *you,* don't you call *me!*"

In 1908, when *Variety* panned the gals, they replied with a steaming hot letter which *Variety* printed:

"In your issue of March 21, you had an article which was one of the most malicious, violent and untruthful writings we have ever read. The person who wrote it is not deserving the name of a man, but is instead a contemptible cur. You said in your paper that we advertised ourselves 'the worst show on earth,' which makes you a liar, point blank. We have always advertised ourselves as one of the best, and we would not be far from the truth if we said the best. . . . Although we have the best act in vaudeville and are the best drawing cards on the stage, we have no swelled heads, as some others have. We have had more knocking since we went into the theatrical business than any other act in the history of the world, and we have come to no other conclusion why this is done except that we are not of the character of these unprincipled editors and managers who have done the knocking and slandering."

The girls lived to a ripe old age. I honestly believe that they thought they were great! And they were great as the worst act in vaudeville!

My old friend Bernard H. Sandler, the noted attorney, in researching some law on a libel suit, came across the following decision, which I think will give you a pretty good picture of these gals and maybe hand you a laugh, SEZ

Your pal,

LEFTY

"In *Cherry v. Des Moines Leader* (114 Iowa, 298, 86 N.W., 323) an action brought by one of three public performers calling themselves "Cherry Sisters" upon the following writing; 'Effie is an old jade of 50 summers, Jessie a frisky filly of 40, and Addie, the flower of the family, a capering monstrosity of 35. Their long skinny arms, equipped with talons at the extremities, swung mechanically, and anon waved frantically at the suffering audience. The mouths of their rancid features opened like caverns and sounds like the wailings of damned souls issued therefrom. They pranced around the stage with a motion that suggested a cross between the danse du ventre and fox-trot—strange creatures with painted faces and hideous mien. Effie is spavined, Addie is string-halt, and Jessie, the only one who showed her stockings, has legs with calves as classic in their outlines as the curves of a broom handle.' The defendant showed that he was not actuated by malice and was merely criticizing a coarse public performance and it was held proper to direct a verdict against the plaintiff."

Three Meals a Day—and a Bluff

Dear Joe,

When me and Aggie read about the big shots (usually ex-vaudevillians) of pics, stage, radio, TV, night clubs, oh yeh, and records coming to New York and stopping at the swank spots like the Waldorf Astoria, Sherry Netherland, Plaza, Gotham, Astor, etc., with a suite of rooms and plenty of service, it kinda brings back memories of the old vaude days when the actors weren't so particular where they "pecked and padded." The only worry was the price, and the price in the old boardinghouses was a buck a day for the use of a near-Ostermoor, three meals, and in some places even a "bluff," which meant a sandwich and a bottle of beer after the show at night.

Nearly everybody on the bills stopped at the boardinghouses, except maybe some legit headliner who felt his position demanded his stopping at the "big" hotel (maybe for two bucks a day) where he wasn't wanted and was damn lonesome (unless he could read). The regular acts (even those making good dough) would stop with the gang for three reasons: one, so their fellow actors wouldn't think they were getting "high hat"; two, because they wanted to be with the gang after the show for laughs; and three, the most important, it was cheaper! They would always kick and complain and make excuses why they weren't stopping at the hotel. Many carried a dog, and used it for an excuse: "They wouldn't let us in with Trixie, so we came here. If they don't want Trixie, they can't have us." Others would say that they stopped at the hotel the last time and "the service was lousy," or "They don't let you have company in the room after the show," or "There's a lot of old fogies there; if you flush the toilet after 10 P.M. some guy complains you're making noise," or "When me and the wife walk through the lobby, you can hear 'em all whispering to each other, 'I wonder if them actor folks are really married?'" And of course the "loyal" guy's excuse, "I stopped with Mom Smith when I first started and I wouldn't hurt her feelings stopping at the hotel now that I'm a somebody!"

Out West when playing the Orpheum, Sullivan & Considine, or Pantages Circuits, the boardinghouses and theatrical hotels would send out "runners" a week or two ahead to book up the people from the show for their rooms. They'd make all kinds of special offers (the competition was big). They would first try to get the headliner by giving him or her a special rate and the best room in the house. This was done because the rest of the bill would usually follow the headliner; it would make them feel they were living as good as he was. The boardinghouse keepers would go to any lengths to get the troupe. They bribed stagehands, doormen, and managers to boost their place to the actors. They even furnished cabs to bring them from the depot to their doors before some of the opposition could make them change their minds. They had ads in the trade papers reading, "Home cooking, good beds, lunch after the show, home atmosphere," and then there would follow a long list of well-known performers who had stopped there, all this signed by "Mom" Something-or-other. All boardinghouses were run by "Moms" or "Mothers." After living in many of their homes, me and Aggie figured most of 'em were stepmothers!

All the theater dressing-room walls had stickers advertising boarding houses, hotels, and restaurants all over the country. The actors would write their personal opinions about the places all around the stickers. Here are some of the remarks we saw written on dressing-room walls: "Lousy." "Terrible, flies get in the soup." "Do not stop here unless you have your mother-in-law with you." "You get pork Monday and every day thereafter until Friday, then you get fish and soup, and pork goes on the bill again Saturday!" "Stop here, she is the manager's aunt, if you don't he'll send in a bad report on your act." "This place gives you all the eggs you want but you don't want more than one." "Stop here because the stage manager gets a rake-off; if you don't your drops won't be hung right."

These notes acted as a sort of "underground" information bureau for actors. They wrote about laundries, managers, actors who stole material, stagehands, musicians, agents, and bookers. Some were in poetry, some in fine prose, but most of 'em were to the point! If anybody had copied all the "wall tips" he would have had the makings of a "Vaudeville Confidential!" It wasn't all panning. Some kindly souls would write, "This is a good place to eat," and sign their names. Somebody would write under this, "Since when does so-and-so know good food?" and sign his name, to which some actor would add, "He may not know good food, but he knows good material; he stole a dozen of my best gags," and the topper would be, "You never had a dozen good gags!"

A gimmick used by most of the boardinghouses was to serve the troupe a fine chicken or turkey dinner on arrival and a fine dinner on the last day. In between the food was awful, but Mom figured the first dinner kept 'em from checking out and the last dinner made 'em forget all about the bad "in-betweenies." Many of the boardinghouses served real good meals. You wouldn't think that it would pay Mom to give you food and room for a dollar a day, but many retired with a mattress full of dough and a big collection of pictures autographed, "To our pal, Mom Smith, better than home." And maybe to many it was!

The boardinghouses, theatrical hotels, and rooming houses were as well known to actors as the swanky hotels were to people who could afford them. Of course in the heyday of vaude, when people were making dough, they swamped the finest hotels, and the finest hotels began catering to them, some even giving a special rate to the profession, because they found it was a good advertisement for the place to house celebrities. But I am talking about the pioneer "tents" nearly all of us lived in before the golden pay-off!

I'll just try to tell you about the more famous ones. They were really fabulous joints! There were Tobin's Flats and Cook's Place on East Fourteenth Street, that served continuous breakfasts from 7 A.M to 1 P.M., single meals, 25 cents, $5.50 to $6.50 a week. (Jolson lived there.) Frank Cook also owned a place on West Thirty-ninth Street. Phoebe Cramer bought him out later. They mostly catered to foreign acrobats, and you hear the shouts of "Allez oop" all through the day. Mountford's was also a great spot for acrobats and dog acts. Mrs. Martin's, on West Forty-fourth Street, was a nice place. The Edmund's Flats on Eighth Avenue between Forty-seventh and Forty-eighth streets on the east side of the avenue were furnished apartments, where a lot of married folks and troupes lived; they did their own cooking and many a small three-room apartment held five or six people. If they were acrobats, they'd sleep three-high! It was O.K. unless the understander took in boarders. If you had no place to sleep, or needed a bite or even a nip, you were sure to find it there among the show folk.

Mrs. Silvers had a nice rooming house on West Forty-eighth

Street next door to the firehouse. Some of the actors living there tried to make a deal with the firemen not to answer an alarm until noon! The old Palace Hotel on West Forty-fifth Street was where Willard Mack & Marjorie Rambeau lived long before they became stars; William Anthony McGuire and his lovely wife Lulu also lived there long before he wrote *Kid Boots* and many more hits. One of the greatest of the real theatrical hotels was the Somerset on West Forty-seventh Street next door to the Palace stage door. Joe Frieberg was the manager. He was maître d'hôtel at the Astor for sixteen years before he leased the Somerset for $125,000 and made a profit of over a quarter of a million in six months. He catered to every whim of the actors for many years until the whims ran into piles of I.O.U.s and he had to give up the hotel, but he left with great memories. He claimed the laughs and enjoyment he got all those years were worth more than all the I.O.U.s! He was a real great guy who would go for "sad routines" when he knew they were phony. It was at the Somerset that Meyer and Ella Gerson had a restaurant where they took care of many a broken-down actor with a stomach to match. They first started on Broadway with a tiny cigar store on Forty-seventh Street and Broadway (right underneath the big Pepsi-Cola sign), then opened Mother Gerson's Fudge Shop, which was known from coast to coast by everyone in show biz, then the restaurant at the Somerset. It was the clearinghouse for vaudeville gossip. All the big and small-time bookers would lunch there, and naturally the actors would "stroll in" to be seen, and many a time got a date because of it. "Basil" and Ella Gerson and Mother Bartholdi were the tops!

The Bartholdi Inn, on Forty-fifth Street and Broadway, was the greatest of all theatrical hotels in America! Mother Theresa Bartholdi started with two upper floors of 1546 Broadway in 1899. After five years she took over the corner of Forty-fifth Street and Broadway and the two adjoining buildings. In 1906 two more houses were added on Forty-fifth Street, and the Inn had 110 rooms. She never had more than a ninety-day option on her lease. It was all half-soled and heeled—and you had to know your way to find your room. Rooms were rented by the week, not by the day, and had no transients. Madame Bartholdi acted as banker and advisor, advanced fares and money to actors, let them run up bills into the thousands, and told me she never lost a penny! In 1916 the Palmer Estate (who owned the buildings), instead of raising her rent, as landlords all over the country were doing, reduced her rent. There were many little fires in the place, because there was careless cooking in the rooms, and the throwing of cigarette butts out of windows; they set *Variety's* awning (it was on the first floor) on fire so many times that an extinguisher was kept handy at Sime's desk, at all times. The Inn had a real bohemian atmosphere; the tables had lighted candles and beer was served in small glass pitchers.

The greats of all branches of show biz stopped there when they weren't even near great. Some of the alumni were Pearl White, Mack Sennett, Harry Kelly, Charlie Chaplin, D. W. Griffith, Eva Tanguay, Nat Wills, Dorothy Dalton, Tad, Harry Hershfield, Tom McNamarra, Laurie & Bronson, Polly Moran, and so many many more. Polly (Pickens), Madame Bartholdi's daughter, helped her mother manage the place and also helped King Baggott and Dell Henderson start the Screen Club, which used rooms at the Inn for headquarters. Gena Cochi was active manager from 1917 to 1920, when they had to move to make room for Loew's State Theatre. There never were as many laughs on the stage of Loew's State as there were in the Bartholdi Inn!

Polly took over the Princeton Hotel, which at one time was a swanky gambling and fancy house. She made it into a great spot that almost had the atmosphere of the Bartholdi. There were a lot of hilarious evenings at the Princeton that will long be remembered. Mother Bartholdi left over a million in cash and real estate when she died. Her husband Louis was a sculptor. She had two daughters, Edith and Polly. The old man got married again, which led to a fight for the estate in 1923.

There were so many great places where show folks lived. The Cadillac (Forty-third Street and Broadway) was first called the Barnett House (where Eugene O'Neill was born), then Wallack's, and in 1915 became the Cadillac. It was taken over by the Claridge Hotel (which opened as Rector's). There were the Remington, the Hermitage, and the St. James. The St. Kilda was owned by Pauline Cook (an ex-sharpshooting act) and Jennie Jacobs (one of the few great lady vaude agents). Mrs. Ehric's place, where the Three Keatons made their headquarters, the Hildona Apartments, Astor Court, Yandis Court (which Lou Holtz owned long enough to make $100,000 profit), Irvington Hall, Henri Court, the Bertha, the Adelaide, and the Duplex were all furnished apartments catering only to the theatrical profession.

Philadelphia had some swell hotels, boardinghouses, and rooming houses. Mike Tuller's, where the Four Cohans and many of the better acts and burly people lived, charged just a few dollars more a week, but set the finest table in the country. There were also Mother O'Brien's, Flossie LaVan's, Cavanaugh's, the Hurley House, Irving House, Zeiss's, St. Cloud, Cook's, and Green's. Mother Green was an old circus gal and when the store shows were in Philly the freaks would all come to Green's to eat. It wasn't very appetizing to have a fat woman on one side of you, a bearded lady on the other, and a giant in front of you, but it was damn interesting. Mother Green would never turn them down. She said, "They are my old friends, and somebody's got to feed them." There were also the Sylvania, the Vendig, and of course Dad's, where everybody would meet on Friday nights after the show in the "Peanut Room," where they'd drink beer and eat peanuts; the floor was knee high in peanut shells. The show folks would entertain themselves. I've seen Jack Barrymore get up and read the Ten Commandments from the Bible and have that audience spellbound, and when he finished he'd say, "Oh, by the way, I forgot to tell you I stole this Bible from the Bellevue-Stratford Hotel!" Dad Frazer's was a great spot!

Chicago had its great spots, too. The old Revere House, which burned down, the Saratoga, the Grant (run by Leonard Hicks), the City Hall Square, and of course the Sherman, with the Byfields as hosts, and the Bismarck and Congress hotels, which always catered to the profession.

Baltimore had Kernan's, which was owned and run by the owner of the Maryland Theatre, Fred Shanberger. The two most popular boardinghouses in the country were in Baltimore, Sparrows and Mother Howard's. The latter was the originator of "three meals a day and a bluff," and if you happened to live there during the racing season, she would throw in a tip on a "hot horse." A great gal.

There were Reilly's in Newark, Smith's in Portland, Oregon, in Cleveland the Winston, Olmstead, and the Hollenden. In Washington, D.C., there were Mother Schroder's (next to the Casino Theatre) and Gus Bucholtz's Occidental, where there was many a great poker game in that front suite facing Pennsylvania Avenue.

The Coast had many furnished apartments priced very reasonably with much better furniture and accommodations than the ones back East. We usually played Frisco, Los Angeles, and Oakland for a two-week run, so it would pay the act to get a furnished apartment and get some home cooking for a change.

But the majority of the actors would go to the Continental Hotels in Frisco and Los Angeles, owned by two of the craziest guys in the business. They advertised, "We get the stars on the way up and on the way down again." They signed everything, "Shanley & Furness, 50-50." They would take turns in managing each hotel six months a year. They would turn away commercial trade and transients; many a salesman would have loved to live there because of all the fun and laughs. It wasn't run like a hotel, but like a "fun-house." It was no surprise to have a juggler wait on you (paying off his tab) and maybe juggle a few plates before he served you. Somebody was always playing a joke on some one, and Aloysius Shanley was the instigator of most of them.

Al Jolson used to stop there when he first played on the S. & C. Circuit. Then when he came there for the first time as a star, Shanley organized a band to meet him at the station and they paraded up Market Street with Jolson leading the parade, and Al made them stop outside the St. Francis, where he went in to register (it was his gag on Shanley), but came out again and marched to the Continental, ordered a half a dozen rooms, where he held court in the evenings and then went to sleep at the St. Francis. Many acts did that when playing Frisco and L.A. in loyalty to those grand guys. They worked up to a chain of seven hotels, but when the crash came they lost 'em all except the Yorkshire, in L.A. (but it never had the atmosphere of the Continentals). They were together for over thirty years and then for business reasons had to split. It was a great loss for show folks.

Yes, there were boardinghouses and theatrical hotels everyplace vaudeville was and vaudeville was everyplace. After the show the troupers would gather and play cards, drink a little beer, lie a little about how good they were doing, exchange theatrical gossip, and have laughs. The rooms, food, and beds weren't much, but young, ambitious people don't need much, and the laughs paid off for all the shortcomings. Remember, it was only a buck a day for room, three meals, and a bluff—and laughs!

The theatrical hotels were much different than the boardinghouses. They usually started as first-class hotels; then when the neighborhood ran down, the hotels became a bit careless about service and furnishings. They could afford to give a rate to theatrical people, who were pretty permanent and didn't expect first-class service. As long as the hotel let 'em make a little coffee in the room, gather in each other's rooms and gab until all hours in the morning, play a little cards, sing, do a little nose-painting, play a uke, and kept the chambermaids from bothering them until late afternoon, they would be satisfied with elevators that developed paralysis between floors, bellhops who got fresh, and clerks who kept asking for room rent. The managers of these hotels understood actors and many times entered into the spirit of their fun. Many of them would keep the hotel exclusive for the profession, barring "towners" and "salesmen." The clerks, bellhops, chambermaids, and porters all knew and spoke show biz, and many of them helped many an act with money when some of the "guests" were going over the rough spots.

There were a few different type theatrical hotels, like those that really let themselves run down and naturally charged cheaper rates and got many acts whose bankrolls wouldn't allow them to live at the better places. The Saratoga in Chicago was that kind of a spot. You could buy anything—a double routine, parody, tip on a horse, hot jewelry or even some "nose candy" right in the lobby. The only rule strictly enforced in this type hotel (known to the profession as "buckets of blood") was "No smoking of opium in the elevators!"

The Rexford in Boston was New England's answer to the Saratoga. The Rexford was a massive building in the heart of Boston's tenderloin. They had bars on the windows, like in a jail, which saved many a guy and gal from falling or being thrown out. The sheets and pillowcases and even the blankets were stenciled with large black letters, "Property of the Rexford." At 3 A.M. a big bell would ring, which meant it was time for everybody to go to his own room. The fun was over. Or was it? On hot summer nights some of the actors would sit on the roof and rush the can. They'd chip in a dime, put it in the can, which they would lower to the street with a long piece of string. There a stooge would take it and have it filled with beer, take a good drink (which was his commission), and the boys would heist it back to the roof. It was all so homey and nice, but kinda rough! They catered to more burly people than vaude, but it was very handy for the vaude acts that played in the olio at the Old Howard, Waldron's Casino, the Scollay Square, etc. It was sold during the war to the Salvation Army, who used it for soldiers and sailors. It was opened with prayer as the Arcadia.

The Alamac in St. Louis was on a par with the Rexford. They too catered mostly to burlesque people, and later became the hangout for bootleggers and gangsters. They never bothered the actors and the actors wouldn't bother them, except maybe for a few bottles.

New York had many theatrical hotels. The Knickerbocker on Forty-second Street and Broadway was where Caruso and many big stars lived. It was turned into an office building which didn't allow any theatrical tenants! The Metropole on Forty-third Street and Broadway, where Rosenthal the gambler was shot, started as Joe Adams' Hotel, a great hangout for vaude and burly people. Later it became the Comedy Club and now is Rosoff's, a very fine hotel and restaurant. The old Continental on Broadway and Forty-first Street was the place the circus and outdoor-racket boys stopped.

There were few good boardinghouses down South. Mother Pettit's, in Richmond, Virginia, was about the best. Actors would usually stop at rooming houses and eat out at the "greasy spoons." In the early days the food was terrible in the South; the big hotels were too expensive, and besides, they didn't care for the theatrical trade. The saying among actors was, "Just saving enough dough to have an operation on my stomach when I get back North." But now the South boasts of some of the finest restaurants in the country.

Living was a problem for acts playing the smaller towns. Every town in those days had a Mansion House, American Hotel, or Commercial House; a Eureka Restaurant, Modern Lunch, or Wagon Lunch, and a Reliable Laundry. The theaters were usually named Globe, Palace, Keystone, Gem, Hippodrome, World in Motion, and, of course, the "Opry" House!

At the old hotels in the small towns you came in and were greeted by a pimply-faced clerk with as much hospitality in his voice as a bulldog that got its tail stepped on. He'd swing the big register around to you (all registers were on swivels), take a pen out of a glass of buckshot, dip it in the large inkwell, and hand it to you. While you wrote in your best Spencerian, the pen would catch on the cheap paper and throw a blot on "and wife" of the guy who registered ahead of you. You'd always put "New York" and "theater" after your name. The clerk would read it and give you a nod of nonrecognition, turn his back to look at the rack for five minutes (nearly all the rooms were empty, but he did this to look important), then tell you he was sorry he couldn't give you a better room because they were all filled (and charge you more than anyone else was paying). He'd bang on a big bell on the desk to call the bellboy, and while waiting for the boy to wake up, you'd take a toothpick out of the glassful on the counter and start picking your teeth to kinda act nonchalant. The boy, an old man of sixty, would finally show up, take your bags and get you in an elevator that would whiz you up at about half a mile an hour. He'd show you into a break-a-way room with a five-watt light (that's why most actors carried their own light bulbs). He would of course ask you how the show was, and be disappointed when you didn't ask him to sit down and tell him jokes.

At night after the show you'd sit around the lobby with a couple of salesmen (they always seemed to come in pairs), and maybe they'd tell you some jokes they just heard at Hammerstein's before they left New York. (The next night you'd try them in your act and find that an act the week ahead of you had already used them.) You'd sit around with the salesmen, listening to them lie about the big sales they'd made, while you countered with how big your act went in New York. You'd flirt with the chambermaid so you could get extra towels, and flirt with the waitress to get extra portions. The night clerk would listen in to your phone conversations (listening to the chorus girls was how he became adult). After a few of these "mortuaries" you'd even hanker for one of those "bucket of blood" hotels. At least there you would know that the country was still alive!

The Hotel Astor on Times Square, although not strictly a theatrical hotel, has always catered to the tops in show biz. Will Rogers never stopped anyplace else when in New York, and Jimmy Durante gets his same suite year after year whenever he hits town. The Hunting Room at the Astor, when show biz was in full blast, had the greatest managers and actors dining there, and when the picture biz was in its infancy, all the future tycoons wrote figures on the tablecloths running into millions. Weber & Fields, the Shuberts, Charles Dillingham, Ziegfeld, Cohen & Harris, Bill

Brady, Marcus Loew, Adolph Zukor, William Fox, Jesse Lasky, Sam Goldwyn, and Sime Silverman would lunch there daily. The Algonquin has always been a hotel for stage folks, artists, and literary greats, and it still carries on the tradition of the late Frank Case.

Boston had its Adams House, Richwood, Healey's, William Tell House, Mother Thomas's, Avery, Touraine, Hollis Chambers, and Jacob Worth's—and not forgetting Pie Alley Strip, where you bought tickets to get coffee for two cents and pie for three cents; coffee and beans were eleven cents!

The actor's living and eating habits have come a long way since the days of Mother Howard's. They now live in plush hotels with clean rooms, excellent service, fine food—but *no laughs!* SEZ

Your pal,

LEFTY

You Mustn't Say That!

Dear Joe,

It was around 1927 that the boys and gals and execs of vaudeville forgot the rule that Tony Pastor and B. F. Keith laid down, "Keep it clean"! They began sneaking gags into their acts that were blue even in the old honky-tonk days! It was one of the poisons that helped kill vaudeville!

It all started slowly (like a cancer). The heads of vaude were more worried about the stock-market quotations than what was going on on their stages (which made it possible for them to dabble with the market in the first place). One act would get a yok with an off-color gag or a blue piece of business (usually a headliner first), so another act would sneak one in. Managers would let the headliners get by with it, but cut it on the smaller acts. Actors, when asked to cut a blue gag, would give the manager an argument, "Why, I used that gag at the Palace," or "on the

Orpheum Time." The manager by then was just a messenger boy and didn't feel that he had the authority to make the acts cut it out; the act was getting ten times his salary and so he was impressed—and let the gag get by.

It was when the managers all over the circuits received letters from their patrons complaining that vaude was no longer a "family amusement" that the trade papers, especially *Variety*, wrote editorials about it and demanded that the managers and circuits start censoring their shows. It was only then that the heads of the circuits finally issued orders to cut all blue material and for each manager to send in a copy of the gags he cut. These reports in turn were sent to all the managers with names of the acts and instructions to cut the gags listed, and to cancel the act if it insisted on using them. That looked like they meant business and would surely cure the evil.

But the "cancer" was all set to eat vaude away. The actors would leave out the gags mentioned on the "cut sheet" and replace them with worse ones. (You see, the acts were getting yoks and couldn't get used to the "nice laughs" they got with clever and clean material.) Some of the acts would use stuff on the opening show that would have been cut in the worst burly show. But they didn't care, they got laughs (and the people that laughed loudest were the first to complain to the manager), and the newspapermen were in for the first show and saw them a hit! So when the local manager cut the stuff they used at the opening show, they would stick other gags in just as blue, and all week it was a contest between the manager and the act. They couldn't have done this if the circuit heads had really cared, because you can cure any actor by taking his route away. But at that time the Big Brass of vaude had their minds on stocks and golf, and as long as they heard the clink of gold at the box office they didn't care. A new low was reached when a gal was "goosed" at the Palace, the cathedral of vaudeville. B. F. Keith must have turned in his grave in blue-earthed New England!

Through the many manager friends me and Aggie had, we collected those "cut sheets" that were sent out. The acts that used the gags will recognize the sword that cut off their income, and a lot of new comedians will be interested in the cut; they may have forgotten the gags and pieces of business and will now put them in on radio and TV—which may bring vaudeville back!

Here they are, Joe. (Maybe a lot of laymen won't understand many of them, but I am sure they'll get the idea. Most of them are very unsubtle!) We don't give the names of the acts that used them—we are sure they will recognize them.

CUT:

Business of girl raising skirt, saying, "I'm a *show* girl."

"The act's all shot to *hell!*"

(After showing leg almost up to thigh) "I'm not going to show you *everything* at these prices!"

Hitting girl in rear with book, girl reaching back, saying, "Oh, my nerves!"

(Time of Arab-Hebrew trouble) All references to Arabs.

Looking skyward and then brushing top of hat.

References to Polacks and Guineas.

"This dog does tricks all over the place."

Orders in restaurant, "I want steak." Waiter yells, "Steak me." "I want a glass of milk." "Milk me," sez waiter.

Story of girl in picture show with man. Girl saying, "Someone is fooling with my knee." Man says, "It's me, and *I'm not fooling!*"

"About a girl taking a tramp through the woods."

"Close those double-breasted lips!"

All references to Mayor Walker and LaGuardia, although used innocently enough. Unfavorable comments have been received by our patrons.

Remarks about Daddy Browning and Peaches.

Words, "Cockeye," "Dirty," "Wop." [Keith cut out "cockeye" in 1895.]

Business of tearing off woman's trunks.

"What's your name?" "Murphy, and don't let the *nose* fool you!"

"Mother and father are fighting." "Who is your father?" "That's what they're fighting about."

Two nance bits: Man kissing woman, other man sez, "What about me, don't I appeal to you?" And, after man does nance walk, "Why, a businessman don't walk that way!" "You don't know my business!"

"Lord Epsom, Secretary of the Interior."

"Kindly see that the girls' navels are covered."

"There are no flies on me." "No, but there are spots where flies have been."

"She had two children by her first husband, two by her second husband, two by her third, besides *two of her own*."

Girl claims she hurt forehead, man kisses it. Then she claims she hurt her finger, which he also kisses, etc. Finally she takes a prat fall and says she hurt herself again!

Girl whispers in mother's ear and moves around the stage, crossing her legs, etc. Finally Mother says, "Go and tell your father."

"You leave a book around the house and some animal punctuates it!"

"I took a girl to see 'Ladies of the Evening,' so now I can speak freely."

All Kip Rhinelander gags. (He married a Negro.)

Story about man looking through transom at woman in the bathtub.

All gags about Peaches Browning and Earl Carroll.

Jokes about De Russey's lane (Hall-Mills murder) and the pig woman.

Gag about auto troubles, saying, "It was sunk-in-the ditch," making it sound like "sonofabitch."

Lady headliner does gag about Spanish fly. Tells about going to make a new picture called "My Wedding Night" with sound effects!

Three big comics doing nance bit at the Palace, with one at finish saying, "It must be the tomboy in me."

Cut all pansy stuff and giving of the raspberry.

Big comic in Boston censored, refused to cut, and was called on the carpet. (He cut.)

Test tube scene (can't cut because whole act depends on finish).

Hitler gags where he appears as a nance.

Wiping perspiration from under arms, legs, etc., and all maneuverings of lady's skirt.

"I thought I picked a skirt, but I picked a bloomer!"

"I believe in companionate marriage; that means 'open shop.' "

"Are you looking at my knee?" "No, I'm way above that."

Word "rabies" in the line "dog had rabies."

Reference to the little cottage behind the big one.

"I like to take experienced girls home." "I'm not experienced." "You're not home yet!"

Picking John Gilbert's nose.

Speaking about a girl as a "broad."

"Children look more like their fathers since we have Frigidaires."

"One flight up and turn to your right, madame" (after she whispers in his ear).

"Panama Panties completely cover the Canal Zone."

"Cow drinks water and gives milk—baby drinks milk and gives —"

"That was when Fanny was still a girl's name."

"I said good-by to the train and jumped on my girl."

"Walking sticks were invented when Eve presented Adam with a Cain." "I didn't think you were Abel."

"She thinks 'lettuce' is a proposition."

"Statue of Liberty is surrounded by water because she raised her hand and teacher didn't see her."

Feenamint gags.

"I slept with the twins during the rain storm, but I might as well have gone home."

Cut names of Pantages and Aimee Semple McPherson.

"I'm going to the livery stable for doughnuts."

"Little Willie Green from Boston, Mass., waded into the water up to his—knees!"

After girl rubs man's chest, he says, "Now let me do that to you."

Boy asks girl's father for permission to marry his daughter. "I'm making $65 a week and that's enough for two to live on." "Supposing you have children?" (Boy knocks on wood.) "We've been lucky so far."

"Didn't I meet you under the bed at the Astor Hotel?"

"I knew you when you didn't have a pot to—*cook in*."

"He's the father of a baby boy, but his wife doesn't know it yet."

"I'll never marry a girl who snores." "You're going to have a swell time finding out!"

Men grabbing partner by seat of trousers, latter crying, "What encouragement did I give you?"

Holding partner's nose, then wiping hand on shirt, saying, "You have a cold."

(To flute player) "Hey, that thing is sticking out again."

"Boy is so small because his father was a Scotchman."

(Man to girl) "Are you married?" "No." "Any children?" "I told you I'm not married." "*Answer my question.*"

"Hurry, you're a little behind, Fanny!"

(To groom) "How do you like married life?" "I'll tell you better in the morning."

"I said, 'Relax,' not 'Ex-lax!' "

Rhyme about girl's haircut, inferring it looks like a man's behind.

Girl walking on stage with a pair of oars, saying, "I just made the crew."

Business of partner trickling sprinkling can on man's leg; he then kicks dog.

Dog appears to be whispering to man. "Sure, it's at the end of the hall."

"He buried his head in my shoulder then *plowed his way through.*"

"I get a thrill when I look up at her balcony."

"If you don't get married, your children will hate you when they grow up."

"Out of 50,000 people, the pigeon had to pick me out."

"Your father is in Kansas City." "He isn't. He is dead." "Your mother's husband is dead, but your father lives in Kansas City."

"He's in the automobile business. He gave me an automobile last night, and tonight he's gonna give me the business."

"Did you pay a green fee?" "No, we were in the rough all day."

"He uses sign language. He expresses his feelings with his hands."

"I have fourteen children and I'm afraid my husband doesn't love me." "Hell, think of what might have happened if he loved you."

"Magician had me in the hallway, the hand is quicker than the eye."

Gag about woman barber nursing baby and saying, "You're next."

Business of apparently spitting in each other's faces.

Vulgar suggestions while dancing with girl (looking down her breast).

"If Nature won't, Pluto will."

Squirting Flit under the arms.

"Out West where men are men and women are double-breasted."

"The next movement is from Epsom."

Business of touching man and saying, "Are you nervous?" (touching rear) "Only around the second chucker."

Name of President Hoover or any state, city, or national official.

Reference to Protestants.

"Old woman who lived in a shoe had so many children she didn't know what to do." "Why did she have so many children?" "Because she didn't know what to do."

Gag with girl from the audience. "Anything else you'd like?" "Nothing you can throw from the audience."

I'll bet you don't believe that all this was pulled on the Big Time, but it was. It only goes to show you how low vaude got toward the finish. It was like an old guy slapping a young gal on the fanny! The brooms, soap and water, and mops used by Tony Pastor and B. F. Keith were all worn out.

These were the things they were told they must not say, but they *did*, until there were no more vaude theaters they could say them in. SEZ

Your *pal*,
LEFTY

P.S. Hey, radio and TV . . . take a hint.

Theatrical Clubs

Dear Joe,

I wrote you about the half a dozen actors who started The Jolly Corks, which later became the Benevolent Protective Order of Elks. In 1898, at Seattle, Washington, a few more showmen started a social club for themselves and called it the "Order of Good Things." The showmen were John Cort, John Considine, Harry Leavitt, Mose Goldsmith, and Arthur Williams. After a few weeks this little club's name was changed and soon became the big fraternal order called the "Eagles." So you see show folks are responsible for two of the biggest benevolent organizations in America!

There was a saying in show biz that whenever three actors got together, they'd start a club. They were always seeking sociability, to swap stories, have laughs, and make touches. But they insisted on being with other actors who understood their language.

The oldest theatrical club in America, up to 1944, when it disbanded, was the Actors' Order of Friendship, which was organized in 1849. It was strictly an actor's club. The mother lodge was in Philadelphia, and New York had Edwin Forrest Lodge No. 2, which was organized in 1907, with a clubhouse at 139 West Forty-seventh Street. Later they joined with the Green Room Club, and when it broke up, the eleven surviving members of the Actors' Order of Friendship sold the clubhouse building, receiving about $2,000 apiece, and disbanded.

The Green Room Club was organized in 1902 and it was then called the Theatrical Business Club. James O'Neill was the first prompter (president). From 1902 to 1904 they met in a house on West Forty-seventh Street, where the Palace now stands. They then joined the Actors' Order of Friendship, whose members didn't have to pay dues, because they gave the Green Roomers the use of their clubhouse. In 1923, when the A.O.O.F. leased their house (later selling it), under the guidance of S. Jay Kaufman the Green Roomers took a ninety-nine-year lease on a beautiful building at 19 West Forty-eighth Street. They were doing very well when financial trouble developed after one of the officers helped himself to a big chunk of the till. Also in 1911 they had had some internal trouble and seventy-five of the insurgents had joined the Friars without having to pay an initiation fee. But for a long time the Green Roomers really had a swell club with a fine membership. They gave Revels at the clubhouse and also for the general public. S. Jay Kaufman as president worked very hard to help the younger actor. He started a dormitory where the young actors could sleep for very little money. Some of our present-day stars were "boarders" in the dormitory when things weren't breaking so well for them. It was a small but very warm club, and it was a shame that it never was reorganized.

The second oldest theatrical club is the Players, which was organized in New York in 1889 and took up quarters on Gramercy Park at the home of the immortal Edwin Booth, who endowed the building to them. His bedroom still remains as it was. The roster of the Players contains mostly legit actors, but nearly all well-known legits played vaude at some time or other in their careers. There are also many fine artists and writers among the membership. A very distinguished theatrical club is the Players!

The first real social club made up of vaudevillians only was the Vaudeville Comedy Club. The idea originated with Louis Simon (remember him in a comedy sketch, "The New Coachman"?) and a few others, while gabbing in the offices of Meyers & Keller, the agents. The first meeting was held at the Empire Hotel in 1906. Frank Byron ("The Dude Detective") gave $10 for expenses. Carlton Macy (Lydell & Macy), suggested the name, Comedy Club, but when they found there already was a club by that name, they changed it to the Vaudeville Comedy Club. Will Cressy, (Cressy & Dayne) was made president. The idea was to have the club for comedy acts only. James J. Morton ("The Boy Comic") was the secretary, and it was through his hard work that the club really got over. It started out as a club for laughs, but they also worked for better conditions backstage and started a protective material department. In 1907 they moved to 147 West Forty-fifth Street (next door to the Lyceum Theatre) and in 1909 they moved to 224 West Forty-sixth Street. It was here the famous Clown Nights started, with Big Jim Morton as M.C. Jim did such a good job that he later became the first professional M.C. in America.

The club did a lot of good work. It supported Percy Williams in his fight against E. F. Albee, and when Albee saw that Williams, with Comedy Club support, would control practically all the comedy and next-to-closing acts, he made peace with Williams, who later sold his circuit to Albee for about seven million bucks. The club stuck to Williams so there would be some opposition in vaude. The start of the downfall of the Comedy Club was when they began to take in managers, agents, and lay people, and soon, through inner dissension among "cliques," they were on the verge of bankruptcy.

At this time Gene Hughes (not yet an agent) was the club's

president, and he called a special meeting to announce the bad news. During Gene's speech there was a hush all over the room and the members were feeling very bad about the turn of events. At this point Harry B. Watson (Bickle, Watson & Wrothe), wearing a checkered suit, gray derby, spats, and carrying a cane, entered. Johnny Stanley (a great ad-libber) looked up, saw Watson, and yelled, "Go back. You're not on for an hour yet!" Everybody got to laughing and Gene Hughes couldn't get them back to order. So what happened? Yep, we went bankrupt! The club was reorganized and started again at the Metropole Hotel, on West Forty-third Street (where Rosenthal was shot), and again the club broke up. Some of the members tried to revive it as the Jesters, with Frank Conroy (Conroy & LeMaire) as president. Al Jolson, J. J. Morton, Harry Fox, Irving Berlin, and Bernard Granville were a few of the revivers, but it just didn't revive. We then had a floor next to the Palace and for awhile it looked as if it would go, but it didn't, and so the Vaudeville Comedy Club and the Jesters closed their doors after about eight years of a lot of laughs. There'll never be another club like it!

In 1906 circuses had a couple of social clubs. The Robinson Show called their club the Elephants, while the Barnum & Bailey show called theirs the Tigers.

In the fall of 1904 an organization called the Press Agents' Association was formed to stop the free-pass frauds. Nearly everybody in and out of show biz was working some gimmick to get a free pass. The first meeting was held at Brown's Chop House, in response to a call by Charles Emerson Cook (then a press agent for Belasco). Channing Pollock was first president, John W. Rumsey, treasurer, and John S. Flaherty (manager and P.A. of the Majestic Theatre) was secretary. A blacklist of phonies was made up and the practice was broken—and with it the interest of the association.

In 1906 Will Page and Joe Plunkett sent out a call and the membership was enlarged to include press agents and actors all over the country, and actors soon became the majority and changed the name to the Friars (originated by Frederick F. Shrader). Charles Emerson Cook was made Abbot (president), Frank J. Wilstach, Dean (vice-president), John Rumsey, treasurer, and Wells Hawks, secretary. They were the first actors' club to give dinners to prominent people. Clyde Fitch, the famous playwright, was the first honored guest at the Beaux Arts Café. At the Victor Herbert dinner, the famous Friars' song, by Cook and Herbert, was born. These dinners had a new twist to them; instead of eulogizing the guest of honor, they appointed an "agent" (supposedly a press agent) to introduce the honored guest. He would pan the guest instead of boosting him. (The late Ren Wolf was the greatest.) It was a novel and welcome change from the regular routines.

The Friars were incorporated in 1907 and held meetings at the Hotel Hermitage. They got a house at 107 West Forty-fifth Street in 1908. Their annual public affairs were first called Festivals, then later Frolics. In 1916 they moved to their own large clubhouse at 110 West Forty-eighth Street. It was called the Monastery. George M. Cohan, then the Abbot, headed a parade to the new clubhouse, where he opened the door and threw the key away. The place remained open until 1933, when bankruptcy closed its doors. They moved to new quarters atop the Hollywood Theatre, and after a short stay again broke up and took a few rooms at the Hotel Astor in 1936 under a reorganization. Then to the Hotel Edison Annex, where they stayed until 1950, when they moved to their own clubhouse at 123 West Fifth-sixth Street. It is really not the original Friars, but they still have many members of the old Friars, and are a very important and successful actors' club (with Milton Berle as Abbot).

But I want to tell you about the fabulous *old* Friars Club on Forty-eighth Street. It was a beautiful clubhouse. Most of the membership were vaude actors, and everybody seemed to have money (we often collected $1,000 for some cause or other in less than an hour). The place was run for laughs. When the club needed money (which was often), George M. Cohan would get the boys together and give a Frolic, which made $50,000, then everybody relaxed until the finances ran down again. The things that happened there are fantastic!

At one time there was a man who took a great interest in the club. He had the pool tables recovered and new cues and balls bought. He then took up the problems of the dining room and had the menu and prices changed. (We had one of the finest dining rooms, serving great food, which by the way, lost $50,000 a year.) This gentleman certainly ran things for about four months. One day he got into an argument with Charlie Pope (husband of Stella

Hammerstein and a terrific character in his own right). Charlie
turned to someone and asked who the fellow was. Nobody seemed
to know; some said he was the head of the House Committee;
others thought he was on the Board of Governors; nobody knew
for sure. Charlie investigated and found that the guy wasn't even
a *member*! He had come in on *a guest card*!

Another time some of us were standing outside of the club
when a van drove up and two huskies said they had come to pick
up a piano to be tuned. They went in and brought it out and a
few of the boys even helped them put it in the van. A few nights
later someone wanted to play the piano and was told that it had
been taken out to be tuned. He looked puzzled and said, "Since
when do you have to take out a piano to have it tuned?" The
piano was never returned.

You think you've heard of funny things? How about having a
steam pipe running through the icebox for years before they found
it out? And it wasn't until we moved from the Monastery that we
found out we had had one of the first air-conditioned clubhouses, via
vents. But they were closed for the more than fifteen years we were
there and in summer we had the hottest clubhouse in New York!
But what a great club for laughs!

I must tell you one more story (out of fifty I know) about the
old Friars to show you the kind of crazy lovable guys we had as
members. Rube Bernstein (one of our great managers), a real
pixie, would go to any lengths for a laugh. We had a member, Bill
Wilder, that walked with a slight limp and carried a cane with a
rubber tip on the end of it. He was a daily card player, and would
hang his cane next to him on the table. One night when he was
very interested in the game, Rube took the cane, removed the
rubber tip, got a saw, and cut off about an eighth of an inch, put
the rubber tip back, and hung the cane on the table in its regular
place. He did this for two weeks, each day cutting off a tiny piece.
One day Bill came into the club leaning way over. Rube asked him,
"How you feeling?" And Bill said, "I'm getting worse and worse,
Rube. I can't walk straight anymore!" That gives you an idea of
some of the many laughs we had in those days. "Let's drink a
deep toast, to the ones we love most, a toast to all Jolly Good
Friars!" That's the finish of the Friars' song. I'll buy that—and
that goes for the *new* Friars!

In 1898 the Negro performers started a social club, the Greasy

Front. It was run by Charlie Moore and there was a restaurant in the basement run by Mrs. Moore. In 1908 they organized a club called the Frogs, with the immortal Bert Williams as president. It lasted a long time. They also had the Clef Club, a social and protective association for colored musicians.

In 1908 there was the Golden Gate Professional Club, which lasted about five years in California. Mrs. Beaumont Packard was president. There was also the Benevolent Order of Upholders, which didn't last at all. In 1910 the Variety Artists League started to buck the White Rats (no go). In 1911 Billy Gould started the American Vaudeville Artists, which didn't last over a minute. (That, too, tried to buck the White Rats.)

In 1913 there was one of the greatest show-folk colonies in the country. It was at Freeport, Long Island. Nearly every home in the colony was built with vaudeville money. Those were the days when vaude acts would lay off in the summer, as most of the theaters closed because of no air conditioning. Hanging around Ed Rice's garage, the boys would chew the fat, get a half a keg of beer, and swap lies and laughs. The gang got so big that they decided to build a clubhouse. They called themselves the Long Island Good Hearted Thespians' Society! (Anything for a laugh.) It finally ended up as the Lights (taken from the first letter of each word. Maybe this gave the Government the idea of all those initial departments like NRA, NLRB, etc.). It became really one of the great actors' clubs in America, organized and run by actors. All the show folks would come from New York for the week end to get laughs, seeing and listening to the greatest ad-libbing and clowning ever heard or seen anywhere! Victor Moore was the Angel (president).

Every summer they would make a Cruise (like the Friars' Frolics and Lambs' Gambols, Greenroom Revels, White Rats' Scampers, etc.) to raise money. They built a beautiful clubhouse right on the bay. The shows on week ends were just terrific! Henry Bergman, Eddie Carr, Tommy Dugan, Frank Tinney, Jimmy Conlin, George P. Murphy, and George McKay were just a few of the great entertainers that ad-libbed their way to the greatest floor-show entertainment you ever could see. The wives started a club of their own, using the rathskeller of the club, and called themselves the Pigs, why, I will never know! But it certainly was a big success.

When things got tough, someone suggested taking in lay members. That was the beginning of the end (as in mostly all theatrical clubs). Soon the actors couldn't even get seats in their own club; all they were wanted for was to entertain the lay members and their guests. These children of fun couldn't stand this very long. They stopped entertaining—and soon the Lights went out! A great loss to the fun of America.

But still the actors weren't cured of "clubitis." In 1914 Chicago saw the organization of the Old Friends, later called the Strollers. A swell guy by the name of Sam Mayer, who went "upstairs" in 1914, left a collection of 1,265 framed pictures of prominent show folks. (Some of the frames had as many as forty pictures.) Charles E. Ellis, Robert Sherman, and F. P. Simpson were responsible for buying this collection. Others aiding were Frank Gazzolo, Ed Rowland, and E. E. Meredith (*Variety* man in Chicago at that time). Gifts came from Amy Leslie and Mrs. Gardiner (widow of Frank Mayo's manager). This collection, bought by Robert Gould Shaw, finally passed to Harvard University, which furnished a building for its housing. Ralph Kettering, playwright and producer and member of the Strollers, tells me that Mr. Shaw was the son of the man who organized the first Negro regiment in the Civil War and was the first husband of Lady Astor. This club lasted only a short time, but they had a lot of fun while it lasted.

Many years later there was a Comedy Club in Chicago, with clubrooms above the Chicago Lindy's (no connection with New York's famous Lindy's). Membership was made up of show folks and music publishers, who did a great job of keeping the laughs going for visiting vaudevillians. In 1914 there was a club made up of women legits called the Gamut Club. I have no idea what ever became of it. Then there was the Lox Club, an offshoot of the Burlesque Club (which had many vaude members).

Which brings me to one of the most unique clubs in America, or even the world—the Burlesque Club! It was organized when burlesque was going real strong all over the country, and the members bought a clubhouse at 237 West Forty-seventh Street. They invested some of their funds in a coal mine in Pennsylvania, which in turn was leased to a company that paid them royalties. When burly went bad and some of the members needed money, the club distributed $600 to each member, and as the membership grew less and less (due to burly being banned in many places), they sold the clubhouse (to Leone, who built an addition to his famous

Italian restaurant). The club then took a couple of rooms at the Forrest Hotel, and after a few more years they didn't even need two rooms, so just held annual meetings. Henry Kurtzman, who has been secretary for years, has really kept the organization alive. There are only about a dozen of us left. Bobby Clark (Clark & McCullough) is president, and Rube Bernstein, Emmett Callahan, and Herman Becker are the directors of the only actors' club that has ever paid dividends to its members!

There have been many show biz clubs in California—the Photo Players Club in Los Angeles, the Writers' Club, the Uplifters (which really wasn't an actors' club, but had many of them as members), and the Bohemians. And of course the Lakeside and Hillcrest Golf Clubs, although not organized as actors' clubs, have a majority of their membership from the profession, including many of the greats from vaude, radio, TV, stage, and pics. They are laugh exchanges!

There is an old organization called the Theatrical Mechanics Association, better known as the T.M.A. It was founded in Boston by the stagehands in 1882. Many actors joined this organization (and in later years were glad they did, because they made a good living as stagehands). They did a lot of charitable work and had branches all over the country.

There were many "goofy" clubs. In 1916 Felix Adler (a very funny man, besides being an actor-writer) organized the Musties. The meetings were held in back of a saloon on Sixth Avenue. Those gathered would put a dollar in the kitty and the president would appoint a committee of one to go out shopping for sandwiches, then another committee of two to watch him to see that he spent the money honestly. Then another kitty would be collected for the "musty ale." Little Billy, the midget, was president. He was offered a quarter for his presidency by George M. Cohan, but he held out for thirty-five cents, which Cohan refused to pay, so Little Billy remained the prez. This was just a gang get-together, made up mostly of Friars. Plenty of laughs!

In 1918 the Lookers was organized as a social club and their first and only meeting was held at Terrace Garden. The organizers were Jimmy Hussey and George Whiting (Whiting & Burt). The club was disbanded because E. F. Albee thought it might become another White Rats, and he didn't want any opposition to his N.V.A.

There was a legit club calling itself the Thespians which didn't last very long. In 1925 the Professional Entertainers of New York, called the Peonys (from the first letters) was organized. The membership was made up of vaude actors and entertainers who played clubs, a large and important part of show biz and a great source of income for many entertainers. The Peonys have lately celebrated their silver anniversary, and are still going very strong. Besides being a social club, they do a great deal of charity work.

The Masquers is one of the most important theatrical clubs of the West, originally started by members of the Lambs who went out to Hollywood for pictures. They asked for a charter from the Lambs, but were refused because it was felt that all those members would be back in New York soon. So, after waiting a few years, the boys organized their own club and called it the Masquers. At first only Lambs were admitted, but then the membership was widened and today includes all the big names of pics, radio, and TV. They have a beautiful clubhouse in Hollywood and run some very fine affairs (called Revels). They are a very important organization and have contributed a lot to Western theatrical clubdom! (The Lambs now have monthly meetings on the Coast with about 100 attending.)

There were many clubs started just for laughs, like the Double Crosses, organized in Gerson's, with ten-cents-a-day dues. Another one organized at Gerson's Restaurant at the Somerset Hotel was the Kockamanias, with Marie Hartman as president. Monthly meetings were held in the Headliner's Room back of the restaurant, which was closed to the public. We would put on a show, with costumes and special music, lyrics, and book, for which the actors would rehearse for a week (and all paid for by "Basil" and his wonderful wife Ella). All they wanted was laughs, and they got plenty!

At one time some of the boys wanted to revive the Lights Club, and called themselves the Blitzes, but it didn't last long. Olsen & Johnson started one, the Ancient and Honorable Flealess Order of Pups, with Ole Olsen as Barking Knight (president). They met whenever and wherever they could. Al Trahan was organizer and president of the Royal Order of Cutthroats, which was short-lived.

The Ramblers was organized as a press stunt to boost the Clark & McCullough show of the same name, and it became very big, with members from all over the country. No dues, no clubhouse, just get together every once in awhile for some laughs and beer drinking. When Paul McCullough died, the Ramblers died also, as he was the mixer of the team and took charge of the get-togethers.

Another fly-by-nighter was the Wildcats; the officers were called Tom Cat, Tiger Cat, White Cat, and Black Cat, and members were called kittens. It expired when there was no more milk in the saucer (treasury). Another goofy club organized in the old days of the Palace was organized at Mark Aaron's Bar next door. They would get new members as they came in the door. The password was "I will," and they would ask the new member, "Who's gonna buy?" to which he would have to give the password, "I will." (It was always good for one round of drinks, anyway.)

The Cheese Club was one of the great luncheon clubs of New York, with actors, press agents, critics, and newspapermen as members. Harry Richenbach, the famous press agent, was president once; then Harry Hershfield (the raconteur and cartoonist) took it over and remained president for many years, until they broke up. In fact, Hershfield is still president! He claims that to get rid of a president they have to give him a party and a watch, and right now none of the Cheese Clubbers can afford it. This was one of the first lunch clubs to kid prominent guests. The Cheese Club had the distinction of being invited and thrown out of more restaurants in New York than any other organization in America. There were no membership dues, no initiation, no nothing! The members brought guests, and if you were a stranger you could still wander in, if you took care of your own check!

Which leads me into a story about a certain big night-club owner and great entertainer whose name happens to be Vincent Lopez! After attending one of the Cheese Club luncheons, he applied for membership! The boys started to go "on the rib," and they told him it would be tough to get in. To get good will he invited all the members and their wives and sweethearts to his famous night club as his guests. They all came, the food was wonderful, the wine flowed freely, and the check was terrific! At the end of the evening Arthur Caesar (a great wit and writer) managed to get up and said, "This has been a wonderful evening, but we don't want a schmoe (he didn't say schmoe) in our club who would spend all this money on people like us!" It was a rib, but Vincent never did get in the club, although he attended all lunches. I would write you more about the laughs we used to have there, but I'm sure my pal Harry Hershfield will write a book about it some day. He should.

The Coast has an organization called the Troupers, consisting of pic, legit, and vaude actors, who hold regular meetings and do much charitable work. The Comedy Club in Hollywood is made up of old vaude actors, standard and headline acts, who have now settled out there. They put on a vaudeville show every year that is the talk of the town. Louis Mosconi (Mosconi Bros.) is the Headliner (president). They prove that quality is always in style.

The ladies of the profession also have clubitis! The Twelfth Night Club is practically (not officially) the feminine branch of the Lambs, as most of their wives and sweethearts belong to it. They even put on many of the sketches used by the Lambs at their Gambols. It is really a great club with a fine membership of actresses, writers, artists, and housewives. The Dominoes, the lady branch of the Masquers (also not officially), is a lot like the Twelfth Night Club in membership and activities. The Ziegfeld Girls Club is made up of principals and chorus girls who were in the Ziegfeld shows. They take care of many of the old show gals that find the going a bit rough. They give an entertainment every year which is a "must" for all show biz to attend. The Troupers in New York (no connection with the club by the same name in Hollywood) is a woman's theatrical club with a membership made up of the wives of many of the night-club entertainers, disk jockeys, and radio and TV actors. They do a fine job of charitable work. A young organization, but a very efficient one.

During Prohibition the actors just had to start another club, and while it lasted it was the funniest spot in town. It was called the Fifty-Fifty Club, and its Chef (president) was Hal Beach, the famous art connoisseur. The membership was the elite of show biz. Like the Lights, they would get up and entertain each other. With Harry Ruby (the famous composer) at the piano and Eddie Miller singing and the choice comedians comedianing, you were sure of a great night's fun. The members had private lockers that held their own supposedly prewar liquors. No laymen broke up this great fun spot as they did the other actors' clubs. The blackout on this one can be blamed on the wives!

I should also tell you about the many Actors' Guilds, which are definitely a part of show biz. Although they are not social clubs, they all do a great job of helping so many of our profession. The Catholic Actors' Guild, the Episcopalian Actors' Guild, the Jewish Theatrical Guild, and the Negro Actors' Guild all operate without regard to race or creed. The Actors' Fund is the oldest of all actors' charitable organizations. They have taken care of the aged and sick and needy for over half a century, besides providing a home for the aged. These are all great organizations, but don't come under the heading of theatrical clubs.

The treasurers have the Hellraisers' club. Another club with membership consisting of managers, agents, press agents, treasurers, and businessmen of the theater is the Hot Air Club (first started in 1899). They run a clambake at Price's Place at Pleasure Bay on the Shrewsbury River every year. There are no dues, no meetings, only get-togethers once a year and a member can bring a guest (usually an actor or a showman). I asked my old friend Elliott Foreman why the name, Hot Air Club? He said, "Because it has always been rated the ruling commodity of Broadway. While the quality has been steadily lowered during the process of orientation, the quantity of the supply or its free usage upon the Rialto has never slackened." Which is a good enough reason for any club!

As for the Lambs (now the oldest and greatest of all actors' clubs) and the White Rats, I will write you about them in another letter.

A coupla actors just dropped in on me. I think we'll start a Club! SEZ

Your pal,

LEFTY

The Lambs

Dear Joe,

The oldest theatrical club in America today is the Lambs. It was Christmas Day in 1874 that five guys who were having supper at Delmonico's Blue Room, in New York, decided to start a supper

club, which Henry J. Montague named the Lambs. There was a
club in England called the Lambs, supposedly because in London
actors used to gather at the home of Charles Lamb and his sister,
Mary Lamb, and the line among the actors was, "Let's go around
to the Lambs'."

There was another version given by Henry J. Montague, who was
one of the original Lambs in London and who I think should really
know. According to him, a few actors in England occasionally took
a dip in the sea near Dover, in the South of England. Sheep raising
was an important industry in that section of the country, and the
shepherds used the spot as an ideal place to wash their flocks. This
gave the little group the thought of calling themselves the Lambs,
and suggested that the head of the organization be called the
Shepherd, the entertainments be called Gambols, and the big event
be known as the Wash (which is an annual outing given by the
Lambs). Take your "cherce" as to which is correct. But we do
know that Henry J. Montague became the first Shepherd of the
Lambs in America!

It was at the Maison Doree Hotel that the first meeting was held,
and in less than a year the Union Hotel was the site of the first
private supper room. In 1877 they moved to the Matchbox, at 848
Broadway (next to Wallach's Thirteenth Street). The next stop
was the Union Square Hotel, and as the membership grew they
again had to move, this time to the Monument House at 6 Union
Square (Fourteenth Street was then the Rialto). By now they had
about sixty members.

In 1878 the Lambs moved "uptown" to 19 East Sixteenth Street.
They had a little over $80 in the treasury and J. Lester Wallack
was elected Shepherd and served for seven years. Moving two blocks
away from Fourteenth Street gave the boys courage, so in April
1880 they got their own clubhouse at 34 West Twenty-sixth Street,
which in those days was way uptown. It was here they started the
Gambols. The first Gambol took place in 1888 with Edmund S.
Holland (one of the five original Lambs) as the collie (which
means he produced the show and was the top man of the night,
and also means you go a month without sleep).

A couple of years later the dough ran out and the boys moved to
the Gilsey House and in three years paid off all their creditors. In
1895 they were going strong again with 272 members. The next
year they had plans for another clubhouse, still further uptown

(where show biz was moving to), 70 West Thirty-sixth Street. It was May, 1897, that they moved into their new clubhouse (they call it the Fold). It was the same year that the London Lambs broke up, and the surviving members were made Honorary Lambs in America. Sir John Hare, the founder of the Lambs in London, was made Shepherd Emeritus, and he presented the club with the original crook and bell and other tokens of office of the London group, which are still used at our Inauguration Gambols.

By 1902 the membership grew so much they had to get a new clubhouse. They first took an option on a hunk of property on West Forty-eighth Street (where the Playhouse was built later), then they switched to where they are now, 128 West Forty-fourth Street. That was in 1904 and in 1913 they bought a couple of buildings west of their quarters and the western half of the Lambs building was built. They used Keen's Chop House as temporary headquarters while the club was being built. The architect was the famous Stanford White, who later was fatally shot by Harry Thaw (not for building the Lambs).

The building contains many valuable paintings presented to the club by artist members, great names in art like Frederic Remington, Edward Simmons, W. L. Metcalf, James Montgomery Flagg, Howard Chandler Christy, Henry Inman, and Maj. Victor Guinness (the official Marine Corp painter). There are a lot of valuable photographs and old programs and stage memorabilia. A shrine to Lambs who served in two world wars holds a bronze draped figure, the work of Robert I. Aitken. An annual service is held before it, with big brass of all services attending. The Lambs did great service during both wars. Under the chairmanship of Joseph Buhler, Phil Green, and Sam Forrest, each member would donate a check covering the weekly entertainment of service men from all countries at the clubhouse. Some of the GIs saw their first show at the Lambs. It was during one of these entertainments that a GI from the South was asked how he liked it. He said, "I've never seen 'round actors' before." (Only pics.)

One of the outstanding curios is the fife rail of the Spanish cruiser *Mercedes*, removed before it was sunk in Santiago Harbor on July 4, 1898. It was first used as the front of the bar on Thirty-sixth Street, but now is at the main desk. The mantel over the present huge fireplace in the Grill was presented by Stanford White. It was rumored that it came from Pompeii, but it really came from Florence, Italy. No matter where it came from, it really is beautiful. The Buddha sitting on top of the fireplace was presented by Lamb Joseph Keegan, world traveler (especially in the Orient), who will tell you fantastic stories of how the Buddha was stolen and finally smuggled into the country. There is a huge silver bowl on the large library table, depicting the career of Joseph Jefferson in his famed role of Rip Van Winkle; it was presented to him as a testimonial and he in turn gave it to his favorite club.

There were many memorable hours in the Lambs. It was an ordinary occurrence for Victor Herbert to play the piano or cello, and for Caruso to sing, "Has Anybody Here Seen Kelly?" Singers around the piano might include Chauncey Olcott, John McCormack, and Andrew Mack. Dancers like Harland Dixon, Johnny Boyle, and Jack Donahue would be dancing to the tune of *Rhapsody in Blue*, played for them by the composer, George Gershwin. A swell little guy would go to the piano and the gang had to listen real close to hear him sing his latest hit—Irving Berlin. Great stories were told by great storytellers. Members included writers, poets, artists, doctors, lawyers, priests, ministers, mayors, governors, cabinet members, admirals, generals, flyers, and now our President, *Dwight Eisenhower!*

The "fun nest" in any club is at the bar. The Lambs is no exception. There were so many funny things that have happened at the famous Lambs bar that it would take a book to record 'em all. But the one that is always told to Lambkins (freshman Lambs) and guests is about the funny, talented, and lovable Dick Carle.

As you know, Richard Carle was a musical-comedy star, writer, and fine comedian. By the way, Dick told me and Aggie how he became a comedian. He was very nearsighted and naturally had to wear glasses. He was in a show in which he played practically a straight part. As he was about to make his entrance he dropped his glasses. Instead of making his entrance through the door, he did it through a window (which he thought was the door). He got a great laugh, took advantage of his mistake, and gave a comedy performance instead of the straight role he was cast for. From that day on he was a comedian—and a great one!

Now to get back to the story. At one time bartenders would decorate the backbar by stacking shiny glasses in fancy designs. One day while Dick Carle was at the bar drinking with some brother Lambs, he told a story, and when he got to the climax, he illustrated it by taking his cane and with a wide sweep, knocking all the glasses off the bar! He was suspended for ninety days. (The members call it being sent to Siberia—which was Pat Finn's thirst emporium next door, which catered to the exiles.) When the three months were up, Dick came in and was greeted by the gang, and of course Dick started celebrating his homecoming with tonsil soothers. He was there a couple of hours when a member came over and asked him why he hadn't seen him around the club in months? "I was sent to Siberia," said Dick. "Is that so?" said his companion. "What did you do, Dick?" "Nothing. All I did was take my cane and do this!" And with that he took his cane and illustrated by knocking all the glasses off the bar again. We didn't see Dick at the club for another six months, unless we looked in on Siberia!

There is a fully equipped theater on the third floor that seats about 300. It is here we give the famous club Gambols; many of the sketches written for them later became Broadway shows. *The Squaw Man, Her Way Out*, with Jim Corbett, *The Littlest Rebel* (also played in vaude as a sketch), *Experience, As a Man Thinks, The Witching Hour, Harvest Moon*, and *The Copperhead*, in which Lionel Barrymore starred, are just a few. Lately *Stalag* 17 was first shown at the club, and Jose Ferrer saw it and decided to produce it on Broadway, where it was a big success. It was at these club Gambols that you would see a great star like John Drew play the part of a butler, with maybe one line, and some youngster have the star part. A Lambkin must play "dame" parts his first year (as no women are allowed in the club). Some of these who were really great in make-up and performances were Stanley Ridges, Joe Santley, Effingham Pinto, and Bruce Evans.

Tommy C. Lamb (C. stands for Casanova), who was the club's mascot for many years, was truly a remarkable cat. Merely an alley cat when he first came to the Lambs, he blossomed forth as one of the most beautiful cats you have ever seen. There wasn't a pregnant cat within a radius of six blocks that didn't blame it on Tom. He really was remarkable. When anyone in the dining room would order fish (just order it, mind you) he would get up from his spot on the bar and come to the dining room, right to the table where the fish was to be served. This has been proven to skeptics time and time again.

The Gallery Boys (which was a fun-club within the Lambs, like the Shriners in the Masonic Lodge) with Joe Laurie, Jr., president, Jack Norworth and Fred Hillebrand, board of directors, and a membership which paid from 25 cents to $5.00 initiation fees, once gave a dinner to Tommy Lamb. Everybody wore evening clothes, speeches were made by great after-dinner speakers, while Tommy stretched out on a special throne, with loads of catnip around him, paying no attention to the catnip or the speakers, and when it was all over got up, stretched, yawned, and walked away.

There was a fraternity next door that had a cat that was altered. The president of the fraternity asked the head of the Gallery Boys would they invite their cat (to the Tommy Lamb party), seeing we were neighbors. He was told that ladies weren't allowed and neither were "nances." He immediately wrote to the New York *Times*, telling them his "beef," which Laurie answered, and the columns lasted for two weeks. People from all over the country sent gifts to Tommy, bales of catnip, women knitted shoes and sweaters, sent dishes, etc. Mickey Walker brought a set of boxing gloves for him (still hanging in back of the bar). James Montgomery Flagg did a swell painting of him, as did a gentleman whose name I am sorry escapes me for the moment, but who is one of the great animal painters of America. Tommy has long since gone to where all good cats go, but he left a grandson that carries on; he is even more talented than his granddad. Under Willie the waiter's training (Willie has been with us over thirty years), he sits up with a cigarette in his mouth, wears glasses, holds a newspaper in his paws and won't move until Willie tells him to. When he gets on the pool table, the rules are that you must shoot around him; nobody is allowed to chase him off.

There are three great characters in the Lambs' employ—Murphy (Biagio Velluzzi), the bootblack, Sammy Pinsker, the night man, and, of course, Margie Henley, the chief telephone operator. All have been with The Lambs over thirty-five years. At one time Gene Buck, who helped produce over fifteen *Ziegfeld Follies* and who was the president of ASCAP for many years, dressed Murphy up in white tie and tails with a red ribbon across his shirt front and a couple of medals and brought him over to the Ziegfeld *Midnight Frolics* where he and Leon Errol introduced him as an Italian count to the girls (and whispered that he was loaded with dough). The girls all made over him and he ended up with a half a dozen phone numbers slipped to him during the evening. On opening nights he puts on his high hat and tuxedo and personally delivers a scroll from the Lambs to any member who may be in the cast. Sammy never fails to give you a "God bless you"; he has taken care of many a big and little star with money and doctoring, and is always cheerful and optimistic. Sammy and Murphy know more about show folks than anyone I ever met. We have them appear in many a Gambol and they know their lines better than many of the actors. Two real great gentlemen of whom the Lambs are very proud. The Lambs would be a lonesome place without "God bless you" Sammy and Murphy!

Last year the Lambs had a Ladies Day, the first one in its history. It was fought by many members, but the Shepherd, Bert Lytell, won out and it proved to be one of the really great events of the Lambs, although many of the members stayed away in protest. There are only four living Shepherds: William Gaxton, the present Shepherd, who also served 1936-1939; Fred Waring, 1939-1942; John Golden, 1942-1945; and Bert Lytell, 1947-1952.

The club's constitution makes it mandatory for the membership to consist of three professionals to one nonprofessional, which insures that the club always be in control of professionals. It is the only theatrical club that owns its own building outright—no mortgages.

An actors' club that can last seventy-nine years is a wonder in itself, but the Lambs happens to be a wonderful club. If the Lambs died, the theater would die. SEZ

Your pal,

LEFTY

The White Rats and the N.V.A.

Dear Joe,

Conditions in vaudeville around 1900 were pretty bad. The U.B.O. had things their own way. They had gypping agents, grafting bookers, cancellation clauses in the contracts, and switching of routes, which meant they would lay out a nice route for you, with short jumps which you could afford to take at the salary they offered, then would switch dates where you had to make big jumps that ate up a lot of your salary. Some acts were paying as high as 20 per cent commission. All of these things led George Fuller Golden, one of our great monologists, to suggest to his friends that they ought to have an organization that would not only be social but also try to eliminate these abuses.

So on June 1, 1900, at a meeting in the Parker House bar, the organization was started. George Fuller Golden was the founder and first Big Chief (president); Dave Montgomery, Little Chief (veep); James J. Morton, Scat Rat (secretary); Mark Murphy, Treasurat (treasurer); Charles T. Aldrich, Chap Rat (chaplain); Tom Lewis, Guard Rat (sergeant at arms). The Board of Governors were Sam Morton, Fred Stone, Jim Dolan, Sam Ryan, and Nat Wills (all headliners). The name White Rats was taken from a fine and well-organized actors' club in London called the Water Rats (named after a race horse which a group of actors owned and the dough they won on him was given to charity). Golden had a great regard for them (when he played London they entertained him royally); when they refused to let anyone use their name, Golden called the new organization the White Rats. (Spelled backwards is star!)

They tried to talk Keith and the U.B.O. into cutting out many of the abuses, like the morning tryouts for new acts at the Fifth Avenue Theater, where, when the managers didn't like an act, they had the curtain rung down on it (which naturally got the actors very angry), the cancellation clauses, etc. But Keith wouldn't listen. They held a meeting at their clubrooms, then on West Twenty-third Street over a saloon.

It was at this very important meeting, where they were going to decide whether to strike or not, that a very funny thing happened. One of the members was a "dese, dose, and dem" song-and-dance man, who was a very enthusiastic member and was continually getting up and making one-syllable speeches and being generally laughed at. At this meeting a young man who had just come in from the West got the floor and made a speech that was beautifully languaged, with fine philosophy and reasoning, and the members were spellbound by his oratory. When he finished they cheered and carried him around on their shoulders. It was then that the song-and-dance man got up on a chair and yelled, "That's what I've been trying to tell you dumb bastards for weeks!" The young man who made that wonderful speech, which they claim really decided the White Rats to declare a strike, was J. C. Nugent!

The strike was a bust, because many of the actors were double-crossing each other. The U.B.O. knew the key men of the club and would offer them nice long routes at better money than they had ever received, while others were turning down routes and fighting for their cause. They took the routes, left town, and so weakened the White Rats. Many acts were blacklisted and driven out of the business. The Rats were practically dead for seven years, until a young Englishman with a terrific gift of gab, by the name of Harry Mountford, took an interest in it and soon had an enthusiastic bunch of vaude actors following him. When the U.B.O. found that they couldn't buy him off, which they tried many a time, offering as high as a quarter of a million bucks (by the way, Mountford died a very poor man), they started pounding the guy in the trade papers, charging him with everything in the book, burglary, rape, bigamy, and mayhem. And when he got Samuel Gompers, the head of the American Federation of Labor, to give the White Rats a charter, the Rats turned from a social club into a fighting labor union. They left their small quarters at 1439 Broadway, and leased the upper part of Churchill's Restaurant on Forty-sixth Street and Broadway, where they had a few sleeping rooms, large meeting hall, pool tables, etc. That was in 1907.

Members were pouring in, as conditions in vaude was getting worse than back in 1900. The Keith-Albee boys were getting worried and declared a blacklist of some of the White Rat leaders. Mountford started the White Rats' own weekly magazine, called *The Player*, in which he kept writing hot editorials telling about the terrible things the U.B.O. was doing to vaude and its actors. The union also bought an interest in the Mozart Circuit, which had small-time vaude houses in Pennsylvania and New York State. (Did you know that Woolworth had a theater in Lancaster, Pennsylvania? It was one which they booked.) They could give a small-time act about thirty weeks. The small-time managers looked with favor on the idea of the Rats running an independent circuit, for it gave them a freedom they couldn't get elsewhere, even with a payment of a weekly fee to the booking office (and a side fee to the booker—to insure good service) which the union didn't charge.

The Player started out with a lot of advertising, but soon the acts (and even the commercial people) started to withdraw their ads because of the fear of being blacklisted. The blacklist was a horrible weapon, which was used freely by Mr. Albee. An act would suddenly find itself turned down by agents and managers, and yet didn't know it was blacklisted. There were a half a dozen acts that swore they were going to kill Albee for taking away their livelihood. They were talked out of it by their fellow actors. Albee had many spies in the White Rats, who reported everything that was said and done. He also had spies on bills who sent in reports on the acts as to how they felt toward the White Rats and the booking office; they were paid off with steady bookings. The White Rats knew who these people were, as there were people in the booking office that didn't like Albee and were tipping the Rats off to what was going on in the office. (A pretty mess, eh?) None of the White Rats would wear their buttons; that was a sure invitation for the blacklist.

After four years they had to give up *The Player*, and *Variety* offered them a few pages every week to tell their story and announce meetings, etc., without any charge and also without in any way changing their own editorial policy, which was anti-White Rat, although it was Sime who originally told the actors to organize to fight the U.B.O. But Sime never liked Mountford, whom he thought too much of a rabble rouser and a hothead, and wanted to see somebody cooler leading the actors. It was funny reading the *Variety* in those days, first reading a few pages panning Albee, the V.M.P.A., and *Variety*, then you'd turn a few pages and read Sime's editorial against the White Rats, then a few pages of ads from the U.B.O. and V.M.P.A. telling how good they were and how terrible the White Rats and Mountford were.

In 1912 the White Rats were very powerful and had a large enough membership to open a new clubhouse on West Forty-sixth Street, which was financed by many of the members buying bonds. It was one of the finest clubhouses in America. Everything was going along fine. The Rats had a 5 per cent commission bill passed at Albany, gave a lot of Scampers (that's what they called their entertainments), and kept taking pot shots at the managers, until 1916, when the lid finally blew off!

They called a few strikes, one in Oklahoma, then in Boston, and then in the Loew theaters in New York City. They helped the stagehands by walking out when they were fighting for a union shop. When they got it they walked back to work and left the White Rats in the cold. There was a lot of rough stuff, stink bombs, etc.

A funny thing happened at the Scollay Square Theatre in Boston during the strike there. The management got a lot of "coast defenders" (actors who just played clubs, etc., in and around Boston) and told them that they would be set for a big route at big dough if they would go on. There was this one guy who hadn't been on the stage for years, and it all sounded good to him. In the front row there were a dozen big husky acrobats waiting for the scabs to appear. This fellow opened with a song which started, "Well, well, well, I just came from the West . . ." when he saw the acrobats sitting glaring at him from the first row. He took one look and sang, "*And I'm going right back again!*" He walked off the stage and right out of the stage door and never came back! But there were plenty of scabs who didn't scare.

The strike was a bad flop!

It cost the managers a couple of million dollars to break the strike. So they started to organize a vaude actors' club to fight the Rats. It wasn't very hard to get some actors to "front" it. They used the finest bait in the world, "a good route at good money" . . . few could resist biting. They called it the National Vaudeville Artists, better known later as the N.V.A. (some wag said N.V.A. stood for Never Vex Albee). To make sure of getting members, Albee issued an order that before you could get your contracts for any of the V.M.P.A. (Vaudeville Managers Protective Association) houses (which practically covered all of vaude), you would have to give up your membership in the Rats and be a member in good standing in the N.V.A. To make it double sure, they hired an apartment directly opposite the White Rats' clubhouse, checked all those who were going in, and quickly put them on the blacklist.

Soon the members got wise to what was being done, and little by little the attendance fell off, the dues stopped coming in, and the club had to take a mortgage of $5,000 on its furnishings. That soon was spent, and the bank made them a proposition: they had a "certain party" that would take over the property and even pay the clubhouse debts. The Rats had to take it. It turned out later that the "certain party" was Albee, who paid off the bondholders

(which legally he didn't have to do, as the Rats were bankrupt).
He also supervised a complete renovating job on the already beautiful clubhouse, and in about six months they had a new opening
of the N.V.A. clubhouse. He really had made it even more beautiful than it was, a lot of spic and splendor, plenty of red and
marble. It had 106 sleeping rooms which rented for $1.50 to $3.00
a day, swimming pool, etc. It was so swanky that they claim the
acrobats came in walking on their hands!

Everybody in show biz was there opening night. You just *had* to
be there, as noses were being counted (especially the noses of the
"name acts"), and if you didn't show up, you stood a good chance
of losing your route (if you had one). It was funny that the only
picture in the whole place was a picture of George M. Cohan with
an autograph reading, "To my first Boss, with all kinds of good
wishes—George M. Cohan, March 17, 1919." I say it's funny that a
picture given to Albee should be shown, when it was supposed to
be an *actors' club*!

As secretary Albee stuck in an old vaude actor, Henry Chester-
field, who ran the club as per Albee's orders. Albee gave the actors
a play-or-pay contract, with plenty of fanfare. A few months later
he put back the cancellation clause—without fanfare. He set up a
committee of actors and managers to hear the actors' beefs against
the managers and the complaints of actors against other acts that
stole their material. (The decisions were mostly against the managers in the cases concerning them.) Albee gave tremendous benefit shows, running in four houses at one time with hundreds of top
acts. He had the baskets passed in every vaude house in America
during the N.V.A. week, when extra acts would go on for free
(advertised and boosting biz) and make a plea to the audience to
give to the N.V.A., which was taking care of the poor actors. (Can
you imagine making the public support his company union?) He
made the actors advertise in the special programs for these affairs.
They had to take space according to their salaries. All these things
brought in millions of dollars. In 1916 there was $3,500,000 in the
Fund from these benefits, collections, and programs. A private
joke among acts those days was that after the N.V.A. collections
all the managers and ushers had new suits. You see, there was no
check-up; the ushers would go through a dark theater with an open
basket after each show, which they turned over to the manager,

Lefty's Letters

who in turn sent it to the main office, who in turn turned it over to the N.V.A. Nobody checked what the main office received—catch on?

Albee gave members a $1,000 death benefit. (Duffy & Sweeney wired the N.V.A., "We died here at the matinee, please send $1,000.") Albee would sign the check (he had no official office in the club, in fact at that time he wasn't even a member), and have it photostated and printed in all the trade papers, with a copy of the letter of condolence he sent to the nearest of kin. In 1930 he opened the N.V.A. lodge at Saranac (original idea of William Morris) which was for members of the theatrical profession suffering from TB. He also started the *Vaudeville News*, with Walter Winchell as a columnist (his first job as such), which he believed would put *Variety* out of business. (He also backed the *Star*, a trade paper, to fight *Variety*.) Albee spent all this dough without consulting the board of directors; it was a one-man organization. He later decided to admit lay members and agents and bookers and managers and their friends. They were blackjacked into membership as the actors had been. It got so the members were afraid to talk in the clubhouse because they feared there were dictaphones in the joint. There were—human dictaphones!

In 1934 the White Rats, who went "underground" and tried to get by with a 5 per cent levy on the salaries of the few faithful, had to call it a day, as they couldn't show the AFL any dues-paying members, so they gave up their charter to Equity. Years later the American Federation of Actors (which originally started as an anti-benefit group—you were veep, so should know about it) received the charter from Equity for vaudeville and night clubs; it was the first vaude actors' union in fifteen years. (Now it is called the American Guild of Variety Artists and has jurisdiction over night clubs and what is left of vaude.)

When vaude got real bad, Albee lost interest in the N.V.A.; he didn't need it anymore, and neither it nor anything else could hurt vaude any more than it was already hurt. The N.V.A. had to give up its beautiful clubhouse and take up quarters a few doors up the street, and after a few years they took over the Friars' rooms in the Edison Hotel Annex Building, when the Friars moved to their new home on West Fifty-sixth Street. The N.V.A. walked out of their clubhouse cursing Albee. He never forgave them for it, and when he died he didn't leave them a penny.

The N.V.A. managed to get along without Albee, not in big-time style, but with more self-respect. They give a show annually that brings in enough dough to keep themselves going. The dues are reasonable and they enjoy playing cards and checkers, and exchanging memories. It's a great place for the old-time vaude acts, many of whom were originally White Rats. Funny, eh?—or is it? SEZ

Your *pal*,
LEFTY

Firsts

Dear Joe,

To say that somebody in vaudeville was the first to do a certain act, gag, or piece of business is sticking your neck out further than a giraffe! It is a lot different in show biz than in any other business where you can definitely trace the beginning, like a patent. The same goes for law and medicine, but in vaude you can go back in research just so far. You don't have much chance of tracing back to someone who originated something and didn't get to New York with it (which is practically the patent office of show biz) to show it to the bookers, audiences, and actors. Somebody else who beat them to it would have received credit for being first, because he had a chance to show it on Big Time, while the originator was doing it on small time and wasn't seen or noticed.

There have been many instances where the originator had to cut his own material out of his act to keep from being called a pirate. Taylor Holmes is a case in point. He was one of the first to do Kipling's poem, "Gunga Din," and he did it very well. He was asked by the Keith office to please cut it out of his act on the circuit, because Clifton Crawford, a new headliner, depended on the poem for the finish of his act. Naturally, Taylor Holmes cut it out (rather than maybe lose his route) for about six months, and then decided to put it back in his act, and everybody (including trade papers, who should have known better) accused him of "copying" Clifton Crawford, who by now was identified with "Gunga Din" (which, by the way, he really did great). Taylor Holmes stopped using it.

What you can do in mentioning "firsts" is to say that a certain act was identified with it. There is no doubt that many acts known for such special things were the originators. Naturally they, like anyone else, must have got the idea from something else, because there are very few things new, especially in show biz!

Will Mahoney's dancing on a xylophone with hammers fastened to his shoes was new, because there is no record of anybody doing that particular thing before him; but there were dancers who danced with brushes on their feet, also with buckets and snowshoes. Nothing like dancing on a xylophone, you say? But to a showman that would be merely a "switch," to which me and Aggie don't agree. Stair dancing was done years before Bill "Bojangles" Robinson, but Bill put a new twist to it and added great showmanship, and all the others are forgotten. If Al Leach (a great artist) could come back today and do his stair dance (which he did about twenty years before Bill), everybody would accuse him of taking it from Bill. Harry Richman, who was on radio many years before Jolson, established himself with his own style of singing, and when Jolson went on the radio, he was accused by many people of "copying" Richman's style. Edison invented the phonograph in 1877, but there was a guy called Leon Scott who invented a "phonautograph" in 1857. Edison improved on it and nobody ever heard of Scott. See what I mean?

So when I mention the following firsts, you will know what I mean. Many of them originated what they were doing, many of them revived something that had been forgotten for twenty-five years or more and so were credited for being original, but most of 'em put a new "twist" to it which made it practically an original. After years of research, I want to say that you'd be surprised to learn how few things are "original" in show biz today!

Here are a few that you may find interesting.

1792: Team of Placide & Martin did somersaults over tables and chairs.

1850: Bibs & Bibs known as "Family Affairs," was the oldest comedy skit. Later revived by Mr. & Mrs. Harry Thorne, the first to do it in variety.

1864: Nick Norton & Billy Emmett and Sheridan & Mack were the first to do a double Dutch act. The latter did "Heinrich's Return" or "The Emigrants."

1865: First real double Irish act was done by McNulty & Murray, "The Boys from Limerick" (long before Harry & John Kernell).

1869: Jim Kehoe invented the Kehoe Clubs (used in swinging contests).

1870: Harry Montague did the first double-entendre act.

1872: Walter Wentworth did the first contortion act in variety.

Hugh Dougherty and Ad Ryman were the first to do "stump speeches" in variety. (Done earlier in minstrel shows.)

Colonel Burgess was the first to wear big comedy shoes.

Sam Rickey was a bit ahead of the original Pat Rooney as the first well-known Irish comic, but Pat Rooney was the first to be recognized as a star.

1873: Maggie Weston introduced the first "Irish biddy" in variety.

Sandford & Wilson were one of the first comedy musical acts.

The French Twins and the Raymond Sisters were the first sister acts.

The first blackface quartette was called the "Hamtown Students."

John Le Clair was one of the first single jugglers in variety.

The original comedy acrobatic act was performed by Johnson & Bruno.

1874: The first German comedians appeared; they were Gus Williams, George S. Knight, and Lew Spencer. (Gus Williams was tops.)

De Witt Cook did a club-juggling act.

1876: E. M. Hall was considered the greatest of all banjo players.

Frank Bush, Howard & Thompson, and Sam Curtis started the "Jew comic" craze. (All were non-Jewish.)

Jimmy Bradley originated the sand-jig dance and Kitty O'Neill was first woman to do it.

1877: First real sketch artists were John and Maggie Fielding, followed by Charles Rogers and Mattie Vickers.

1877: The Original Four Kings, Emerson, Clark, and the Daly Bros., were first to do kicking at objects, such as hats, cigar boxes, tambourines, etc.

The Poole Bros. did the first acrobatic clog dance.

1878: Gus Hill was the first outstanding club swinger.

Jap & Fanny Delano were the first outstanding man and woman talking act.

First water-tank act, such as eating under water, was Wallace, the "Man Fish."

Lurline was the first woman performing an underwater tank act.

1879: Maggie Cline was the first single-woman comedy Irish singer.

Fanny Beane, Millie, and the Barretts did the first "lady" song and dance acts.

First variety children stage artists were Baby Rhinehart, Little Rosebud, Baby McDonald, and Master Dunn.

First male singing trio was the Three Rankins.

Bunth & Rudd did a double comedy magic act.

1880: Imro Fox was the first single comedy magician.

James F. Hoey ("Old Hoss" Hoey & Evans) was the first "nut" comedian.

Ryan & Ryan did a burlesque boxing bit; so did McNish & Johnson, Gallagher & Griffin, Casey & Reynolds, and McCabe & Emmett. Miller & Lyles came years later and revived it. Moran & Mack took it from them.

1881: Carrie Swain was the first woman in blackface to do a knockabout acrobatic act.

1884: Weber & Fields first did an Irish act dressed in short breeches, including paper tearing, and clog dancing. They appeared between acts of a melodrama at the old Windsor Theatre on the Bowery.

1885: Leon, William Henry Rice, Charles Heywood, and Lind? were the first of the female impersonators.

Lottie Gilson was the first to have a singing "plant" in the audience, also first to sing to a "baldheaded" man in the audience, later shining mirror on his head, etc. (She did this act up to 1905.)

1886: Johnny Lorenze (Cook & Lorenze) did first turkey trot in barrooms with Guy Hawley. Guy Hawley was the first to do a "break" on the piano.

1886: First buck dancing done in burly by Johnny Jess (he also played in variety).

Bert Williams first to pull expression, "It's a bear"; he danced on sidewalks of Denver, when the turkey trot was called the "Denver Drag."

Rocking table first done by Caroll & Nealey, the "Nickelplated Coons"; they used two tables and a barrel. Afterwards done by Sully & Nealey, also Buckley & Dwyer. But it was Bert Melrose who made it famous.

First comedy piano act done by Charlie Thatcher; he did it as a specialty in the pit for his overture in Denver. Will H. Fox was the first to do a comedy piano act on the stage, followed by Tom Waters.

1888: Blockson & Burns did a comedy perch act (suspended from a wire, doing all kinds of impossible stunts). Collins & Hart came later and made it famous all over the world.

The American Four were considered the greatest quartette; it consisted of two famous two-man acts who doubled up. Wayne & Lovely, Cotton & Bedue; and the Big Four, same type of act, came later and also were great, with Lester & Allen and Smith & Waldron.

The first "kidding" act and "topical songsters" were Lester & Allen.

Lew Randall was the first buck-and-wing dancer.

Dainty Katie Seymour (of London) was the first "skirt" dancer.

Charles Guyer & Nellie O'Neill were the first "roughhouse" dancers.

Delahanty & Hengler were the first to do "neat" Irish song and dance.

Professor Davis and Trovollo were the first ventriloquists to introduce the mechanical walking and talking figures.

The first "electrical clown" was Herr Tholen; he sang with a poodle.

Topack & Steele were the first knockabout comedians.

Major Burke was the original lightning-drill artist with musket and bayonet.

Melville & Stetson, a sister act, were first to do imitations.

Lester & Williams, Arthur O'Brien, Lew Carroll, Joe Flynn (he wrote "Down Went McGinty") of Sheridan & Flynn, and Harry & John Dillon started the parody craze. (Hoey & Lee came later.)

Caron & Herbert were the first acrobatic clowns in variety.

The Borani Brothers (Englishmen) were the first to do a certain somersault known as the "Borani somersault."

The Garnella Brothers were first to do the "shoulder to shoulder" double.

The Sigrist Family were the first American acrobatic troupe.

The Bohee Bros. were first to do a double banjo song-and-dance act.

Harper & Stencil were the first double one-legged song-and-dance men. Harper had his right leg off, while Stencil had his left leg off. They wore the same size shoes and would buy just one pair for both of them.

Yeamans & Titus (Annie Yeamans' daughter) did one of the first piano acts.

Jolly Nash and John W. Kelly were the first extemporaneous singers.

George Cain did the first "smoke" singing; he would put the full lighted cigar in his mouth while singing, and the smoke would come out of his mouth. The song he sang was "While I'm Smoking."

George Wilson introduced the first "laughing song."

Harry G. Richmond was the first to do a "tramp" act.

Kelly & Murphy did the first boxing act on the stage in variety.

1895: Lumiere's Motion Pictures were first shown in Keith's Union Square Theatre.

1898: First continuous vaude at Keith's in Boston. Next year Proctor did it at the Twenty-third Street Theatre, beating Keith to it in New York.

1906: J. Royer West and Van Siclyn used sandwich men to advertise their acts to agents in front of the St. James Building and in front of Hammerstein's. Laurie & Aleen did it years later at the American Theatre, as did Bob Hope and other acts.

1907: First "family vaudeville."

Harry Sefton and O'Brien Havel were among the first to do "drunken" acrobatic rolls.

George Primrose was the first to wear different colored evening clothes.

First barefoot dancer in vaude was Mildred Howard De Gray.

1908: The Hawaiian Trio (with Toots Papka) was the first to introduce the steel guitar.

Toots Papka was the first Hawaiian dancer in vaude.

1909: Chuck Conners, in an act at Loew's Columbia, Brooklyn, first used the expression, "gorilla," meaning a tough guy or hoodlum.

Harrison Brockbank was first to do Kipling's *Barrack-Room Ballads* in New York.

Henry E. Dixie was first comedian to do a burlesque on ballet.

Bickle & Watson were first to do burlesque music.

Billy Gould was first to do "conversational song and dance," telling gags while dancing with gal.

1920: Belle Baker was first to do "Eli, Eli" in vaude. Allan Rogers was the first tenor to do it in vaude.

Brendel & Burt were first to do duet with phonograph record; Brendel did lip movements to Tetrazzini's singing.

The first act doing double talking with a phonograph was done by Richard Craig, Sr.

1921: Reeder & Armstrong were about the first double piano act.

1922: Aileen Stanley was first on stage with a radio outfit and amplifier.

1924: Roland Hayes was first Negro to do a concert. (Jules Bledsoe of Francis & Bledsoe was second.)

1929: Charlie Freeman was the originator of the intact rotating units for the Inter-State and Keith Circuits.

And here are a few odds and ends:

The Barlow Brothers and Girard Bros. were the originators of the double sand-jig dancing.

Fred Hillebrand (& Vera Michelina) was the first to use, "Give the little girl a hand!" It was taken by Texas Guinan, who said, "Give the little girl a *big* hand!" and became famous for it!

Shooting finishes and black-outs, which so many acts and revues used, was done by the Byrnes Bros. in "Eight Bells" way back in the '90s.

Joe Hyman (Hyman & Franklin) was the writer of and the first to do "Cohen on the Telephone." This American act spent over forty years playing in England, where it is still a big hit.

Benny Fields (*not* Rudy Vallee) was the first to sing through a megaphone on stage.

Blossom Seeley was the first to start the finger-snapping style of singing syncopation.

Clarice Vance had the first mirror dress. Mindil Kingston (World & Kingston) wore a cloak with mirrors in *Follies* of 1910. Miss Vance sued. Miss Kingston claimed her father invented it over 40 years before (1870), that mirror dresses was the natural evolution from mirror held in the hand against a spotlight for flirtation numbers. Miss Vance won, by proving there were no spotlights in those days.

Jack Norworth was the first actor to write a column for V*ariety*.

This will give you an idea of some of the "firsts" in variety and vaude. I mentioned many more in my other letters to you, which you can add to this list if you want to.

There were many arguments in vaude as to "firsts." There were two acrobats who claimed they were the first to use *colored* handkerchiefs to wipe off the perspiration, instead of the regular white ones used by all other acrobatic acts. So you can just imagine.

Me and Aggie never did hear anyone claim that they were the first to kill vaudeville, and believe me, a lot of 'em could have claimed it and been right. SEZ

Your pal,
LEFTY

Accompanied by . . .

Dear Joe,

If you were any kind of a vaude fan, you must have heard some act reciting Robert W. Service's "Spell of the Yukon." With an amber spot and a red bandana around his neck to lend atmosphere, he'd go into:

> "The Ragtime Kid was having a drink,
> There was no one else on the stool,
> And the stranger stumbled across the room
> And flopped down like a fool.
>
> In a buckskin shirt that was glazed with dirt
> He sat and I seen him sway,
> With a talon hand he clutched the keys,
> God, but the man could play!"   Etc., etc.

The audience would settle back and recite word for word with the actor.

Hartley Claude Myrick was the original "ragtime kid" of the poem; he passed on a few years ago in Seattle, Washington, at the age of 65. When he was a young man, he played piano in all the honky-tonks from Nome to Chilkoot Pass and was known as the Ragtime Kid. His passing brings to mind many of the "ragtime kids" who were so important to vaude in its heyday. They first started out as just piano players; then when they got a bit more important they were billed, "at the piano, Mr. So-and-So," and when vaude got real classy, it copied from the concert stage and billed them as "accompanists." Often they became part of the act and sometimes the best part of it.

Back in the 1920s it was estimated that one third of all the vaude acts had a piano player. Many times there were so many piano acts on one bill that they followed each other, which made it nice for the second piano player, who inherited warm keys.

At first the piano player got no billing; he would sneak onto the stage in the dark while the act he was playing for was in the spotlight, and at the finish he would sneak off the way he came on. Some of them were loaned to the star by the publishing house to help put over its songs. Then when single singers found it was better to carry a piano player than to depend on orchestras, they started to bill them.

Where piano players came from and where they went to, no one knows and no one seems to care. About one in every ten piano players in vaude was a musician or entertainer, whose business was piano playing. Many of these later became recognized composers, mostly of pop songs. But many of them played by ear, and when they didn't do that, they knew enough "classical" music to get by with the audience. While the gal was making a change, the piano player had to do a solo or specialty. Some were tricksters, like playing with one hand, or playing standing on their heads, or playing "Dixie" with the left hand and "Yankee Doodle" with the right, "both simultaneously," as they would announce it. And others would play "Alexander's Ragtime Band" as different composers might have written it.

Piano players were an easy lot. They didn't care if the piano was set in a wood scene or at the end of a stream or even a street; the backdrop was immaterial to the piano player. He could play anywhere. He was satisfied as long as the gallery boys left him alone, which was sometimes hard for a gallery to do, especially when he was dressed in tails or a near-fitting tux to kinda classy up the act. When playing at the Jefferson on East Fourteenth Street, Loew's Delancey Street, or the Colonial, a piano player would take no chances and would wear street clothes, which many times was just as funny!

Single women used up more piano players than anybody else. With a single woman he had a heavier job than just accompanying. He would take care of the railroad and hotel reservations, check the baggage, collect the salary, pay out the tips, take care of the rehearsals and props, and maybe bring up coffee to the lady with the morning mail, and sometimes ended by marrying the gal.

Nora Bayes had about the most piano players of anyone during her vaude career. She had such great accompanists as Harry Akst (who accompanied Al Jolson on all his GI tours), Lou Alter, Gus Klienecke, Bernard Fairfax, Seymour Simon, Robert Goldie, Abel Baer (writer of "Mother's Eyes"), the great George Gershwin, Ted Shapiro, Edmund Goulding (later to become a famous Hollywood director), Eddie Weber, Leo Edwards, Dudley Wilkinson, and Dave Stamper (composer for many *Follies*). Irene Bordoni was her closest runner-up, using Lou Grandi, Mattie Levine, Lou Alter, Leo Edwards, Gitz Rice, Eddie Weber, Leon Vavarra, and Melville Ellis to play for her. Anna Chandler had Eddie Fitzgerald, Lester Lee, Arthur Samuels, and Sydney Landfield (now a Hollywood producer). Marion Harris had Billy Griffith, Jessie Greer, Phil Goldberg (her first husband), Lou Handman, J. Russell Robinson, and Eddie Weber.

Eva Tanguay started in 1896 with George M. Fenberg; he was her director-pianist. She never used a piano on stage, as she needed all the room she could get. Her piano players would work in the pit, mostly as director, and of course would play for her rehearsals. She had Jack Stern, Charlie Seville, Al Pardo (her husband), and Eddie Weber, who played for her for ten years—a record with Eva! Sophie Tucker had Slim Pressler, Al Siegel, Jack Carroll, and Ted Shapiro. Ted has been with her for over twenty-five years, which makes him the dean of all accompanists of lady singles.

Among the men singles, Frank Fay used up plenty of ivory ticklers, like Harry Akst, Adam Carroll, Dave Dwyer, Clarence Gaskill, and Gitz Rice. And Harry Fox as a single (and when playing with Beatrice Curtis) had Harry De Costa, Harry Gray, Lew Pollack, Jean Schwartz, Charlie Seville, and Eddie Weber.

Leo Edwards and Eddie Weber are about tops for the number of acts they played for. Leo's list has names like Lillian Russell, Andrew Mack, George Primrose, Ralph Hertz, Clark & Bergman, Grace LaRue, Fanny Brice, Kitty Gordon, Orville Harold, Marie Dressler, Cissie Loftus, Bunny Granville, Marie Cahill, Adelaide & Hughes, Bessie Wynn, Mabel McCane, Nora Bayes, John Charles Thomas, Marie Tempest, and Irene Bordoni to his credit. Eddie Weber is right up there with names like Eva Tanguay, Adelaide & Hughes, Harry Fox & Beatrice Curtis, Whiting & Burt, Marion Harris, Fanny Brice, the Cameron Sisters, Karyl Norman, Ruth Roland, Irene Bordoni, Carter De Haven & Flora Parker, Nora Bayes, Cross & Dunn, John L. Fogarty, Fanny Ward, Ann Seymour, Frank DeVoe, and Estelle Taylor.

You will notice that the vaude piano players were interchangeable and had a great turnover. Some only wanted to play for acts around New York. Acts would change piano players because of temperament, or with single women because "love" had entered the picture, or for a dozen other reasons. When an act went bad, they'd always blame it on the piano player, but in the old days a good one could always get a job.

To mention just a few of the boys who were tops at "thumping the box," there were Clarence Gaskill, Harry Akst, Jerry Jarnegan, Burt Green, Mike Bernard, Lou Alter, Ernie Ball, Lew Pollack, Lou Handman, Harry Richman, Harold Arlen, Martin Broones, Halsey Mohr, Jimmy Steiger, Andy Byrnes, J. Fred Coots, Adam Carroll, Abel Baer, Con Conrad, Fred Clinton, Harry De Costa, Vincent Lopez, Joe Santley, Raymond Walker, Elmore White, Harry Tighe, Willie White, Clarence Senna, Eddie Moran, Harry Carroll, Joe Daly, Sidney Franklin, Mel Morris, Martin Freed, Billy Griffith, Jack Joyce, Arthur Johnson, Gitz Rice, Charlie Straight, Cliff Friend, Al Siegel, Jack Denny, Cliff Hess, Arthur Freed, Abner Silver, Henry Marshall, George Gershwin, and Jerome Kern, who played for Edna Wallace Hopper when he was a publishing-house staff writer, salesman, and piano player!

Among the women accompanists were Emma Adelphi (the late Mrs. Jack Norworth), who played for Jack, Billy Glason, and was the partner of Janet Adair. Mildred Brown played for Rae Samuels and Marguerite Young; Edyth Baker played for Harry Fox; and the great Hildegarde played for Wait Hoyt, Mickey Cochrane, Dora "Boots" Early, and the DeMarcos, until she decided to play and sing herself into stardom. Lou Silvers, Mlle. Henrietta Henri, and Florence Kingsley played for Eddie Miller. Dolly Jordan had Theo Lightner (who was also part of the Lightner Sisters and Alexander act) play for her. Rae Samuels had Mildred Land and Bea Walker as pianists. The gal stuck to their jobs longer than the average male accompanist.

When vaude fell apart, many of the piano players did very well writing hit songs, and others spread around cafés and night clubs. Many, too many, have changed their piano for a harp!

Of all the old-time vaude accompanists, there are still two who are working at their trade and doing great. Ray Walker (writer of "Good Night, Nurse" and other songs), who played for Sophie Tucker, Mae West, and Marie Fenton when they first started, and who has played everything from the Chatham Club in New York's Chinatown to vaude and then to night clubs, now at the age of seventy is still accompanying the future greats in the plush cafés of Florida. The other is Ted Shapiro, rounding out over a quarter of a century with the indestructible Sophie Tucker.

They were a great bunch who helped many an act to get over, playing on vaude pianos, some of which were tuned, and what would us guys have done when we went out after the show at night for fun if we hadn't been "accompanied by . . ." the boys who furnished the "mood music"? SEZ

Your pal,

LEFTY

2

THESE WERE
THE KINGS,
RULERS, AND
CZARS OF
THE NOW-
FORGOTTEN
KINGDOM OF
THE TWO- AND
THREE-A-DAY

Tony Pastor

Antonio (Tony) Pastor, known as the godfather of vaudeville, was born on Greenwich Street, New York City, on May 28, 1832. Some claim he wasn't Italian but was of New England stock on his mother's side and had a Spanish father who was supposed to have been a great violinist. Nobody ever really knew and Tony Pastor never spoke about it.

We do know that his first appearance was at the age of six, at the Dey Street Church, singing duets with C. B. Woodruff. In 1846 he joined Barnum's Museum, where he corked up and played tambourine and was in the minstrel band. The next year he became a minstrel man, then followed that by becoming an apprentice with John J. Nathan's Circus. It was in this circus that he first sang comic songs. He made his debut in the arena that fall at Welsh's National Amphitheatre in Philadelphia.

When the ringmaster, Neil Jamison, died, he was succeeded by Tony, who became the youngest ringmaster in all of the circus biz! He wrote an act called "Peasant's Frolic," which later became popular under the name of "Peter Jenkins." It was a rural character acting stewed who, after a lot of cross-fire talk with the ringmaster (or some other performer) and many prat falls, finally stripped to tights and did a riding act. (This bit was used in circuses for many years.) He also tumbled with the acrobats and danced "Lucy Long" in the minstrel show. (All circuses had minstrel shows in those days.) In 1851 he was at the Bowery Amphitheatre at 37 Bowery, where he was ringmaster and also acted in dramatic skits for the first time. In 1857 he became a clown at the Nixon Palace Gardens in New York.

In 1860 he made his variety stage debut at Frank River's Melodeon in Philadelphia, and decided to quit the circus and adopt variety as a permanent profession. Back in New York, he was a comic vocalist at the Broadway Music Hall (formerly Wal-

ACK.ry

lack's Theatre, on Broadway near Broome Street) when it was first opened on March 22, 1861. Tony stayed there for a year. He then went to his own place at 444 Broadway and stayed until 1865. It was a honky-tonk, offering beer, wine, liquor, and a few hostesses. The only name the place had was 444! In 1865 he and an old minstrel man by the name of Sam Sharpley took over Volk's Garden at 201 Bowery. They fixed it up and named it Pastor's Opera House, and successfully managed it for ten years.

At that time the East Side of New York was the popular residential section and more purely American than any section in the city. The door plates of the old Knickerbocker families were on thousands of homes. Pastor invited the women to come in to see his variety show. Up to this time variety had played to strictly stag audiences and some of the gals who came in "to rest their feet"; it was pretty hard to get nice women and children to see Pastor's show.

Tony tried coaxing 'em in by giving out bonbons, dolls, and flowers, and set Fridays apart as Ladies' Night, when husbands brought their wives and young men their sweethearts free of charge. This didn't get over so good, so he tried more material arguments, giving away bags of flour, packages of coffee, tons of coal, hams, and even sewing machines, but this didn't get the gals either. But when he announced that on a certain day he would give away twenty-five silk dresses—he got 'em! Macy's on a bargain day wasn't in it! You could always reach a woman with a dress (of course you could do pretty good with a mink coat, too). The next thing Pastor gave away was bonnets; with the aid of some milliners he displayed twenty-five hats of the latest fashion, and it took twenty-five cops to keep the gals in line. There was no vaudeville about that—it was just plain variety. His business prospered. (Funny that almost seventy-five years later other showmen thought of the same idea, when they ran Country Store Nights, Bank Nights, Dish Nights, etc., and radio and TV weren't far behind with their Break the Bank, Winner Take All, and even once gave away an announcer for a week end. New stuff, eh?)

It was at this time that Pastor got the idea of organizing a variety road show while his house was closed for the summer. He started out at Paterson, New Jersey (his first trip as a manager), with Tony Pastor's Own Company. There were other traveling companies at the time, but Pastor had a real fine variety show with plenty of comedy, and it was a big success playing high-class theaters at high prices. He increased his annual tours from three months to six months and played every prominent town on the map. He first visited New England, then extended his tours to the West, and finally to California. While in New York he played two weeks to big biz at Laura Keene's former house, the Olympic, several weeks at the Grand Opera House, the Academy of Music, and Hammerstein's Columbus Theatre in Harlem. (This later was known as Proctor's 125th Street.)

Having thus opened the way in getting first-class patronage, his lead was quickly followed. John B. Haverly, one of America's greatest showmen, established a grand variety house in Chicago, the Adelphi; John Stetson, the Howard in Boston; Colonel Sim, the Park Theatre in Brooklyn; and many more.

It was on October 24, 1881, that Pastor opened his Fourteenth Street Theatre in the Tammany Hall Building. New York never had a theater just like Pastor's. There was something about it, call it atmosphere or whatever you want, but it was "different" than any other theater in America from 1881 to 1906. The theater really was opened in February, 1881, with parodies on Gilbert & Sullivan, like "The Pie-Rats of Pen-Yan," but they didn't prove successful, so Pastor opened in October with a straight variety show that was as clean as a hound's tooth. The theater had a special distinction, a lot of which was contributed by Tony himself. He was a little man who wore boots with high heels and an opera hat, which he would open up with a snap and put on "cockily." He did it mostly to kinda cover up when he forgot his lyrics. He knew 1,500 songs. (I have never heard of a singer before or since that had that large a repertoire; Tommy Lyman is supposed to have 500 songs that he can sing at a moment's notice.)

Tony Pastor had a very pleasant personality and loved variety actors and show biz in general. He was the only manager who was an honorary member of the White Rats. During all the forty years of his managerial career, Pastor never *closed* an act, and that was long before play-or-pay contracts. If a very bad act knew enough to quit at Pastor's, they were always paid in full! Tony was a very religious man (had a shrine backstage). He didn't pay big salaries unless he had to, and then it was only big for him and not comparable to what other managers had to pay for the same acts. He couldn't very well compete with other managers, because his was a tiny house with less than 300 seats.

If he liked your act, he would tell you that you could bring in your trunk any time you wanted to, and many did when they had an open week. They would just show up, and he would tell the boy to put out the name in the billing and on the stage cards. (Each act was announced by a card on an easel on the side of the stage.) James C. Morton (Morton & Moore) started as a card boy at Pastor's. Acts working at Pastor's didn't interfere with any other circuit, and Tony was particularly great for giving newcomers advice, encouragement, and a chance. Pastor's in the early days was a very important "showing spot" for a new act. All the actors, agents and managers would be out front (the same as at the Palace and Hammerstein's in later years). All this made it possible for Pastor to get acts for much less than anybody else.

When B. F. Keith opened the Union Square Theatre just a few blocks from Pastor's and charged 50 cents for a good seat in a beautiful little theater with many headliners and top acts, Pastor had to cut his prices from $1.00 down to 10-20-30 cents, and he never could raise them again. Even at those prices, biz fell off; his old customers started to patronize the theaters uptown, but Pastor never could raise them again. Even at those prices, biz fell off; his Proctor, and "all those other fellers stand all that worry, running those big chains." (He always used the expression, "Jimenety," when he was excited; he never cursed.)

This little gentleman who was so ambitious when a youngster had "cooled down" and had no ambition for big theaters and big dough. He was satisfied with his tiny theater and to be able to go on once in awhile (toward the finish of Pastor's, he would only appear when he felt like it) and sing his songs. There were only six big vaude managers who had stage backgrounds: Martin Beck, who gave it up early and made a fortune; F. F. Proctor, who started as an acrobat, and also made millions; Percy Williams, who acted and also wrote plays but not for long, and left millions; Wilmer & Vincent, who spent about twenty years as variety artists and writers, then went into management and made many millions; and Tony Pastor, who made it possible for all of them to cash in with his idea of clean vaudeville, and who died on August 28, 1908, and left less than $6,000!

He left more than money; he left a good feeling in the hearts of all the people who knew him.

There never lived, then or now, in or out of vaude, any better liked theatrical manager than Antonio (Tony) Pastor!

Benjamin Franklin Keith

Benjamin Franklin Keith, born in Hillsboro Bridge, New Hampshire, in 1846, was said to have been originally a purser on a steamer, getting over into the show biz through the candy concession on a circus for which E. F. Albee was the legal adjuster or "fixer." Laying over in Boston one winter (about 1883), he (in partnership with Colonel Austin) exhibited a prematurely born Negro baby, perhaps the first of the incubator baby shows, though there was no incubator available for the puny infant. When the child grew too large to appeal to the curious, Keith suggested to his partner, George H. Bacheller, that they fit up the store into a dime museum. The venture was immediately successful, for the dime museum was then in its heyday of popularity.

The layout of the museums was always the same: a curio hall in which the crowd gathered for the next show, and a theater, where an hour's performance was given. There was magic in the name of "museum," for the very religious customers salved their consciences by pretending that it was really the museum they came to, and the theater, "that abode of the devil," was merely incidental. Barnum had found that out years before, and the Boston Museum, eventually to become the home of classical drama, was already in the field, giving full-length plays (including one that has been running for the last sixteen years in California, *The Drunkard*). The plays did two shows a day. Keith favored vaudeville with a show running an hour.

Keith found that many persons would ask at the box office when the next show started and, on being told that there would be a wait of half an hour or more, would turn away, unwilling to spend the waiting time in the dreary curio hall. One Sunday morning he took space in the Boston papers to advertise the continuous performance. "Come when you please; stay as long as you like." The idea was so revolutionary that even his stage manager and lecturer, Sam K. Hodgdon, could not grasp the idea. Keith told him to go ahead and he would show him how it worked.

Hodgdon opened the show with a brief lecture on some relics brought back by the Greeley Relief Expedition from the Arctic. When the first show was over, Keith told Hodgdon to go on again without clearing the house. Hodgdon protested that most of the people who had just seen him would walk out. "I hope they do," was Keith's reply, and Hodgdon got the idea. This made Sam K. Hodgdon the first "chaser" act in the business. Of course Barnum had a pretty good idea of how to get rid of many customers (many years before Keith) by putting up a sign reading "This way to the Egress"—many of his customers thought it was some kind of an animal and, walking through the door, found themselves out on the street.

Keith's idea worked well except on holidays, when the crowd had plenty of time and could stick around. It took a pretty strong guy to stand two hours of the sort of show Keith put on in those days, although he used a fair grade of acts, one of the most popular being Jerry & Helen Cohan (father and mother of Josephine and George M.). With growing prosperity, Keith elaborated his show and put on a comic opera troupe, handled by Milton Aborn (who was the leader in tablo'd opera). The productions were mostly of Gilbert & Sullivan works, which were in public domain (no copyright laws then). The idea clicked, but not as well as it should have, and Keith flashed an appeal to his old friend Albee to come and see what he could do. Albee cleaned up the front of the house (which had cages full of smelly animals) and business picked up. It p'cked up so well that Albee decided to try out his idea of a de luxe theater. Keith shied away (being pretty close with a buck). Albee proposed building nothing short of a palace, and Keith could not see where the money was coming from.

Always the dominant personality, Albee moved in on Keith, took the reins out of his hands, and arranged to build, mostly with money borrowed from the wealthy Catholic Diocese of Boston. To get this dough he had to assure the churchmen that the performance would be clean and unobjectionable. Keith's Colonial, Boston, was opened in 1893. It was Albee, rather than Keith, who carried cleanliness to an almost fanatical degree. Profanity and vulgarity were rigidly censored. It was reported that a well-known elocutionist, playing there, was ordered to cut from a Shakesperean selection the phrase, "And straight from the mouth of hell let loose the dogs of war." She was told to substitute "hades," though she protested that she had read the lines, without protest, at hundreds of church events. It might be good enough for the churches, but Keith's was Keith's and Hell was Hell and never the twain should meet! (Or at least, not until many years later.)

To insure supervision, the superintendent of one of the leading Sunday schools in Boston was hired to stand at the rear of the house, and any minor infraction resulted in a note being sent backstage to the act and the stage manager. Church people approved, and the idea was plenty profitable until the era of nudity brought about an almost complete reversal of form.

The Keith idea was extended to Providence, to Philadelphia, and eventually to New York, when Keith took over the Union Square Theatre, which up to then was the home of the legit stage.

For a long time the out-of-town houses were no match for the sumptuous and beautiful Boston Theatre, but as Albee became more firmly entrenched in the saddle, he went upon an orgy of building, the Chestnut Street Theatre in Philadelphia being the second. And it was here that Keith and Albee met one of their few defeats. The old Bijou on Eighth Street was managed by a relative of Albee's, a fussy old guy whose chief complaint was that he could not train the people from Camden to use the aisle in making their exits from the gallery. They went over the backs of the seats, to his great distress. He had no drag with the newspapermen. But his assistant, Harry Jordan, was tremendously popular. Keith was having trouble with his building permit for the Chestnut Street house, and he propositioned Jordan to grease the wheels, in return for which he was to be made the house manager.

Jordan did a great job, but as the house neared completion, Keith told him regretfully that he was too young to be entrusted with so important a theater. Jordan said nothing, but in a week or two a law was introduced in the Pennsylvania legislature that all theaters not yet opened must have a lobby width equal to that of the rear of the auditorium. This would mean no license for the Keith house, which had but a single frontage on Chestnut Street, and no chance to buy on either side. Jordan was called in again, the law was pigeonholed, and Jordan moved in as manager.

Keith and Albee respected Jordan because he had licked them. They never had reason to regret his appointment. He stayed there until the finish of the two-a-day and became the best-liked manager on the circuit by the actors who played for him. He had a great idea to stop arguments about the star dressing room by naming them after states. There was no star dressing room at Keith's Chestnut Street, in Philadelphia. (It was also the first vaude theater in America that had the stage manager dressed in evening clothes —long done in England.)

Keith was a little man, both in stature and mentality. He had a curiously cold and colorless personality and he was petty in little things. He had no use for the people he could not buy and small use for them when he bought them. Epes W. Sargent (Chicot), the famous critic on *Variety*, refused a $100 bill offered to him by Keith and completely lost Keith's approval. If he could not be "tipped," he was to be feared!

For years Keith hated F. F. Proctor, who had beat him into New York with continuous vaude. When the booking office was in the process of formation, Keith insisted that the meetings were to be held in Boston. The deal was practically set up when some of the managers insisted that F. F. Proctor be included. Keith refused, but eventually gave in, and Proctor was invited to come to Boston. Proctor said no, and it took a couple of more days to get Keith to consent to go to New York. Later, when the company was formed, Keith suggested to a newspaperman that he dictate his story in the Keith apartment, so he might supply any missing details. The invitation was accepted (the man was Chicot) and all went well until the writer dictated, "At this point, adjournment was taken to New York, to include F. F. Proctor in the negotiations." Keith was on his feet in an instant. Two hours later, this compromise line was agreed on: "At this point, Mr. Keith having business in New York, adjournment was had to that city and F. F. Proctor was invited to sit in with the others." Keith's face had been saved, though everybody in show biz knew that Proctor had forced the change.

When the first Mrs. Keith (Mary Catherine Branley) died in 1910, she left $500 each to four Catholic institutions and the rest of her estate went to her son Paul. (She was a very devout Catholic, and contributed a lot to charity when she was alive.) In the early days when B. F. started, she ran the boardinghouse for the actors working at the museum and theater. After her death B. F. gave his son two million bucks before marrying the daughter of P. B. Chase (owner of the Chase Theatre, Washington, D. C.). He suffered a nervous breakdown on his honeymoon traveling around the world in his yacht. He was never quite himself again and gladly turned over control of the organization to Albee (who had it anyway); the old gent was willing to take the credit, but took no active part. Eventually nobody paid any attention to the boss, Keith. Any order he gave required an O.K. from Albee—and B. F. gave few orders, being content to "play" manager of the little Bijou, his original Boston house.

He died shortly after his second marriage, cruising on his yacht in Florida waters. His death caused scarcely a ripple in vaudeville, because he had become a nonenity. He left the bulk of his property to his son Paul and Albee long before his death to get away from the inheritance tax. His estimated fortune was from eight to ten millions. His second wife, Ethel Chase Keith, got a prenuptial settlement of half a million!

Besides the dough, he left the name of Keith, which was known all over the world, but it was just a name, because he cut but a small figure in the actual development of vaudeville. The only thing he could lay claim to as an originator and contributor to vaude was the continuous performance idea.

In the last years of vaudeville, when they got away from the clean, refined, wholesome entertainment that had made the name of Keith famous (although it was Pastor who really started it) and allowed profanity, nudity, and dirty gags to sneak in, even the great name of Keith was forgotten!

Edward Franklin Albee

From an "outside" ticket man and a "fixer" with a circus to being the czar of all vaudeville! That's what happened to a kid born in Machias, Maine, in 1857, by the name of Edward Franklin Albee! His work with circuses gave him the shrewdness and the motto, "Never give a sucker an even break," which carried him through as top man in a fantastic era of show biz!

Meeting B. F. Keith, who was a candy butcher with one of the circuses that Albee was a "fixer" with, was his springboard to being top man some day. When Keith opened his little museum in Boston, he called on Albee when he was in a jam or needed showmanship advice. When Keith became partners with Mr. George Bacheller, it was on condition that he meet Bacheller's bankroll of $10,000. Keith called Albee, who came to Boston with the circus bankroll, matched Bacheller's money, and a couple of days later got his money back. The venture was a success with Bacheller's money alone!

The story became authentic with the next move, for which Albee is the authority. Keith and Bacheller split. (Bacheller went to Providence, Rhode Island, where he owned and managed the Westminster Theatre for many years.) Keith continued in Boston, and when the museum was petering out, he called on Albee again.

Albee made another trip to Boston. Coming down Washington Street on a hot day he came to the Bijou, an upstairs house to which Keith had moved. In the narrow lobby was a cage containing a number of animals, a couple of raccoons, a monkey, and a few more smelly citizens of the forest, which Keith regarded as a business attractor, but which Albee no liked. Keith was offering Gilbert & Sullivan and other nonroyalty-paying musicals. Albee figured the class of women patrons to whom the bills most strongly appealed would be kept away by the smelly menagerie. So he took the animals out and redecorated the lobby with gay-colored fans and Japanese umbrellas. Business jumped away up—and Albee moved in!

Eventually he sold the timid Keith the idea of building a real theater. The adjoining property could be bought cheaply, but Albee's ideas were far from cheap. He wanted a theater as magnificent as the Tabor Grand in Denver. That was the most magnificent theater in the country at that time. They could swing the land deal. Much of the construction money came from the Catholic Church. There was method in Albee's financial scheme. Boston was a strongly Catholic town. The Diocese was rich. If their money was invested in a theater of the sort Albee outlined, the church would get behind the enterprise, not only to encourage clean shows, but to get its money back. The Protestant angle was taken care of by the engagement of the superintendent of one of the fashionable Sunday schools; he was a sort of reception committee and floor manager, who also listened for any blue material pulled on stage. Had Boston boasted a larger Jewish population, it is certain that Albee would have worked a rabbi into the scheme of things.

With a really beautiful theater presenting smart and clean vaude and miniature operas staged by Milton Aborn, the Keith Colonial got away to a runaway start and its fame spread throughout the country. To have visited Boston without having gone to Keith's was like coming to New York and not seeing Broadway! The customers were taken on tour and the cellar was as spic and span as the auditorium. It was Albee's idea to spread an $89 red rug in front of the white-washed coal bin! It was a sensation and was talked about more than the show. The locals were steady in their patronage. Keith was on the crest of the wave, and Albee was making the waves. Other houses were soon opened, in Philadelphia next, then in New York.

When Albee moved over to New York, he still retained his office in Boston. Although he was practically the head of the circuit, he was to all but a few insiders just a name. He never was a good mixer, but he made an effort to impress and one of his appeals was his stories of the old circus days. He had a raft of them, and one of his favorites was the one about the efforts of a Texas sheriff to put a lien on the show. He boarded the train at the first stop this side of the Texas line, intending to serve his papers as soon as they reached Texas soil. On the excuse that the privilege car was too crowded, Albee coaxed the sheriff into the baggage car, where there was no window to look out of. With a bottle and a line of chatter he kept the law man occupied until a train hand gave "the office" that they had crossed the Texas Panhandle and were now in Indian

Territory (now Oklahoma). So they stopped the train and dumped the sheriff on the right of way between stations.

As the job grew, Albee grew into an appreciation of the importance of his position. His circus stories became fewer and fewer and even the mention of the tents was taboo. Albee wanted to forget those days, for now he was not only the general manager of the expanding Keith Circuit, but also head of the United Booking Office. He was in a new and higher social set—and wanted to forget the circus.

In those days he was an odd mixture of shrewdness and unsophistication, and was like a boy when someone suggested he go one evening to see the show at Sam T. Jack's (a burly house). In Boston he did not dare to be seen in the Old Howard, and on the road he had no time for burly shows. I will let Epes Sargent tell you what happened.

"Sitting too long over dinner, we did not reach the theater until after curtain time, and as we climbed the steps of what had been the Princess Theatre (next to the Fifth Avenue) the strains of a gospel hymn came down the stair well and Albee stopped in his tracks. 'It's a damn poor idea of a joke,' he reproved. (He thought he was being steered into a gospel meeting.) But a moment later the tune changed and he recognized 'Old Jim's Christmas Hymn,' into which was worked 'Jesus, Lover of My Soul.' He enjoyed the performance, which was an absolute novelty to the man who controlled a large slice of show biz, and two of the olio acts owe their getting out of burly into vaude on the Keith Time to this visit. One of the acts was Fonte-Boni Bros., the other escapes my memory." Epes Sargent was with him that night and told me about it years later.

In Boston, Albee's hobby had been driving, for he had a New Englander's love for good horseflesh, and his mare, Hilltop, was a beautiful animal. He brought her to New York, but soon had to give up his early morning drives and use his big automobile. It was one of the prices he paid for his big position in the show world.

Always with a mind to profits, he promoted the Boston Fadettes, a woman's orchestra under direction of Caroline B. Nichols. He booked them into all of the affiliated houses, taking his cut on the salary. He also toured a sort of fair or carnival staged in Boston and which was made an annual event for several years, but only in the Keith houses. Later Martin Beck imported the Hungarian Boys' Band, under Schilzonyi, and this gave Albee the idea for the Keith's Boys' Band, formed in part of employees of the New York houses. It was not used as an attraction, but was loaned as an advertisement. It disappeared when the retrenchment era set in.

The night that the formation of the United Booking Office was finished and announced, Albee declared that a new era had arrived. For several years the actors had been upping their salaries, often without changing their acts, and it galled the man from Machias that he could do nothing about it. Now the whip was suddenly placed in his hands, and he rejoiced!

"Those damned actors have been sticking it into me for many years," he declared. "Now I'm going to stick it into them—and harder!" He tried it, but Percy Williams proved a stumbling block. It was useless to ask an act to take $350 if Williams would pay them $500! Eventually Keith bought Williams out at a sum said to be around six millions, then they started cutting acts' salaries, and they were drastic cuts. They could now do it, for the Keith Time, with the exception of a few weeks booked by William Morris, was the only opening in the East and Midwest. On the Coast Pantages was making trouble, but playing small-salaried acts. Vaudevillians had to take what the booking office offered or do the best they could with a few pick-up dates, mostly at even smaller money.

It was reported around Broadway among show folks at one time that this price cutting had reached such a scientific point that private detectives investigated new acts the office wanted. The investigators reported what the actor paid for rent and food and what he needed to support maybe a couple of children. With that info at hand, the booking office could offer a figure slightly higher, but still much less than it would have probably set without this information. The story may have been a lie, because it was never definitely proven, but certainly the offers made showed an uncanny knowledge of just how much money an act needed to live on. (They claim this procedure has been followed in Hollywood; when finding that an actor is stuck with a big home, swimming pool, debts, etc., they know they can offer him a cut.)

Even standard acts were cut and sliced until at one time Variety reported that 1,200 turns were booking only from week to week, not willing to commit themselves for a season at the figures offered.

The office may not have gotten back all the dough paid Percy Williams for his circuit, but it was certainly able to write off a large slice of the investment. Albee was "sticking it in" to a fare-thee-well, and was aided by his fellow managers, all of whom resented the growing costs of bills.

It put Albee in a great spot, and for a time he rode high in the saddle. But someone slipped a burr under the saddle. John J. Murdock was the burr. He was still smarting from the deal Albee worked on the Western Vaudeville Association. Murdock sensed Albee's weakness. Albee was giving more time and thought to the building of new theaters than to the entertainment which was gonna pay off the contractor's bills. He was enjoying an orgy of planning theaters, buying oil paintings, antiques, and decorations for them, and forgetting vaudeville.

With the death of B. F. Keith and later A. Paul Keith, Albee was able to discard the fiction that he was acting for Keith. From a hired hand he became a dictator, and became drunk with a sense of power. He formed a company union of actors, and bankrupted the White Rats. (See my chapter about the White Rats and the N.V.A.)

Albee certainly had built the finest theaters in the world for vaudeville! Beautiful lobbies with oil paintings that cost thousands of dollars, rugs that cost more thousands, dressing rooms with bath that compared to the finest hotel suites, and he even furnished large turkish towels to the actors. A green room that any millionaire's home could boast of. The Albee in Brooklyn, the Palace in Cleveland, and the Memorial in Boston—they were cathedrals! As a showman he was proving himself one of the best architects in the country. This down-East Yankee had a genius for color and decoration that would be the last thing you'd expect from him. His taste leaned too strongly to marble, red drapes, etc. (the old circus influence) but he had plenty of ideas. He designed the "mushroom" system of theater ventilation, which later was adopted by the engineers for both houses of Congress in Washington. He improved on the old idea of passing air through an ice chamber, developing the idea of present-day air-conditioning systems. He dotted the Eastern country with theatrical monuments to his architectural skill, but many of the houses proved costly to the circuit and helped a lot in pushing vaudeville down the hill. If he had remained the great showman (which he undoubtedly was) instead of becoming an architect, there still might have been good vaude, or at least it might have lasted a bit longer.

While speaking about Albee's building ideas, I must tell you another story my friend Epes Sargent told me. It was after Keith had built Keith's Colonial Theatre that Sargent dropped in to see J. Austin Fynes, who was F. F. Proctor's general manager (and who didn't like Albee at all). Fynes said to Sargent, "I hear you are go'ng up to Boston to see the new Keith Theatre. Well, you'll find Ed Albee one of the best sanitary engineers in the country" (he didn't say sanitary engineers). Next day Albee took Sargent for an inspection tour of the only de luxe house in the country. "The house is not ready as yet," said Albee. "Suppose we look over the sanitary arrangements?" They were magnificent, and J. Austin Fynes' words came back to him!

A year later when Sargent went to interview Mr. Keith, the old man suggested they drive out to Marblehead where he (really Albee) was reconstructing a summer home he had bought. All along the road there were cottages being redone, but Sargent pointed ahead to a place and said, "That's yours." Keith said, "I didn't know you knew this country." Sargent didn't, but he saw three crated toilet-fixtures on the lawn and knew Albee must have ordered them!

In his later years Albee did many nice things. He contributed and raised a lot of dough for Bishop Manning to build St. John's Cathedral. He left about $100,000 to the Actors' Fund and a few bequests to English actors' organizations. He didn't leave very much to the American actors, because they broke his heart (like he did theirs).

There is no doubt that E. F. Albee took variety out of the kennels and placed vaudeville in the palaces he constructed, but he never seemed to realize that it was vaudeville itself that was more important than the theaters which housed it. The beaut'ful houses did a lot to dignify vaude, but beautiful theaters can't entertain.

Edward Franklin Albee tried to make vaudeville a one-man business, and he was not a big enough man to run it. After all, vaudeville meant variety—even in managers!

John J. Murdock

John J. Murdock, the last survivor of the great pioneers of the kingdom of Vaudeville, died on December 8, 1948, at the St. Erne Sanitarium in Los Angeles, California. He was eighty-five years old.

The life of John J. Murdock is the history of American vaudeville. No leader of the industry was so conspicuous in the organizing and developing of variety as Murdock. As a promoter of chains, builder of theaters, and arbitrator of warring factions in labor and management, his hand was always that of the quiet dealer, his brain the one that hatched the better ideas, yet his name seldom was seen in print. He said to reporters, "I'll give you the story, but keep me out of this." He was content to manipulate the strings backstage and let E. F. Albee take all the bows. (Like Albee did with Keith.)

Murdock, a man of Scottish drive and business sense, started in the late '90s as a stage electrician. He soon owned a stock company in Cincinnati. Coming to Chicago he made the Masonic Temple Roof an outstanding vaudeville theater. His competitors at that time were Charles C. Kohl and his partners George Castle and George Middleton, who ran the Chicago Opera House, the Olympic, and the Haymarket. Kohl and Middleton had been buddies with the Barnum show and controlled the dime museums and cheap variety in Chicago, Milwaukee, and St. Louis. Castle did the booking for the Haymarket and Chicago Opera House.

Castle's idea of a headliner was far from Murdock's, who circused "Little Elsie" (Janis) and promoted a wild story that he paid the Four Cohans $5,000 for their farewell appearance in vaudeville. Murdock liked music and saw that his patrons got the best the market could afford at that time. When he ran short of class acts, he created them, as in the case of Grace Akis, "The Girl with the Auburn Hair," who later became Mrs. Murdock. She posed with drapes before a group of choir boys who sang semireligious and seasonable songs. She was one of the first of the living picture acts, and became a headliner.

About the turn of the century, Kohl, Castle, Middleton, and

Martin Beck made their offices in the old Ashland Block at the corner of Clark and Randolph streets over the old Olympic. They brought in Murdock, who developed the Western Vaudeville Managers Association. Murdock picked up Jake Stenard and several other independent booking offices and in a short time was servicing twenty amusement parks with outdoor attractions, bands, and free shows. This was followed by the first million-dollar theater, the Majestic, Chicago. Built by the Lehman estate, owners of the Fair department store, it opened on January 1, 1906. Murdock promoted this beautiful vaudeville house, which was also a twenty-two-story office building. It was a far cry from the old dime museum! It was the job of Murdock to obtain attractions which would draw the Chicago elite to variety shows.

He brought in Lyman B. Glover to "front" for the place. Glover had been Richard Mansfield's manager and was dean of the dramatic critics covering the theater for the old *Herald*. Murdock, who started as a stagehand at the old Pike Opera House in Cincinnati, was doing all right for the museum boys and plenty good for himself.

Martin Beck, who at one time booked Chicago beer gardens, graduated to general manager of the Orpheum Circuit. All of the office staff was moved to the Majestic building in 1906 and a family department was established. This brought in the baby Gus Sun Circuit (which later developed into more than 1,000 houses), the Butterfield Circuit, and the John Hopkins Louisville Theatre and Parks. The houses in Cincinnati and Indianapolis were controlled by Max Anderson, the Cox-Rinock people, and the Inter-State Circuit in Texas. Later the Finn & Heiman Circuit and the Thielan Time were added. The Middle West gave plenty of work to actors then. Murdock did a "Branch Rickey" with his farm circuits in order to develop big-time talent. Many famous names first played the Western Time as beginners, then graduated to the Orpheum Circuit, and eventually played the New York Palace!

Coming East to join Albee, who placed a trust in him that others considered unwarranted, Murdock was feared and was taken into the fold to eliminate him. His associates soon learned that he was the one man who could assemble theaters and make vaude pay off in millions. He was cagey, hesitant, and it was almost impossible to get a definite answer out of him. He would sit cross-legged and pull out a desk drawer containing knickknacks. He always had a bottle of Kumyess (goat's milk) and a large hunk of honey on his desk. While you were trying to make your point, he would take a sip of Kumyess and a bit of honey, take a piece of film out of the drawer, hold it up to the light, inspect it, ask how you liked a certain shot, and then he would snip off a piece of film with the scissors.

One of Murdock's greatest weaknesses was his "chair cooling" idea. He seldom made an appointment, but when he did, he kept it promptly. He always made callers sit a long time or come back.

At one time a prospective builder of a theater down South called on Murdock to declare him in on his proposition for a franchise. He arrived only to find Murdock at a meeting. It was the custom at the time to call a boy and take a prospective partner into the dress circle of the Majestic Theatre to see the show and be impressed by Murdock's organization. From the reception room on the third floor the callers were taken down a long narrow hall, led past the executive office, through the large directors' room, into the dress circle, and then asked to wait. Some could have read *Anthony Adverse* before being called into Murdock.

Once Murdock and Marcus Heiman (who at one time was head of the Orpheum Circuit) made a date to meet the top people from Universal Pics to discuss a ten-million-dollar deal. When they got to the meeting they had lunch. After lunch Murdock said, "Gentlemen, I left my glasses at home; I also left my notes at home and without them I am lost, so let's call this meeting off until tomorrow." When Marcus Heiman asked him later what the idea was of calling a meeting and then calling it off, Murdock replied, "I felt tired after lunch, and I was afraid I couldn't think fast enough for those fellows—so I postponed it."

Once he sent for one of his managers. The man arrived at the Palace in New York. J. J. was notified and sent word to the man to come back to his office after lunch. He returned and was told that J. J. was at a meeting. He came back at 4:30 and was told that Murdock was gone for the day. So he called early next morning. When J. J. arrived he said, "I asked you to see me yesterday, where were you?" The manager replied, "I just got here." Murdock saw him the next day.

Most of Murdock's deals brought houses into the Eastern and Western Circuits on contracts calling for his firm to operate on a 50-50 basis. He did the hiring and firing, but, most important,

booked and charged for various services which go with the supply-
ing of attractions. Millions rolled in as a result.

As a diplomat, he never was too one-sided. He was friendly with
his superior's (Albee's) worst competitors and enemies. When
Variety was barred in the United Booking Offices by Albee, Murdock was caught reading it. He was asked, "What's the idea of not
only having but reading Variety when Albee's orders are to bar it?"
"Why, this is Albee's copy! I took it off his desk!" said Murdock.

On Saturday afternoons J. J. loved to browse around old furniture
stores, antique shops, and quaint holes. One day on his way home
to Westchester he dropped into the Alhambra Theatre at 126th
Street and Seventh Avenue. Across the street from the stage door
he spied a secondhand furniture store and decided he wanted certain pieces he saw there. He called Harry Bailey, the manager of
the theater, gave him the list, believing Bailey could make a better
deal, and departed. Bailey, in turn thinking that his prop man
could do even better, sent him over to price the stuff. To the manager's surprise and to Murdock's chagrin, the prop man learned
that most of the pieces were sold to the dealer by Murdock's
brother-in-law, who had taken them from one of Murdock's old
farm buildings!

Murdock had a marvelous sense of loyalty to his employees.
"Tink" Humphries was a favorite, as was Billy Jackson. He did not
go for everyone, but if he became intimate with someone it was
because he was certain of him and was not afraid of his judgment.
Should an employee make a mistake, Murdock would fix it, move
the man around, but very seldom fired him. He was a true and
tricky friend. He did object to any of his managers having interests
in other theater projects. When he discovered this "disloyalty,"
out went the manager. Many boys in his organization were raised
from a pup by J. J. He liked giving kids a break and some of his
boys developed into well-known showmen and bookers.

Before coming East with Albee, Murdock lost out with the Western bunch. He played around in the pic industry and was active in
breaking the motion pictures' Patent Trust with Carl Laemmle.
He was once managing director of the American Talking Pictures
Company, and was thrown out by Edison, who took it over and
changed the name to the Edison Kinetophone Co. That was back
in 1913.

He fought labor and won and broke many a strike by stagehands, musicians, picture operators, and actors. In 1926 the musicians and stagehands were going to strike in Frisco. Murdock got them and the managers on the phone from New York and spoke for five and a half consecutive hours and averted the strike. The bill—$2,157.80— was split between labor and management.

Time after time Murdock advised Albee to enter the picture business, but Albee didn't listen. He also tried to interest the Eastern managers, but they too failed to listen, while Fox, Loew, and Moss did and made millions.

In 1926 J. J. was told by his doctor he had cancer. He thought honey was a good cure for it to build a lining for his stomach, and he became a fanatic on the subject. He studied bees and raised his own honey on his Mamaroneck farm. He backed doctors in trying to find a cure for cancer. Their theory was to perfect serum from blooded horses, and J. J. went for over $800,000 buying blooded horses to bleed, etc. He gave millions for cancer research and was very angry when this became known. But he outlived all his doctors!

When J. J. Murdock came to New York, he had about $100,000 in cash. He started with Keith at a salary of $6,000 a year. (He set the salary himself, with a proviso that his commissions be raised if he increased earnings for Keith. His salary stayed at $6,000 until the day he retired, but his commissions ran into millions. At one time he was rated at eight million.) Besides adjusting labor troubles for the circuit, he made deals for the construction of all theaters, trades, mergers. He also directed all agents, which alone was a five-million-dollar-a-year business.

Sime Silverman, the publisher of *Variety*, took many a punch at Murdock. He asked B. F. Keith to investigate the activities of Albee and Murdock, he printed cartoons against Murdock, and still Murdock became one of Sime's greatest friends. It can be told now that it was Murdock who tipped off Sime to all of Albee's moves. Murdock was hard in business, but soft inside. He was an iron man who never looked back, a terrific showman who had definite likes and dislikes. He helped many an actor and hurt many more. He okayed the booking of stool pigeons who reported by letter almost daily the backstage gossip, a practice which led to the blacklisting of many of the acts.

He was never a theater owner while with Keith's. He stuck to Keith's, saw it become the Keith-Albee Circuit, and finally the Radio-Keith-Orpheum. He arranged for the purchase of Pathé Pic-

tures and became board chairman of Pathé before he retired in
1929. After his retirement he was property poor. All his money was
tied up in real estate back East. In his last years he saw very few
people except his old friend Colonel Levy of Louisville, who spent
his winters in California.

With the passing of J. J. Murdock, there also passed an era in
show biz.

Percy G. Williams

Like most really big showmen, Percy G. Williams cared little or
nothing for self-popularity. He was in the business of selling shows
on their merits and he felt that the glamor of his name meant little
to the man that was seeking amusement. As a result, the number
one showman of the golden era of vaudeville is less known than
the lesser lights with bigger bumps of egotism. To Williams, showmanship was procuring the best possible programs and selling them
to the greatest possible advantage. He excelled in both these things.

Seated in a crowd, Williams would never have been picked out
as a leader or as a showman. He had a retiring modest personality
and was soft-spoken. Slightly under average height, he did not stand
out. He was well informed and very seldom used "I" in his conversation. He seldom bragged about what he had accomplished, unless
it had a humorous angle. He gave personal attention to all booking
matters and saw that each act contributed to the general effect of a
good show. He wore "quiet" clothes and, instead of the regular
manager's diamond ring, he wore an Egyptian scarab. He never
bragged about the money he accumulated, but one time when he
was giving bond for a friend taking out letters of administration,
he was asked what security he had to offer. He drew from his
pocket a list of some twenty or thirty properties. "Take any one you
like," he said. "None of them is mortgaged!"

Born in Baltimore, Maryland, in 1859, he was brought to Brooklyn, New York, when a very young kid. He started his career in the '80s as an actor in a cheap touring combination. He got the idea of a liver pad, bag, or belt, which was a red flannel contraption stuffed with aromatic herbs (originally made up by his dad, who was a doctor). The argument was that, worn about the body, it would permit the pores to absorb the medicament in the herbs. In later years he improved on the liver pad; he had an electric rheumatism belt. He would send a man ahead to pick out the most rheumatic man or woman in town and ask them to wear the belt. "No money, no obligations, you have nothing to lose and everything to gain if it cures you." In a few days Williams would come along with his show. He did a "high pitch" (from a wagon). After a few specialty acts of blackface, banjo playing, dancing, and a few jokes, Williams would make his spiel and ask the man or woman to step up. The townspeople would be surprised to see the cripple actually walking for the first time in years. They knew it was no fake because the man or woman was a solid citizen. Williams would sell the belts like hot cakes. Of course, the gimmick was that there was such a terrific battery charge in the belt it would make a dead man move. Still, they cured a lot of people who thought they had rheumatism!

Williams had noted that medicine fakers working a high pitch (from a carriage or wagon) used banjo or other instruments to attract a crowd. He bettered the idea by forming a small show and playing in a tent. He headed his own troupe, selling the belts between the acts, but the idea proved so successful that he put someone else in to take his place and opened a headquarters from which he organized and sent out other troupes, some of them on his own, but mostly in partnership with some enterprising showman. He was said to have sixty companies out at one time in the United States and Canada, and some of these outfits brought in as much as $20,000 net profit on the season.

When the country was properly supplied with belts, and the Indian Sagwa Troupes started to cut into his takings, he let the matter drop. He soon tied up with Thomas Adams, Jr. (then the Tutti-Frutti Chewing Gum king), and invested in a project on Jamaica Bay—three hundred acres of swampland. They intended to build it up as a real estate development, but the mosquitoes were so thick that whisk brooms hung beside most screen doors to brush off the pests before entering the house. But Williams took a page from his medicine show experience and started a small amusement venture known as Bergen Beach. This consisted of a boardwalk, a casino, a bathing pool, a dozen small buildings for sideshows, and an open amphitheater on the edge of the bay with a stage on the water on which he gave performances of *Pinafore*. (It took almost fifty years for them to copy this one, which they are now doing all over the country.)

At one time he thought he'd boost business by staging an underwater explosion of a charge of dynamite, but this was dropped on demand of the Federal authorities when the first blast practically covered the bay with stunned and dead fish. After that he concentrated on the Casino (later called it the Trocadero), where he presented light musical comedies, most of them written by himself. It was pleasant enough entertainment, after a ride in the cool of the evening on the Flatbush Avenue trolley, the last half of the journey being made through practically open country. It is all built up now, including the beach itself. Many of the original investors in lots were actors; and none of them failed to make a good profit on his investment.

One season Williams brought up from the South the first showboat to enter metropolitan waters in a couple of generations. He moored it in the bay, but never figured any use for it, so resold it and it went back down South. Had he thought of it, he might have written that chapter of amusements which started nearly a generation later with kidding performances of *The Drunkard*, but maybe in 1900 they would have taken it seriously.

To show his sense of humor, I must tell you about the time one of those chronic "pass chasers" came to his table in the pavilion and asked for a pass to the show. Williams told him he was sorry that the Casino was sold out. "Well, give me a pass for something, anything," said the grafter. Williams gravely wrote out something on a slip of paper and handed it to him. "Pass bearer to fish in Jamaica Bay," read the grafter. "Where do I get the boat?" "You *hire* one," explained Williams. "That's just a pass *to fish*!"

In the winter Williams ran a small show on the East Side in New York in what had been known as Zip's Casino, a third-rate beer garden. In 1897 he took over the old Brooklyn Music Hall (Gotham), then took over the Novelty on Driggs Avenue, in Williamsburg. He had the acts play *both* houses, taking them from one house to the other in carriages and tallyhos, which received plenty of publicity. (First time "doubling" was ever done. Many years later small towns exchanged acts, and the Big Time "doubled" acts when there was a shortage.)

These theaters were so successful he decided to tackle downtown Brooklyn and bought a plot at Fulton Street and Rockwell Place. It was in 1901 that, with Otto Huber Brewing interest and Adams, the chewing-gum king, Williams built the Orpheum Theatre. Hyde and Behman had a monopoly of the theater business in Brooklyn, largely through a political pull. They made desperate efforts to prevent a building permit being issued for the new venture, but it didn't work. Williams, Adams, and Huber also knew politics and pulled the right strings, so the Orpheum opened on time and Hyde and Behman cut their prices at their Adams Street house to half a buck. Williams started the Orpheum with the first ten rows at a dollar top, but was forced to move the dollar section back five more rows. People asked for dollar seats and, when told there were no more, turned away. They didn't want the 75 cents ones, but would gladly pay a dollar for the same seats. It was a dollar crowd and they wanted dollar seats.

The Orpheum became one of the greatest subscription houses in America. Families had their reservations for years and years. There were three houses of this type, the Majestic in Chicago, the Orpheum in San Francisco, and the Orpheum in Brooklyn. They could tell you their gross weeks ahead. Many of these subscriptions were handed down to sons and daughters as an inheritance. That's how important vaude was in those days.

Percy Williams presented the best programs he could get and was willing to pay the price to get what he wanted. He was known as the father of big salaries in vaude. If the Keith office was stalling an act in the hope of getting them more cheaply, Williams would come through with the dough the act wanted, and get it first. That established their salary, which Keith had to pay later. On one occasion he got a chance to put in the then popular Kilties' Band. It was a sensational booking and became more of a sensation when Williams threw out the first half of the bill already engaged (and paid them) and played his headliners for the first half of the show. It never had been done before. "It will cost you a lot of money," a friend told him. "Mebbe so," agreed Williams, "but it will pay in the long run. I expect the Kilties to bring in hundreds of people who never before saw a vaudeville show. I want them to see what

my usual shows are like, so I put the headliners in the first half;
they'll like it, and will come back for more after the band is gone.
I'll get my money back." And he did. (Martin Beck booked Sarah
Bernhardt on the same idea.) Actors played to the same audience
at the Orpheum week after week and year in and year out. It was a
gold mine! Besides being one of the greatest audiences of vaude
fans in America!

The success of the Orpheum led to Williams taking the Circle
Theatre, on 59th Street and Columbus Circle, his first New York
theater, and then the Colonial, which was originally built by
Thompson and Dundy (the famous builders of the New York
Hippodrome later) to be run on the lines of an English Music
Hall. They didn't know that kind of business (they were really
carnival and circus people) and were glad to drop it. Williams took
it over and put it on its financial feet. Then he built the Alhambra,
at Seventh Avenue and 126th Street. Harlem had not felt the
Negro invasion and was able to play to a class audience for many
years.

With four theaters going big, he built the Greenpoint in Brooklyn in 1908, the first real theater for that section, then that same
year took the Crescent Theatre and moved it 600 feet from its
original location on Fulton Street. (It was the first big-building
moving job.) He built the Bronx Opera House and ran vaude in
Boston and Philadelphia in opposition to Keith, because they
wouldn't let him in the United Booking Office. But he now became
a thorn in the side of the U.B.O. (practically Keith's). They were
about to close in on him when the Comedy Club, an organization
of the great comedy acts of vaude, promised to stick to Williams.
(They wanted an opposition circuit.) Keith couldn't buck that, so
got him in and finally bought him out for about six million bucks.
Williams was ready to quit; he had made a fortune and already was
feeling the effects of the cirrhosis of the liver which eventually
carried him off.

It was the talk of the town that the Keith people got the purchase price back in a few years through salary cuts, but I don't
believe that's true, because six million bucks is a lot of bucks to get
back; but the Keith people did pretty good.

Under the Keith operation the shows were cheapened and so
were the standards. Within a year after the sale it became necessary
to put special officers in the balcony and gallery of the Colonial

Theatre to keep the patrons from becoming too demonstrative. The famous Colonial claque caused plenty of trouble (even in the days of Williams); when they didn't care for an act the entire gallery would clap their hands in unison. It was equal to a Bronx cheer, only louder. The class patronage Williams gathered soon scrammed. But I must say that even Williams was afraid of the Colonial gallery. When he booked Bransby Williams, who did delightful impersonations of Dickens' characters, and was what was called a "quiet act," he shut down the gallery with a sign "Under repairs," to save trouble for Bransby Williams. It meant a loss of a lot of dough, but Williams was that kind of a guy. Anyway, the Colonial gallery got more unruly under the Keith management, and so the house lost its class patronage. They wanted the best (without annoyance), and the Keith's best wasn't good enough.

It wasn't generally known that Williams took a flyer in melodramas written by himself. He openly sponsored only one, *Tracy, the Outlaw,* based on a sensational escape and recapture of a Western convict. This had dramatic angles, and showed what a showman Williams was. He was out West at the time and wired his office that he had bought the bloodhounds employed in tracking Tracy and would use them in a play based on the escape. What he brought back were a couple of "tom dogs": great Danes which were always used in performances of *Uncle Tom's Cabin* because they looked fiercer and more dramatic than bloodhounds. He later confessed that he picked up the pair for little dough from a stranded "tom show" and that this gave him the idea for the play. Before he wrote the script, he was sitting in the Orpheum one night with William Morris. Vitagraph, who supplied his houses with motion pictures, threw on the screen a French picture showing a sledge-hammer battle between two men in a blacksmith shop. Williams turned to Morris and said, "Keep your eye on that film, Bill; I'm going to want it in August." When August came he set his actors in front of the screen, ran the picture over and over until they had memorized every move, and "the fight in the forge" was the big noise in his show. Just quick thinking.

Before "chain management," where managers are practically office boys, most theaters reflected the personality of the manager. The Williams houses were friendly, comfortable, and without any such snobbish pretense as many theaters put on today. For a long time the Colonial had a patron who came in two and three times a week and never saw a full show. He bought an admission ticket, went straight to the lounge, and sat there reading his paper. He explained it was more cheerful than his bachelor apartment and more comfortable than his club. That was the keynote of Williams' success. He made people want to come. That was showmanship.

J. J. Maloney, who started with Williams as a bookkeeper, became his confidential secretary and remained with him throughout the years. Williams was the Exalted Ruler of the Brooklyn Elks (he was one of the first sixty members of that lodge). In 1905 he was pinched for giving Sunday shows; he took it into the court, and a year later took it to the Supreme Court and won from the city.

When Percy Williams died in 1923, he left his beautiful estate in Islip, Long Island (and the money for its upkeep), as a home for aged actors (the only manager in the world to do this). In his will he appointed members of his beloved Lambs as trustees with trustees of the Actors' Fund to see that the actors have everything they wish for, because, as he said before he died, "It was the actors who helped me make all my money, and I want them to enjoy it."

Percy G. Williams died a gentleman of the theater very much mourned, loved, and respected by both actors and laymen. Could you ask for anything more?

Martin Beck

Almost everybody likes to say, "I knew him when . . ." Especially actors. And nearly all the old-time vaude actors like to say, "Why, I knew Martin Beck when he was a waiter!" They tell you this and expect you to fall over in surprise. So what? He never denied it. I know a waiter that once was a headliner!

The truth is that Martin Beck came to the United States when he was about sixteen, as a member of a small troupe of German actors. They first played in South America and then came to the

U.S. W. Passpart (who later became the European representative
of the Orpheum Circuit) and Charles Feleky (who became the
head of the Orpheum Producing department) were also members
of this troupe. There are no records of how good or bad an actor
Martin Beck was, but we do know the troupe didn't do so well
and broke up. Beck and Feleky went from door to door selling
crayon pictures and took any odd job to keep from starving.
Soon Beck landed a job as a waiter at the Royal Music Hall on
North Clark Street, Chicago, for $12 a week (and tips). That was
the year of the World's Fair in Chicago, 1893. With his knowledge
of the show biz he soon was helping around as manager, stage
manager, cashier, auditor, barman, and waiter for which he was
raised to $20 a week. The Royal was next to Engel's, the best-
known concert hall in the city. After a year at the Royal, Beck went
to Engel's and remained there for two years. He became a partner
and opened another place on the South Side. He would make the
trip from one house to the other on a bicycle (to save expenses) to
make change, pay off the help and check the receipts. He was doing
pretty good when the crash came and ended Beck's career as a
concert hall waiter, bookkeeper, manager, cashier, etc. He took his
apron off and joined the Schiller Vaudeville Company on a trip
to the West!

While playing in San Francisco he met Gustave Walters, who
owned the Orpheum Theatre, a saloon concert hall there. He also
owned one in Sacramento. Walters broke up the Schiller Vaudeville Company, using two acts for his houses, and offered Beck a
job as manager and booker. Walters was strictly a saloon man and
knew very little about variety shows. He also owed a $50,000 liquor
bill to two gentlemen by the name of Morris Meyerfeld and his
partner Dan Mitchell. He couldn't pay the bill, so the two gentlemen took the place over. They knew even less about show biz than
Walters, so it wasn't long before Beck took over and soon was
promoting a new Orpheum with Martin Lehman, who owned a
theater in Los Angeles, and they made Charles E. Bray the secretary. Beck, Lehman, and Bray were all good showmen, but Beck
also was a cute real estate operator and picked the sites for the
many theaters the Orpheum started promoting. He was said to
have had 10 per cent interest in the circuit at that time. All the
theaters were promoted with local capital, which made the townspeople interested in the theaters. They were all fine, clean, well-

appointed theaters, running clean shows, and were a credit to the towns.

When the Orpheum Circuit only had three theaters out in California, they had to play an act three weeks in each house and pay the act's fares and excess baggage, because very few acts wanted to make that long jump for a few weeks' work.

It was through Martin Beck that the Orpheum Circuit joined the great Middle West vaude powers, Kohl & Castle, in Chicago, and started the Western Vaudeville Association. They controlled all the vaude bookings in the Middle West. Before the organization of the W.V.M.A., the managers would book through the powerful United Booking Office in New York, where the Orpheum representative was Robert D. Girard. About 1905 Mr. Meyerfeld started to relax and practically turned over the running of the Orpheum Circuit (now a very big organization) to Beck. He came East and opened up his office in the St. James Building, where the mighty United Booking Office had their headquarters, and Mr. Beck soon got in with Albee and the rest of the tycoons of vaudeville.

Beck was a pretty gruff man in business; he liked things done his way. He could even outfox Albee, which took plenty of foxing! But he gave everybody a square shake. He was an easy touch, liked nice things, and was loyal to his friends. He spoke about five languages and was a well-traveled and intelligent man, also a very stubborn one. When his office was at 609 Ashland Block in Chicago and he was booking Kansas City (that was about 1899), Montgomery & Stone asked $250 to play there. Beck told their agent, "Not as long as I live will I ever pay Montgomery & Stone $250 a week in Kansas City." (He never did.) He had an uncanny memory, could tell what he paid actors years ago, and could quote parts of their acts. I heard him tell a certain big-time agent on Broadway, "I will never buy an act from you until you pay me back the $15 I loaned you twenty years ago when you were a hoofer, to get you out of town." The agent looked surprised and apologetically said, "Oh, Mr. Beck, I forgot all about it." Beck said, "I didn't!" He got the money and slipped it to a beggar.

While I was in his office one day talking to him about making an Orpheum tour, his secretary came in and told him that a certain act he wanted to see was in the office. "Send 'em in," said Beck. It was a foreign acrobatic act, two men and a woman. He asked them if they had signed their contracts? They said yes. "Do you know for how much?" "Yes, for $175 a week." Beck glared at them and yelled, "How the hell are you three going to live on $175 a week, with all that railroad fare you have to pay?" "The best we can do, Mr. Beck." "Do you realize what hotels and meals cost?" The acrobats were panicky. "We do the best we can, we really need the work." Beck still glaring, tore up the contracts and said, "I can't have my actors living like bums and dressing like tramps. When you are hungry you can't work properly. I must have actors that work good for me." By now the act was almost in tears. Then Beck said, "Tell the girl to make out new contracts for $350!" That's the kind of a guy Beck was, scare you to death, then do something nice. He didn't like anything cheap, and he liked class.

Beck was the man who really put class into vaude. He would pay big salaries to fine concert musicians and ballet dancers (he first booked the Albertina Rasch Dancers). He didn't care if those kinds of acts went over with the audience (many of them were away over the heads of the vaude patrons of that time). When they would flop, Beck would shake his head and say, "They got to be educated." (Meaning the audience.) I asked him why he booked that type act, when the majority of people didn't like it. He replied, "Listen, in a vaudeville show everybody on the bill can't wear red noses, baggy pants, and take prat falls. A bill must have variety, change of pace, and have something that appeals to everyone. You know, there are a lot of people like good music. If one man out there liked that fine violinist, I've made a customer!" His booking of Sarah Bernhardt for $7,000 a week (highest salary ever paid up to that time in vaude) proved his point. She did a terrific business for him when she first opened in Chicago and of course put the Palace on the map.

E. F. Albee was always afraid of the ambitious Beck, and through agreements and threats he kept the Orpheum Circuit west of Chicago, and the U.B.O. stayed East. But Mr. Beck felt he was too big to be confined to a certain territory and wanted to get in New York. He bought a plot of ground and built the Palace. He had strong financial backing from a very wealthy Westerner, who remained in the background. The building of the Palace caused a panic among the Eastern vaude managers, especially E. F. Albee. Hammerstein showed his U.B.O. franchise, giving him all vaude rights to the territory from Forty-second Street to Columbus Circle, which meant that Beck couldn't get any acts from the U.B.O. (which had all the great standard acts). His backer got cold feet and didn't go through with the deal, so Beck had to do business with Albee. When the smoke cleared, Albee had the Palace, so eliminating a threat of opposition, Beck retained 25 per cent of the stock, and the booking of the Palace went through his office. Albee had to pay Hammerstein's $200,000 (he was offered a big block of stock, but Willie Hammerstein took the cash, saying the Palace wouldn't last two years, it was too far uptown). He wasn't the only one who has made bad predictions. Didn't we see master showmen say that pictures wouldn't last, that talkies were just a passing novelty, radio was a toy, and TV a gadget?

Here is a story about Beck signing up Sarah Bernhardt that has never been told. He went to Paris to get Mme. Bernhardt, and she signed willingly; he didn't have to hold a gun to her head or break her arm when he offered her $7,000 a week. When Beck got back to his hotel, he became very nervous and started to pace the floor. His wife asked him what was the matter? "I forgot to tell her that she had to work on Sundays in America." All night he pictured how she would explode her temperament all over the place when he told her about Sundays, how she would tear up the contract, etc. etc. It was a sleepless and very nervous Martin Beck who called on Mme. Bernhardt the next morning and tried to break the news to her gently. Instead of flaring up, Bernhardt patted him on the cheek and said, "Why, don't worry. I have no other place to go on Sundays, the theater is my church and home. I'll be happy working there on Sunday!"

Martin Beck was the first to give out fine booklet programs instead of the one small sheet that all theaters used. He was also the first to build a mortgage-free theater; he owned every brick of his Martin Beck Theatre on West Forty-fifth Street. He was also one of the first to build a theater "off Broadway." West of Eighth Avenue was practically out of town. He opened his theater with *Mme. Pompadour*, which he produced with Charles Dillingham with Wilda Bennett in the lead. It first opened out of town with Hope Hampton (the beautiful wife of the late Jules Brulatour, who got a commission on every foot of film sold in America). Beck canceled her and replaced her with Wilda Bennett, and had to pay Hope Hampton too. He spent a fortune on the production, and it was a magnificent flop. I asked him once why he did it? He shrugged his shoulders and said, "It was beautiful. *Bad*, but beautiful!"

In later years when vaude was going on the rocks he again took charge, but it was too late for a doctor; not even a specialist could help it. He then became advisor to RKO (Very few people knew this.) He had a peculiar assignment. When the Radio City Music Hall was being built, his job was to keep his eye on Roxy, who was spending a lot of money; everything he saw that he felt would make the theater better he would buy, and even the Rockefellers couldn't stand his mad spending of the RKO dough. Once in Paris he was shown a beautiful organ. Roxy immediately ordered a half a dozen, which ran into quite a large sum. After Beck talked to him, he cut the order down to *four*!

There are many stories about Martin Beck told among actors, one especially which was repeated time and time again whenever actors were reminiscing. I was surprised one day when Beck asked me, "Did you ever hear the funniest story told about me?" I immediately thought of *the* story that I'd heard for years, but didn't dare say anything about it to him. So you can imagine my surprise when I said no, and he went right into the story that I was thinking of.

"A fellow I didn't book, because he had a very bad act, swore he would get even with me some day. Years later, when he still had a bad act, he blamed me that I was keeping him from bookings, which I never did. Anyway, one day he got a broken-down horse and wagon, drove up in front of the Palace Theatre just before matinee time, when there was a big crowd of agents, actors, and bookers, and started backing up the wagon, while he yelled to the horse, "Beck, you bastard, Beck, you S.O.B., etc." It got a big laugh from the show people, and you want to know something? when I heard about it, I laughed too. I only wish he was as funny on the stage. Maybe he should have worked with a horse?" So Beck did have a sense of humor!

He died leaving his charming wife Louise to take care of his many theatrical interests. She in her own right rates high in show biz as a prominent and tireless worker with the Theatre Wing and all theatrical charities.

Actors told a lot of gags about Martin Beck, but they liked him;

they knew there wasn't a vaude circuit in the world that gave them fairer treatment than the Orpheum Circuit. And the Orpheum Circuit reflected its head—Martin Beck!

F. F. Proctor

Frederick Freeman Proctor was born in 1852 at Dexter, Maine. He left school at an early age on account of the death of his father. He worked for awhile in the R. H. White's Dry Goods Store, in Boston, as an errand boy. Being fond of athletics, he joined the Y.M.C.A. While practicing there, he was seen by a performer by the name of Levantine, who was using the gym at the time, and soon joined him in an acrobatic and juggling act. They juggled barrels with their feet. He later worked in a circus and variety shows with different partners. He finally did a single and made a successful European tour under the name of his first partner, Levantine. He stayed in vaudeville for a few years and then decided the other end of the business was where he belonged.

In 1880 he opened his own theater, the Green Theatre, in Albany, New York. His partner was H. Jacobs. They soon split and Proctor became his own boss and stayed that way until many years later, when he hooked up with B. F. Keith, and eventually broke away from him. He named his first theater Levantine's Novelty Theater.

From 1880 to 1889 he and Jacobs opened theaters in Rochester, Utica, Brooklyn (Novelty and Criterion), Boston, Buffalo, Syracuse, Troy, New Haven, Bridgeport, Hartford, Lancaster, Worcester, Lynn, Wilmington, and finally in 1889 opened Proctor's Twenty-third Street, New York. He started continuous performances in New York City, a copy of the Boston policy of Keith, who at that time couldn't find a good theater in New York. Proctor's advertising read, "After breakfast go to Proctor's—After Proctor's, go to bed." He formed a sort of a partnership with Charles Frohman and ran the noted Frohman Stock Company.

When Jacobs and Proctor were partners, their theaters dotted the middle section of New York State. Many people credit Jacobs with being the originator of the 10-20-30 school of amusement. In reality it merely followed a popular lead, but he made it his own in a way through advertising. It was the year Grover Cleveland had been elected the first Democratic president in years, and manufacturing leaders feared the effects of his free-trade policies. Even before he was inaugurated there was a healthy panic which was reflected in the theater, and all over the country managers were finding it necessary to cut their prices of admission from 50 to 75 cents top to a 30-cent orchestra seat with perhaps a row or two of four-bit seats to kinda save face. Jacobs didn't want to save face. He made a virtue out of necessity, and the Proctor and Jacobs theater ads bragged about the 10-20-30 price, and the figures were lighted up on their house fronts. It caught on, and for a time the firm made plenty dough. Eventually, however, the circuit grew too large to handle intelligently and broke of its own weight.

Both partners came to New York, and Jacobs became manager of the Third Avenue Theatre, while Proctor took the out-of-the-way house on West Twenty-third Street, between Sixth and Seventh avenues. The house played a few melodramatic hits like *The Lost Paradise* and *The Long Strike*, but it was too far from Broadway to draw any transient trade. It was then that Proctor decided to try Keith's idea of continuous performances, which had not as yet been introduced to New York. Keith couldn't get a spot, so it was virgin territory for that policy.

Profiting by the lesson learned from Jacobs, Proctor decided to sloganize the town with thousands of one-sheets, snipes, and newspaper ads, all shouting "After Breakfast Go to Proctor's." This caught on and got the house off to a good start. In Boston, Keith and Albee were frothing at the mouth. (Keith never really forgave him for it.)

It was a couple of years before Keith took over the Union Square Theatre, which was the home of English melodrama. Keith cut down Proctor's lead in the town through giving better shows, particularly on the so-called "supper show." That was a show given from 5.30 to 7.30 P.M. The headliners did not appear at this show; they only did two a day, while the supper show acts did three. Proctor loaded this section of the bill with serio-comics who would work cheaply. Keith varied his programs more and set the rule that

$35 single and $50 double was the least to be paid for this type of act. It cut down the Proctor's distance draw, but there were enough locals to still show a profit for Proctor.

Proctor made enough money from the theater to start his second venture, the Pleasure Palace, at Fifty-eighth Street and Third Avenue. This was looked on as the start of a new type of show biz, a sort of department store of amusements. There was an auditorium seating better than 2,500 with a roof garden and a rathskeller. The rear stage wall was an asbestos curtain and it was planned to raise this and let the patrons of the beer garden enjoy the same show. The idea never clicked, because the acts didn't know which audience to face. (So the "theater in the round" is new, eh?)

They finally walled up the passageway from the rathskeller to the billiard and pool room in the basement of the beer garden, and the Palm Garden was rented out for dances and weddings. The roof garden never clicked, running only for a couple of seasons, and the rathskeller was a total loss. Instead of going downstairs after the show, the few who were thirsty and looking for fun went across the street to the Terrace Garden. The rathskeller too was closed and the whole ambitious idea put an awful crimp in the Proctor bankroll for a time. Some years later the house was gutted and changed to a fine theater, with only one balcony, and the former Palm Garden space added to its capacity, and still later it was again changed to the modern theater it is now.

Proctor added the Columbia Theatre, the first house built in Harlem by Oscar Hammerstein, and renamed it Proctor's 125th Street. He later took over the Harlem Opera House, also built by Hammerstein, and then got the Fifth Avenue Theatre at Broadway and Twenty-eighth Street, which, like the Union Square, had been left behind in the uptown march. He kept the Albany house for a time and also built the first Proctor's in Newark.

These extra spots that Proctor opened were burning Keith and Albee, who as yet hadn't started their expansion program. Keith had been using a four-leaf clover for a design, sort of emblematical of his four theaters. Proctor used a series of linked wreaths, sort of suggesting the Keith emblem, but larger!

When E. F. Albee went gunning for complete control of the Keith enterprises, J. Austin Fynes, who had managed and "made" the Union Square, slipped out from under and went with Proctor as his general manager. He never could make Proctor spend as much for talent as Keith was doing, but he made a decided improvement in the Proctor enterprises.

When the first White Rats strike (1900) disorganized the vaude biz, Fynes put stock companies in the houses, with Hugh Ford (later a great pic director) as general producer, and the theaters began booming. The 125th Street Theatre was a gold mine, with Paul McAllister and Jessie Bonstelle as headliners. William J. Kelly became a terrific matinee idol there later.

F. F. Proctor married Georgena Mills, whose stage name was Georgie Lingard. (Lingard, her uncle, owned the Bowery Theatre and played the original part of Uncle Tom at the Bowery Theatre in 1866.) She was a soubrette and rope dancer. They started for the St. Louis Fair by auto. He was ditched near Pittsburgh and broke his legs, and was taken to Pittsburgh for hospitalization. During his convalescence Proctor started to pal around with Harry Davis. To Proctor nothing of his own seemed as good as the other fellow's, and he grew discontented. He thought the Davis stock company was much better than his and wrote Fynes demanding a stock company "like the one here." Hugh Ford showed Fynes applications from nearly every member of the Davis Stock Company asking for a job in his stock company, and told Fynes why he didn't hire them. Ford was the number one stock producer of the day and knew his biz, but couldn't satisfy Proctor and got out.

Proctor then wanted to know why he couldn't get as good vaudeville acts as Davis was showing in Pittsburgh. Instead of telling him it was because he would not pay the money, Davis told him that he did not book through Jules Ruby (Proctor's booker), who was getting gray trying to chisel five and ten dollars off actor's salaries to get within the Proctor limit. Ruby quit too. And when Proctor came back, he made things so tough for Fynes that he quit even before his contract ran out.

Fynes knew that the lease on the Fifth Avenue was about to expire, and tipped Keith off, with the result that Keith leased the house over the head of the unsuspecting Proctor. This eventually led to the formation of the Keith & Proctor Company, with the Proctor houses thrown into pics. Some years later when the company was dissolved (through a lot of litigation), Fynes told Epes Sargent (who in turn told me) that he testified in Proctor's behalf through sheer pity. He expected Proctor to be trimmed. He wanted him to be, but he did not expect the complete scragging Proctor

got. It was largely through Fynes' testimony that Keith had to give
Proctor back his houses and some of the profits.

Then began a new era for Proctor. His biz manager, George
Wallen, a very smart cookie, convinced Proctor that he had the
right idea. Instead of New York expansion, he went into the small
towns, building combined theaters and office buildings (which
New York managers are now fighting for), which gave Proctor
his auditoriums practically rent free. Instead of pointing up the
current headliner, managers were told to sell the Proctor *show*,
week in and week out. When there were no big headliners, the
people came anyway. The show was profitable because the office
building paid the rent. Proctor had gone into the Keith booking
office, and let Albee build the Eighty-sixth Street Theatre, the first
theater in the country to be fitted up for light housekeeping backstage. Wallen, as Proctor's general manager, watched the operations of every phase of the building, and when RCA bought the
Keith outfit, Proctor got plenty on his setup. He had Wallen to
thank for the fact he left a big estate.

Proctor had a colorless personality. He was in no sense an out-
stander and made few friends. He very seldom went backstage to
meet any of the acts; he always watched the front of the house and
the box-office till. Very few actors knew Mr. Proctor personally.
Toward the last he had a terrific objection to meeting new people
or even contacting those whom he had known but had lost touch
with. It was almost a phobia.

He hated drinking men, and those who worked for him around
Proctor's Fifth Avenue (where he made his headquarters) were
afraid to be seen going into a saloon on Twenty-eighth Street. But
a scene door, connected with a scenic studio on what had been the
stage of the old theater, made it possible for the boys to slip out
on Twenty-ninth Street without a chance of being caught by the
boss. The stage doorman was tipped off and when Proctor asked
for a delinquent, he was told the man was on the stage. Then the
call boy would rush out and get the man wanted from the bar.

F. F. Proctor was the first to give his employees insurance; first
to do dramatic shows with vaude in between; first to reduce admission prices between 10 and 11 A.M., 25 cents admitting to orchestra
and balcony seats. (You thought it was practically a new idea, eh?)
He established full orchestras. He was first to recognize the value
of pics and first to play a feature in a first-class theater. He dis-

continued vaude at the Fifth Avenue in 1912 and put in a ten-reel feature, *Intolerance.* He pioneered in furnishing nice dressing rooms for actors, and was the first to share his profits with employees. He was also the first to start advertising in "box style" all his theaters.

Essentially, Proctor was a one-man institution. He was successful only through the efforts of others and then only when he would let his advisor set the pace. In 1929 he sold his interests to RKO, transferring eleven theaters for an estimated value of sixteen to eighteen millions. Clarence Wallen and brother worked for him for over forty years. At one time Proctor had fifty theaters!

When he died at the age of seventy-seven, on September 4, 1929, he remembered over 300 persons in his will, and gave $100,000 to the Actors' Fund. He was a definite part of big- and small-time vaude, one of the great pioneers, but was colorless.

Frederick Freeman Proctor came a long way from being an acrobat in a circus to being one of the top managers and theater owners of American vaudeville!

William Morris

He was a kid who couldn't talk English and who received very little schooling, who delivered papers before school and after supper clerked in a grocery store. In the afternoons he carried big bags of coal and delivered ice for just a few cents a day. To help support the family he worked as an office boy on a cloak and suit trade paper, and by the time he was twenty, he was earning $15,000 a year via commissions by soliciting ads. They were about to put his name up as a partner, but the 1894 panic came and put the paper out of business, and with it, William Morris.

That was the early career of the man who, born Wilhelm Moses in Austria in 1873, later became the greatest independent showman of our time!

He always had a hankering to get into the business end of the show biz. To him it was a dream world with dream people, so different from the people in the cloak and suit business he knew. After being turned down by Mike Leavitt (a big showman at that time), Bill Morris swiped one of his letterheads and wrote to George Liman, who was the leading variety agent, telling him "confidentially" that he was seeking a new connection. He got an appointment and told Mr. Liman that he had a lot of experience in the agency business and Liman, impressed, offered him $8.00 a week. Bill turned it down flat and finally settled for $9.00 a week. With the okaying of the salary, Liman gave him a list of acts and houses and told him to "book 'em"!

Bill got the office boy to tell him about the business, talked to actors and managers to get the lowdown (without tipping his mit that he was a tyro), and in about a month was made general manager of the oldest variety agency in New York! (Sounds Horatio Algerish, doesn't it? But true.)

Morris helped the managers with his great ideas; he put single acts together and made them into valuable doubles instead of mediocre singles. He looked for novelties, he balanced his shows, and they proved money-makers for the theaters he booked. But his thoughts ran to big things and big money, and booking Eva Tanguay for $35 a week, and she was closed, or booking Emma Carus for a Sunday for three bucks, on which he received 15 cents commission, didn't appeal to young Morris. When George Liman died, his widow got rid of Bill, thinking she could run the business herself. So within a month she was out of biz and Bill bought up the office furniture for four dollars and stuck his own name on the door, the W and M crossing, which became his trade-mark and was used on every office door William Morris ever had. (And he had plenty of them.)

By 1900 he was running the biggest independent agency in the country. In 1904 he booked twenty-nine weeks and the next year he booked the houses of Percy Williams, Proctor, Hammerstein, Weber & Rush, Poli, Sheedy, Keeney, and many more. He taught Willie Hammerstein showmanship while also teaching him how to play pool. He would lay out a bill and ask Willie how he would lay it out and how much he would pay each act? And then show Willie where he was wrong. In 1906 he could book an act twelve weeks in New York City without a repeat.

Bill was getting real big, when Albee stepped in and offered the managers membership in the United Booking Office, which charged commission to acts for playing their own houses, and also split that commission with the managers of the U.B.O. It amounted to a lot of dough and was great bait. Bill Morris was making a quarter of a million a year on commissions; Bill didn't split commissions. So one by one the managers, whom Morris had helped to make rich, left him to join the U.B.O., where they could partake of this unholy graft. With nothing to book, he incorporated for $500,000 and became a manager and also a deep thorn in Albee's side. Albee hated Morris but respected his showmanship!

It was Morris who masterminded and did the booking for Klaw & Erlanger when they decided to play Advanced Vaudeville in opposition to Keith. What Morris didn't know was that they and the Shuberts were only in the vaude business to get a big price from Keith to quit. They were offered a lot of money to quit in the first few weeks, as they were making it expensive for Keith to get acts, because Morris was signing up acts for almost double what they could get from Keith. K. & E. refused and held out for more dough, which they finally got, and quit, leaving Morris high and dry. Morris could have sued on his contract with K. & E., but tore it up in front of Erlanger (who looked at the torn contract to see if it wasn't a phony). He couldn't believe anybody would do such a thing, but he didn't know Bill Morris.

Never licked, Morris signed Harry Lauder, whom he had booked for K. & E. for $2,500 a week and who broke all records. He gave Lauder $3,000 a week and also paid the English managers for dates that Lauder didn't play there for which he had contracted. (It's play or pay in England.) He toured Lauder all over the country, with one of the finest publicity campaigns ever given a vaudeville performer, and broke all records on the road. With Lauder as anchor man, Bill started his own circuit. He got the Boston Music Hall (Keith had it, but forgot to exercise his option). He also took over the American Theatre on Forty-second Street and Eighth Avenue (a dead theater at the time), where he made his headquarters. He had theaters in Chicago, Boston, and Brooklyn—all profitable. The U.B.O. blacklisted every act that played for Morris, which made it plenty tough, but he was doing great in spite of it. The American was making $125,000 a year profit, but when the Keith squeeze started to work, there was a dearth of new acts and especially headliners. It was then that Morris started the twenty-two act shows, and sold the public big shows instead of headliners. It worked out great for a while, and then his great friend and right-hand man George M. Levebritt died suddenly and Morris began having financial troubles. Martin Beck was going to buy out the circuit and take over the debts (which Morris insisted on) which would have given him the foothold in the East he always wanted, but the deal fell through. Finally Marcus Loew stepped in and took it over. (Albee wanted to buy Morris out with the proviso that he could never go back in the business again, to which Morris said *no*.)

By now Bill was a pretty sick man, but he didn't give up. He leased the New York Theatre Roof and put in a Coney Island idea right on Broadway, which he called Wonderland. He had everything from a carrousel to all kinds of concessions. He ran contests, cakewalk, etc., and gave out fabulous prizes which he got for free from the manufacturers for just mentioning their names (à la Tony Pastor, radio, and TV). It didn't pay off, so he gave it up and devoted all his time to managing Harry Lauder on his many tours. His opposition to regular vaude with his great attraction was still bothering Albee and Beck (whose territory he often played).

It was in 1920 that Morris broke into the *Christian Science Monitor* with a theatrical ad (the first). Their policy not to advertise shows with murder or immoral topics of any sort had kept all theatrical ads out until Morris broke the tradition with one for the Lauder show. (The New York Hippodrome was second.)

In 1925 Morris got the idea for a home for show people stricken with TB. It was first called Adirondack Tubercular Fund Northwood Home, with E. F. Albee as president, Morris as V.P., and Col. Williams as treasurer. Later Albee managed to take it over and named it the N.V.A. Sanitarium (after his company union) and N.V.A. funds were used for its upkeep. When vaude folded, so did the N.V.A.'s funds, and the picture people took it over, renaming it the Will Rogers Memorial Hospital. They too gave it up and now it is one of the favorite charities of the famous Variety Clubs of America.

Bill Morris was also the founder of the Jewish Theatrical Guild.

He left a foundation of good will to his son William Morris, Jr., and his daughter Ruth, built up by the most profitable and important artists' agency in the world, handling the foremost attractions. William, Jr., has retired as the active head of the agency and is now chairman of the board. The agency is headed by Abe Lastfogel, who was raised from a kid by Bill Morris, Sr., who taught him show biz from A way past Z. He is considered one of the greatest of all-round showmen in the country today. He is nearly a William Morris, which is the highest compliment I can pay him.

On the death of William Morris (November 2, 1932; he fell over with a heart attack while playing cards at his favorite club, the Friars), Jack Lait (once press agent for William Morris' Lauder attraction, an old *Variety* mugg and now editor of the New York *Daily Mirror*), wrote an obit in *Variety*, part of which I would like to quote, because he summed it all up by saying:

"William Morris towered above the personalities and significance of most of the figures in the theatrical world. He has sounded the depths and the rarified air above the clouds of theatredom; he has been the general of battles that will be told for many years, often the general of an army of one; he was beholden to no one, was respected and beloved and carried on his inspirational life purpose, charity, welfare, tolerance and love until he died. He cried only for the griefs of others, for himself he only chuckled. His conscience was clean and when his books weren't they were messy only from wiping off the debts others owed him. A great man of the theatre, and the world!"

That was Jack Lait's tribute to a great human being. I would like to add a salute for myself and all the actors he helped directly and indirectly by his independence and charity and as one of the vaudeville managers who didn't sell out their consciences!

Marcus Loew

Marcus Loew at the age of thirty-six was in the fur business; so was John Jacob Astor many years before him. Astor did much better than Loew but Marcus didn't do so bad for a kid who was

born in a windowless room on the lower East Side, at Avenue B
and Eighth Street (where he later erected a million-dollar theater).
His ambition was to be like his dad, who came to America, married
a German girl, and became a headwaiter. So to become a headwaiter would be good enough for Marcus. As a kid Marcus did all
kinds of odd jobs to help support the family. He worked in a map-
printing shop for 35 cents a day, peddled newspapers, and did other
jobs, and finally got into the fur business as a salesman. He saved
a few bucks and bought himself an equity in an apartment house
in Harlem.

At that same time David Warfield, a great comedian with the
Weber & Field's Company, was doing big and figured it wouldn't
last long, so stuck about $50,000 in an apartment house right next
door to Loew's. Marcus went down to see Dave to tell him that he
could run his apartment house better than the way it was being
run. Warfield made him his real estate agent and it was the beginning of a lifelong friendship which made them both millionaires!
Warfield made more money with Marcus Loew than he did in all
the years he spent in show biz as a star getting big money under
the management of David Belasco!

One of Loew's neighbors up in Harlem was Adolph Zukor, who
was also in the fur business, and they too became pals. In 1906
Loew saw Zukor, Aaron Jones, and Morris Cohen turn a store into
a penny arcade, so they could use the penny slot machines they
were interested in. These arcades were filled with "peek machines,"
where you put in a penny, turned the crank, and saw moving pics
like "Beauty and the Beast," "In My Harem," "Her Beauty Secret,"
etc.—get the idea? You could also put a penny in a machine, put
earphones to your ears, and hear a record! Marcus joined forces
with Zukor and his partners and also got Warfield interested. The
two of them soon quit Zukor and went in for themselves and
opened their first arcade on Fourteenth Street. Mitchell Mark (who
later built the first de luxe picture theater in America, the Strand,
on Broadway) joined Loew and Warfield and in a short time they
owned four arcades.

Loew heard of an arcade in Cincinnati (the Hippodrome) that
wasn't doing so well and was for sale. He bought it and fixed it
up and soon it was doing fine, and it was really this house that put
him on the show biz road. He heard about a fellow in Covington,
across the river, who had a picture machine and who charged five

cents to the natives to look at the pictures. Loew went over to see it, and saw a small room with about twenty-five people watching these pictures, with the owner explaining them, saying, "Now watch him fall," "Now he's going to hit him!" etc. After the showing of the picture, the colored boy who cranked the machine did a few jig steps. That's what put the "picture bug" in Marcus Loew's ear.

He bought a pic machine and put it in a small room above the Cincinnati Arcade and ran pictures. The first one was "Hot Chestnuts"; it ran about four minutes. People started to come in, eighty seats at a nickel a throw; he did over $500 the first week. (The first nickelodeon was run by Harry Davis in Pittsburgh, who was jamming them in; no seats—they had to stand up.) Loew soon came back to New York and opened his first picture show on Twenty-third Street, which was one of the first nickelodeons in the city. He begged Jake Lubin, who was then manager of Miner's Eighth Avenue, to go in with Warfield and himself, but Jake laughed about it, and gave Marcus plenty of good show advice and even some old wiring he had in the theater, which Marcus used to wire up his house. Some years later Jake Lubin became the head booker of the Loew Circuit, which position he still holds.

In six months, with Warfield as a partner, Loew had forty nickelodeons returning 40 per cent on the investment. It was in 1908 that an unemployed actor was sent to him by Warfield for a job. There was no opening for an operator, cashier, or ticket taker (that's all the help he used in each store), so he asked the actor could he recite "Gunga Din" and "The Road to Mandalay"? The actor could. "O.K., go on between the pictures and recite," which meant about twenty shows a day. The audience liked it, and he took the actor around to all his places and found the box-office receipts better with "Mandalay" and "Gunga Din" than without them, so that was practically the beginning of vaudeville with Loew. (Years later actors almost ruined vaudeville by reciting "Gunga Din.")

It wasn't very long before booking acts in his theaters was big business and Joe and Nick Schenck, owners of the Palisade's Amusement Park in New Jersey, joined the organization and Joe became head booker, while Marcus Loew was buying up new sites for big picture houses, where he now charged 10-20-30-cent admission and business was just terrific!

He was forced to go into the picture business, as he needed a large supply for his many houses and there was plenty of competition. When Warfield heard about Marcus going into the pic business, he wanted to pull out of the partnership, feeling that Marcus was going too far, but Loew told Dave he couldn't draw out because they were life partners. Dave stuck and made an extra ten million! In 1917 Loew controlled seventeen theaters in France and many in Germany (under cover), besides his many theaters in New York. The first big picture he was interested in was *The Big Parade*. When he bought the picture company, he couldn't put the name of Loew on the films because the other exhibitors refused to advertise Loew on their screens, so the company was called Metro-Goldwyn-Mayer, or M-G-M.

He really learned show biz when he got his first picture house at Pearl and Willoughby streets in Brooklyn, which Lew Fields told him he could get cheap. It was known as Watson's Cozy Corner, a burly house that had been raided by police because of dirty shows and had a bad name in the neighborhood. It seated 2,000. Loew at that time was used to 200-seaters and this was a big proposition for him. The first thing he did was to book an Italian company doing Shakespeare, to get the "stink off the joint." He lost dough for a few weeks, but when the house reopened as the Royal Theatre, with vaude and pics, the neighborhood had forgotten about Watson's Cozy Corner. He raised his price to 10 cents (up to now he had only had nickel theaters). The first day's receipts was exactly 10 cents! Only one customer came in, out of curiosity. Loew had forgotten to advertise he was going to open! The stagehands went out on strike and started picketing the theater day and night; they sent out letters all over the neighborhood about the strike at the Royal, and people became curious and came in. Loew cleared $65,000 that season.

In 1910 he opened his National Theatre in the Bronx, a beautiful theater for that time. It was here that Loew got some of the great Broadway stars, like Marie Dressler and the Dolly Sisters, to make an appearance on Surprise Nights; some just took a bow, some did a song or a dance, and they did it without pay just for the love they had for Marcus Loew and Joe Schenck. Eva Tanguay went on under the name of Dora Doone and was a riot. Loew offered George M. Cohan $10,000 for one week: Cohan refused. (This is the place the Bronx cheer started.)

One of his first big houses was Loew's Delancey Street, which was in the heart of the ghetto. One summer day Loew went down to see how things were going in his beautiful playhouse and was horrified to see men going in without coats or ties. He told Mike, the doorman (a big Irishman), not to let anyone in without a coat or tie, they weren't going to make a dump out of his new beautiful theater. The next day the manager received a lot of complaints about Mike; in fact, some of the patrons were ready to lynch him. After investigation it was found that Mike was carrying out Mr. Loew's orders a little too harshly, grabbing a patron's long beard and lifting it up to make sure he had a tie on. The order was rescinded! It was at this house where a monologist, while doing his act, saw a mother nursing her baby at the breast; the kid started to cry and the lady said, sternly, "If *you* don't take it, I'll give it to the hector!"

When Loew bought out the Sullivan & Considine Circuit to extend the Loew Circuit from coast to coast, he tried to put in his regular policy of vaude and pics with continuous performances. The Western people were accustomed to a matinee and two shows at night. They liked to go home for their supper and then come to a fresh theater. Loew believed he could educate them to his way. He was about a million dollars wrong, and after a year of experimenting, he gave the theaters back to S. & C. (He was just ahead of the times, as some years later the West was full of continuous houses.)

E. F. Albee at first paid no attention to Loew and his circuit, but as Loew got bigger and bigger the old man became a bit nervous, realizing that he was already a threat to his small "family" time and maybe if he got too ambitious he might get an idea to enter the Big Time. Loew did play a big-time act as a feature; it didn't bring any more money at the box office, but it was sort of a present to the loyal audiences he had built up. The audiences liked it because it smelt of "class," but it was really the picture that counted in those days. Orville Harold, a Metropolitan Opera tenor, was offered booking on the Loew Circuit for $5,000 a week. He said he would take it on condition that Mr. Loew sign his contract personally. It took Mr. Loew weeks to get around to it and when he finally did, he asked Orville why he wanted him to sign the contract personally? Orville, with a triumphant smile, said, "Because I worked for you years ago for $40 a week and when I asked you for $50 you wouldn't pay it, so I quit. Now you're paying me

$5,000 a week!" Loew smiled and said, "Believe me, Orville, I would have paid you $50 if you were worth it."

Sime, the publisher of *Variety*, had something in that bible of show biz that caused Marcus Loew to get very angry. (He and Sime were great pals.) When he met Sime he told him how wrong the article was and that he was real mad about it. Sime said, "Why don't you take a page ad in *Variety* and tell your side of it?" "How much is a page?" asked Loew. "$400," said Sime. *"That mad I ain't!"* said Loew.

Marcus Loew didn't look like a showman; he looked more like a semiprosperous furrier or tailor. He never wore any jewelry, and although his clothes were of the best, they didn't make him look distinguished. He was a very modest and mild-mannered man. He treated the smallest actor like he did the biggest star, with courtesy and kindness. Actors never had any contract trouble with the Loew Circuit. Joe Schenck and later Jake Lubin and Marvin Schenck, the bookers of the circuit, were square guys who followed the Loew code: their word was their bond!

At a testimonial dinner given to him by the White Rats, Loew was introduced by Will Rogers as "the Henry Ford of show business." In 1926 he was the first in show biz to receive France's Legion of Honor decoration. He loved to play pinochle with his cronies, and when he won he would accidentally knock over the table and the chips would get all mixed up and nobody had to pay off. He bought the famous Penbroke Estate at Glen Cove, Long Island, for a million dollars (a few months later he was offered five million for it). It was really a big castle with some forty odd rooms. On week ends there were 100 to 150 people there, guests of his twin sons, David and Arthur (both fine showmen) and his wife. Marcus wouldn't know a half-dozen there, and would usually go up to his rooms with some old friends and spend the week end playing pinochle.

Loew's early methods didn't set well with the older showmen, particularly his scheme of giving away thousands of free passes through department stores, but it put his new houses on the map. He was without a doubt the big power of the small-time show biz. He built 150 theaters, 125 of them de luxe; he built twenty-eight in a single year. But his State Theatre on Broadway and Forty-fifth Street, New York, was his dream baby. When the State was in the course of construction, he would watch every day from the windows of his office in the Putnam Building (where the Paramount now stands). One day he turned to Jake Lubin and said, "Jake, I'm going to give you 3,000 shares of stock in the company." Jake beamed. "And," continued Loew, "I'll take so much a week out of your salary." Jake unbeamed. He beamed again years later when he sold some of his stock for $60,000.

In spite of the State being classed small time as against the Palace Big Time, some of the tops in vaudeville played there, including Eva Tanguay, Jack Dempsey, and Jack Benny, who acted as M.C. (doubling with the Little Club). Milton Berle played the No. 3 spot and later made his first real big hit at the Palace, just a few blocks up the street. Clayton, Jackson & Durante made their first stage appearance there, as did nearly all of the top columnists and bands.

Loew never drove a bargain in which the other fellow lost. He was loyal to his employees and they in turn were loyal to him. In the Loew organization today over 50 per cent of the personnel have been with it thirty years or more.

Marcus Loew died in 1927, at the age of fifty-seven. A friend said he was burned out with worrying about his friends and others who had invested in his business. He was a sweet, kind, charitable gentleman, who tried to give everybody a decent shake. He may have been the king of small time, but he personally was strictly Big Time!

It Runs in the Family

Show business and the public today both know almost all about Oscar Hammerstein, 2d—that he made four million dollars on Broadway by his lyrics and plays.

Even some of the show biz newies must know about Oscar 2d's uncle, Arthur Hammerstein, whose musical-comedy successes of the 1920s, such as *The Firefly, Naughty Marietta, High Jinks, Rose Marie, Sometime, Blue Kitten, Song of the Flame,* and

Golden Dawn, are just a few that made theatrical history. And of that era, many of voting age will also recall the beauteous and talented Elaine Hammerstein, silent screen star, who was Arthur's sister. As for the saga of the first Oscar Hammerstein, who came to America from Berlin when he was about fifteen, started as a cigar maker, and became one of the greatest impresarios of grand opera, that is now theater lore.

It is mainly of Oscar's son and Arthur's brother and Oscar 2d's father, the fantastic Willie Hammerstein, that I want to tell you, because he was so close to vaudeville, but a reprise of the Hammerstein dynasty proves that genius certainly runs in the family. (Incidentally, today's Williamson Music Company is a tribute by Richard Rodgers and Oscar Hammerstein, 2d, to their fathers, both of whom were first-named William. But whereas the composer's dad was formally Dr. William Rodgers, Oscar's dad was always most informally Willie Hammerstein!)

It was through his management and great showmanship that Hammerstein's Victoria Theatre became the greatest and most colorful vaudeville theater in the world. In its seventeen years it grossed twenty million and made five million profit for Hammerstein. (It was only a 1,250-seater.) However, it isn't the money but the "fun" Willie had making it that I believe will interest you. Talent and showmanship were never rationed in the Hammerstein clan.

In his day, Oscar 1st discovered more musical and operatic talent than any of his contemporaries. But among the old vaude fans and actors, he will always be remembered for building the famous Hammerstein's Victoria Theatre and Music Hall. On the site of an old barn, on Forty-second Street and Seventh Avenue, he built this "freak" house with old building materials, because of his shortage of cash (one of the many times). It was a combination theater and music hall and roof garden, playing the great dramas and musical and variety shows. Drinks were served during the performance; the bar was never closed during all the time Hammerstein's was open. (There were bars in only two New York theaters; the other one was, and still is, at the Metropolitan Opera House.) The last show at this house was on April 26, 1915, just beating Prohibition by a couple of years.

The Victoria was Oscar's fifth plunge in theater building. His first was the city's first theater north of Central Park, the Harlem

Opera House, built in 1889. He then built the Columbia on East 125th Street (also known as Theatre Comique and Harlem Theatre), which was bought in 1900 by F. F. Proctor for his continuous vaudeville and stock companies. Hammerstein built the Manhattan Opera House, at a cost of $350,000, on Broadway and Thirty-fourth Street (now Macy's), which opened as Koster and Bial's Music Hall. (Hammerstein was their partner for a short time. Their original saloon-concert hall with the famous cork room was on Twenty-third Street and Sixth Avenue.) In 1889 Hammerstein's fourth plunge was the Olympia Theatre (later called the New York Theater) on Broadway between Forty-fourth and Forty-fifth streets on the east side of the street. The space was originally occupied by the 71st Regiment Armory. (Times Square was known as "Thieves' Lair." Broadway from Forty-second to Fiftieth streets was lit by gas light and was deserted at night.) Everybody said Oscar was crazy. The Olympia was a combined music hall, theater, roof garden, Oriental café, and billiard hall, with lounging, smoking, and cloak rooms, all for a 50-cent admission. The music hall was devoted to vaude. The opening bill had Yvette Guilbert, who was a big hit. The building also housed the Criterion Theatre (originally called the Lyric), where they played legit. It was on the New York Roof that Ziegfeld first played his *Follies*. The opening of the Olympia was the talk of the town. Oscar lost it when the New York Life Insurance Company foreclosed on a $900,000 mortgage.

Again Oscar was broke. On June 29, 1898, the day the Olympia was being sold, there were benefits given for him at the Garden Theatre, Harlem Opera House, and the Columbia Theatre, which raised about $8,000, and a few months later the first dirt was shoveled for the Victoria. In 1900 his sixth plunge was erecting the Belasco Theatre (west of Hammerstein's on Forty-second Street). It was on the site of the ill-famed McGory's Dance Hall. The Belasco was later called the Republic, playing dramas, and years later received national publicity when Minsky's took it over for their burlesque and strip-teaser. It is now a grind picture house. In 1904 Oscar built the Fields Theatre, on the south side of Forty-second Street, and leased it to Lew Fields for his stock company. It was a duplicate of the Republic Theatre. In 1905 it was named the Hackett, and six years later the Harris, then Wallack's, and finally the Carroll (Earl Carroll owned it by then).

Hammerstein's next plunge was to build the Manhattan Opera House on the north side of Thirty-fourth Street between Eighth and Ninth avenues. It was originally called the Drury Lane, and was built on the old piano factory site of Decker & Company, which Oscar bought for $200,000. Oscar started building it in 1901, and as the money came in he would go ahead. When Fregoli, the great protean artist, was at the Victoria, business was very good, and it was said he "put the roof on the Manhattan." It was at the Manhattan that Oscar first circused grand opera, selling a ticket for $6.00 which entitled the holder to see two operas in one day—*Elektra* at the matinee and *Salomé* in the evening. He went along with his operas until he had a fuss with Mrs. Clarence Mackay, who gathered her wealthy friends and walked back to the Met. Oscar said, "She took the roof off my opera house."

In 1910 at this same opera house he inaugurated a twenty-four-act vaude bill, the first and only three-ring vaudeville. It started at 7:30 and lasted until midnight, and then the picture went on! Maggie Cline, the headliner, said, "The walk across the stage from Eighth to Ninth Avenue will be the death of me." Years later, Frisco said about the Roxy, "Don't get caught on the Roxy stage without bread and water." At 8:20 the eleventh act was on. Dumb acts were shoved on three at a time. Lightning Hopper, a cartoonist, Chester Johnston, a cyclist, and Edith Raymond, on the wire, were on all at once, as was Saona with impersonations, the Juggling Jewels, and Arusa, hand balancer. It was a financial failure.

When Hammerstein was trying to sell the Manhattan, Marcus Loew came around to dicker for it. "I'll pay you $100,000 down and $100,000 for four years. After the first year if I find I don't want the house I'll turn the key over to you." Oscar looked at him and said, "Mr. Loew, just around the corner is Ludwig Baumann's furniture store. Go deal with him. I don't sell theaters on the installment plan." So Loew left, and built the Greeley Square, at Thirtieth Street and Sixth Avenue!

There were many stories told about Oscar when he was in opera. The employees knew when he showed up with a slouch hat that it meant trouble, but when he wore his high hat, everything was O.K. He paid Mischa Elman $1,000 to play the "Meditation" from *Thaïs*; Elman was not a member of the Musicians' Union, so Oscar put a chair in the aisle next to the musicians for him.

In 1906, when he went to sign Melba, he couldn't get a definite answer from her. Throwing thirty $100 bills on the floor, he said, "If you're afraid of your salary, I'll pay you in advance." "Wait," said Melba, "I will sing for you for nothing." In 1908 he built an opera house in Philadelphia at Broad and Poplar streets. Melba was supposed to open but was sick, and Tetrazzini filled in and was a riot. He built an opera house in London and the Lexington Opera House in New York, which opened with pictures because by the time it was finished Hammerstein had sold out to the Metropolitan Opera Company for more than two million dollars and was forbidden to have anything to do with grand opera for twenty years.

Oscar was a very versatile man and, contrary to popular belief, he did not speak with an accent. He played violin and piano pretty well. In 1893 he made a bet with Gustave Kerker (director of operas) that he could write an opera in forty-eight hours. He shut himself in the Gilsey House (Broadway and Twenty-ninth Street) and wrote *The Koh-i-noor Diamond!* Kerker refused to pay the bet, saying it wasn't what an opera should be. Oscar produced it at the Harlem Opera House to a gross of $400, but he had fun!

The first Mrs. Hammerstein (Rose Blau) was mother of Harry, Arthur, William, and Abe. When she died Oscar married Malvina Jacoby, by whom he had two daughters, Stella and Rose. He divorced Malvina and married Mrs. Emma Swift (he was sixty-four; she was thirty-two) in 1914, after losing three of his four sons within a period of five months. Harry, the oldest, went to New London with his regiment and died that night. Abe was always sickly, and Willie went suddenly. The only son left was Arthur. When Malvina died he paid the alimony to his two daughters.

Making money was a pastime for the elder Hammerstein; handling it was a nuisance. Many is the time his son Willie had to shove a $5.00 bill in his dad's pocket. Willie also would take the money out of the till, because his dad would think nothing of taking it all with no accounting. He paid his bills if there was money in the box office; if there wasn't, he would just let it go until there was.

Truly a fantastic figure was this Oscar Hammerstein, who made theatrical history with a deskless office, a bookless bookkeeper, a reversible plug hat, a gold-headed cane, and a Van Dyke beard. He invented many work-saving devices for the cigar business, which kept him in fresh money. The management of the Victoria was turned over to Willie to run as he liked and he liked to run it. When Oscar was in the grand opera business, he would spit at the Victoria's box office and say, "Phooey on this cheap business!"

And so this is the character of the father of Arthur and Willie, Stella and Elaine, and the grandfather of Oscar 2d, a great showman!

In the twenty years that Willie Hammerstein managed the Victoria, he brought more new ideas and received more newspaper space for his attractions than any manager in our generation! He violated all managerial traditions by coming to work at 8 A.M. and quitting at 9:30 P.M., when he would go right home. He was known by everybody on Broadway, but he never went for the night life of the Big Street. His home was entirely separate and distinct from his theater life. With the exception of a very few intimate friends, he never invited anyone to his home. In his twenty years as manager, he never saw a play at any other theater and only once did he drop in next door at the Belasco to see part of an act of *The Girl from the Golden West*. His only office was the lobby of his theater, sitting in a crooked chair surrounded by his cronies— actors, press agents, playwrights, managers, wine salesmen, vaudeville agents, bookers, gamblers, and screwballs. He loved these characters who would gather in the lobby while the show was going on. From them he would get the gossip and new stories of Broadway. The admission to this inner circle was being funny or interesting. Willie possessed a grand sense of humor and was a great practical joker (all done with a dead pan).

Before he got to the Victoria, he opened the Imperial Gardens with George Blumenthal (who later became a manager and pal of Oscar's) as his partner. The beer garden was on 110th Street, next to Dietrich's. (Willie started his vaude career there.) The place was backed by Ruppert's. Harry Pilcer was call boy and kept the stage and dressing rooms clean, besides helping sling beer; he would also go on and do a dance and a short act. Willie hired John Rynland, the Negro superintendent at the Empire Theatre, to press-agent the place by riding a bicycle and doing stunts; he had a funny laugh. He'd start at Ninety-sixth Street and bring crowds to the Imperial Gardens. He got 50 cents and all the food and beer he could consume. The partners then took over the Criterion Theatre, Brooklyn, to do stock. They paid $100 a week rent and had to borrow the first hundred. They divided with the actors 50-50.

You could always get "peck and pad" money from Willie. He was a soft touch. As a youngster he was an advance agent for a Davis & Keogh melodrama, went broke, and knew what it was to face long summers without money on Broadway. He never refused the courtesy of the house to any show people. He anticipated a request for an Annie Oakley; he would size you up as you approached him and say, "Sure, step right in and grab a seat." If you couldn't find a seat, you'd stand up with the "rail birds." They were the inner circle of Hammerstein's. They would drop in and stand back of the orchestra, see an act or two, or maybe just part of some act they particularly enjoyed. They would make wisecracks for or against the acts. There were more wisecracks and "nifties" pulled at Hammerstein's in a minute than one now hears on Broadway in a week. The wits and their half-brothers liked to stand behind the rail; it made them one of elite—and show-wise!

"Characters" were attracted to Hammerstein's like Damon to Pythias or Winchell to Runyon. There was little Jimmy Bell, a screwy boy tenor, who would amuse the gang by standing on one foot while singing, and for a few extra pennies he'd even shut one eye, "to make it harder." One of the famous characters on Broadway in those days was Doc Steiner, a vaude agent with a thick German accent that matched his thick eyeglasses. He not only wore glasses, but he liked to empty them. He wasn't a funny man, but was a great foil for Willie, whom he adored. I remember the time when Willie and Houdini, the world's greatest escape artist, framed the Doc. Willie one night started to argue with Houdini, in front of the gang, that he couldn't release a man from a pair of handcuffs if Willie furnished them and the man. Idea was that there would be no collusion with Houdini and no pretampering with the cuffs. The argument grew long and loud and finally they both put up $100. Willie said the only man he could trust was his pal, Doc Steiner. He sent him to the West Forty-seventh Street police station to get a pair of handcuffs, and when he returned, he said Doc was the only man he'd trust not to double-cross him with Houdini. Doc was flattered. The cuffs were placed on one of Doc's wrists and the other end was locked to the radiator pipe in the lobby. The radiator was plenty hot! Houdini started working on the cuffs and the more he tried to open them the madder he got. Everything seemed to go wrong. One by one the bystanders walked away. Finally Houdini, disgusted with his failure, also walked away.

Doc was left alone, handcuffed to the radiator pipe. It was hours later that a detective walked in and released him. The Doc lost five pounds. After a good laugh and a few drinks, Doc once again was ready for another of Willie's practical jokes!

Another time a screwball made an application for a tryout. He told Willie that he not only could sing better than Caruso, but louder! "How much louder?" asked Willie. "I can make my voice carry for three blocks," said the lamster from a nut factory. Willie told him to go over to the Times building across the street and sing as loud as he could, and if he heard him he would wave his hand. The fellow walked over to the Times building, the noisiest spot in town, and started to sing at the top of his voice for nearly half an hour without seeing Willie wave his hand. By this time he had a mob around him and almost got pinched for obstructing traffic. He finally came back for a decision from Willie, who asked him, "What's the matter, did your voice go back on you?"

His sense of humor and of the ridiculous just fit him for the task of managing Hammerstein's. As a headline hunter he had no equal. He inaugurated the "freak act" in vaudeville. He booked all the prominent fighters, wrestlers, and bicycle and running champions. He played the killers and near killers. A couple of comely girls, Lillian Graham and Ethel Conrad, shot at W. E. D. Stokes, a socialite realtor. The bullet struck the three-initialed gentleman in the leg and he promptly had the gals arrested. The newspapers were filled with the accounts of the shooting. Willie went bail for the girls and booked them for Hammerstein's, billing them as "The Shooting Stars." They couldn't sing, dance, or act, but jammed the house. After seeing the act, Junie McCree (a noted wit) remarked, "They'll be lucky if they finish the week without someone taking a shot at *them*!"

Hammerstein also played Nan Paterson, who shot Caesar Young in a cab, but didn't kill him. Willie paid her $500 a week. A little lady by the name of Beulah Binford didn't kill, but a man killed his wife for her, which she figured should make her a headliner, but that was too raw even for Willie, so she hired the Garden Theatre and played a maid in a sketch. There were forty-nine people one night who showed up to see her; that was her top attendance for a week at 10-20-30 prices. She gave up. Florence Carmen, the wife of a Long Island M.D., accused of shooting at a woman patient of her husband's through a window in her Freeport, Long Island, home, got booked. She sang "Baby Shoes."

A freak engagement is made with the deliberate object of promotion, the financial profit being secondary. People come to the theater who have never been there, or have been there very seldom. They see the rest of the show and like it, thus becoming a customer. Willie made Hammerstein's an institution, and as my friend Channing Pollock once said, he took care it wasn't an institution for the blind. He taught the public the danger of trifling with a young girl's affections. He booked Mae Sullivan, who won fame by suing a certain rich man for breach of promise. Her talents seemed limited to love and litigation. Willie once said, "The clamor is for novelty. You can't class this house as a vaudeville theater. Get a new name for it. The agents can't supply the demand for novelty, so you must invent and furnish it yourself."

Hammerstein's had some of the greatest press agents in the business! Willie gave them plenty of leeway. Abe Levy, Ann Marble, Nellie Revell, John Pollack, Joe Flynn, and Morris Gest were all tops and could cook up many novel ideas of publicity, but Willie was the commander in chief!

The Roof was an institution in itself. It occupied the roofs of both the Republic (nee Belasco) Theatre and Hammerstein's. It was originally called the Paradise Roof, and was later changed to Hammerstein's Roof Gardens. He billed the attractions up there as "Hytone Vaudeville." It opened in 1900 as a circus, but when it rained there was trouble getting the animals downstairs. The city wouldn't let Hammerstein put up the skeleton roof he wanted. He finally did it little by little, and the city let him get away with it. Willie had a farm up there, cows and beautiful milkmaids, a man with a 17-foot beard, and Sober Sue, whom nobody could make laugh. Willie offered prizes to top comedians if they could make her laugh. There was a gimmick; the poor colored gal had paralyzed facial muscles and, though she could laugh inwardly, she never showed it. They had acts, music—it was a great hangout for those who had to stay in the city in the hot summer days. The stage was like a fight arena; acts made their entrance through the audience. (Theater in the round?)

The Roof was enclosed in glass, and you can imagine how hot it was after the sun had beat down on the glass all day. There was no cooling system in those days. But Willie thought up a great idea. He had the elevator that brought you up to the roof heated, and when you got out on the roof it seemed at least 100 per cent cooler. He tried all kinds of experiments on the roof, including amateur nights, and special nights where all the actors playing downstairs would play an afterpiece for fun. Aaron Kessler, who was Willie's able assistant, put in small-time acts with pictures and a Negro orchestra to whose music people tangoed. He booked Mlle. Polaire and billed her as the ugliest woman in the world with the smallest waist, and business was so good he switched to $2.00 vaudeville with her.

Hammerstein's played a great list of attractions; the body of his shows consisted of standard acts, then he'd play some fakes, some real novelties. The late Morris Gest, who started as a sidewalk ticket speculator in front of the Victoria (some said he was Willie's private spec) and finished as one of the real great producers of Broadway, became a scout for some of Willie's "dream acts." (He'd dream up some fake.) Gest told me about the time Willie sent him to Europe to dig up a Turkish attraction. At that time there was a lot of talk about a Turkish Republic; the young Turks were on the verge of a revolution, and the newspapers were full of it. Willie figured anything Turkish would bring 'em in. Gest's instructions were to get a Turk with three wives or a reasonable facsimile.

At a small variety house in Lucerne, Gest saw an artist who did quick oil sketches. His name was Adolph Schneider, and he was a very intelligent fellow who spoke four or five languages (but no Turkish), and had a wife, daughter, and sister-in-law traveling with him. Gest unfolded Willie's plot, and it was easy to talk Schneider into coming to America for a salary he had never even dreamed of. They went to Adrianople and were outfitted with complete Turkish outfits for the three "wives" and himself. They learned a few Turkish words and were coached as to their actions and behavior. Then they notified the New York *Herald* correspondent in Paris that Abdul Kadar (Schneider's new name), court artist of the Turkish Sultan, was en route with his three wives to New York.

They played in Paris and created a sensation, and their coming to America was cabled and played up by the New York papers. On the boat whenever passengers asked them a question they sank to their knees and prayed to Allah. It kept them from having to answer. They became the passengers' pets when the ships' reporters came aboard. Immigration officials sent the entire outfit to Ellis

Island, where they were detained while the official status of the
three wives was referred to Washington. (Willie, under a different
name, made the complaint to the authorities.) The conflict with
the Immigration officials got plenty of newspaper space. Willie
finally put up a bond guaranteeing that the Turk and his wives
would leave the country in due time and that they wouldn't be a
financial burden to the good citizens of the U.S.

He sent them to the Waldorf-Astoria for accommodations. They
were refused (a guy with three wives—and only one house detective in the place). They then went to several other big hotels with
their forty pieces of baggage, and of course a parade of newspapermen and photographers, and they were turned down by all the big
hotels. Willie finally put them up in a swanky furnished apartment
(which he had ready all the time). Abdul Kadar and His Three
Wives appeared at Hammerstein's; he painted quick sketches in oil
while the "wives" graced the stage, doing nothing except to remove
the sketches when he finished. He was a sensation for many weeks
and when he finished his engagement he bought a home in Atlantic
City and lived there under his real name with his family for many
years on the profits he made at Hammerstein's!

The biggest receipts at Hammerstein's were from Evelyn Nesbit's
engagement. After the sensational testimony and the notoriety she
received in the famous White-Thaw case, no manager would give
her a job. Willie sent her to London, where she played for a few
weeks (the English were very polite to her), but cables came to
America about her tremendous success as a dancer. Newspapers
those days would accept news from abroad and feature it, but
wouldn't touch the same story (especially theatrical stuff) if coming from America. When Miss Nesbit came to New York, she was
an object of great curiosity. Willie had her billed as Mrs. Harry
Thaw, to which she objected and made him change it to Evelyn
Nesbit. The first week she played Hammerstein's, luck was with
Willie from a publicity standpoint. Harry Thaw escaped from
Matawan. Instantly Evelyn became the center of attention by de-
claring in a dramatic manner that she feared for her life, now that
Harry was free. Willie got a detail of police (in uniform, of
course) to guard her day and night. Some people even accused
Willie of engineering Thaw's escape! Evelyn became the most
talked-of woman in the world. Hammerstein's made an $80,000
profit on her eight-week engagement and paid her $3,500 a week.

Jack Clifford was her dancing partner. She went on tour and became a big box-office draw. Morris Gest managed her, and he and his associates made $100,000 on her tour; even the conservative Keith Circuit played her for many seasons.

Another attraction Morris Gest told me about was Machnow, an ignorant Russian peasant, who was 9 feet 2 inches tall. Circus and freak shows tried to get him to America, but he feared the ocean voyage. Willie sent Gest to get him. He got him to sign a contract easily enough, but on the day of sailing he refused to go. Gest got two hotel porters in showy uniforms, introduced them as police officers, and Machnow was told they had to take him to the Captain on a warship who was in command of the city. He got on the ship, and when it started to move it took ten sailors to hold him down. He had a terrific appetite; ten bottles of soda and thirty oranges was a good lunch. He slept in the private passageway on the floor as the berths were too small. Arriving in America, there was more trouble with the immigration officers; they not only refused him admittance but ruled he was an imbecile. Willie put up a bond and Machnow opened at Hammerstein's and was a sensation—doing absolutely nothing! Later needing more publicity, Willie had Machnow pinched for walking on the grass in Central Park. He wouldn't fit in the patrol wagon—more publicity, more pictures, more business.

Ann Marble, then Willie's press agent, went to Washington and telegraphed to Willie in the name of Teddy Roosevelt that he wished to see the giant. Through influence, Ann Marble finally got the O.K. from T.R., and Willie chartered a special train for newspapermen. The giant met the President and turned his back on him, claiming that they were playing a joke, that it wasn't really the President of the United States. How could he be? There were no soldiers around him and he didn't wear a uniform. He was finally convinced and the story went all over the world, which made Machnow a great attraction for many more weeks. He took enough rubles back to Russia to finance a private revolution.

Willie believed that one of the greatest attractions he ever had was Gertrude Hoffman as Salomé. The Salomé craze was at its height in Europe, and Willie read a description of the dance that Maude Allen was doing in London at the Palace Music Hall. Seeing Gertrude Hoffman seated in a box with her husband and musical director, Max, he convinced her that she should be the first to do it here, as she already had a big name in vaude and this would make her bigger. It didn't take Willie long to convince anybody and in a few days she and her husband sailed under the name of Mr. and Mrs. Adams, as they didn't want anyone to know they were going over to see Maude Allen. It didn't take her long to see what Miss Allen was doing and she returned to America. When she put the act in rehearsal here, Oscar heard about it and objected. "I have just engaged Mary Garden to sing *Salomé* at my Opera House; we cannot have two of them." This tied the act up for awhile, but soon he gave his O.K. and "A Vision of Salomé" was put on and was positively sensational. It ran for twenty-two weeks, which was the longest run for any attraction at Hammerstein's. There were literally hundreds of Salomé acts after this.

Willie could make an attraction out of almost anybody. With his genius for publicity and sensing what people wanted, he could make a money-maker out of an obscure person. There was a girl by the name of Flossie Crane who worked in Smith's Café at Coney Island, which was one of the best-known and popular resorts of the Island. She was a raw-looking, gawky gal, strictly country style. She seemed to have two voices, changing from baritone to soprano. The crowd would laugh. Willie sent for her. It took a long time for him to convince her that she wasn't being kidded when he offered her a job at his theater. She rehearsed an act and Willie billed her like a circus—"New Discovery, Flossie Crane, the Girl from Coney Island."

"You know, people like that," said Willie. "People like to discover talent, especially a poor girl from a saloon; Cinderella stuff always gets them." She went on and did fairly well, proving a good drawing card while she lasted. Hammerstein had her under contract for $50 a week, and got her other dates for $250 and made the difference.

He took Rajah, a snake charmer at Huber's Museum on Fourteenth Street, had her put on a dance with a snake, and she became a headliner for many years. Ruth St. Denis, the famous art dancer, first was presented at Proctor's Twenty-third Street under the name of Radha and was a failure at $750 a week. A few years later Willie hired her, changed her name, publicized her, and paid her $2,000 a week for almost the same dance, and she became one of the country's most famous dancers!

Lady Francis Hope, originally May Yohe, who married the

owner of the famous Hope Diamond, was once booked at the New York Theatre, to sing a few songs and show the famous $100,000 Hope Diamond. When she played for Willie later, he put in the contract that Lord Hope had to stand in the lobby; for this he paid them $1,500 a week. He later played her for $1,000 a week, and much later, when bad times hit May and there was no Hope (having been divorced), he played her for $75 a week. She was then married to Jack McAuliffe, the fighter.

Willie booked the famous Dr. Cook, phony North Pole explorer, who claimed it was he, not Admiral Peary, who discovered the Pole and had a lot of publicity about it. He made two spiels a day and received $1,000 a week, but he didn't draw. Bessie DeVoie, who gained much publicity for getting love letters from millionaire Frank Gould, also flivved.

Don, the Talking Dog, who could say "Hunger" and "Küchen" and that's about all, was a great attraction at the Corner because of Loney Haskell's monologue on him while the trainer tried to make him talk. Countess Swirsky made them laugh at a classic dance she did (they weren't supposed to laugh) for $750 a week and jammed them in.

Willie heard about a Hindu playing a small music hall in London, had him dressed up as a "titled" Persian, provided him with a retinue of native servants, and the ship news reporters went hook, line, and press release for him. He was billed as "Shekla, the Court Magician to the Shah of Persia." He was a big hit for a whole summer. Most of the "freak acts" had no specialty, and that was where Loney Haskell, an old monologist, and then working as assistant to Willie, came in. He would go on, make the pitch, answer questions, get laughs, etc., for the acts that didn't do anything.

The biggest fake attraction at the Corner was Carmencita, the dancer. Way back in 1894 when Koster and Bial's Music Hall was the center of gay life in New York, there had been a famous dancer named Carmencita. She was the idol of the wolves of that day and was a sensation. When the original Carmencita had been dead for over six years, Willie engineered a "farewell' appearance for her. Next door at the Belasco, *The Rose of the Rancho* was playing, and in the show there was a former chorus girl who interpreted a Spanish dance in the drama. She became Willie's "Carmencita." He signed her to a contract, sent her to Europe, and agents there cabled about her success. She came back to America, grabbed lots of newspaper space about her old triumphs (nobody bothering to check up that she had been dead six years), opened at Hammerstein's, and was a riot! Billed as "Reappearance of the famous dancer, Carmencita, after an absence of ten years." All the old-timers and tired wolves came to see her once more. Nobody ever discovered that she had been an obscure dancer next door to Hammerstein's only a few months before.

Al Jolson first played Hammerstein's as a single in New York and proved one of the biggest hits that ever played the house. He went back to Dockstader's Minstrels for much less money, but he liked it. The aristocrats and the blue bloods of vaudeville all appeared at Hammerstein's!

Like Tony Pastor, you didn't need a contract with Willie. When he said, "O.K., you play here week of so-and-so," that was as good as a contract. One week he would book an act that drew a lot of women who acted like men, and the next week he'd book an act that drew a lot of men who acted like women. Willie was neutral; anything for a laugh, especially if it would jam 'em in.

Between packin' 'em in and dreaming up headliners and playing practical jokes, Willie found recreation playing horses, poker, pinochle, and shooting craps. He once said, "Years ago I lost $50 in my first crap game and I've been trying to get it back all these years." He only played with his own particular friends. At one time the backstage crap game at Hammerstein's was one of the biggest in town. It got so big they had to transfer it to the Hermitage across the street. Thousands were lost, and won.

In 1911 Willie had an argument with his dad and left the theater. You never saw such a change in a theater overnight. The house dropped plenty; on a Saturday night they only had $400 in the till! He returned two months later (two terrible months for Hammerstein's) and put on a seventeen-act bill and brought biz back overnight. He billed it as "Colossal Vaudeville." Frank Jones replaced Aaron Kessler as assistant manager; Aaron became a big-time agent. The head usher there for many years was Dick Abernathy, the bartender was Davy (I doubt if anybody knew his last name), George May was the leader, Mike Simon the stage manager (later Mark Nelson replaced him), Charlie Jones was in the box office with Brady Greer as his assistant (Allan Schneebe followed Jones), and the theater's cat's name was Thornton. What a family!

Willie never spurned a "freak attraction" that had been advertised in the headlines; they all meant one thing to him—box office! Willie was unlike the typical showman. He didn't have the glamor of his dad; he was cold, reserved, and cynical. He would unbend only among his close friends, but in the main he was unresponsive. He was generous with passes but never used a pass pad, merely scribbling a circle number and W.H.; sometimes he added a date. It seemed very simple for he used any scrap of paper that was handy, but it is said that there were practically no forgeries passed at the box office, though many tried. (It was a practice of many pass-hounds to even forge them for different houses.)

Willie booked shrewdly but fairly, and if he felt that an act would bring in big returns, he was willing to pay big money, but he wanted value received for all he paid out, and he generally got it. He paid many acts "show money" that wanted to be seen at the "Corner." Many a turn owed its professional life to the build-up he gave them when others were afraid to take a chance, and he was not afraid to put an act in for a run if he felt it would hold attention. Often he offered suggestions that made the difference between failure and success.

Willie never showed emotion and his own personality was completely different than the personality he gave to the theater. The "Corner" was a genial, friendly spot, loved by the paying patrons, and the gathering place of the show folk and the sporting element of the city. While Willie was manager, actors loved to play there; it was the Palace of its day. Hammerstein's was billed as the "stepping stone to Broadway." It was the fantastic Willie Hammerstein who helped many an actor step on that magic stone to Broadway, fame, and fortune!

So it was with a heavy heart that show folks heard about the passing of Willie Hammerstein. He died at the age of forty-two, in 1914. He was married twice. His first wife (mother of Oscar 2d and Reggie) died in 1910. Willie then married her sister (Anna Nimmo).

After Willie's death, his brother Arthur and Loney Haskell and Lyle Andrews took over the management. The Palace was cutting in terribly. The "Corner" just wasn't the same without Willie. The place seemed to have a reversal of form. Admissions were reduced

Freaks were not so popular. Mrs. "Gyp the Blood" and Mrs. "Lefty Louie," whose husbands had been electrocuted for the murder of Rosenthal the bookmaker, wanted a job, although not keen to do an act; they were turned down. Later Arthur booked a few freaks; it paid off. He made many changes. The colored male ushers were changed, after fifteen or twenty years, to colored girl ushers. It was all a different show biz than when Willie was alive. The Palace was ushering in a new era. It wasn't Arthur's fault he couldn't make the "Corner" pay off.

Hammerstein's went up for sale for $125,000 yearly rent for remainder of a ten-year ground lease; it stood Hammerstein about $50,000 a year rent and taxes. Arthur Mayer and his associates bought up the lease, rebuilt the old place, and called it the Rialto (1916). The last bill at the Victoria was the week of April 26, 1915. The bill was: Overture, Althea Twin Sisters, Dainty Marie, Harry Breen, Exposition Four, O'Brien Havel Co., Intermission, Will Rogers, Ruby Norton & Sammy Lee, Frank Fogarty, Princess Rajah (funny she should be on the last bill in the theater that made her a headliner), and a Charlie Chaplin comedy picture—and the *exit march*! As an afterpiece at the last show there was a special minstrel show with Frank Fogarty as the interlocutor.

Arthur tried to start vaude again with William Morris at the Forty-fourth Street Theatre, but was refused bookings by the U.B.O., which claimed that his franchise applied only to the Victoria. The Forty-fourth Street idea didn't last long after that, although he had a few real big vaude shows.

Oscar Hammerstein, 1st, died August 1, 1919, a great showman. He lived to see his sons become great showmen like himself, his daughters fine actresses, and one of his grandsons (named after him) one of the great lyricists, poets, and producers of our time. There are a few more Hammersteins to carry on: Teddy (Arthur's son), Reggie and Oscar (Willie's sons). Abe and Harry had no children.

Hammerstein's Victoria died when Willie died. It may be generations before anyone achieves the same measure of friendliness for a theater as Willie did for his Victoria, at the "Corner" of Forty-second Street and Seventh Avenue!

Sylvester Z. Poli

One of the most colorful romances of the days of real vaude is the story of Sylvester Z. Poli, who ran a small group of wax figures into a multimillion-dollar amusement enterprise. He was a genius in his way and yet a modest and unassertive personality who enjoyed the respect of the entire business.

He was brought to this country by the Eden Musée, when their waxworks show opened on West Twenty-third Street, over half a century ago. He was a sculptor of sorts and it was his job to keep the exhibit up to date. Some of the figures, such as the group of crowned heads, were more or less permanent (they were permanent in those days), but the Musée's "change of bill" consisted of offering effigies of the latest murderers, bank robbers, and others in the public eye. When a figure became outdated, it was Poli's job to melt the wax head down and recast the material to some newer public figure.

On the side he made a few figures for himself and when he got a couple of dozen, he quit his job and opened a side show at Ontario Beach, a resort near Rochester, New York. He moved around with the seasons, but finally came to rest in New Haven, Connecticut, where he found an upstairs hall which could be rented cheaply. He set up his waxworks museum and soon added a few variety acts (as all museums did those days). Eventually the variety show became so important that he got rid of the wax figures and ran just variety. Where other theaters worked the two- and three-a-day schedule (with the big acts doing two), Poli played his more important acts doing three and the lesser acts doing four. Acts that flatly refused to do a "supper show" for Keith would go to New Haven and do it cheerfully for Poli. Some of the tops of old variety did three-a-day for Poli, at New Haven.

With a small seating capacity he could not afford to pay the acts their regular salaries and they knew that they would have to take a cut (and a good one) to play the date. Generally, the big acts booked in only when it was not possible to get other and financially better bookings. Poli never knew until Thursday (sometimes Friday) the show he was going to have on Monday. And sometimes it was even Monday morning when he knew his complete bill. Acts playing Poli's figured it was better to play the week at a big cut than not to play at all. But most of them waited until the last minute in the hope of picking up a full-price date. In other words, they used Poli as a convenience. They also played for him because he was an independent, was out of town, had no opposition, and, best of all, nobody knew the salary he was paying.

In his booking, Poli was largely helped by William Morris, who had plenty of full-pay-time bookings, but tucked Poli in as a rider. Morris acts felt they were more or less obligated to play for Poli, though Morris never made them do it (as many other bookers did). He used one argument, "Why lay off? Cop this dough," and so Poli gave as good a show as many a big-time house in New York. It was tough to advertise a show that was not set, but the town sensed the difficulties of getting acts to come to New Haven and figured that Poli would have a good show, no matter what the ads said, so they came. And anyway those Yale students would go any place to duck classes!

I recall the time when Poli asked the famous Jim Thornton to play for him. He told him that his theater was a small one, the town was small, the orchestra was small, the seating capacity was small, etc. After Thornton heard this, he turned to Poli and said, "Mr. Poli, why don't you book *midgets* for your house?"

It was a number of years before Poli tried to expand. There was plenty of open territory, but he held off until he felt that if he didn't, some other manager would. He opened houses in Bridgeport, Waterbury, and other near-by spots, and did so well he built a real theater in the home town, the Palace.

S. Z. Poli is probably the only man in this country who built a vaude theater without a single mortgage or lien. (Martin Beck was the only one that built a legit theater without a mortgage.) Poli paid as he went, and the house opened absolutely free of obligation. It was really a handsome house for its time. As a sculptor Poli brought in all the Italian marble duty free and used plenty of it. But building a theater very nearly proved his undoing.

When the Keith Booking Office had been formed, every effort was made to get Poli in line, but he dodged. Once Phil Nash actually talked him into joining and got his check for membership dues. Poli went down to lunch with William Morris. Nash told the

actors gathered in the reception room that Poli had come into the
Booking Office, and showed the check to prove it.

That time Morris and Poli, breaking their usual custom, went to
lunch at the Morton House, taking a table at the window level with
the street. Soon an actor spied them and told Poli he wanted to
cancel a date he had made for a few weeks later. "I'm not going to
let you tell the booking office what you're paying me." A little later
another actor canceled; then a third. "But I'm not in the United
Booking Office," insisted the frightened Poli. "You can tell everyone." So the actor raced off and the first one he told was Nash,
who laughed and waved the Poli check. He didn't laugh two days
later when the check came back marked, "Payment stopped."

When Poli had only one house the U.B.O. let him alone; it was
after bigger game. But when he expanded and the office learned of
his financial setup, it moved in. Poli sought banking accommodations from his usual sources and was refused. He went to other
banks, but got the same results. No credit! Then a friendly banker
advised him that every financial institution in the state had been
warned that if Poli opened up any more theaters without U.B.O.
consent, Keith would build an opposition in every spot. So what
happened? Poli left Morris and joined the U.B.O., much against
his will, but he just had to.

With the financial bar removed, Poli expanded his holdings. He
had to pay more for acts, but not as much as he had feared, and
he was able through thrifty management to make a nice profit.
He later sold out to William Fox at a big profit, though some of
the dough is said to be still unpaid, being represented by stocks
and bonds. Still he made enough cash to retire to a life of luxury
and to marry his daughters into Italian nobility.

Personally he was tall, heavy-set but not fat, with jet black hair
and mustache. He never lost his heavy Italian accent, but it was
not the accent of the stage comedian. He was jovial and was good
company and he had the respect of his fellow managers who booked
through the Morris office. Often when a business question arose at
meetings, Willie Hammerstein or Percy Williams would suggest,
"Let's leave it until Thursday when Poli comes to town." He was
then still in the one-house stage, but the big-time men had a
healthy respect for his knowledge of show biz.

For years he personally booked his shows, coming to New York
on Thursday and again on Friday if necessary. Later, when the

circuit expanded, he sent his nephew, P. Alonzo Poli, down to New York to represent him. Shortly after Alonzo started, a friend asked Poli how Alonzo was doing? Poli shrugged his shoulders and said, "Pretty good. Of course he makes some mistakes, but he'll learn from them. I'd rather lose money from his mistakes than put in a clever guy who would not make mistakes but would graft. When Alonzo learns, he'll make no more mistakes. The clever guy would keep on grafting." He was right about Alonzo, who became a fine booker.

Poli was a natural-born mixer, and Sylvester dressed in a green sash and plug hat marching in the St. Patrick's Day Parade of the Ancient Order of Hibernians was one of the local sights. He saw nothing odd in his membership in an Irish Society. They liked him and he liked them. He was happy to accept their invitation to join, and he always did his bit.

When he made his first trip back to Italy, he was given a send-off banquet at which the Mayor of New Haven acted as toastmaster. The "Who's Who" of New Haven and the state were guests at that party.

The tip-off on Poli is an incident that happened at the opening of his Bridgeport house. Several friends came down from New York and he met them at the station. They went to dinner, then to the theater, where they tried to get in through the front door, the doors not yet being opened. The doorman stopped them, explaining he had been told to let no one in. "But I am Poli," the host protested. "I don't know that," said the doorman. "You'll have to see the manager." Without a word Poli led the party around the block to the stage door, where he was recognized. "I suppose you'll have a new doorman tomorrow?" said one of the party. Poli looked surprised and said, "Certainly not. The man was just doing his duty. He never saw me before. I might not have been Poli!" And that was that. As long as a man did his duty, he was sure of a job with Poli. He was too big a man to resent being turned down at the front door of his own theater.

When S. Z. Poli died, he was honestly mourned by actors and managers and neighbors. He left about thirty million bucks, and the Government got the last laugh, when they *cut* Poli!

Alexander Pantages

Born in Greece in 1871, Alexander Pantages came to this country as a young man, and when the gold rush was on he struck out for the Klondike. They say he ran the honky-tonk owned by Klondike Kate, but the truth is that he started as a waiter and signed contracts with the gambling houses to clean, sweep, and wash up the floors at night. From the sweepings, he extracted the gold dust dropped by players during the gambling hours; this added up to quite a bundle.

From the Klondike he came to Seattle, Washington, and opened up a combination bootblack parlor and fruit store adjoining the Sullivan & Considine theater. The actors playing the theater patronized his store and he became a favorite with them. In 1902 he sold the store and opened up a 10 cent theater, did very well, and opened some more and soon he had a chain. He was now opposition to Sullivan & Considine and he and John Considine became real enemies. The feud lasted for many years and only stopped when his daughter Carmen married John W. Considine, Jr., who is now a big producer in Hollywood.

Pantages' success with his few theaters led him to enter the sacred Orpheum Territory down the Pacific coast. He was so successful that he got the idea for a national circuit on a big scale. He opened booking offices in New York and Chicago and routed his shows westward. He got as far east as Birmingham, Alabama. Most of his holdings were in the Middle and Far West. He overexpanded with vaude-film and in the 1929 crash was hit hard. He disposed of most of his holdings and sold six of his principal properties to RKO, Tacoma, Portland, San Diego, Spokane, Frisco, and Salt Lake City, for three and a half million dollars. (A few years before he had asked eight million for them.) He got part in cash and part in bonds. (He lost the bonds, as did RKO, when the company went into default, receivership, etc.)

At the peak of his career he operated thirty theaters. He tried a comeback in 1933 by leasing theaters in Hollywood, Seattle, and Salt Lake City. It failed because the jumps were too big. At one

time he was one of the most important inde circuits in the country
as to most weeks offered and territory covered. He road-showed
his shows (à la Orpheum and S. & C.) and issued contracts for
thirty-two weeks (with a catch; all contracts read fourteen weeks
or more). At the end of six weeks the act would reach the Coast
and six of the remaining eight weeks would go to 25 per cent cuts,
take it or leave it; most of the acts took it to keep from being
stranded way out there. When the Orpheum and S. & C. circuits
bought up all the good acts, he booked European acts who would
never have played in America if not for Pantages. Personally he
favored acrobats and played at least one on each bill, sometimes
two. He had a habit of breaking up "flash acts" and taking out certain singing or dancing girls or teams and playing them on his
circuit.

He liked to book acts direct but let the actual bookings go
through the agents; he took the word of the act instead of the
agent. He even used some acts as spies to send in reports on the
shows, house, and management. He didn't even trust his managers!
Pantages never learned how to read or write. He had his employees
read his telegrams, and his wife handled his personal affairs. But he
had a remarkable memory (like Martin Beck); he could remember
salary, position on the bill, when the act played for him, and how
they went over. He created "office" acts, that is, girl acts or flash
acts in which one of his bookers or agents had an interest; in that
way he knew what it cost and what the overhead was. He played
one office act against the other, each one watching the other's
mistakes and watching out for graft.

Pantages played many big-time high-salaried acts as headliners,
but he never went Big Time. Unlike Marcus Loew, he considered
vaude more important than pictures, and was a very good vaude
showman. During the war in 1914 he put up a wireless on the roof
of his theater in Edmonton, Canada, so the latest war messages
could be read between acts. It was seized by the army and dis-
mantled. He leaned a lot towards the Willie Hammerstein school
of playing freak acts, although never was the showman Willie was.
He played a number of convicts and also in 1924 gave Fatty
Arbuckle a chance to make a comeback when nobody would touch
him after the bad publicity he had received. When Arbuckle
walked on the stage in San Francisco he received a two-minute
ovation. Pantages played many fight champs and did big business

with them. In 1930 he introduced at his Minneapolis theater a new idea in picture trailers. He had two actors who were playing on the bill act out big moments of the coming film in an interior set.

He was more or less retired at the time of his death (he died in bed from a heart attack, 1936); he was in a partnership with RKO with his houses in Hollywood, and the Hill Street, Los Angeles, which his son Rodney operated. Pantages went through several fortunes. In later years he had a great interest in race horses; his son Rodney, partnered with Harry Rogers, handled the theaters and the booking office. Pantages made a lot of money in oil and investments.

He would play acts he liked over and over again on his circuit. He figured himself a great ladies' man and liked to book girl acts.

The only thing that Pantages contributed to vaudeville was the opposition he gave to the Orpheum and S. & C. circuits, which made it possible for the actors to dicker for the salaries they wanted. He certainly played a big part in small-time vaudeville!

James Austin Fynes

I feel that I should tell you about J. Austin Fynes, because he contributed a great deal to putting early vaudeville on a solid foundation. I realize the name is strange even to vaudevillians and practically unknown to the layman. But he really was a very interesting personality. I didn't know him, but from the stories told to me about him by Sime Silverman, Chicot (Epes Sargent), J. C. Nugent, and George M. Cohan, I believe I can give you a pretty good picture of this gentleman.

Had he been six inches taller, the probabilities are that James Austin Fynes would have written his name more boldly in the book of vaudeville, for he suffered an inferiority complex that crabbed his disposition and to some extent limited his usefulness. He always had a dread that some third-rate actor would hold him up on the street and bawl him out for not booking his act. For that reason he always carried a heavy cane for self-protection. He never had to use it, but he figured there was always a chance. He was very sarcastic and quick to find offense where none was intended, and this kind of narrowed his friendship circle.

For some reason he disliked his first name. His close friends called him Jack, though that name really belonged to his brother, John T. Fynes (a press agent). To all others he was J. Austin Fynes, and few knew what the initial stood for. (To this day nobody knows what the R. H. stood for in the late R. H. Burnside's name.)

Fynes started as a Boston newspaperman, then came to the New York *Sun*, doing dramatic criticism as a side line for $5.00 a story. When Frank Queen, owner and editor of the *Clipper*, died, Fynes was given the editorial post and made good. But Albert Borie, the business manager, was out of step with Fynes' advanced ideas, and Fynes tried to buy the paper from the estate, getting the cash from B. F. Keith (whom he had known when he was a Boston newspaperman). The deal was just about to go through when Borie got wind of it and went to Philadelphia to talk the heirs out of the deal.

That left Fynes out on a limb and Keith suggested he take over the management of the Union Square Theatre, which he was about to open. Fynes grabbed at this offer and did a great job. In those days each manager selected his own program, subject to a budget limit, and was practically an independent operator. Fynes used his acquaintance with the legit actors to get many of them to take a flyer in vaude. Until that time only one legitimate sketch (Redding & Stanton) had tried vaude, and it was their success which gave Fynes the idea.

He made a start with Charles Dickson and his wife, Lillian Burkhart, and followed them with Mr. and Mrs. Drew (Gladys Rankin), and then John Mason and Marion Manola. Only the Drews and Miss Burkhart lasted in vaude. The others went around once and were through. Fynes naturally wanted entertainment, but he would book a big name in a poor sketch for the sake of the people who would be attracted and get a liking for vaudeville. Now and then he varied the dramatic sketch with some concert artist, Camilla Urso and Edouard Remenyi being outstanding.

This kind of act upped the box-office receipts and made the Union Square an important house. His success came to the attention of E. F. Albee, Keith's general manager, who figured that this former newspaperman was a real rival. He cut down the activities of the resident managers of all Keith houses and put the booking of the entire circuit in the hands of S. K. Hodgdon, who up to that time had booked only the Boston Theatre's shows.

Via grapevine (which they have in show biz as they do in the underworld) Fynes learned of the move and was ready for it. At the same time as the announcement of the Keith change came the announcement that Fynes had signed with F. F. Proctor as general manager; he was now in a position to thumb his nose at Albee, since his own position was just as big as Albee's. To get even with Keith and Albee, Fynes began raiding the Keith personnel. Fynes could have found others just as good, but he wanted to irritate Albee and he certainly did. He had both Keith and Albee nuts!

At Proctor's he had a great freedom. When he was with Keith he had to stick on the job. On the Proctor end he could do his work when and how he wanted. He was a master of detail, and got rid of a lot of work in a short time. He showed up at his office at 8:00, went over his mail, received his assistants' reports, gave his orders, and by noon was ready to go to lunch, leaving his desk clean. He liked to go to the race tracks or around a horse room for the winter betting, then go back to his office to clean up the business of the day.

He made instant decisions and was very seldom wrong, and when he was he never passed the buck to the one who originated the idea. If Proctor complained that so-and-so shouldn't have done such-and-such, Fynes very quietly would say, "I told him to," and head off further debate. He always stood behind his staff and his staff loved him for it.

It was Fynes with Hugh Ford who developed the highly successful stock companies and who put into practice the English idea of doubling. The nearness of the Twenty-third Street Theatre to the Fifth Avenue house made it possible to give a headliner a double job at a salary and a half. He once even tried to do a triple booking, playing Blanche Ring at the Newark Theatre in addition to the Twenty-third Street and Fifth Avenue, but it was too tough on the artist. It never was repeated.

Fynes was never able to make Proctor theaters contenders with Keith's because Proctor would not spend the money, but he did make a very good profit for the circuit. Fynes left Proctor before his contract was up because of friction, and was soon heard from in the picture field. The pic store fit-up had just about hit New York, and Fynes was shrewd enough to see its possibilities. The small scale of costs and receipts didn't appeal to him, but for a time he started these shows and sold 'em out as going concerns. For example, he revamped an old church in Harlem, got his costs back the first week or so, and sold the place for $1,500; it was a profitable business while it lasted. (It required only an empty store, picture sheet, cheap chairs, and a papier-mâché front with a few big incandescent lights.)

A couple of years later he made his last stand in the amusement field and met his first defeat. He had popularized the legit artist in vaudeville; now he tried to get the picture producers to use these same names. But the producers were not yet ready for this. They got nine cents a foot, net, whether the leading actor was John Jones or a name star. They couldn't see any advantage, in money, in using big names, and Fynes dropped the idea in disgust, going back to the real estate business, in which he had dabbled for years. A few years later he saw his headliners scheme adopted by the pic people, but he made no fresh efforts to get into the game. He had met the producers and felt they did not speak his language. Had he lived, he might have become Hollywood's first and greatest ten-percenter, but he passed on without making the try.

J. Austin Fynes did a lot for vaudeville and added a lot of firsts from the managerial end. Besides getting the top legits to go into vaude, he practically started the "freak act," not as strenuously as Willie Hammerstein, but he booked Mrs. Alice Shaw, a society gal who was a whistler, and she brought the carriage trade to the box office.

J. Austin Fynes was one of the few men who accomplished something really constructive in the vaudeville business when vaudeville needed it most.

And Not Forgetting . . .

One of the very important figures in small-time vaudeville was
Gus Sun. Born Gus Klotz in Toledo, Ohio, in 1868, he started as a
juggler and equilibrist in variety, then joined the Sells-Foley Circus
(later known as the Sells-Floto). He became treasurer, then circus
manager. Gus had three brothers, John, George, and Pete. With
only $200 they launched the Sun Bros. Circus in two wagons, with
the four boys and a 50-foot round top. In its seventeenth season
they shifted from wagons to sixteen railroad cars carrying 250 people. Gus gave this up to become a vaude manager and booker.

He started with a theater in Springfield, Ohio, which he made
his headquarters. In 1906 he booked three houses and by the next
year he controlled 70 houses in Ohio and Pennsylvania and booked
100 others. In 1909 he booked 200 houses and by 1926 was booking
over 300.

The Sun Circuit was more potent even than the smaller managers and agents credited it with being. On the circuit there were
many important cities. He could play a medium-priced act, say
from $250 to $350 weekly, for ten to fifteen weeks in two- and
three-a-day houses. Of course he would use only one of this type act
on the bill and naturally headline them. Many acts didn't care
what they received, as they were breaking in their act for the Big
Time, and for Sun they would play towns that didn't interfere
with the big-time bookers. Gene Tunney and Jack Dempsey broke
in their acts for Sun. Of course the rest of his houses were small
theaters, airdomes, store shows, and were real small time.

Gus Sun introduced many things to vaudeville that didn't help
it any. He was the first to play "split weeks," which meant three
days in a town instead of a week, and he also was the first to have
the cancellation clause in his contract, where the manager could
close an act after the first show without paying the act a dime.
He also was the first to pay an act six-sevenths of a week's salary for
a six-day week where they didn't work on Sundays. (Many managers
in the East followed his example.) He would book an act on
photos, ads, and letterheads. When you put comedy in your ads,

or sent him good-looking letterheads and clean photos, he would say, "It must be a good act." He had the reputation of wiring his acts (instead of writing to them) on the least provocation. Acts would figure at least three to five dollars a week for telegrams. (He always sent them collect.) It got so actors called a messenger boy on a bicycle, "Gus Sun's Bicycle Act." The Western Union did more business in their Springfield, Ohio, office than they did in many big cities. It was said that Sun had plenty of stock in the company. They tell about the time he wired an act, "You play Scranton, Pa., next week. Confirm." The act wired back (prepaid), "Scranton O.K. next week." To which Sun immediately wired back (collect), "Not Scranton O.K. Scranton P.A. Wire confirmation."

There were many cancellations on the Sun Time; the managers were new to the business and very cheap and took unfair advantage of the cancellation clause in the contract. By canceling an act or two, they would have a new show at night, which brought in some repeaters. One manager who played five acts had a slide put on the screen even before the show went on reading, "All new show tonight!" He would cancel his whole show, good or bad. The actors didn't get wise for months. Van Hoven, the great comedy magician, was closed more often than the cash drawer at Woolworth's.

Gus Sun at first restricted his operations to the Middle West, but little by little he spread to the South, Pennsylvania, New York State, and even New England.

The best you could say about most of the Gus Sun Circuit was that it was the proving grounds for many acts; the good ones and the ambitious ones left it as soon as they could, and the ones that kept playing the circuit season after season could never brush off that "small-time dust."

I will say that hundreds of acts on the Sun Circuit who never got off it saved more money than some of the big-time acts. Many of them saved enough money to buy a farm or a business or were able to retire and live in comfort. Gus didn't pay big salaries, but the jumps were small, many of them being just ten-cent electric car rides to the next town, living was cheap (usually with some private family), and the stage costumes didn't have to be expensive (usually made by the wife) and lasted for many seasons. The act didn't have to dress up in the small towns, so their street wardrobes didn't amount to much. And there were few places to spend any money. So the grouch bags on the Sun Time grew fat by the end of the season.

At one time Gus Sun booked more theaters (?) than the Keith Circuit, but that's like saying a "pitchman" on Forty-second Street sold more phony pearls than Tiffany did real ones! Gus at this writing has retired and earned the fun he is now having with his grandchildren, as he was a nice guy and never left his business a minute in all the years he operated. It was too bad he was pioneering vaude when he had to deal with yokels who went into the "new" picture-house business they "heard" about. Those days they opened pic houses like they did gas stations years later, or like the city chaps that went into the chicken-raising biz!

There were many managers who helped vaudeville reach the Palace—managers who did the spade work that dug the foundation for the Palace—men who were respected and honored in their communities and by the actors who played for them. Space doesn't permit giving full details about all of them, but no story of vaudeville would be complete without mentioning some of them.

Harry Jordan of Keith's, Philadelphia, was a very important part of vaude; he not only was the manager of one of the finest vaude theaters in America from the day it opened to the day vaudeville was discontinued there, but he had a lot to say about the booking of acts for his house. He helped good acts get routes by going to New York on booking days and putting in a plug for the acts that had made good for him, and his judgment was respected by the bookers. A real fine gentleman whom the actors all loved.

John Royal, manager of Keith's Palace in Cleveland, was like Jordan. He was a pioneer manager for Keith and practically ran his own theater, and his opinion on acts was also highly respected in the New York office; he too helped many an act get a break. He now is one of the great consultants on radio and TV for NBC. He also was the head of their talent department when it started, and with his great experience in vaudeville I believe knows more about acts in these two branches of show biz than anyone else. He is liked by actors, which is a tip-off on a nice guy. I believe that John Royal today is one of the few pioneer vaude managers that carried on his great experience to radio & TV.

Then there were Wilmer and Vincent, two actor-writers who played vaude and wrote many acts and finally ended up as managers and owners of a chain of theaters. Mr. Wilmer died many years ago. Walter Vincent, one of the finest gentlemen of the theater I have ever met, still has a great circuit of houses in the South, which are run by old bookers and agents and managers of vaudeville with whom he worked for many years. Walter for over twenty-five years has devoted his time, money, and heart to the welfare of the actors he worked with and who worked for him and all those that have followed them. He is now the president of the Actors' Fund, following in the hallowed footsteps of Uncle Dan Frohman, who was president for a half a century. A fine showman and fine gentleman is Walter Vincent.

William Fox started with small-time vaudeville, and I started with him, not as a partner but as an actor. I remember the tiny office in the lobby of the Dewey Theatre on East Fourteenth Street (directly opposite the famous Tony Pastor's). This tiny office could only hold a trio; if a quartette wanted to do business, the tenor had to stay outside. There were no contracts; they just gave you a slip of paper with the name of the theater you were to play. Everyone knew the salaries, $20 for singles, $40 for doubles, $60 for trios, $80 for quartettes, and if you happened to have five people in the act they would add on a $5.00 bill.

William Fox was a great factor in early small time. Joe Leo, his son-in-law, was his first booker, then Mr. Norris took over, followed by Edgar Allen, and finally Jack Loeb, who was a partner of Fox in a few theaters. Bill had quite a number of small-time houses and was getting very important, but became picture-conscious and before you knew it was the head of Fox Pictures and one of the tops in the business, so forgot his vaudeville interests and let Marcus Loew step in. At one time Fox (an old furrier) owned more theaters than anyone in show biz. He was buying up whole circuits; he had an ambition to control all the theaters (nonlegit) in America, and he almost made it, but a lot of financial troubles piled up on him which ended up in bankruptcy. He still managed to leave many millions when he died.

He spent the last years of his life playing pinochle in the little shed in the parking space back of the Roxy Theatre (which he owned, as he had owned the Roxy at one time). He was very loyal to his old friends; he made Ed Keeley, a cop he knew when he had the Dewey, his booking manager, and later gave him a life job at the studio. He became a partner of Keith in the Riverside Theatre, New York, which made him familiar with big-time actors' salaries, and so helped his booker get the acts at the right price. The Fox office had lots of trouble with actors in the breaking of contracts, etc., and at one time the V.M.P.A. gave him warning that if he didn't mend his ways they would have to throw him out. This, with the trade papers and actors also against him, made him issue a new contract, the first one of its kind—he even put down what spot the act had on the bill (never done before). But Fox's mind wasn't on vaude; he was in for much bigger money in pics. He got it. However, you must count him as an important pioneer in small-time vaude.

Then there were Sullivan and Considine. The Sullivan was Timothy D., a New York state senator and political boss of New York City. He was an East Side product and knew his way around. But one time he was fooled was when, in partnership with William Fox, they built the City Theatre on Fourteenth Street. They knew that the city was going to condemn the property in order to cut Irving Place on through, so they built the City Theatre right in the middle of the right of way, figuring the city would pay a big price in condemnation proceedings. Well, it just didn't happen, and the City Theatre is still there! You would think, with his great power and his knowledge of inside stuff, that Timothy D., or "Big Tim," as he was called, could have put it through, but he didn't. He was part of the theatrical firm of Sullivan, Woods & Kraus (later Sam Harris joined the firm); they did melodramas (no doubt Sullivan was declared in for his power in the city). Then he joined John Considine and started the Sullivan & Considine Circuit.

The S. & C. Circuit was not considered by the big or small time as opposition. (Could it be the big guys in the East were afraid of Big Tim?) They flourished in the West, and gave the only theatrical contract in America you could borrow money on; it was the first real play-or-pay contract. They treated the actors swell.

John Considine was the showman and ran the circuit. He started with his brother George running the Comique in Seattle, Washington, in 1889. It was a combo music hall and dance hall for miners, sailors, and Chinese—these were the days of the honky-tonks, dance halls, and gambling joints that catered to the adventurers flocking to Alaska's gold rush. It was something of a slave market. "Come in and pick one out—they're beautiful," was the sign outside. John Considine was one of the most colorful characters in show biz. He could handle a gun like Wild Bill Hickok and could play pool like Hoppe. His activities reached into various fields of sports —horse shows, harness-horse breeding, setter-dog kennels, and boxing promotion. He ended up as the owner of the most famous saloon in America in the 1900s, the famous Metropole on the busiest corner in the world, Forty-second Street and Broadway! Many people think that the old Metropole was the spot where Rosenthal the bookmaker was killed, but it was after Considine's was closed and his new place on Forty-third Street (now the famous Rosoff's Restaurant) was where it happened. It was at the old Metropole that you could meet all the famous figures of the stage and sporting world, and John knew every phony and real guy.

John Considine was the active member of the firm of Sullivan & Considine, and was the first manager to offer a full season's route through the West. It was the first circuit that Al Jolson worked for as a single. Freeman Bernstein was one of the first bookers of the circuit, followed by Chris Brown and Abe Feinberg. Little Meyer North served his apprenticeship as an office boy. They played some of the biggest headliners when they were through with the Orpheum Circuit. John was loyal to the acts that started with him and they could play the circuit any time they wished.

John retired from active show biz about 1928. (Big Tim was declared insane.) John was a great giver to old and new friends; his word was better than a bond. He claimed he never lost a dime in loans, never sued an actor, and never was sued by one. He would carry as much as $20,000 in cash on his person. When asked why, he said, "Never know when you meet a sucker." Sullivan and Considine were two top guys who ran a top circuit, and contributed to vaudeville by giving it a play-or-pay contract and clean business methods!

Before space runs out, I must tell you about the most colorful and nicest guy of all the owner-managers of vaudeville. Mike Shea, of Buffalo, started from scratch in the early 1880s and nursed vaudeville from the museum to the most popular form of amusement of its time! He believed in talent and independent and individualistic showmanship.

Mike Shea became a showman in 1883 when he was twenty-five years old. He had been a sailor on the Great Lakes, an iron-foundry worker, and a stevedore. He made his theatrical debut as the owner, operator, booker, bouncer, and entire staff of Shea's Music Hall in Buffalo. He was destined to become Show Business itself, as far as

Buffalo was concerned. No man had greater influence on the theater of any large city than Mike Shea did in his home town.

In 1883 there was no central booking office on which an inde theater operator could depend for his show. It was a matter of picking up the acts when and where possible, mostly by correspondence, with the operator acting as his own booker. Having once acquired the habit, Mike never lost it. His theaters were listed on a circuit's books, but he came to New York regularly to personally oversee the penciling in of every act for his houses. He set his own salaries, which the Keith people didn't like. He'd pay an act $100 more if he thought it was worth it and the booking office would squawk because the higher salary he placed on an act would set a precedent, and they too would have to pay it.

He operated the Music Hall for twelve years, and the only thing that could stop him did—a fire! It burned the two-a-day 50-cent-top show house of specialty acts to the ground. So Mike built himself another one, the Garden, and when that went out of date he built the Court, which he ran for twenty-five years with straight high-grade vaude and in November 1926 he went to Vitaphone. He kept building theaters, the Buffalo, Great Lakes, Hippodrome, Shea's, Seneca, Century, Community, Park, Bailey, and a half a dozen others, all in Buffalo and its suburbs. He also built a pair of theaters in North Tonawanda, New York, a near-by town, and one in Toronto, Canada. He ran them all himself, except the one in Toronto, which his brother Jerry ran. He had a general manager, Vince McPhail, who was with him for thirty-one years, and Tommy Carr (Mike's brother-in-law) replaced him and stuck to the finish. Mike's New York office was wherever he happened to be buying pictures or talent. In Buffalo, his office was adjoining the top balcony, three flights up, no elevator. When asked what was the idea, he said, "I like to see the bankers walk up the stairs—it winds them." He personally kept in great shape playing handball, even when he was well over sixty-five.

In 1908 Mike stopped booking with Keith. Mr. Albee went to Buffalo and told newspapermen that he had bought a large plot of ground for a new vaude house. Next day Mike saw carts of dirt going by with small American flags and signs on them reading, "This is the dirt from the site of the New Keith Theatre." Shea went back to Keith bookings. It was Mike Shea who, against orders, booked the Ponselle Sisters for $400 a week, when Keith refused to raise them from the $350 they were then getting. They broke up the act after the Shea's booking, and Rosa went with the Metropolitan Opera Company. Many times Mike would figure you weren't getting enough money for your act and would slip an extra $50 in your envelope. He liked to go backstage and talk to the actors.

In 1931 he went 50-50 with Publix on his twelve houses and made a lot of money; then when Publix failed he had to take his houses back at a big loss. When pic and vaude booking became big he had to come to New York very often, so bought a house at Sheepshead Bay, and from then on he and his wife (only had one) divided their time between their New York and Buffalo homes. Mike died at the age of seventy-five in 1934.

There never was a rougher, tougher, sweeter, and nicer Irishman than Mike Shea! And a great showman!

There are a few more I'd like to tell you about, like my pal Johnny Galvin in Wilkes-Barre, Harry Bailey at the Alhambra (New York), Ed Fay in Providence, Ben Piazza (of all over), and Doc Elliott in Youngstown, and Grady in Boston, but they keep yelling at me, "We're running out of paper."

And so, these were the kings, czars, and rulers of the kingdom of Vaudeville, the fatherland of song, dance, and story.

3 PAGES TORN OUT OF OLD VAUDEVILLE

Following is an introduction written by Epes W. Sargent before his death in 1938. Sargent was one of Sime Silverman's associates at the time Variety *was founded. Known on the paper as Chicot, he was feared but respected by all vaudeville performers. His knowledge of vaudeville was encyclopedic and, like Umpire Klem, he "called 'em as he saw 'em" and played no favorites.*

Chicot and I often talked for hours in the Variety *office about show biz, and it was he who urged me to write the story of vaudeville. When he read some of my early chapters he asked, "Joe, would you allow me to write an introduction to your book?" This, coming from Chicot, was the greatest compliment ever paid to my scribbling!*

SEZ

JOE LAURIE, JR.

Back down the years, so long ago, in fact, that only the most venerable of the old-timers can recall, Hyde & Behman were the absolute czars of the Brooklyn theaters and Percy G. Williams had not even started to popularize his Bergen Beach resort. And the Hyde & Behman Adams Street Theatre was a temple of variety second only to Tony Pastor's latest house in the old Tammany Hall. They played the best acts to be had and wound up with the traditional afterpiece, colloquially known as "nigger acts."

417

Louis C. Behman conceived the idea of making a collection of these sketches, few of which have ever been committed to paper. They needed no book. All actors knew them and could play them in any part at a moment's notice. It was Behman's thought that the actors were getting no younger and it might be interesting to get a permanent record. Week after week a new afterpiece was presented, little better than a dress rehearsal at the Monday matinee, but going full swing toward the middle of the week, when half-forgotten bits were recalled and inserted. Friday nights Behman put a stenographer in one of the boxes and obtained a shorthand record, probably the first and very likely the only written transcript of "Stitch, the Tailor," "Forty Miles from Nowhere," and kindred titles. By the end of the season he had the basis of a priceless library.

Then came a fire, the playscripts were destroyed, and Behman lost heart and interest. It is probable that few of these old-timers could be played today with anything approaching fidelity. Most of them have been forgotten, though their component elements still survive in musical comedy and on the radio.

Probably such playbooks would possess only an academic interest today, for tastes and styles have changed, and patrons reared on smutty songs and strip teases would give but a negative reaction to the wholesome humor of the bygone day, but it would be of interest to have them to compare with modern vaudeville and burlesque.

No similar fate will befall the old-time acts, for Joe Laurie, Jr., has spent his time and energy in the collation and collection of type sketches, originally appearing in *Variety* but primarily designed for the purpose of the present publication. Unlike Behman, he has not sought to reproduce in toto the act of any one team or combination. Rather he has striven, and with singular success, to arrive at a norm which is representative of an entire type rather than a single turn. Most of the bits are from actual offerings, as the old-timers will realize, but each division is more typical of its genre than any single act could be. He has sought the norm of that classification rather than the reproduction of a single example.

The result is a compendium of the old-time talked vaudeville that is truly representative of its day and which, as time passes and with the time the players, will be an authentic source of information for the student of popular entertainment. It has been a labor of love with him, and this book is the result of deep study and exhaustive research, simple as the results may seem to be. He has been at pains to go to original sources for the material. He has not merely paraphrased or adapted material. He has dug out actual examples, authentic repetitions, giving a picture of that vaudeville which was in its heyday in the late '90s and early in the present century. Only those who were familiar with that period can realize how well and thoroughly he has performed his self-imposed task.

None of the examples is given in full form. Most of the acts represented under these headings ran from twelve to fifteen minutes. He has not sought to cover the matter exhaustively, but has cunningly contrived to give the full flavor of each style in curtailed form. To endeavor to do more would be repetitious. Each example is truly typical of its style and will give a clear and exact picture of what they used to laugh at a quarter-century and more ago. But it must be remembered that old vaudeville was more a matter of style than material. It was not so much what they said and did as how they said and did it. The compiler can give the words. He cannot add the saving grace of personality.

In added chapters he has captured the flavor of the typical vaudeville actor's shoptalk, and has made lengthy lists of the old favorites, very nearly complete catalogues of the old-timers, but here too the limitations of words prevents the transfer of the full flavor. Nor can he more than faintly suggest the real flavor of vaudeville, the specialties. Not the most finished word painter can even remotely convey the idea of the real charm of the old vaudeville: the specialties.

Who can put in cold type the grade and daring of the triple bar act of Frank Marlom and Ben Dunham, for example? They can be mentioned, but not adequately described. Similarly no words can be found for the droll antics of Frank E. McNish in his acrobatic "Silence and Fun," nor tell the grace and finish of the Four Bards in their more stylized acrobatic act or the flashy and finished work of the Cragg Family. No pastel in prose can adequately tell of the elaborate "class" of a Billy Emerson song and dance or glorify the remarkable feats of Alcide Capitaine on the trapeze. All that can be done Laurie has done, and adequately, but the bigger and better half must forever remain untold because telling is not possible.

Vaudeville as we used to know it is as dead as the ancient line of Caesars and its carcass bears as many stab wounds as the coroner found on the body of the late and lamented Julius of that ilk. The motion picture administered the *coup de grâce*, but vaudeville might have survived merely the pictures. The more insidious wounds came from its friends. Even Percy G. Williams pushed in the knife when he sold out his interests to the Keith office and the Keith people promptly cut salaries to retrieve the purchase price. The influx of nudity which then followed the introduction by Eva Tanguay of the Dance of the Seven Veils did much to lower the standards. A growing disregard for cleanliness was another insidious blow, for one does not have to be clever if laughs can be more easily won through the shock of impropriety. Vaudeville today is a matter of four-figure headliners. It seldom happens that a vaudeville show today draws money because of the correlated presentation of eight or ten acts of entertainments. The "name" draws and the rest is merely a filler. The name still applies to a certain form of entertainment—but it isn't vaudeville, and it never will be again.

Which is what will presently make this little study of what was of interest for comparison with what will be, whatever that may be. This book is a chapter of the past, speaking with no uncertain voice. It is a more important contribution to the literature of that stage than it may appear to be for the moment.

EPES W. SARGENT (CHICOT)

The Monologist

Enters to good lively music, music stops when he starts talking. He is dressed in Prince Albert and has a newspaper in his hand.

Well sir, I just came to the theater on a streetcar. There was only *three* of us on the car, a blind man, a policeman, and myself . . . and I *lost my watch*. I asked the conductor, "Does this car stop at the Battery?" and he said, "If it doesn't, we'll all have to swim." We went along a little further and I saw the conductor acting very peculiar; he was throwing a handful of nickels to the top of the car. I said, "My good man, what is the idea?" and the conductor said, "I throw up all the nickels and the ones that stick on the bell rope, the company gets." Yes siree.

Which reminds me of my wife, God bless her. Whenever I talk about my wife, I say God bless her; of course sometimes I say God . . . But speaking about the wife, I believe every man should take a wife, but be careful of whose wife you take. I'll never forget the time I proposed to my wife. Boys, did you ever notice when you propose to a girl she hangs her head and hardly knows how to answer you? Before you're married a week, she'll know how to answer you. . . . Yes siree. I think everybody should take a wife, and if you have a deep grudge against yourself, marry a widow. I did. I told her I would be the captain of her ship so we could sail down the tossing sea of life together. She said I was too late for captain, but I could become her second mate. I did. I married her because I thought she had money. And right here let me tell you folks that a man that marries for money has a hard time collecting his wages. Yes siree.

I'm glad to see the ladies looking so fine, bless their dear little hearts. For that matter, they alway do look fine, especially in the morning when they are watching the eggs boil, with their hair full of curl papers and their mouth full of hairpins. And have you noticed how the ladies are taking part in politics lately? Why, we'll soon have lady policemen, and I suppose if we have lady policemen we will have lady pickpockets; well for that matter we have lady pickpockets now. I know; I'm married. But there is one thing we will never have in this country, that is a lady President. Not that any one of you ladies would not make a good President, but the Constitution of the United States says that anyone to be President of the U.S. must be over thirty-five years of age. Now tell me, where are you going to find a woman that will admit she is over thirty-five? No siree. At that, some day we will wake up and find a woman President. . . . Well sir, that's the morning I want to oversleep. Yes siree.

I know my wife won't tell her right age. Last week was the anniversary of her birthday; she was twenty-six for the twelfth time. No wonder everybody says she holds her age well. But there's one person she couldn't fool; that's the census-taker. She has to tell him her right age or go to jail. But *my* wife got the best of him alright. She asked him did the Hill sisters who live next door give their age? And he said, "They certainly did." And she said, "Well, I'm just as old as they are!" and the census-taker wrote down that my wife was as old as the Hills. Yes siree.

My wife is a frail little creature. She weighs 300 pounds. That's two pounds less than a horse. I'll never forget the day of our wedding. No siree. The minister looked her over and then turned to me and said, "Are you doing this of your own free will?" and Truck 6 said, "I'd like to hear him say he isn't." Then the minister said, "This don't look like an even match to me. You are giving away too much weight." Then he pronounced us man and *wives*. All the women started to cry, too. None of my folks attended the wedding; they said they wanted to remember me as I was in life. Yes siree. My wife comes from good stock. Her father is a fine old German; his name is Shamus O'Brien. He said his daughter was too good for me. I didn't know what he meant until I had my first scrap with her. Then I found out he was right. Yes siree.

On my way to the theater I wanted a bite to eat so I walked into a restaurant and I ordered two eggs. When the waiter brought them to me he opened one of them and said, "Shall I open the other one?" I said, "No, open a window." Then I ordered cocoa and when he brought it I said, "Waiter, my cocoa's cold." And he said, "Put your hat on and it won't be cold." Then I said, "Have you frogs' legs?" and he said, "No, my corns make me walk this way." I never was so disgusted with a waiter in all my life. No siree. Coming out of the restaurant I felt a little thirsty, so I walked into a saloon. I said, "Bartender, give me two glasses of beer." I drank one glass and started to walk out when the bartender said, "Say, mister, you didn't pay for your drinks." I said I only drank one beer and I left the other one to settle. The laugh was certainly on him. Yes siree.

While walking down the street I met a little boy. I don't believe he was over eight years old. He looked very bright so I said to him, "Young man, I'll bet you don't know how many letters there are in the alphabet?" And the little fellow looked up and said, "I'll bet you that you don't know how many letters there are in the post office." Well sir, he had me there. Yes siree.

I noticed that you folks have been looking at my diamond ring; two more payments and it's mine. Yes siree. Well I feel a song coming on, I will sing a little song entitled, "Mama, Get the Hammer, There's a Fly on Baby's Head." All right, Professor.

(After Song—Exit)

The Man and Woman Act

Street Scene . . . in One. Enter at opposite sides of stage and as Man approaches Woman, he tips his hat and sort of flirts with woman.

w.: (*Angrily*) What do you mean by tipping your hat to me? You don't know me.

m.: This is my *brother's* hat; *he* knows you. Say, you know I like you.

w.: Is that so?

m.: I sort of have a *"heart"* affection for you.

w.: Have you had it *"lung"*?

m.: Oh yes. And I feel I will *"liver"* troubled life without you.

w.: Then you better *"asthma."*

m.: Say, you're a pretty smart girl. What's your name?

w.: Helen Summer.

m.: What is it in winter?

w.: Oh, a pretty smart fellow, eh?

m.: How old are you?

w.: Sixteen.

m.: How old?

w.: I've told you twice, sixteen.

m.: Oh, *twice* sixteen; that's more like it.

w.: Oh, a pretty smart fellow eh? Where were you going just now, Tom?

m.: How did you know my name was Tom?

w.: Oh, I just guessed it.

m.: Then guess where I'm going.

w.: Oh, a pretty smart fellow, eh?

m.: I'm very smart. You can ask me any question about the sea.

w.: Is that so? Well, why don't fish have a good time?

m.: You're wrong. Fish have a very good time.

w.: Yes? How do you make that out?

m.: Didn't you ever hear of *fish balls*?

w.: Pretty smart. Now tell me where you were really going?

M.: I was going down to the depot to meet my friend's mother-in-law. He promised to give me a dollar if I meet her.

W.: Supposing she doesn't come?

M.: Then he promised to give me *two dollars*.

W.: You talk like you are against marriage.

M.: No, I'm up against it. (*Someone applauds in audience*) There's another poor fellow in the same boat.

W.: The way you talk you'd think everybody out there is against marriage.

M.: Well, most of them are.

W.: Oh, that's preposterous.

M.: I'll prove it to you. You take one side of the house and I'll take the other.

W.: Alright. I'll take these lovely ladies and gentlemen down here. (*She points to the orchestra*)

M.: Alright, I'll take the boys up on the shelf. (*Points to gallery*) Those are my boys. I used to be a newsboy right in this neighborhood.

W.: Don't you know that a good wife is the most unselfish creature in the world? Why, every minute that her husband's awake she tries to help him. (*To audience*) Am I right, girls? (*Wait for applause*)

M.: Yes, and after he's asleep, she helps herself. (*To gallery*) Am I right, boys? (*Wait for applause*)

W.: The very idea. Why, woman is the *soul* of honor. (*To audience*) Am I right, girls? (*Wait for applause*)

M.: Yes, and she's made many a *heel* out of a guy. (*To gallery*) Am I right, boys? (*Wait for applause*)

W.: Why, my boy, woman is a gold mine. You never know her true value. (*To audience*) Am I right, girls? (*Wait for applause*)

M.: Yeh, and there's many a sucker went broke *prospecting*. (*To gallery*) Am I right, boys? (*Wait for applause*)

W.: A woman will stick to you through thick and thin. (*To audience*) Am I right, girls? (*Wait for applause*)

M.: Yeh, and the longer she sticks, the thinner you get. (*To gallery*) Am I right, boys? (*Wait for applause*)

W.: You're positively insulting. I wish God made me a man.

M.: Maybe he did and you haven't found him yet.

W.: Enough of this. (*Turns away in disgust*)

m.: (*To gallery*) Well, boys, looks like we won. (*Wait, as there should be more applause on this*)

w.: Come to think of it, didn't I see you come out of the barroom yesterday?

m.: Well, I had to come out sometime.

w.: Don't you know that every time you go into a barroom the Devil goes in with you?

m.: Well, if he does he will have to buy his own drink.

w.: How did you get so drunk?

m.: I didn't know what I was doing.

w.: Why didn't you know what you were doing?

m.: You see, I was under the influence of liquor when I started. Say, do you know there is something I like about you?

w.: (*Coyly*) Yes? What is it?

m.: (*Placing arm around her waist*) My arm. Will you marry me?

w.: (*Laughing heartily*) Marry you? Why you're a joke.

m.: (*Mimicking woman's laughter*) Can't you take a joke? Come on, be a sport, give us a kiss.

w.: (*Indignantly*) Why, I don't even know you.

m.: Well, I'm taking as many chances as you are. Give us a kiss.

w.: Don't you know some terrible things can be caught from kissing?

m.: Sure. You should see the poor fish my sister caught. Come on, marry me.

w.: Ha. The man I marry must be straight, upright, and grand.

m.: Say, you don't want a man, you want a piano.

w.: I don't think I'll ever marry, I love my automobile too much.

m.: (*To audience*) Another case of man being replaced by machinery. (*Back to her*) Come on, marry me. Don't you think you can marry a man like me?

w.: (*Hesitatingly*) Why . . . yes . . .

m.: (*To audience*) Oh boy, I have won her at last.

w.: That is if he wasn't too much like you. (*Laughs*) Anyway, I wouldn't marry a man unless he was able to wheel a baby carriage. Can you wheel a baby carriage?

m.: I ought to. I spent two years in Wheeling, West Virginia.

w.: That's great.

m.: We're all great in our family. My old man was a great man.

w.: What did your father ever do that was great?

M.: (*Turning around like a model for clothes*) Look me over, kid, look me over.

W.: What do you do for a living?

M.: I'm a director for a railroad.

W.: Is that so? So you're a director for a railroad?

M.: Yeh, I stand at the depot and direct people where to go. By the way, did you know that the cars were going to issue clothespins instead of transfers?

W.: What's the idea?

M.: Because clothespins are good on any line. Aw, come on and marry me.

W.: Why you don't even know how to propose.

M.: Is that so? Why I know how anybody in any line would propose.

W.: Alright, I'll try you. What would an undertaker say when he proposes?

M.: He'd say, I'm *dead* in love with you.

W.: That's very good. How would a jeweler propose?

M.: Why he'd say, Darling, you are my *pearl* of creation.

W.: Now here's a hard one. How would a sailor propose?

M.: That is a tough one. (*Thinks a minute*) I got it. He'd say, Let me be the captain of your ship and we can brave all the storms of life together.

W.: Well, you are pretty smart. I think you must have had a lot of experience. Didn't I see you buying a cradle the other day? What made you do that?

M.: Oh, I just did that for a kid. Come on, give us a kiss.

W.: You know I'm a good girl.

M.: Do you know where all the good little girls go to when they die?

W.: Why, they go to Heaven.

M.: That's right. And do you know where all the bad little girls go?

W.: Why no, where do all the bad little girls go?

M.: They go down to the depot to meet the traveling salesmen when they come in.

W.: Pretty smart, eh?

M.: Say, will you meet me tonight at the post office? I'll take you out to see a movie.

W.: What time shall I meet you?

M.: If I get there first, I'll make a chalk mark.

W.: Ah, but supposing I get there first?

M.: Ah, then you *rub it out.*

(*Finish Act with Song and Dance and do a few jokes while dancing*)

The School Act

SCENE: *Schoolroom with desks and seats. Teacher's desk stage Left. Blackboard on walls with funny pictures of teacher on it, tick-tack-toe, etc. etc.*

CAST:

Percy Harold—SISSY

Jesse James—TOUGH

Tony—ITALIAN

Gladys Umpah—LISPING GIRL

Skinny Jones—FAT BOY

Abey Maloney Goldstein—JEWISH BOY

Rastus Johnson—COLORED BOY

AT RISE: TEACHER, *who is a Dutchman with chin piece, Prince Albert coat, small brown derby hat, enters with books under his arm. Music plays "Schooldays" until he picks up large bell on his desk and rings it. Then music fades out as* PERCY HAROLD *enters.*

PERCY: (*Singing*) La La La La . . .

TEACHER: That must be one of the girls.

PERCY: Oh, you go on.

TEACHER: I'm the new teacher. Vot's the meaning of dis la la la la business?

PERCY: It's none of your business.

TEACHER: Oh, ist dot so? I am going to make it some of my business. Where ist the rest of my pimples?

PERCY: Downstairs playing a game of pinochle, teacher.

TEACHER: Pigsnuckles, eh? What a fine bunch dis must be. I'll bring the rest of 'em here. (*Rings bell. Pupils rush in like a football team, grab teacher's hat, and throw it around as if it was a football.* TEACHER *gets all excited chasing them etc.*) Say, what do you think dis ist, a feetball game?

TOUGH: Hey mug, I'm in.

TEACHER: I'm glad oft dot. Where voss you?

TOUGH: Downstairs playin a game of ping-pong.

TEACHER: Stick out your hand. (TOUGH *does so and* TEACHER *hits him over the head with umbrella*) Zit down. The pimples will please be seated. We will open up the class wit singing the national antem. (*Everybody sings "How Dry I Am"*) Dot voss nice. Now I will open the school by calling the roll.

PERCY: Oh, teacher.

TEACHER: Vos ist the madder wit you, you sick?

PERCY: We had them this morning for breakfast.

TEACHER: Vot did you have for breakfast?

PERCY: Nice Vienna Rolls.

TEACHER: Who said anything about Vienna Rolls? I mean rolls the names of the pimples, vot ist here in school. The first name ist Percy Harold.

PERCY: Here teacher.

TEACHER: Tony Baccicolupe.

TONY: Here I am, boss.

TEACHER: Gladys Umpah.

GLADYS: (*Lisping*) I'm here, teacher.

TEACHER: Skinny Jones.

SKINNY: Can't you see I'm here?

TEACHER: Rastus Johnson.

RASTUS: Here too. Here too, teacher.

TEACHER: Abey Maloney Goldstein.

ABEY: I'm in the place.

TEACHER: What's the idea of Maloney in the middle of your name?

ABEY: I use it for protection.

TEACHER: Jesse James.

TOUGH: Couldn't come today.

TEACHER: Don't say you couldn't come when you are sitting here. And face about, vot you think, I can talk to the front of your face behind your back? Vell, I am glad all the pimples are present. Ve vill start with the first lesson this morning in geography.

EVERYBODY: Oh.

TEACHER: Cut it oud. Oh, ist not in the lessons. Vot ist an island?

TONY: An island is a pimple on the ocean.

TEACHER: No, it's no pimple on the ocean. Stick out your hand. (*Hits* TONY *over head with umbrella*)

PERCY: I know, teacher.

TEACHER: You're so smart, what ist an island?

PERCY: An island is a keg of beer surrounded by (*local*) policemen.

TEACHER: Hold out your hand. (*Hits him on head with umbrella*) Say, tough mug, name me some of the principal oceans.

TOUGH: Atlantic and Pacific.

TEACHER: Dem's not oceans, dem's a tea company.

TOUGH: Oh, you mean oceans. Alright, Montreal, New Hampshire, and Sigel and Coopers.

TEACHER: Dem's not oceans, dem's mountains.

TONY: You mean oceans? I got a notion in my head.

TEACHER: (*Hitting* TONY *on head with umbrella*) Now you got water on the brain. Just for dot, Tony, you gotta sing a song. (TONY *sings a song. After song by* TONY) Dot vos very nice, Tony. Now Skinny, vot ist a cow?

SKINNY: My mother.

TEACHER: Vot its dot foolishness? Vot makes you say your mama's a cow?

SKINNY: I heard my daddy say to her this morning, "You're as big as a cow."

TEACHER: A cow ist an animal with four legs, one on each corner. Now Gladys, can you tell me the use of cowhide?

GLADYS: Sure I can. It keeps the cow together.

TEACHER: Now pimples, can anyone tell me the greatest invention in the world?

SKINNY: The telephone.

GLADYS: The automobile.

TONY: The radio.

PERCY: The airplane.

TEACHER: You are right, poys and girls. They were great inventions.

ABEY: Say teacher, the fellow dot invented interest was no slouch.

TEACHER: Just for that ve will have a dance by Rastus Johnson.

(JOHNSON *does a dance. After dance*) Dot voss very goot. Now for the spell-ink lesson.

EVERYBODY: I-N-K.

TEACHER: I didn't say ink. I don't mean ink vots here in the ink well, I mean spell-ink vot ist here in the book. Jesse James, how do you spell giraffe?

TOUGH: G-I-R-A-F-E.

TEACHER: In the dictionary they spell it with two *f*s.

TOUGH: Well, you ast me how did *I* spell it.

TEACHER: Put your hand out. (*Hits him on head with umbrella*) Tony, make for the teacher a sentence mit the word delight on the inside.

TONY: The wind blew so hard it blew out de light.

TEACHER: Yes, and I'll blow out your light. Cut out dese nonsense. Ah, dere's a goot vord—nonsense. Skinny, give me an example of nonsense.

SKINNY: An elephant hanging over a cliff with his tail tied to a daisy.

TEACHER: Just for that you will haf to sing a song. (SKINNY *sings. After song*) Dot voss very goot. Vot ist the great American desert?

EVERYBODY: Prunes.

TEACHER: Abey, can you tell me where Pittsburgh ist?

ABEY: They are playing in Chicago.

TEACHER: Percy, when was Rome built?

PERCY: At night.

TEACHER: Who told you dot?

PERCY: You said Rome wasn't built in a day.

TEACHER: Put out your hand. (*Hits him on head with umbrella. Sees* RASTUS *raising his hand*) Vot do you want, Rastus?

RASTUS: I want to leave de room.

TEACHER: No. You stay here and fill up the ink wells. Gladys, vot ist the opposite of misery?

GLADYS: Happiness.

TEACHER: Dot's right. Now Abey, tell me vot ist the opposite of woe?

ABEY: Giddap. (*Puts head out to get hit with umbrella*)

TEACHER: Has anybody else got any questions?

TOUGH: Yeh, what time is it?

TEACHER: I'll show you vot is it. (*Goes after him; pupils all go after teacher—free-for-all fight*) Vell, if you don't let me be the teacher I may as vell be one of the gang. School ist over, boys and girls . . . Now let's sing and dance. (*Finish with everybody singing and dancing as Curtain descends*)

The Storyteller

Enter to Music which Dies down as You start speaking. Costume should consist of Prince Albert coat, striped trousers, and puffed tie. If you can not obtain these clothes, a plain business suit can be worn.

(*Laughingly*) We have a colored girl working for us at our house and her name is Mandy Brown. Well, the other evening she came home all excited. "What's the idea of all the joyousness, Mandy?" I asked her. "Why, I'se goin to git married," said Mandy. "Why Mandy, I didn't even know you had a beau," said I. "I ain't exactly had one, Mister (*use your name here*), but you know the fun-ral I'se went to last week; well, I'se goin to marry the corpse's husband. He says I was the life of the fun'ral." (*This should be done with a Negro dialect when coming to the colored girl's part of the conversation, and in your own natural voice when doing the straight stuff*)

Which reminds me of the time my friend Si Slimkin from up in Maine came to New York. When he landed in the Big City, the first thing he noticed were some laborers digging up the streets. He walked over to the excavation and looked down the deep hole in the street, and could see some of the men working. (*In rube dialect*) "Hey, there," shouted Si, "what are you doing down there?" "Building the subway," came the answer from below. (*This should be done in Italian or Irish dialect*) "How soon will it be finished?" asked Si. "In five years," they shouted back. "Well, never mind, then. I'll take the elevated train," said Si as he walked away.

I must tell you about my good friends, Pat and Mike. Mike was sick in the hospital and Pat thought it was his duty to visit Mike in the hospital and make him forget his pains by telling him funny stories. Before going to the hospital Pat stopped off in a few thirst emporiums and by the time he reached Mike's bedside he had a nice brannigan on. When he finally reached the hospital and got to Mike's side he told him a story of what happened to him at church the past Sunday. "Ah," sighed Mike, "will you tell me that story again?" Pat repeated the story. "Would ye mind leaning over a bit, Pat, me hearing ain't what it used to be, and tell me that story again," said Mike. And Pat repeated the same story again. "Tell it again," begged Mike, and after Pat told the same story a dozen times, he said to Mike, "Mike, that story ain't so good as to be worth me tellin it to ye so many times, is it?" "Sure it ain't the story," sez Mike, "it's your breath that is like a whiff from Heaven." (*This story should be told with two different Irish voices. A thin voice for Pat and a deep voice for Mike, or vice versa*)

And speaking about Mike reminds me of the time he sent his young daughter Bridget to Sunday school for the first time. Mike instructed her in case the teacher should ask her some questions. Mike said, "Now, Bridget, if the teacher asks your name, say Bridget Doolan. If she asks you how old you are, say seven years old. And if she asks you who made you, say God made me." Well sir, when Bridget got to Sunday school and was questioned by the teacher, she made the correct responses to all the questions until the teacher asked her who made her and she answered (*in a kid's voice*), "Papa told me his name, but I've forgotten."

I believe I'll lay off the Irish and tell you a story about my old friend Ikey Cohen. Ikey was a pretty rich man and he was showing his daughter the family jewels that were kept in a large trunk at the house. The daughter was admiring a particularly valuable necklace when two burglars rushed in, brandished revolvers, and carried the trunk out of the door. "Oy, Oy," shouted Cohen. "Gone, our jewelry is gone. Everything is lost." "Not everything, Papa," said his daughter Sadie. "Look, I still have the pearl necklace." "Sadie, mine child, you saved the pearls. How did you manage to do it?" "Easy, Papa," said Sadie. "When the burglars came in, I just put the necklace down and sat on it." "Oy, Sadie," sighed Cohen, "if your mama was here we could have saved the whole trunk." (*This story should be told in Hebrew dialect when the Hebrew characters are speaking*)

Ikey had a brother named Jake who went one evening to visit his oldest sister, who was married and had young triplets. Before Jake started for home a heavy storm blew up. "You can't go out in this awful rain, Jake," his sister said. "You'll get all wet. Better you stay here tonight. You can sleep in the next room with the triplets." So Jake did, and the next morning she asked him if he had a good night's rest with the triplets. "Oy, I slept alright," said Jake, "but I may as well have went home through the rain."

A few days ago my friend Bill Tomkins had a few drinks too many and was driving down Broadway and in attempting to turn around in the middle of the street was side-swiped and upset by a hook-and-ladder truck. Walking over to Bill's overturned flivver, a traffic officer poked his head through the window and said (*in Irish dialect*), "What do you mean by blocking traffic like this? Come outta there, you're pinched." (*Speaking as if you're under the influence of liquor; muss your hair up a little*) "Shay, offisher," sez Bill, "how did I know them drunken painters were going to run into me?" (*Hic.*) (*Rearrange hair and bow as music plays "Auld Lang Syne" for Exit*)

The Dramatic Sketch

SCENE: *A richly furnished drawing room with French doors center . . . leading out to small balcony. The room contains a bookcase (with books), a sideboard with decanter and glasses on it. A few big easy chairs. A flattop desk (stage Left) with papers and law books on it. Chair at desk is directly in front of a radi-*

ator, and a small piece of the steam pipe is shown leading off into another room.

AT RISE: JUDGE DEBECK *is discovered seated at desk working over some papers.* MRS. DEBECK *is seated (stage Right) in a large easy chair, with floor lamp shining on her. She has a work basket in her lap, and is sewing.*

JUDGE: (*Looking up from his work*) Dear, you will hurt your eyes sewing so much. Why don't you go to bed? It's very late.

MRS.: I think you're right, Tom. I didn't notice it was so late. How about you, will you be finished soon?

JUDGE: In a little while, dear.

MRS.: Still on that Logan case?

JUDGE: Yes. It comes up in the morning.

MRS.: Tom, in the years we have been together I have never discussed any case with you on which you had to render a decision. But somehow I feel this boy is innocent.

JUDGE: I guess you are interested in the case because the boy has the same name as you have. I admit it's all circumstantial evidence against him, and I also believe that . . . (*Pauses*) But look here, my dear . . . this is unethical. A judge discussing a case before him. (*Laughs*) I'll have to fine myself for contempt of court. (*Gets up and goes over to her and kisses her*)

MRS.: Will you try and come home early tomorrow?

JUDGE: Why certainly. You think I have forgotten that tomorrow is our third anniversary?

MRS.: You're a dear. You never forget. Are you happy, Tom?

JUDGE: The happiest man in the world. And are you happy, dear?

MRS.: It's been one continuous honeymoon. It doesn't seem like three years to me; it's more like three days.

JUDGE: You remember me when I courted you?

MRS.: (*Laughingly*) I'll never forget it. I was working as a telegrapher at a little railroad station back home and you came in to send a wire.

JUDGE: Yes, it was a case of love at first sight. I thought it was funny for one so young and . . . pretty to be a telegrapher.

MRS.: Those were grand days when you were courting me. I taught you the Morse Code and when you were sitting on the bench in court, and I would watch you so proudly, you would tap out love messages to me with your pencil on the desk, "Do you love me?"

and I would nod yes, and nobody knew that the honorable judge was making love while listening to a case. (*They both laugh*)

JUDGE: I was saving this surprise for you for tomorrow, but it's after midnight now so it's practically tomorrow. Here . . . (*He takes out a beautiful pearl necklace with a locket attached to it and puts it around her neck*)

MRS.: Oh, it's beautiful. You took my mother's locket and had a pearl chain made for it. Oh, this is a surprise. (*Kisses him*) I have a surprise for you too, Tom. (*Goes to sewing basket and takes out something*) Now, close your eyes until I count three. (*He closes his eyes*) One . . . Two . . . Three. (*He opens his eyes and she holds up small baby's shirt*)

JUDGE: (*Looking in amazement*) Oh darling! (*Hugs and kisses her*) I've always wanted a son to carry on my work and my name.

MRS.: Maybe that is why I am so interested in that Logan boy. When I have a son, I wouldn't want him to get into any trouble.

JUDGE: Well, dear, you'd better go to bed. You must be very tired. Good night.

MRS.: Good night, dear, and please, dear, don't stay up too late. (*Kisses him and exits*)

(*The JUDGE returns to his papers on desk. We see a flashlight on the outside of balcony leading to the French doors. As the JUDGE is engrossed in his work, door opens and MAN enters with gun in his hand*)

MAN: Hold steady, Judge. I wanna talk to you.

JUDGE: (*Looking up*) A burglar.

MAN: No, I'm no burglar. I'm Bill Logan's father. I come to talk to you about my boy.

JUDGE: Does one usually come to a man's house with a gun in his hand to talk?

MAN: That's the only way I could get to you. They've refused to let me see you, so I took this means. You mustn't send my boy away, Judge.

JUDGE: My good man, this is no place to discuss this case . . .

MAN: But it's all circumstantial evidence. I tell you, my boy didn't do it.

JUDGE: They found the gun in his room, also a bloody handkerchief with his initials . . .

MAN: I tell you he met a man and it was he that did the shooting and threw the gun and handkerchief in my boy's room. My boy is innocent!

JUDGE: Then how do you account for the initials on the handkerchief?

MAN: He had the same initials as my boy's, his name is Ben Landau.

JUDGE: That's where your case is weak. Why don't you produce the man?

MAN: Because we can't find him. He has disappeared . . .

JUDGE: Well, you will have to leave. I can't discuss this matter any further. (*While the* JUDGE *has been talking he has been tapping with his pencil on steam pipe*) Justice will be done.

MAN: Listen, I'd rather commit murder than see my boy sent up for something he didn't do. Justice! (*With a sneer.*) You don't know the meaning of the word. Sending an innocent boy to the chair. I wish your boy gets a deal like this some day. I tell you this is driving me crazy. I'll kill you and then shoot myself. I can't live to see my boy disgraced. (*He acts crazily.* POLICEMAN *enters behind* MAN *with gun in his hand*)

OFFICER: Drop that gun. I've got you covered. (MAN *drops gun and turns around. As* COP *picks up gun,* MAN *drops.* MRS. DEBECK *enters and runs to* JUDGE)

MRS.: Are you hurt, dear?

JUDGE: No. So you got my message?

MRS. Yes. I was getting ready to go to bed when I heard your message over the steam pipe, and I phoned the police and Officer Grogan came right away.

OFFICER: What do you want done with him, Judge?

JUDGE: I think you had better put Mr. Logan under observation; the strain has been too much for him.

MRS.: Mr. Logan? Is this . . . ?

JUDGE: Yes, the boy's father.

MRS.: Wait a minute. You look very tired, Mr. Logan. Sit down. (*She sits him down and goes to sideboard and gets him a drink*) Take it, Mr. Logan. It will do you good. It's just a little sherry.

MAN: Thank you, Mam. (*Drinks and sees locket*) Where did you get that locket?

MRS.: Why, this? (*Points to locket*) I got this from my mother when I was a little girl.

MAN: (*As if to himself*) I have never seen one like it since. May I see the inside?

MRS.: Why certainly. It's a picture of my mother. (*Opens locket and shows it to* MAN)

MAN: (*Excitedly*) It's true. You come from Circle Leville?

MRS.: Why, yes.

MAN: Did you ever hear your mother talk about her brother Fred?

MRS.: Why yes, she had a brother Fred who ran away from home years ago. They never did hear from him again.

MAN: I am Fred. . . .

JUDGE & MRS.: What? You are Fred Logan?

MAN: Yes. I got into a little scrape back home and ran away. I went to the Klondike and made and lost a fortune. I got married and drifted around all over the country. And then I heard my sister—your mother—died, leaving a daughter. I came all the way from the Coast to get the daughter, but I was too late. She had been sent to an orphan asylum. On my way over there I was hit by a truck and was laid up for nearly a year. When I got out of the hospital the kid had been discharged from the orphanage and I couldn't find any trace of her.

MRS.: Tell me, how did you know about the locket?

MAN: You see, it was my mother's wedding present to your mother.

JUDGE: Officer, I don't think we'll need you. Have a drink?

OFFICER: I never take a drink when I'm on duty, your honor, and anyway, I don't like sherry.

JUDGE: And Grogan, not a word about what happened here to-night.

OFFICER: And sure I'm deaf and blind, your honor. I don't know how I ever got on the police force. (*Winks broadly*) Good night. (*Exits*)

MRS.: What will we do, Tom?

JUDGE: We'll fix all that in the morning. Don't worry, dear.

MAN: Then you mean my boy will be free?

JUDGE: A judge can't give his decisions outside the court, but to-morrow you both come here and live with us.

MRS.: Oh, you're a darling. This is the greatest anniversary present you could have given me.

JUDGE: (*During this talk has poured out a drink for the* MAN *and himself. Raising glasses*) I'm sure *my boy* would approve of this, eh, Uncle Fred?

(*All hold picture for Curtain*)

The Stump Speech

(*Enter dressed as old colored preacher, with large book under arm. Old hotel register is best for this purpose, or else any large book or even a phone book. Place book on table center stage, and face audience from behind table, as if table is a pulpit.*)

Brethern and Sistern, I have decided to divide my sermon in three parts. The first part I'll understand and you won't. The second part, you will understand and I won't. The third part nobody will understand. You will notice I have arranged everything in my sermon for simplicity. For in the first part, I tell you what I'm going to tell you, and the second part I'll tell you, and in the third part I'll tell you what I has told you. (*Bang open book with hand*)

Now, Brethern and Sistern, let's open the little red books and sing (*To music of "St. Louis Blues"*):

> Ashes to ashes
> Dust to dust
> If the black gals don't get you
> The high yallers must.

Very good, very good indeed. The subject of tonight's course is Woman. The word woman is derived from the Latin by adding woe to man, and she's been adding woe to man ever since. (*Bang book with open hand*) Adam bit into the apple because he was tempted by a peach, and man's troubles have been coming in *pears* since. And although woman was evolved from man's rib, she refused to be a side issue. (*Bang book with open hand*) Woman is indeed a conundrum; she keeps us guessing and yet we hate to give her up. A woman has twenty-four ribs and an umbrella has thirty ribs, and yet see how much easier it is to shut up an umbrella. And then again on a rainy day, a good wife is more likely to remain at your side than an umbrella. (*Bang book with open hand—or umbrella*) When I pick up a newspaper in the morning, the first thing I look at is the engagements, then I look at the marriages. And last of all the matrimonial squabbles. I like to see who is being hooked, booked, and *cooked*. (*Bang book with open hand*) There are thousands of farmers down South clamoring for wives; they must be farmers or else they wouldn't be so anxious to get married. I believe that lots of men would get married if they only knew where to get good helpmates. Why doesn't some big department store open up a wife department? Great idea. Green trading stamps with every purchase and *double* trading stamps with females over forty. (*Bang book with open hand*) Customers at a distance could order wives by mail. Just send for catalogue. If you want a young wife, look under peaches, if you want an old maid, look under dried fruit. (*Bang book with open hand*) Wives to suit every pocket. Even if they don't know much about your pocket, they will soon get their hand in. Just pick out the wife you want and the rest is easy. She'll be shipped by express to you. The box will be marked "Contents brittle and liable to *break*—any man." (*Bang book with open hand*)

Women are not what they used to be; they used to be girls. She's only a rag, a bone, and a hank of hair, but all the boys want to become junk dealers. All women don't talk, some of 'em *holler*. Women don't talk oftener than men, but they talk *longer*. (*Bang book with open hand*) Can you imagine a barber trying to shave a woman's chin? All he would have to do is to hold the razor to the chin and she would talk so much that the chin would shave itself. The greatest calamity I ever seen was a two-faced woman who talked to herself and tried to have the last word. You never can tell about women; even if you can, you shouldn't. (*Bang book with open hand*) The best way to approach a woman with a past is with a present. Women are like olives; you must get used to 'em. As I said before, woman was made from man's rib, but today she is usually made from something from the hip. I don't believe in clubs for women; take an *axe*. All great temptations are circular in form. A bottle is round; so are women's waists and garters. (*Bang book with open hand.*)

Now, Brethern and Sistern, let's roll over, I mean turn over, another page (*turns page in book*) and skip the next three pages (*does so*) and see what it sez. A good wife is the sunshine of the home. And a drunken husband is the moonshine of the home. All women are good, but the wife is a little better, and when she becomes a mother she is still better, all women are better still. Some wives talk all the time, all wives talk some of the time, but *no wife* talks none of the time. (*Bang book with open hand*) A wife can either make or break a husband, she usually does one or the other. Wife means a lot to some men, but some men are mean to a lot of wives. What's become of the old-fashioned wives? They used to roll up their sleeves and go in to the kitchen; now they roll up their stockings and go in the street.

Remember, folks, there is only one good wife in this town, and every married man thinks he's got her. I don't believe in free love; the cash and carry kind is the best. Fifty per cent of the people fall in love—the rest of 'em are either shoved or dragged into it. Remember, Brethern and Sistern, the sweetest love is a mother's, the longest is a brother's, the dearest a man's love, and the sweetest, longest, and dearest love—is a love for money. And speaking about money, I will now pass around the contribution basket, but I wish to call your attention that the basket is passed around for my benefit; last time it was passed around I noticed one of the brothers threw in five cents and took out eighty cents change, and the worst part of it was that the nickel he threw in had a hole in it. (*Bang book shut . . . and walk off*)

The Ventriloquist

SET: *Interior in Two with Table and Chair, Center. Large drinking glass, package of cigarettes, and bottle of liquor on table. (This is Very Important) There is also a small box or trunk stage Left.*

Music plays Forte and Dies Down as Ventriloquist enters and gets seated at table, with his dummy on his lap.

VEN.: Well, Tommy, how are you feeling this morning?

TOM: I feel like the house. (DUMMY *looking around and up at gallery*)

VEN.: And how's that?

TOM: Half full.

VEN.: (*Laughs*) How have you been in school lately, Tommy?

TOM: Oh, I'm the head of the class.

VEN.: Well, that's very nice. So you're the head of the class?

TOM: Yeh—when the recess bell rings. (*Winks at audience*)

VEN.: I'll see how smart you are, young man. Do you know anything about geography?

TOM: Gelolopi?

VEN.: No, my boy, geography.

TOM: Oh sure. I thought you said geography.

VEN.: I did say geography. What is the shape of the world?

TOM: It's in very bad shape.

VEN.: Now quit your stalling. What is the shape of the earth?

TOM: (*Looks puzzled and mumbles to himself as ventriloquist busies himself with some things on the table.*) It's—it's oblong.

VEN.: No. No. Why, any fool knows what the shape of the earth is.

TOM: Do you?

VEN.: Why, certainly. (*Catches the idea and pushes* DUMMY, *who winks to audience*) Now look, I will help you. Now what is the shape of your father's cuff buttons?

TOM: Oh, that's easy. They're square.

VEN.: No, no. I don't mean the ones he wears on week days, I mean the ones he wears on Sundays.

TOM: Oh, the Sunday ones, they're round.

VEN.: That's right. Now, what's the shape of the earth?

TOM: Square on week days and round on Sundays.

VEN.: (*Pushes* DUMMY) The very idea.

TOM: Why, ain't that right?

VEN.: What did you say?

TOM: I said, ain't that right?

VEN.: Ain't? I'm surprised at you. Don't you know that isn't very good English? Ain't. Why, where's your grammar?

TOM: She's home with my grandfather.

VEN.: By the way, Tommy, how are things at your house?

TOM: Say, did you know we had a goat at our house?

VEN.: Now, Tommy, you aren't going to tell me that old one about the goat that hasn't any nose?

TOM: Oh, this one has a nose.

VEN.: Then it's the one about the goat that has four legs that reach the ground?

TOM: No, this is a goat we sleep with.

VEN.: You mean to sit there and tell me you sleep with a goat?

TOM: (*Mocking* VENTRILOQUIST) Yeh, that's what I mean to tell you.

VEN.: Well, how can you stand it?

TOM: Oh, he's getting used to it.

VEN.: (*Aside*) He's getting used to it. The very idea.

TOM: And did you know we had two barrels of whisky in our cellar and some Democrat stole one of them?

VEN.: How did you know it was a Democrat that stole one of them?

TOM: 'Cause if it was a Republican he'd a stole *both* of 'em.

VEN.: By the way, what is your father, a Republican or a Democrat?

TOM: He is a Democrat.

VEN.: What are you?

TOM: Well, my father is a Democrat so I'm a Democrat.

VEN.: Supposing your father was a horse thief?

TOM: Then I'd be a Republican.

VEN.: I have to hand it to you, Tommy. You're a pretty smart lad.

TOM: Oh sure, my father and I are the smartest people in the world.

VEN.: How do you make that out?

TOM: Because between my father and me we can answer any question you might ask.

VEN.: Is that so. Well, who is going to be our next President?

TOM: (*In deep thought for a minute*) Well, that's one of the questions my father can answer.

SAM.: (*Negro voice from small box*) Let me out. Let me out. (*The* VENTRILOQUIST *and* TOMMY *look toward the box*)

TOM: The naigur wants to get out.

VEN.: Why, I'm surprised at you calling him a naigur. His name is Sambo. He is the same kind of a little man that you are; only he is of the colored race, and you are of the white race. In fact we all belong to the human race. (DUMMY *laughs*) What are you laughing at, the human race?

TOM: Yeh. (Ha, ha, ha) You're not in it.

VEN.: Just for that you sit here and I'll get Sambo. (*Sits* TOMMY *down and goes over to the small box, or trunk, gets* SAMBO *out, then places him on one knee and* TOMMY *on the other*)

TOM: (*To* SAMBO) Hello, eight ball.

SAM.: Hello, Irish. (*Fight starts*)

VEN.: Here, boys, if you don't stop your fighting I'll put you back in the box.

TOM: If you do, how are you going to make a living?

VEN.: Oh, is that so? I'll have you understand I have a trade. I'm a cooper.

TOM: A copper?

VEN.: No. No. A cooper. In fact, my father is a cooper too. Do you know what a cooper is?

TOM: Yeh. What is it? (SAMBO *laughs*)

VEN.: A cooper is a man that puts heads on barrels. (TOM *laughs*) What are you laughing at?

TOM: (*Still laughing*) You say your old man is a cooperer?

VEN.: Why yes.

TOM: Well, he certainly put a bum head on you.

VEN.: I'll have you understand I have something in my head.

TOM: Yeh, I noticed it. You better take something to kill 'em. (SAMBO *laughs*) What is ink spot laughing at?

SAM.: My pappy. The other night we were going to have company in the house.

TOM: You don't live in a house, you live in a tree.

VEN.: Keep quiet, Tommy. Go ahead, Sambo.

SAM.: We were going to have company in our house and Pappy started scratching his head and I said, "Guess the company has arrived,"—so we had to kill the company.

TOM: Do you know the trunk I travel in?

VEN.: Why yes.

TOM: Well, coming to the theater the expressman threw me around something terrible.

VEN.: He did?

TOM: I'll say he did.

VEN.: Why didn't you give him a piece of your mind? In other words, why didn't you talk back to him?

TOM: How could I when you were at the hotel? (*Winks at audience as* VENTRILOQUIST *acts embarrassed*)

VEN.: Now, that will do. I want you boys to sing a song.

TOM: You mean both of us?

VEN.: Yes, you and Sambo. I want you, Sambo, to sing like your little sister sings, you know, soprano. And you Tommy, sing alto.

TOM: Hey, let me whisper something in your ear.

VEN.: (*Puts* TOMMY *to his ear and acts as if* TOMMY *is whispering something to him*) Why no, of course not. I don't want you both to sing at the same time.

TOM: I thought not. (*Winks at audience*)

VEN.: I want you to sing one line and Sambo the other.

SAM.: Yas sir. What you all gonna be doing while we're singing?

VEN.: Why, I will smoke a cigarette, eat a banana, and drink a large glass of whisky.

TOM: We got to do all the work while you have a good time?

VEN.: Now, that's enough from you. Go ahead.

TOM: (*Looks at leader*) Alright, Professor.
(*Orchestra Plays Introduction of "Schooldays."*)

VEN.: Go ahead and sing. (*He starts choking a little and wipes mouth with handkerchief*)

TOM: How can we sing when you're choking?

VEN.: Go ahead. (*Sing "Schooldays" and finish walking off with heads removed from* DUMMIES)

The Double Dutch Act

The Team consists of a STRAIGHT MAN *and a* COMEDIAN. *The* STRAIGHT MAN *should be tall and wear a large-checkered suit, with the coat short and with large pearl buttons. He wears a small brown derby hat, large collar, loud tie, big squeaky tan shoes. The* COME-

DIAN *has a "belly pad" which makes him look short and real fat. He wears a wide-striped suit, flat-brown derby, large shoes. They both wear chin pieces.*

Open with a popular song, of which they only sing the Chorus; on last few notes they strike bum harmony as the orchestra plays a discord.

BOTH: (*Shaking hands*) By golly, dot vos alright.

S.M.: Hey Miller, I hear your uncle vot ain't dead yet left you a lot of money.

COMIC: (*Showing big roll of bills*) Sure, here 'tis.

S.M.: Vot are you going to do mit it?

COMIC: I don't know. I dink I'll sell it to somebody.

S.M.: Don't do dot. I got a idea. Let's open a restaurant mit it.

COMIC: Vot? I put in all dot money and vot do you did?

S.M.: Vy, don't you sees it? I vill let you be the vaiter and I vill be the boss. Dot vay you get all the money and the tips, vot comes in first, den all you have to do ist to hand it to me.

COMIC: Py Gollies, dot listens easy. How much costs it to open this dump?

S.M.: Vell, how much have you got?

COMIC: All I got ist $60,000.

S.M.: Dot's hardly enough but I think it will do to staht mit.

COMIC: Oh. Ve could staht someding mit it, by golly.

S.M.: Now, do you dink you can be a schvell vaiter?

COMIC: They couldn't make 'em any schveller.

S.M.: Goot. Ve vill now open the restaurant.

COMIC: Goot. Here ist where ve eat. I luv to eat. Excuse Phillip till he moves in. (*Pushes* S.M. *aside*)

S.M.: Don't push. Now dis ist a schvell café und you are a handsome vaiter. Now, ven a schvell lady comes in, vot do you do?

COMIC: Vy, I rush oud and get a schvell vaiter.

S.M.: No, no. *You* are a schvell vaiter. Now I vill be a schvell lady. I am coming to eat somedings. Get ready.

COMIC: Business ist now open. (STRAIGHT *enters like a woman would*) Oh, vot a rotten shape.

S.M.: (*As if talking to porter outside the door*) John, gif my horse a bucket of champagne und some strawberry shortcake.

COMIC: Oh, vot a schvell jackass dot ist. (*Use "horse" if they don't allow you to use "jackass"*)

S.M.: Und John, take the carriage to the insane asylum.

COMIC: Insane asylum?

S.M.: Yes, von of the wheels ist off its nut.

COMIC: Oh, he ist getting loose house.

S.M.: Vaiter, Vaiter.

COMIC: Yes sir, yes sir.

S.M.: Not yes sir to me, I'm a lady.

COMIC: Oh, git oud, you ain't no lady, you're de boss.

S.M.: No, no, I ain't the boss no more.

COMIC: Oh, you quits?

S.M.: No, I didn't quits. I am de boss.

COMIC: Yes sir.

S.M.: I vos de boss, but now de boss ain't und de boss vot ist not, ist now, vot am I?

COMIC: I dink you're a cockeyed liar. (*Use "piece of cheese" if they don't allow "cockeyed."*) Vell, vot do you vont to eat?

S.M.: I don't know. Give me the menu.

COMIC: De vot?

S.M.: De menu.

COMIC: I know you mean me. Vot do you vont?

S.M.: Menu.

COMIC: Mean me?

S.M.: Ven I say menu I don't mean you.

COMIC: Ach, vot *do* you mean?

S.M.: Menu. (*Pointing to menu*)

COMIC: Ach, de book.

S.M.: (*Looking over menu*) Hav you got any brains?

COMIC: Yes mam.

S.M.: Stop dot. Vot do you think I am, a fool?

COMIC: Yes mam.

S.M.: I am not a yes mam.

COMIC: Ain't you a lady?

S.M.: Yes mam. My Gott, you got me saying it. Now listen. I am going to let you be the schvell lady und I vill be the vaiter und I vill show you how to vait. Can you be a schvell lady?

COMIC: Yes mam.

S.M.: Can't you say anyding but yes mam?

COMIC: Yes mam.

S.M.: Den say it.

COMIC: No mam.

s.m.: (*All excited*) I vill choke all de yes mams and no mams out of you. Now come into the café and act like a lady.

comic: I'll order some liver and milk.

s.m.: Goot evening, madame.

comic: Ist dis a restaurant?

s.m.: (*Disgusted*) Ist dis a restaurant? No, ist a sawmill. Vot did you come in for, a haircut? Vy certainly it ist a restaurant. Go oud und come in like a lady.

comic: Oh, like a lady?

s.m.: Goot evening, madame.

comic: Vy hello, boss.

s.m.: No. No. You are a schvell lady. I am not your boss, don't you understand?

comic: Yes mam.

s.m.: You musn't say yes mam to a vaiter. You must treat me like a dog.

comic: Oh I knock his eyes in.

s.m.: Goot evening, madame.

comic: Shut up, dog.

s.m.: Vot do you vont?

comic: None of your business.

s.m.: Vot are you going to have?

comic: I would like some fishes' eyebrows. How ist your eyebrows today?

s.m.: Pretty goot, how's yours?

comic: Fine. Ist your kidneys alright too. Giv me one of your kidneys and a couple of your pigs' feets.

s.m.: Vill you have them enfinanceree or encasserole?

comic: In castor oil?

s.m.: No. Not in castor oil. I said encasserole.

comic: (*Bewildered*) Hey, Phillip, vot should I say?

s.m.: Say it's immaterial.

comic: Vot kind of material?

s.m.: Don't you know vot immaterial means? Den I vill expire to you. Now, for inkstands, you pick up a handful of mud mit de juice oozing out.

comic: Juicy mud?

s.m.: Yeh.

comic: I couldn't do dot—I'm a lady.

s.m.: You do dot only for inksfands. You pick up the mud mit your left hand, now ven you got dot handful of mud, close up your hand like dis (*Demonstrates*) und you squeeze it. Now, whether de mud comes oud of dese fingers or dose fingers it ist immaterial.

COMIC: Now I sees it.

S.M.: Now you know vot immaterial ist?

COMIC: Sure.

S.M.: Vot is it, immaterial?

COMIC: A lady mit a handful of mud.

S.M.: (*Chokes little fellow*) Ach, you're too dumb to be a vaiter. I'll make an opera singer oud of you.

(*Cue for music. Both sing parody on opera—and exit*)

The Double Wop Act

Both enter as music plays "My Mariutch She Take a Steamboat." STRAIGHT MAN *walks a bit ahead of the* COMEDIAN. *They are both dressed in misfit suits. Comedian has long mustache and bandanna handkerchief around neck. Straight man wears celluloid collar, red tie, big watch chain, yellow shoes that squeak, and is sort of sporty in an Italian way.*

STRAIGHT: Come ona—wassa madder—come ona. . . .

COMIC: Waita one minoots. I no can walka fast. My uncle isa sick.

STRAIGHT: Whatsa your uncle gotta to do wit you no walka fast?

COMIC: I tella you my uncle isa sick.

STRAIGHT: Your uncle isa sick?

COMIC: (*A little angrily*) Yeh, my uncle. (*Points to ankle*)

STRAIGHT: Oh, you meana ankles. Say, whatsa your name?

COMIC: My namesa Tom Giariba Idi Columbo Scabootcha Castella Mascrici, but day calla me Tom for short.

STRAIGHT: Well, Tom is no high classa. I will calla you Tommas.

COMIC: Say, my namesa Tom and you calls me Tommas?

STRAIGHT: Sure. Dots ahigh classa for Tom.

COMIC: I gotta brudder his namesa Jack. What you calla him, Jackass?

STRAIGHT: Say, howsa your big brud Sylvest?

COMIC: Hesa nunga feela so good.

STRAIGHT: Wassa matter wid him?

COMIC: You know Sylvest hesa gotta big ship tattoed on hisa chest.

STRAIGHT: Yeh, I know.

COMIC: Well, de odera days a bigga man come up to my brudda Sylvest and givea him onea punch on his chest and sank the ship.

STRAIGHT: Say, how manna kids you gotta 'em now?

COMIC: I gotta twelve bambinos.

STRAIGHT: All together?

COMIC: No, one at a time.

STRAIGHT: How many girls?

COMIC: Fivea girls.

STRAIGHT: And how many boys?

COMIC: Fivea boys.

STRAIGHT: Dats only ten kids.

COMIC: Fivea boys and fivea girls and two other kids. Mixem up.

STRAIGHT: You workin now?

COMIC: Sure Mike. I'm a politich in an auto factory.

STRAIGHT: What, you mean you're a politician in an auto factory?

COMIC: Sure, I'ma assembly man.

STRAIGHT: I gotta a good job for you.

COMIC: What doin?

STRAIGHT: Manicurin boulevards.

COMIC: How mucha you pay?

STRAIGHT: Twenty-two dollars a week.

COMIC: Twenty-two dollars a week?

STRAIGHT: Yeh—two twos.

COMIC: Datsa nice. Whatsa the hours?

STRAIGHT: You start at eight in the morning and stop at six ata night.

COMIC: Datsa too mucha work.

STRAIGHT: Okay. I makea it easier for you. You start at six anda finish at eight.

COMIC: Datsa nice man. I go now and tella my friend at the city hole.

STRAIGHT: Whatsa your friendsa name?

COMIC: He livesa at the city hole, I nunga remember hisa name. Hisa gotta name somethin like a horse.

STRAIGHT: You don't mean the mayor?

COMIC: Sure, datsa him, the Mare. He's a fine fellow. He invite me to be a polar bear.

STRAIGHT: You got invitaish to be a polar bear? You nunga can be a polar bear.

COMIC: Sure, I gotta be a polar bear.

STRAIGHT: You know whata polar bear is?

COMIC: No, but I gotta be one.

STRAIGHT: Listen—polar bear sits on ice and eatsa fish.

COMIC: Nunga foola me now.

STRAIGHT: I'ma no foolin you. Wasa matter?

COMIC: You know my frienda Guiseppi? He died and hisa family wanna me to be polar bear. I no sit on ice and eat fish for nobody.

STRAIGHT: (*Laughingly*) You mean the pallbearer.

COMIC: Sure.

STRAIGHT: You are astronga man. You can be pallbearer.

COMIC: I'ma strong but my fadder he'sa bigga strong man.

STRAIGHT: Yeh?

COMIC: My fadder he takesa two billiard balls, squeeza 'em together and makes *talcum powder*.

STRAIGHT: Youa stronga man, you wanna be a fighter?

COMIC: Sure Mike. Makea lotta money fighting.

STRAIGHT: First you gotta loin how to block a punch.

COMIC: Whata you mean block de punch?

STRAIGHT: I mean you gotta learn how to stop a blow.

COMIC: Datsa ease. When he hit me it stop himself.

STRAIGHT: Say, howsa your wife?

COMIC: My wifea and me fight alla the time likes United States and Mexico.

STRAIGHT: What do you mean you and your wife fight like United States and Mexico?

COMIC: We fighta on account de boarder.

STRAIGHT: Where isa your wife now?

COMIC: My wifesa in the country with pendicitus.

STRAIGHT: I tolda you she likes Greeks.

COMIC: And I nunga feel so good either, on account of my kid niece.

STRAIGHT: You mean your sister's gal?

COMIC: Whosa talk about my sister's gal? I say my kid niece, my kid niece. (*Points to kidneys*)

STRAIGHT: Oh, you mean your kidneys.

COMIC: Sure. I say kid niece.

STRAIGHT: Where you liva now?

COMIC: I live on not-feeling-good street.

STRAIGHT: What you mean not-feeling-good street?

COMIC: I liva on sick street.

STRAIGHT: Your littlea girl Maria—how's she?

COMIC: She'sa bigga gal now. She'sa gonna geta de pluma.

STRAIGHT: She'sa gonna for de pluma? Wasa matter, your pipes broke?

COMIC: Whatta you talka bout my pipes? I say my gal Maria she'sa gonna getta de pluma.

STRAIGHT: Well if she'sa gonna getta de pluma somethin musta be wrong witha de pipes.

COMIC: (*Angrily*) Listen. My little girl Maria goesa to school and she's agonna getta de pluma.

STRAIGHT: Oh, you mean a diploma.

COMIC: Sure. Can't I understanda what I speak? Well, so long, I'ma gonna get a drink.

STRAIGHT: Ain't you gonna treat me?

COMIC: No, I'ma gonna drinka myself.

STRAIGHT: You selfish.

COMIC: What?

STRAIGHT: I say you selfish.

COMIC: You crazy in the head. I no sell fish, I buy junk.

STRAIGHT: You drive me coconuts. What happened on the boat the other day?

COMIC: Nunga hear? I was on de bigga boat and somethin hit it and madea bigga hole in de front of de boat on the bottom, an the water she com arushin in.

STRAIGHT: What did you do?

COMIC: I'ma smarta guy. I go down to the bottom of de boat and makea another big hole in de backa of de boat.

STRAIGHT: Whata you do that for?

COMIC: When de water comea in from the front, it *goes out in de back.*

(*Finish with parody of "Dorando."*)

The Double Irish Act

MUSIC: *Chorus of "Wearing of the Green" played forte and fast. Music dies out as* STRAIGHT MAN *enters. He wears a gray woolen suit, straight-tailed frock coat, high hat, red-haired wig partly bald, and white gaiters. His face is made up with red nose, red cheeks, and he wears "sluggers." He carries a heavy cane. As he enters he pretends to be angry, looks off at entrance, and speaks.*

PAT: The oidea of callin me a Tarrier. Why, a Spanyard can't walk on the shtreet nowadays widout bein taken for a Mick or a Tarrier. But there's nawthin but trouble in the wurrld. The other day I bought a horse, and the man tould me he'd trot a mile in two minits; and be heavens he could do it only fur wan thing—the disthance is too much fur the toime. My wife and her mother tuck the horse out fur a drive in the park the other day; the horse ran away, the buggy upset, and my wife and mother-in-law war thrun out and kilt. Now, ayther you belave me or not, more than five hundret min have been after me thrying to buy that horse. Well, while I'm waitin for me ould friend Mike Mc-Carthy, I'll sing a bit of a song. (*Sings*)

> "I'm Pat McGinnis
> The Alderman, the Alderman.
> I'm Pat McGinnis the Alderman so gay."

(*Does a short dance and walks off*)
COMIC *enters opposite side. He is dressed in long-tailed frock coat, high vest, short pantaloons, sort of baggy. He wears black gaiters, carries a heavy short cane, and wears a squatty white square-topped stiff hat. His make-up is sort of white with a least bit of red on the nose, heavy eyebrows, and wears "Galway Sluggers."*

MIKE: Now I'm a man can shtand a joak, but whin I go into a barbershop on a Sunday mornin and the Nagur barber pins a newspaper under my chin an hands me a towel to read, it's goin a little too fur. The other mornin I intered a friend's salune.

There were grape shkins on the flure, an I sez to him, "How de you do, Mr. Cassidy? I see you had a party last night." "What makes you think so?" sez he. "Because I see the grape shkins on the flure," sez I. "Thim's not grape shkins," sez he. "Thim's eyes. Some of the byes had a fight here lasht night and you're now surveyin the battle field." But I was expectin Pat McGinnis, a friend of mine, down here. Ah, here he comes now. (PAT *enters*) Pat, how are you?

PAT: I'm well, Mike. What kept you so quick?

MIKE: I'd been here sooner only I couldn't get down any later. Say Pat, where did you go whin you left me tother night?

PAT: I wint down to the maskeerade bawl.

MIKE: I heard you was there. They put you out because you wouldn't take off your mask after twilve o'clock.

PAT: But I didn't have any mask on. Sure it was me own face.

MIKE: That's what I told thim but they won't belave me.

PAT: How long can a man live without brains?

MIKE: I don't know. How ould are you now?

PAT: Say, Mike, do you know what a plate of hash is?

MIKE: Sure, a plate of hash is an insult to a square meal.

PAT: Thin you can shtand more insults than iny man I ever saw. (*Walks to other side of stage while* MIKE *remains center*)

MIKE: Say, Pat, can you tell me the difference between you and a jackass?

PAT: (*Measuring distance to* MIKE *with his eyes*) About twelve foot.

MIKE: No, that's not the right answer.

PAT: Well, I'd like to know what *is* the difference between you and a jackass?

MIKE: No difference. (*Laughs and then gets the idea he pulled the joke on himself. He throws down his hat and cane and "mugs" until the audience stops laughing*)

PAT: Did you hear about the big explosion down to the gas works?

MIKE: No. Anybody kilt?

PAT: Forty Eyetileians and one Irishman.

MIKE: Oh, the poor man.

PAT: An have you heard about McCloskey? He has lo-co-mo-tor at-taxi.

MIKE: Lit him have it. Fur my part I'd rather have a horse.

PAT: Hah, I jist noticed it.

MIKE: Noticed what?

PAT: The black eye, and where did you get it?

MIKE: Some dagoes called me an A.P.A.

PAT: Why the durty, black-hearted, murderin' . . .

MIKE: Shhhh. Don't spake ill of the dead.

PAT: Say, Mike, what would you do if you had a million dollars?

MIKE: Sure I'd put six inches more on me pick handle.

PAT: An how's your brother Dinny?

MIKE: Oh he's a foine lad. You know he had over 50,000 men under him?

PAT: Fifty thousand? Sure he must be a great gineral.

MIKE: Noo, he was up in a balloon.

PAT: I'll niver forget the time back in Ireland I saw a man chased by the Black and Tans for five miles and when he came to a river a mile wide he just jumped right over it. What do you think of that?

MIKE: Sure that's nothin. Look at the shtart he had.

PAT: I don't want to talk to the loikes of you.

MIKE: Phwat's the matter?

PAT: Iny man that will pour hot water down a hen's mouth to make her lay boiled eggs, I have no opinion of.

MIKE: (*Laughs heartily*) Ha, ha, ha, ha.

PAT: Phwat are you laughin at?

MIKE: I saw you try the same thing on a *rooster*.

(*Finish act with song and Irish reel*)

The Straight and the Jew

STRAIGHT MAN *enters and sings a song. After the song, Shots are heard off stage and* JEW COMIC (*with hat over ears, short beard, and misfit suit*) *comes running out.*

S.M.: Mr. Cohen, what are you running for?

COHEN: I'm trying to keep two fellows from fighting.

s.m.: Who are the fellows?

cohen: An Irishman and me. (*After laugh is over*) Say, why don't you pay me for that suit you got on?

s.m.: Well really, Mr. Cohen, I would pay you, only I haven't the money.

cohen: (*Mocking* straight man) Yeh, I'd be a rich man, only I ain't got the money. Can't you pay me something on the bill?

s.m.: How much do you want?

cohen: I'd like enough to hire a lawyer to sue you for the balance.

s.m.: You're a pretty smart fellow. Are you good at spelling?

cohen: You betcha my life I'm a good speller.

s.m.: I'll bet you that you can't spell needle.

cohen: I'll bet you my life I can spell it.

s.m.: I won't bet you that.

cohen: I'll bet you my whole family's life.

s.m.: No, I won't bet you that, but I'll tell you what I will do, I'll bet you ten dollars that you can't spell needle.

cohen: No siree. When it comes to betting money, that's another matter.

s.m.: I'll try you anyway. How do you spell needle?

cohen: N-I-E-D-L-E.

s.m.: You're wrong.

cohen: I'm right.

s.m.: We will leave that to the leader. He looks like an intelligent person. (*Goes over to* leader *of the orchestra*) You heard the argument, George. Who is right?

leader: Why, you are, of course.

s.m.: (*To* cohen) You see? (*To* leader) Do you smoke?

leader: Why, of course.

s.m.: (*Takes cigar out of pocket*) Well, here's a cigar. Try spelling it again, Mr. Cohen.

cohen: (*Looks at* leader *through the business of* s.m. *giving* leader *cigar, etc. Is disgusted with* leader *when he says that* s.m. *is right, after tries in vain with motions behind* s.m.'s *back to make the* leader *say that he is right*) Alright, here I go again. N-E-E-D-D-L. (*Triumphantly*) Now *that's* right.

s.m.: (*Laughing heartily*) Why no, that's worse than your first attempt.

cohen: No, that's spelt right.

s.m.: We'll ask George. (*Goes to* LEADER *again*) Who was right that time, George?

GEORGE: (*Paying no attention to* COHEN, *who is again trying to make motions behind* s.m.'s *back to make* GEORGE *say he is right*) Why, you are right.

s.m.: Have another 'cigar. (*Gives* LEADER *cigar*) Well, Cohen, I will give you one more chance.

COHEN: Needle. Is that the word?

s.m.: Yes.

COHEN: Why didn't you say so? N-I-D-L-E.

s.m.: Wrong again.

COHEN: I'm right.

s.m.: We will ask . . .

COHEN: I will ask him this time. Mr. Musiker, who is right this time?

LEADER: Why, you are, Mr. Cohen.

COHEN: (*Very happy, making faces at* s.m.) See? (*To* LEADER) Do you smoke?

LEADER: Why, yes.

COHEN: (*Hand in pocket as if to take out cigar*) Here's a *match*.

s.m.: (*Laughs*) Mr. Cohen, you are a card. Say, Cohen, I was reading the papers this morning and I see that (*Local town*) has three saloons to one policeman.

COHEN: That gives you three guesses as to where the policeman is.

s.m.: By the way, where is your boy?

COHEN: You mean my boy Abie? He is an eye doctor.

s.m.: (*Surprised*) Why I thought he was a chiropodist.

COHEN: He *was* a chiropodist. You see, he began at the foot and worked himself up.

s.m.: Are you still happily married?

COHEN: Yeh, I don't live with my wife.

s.m.: You know, I've been married since I saw you last. I married a sharpshooter from the Buffalo Bill Show.

COHEN: A shipshopper, eh?

s.m.: Yes, sir. My wife's a very good shot. Why, she can hit a silver dollar at a hundred yards.

COHEN: Dot's nothing. My wife goes through my pockets and never misses a dime. You know, I got a great idea how to get along with my wife.

s.m.: I'd like to hear it; it may come in handy sometime.

COHEN: When I come home I throw things around the house, I put cigar ashes on the floor.

S.M.: Why, what's the idea of that?

COHEN: I get my wife so mad she won't speak to me. Then we get along fine.

S.M.: A woman that doesn't speak, why that's a miracle. Of course, you know what a miracle is?

COHEN: Sure I know what a miracle is.

S.M.: Well, tell, me what is a miracle?

COHEN: Well, if you see a bull in the field . . .

S.M.: Yes, if you see a bull in the field?

COHEN: Dot ain't no miracle.

S.M.: Of course not.

COHEN: If you see a thistle in a field, dot ain't no miracle.

S.M.: Of course a thistle in a field is no miracle.

COHEN: And if you hear a lark singing, dot ain't no miracle.

S.M.: Of course hearing a lark sing is no miracle.

COHEN: But if you see a bull sitting on a thistle singing like a lark, *dot's a miracle.*

S.M.: (*Laughs*) You're a card, Cohen. Will you have dinner at my house tonight?

COHEN: Say, that was a nice dinner we had at your house last week. The salmon was wonderful.

S.M.: Why, that wasn't salmon, that was *ham.*

COHEN: (*Makes funny face*) Who asked you?

S.M.: Say, are you still playing the horses?

COHEN: I played a horse yesterday twenty to one.

S.M.: And did he win?

COHEN: He didn't come in until a quarter past six.

S.M.: By the way, how is your uncle, the one that was so sick?

COHEN: My sick uncle? You know, the Board of Health wouldn't let me bury him?

S.M.: (*Indignantly*) Why I never heard of such a thing. Why wouldn't they let you bury him?

COHEN: Because he ain't dead yet.

S.M.: (*Laughs*) You're a card, Cohen.

COHEN: I'm a whole deck. I'm going to get a drink.

S.M.: What's the idea?

COHEN: Then I'll be a *full* deck.

S.M.: You're incorrigible.

COHEN: Why bring religion into this? I'm going now.

S.M.: Where are you going?

COHEN: I'm going to get my wife a nice dog. He must be able to swim.

S.M.: Why must he be able to swim?

COHEN: You see, my wife holds him on her lap and she has water on the knee.

S.M.: (*Laughs*) I think we better sing.

(STRAIGHT MAN *sings a popular song. Then* COHEN *sings a parody on it. Then they both Exit*)

The Two-woman Act

As music plays the STRAIGHT WOMAN *enters. She is all dressed up in evening clothes. She should be dressed in the latest fashion and should have plenty of style to her manner. Every move should bespeak class in contrast to the* COMEDIENNE *who follows her on. She is dressed eccentricly with tiny hat that has a lone feather sticking up, she wears large gloves, tight skirt, and a mangy fur piece thrown around her neck. As music dies out, the* COMEDIENNE *walks a bit faster and gets ahead of the* STRAIGHT WOMAN.

S.W.: Say, what's your hurry?

COM.: I have a date with an old man and I want to get there before he falls apart.

S.W.: How old is he?

COM.: He is eighty years old.

S.W.: Is he rich?

COM.: He is in the belt-manufacturing business.

S.W.: Why don't you marry him?

COM.: I'm afraid his knees will buckle. (*Makes motion with hand to audience*) For goodness sake. (*As she put other hand to her mouth. This same business is used after each laugh, and should be worked up until it's a scream*) I had a date with a general last night.

s.w.: Major general?

com.: Not yet. (*Hand business*) For goodness sake. (*Etc.*) Do you know, he tried to kiss me?

s.w.: Did you call for help?

com.: No. Witnesses. (*Repeat hand business*) For goodness sake.

s.w.: Well my boy friend wouldn't kiss me unless I allow him to. He's a saint.

com.: Yeh. A Saint Bernard. (*Business with hand*) For goodness sake.

s.w.: (*Looking at ring on* COMEDIENNE'S *finger*) Say, that's a nice emerald you have there.

com.: That's a diamond.

s.w.: Who ever heard of a green diamond?

com.: Give it a chance; it isn't ripe yet. (*Hand business*) For goodness sake.

s.w.: Well, I have to be getting along. I'm going to the beauty parlor.

com.: I was in one of those places yesterday. I asked the doctor should I have my face lifted.

s.w.: And what did the doctor say?

com.: He said if I had it *knocked off* it would be much better. (*Hand business*) For goodness sake.

s.w.: And what did you say when he told you that?

com.: I told him if I wasn't a lady I'd kick his teeth out. (*Hand business*) Say, where did you get that swell-looking dress you have hanging on those bones?

s.w.: Oh, a little thing I picked up at Saks. You know, all smart girls buy their clothes there.

com.: Hah. *Smart* girls don't *buy* their clothes. (*To audience*) Get it, girls? (*To* STRAIGHT) Are you married?

s.w.: I was married. I married a tattooed man from a circus.

com.: I got it. So you could stay up all night and look at the pictures for nothing.

s.w.: I divorced him because he was so old-fashioned.

com.: I guess you wanted a guy with *talking* pictures. (*Hand business*) For goodness sake.

s.w.: I'll have you understand as far as men are concerned, I'm a one-way street.

COM.: You may have been a one-way street, but you look to me like you're open for all traffic now. (*Hand business*) For goodness sake.

s.w.: (*Haughtily*) Why, last summer I said no to seven different men.

COM.: What were they selling? (*Hand business*)

s.w.: Are you married?

COM.: I was married for two years. I just had an option on him.

s.w.: Did the option run out?

COM.: No, but he did. One day he stuck a fork into me.

s.w.: (*Surprised*) Stuck a fork into you? Why, what did that mean?

COM.: It meant that I was done, sister, I was done. (*Hand business*)

s.w.: You should see my boy friend. He is handsome. I have a picture of him hanging in my boudoir.

COM.: (*Mimics her*) Bood wahh?

s.w.: Boudoir, in French, means a place to sleep.

COM.: (*Knowingly*) Yeh? In America it means a playground. (*Business*) But don't get so stuck up with your Boodwahh. My boy friend took me to eat at the Ritz.

s.w.: Say, you couldn't even pay the cover charge at the Ritz.

COM.: I said *eat* there, not *stay* there. For goodness sake. And he is a handsome man too. I think he is an architect. Look at the blue prints he left on my neck. For goodness sake.

s.w.: Did you have a good time?

COM.: Did I? I went out fit as a fiddle and came back tight as a drum.

s.w.: Say, whatever became of the doctor you kept company with?

COM.: I gave him up.

s.w.: What was the matter?

COM.: Every time I got a letter from him I had to take it to the drugstore to find out what was in it. (*Business with hand*) I said some very foolish things to him.

s.w.: Yes?

COM.: That was one of them. (*To audience*) Catch on, girls?

s.w.: That's a very funny piece of fur you have there. What is it?

COM.: I bought it for seal.

s.w.: (*Laughingly*) Seal? It looks more like monkey.

COM.: Don't blame me if someone has been monkeying with the seals.

S.W.: (*Very ritzy*) Now this scarf I have on is the real thing. You know, I had a terrible dream last night, I dreamed that the animal this fur came from was going to chew me to pieces.

COM.: Now don't tell me that you are afraid of rabbits? For goodness sake. Say, you smell awful good. What is that perfume you use?

S.W.: Why that is Coty's Chypre. (*Pronounce it as sheep.*) Five dollars an ounce.

COM.: Is that so? Well, get a load of my perfume.

S.W.: (*Walks over and smells and makes a terrible face*) What is it?

COM.: McCarthy's goat. Ten cents a gallon. (*Business*) For goodness sake.

This should be cue for music. Both sing song, with STRAIGHT WOMAN *making gestures and* COMEDIENNE *copying and exaggerating each one. At finish of song walk off with* COMEDIENNE *saying "For Goodness Sake."*

Double Blackface Act

Music plays "Nobody"—as both enter wearily. One tall lanky "Nigger" type and the other a small dumpy "Nigger" type who acts as comedian while the tall one acts as straight man. STRAGHT MAN *enters ahead of* COMEDIAN.

S.: Come on—Come on. . . .

C.: How much further we got to walk?

S.: Ten miles.

C.: Ten miles?

S.: Man, dat's nothin . . . it's only five miles a piece.

C.: You know that argiment wit dat man tired me all out.

s.: You shouldn't have sed that. No sir.

c.: I didn't sed nothin.

s.: Yes you did. When dat man ast you what your nationality was, what did you say?

c.: What did I sed?

s.: You sed you were a Republican.

c.: Well I *am* a Republican.

s.: I know dat, but he didn't want to know your *religion*.

c.: Well, I felt sick, I didn't know what he was talking about.

s.: Sick from what?

c.: Sick from eatin too much watermelon.

s.. Man, there ain't no sech thing as *too* much watermelon. Nigger, you ain't got enough stomach, dat's all.

c.: I was wit my gal.

s.. You mean Sadie?

c.: Yeh, Sadie.

s.: That black gal?

c.: She *is* black, ain't she?

s.: I'll say she's black. Boy, when she stands beside you, you look like a bottle of milk.

c.: She's a swell gal. She calls me her chocolate.

s.: Say, if you is chocolate, then I must be licorice.

c.: She sent me a letter. Here 'tis. (*Takes out letter and acts as if he's reading it*)

s.: What you doin? You can't read.

c.: What you talkin about, man? Sure I can read.

s.: Then read it to me.

c.: Well, I can't read dat—dat's typewritten.

s.: Why, dat's the easiest kind. What kind ob writin kin you read?

c.: I kin only read lead-pencil writin. I only went to lead-pencil school.

s.: I'll see if you can read. (*Looks at paper*) What letter is dat?

c.: Why, dat's a capital seven.

s.: Why, dat's an *L*—you're holdin it upside down.

c.: Is dat a fact? Well, all I can read is numbers on dice.

s.: You just plain igorant. You kaint spell nor nothin.

c.: Who sez I kaint spell?

s.: I sez you kaint spell. How do you spell Ohio?

c.: Dat's easy.

s.: Well if it's so easy come on and spell it. Spell Ohio.

c.: O-H-ten—Ohio.

s.: O-H-ten. (*Disgusted*) Say, where you spendin most of your time?

c.: Eh?

s.: Where you spendin most of your time? Where do you hang around?

c.: Do you mean where I'm generally at?

s.: Yeh.

c.: The jail.

s.: You ought to be in jail now.

c.: How come?

s.: I saw you knock dat man down and when he was down you blackened both his eyes. The Devil must have put dat in yo head.

c.: The Devil might have put it in my head to knock him down, but those black eyes were my own idea.

s.: You keep on doin dat stuff and you'll end up bein electro-cutioned.

c.: What's dat?

s.: Don't you know what electrocutioned is?

c.: No, but I specs it's better than hanging.

s.: Yeh, dat's cause you is igorant. When they electrocution you, dey puts a bran new pair of pants on you, den they cuts a slit up one leg right up to the knee. Den dey sets you up in a barber chair and ties a wet sponge on yo wrists. Den dey puts a crown on yo head, den a fellow puts his hand on a button on the wall, and *blewy*.

c.: What's that button for an do?

s.: Do? Why it just *ruins you*.

c.: Talkin about doin, what you doin now?

s.: I'se in show business.

c.: Is dat a fact? What you do?

s.: I is the head man.

c.: The head man?

s.: Sure. Did you ever hear of Field's Minstrels? I was the head man of that.

c.: Is dat a fact?

s.: Yes sir. Did you ever hear of the Ringling Brothers? I was the head man of dat.

c.: Sure enough?

s.: Yes sir. Did you ever hear of Adam and Eve?

c.: Yeh, but you weren't *head man of dat?*

s.: Listen, nigger, don't contradict me. When I say I'm right, I'm right, an don't forget it.

c.: Alright, Black Cloud, but I wants to tell you dis, if you was as short as me an I was as tall as you—you'd be wrong as hell.

s.: Listen, baboon. Don't argify wid me. Cause 1-2-3-4 I'll hop right up on you.

c.: Yeh? Well 5-6-7-8 you'll hop right back off.

s.: Yeh? See dat fist, Midnight? When I hit the side of yo face wit it you're goin to see down your back widout turnin yo head.

c.: Is dat so? See dat foot? Once I kicks yo wid dat, everytime yo sit down you'll leave a footprint.

s.: Boy, if you does that, I'll hit you so hard on yo head I'll break both yo ankles.

c.: Last man tried dat on me ran so fast his coattails were standin straight out and his vest pocket dipped sand.

s.: Listen boy, we shouldn't argify like this. We mustn't forgit we are old war buddies.

c.: You were nothin but an old windjammer in yo outfit.

s.: Is dat so? Say, Big Mouth, I waz a better bugler than you were.

c.: How do you make dat out?

s.: Cause when I blew reveille the dead started puttin on their shoes.

c.: Boy, dat's nothin. When I stuck my horn to my face and blowed *soupy*, de cooks had to cover the strawberries to keep em from kickin the whipped cream outta de dishes.

(*Finish act with* STRAIGHT MAN *playing harmonica and* COMIC *dancing, in which* STRAIGHT MAN *joins in last eight bars for Exit*) (*Note: A single number of Bert Williams "Poker Game" can be used by* COMIC)

The Comedy Sketch

SCENE: *Kitchen set of rich man's home. A few potted plants and maybe a gold chair, giving it a tone of richness. Also table Center with meats, fruits, loaf of bread, coffee pot, prop ham on it.*

CAST:
Lucullus Simpson Smith—THE MAN
Percillia Perkins—THE MAID

AT RISE: PERCILLIA *in neat maid's costume is seen dusting a chair.*

PERCILLIA: I hope Mr. and Mrs. O'Casey get home in time because Billy promised me to take me to the opera. (*With feeling*) If there is anything I delight in more than anything else, it's the opera. The Mikado, Little Tycoon, why it's delightful, it's entrancing (*Music cue; Song, "Carissima," by* PERCILLIA. *At finish of song, property man [or this can be done by the male partner] blows letter-carrier whistle off stage and yells, "Letters."* PERCILLIA *acts surprised*) Eh, letter? Perhaps it's from Billy. (*Goes to door calling*) Hi there, give me that letter. (*Opens door and receives two letters—just the hand of the man giving letters to her is all that has to be shown*) Two? Why, let me see. (*She turns letter over and looks at address while coming down Center Stage*) Miss Percillia Perkins, that's me. I'll bet it's from *Billy.* (*Tears open letter and reads*) Dear Percillia: This is to inform you that I can not leave the meat shop tonight. But I love you more than ever. Farewell. I have to stuff a blood pudding with ham. Thine until death, William Thadeus Jinks. (*Brokenhearted, sits on chair.*) After all my plans we can not go to the opera. Heigh Ho. It's too bad. (*Toying with other letter*) I do think Billy might have forsaken the blood pudding for my sake. (*Glancing at letter*) Hello, what is this? Why, as I live, if I haven't opened Mrs. Scroggins' letter. Won't there be a row when she comes in. I'll have to stick it together with some mucilage. (*Looking for mucilage*) Oh, here it is. (*Takes bottle of mucilage*) If Billy would only stick to me like this mucilage, but no (*sobbingly*), he's forgotten me now. Well, I may as well stick up the envelope. There can't be any harm in my reading it, just to see how high-class folks write, then I can stick it together again. (*Opens letter and reads*) Dear Maud: You know the romantic notions of my dear brother, and although I have over and over again asserted your sister's meekness, the dear boy wants to be convinced before proposing to her, and will arrive in your house almost as soon as you get this, in the disguise of a traveling actor. Tell Flora to treat any such she may have call on her well, for no one can tell which might not be the duke. Ever yours, Lady Clive. (*Drops letter in surprise*) Well I never. A real live duke coming here disguised as an actor and Mrs. Scroggins has gone out. (*Picks up letter and fastens it, meanwhile getting bright idea*) I know what I'll do. I'll pretend I'm the missus and receive him. Perhaps he may be stuck on my figure and propose to *me*. And when I'm a duchess, I'll ride past Billy's meat shop and turn my nose up at him. I'll just spruce up a bit and get ready for the duke. (*Exits.*)

(*Shouts of Police—Police off stage as door suddenly flies open.* LUCULLUS *with half carpet bag, one white-gloved hand, green umbrella, mangy fur-collared coat, battered high hat. Face pale, black eyes, and long-haired wig. He rushes in and dives under table, and as the cries outside die away he sticks out his head, glances around, sees loaf of bread, grabs it and eats, gets fit of coughing, spits out bread, sits on the edge of table, drinks out of the spout of the coffee pot.*) "Oh, ouch." (*Business with bread and coffee*)

LUCULLUS: Phew. That's almost as bad as the fate I just escaped. I do believe if those policemen had got hold of me they would have ransacked my wardrobe. (*Shows audience other side of bag, it only being half of one. He discovers sock pinned within*) Confound them, they've shaken me all up, I lost the key of my valise and can't get into it. (*Noise off stage*) What's that? I thought they were after me. I've walked thirty hours on cross ties in the last week. The sheriff came down on me and Lucullus was forced to make a hasty exit. It so happened right in the middle of Shakespeare's sublime tragedy of *Hamlet,* so I was forced to seek shelter in these kingly robes, so I'm *crushed again.*

(*Music Cue . . . Sings.*)

There goes Lucullus Simpson Smith
The Cincinnati Ham
Who by the managers kicked out
Finds solace in a dram.
His clothes melt in a heavy dew
His hat is long since slain
When I bounced out, the boys all shout
Hey Smithy . . .
                    "Crushed again."

(*Spoken*) That's what they used to say, although I could knock
the puddin out of Mansfield and Mantell. Yet, such was the
envy of me rivals I could never get a date at the leading theaters.
But I'll get on my feet and no more will they have cause
to say . . .

            (*Chorus . . . Singing Again*)
He's a *ham*, he's a *clam*, he's the worst of 'em all
To try doing Caesar he shows an awful gall
His Brutus is terrific, his Iago a myth
A regular barnstormer is Lucullus Simpson Smith.
My Cassius is simply grand
But managers won't seize it
Where'er I go they whisper low
Oh nix cull . . . cheese it.
But now I am a manager and star
It causes them much pain
Because you see they all agree
I'll never be crushed again.

(*After song goes to table and eats—as* PERCILLIA *enters, not
seeing* LUCULLUS)
PERCILLIA: There. I've fixed up and put on a ribbon or two, and
    I do believe I could crush the heart of even a duke. (*Sees* LUCUL-
    LUS *and screams*) Here, you beggar, this is no place for tramps.
LUCULLUS: (*Drawing himself up proudly*) Tramp? Vile minion,
    behold in me the last of an ancient and honored race, the
    favored of the earth. (*Panting tragically*) No, I'm no tramp but
    the crushed genius endowed with immortal fire. Call me out-
    cast, ragmuffin, but spare me honor, ask of the four winds of
    heaven who I am and they will reply, Lucullus Simpson Smith,

tragedian. (*Slaps breast and struts up and down stage majestically*)

PERCILLIA: (*Screams*) It's the duke. Oh, love penetrated your disguise. (*Bows extravagantly*) I have recognized your lofty brow even in its mask of poverty. (*Bows*) But be thou spirit or goblin damned?

LUCULLUS: Young woman, don't cuss.

PERCILLIA: Thou comest in such unquestionable shape I'll answer thee.

LUCULLUS: She's stuck on my shape.

PERCILLIA: I'll call you king . . .

LUCULLUS: Good 'nuff.

PERCILLIA: Father . . .

LUCULLUS: Nix, there's six of 'em at home calling me that now.

PERCILLIA: Royal Dane.

LUCULLUS: Young woman, I object. Do I look like a dame? No. I will not bid your sordid huckster for thee, priceless gem. (*Picks up ham from table*) No, there's the sum twice told, blush not to take it, for there's not a coin that has not been bought by a solder's blood.

PERCILLIA: Ah, that voice again.

LUCULLUS: Come to my arms—thy husband. (PERCILLIA *screams and falls heavy in his arms and doubles up quickly*) I said come to my arms, not the pit of my stomach. (POSTMAN *whistles off stage and yells " A letter"*)

PERCILLIA: Another letter? (*Rushes to door and gets it*) And it's to me and in my missus' handwriting. Oh, what if she has found out I'm entertaining the duke? (LUCULLUS *seats himself at table and starts eating fast, while* PERCILLIA *opens letter and reads:*) Percillia, hurry up and get supper as soon as possible. Don't delay a moment for the duke who has been with us all day in the disguise of an actor will be home to supper with us. (PERCILLIA *screams and drops note as* LUCULLUS *goes to her*) Don't touch me, you impostor. You're no duke, you're a tramp. (*Throws ham at* LUCULLUS *and he falls down*)

LUCULLUS: Look out, Queen Elizabeth, you're mistaken. I'm no duke but still no tramp.

LUCULLUS: (*Removing wig*) Your Billy. It's all merely a joke to fool you. (*Rubbing his eye where she hit him with ham.*)

PERCILLIA: Well I'm sorry.

LUCULLUS: Not half as sorry as me. (*Takes hold of her hands*) We are both mistaken. (*Finish with medley or song and dance*)

The Afterpiece

The Afterpiece was played at the end of nearly all old variety shows, and was participated in by the entire company. "Irish Justice" was one of the outstanding of all the afterpieces and has been written and rewritten hundreds of times with as many different versions. If the judge was played by an Irish comedian, it was called, "Irish Justice"; if a Dutch comedian played the lead, it was called, "Dutch Justice"; and if a blackface comedian played the judge, it was called, "Colored Justice." The following is the author's version of "Irish Justice."

SCENE: *Court room. Judge's desk up C. Prisoner's box L. Jury box R. Desk in front of Judge's stand. Chairs R. and L. for lawyer and district attorney.*

CAST: Mike O'Malley .... THE NEW JUDGE
Con .... THE DISTRICT ATTORNEY
Guggenheim .... AN ATTORNEY
Makeem Welcome .... COURT OFFICER
Hooligan .... VICTIM OF HARD LUCK
PRISONERS. WITNESSES. JURY. COPS, ETC.

AT OPENING—*Everybody is in court except the judge.*

CON: (*To* GUGGENHEIM) So now you're a lawyer. How did it happen?

GUGG.: The judge fixed it for me. He wanted someone with him who knew the law so I went through college, and the judge met me outside; now I'm a lawyer.

COP: Here comes the new judge.

(*Music plays "Wearing of the Green" as* JUDGE *enters* L. *While everybody looks* R. *He has large book under his arm and is dressed in black robe and a battered high hat. Everybody cheers as the* JUDGE *gets up on the stand and does funny business with his hat, finally throwing it down.*)

JUDGE: Darn that hat, what's the matter with it?

GUGG.: You got a swell head this morning.

JUDGE: There's nothing wrong with my head. It's been raining; this is one of those hats that shrink in the night.

CON: Oh, you got wet, did you?

JUDGE: I did, inside. Now you cops do a run and chase up some business.

(*Chorus Exits.*)

Begorra, this is a great business. I'm the judge, he's the district attorney, and you're a liar . . . a lawyer. Who's that bum sleeping there?

GUGG.: He's the court crier.

JUDGE: (*Hitting* POLICEMAN *with bladder on head. The* POLICEMAN *wakes up.*) Get a can opener and open this here court.

COP: This court is now open. Hear ye, hear ye.

JUDGE: We hear ye, we ain't blind. What's the first case on the docket?

CON: The first case, your honor, is a case of bigamy.

JUDGE: Bring in Big Annie. (POLICEMAN *executes a grotesque dance and exits. The* JUDGE *just barely misses him with the bladder.*) Say, what is this? A dance hall? (*Enter* POLICEMAN *with* BIGAMIST *who goes to stand*) Who's he been murdering?

CON: Your honor, this man is not a murderer. He has *two* wives and the people demand that he be punished.

JUDGE: Oh, the people are non compos mentis. I'm the courthouse. (*Raps desk with large bung starter, which frightens* GUGG., *who jumps into* POLICEMAN'S *arms—after laugh,* POLICEMAN *drops him*) Have you anything to put before this court before the case goes to the jury?

BIGAMIST: Would $10,000 be enough? (*Takes out roll of bills. Everybody makes a grab for the bills . . . but* HOOLIGAN *enters, grabs money, and exits*)

JUDGE: Are you guilty or not guilty?

BIGAMIST: You guess first, Judge.

JUDGE: Officer, remove the rubbish. He's discharged. (COP *takes* BIGAMIST *off*)

CON: I demand to know on what grounds you discharged the prisoner.

JUDGE: On the courthouse grounds.

GUGG.: But what kind of justice is this?

JUDGE: This is (*Local town*) justice. That man has *two wives*. I have *one*. He is punished enough. (*Raps with mallet as* GUGG. *and* COP *start a fight*) Order in this butcher shop. What's the next case on the docket?

CON: The next case, your honor, is a case of assault and battery.

JUDGE: Bring them both in. (POLICEMAN *exits with another funny dance and the* JUDGE *barely misses him with bladder*) That cop is full of Lydia Pinkham's medicine. (COP *brings man in*)

CON: This man is charged with hitting a cop.

JUDGE: That will cost you eleven fifty for hitting a cop.

MAN: That's cheap. (*Hands up money*)

JUDGE: Say, that eleven fifty means eleven dollars and fifty years in jail.

MAN: But my doctor sez I won't live over twenty years.

JUDGE: Well, do all you can of it. Take him away. (POLICEMAN *has fallen asleep and* JUDGE *hits him with bladder—*COP *runs off*) Next case. (COP *brings man in who is* HOOLIGAN)

CON: This prisoner is arrested for stealing a nanny goat.

GUGG.: I'll take this case. (*Goes to* HOOLIGAN) I'll get you out of this and all it will cost you is the mere sum of ten dollars. (HOOLIGAN *shakes his head yes*) Now when anyone says anything to you, don't say a word, just make a sound like a nanny goat. (*Both imitate goat*) I'm ready for the case, Judge.

JUDGE: Go ahead, I won't listen.

CON: This disreputable specimen of humanity is guilty, your honor, beyond the shadow of a doubt. For with my own eyes I saw him in the company of the aforesaid goat.

GUGG.: You never saw him with a goat.

CON: I did see him with a goat. (*They both wrangle like two kids*)

JUDGE: (*Hitting them both with bladder*) I'll buy you kids a candy horse and if you don't like it you can lick it.

GUGG.: Well, Judge, he is not guilty and I can prove it.

JUDGE: Well, prove it, and I won't believe you.

GUGG.: You see, Happy was going home one bright afternoon in the middle of the night and he found laying in the road a long piece of rope.

JUDGE: Tin or wood?

GUGG.: Glass. He took it home and when he got there he found the goat on the other end of the rope.

JUDGE: To this terrible charge do you plead guilty? (HOOLIGAN *imitates nanny goat*) I say do you plead guilty or not guilty? (HOOLIGAN *repeats nanny goat imitation*) Officer, remove him, he's a nut.

GUGG.: (*Goes to* HOOLIGAN) I got you out all right. Where's my ten dollars? (HOOLIGAN *imitates goat and Exits.* GUGG. *appeals to the* POLICEMAN, CON, *and* JUDGE *and they all imitate nanny goat. Enter* HOOLIGAN *with a ladder*)

JUDGE: Hey, where are you going with that ladder?

HOOLIGAN: I'm going to take my case to a higher court. (*Exits*)

CON: The next case is a man accused of murdering his family.

JUDGE: (*As* COP *brings in man*) Get the Bible and swear in the murderer.

COP: Your honor, the bull pup has chewed up the Bible.

JUDGE: Make the witness kiss the dog. We can't adjourn to get a new Bible. So you murdered your whole family?

MAN: Yes, your honor.

JUDGE: Thirty days.

MAN: Don't be so hard on me, Judge. It was only a small family.

JUDGE: Take him away, there ain't going to be no murderer in my court. (*Enter* HOOLIGAN *and wanders around courtroom*) What are you doing in this court?

HOOLIGAN: I'm a witness.

JUDGE: What trial?

HOOLIGAN: I don't know. But you never can tell what cases come up. (*Exits*)

JUDGE: What's the next case?

CON: A man accused of stealing a jug of whisky.

JUDGE: Bring in the whisky stealer. (POLICEMAN *does funny dance and exits and re-enters with whisky stealer who has jug.* COP *tries to drink out of it.* GUGG. *takes it away from him and hands it to the* JUDGE) How dare you try to drink before the judge? (*Takes drink, makes faces.*) What's that, lamp oil?

GUGG.: Your honor, this man's not guilty. He is simply subject to fits. While meandering down the boulevard he took a fit.

JUDGE: I'll soak him five dollars for that.

GUGG.: While under the influence of this fit his hand involuntarily reached into a window containing jugs of whisky. His hand clutched a jug, he took it home, and it cured him of fits.

JUDGE: You say whisky is good for fits?

CON: But I say whisky is *not* good for fits. (COP *is seized with a fit.* JUDGE *brings down jug and gives him a drink.* HOOLIGAN *comes on and has a fit, is given a drink, then the* JUDGE *has a fit. . . .* HOOLIGAN *turning jug upside down*)

HOOLIGAN: Judge, there's no more whisky.

JUDGE: (*Coming out of fit quickly*) Then there's no more fits. (*Whistle blows, bell rings, as* JURY *all start to go out*) Here, here, where are you going?

JURY: Why, it's lunch time. We want our lunch.

JUDGE: Say, officer, go out and bring in the Jury some lunch. We have a lot of cases before us. And here's a dime and tell Bill the bartender at Schmidt's to fill it up, it's for the judge. (*Hands him coal scuttle and a dime.* JUDGE *lights a cigar or a pipe*)

CON: Your honor, there is no smoking allowed in court.

JUDGE: Say, I'm the judge, ain't I?

CON: Yes, your honor.

JUDGE: Well, the judge can smoke a little. (OFFICER *enters with a pitchfork full of hay and throws it in the jury box and Exits.* HOOLIGAN *comes in with coal scuttle full of beer and hands it to the* JUDGE, *who drinks it all up as everybody is watching him with their mouths watering. Loud noises heard off stage. Everybody looks as* OFFICER *enters with chorus girls, who are dressed in long capes*) What is the matter here?

OFFICER: Your honor, they all were doing the hootchie-kootchie dance in one-piece bathing suits.

JUDGE: (*Raps mallet on bench, puts hat on, and yells*) Court's adjourned.

CON: (*Seeing* JUDGE *going down to the girls*) What are you going to do with them, your honor?

JUDGE: (*Flirting with the girls and holding one of the girls around the waist*) I am going to hold them all for further examination. (HOOLIGAN *hits* JUDGE *on head with bladder from behind, and takes his place with the girls as everybody sings and Curtain Falls*)

The Parody Singers

*Two men made up as Hebrew or Dutch Comedians . . . Enter
with opening introduction. Stand center stage and sing clearly and
distinctly so that the audience will get the "catch lines."*

(*To the tune of "Old Gray Bonnet"*)
Our friend young Jimmy Grady has a girl, her name is Sadie.
They are going to be wed, so he called one morning early
At her home to see his girlie, but her mother to him said,
"To you I must confess, Sir, that my daughter's still in bed,"
"You will have to wait, dear Jimmy, all I have on is my—coat."
Then he sang to his love.
Chorus
Put on your old gray bonnet, with the blue ribbons on it,
For I'd like to see you right away.
She said, "Jim, that would never do to see me this way, why,
You must wait 'till our wedding day."

(*Both Exit. Come back and as music is vamping, say, "We got
some more—you ain't heard nothing yet."*

(*To the tune of "Kelly."*)
To a spirit-rapping party Patrick Casey took his wife.
A lady there went in a trance and brought the dead to life.
The spirits started rapping, at least so the lady said,
And soon the room was filled with shades of people who were dead.
The lady said, "Is there some shade somebody wants to see?"
Then Casey said, "Yes, find one man who owes money to me."
Chorus
Has anybody here seen Kelly? K-E-L-L-Y?
I lent money to Kelly when he was alive.
When a Dutchman dies he's dead alright,
But an Irishman has to be watched three nights.
If anybody here sees Kelly, tell him I want my five.

(*Both Exit—Come back as before and say, "We got some more,
you ain't heard nothing yet."*)

(To the tune of "Dixie")

Way down yonder where the grass is blue
We wrote this song for me and you,
It's good, it ain't, it's fine, we don't believe it.
We'll sing you a song we wrote last night,
Our pen was wrong but we made it write,
Our ink was pink, dot's vy dis song is foolish.
We wish we was in Dixie, we should, vy not?
We wish we was in Dixie land
With three millions in our hand.
We ain't, we are, don't wake us up, we are dreaming.
Don't laugh out loud or the manager will fine us.
We wish we was two Mormons, we would, we could,
We wished we lived by old Salt Lake
With all the wives that we could take,
We'd drown them all and then we'd drown their mothers.
Salt Lake is great, that's where they catch salt codfish.
We wish we was a pickle so sweet to eat,
We wish we vos a piece of soap,
Some girl would wash with us we hope,
Oh joy, oh fudge, we know a girl needs washing,
Dot's how she lives, she's working in a laundry.

(Both Exit—Come back and say, "We got more. You ain't heard nothing yet")

(To the tune of "Dreaming")

Last summer I went on vacation
To the country for sweet recreation.
I found all the rooms had been taken.
A young clerk from Siegel and Cooper
When he found out that I was a trouper
To the landlord said he,
"He can sleep with me," and so I did.

Chorus

Dreaming, dreaming, of his work that clerk he started in dreaming,
One yard or two yards, I heard him repeat,
When I heard a big rip I said there goes my sheet.
Dreaming, dreaming, a smile on my face it was beaming.
But I found out next morn 'twas my night shirt he torn
While dreaming.

(*Both Exit—Come back and say, "We got some more. Say, what do you want for your money?"*)

(*To the tune of "I Love a Lassie"*)
I love a lassie, a bonnie lassie,
She's as skinny as the paper on the wall.
And everytime I meet her, with a hug and kiss I greet her
And she says:
(*Modulation into tune of "Stop Tickling, Jock"*)
Won't you stop your tickling, Jock,
Won't you stop your tickling, Jock,
Then I laugh and to her say,
(*Modulation into tune of "Highland Lassie"*)
Bonnie, my Highland lassie,
For you my heart it pines,
Please do some Scottish dances.
(*Modulation into tune of "Highland Mary Did the Highland Fling"*)
When Highland Mary started in to do the Highland fling,
"Hoot Mon," said Highland Mary as she did the Highland
    fling,
When her foot got tangled in the chandelier
One Scotchman arose and he did cry:
(*Modulation into tune of "Jerusalem"*)
She's losin' 'em, She's losin' 'em,
Then they all got up and sang:
(*Modulation into tune of "Don't Take Me Home"*)
Don't take us home, please don't take us home.
(*Modulation into tune of "Auld Lang Syne"*)
Should auld acquaintance be forgot, to each other they did say,
When Highland Mary said she'd dance for them again some
day.

(*Both Exit—Make change into long linen dusters, goggles, cap, etc., like two automobilists—Look at audience and say, "What, some more?"*)

(*To tune of "Yankee Doodle"*)
Oh we both were very dizzy, from being very busy,
So we decided that we'd quit and lead a quiet life.
First we bought an automobubble
And that started all the trouble

For both of us then we did take ourselves a wife.
Then we went automobubbling walking,
Oh we both felt dandy, like full of candy,
We run, we ran everybody down
Till the machine went in the air,
But we didn't give a care,
We saw all kinds of colors, the red, white, and blue,
We almost saw the star-strangled bananas.

(*Modulation into tune of "We Rambled"*)
We rambled, we rambled, we rambled all around,
In the air not on the ground.

(*Modulation into tune of "Poor John"*)
For the auto took us round to see our mother-in-law,
Our mother-in-law, our mother-in-law.

(*Modulation into tune of "See-Saw"*)
Then she saw she saw, she saw us go up and go down.
We said that we'd visit her that night again
And to be ready to greet us not later than ten.

(*Modulation into tune of "I Don't Care"*)
But we didn't care, we didn't care,
Once we were out of her sight
We wandered all around, we went from town to town,
And we ended up that night

(*Modulation into tune of "Gem of the Ocean"*)
With our auto at the bottom of the ocean,
We were surprised to find it bright.
It was full of electric fishes.
We're here to say it was a wondrous sight.

(*Modulation into tune of "Silvery Moon"*)
By the light of the silvery moon, our wives did swoon,
So we started for home mighty soon.

(*Modulation into tune of "All Aboard for Blanket Bay"*)
We jumped aboard and rode away,
No more with fishes will we play.

(*Modulation into tune of "Come Over to My Yard"*)
We put the auto in our yard
And from there it never will stray.

(*Modulation into tune of "Yankee Doodle"*)
From now on we are walking dandies,
The ground is good enough for us.

If we take a trip again it will be upon a pony.
Hurray for the red, white, and blue.
(*Modulation into tune of "Auld Lang Syne"*)
Our auto trip we'll never forget until the day we die,
We told you all about it—now it's time to say good-by.
(*Exit*)

Odds and Ends

THE ACROBATIC ACT
(*Stop music at finish of act and stand center stage*) Ladies and gentlemen, my partner will now do a double complete somersault from the floor, and is the only man alive ever to attempt this trick. (*This can be said in a German dialect*)

THE DOG ACT
Ladies and gentlemen, little Trixie here will now pick out the different flags of all the different countries, just by hearing the orchestra play the national anthems of the different countries. This is done by Trixie herself and is not worked through any cues of mine. This is all done by kindness. (*See that the dogs don't bark loudly when you whip them off stage, as the audience may think you are cruel*)

FEMALE IMPERSONATION
(*At finish of act remove wig and lift shoulders to make them look big and in as mannish a voice as you possibly can, say*) So long, fellows.

JUGGLER
(*When you are dropping balls, clubs, or any objects you may be juggling*) This is the only act in the world that gets paid for practicing.

(*When woman assistant gives you the different objects*) I carry her so she can hand me things—last night she handed me a black eye. (*Look at her legs*) I wish someone would look at *me* once in a while.

(*Before doing a trick*) I did this trick before the crowned heads of Europe and the bald heads of (*Local town*).

(*When missing a trick*) If I did it the first time, you wouldn't think it was a good trick.

(*Try putting hat on stick while balancing stick on head; after missing it a dozen times, place hat on stick and say*) Well, anyway, this is the way it looks if I did it. (*Exit*)

DANCING ACT

(*Stop music*) My partner will do triples and wings; she is the only lady in the world doing this style of dancing, and we have ten dollars posted with the management of this theater as a challenge to any lady dancer. (*At finish of dance or on the last four bars, yell to leader "Let's Go"*)

MAGICIAN

I have here an ordinary deck of playing cards. I will now prove to you that the hand is quicker than the eye.

I did this trick before President Roosevelt . . . was elected. Has anybody in the audience got a stiff gentleman's hat? I mean a gentleman's stiff hat.

(*Taking rabbit out of hat*) I always use a rabbit, because you know rabbits are smart, they can multiply.

I will now roll up my sleeves to prove to you that there is nothing concealed in them.

I would like to borrow a five-dollar gold piece. (*Look around audience and when nobody offers you the gold piece, say*) Alright, I'll settle for a dollar.

WIRE ACT

(*While walking on wire*) I just received this wire from my agent. Somebody asked me how my business was and I said, "Slack."

CARTOONIST

If the lady in the upper box will take her hand away from her face, I will try and make a drawing of her.

I once drew a chicken so well that when I threw it in the wastebasket, it *laid* there.

I showed a picture of an apple that I drew to my teacher and she said it was rotten.

SINGER

Ladies and gentlemen, I have a special request this evening to sing (*Pick out song you sing best*).

COMPOSER

I will now play you a medley of my compositions. (*Play part of chorus, and between each one say*) And then I wrote . . . .

VIOLINIST

Ladies and gentlemen, I will try and give you a series of imitations on my fiddle. My first will be that of a man speaking to a lady and the lady answering back. If you will pay particular attention, I am sure you will distinctly hear what they have to say. First he meets the girl and flirts with her. (*Play "Oh, You Kid" on G string*) This is what she answered. (*Play "Go To Hell" on E string*)

HYPNOTIST

Ladies and gentlemen, I am about to show you a few interesting experiments in the science of hypnotism. I would like for a committee of about a dozen gentlemen to step up here on the stage and see that I do not use any confederates or plants, and also see that there is no trickery whatsoever in my experiments. I will be very grateful to you gentlemen if you will volunteer for the committee. You will find steps on both sides of the stage and I assure you I will not do or say anything that will offend or embarrass you. (As the committee comes up, you greet everyone with a handshake.) Now, gentlemen, will you please tell the ladies and gentlemen in the audience that you have never seen me before. These men are all strangers to me. All right, we shall now proceed with my first experiment. For my first experiment I shall try suspended circulation. I wish to state at this time that I appeared before the faculty and students of science and medicine last week at Barndy College; my suspended circulation experiment was used in the amputation of an arm. It is one of the first bloodless operations in the annals of medicine. So you see, ladies and gentlemen, my act is educational as well as entertaining.

ENGLISHMAN APPEARING FOR FIRST TIME

(*After act is over*) I love your country very much and I wish to thank you from the bottom of my heart for being so grand to me on this my first appearance in your country. And I am very proud to state that I have already applied for my first papers and hope to be a citizen of your grand and glorious country soon. I thank you.

MASTER OF CEREMONIES

Now folks, give the little girl a great big hand.

PICTURE STAR MAKING PERSONAL APPEARANCES

I can't tell you ladies and gentlemen how much it means to me to
see and meet my audience face to face. I want you to know my *real*
self besides knowing my *reel* self. Contrary to what you read in the
papers, we do not play all day and all night in our beautiful homes.
It is real hard work in Hollywood if one takes her profession seriously. Day in and day out we appear before the camera with nobody
to applaud you when you feel you did something really worth
while. I can't tell you how wonderful you have made me feel this
afternoon with your generous applause. It makes one feel proud
and grand to know that one isn't forgotten. I shall endeavor in the
future to do better work in the pictures and to keep your friendship. I shall go back to the studio in Hollywood with a lighter
heart and appreciative feeling for having met you all in person.
I thank you.

Memories of . . .

The Palace

The Palace Theatre on Broadway and Forty-seventh Street, New
York City, has been glorified in pictures and novels, on radio, TV,
and the stage, and is known all over the world!

The Palace was a very appropriate name, for it was here that the
kings and queens, princes and princesses, of comedy, song and
dance, music, drama, and acrobatics ruled for nineteen years! It
was here that the princes of entertainers and the entertainers of
princes played for the many loyal subjects of the Kingdom of
Vaudeville!

When an actor made good at the Palace, he was knighted with

the golden sword and admitted to the inner court circles of the aristocrats and blue bloods of the kingdom. The Palace maybe didn't play royalty, but it paid royally! If you made good at the Palace, you walked down the three red-carpeted steps on either side of the stage and stepped into the rich fields of musical comedy, drama, movies, and radio. It ceased being the throne room of the kings of Vaudeville in 1932. Talkies, radio, and a dozen and one things crumbled the kingdom, and a few wandering tribes remained. And to this day you can see some of their descendants, but they bear little resemblance to their ancestors of the two-a-day at the Palace! (Especially under glass.)

The Palace was built by Martin Beck, who through it was going to fulfill a life's ambition of bringing Orpheum vaudeville into New York City, where Keith-Albee had ruled for so many years. Beck's backer ran out on him, so he had to give up to Albee, but retained 25 per cent of the stock in the Palace and was allowed to have a little say about some things. Finally in 1928 both the Orpheum and Keith circuits were taken over by Joseph P. Kennedy, the financial genius (later U. S. Ambassador to England) and General David Sarnoff, representing Radio Corporation of America. The new combine was named the Radio-Keith-Orpheum Circuit, or RKO. Mr. Kennedy placed a gentleman by the name of Hiram Brown at the head of his new kingdom. Mr. Brown was a big leather man who knew a lot about leather but nothing about show biz, except what the ticker tape told him, for now the kingdom was ruled by the Wall Street boys!

Beck—Albee—Brown. Blood—sweat—and tears. It was Martin Beck's blood that built the Palace, E. F. Albee's sweat that kept it going as the world's greatest vaudeville theater—and Hiram Brown's tears (when the stock market stopped laughing at vaude) that washed it all away. Beck was the artist, Albee the showman, and Brown the businessman. It was Big Business that helped ruin vaudeville and the Palace!

For the first few months of its existence the Palace didn't do very well. It was when Beck booked the immortal Sarah Bernhardt that the Palace really got on its feet. They even raised the prices, which didn't come down for a long time. Some years later the Divine Sarah played the Palace again, when she only had one leg to stand on. Her other one had been amputated, but her ability as an artist and drawing card hadn't!

The Palace started out with a check on anything that was off color in song, dialogue, or pantomime, as was the rule over the whole Orpheum and Keith circuits. Frank Keenan, the noted dramatic actor (grandfather of Keenan Wynn), played a sketch, "Vindication"; it was about an old Southern soldier who came to see the governor (who had fought on the Union Side). "It's about my boy, Governor; you are going to hang him next week. He never did anything wrong in his whole life. I don't think you know how it happened. You see, this man spit on the picture of Robert E. Lee, and—*God damn him*—my boy shot him!" It was a shock to the audience, who had never heard such language on any vaudeville stage, but it was done so artistically and so dramatically by Mr. Keenan that Mr. Albee allowed him to keep it in and played him over the entire circuit. Mr. Keenan and "the line" received editorial comment, plenty of publicity, and did plenty of business. I believe that Albee was showman enough to realize it would. It was years later, in 1929, that another great artist, Beatrice Lillie, sang a song at the Palace in which her finishing line was, "I see the same *goddam* faces." It was not censored.

The blue and the double entendre were starting to eat away at the bowels of vaude. The worst offenders were at the Palace, where the acts felt they were playing to a very "wise" audience who wanted that type material. They didn't, which was proven by the many acts that didn't use it and were hits. It got worse and worse—dirty jokes, dirtier pieces of business, and very dirty lines for black-outs, all of which was topped by the "goose with the cane"! There were no more signs backstage at the Palace reading, "Remember this theater caters to ladies and gentlemen and children. Vulgarity will not be tolerated. Check with manager before using any material you have any doubt about. Don't use words, hell, damn, devil, cockroach, spit, etc." The signs now were covered with dollar marks!

The Palace was the first and only theater that I know of in which a funeral service was held. It was on the occasion of the passing of a fine gentleman and great showman, Sam K. Hodgdon, who was an executive with the Keith Circuit from the days when Keith started in his tiny museum in Boston to the time of his death. His funeral service at the Palace was jammed with saddened children of vaude who honestly mourned the loss of a good friend. Sam Hodgdon was practically a poor man in the days when the boys on the booking floor were "on the take."

It was at the Palace that Weber & Fields walked off the bill, pleading illness, but the real cause was that they were billed second to Marie Dressler (who used to work for them). It was the first time in their entire noble careers in the theater that they failed to appear in a performance which they were billed for.

It was the Palace that played some of the top single-woman acts on one bill: Marie Dressler, Cissie Loftus, Marie Cahill, May Irwin, and Yvette Rugel, and for good measure Cissie Loftus and Marie Cahill did a "sister act," and they too sneaked in a "bluey," when Marie Cahill asked Cissie Loftus about a mutual girl friend, "She never married, did she?" And Cissie replied, "No, her children wouldn't let her." In 1925 the Palace ran an all-English bill with Bransby Williams, Ada Reeve, Albert Whelan, and Nervo & Knox as the features. A year later they repeated with Daphne Pollard, Arthur Prince, Marie Cahill, Ella Shields, and the Du For Boys. (Cahill and Shields were not English, but had played over there for many years.)

In 1922 someone got a bright idea of running a show at the Palace without headliners. Nobody was featured in the billing. It didn't pay off. (It would have saved a lot of billing headaches for the bookers, if it had worked.) There were no names in lights at at Palace until 1928. The only lighted sign up to then was Keith Vaudeville. Some headliners would have a banner with their names in big letters stretched across the entrance. In 1928 the Keith electric sign was removed and replaced by a new one which read Radio-Keith-Orpheum Vaudeville and made room for the actors' names in lights too. The first ones to be put up were Fanny Brice, Al Trahan, and Fowler & Tamara.

The Palace had many billing and dressing-room troubles, because they booked so many great stars who figured they should get top billing and the best dressing room. Elsie Janis, Fritzi Scheff, and Nora Bayes all walked out at different times because of billing. Eddie Darling, the great booker of the Palace, hit on a cute trick to cut down his dressing-room headaches. When there was a chance of a dressing-room argument, he would instruct the stage manager to put ladders and paint buckets in the downstairs dressing rooms and tell the headliners that they were being painted and so couldn't be used. They would all take the upstairs rooms, which were much roomier and better ventilated, and never make a kick.

The downstairs dressing room for the star dates way back. Naturally one didn't want stars to tire themselves out by climbing stairs, so they got the first off-stage dressing room. But it became a phobia with stars to get the No. 1 dressing room or the one with the star on the door. Jordan in Philadelphia had all the rooms named after states: there were no star rooms. But now, when most theaters have elevators backstage, it doesn't matter much, that is, as long as *one* room has a star on it!

During World War I, there was a mass meeting held at the Palace by all the great names in show biz, with George M. Cohan presiding. It was called to organize volunteer entertainment units to be sent to the front, hospitals, and camps (like our present USO Units), under the auspices of the Over There Theatre League. It was the first meeting of its kind in the history of the theater. When Cohan asked who would volunteer to go overseas and entertain our troops, the whole audience stood up. It was originally E. H. Southern and Winthrop Ames's idea. The Y.M.C.A. would send them over and maintain the actors while there.

At one time Mr. Albee turned the Palace over to religious services on Sunday mornings.

There has been much written about the Palace, and most of it was as wrong as a dame in a Bikini bathing suit in Alaska. So just for the record, let me jot down a few facts. Carlton Hoagland was its first booker, followed by many others. Martin Beck, Marcus Heiman, George Godfrey, Max Gordon, Arthur Willie, Harry Mundorf, Bill McCaffery, Bill Howard, Charlie Freeman, Sam Tishman, and of course Eddie V. Darling (V. stood for Valentine, his birthday), who booked the Palace in its most glorious days. He was a great booker and took charge of most of the big-time houses on the circuit. A good booker could make a fair bill play well by the proper placing of the acts. Of course, in booking the Palace the budget was much larger than for other theaters and so it was easier to lay out a show, but still there were plenty of headaches, as the booker had three and sometimes four headliners to satisfy as to billing and position on the bill. Eddie Darling had a sense of humor and especially loved to "rib" single women. He would drop in to visit them backstage and repeat some piece of gossip he heard about them, etc., and in no time he'd have created an upheaval. The actors liked him, as he was a fair man in his dealings with them.

Frank Thompson was the first manager at the Palace, followed by Doc Breed, William Wood, and Elmer Rogers. The latter came up from the Union Square Theater where he first worked for Keith; he stayed at the Palace throughout its palmy days and resigned when it stopped playing two-a-day (he received a pension). He was tops—a very fine gentleman who knew his business, and his business at the Palace was being not so much a manager as a diplomat with the temperamental actors backstage and the Big Brass who would always be dropping in to see part of the show. He was the reserved-seat vaude manager and dean of 'em all.

Paul Schindler was the first musical director, followed by many real greats of the vaude leaders, like Jules Lensberg, Charlie Dabb, Benny Roberts, Lou Foreman, Milton Schwartzwald, and the "guest conductors" who came later.

The boys backstage, Bill Clark and Bob Altman, were the stage managers for years with a number of deck hands that stuck it through until the finish. The elevator boys, two weird characters, Doc Cook and Morris, knew more about vaude people than anyone in town. They would run errands for 'em, wake 'em up at the hotel, see that they made the shows, etc. They were a lot of fun. Murray Roesdies was chief usher and Mamie McBride was matron from 1920 to the finish.

The great press agents for the Palace were Will Page (he was the first), William Raymond Sill, Walter Kingsley, Mark Leucher, John Pollock, Bob Sylvester, Carrol Pierce, Don Prince, and Dick Maney. They did a nice dignified job. They didn't have the field days that Hammerstein gave to his press agents; that place was a P.A.'s Paradise!

The opening bill, March 25, 1913, matinee:

Eight Palace Girls	Dancers
McIntyre & Hardy	(They left the bill because of conflict with another act and were replaced by Hy Mayer, famous cartoonist of *Judge*.)
Ed Wynn	(Assisted by two men)

The Eternal Waltz	Thirty-person "flash act." Music by Leo Fahl, book by August Hurgon, produced by Joe Hart, with Cyril Chadwick and Mabel Bera among the principals.
Taylor Holmes	Monologue. (He was added to the bill after the matinee.)
Milton Pollock & Co.	In George Ade's comedy, "Speaking to Father."
Four Vannis	Wire act with four people. One of them was dressed like a woman.
Otto Gygi	Violinist. (Was hit of the bill.)
La Napierkowska	Pantomimist and dancer (cooch variety). She was supposed to be stung by a bee, which makes her go into her squirms.

The house was an 1,800-seater, the prices were 25 to 50 cents in the gallery and $1.50 downstairs. The show cost about $7,000, the receipts were $4,000, showing a loss of about $8,500 on the first week of the Palace!

The last bill of two-a-day before it turned to grind policy was on May 7, 1932:

Bill Demarest	M.C. (of Demarest & Colette)
Allan Mann & Dorothy Dell assisted by Helen O'Shea	In song and dance
Ada Brown	Sepia warbler
Henry Santry & Band	(Had performing parrot in act.)
Rosetta "Topsy" Duncan	Of the famous Duncan Sisters
William Demarest & Estelle Colette	Comedy
Floyd Gibbons	Famous war correspondent and fast gabber talked about Sino-Japanese War
Frank Mitchell & Jack Durant	Knockabout comedy
Charlie Jordan & Johnny Woods	Burlesquing radio features

Dave Apollon with his Filipino Orchestra	(Third week)
Albertina Rasch Girls	With four adagio dancers and Goodell & Nora Williams, a warbling dancer

The last bill at the Palace, then doing four-a-day, was November 16, 1932:

Nick Lucas, Hal LeRoy, Sid Marion, Giovanni, Ross & Edwards, Ola Lelith, and the Honey Family.

When vaudeville was real honest-to-goodness two-a-day straight vaude without gimmicks, James J. Morton, "The Boy Comic," was used for a novelty as the M.C. of the show and he maybe came around once a season to a house that enjoyed the idea. But later on, when there was a shortage of top-notch acts and the Palace was using many acts for two- to four-week runs and repeating headliners, they put in a Master of Ceremonies regularly. The picture presentation houses used M.C.s to bolster up a small fair show. It was up to the M.C. to get the audience to applaud acts they would never have applauded; the M.C. would "talk it up," tell how great the act was, how wonderful the girl was, that they were good to their mothers, etc., and so out of many a mediocre show he would make what seemed by the applause he got for it like a hit show. It got so that the Big Time and especially the Palace copied this idea.

The M.C.s would do bits and impromptu gags with the other acts and would do their own act, besides an afterpiece with most of the acts on the bill in it. Broadway seemed to like this. The Palace even tried to revive the famous old Winter Garden Sunday nights. The M.C. would call on prominent actors seated in the audience, some for a bow, and some to get up on the stage and "do their stuff" (for free). Al Jolson had never played the Palace, but was called on one Sunday night by Dave Apollon, the M.C., and he sang a song from the aisle. They even had a blackboard in the lobby and wrote the names of the prominent people on it as they arrived. This was in 1930, when the Palace was trying anything to keep going. An M.C. at the Palace had to be important to be able to get celebs up to take bows or do a number without offending them. Of course, many of the "guests" you didn't even have to ask; they'd jump up ready to do their act even if you looked at them.

James J. Morton was of course the first of the professional
M.C.s. He never worked like the M.C.s that followed him; he
would go through the show without working with anyone. Frank
Fay was undoubtedly the first M.C. at the Palace, and enjoyed a
run of eight weeks there to tremendous returns. (He had George
Haggerty, Patsy Kelly, and Lew Mann as his stooges.) It was his
great success that decided the management on bringing in an
M.C. every week and make it a part of the show. The first Mistress
of Ceremonies at the Palace was Florence Moore. Allen (Fred)
& York with their "joke cemetery" drop (funny epitaphs on the
headstones), would introduce the acts, addressing themselves as
Mr. Fink and Mr. Smith. Jack Benny M.C.'d in 1927; others
who acted as M.C.s were Benny Rubin, Jack Donahue, Bert Hanlon, Taylor Holmes, Julius Tannen, Ken Murray (when he was
with the Harry Carroll act), Lou Holtz (an eight-week run), Ted
Healey, Joe Frisco, Georgie Price, Harry Richman, Lester Allen,
Emil Boreo, Eddie Dowling, and Dave Apollon. Some of these
were after the Palace had already changed its policy to pics and
vaude.

There was always something doing at the Palace. It was here
that a young comic by the name of Bob Hope became discouraged
and wanted to leave the bill and got a pep talk by Harry Hershfield and decided to stay. (I dread to think of Bob having left the
show biz then; we wouldn't be having so many laughs now.)
Wilkie Bard, the great English artist, played Hammerstein's years
before and was a great hit, but when he came to the Palace he
flopped. After rearranging his routine he became a big hit again.

The only agent ever to book a complete show of his own acts
in the Palace was Charlie Morrison, in 1928, the first and only
time it happened not only at the Palace but in all big-time vaude.

The house played very few freak acts, although in 1916 they did
play an act called "The Twelve Speed Maniacs," who assembled
a Ford in two minutes! The Palace also had "Country Store Night"
the same as the smaller-Palaces in Kokomo, Kankakee, and
Keokuk. And in 1928 it also placed an electric piano in the lobby,
just like any honky-tonk, but that didn't help get the customers in.

At one time they had Wednesday morning try-outs at the
Palace, with all the managers, agents, and bookers watching for
future greats, as the talent barrel was running low. There were
about fifteen acts a week at these try-outs; they picked about one

out of seventeen acts that was good enough to play the circuit.

In 1926 there was an acrobatic tumbler by the name of Sie Tahar who opened the show. As he was about to go on, he turned to Bill Clark, the stage manager, and said, "They say opening acts always die at the Palace. Me no die." After his act he went to his dressing room and dropped dead!

It was not until 1928 that Clayton, Jackson & Durante first played there, and they "rocked the joint." Sally Rand, in an act with eight girls, did a toe dance and *Variety* said, "Too much on the gal." (She was a bit plump.) In 1930 the Gaudschmidts (a very funny act), who were at the Palace with their acrobatic French poodles, were reviewed by *Variety*. Sime said, "The Gaudschmidts, lately returned from Paris with their French Poodles; the dogs wanted to behave as though still in Paris—one of those things that couldn't happen again in 100 years on the stage."

When Grock, the famous European clown, played the house in 1920 there was a large printed sign in the lobby reading, "We guarantee him because we set his salary after seeing him." (Grock went on at the Riverside without billing for a few shows to kinda try out his act for America and was a riot, taking over a dozen bows.)

In 1924 they barred bare legs. They also had signs backstage, "You must only take *two bows*." This was because acts at the Palace were getting into a bad habit of jockeying for applause and using all kinds of tricks to get it. Some would take out an instrument for bows, practically asking the audience to "ask me to play it." Jack Kenny (Kenny & Hollis) had a funny one; when bowing he would yell to the audience, "Make me dance," and his partner would drag him off. Some acts would tell the stage electrician to put out the lights as soon as they finished. They would go out on stage for a bow in the dark, then walk off apparently in disgust. The audience, figuring they weren't getting a good break, would applaud, and just as they came on again the lights would go out again; the audience never figured they were being tricked. In this way an act that would ordinarily get two bows "stole" a half a dozen. Many of the acts saved the best of their act for an encore, so that is why the "Two bow" sign, but it did no good, because when a good act only took two bows, the audience kept applauding and the next act couldn't go on. And of course the headliners wouldn't think of taking less than a half a dozen bends, whether they earned them or not, so the two-bow rule in a few weeks just remained a sign. Another good idea of Albee's gone wrong.

Albee issued an order not to play any radio acts, because he felt that radio was terrific opposition to vaudeville. ("Why pay $2.00 for an act you can hear on the radio for free?") Anyway, when Mr. Albee needed a box-office attraction, he would break his own rules. Harry Richman was a big hit on radio and was receiving great publicity, so they booked him with his Harry Richman Night Club floor show, "A Night at the Club Richman." He proved a big hit and a big B.O. draw.

Funny, when the Palace opened in 1913 you saw hardly any actors hanging around outside; they were all around Hammerstein's in those days, figuring Forty-seventh Street was too far uptown. But in 1916 the police handed out summonses to actors for loitering outside the Palace and obstructing traffic, and they were fined $2.00 to $3.00! When Bernhardt opened at the Palace, prices were raised to $1.50, $2.00, and $2.50 (specs moved in later and on Saturday and Sunday nights they would get as high as $10 a pair).

In 1914 the Castles played two houses at one time, Hammerstein's (which was only five blocks away) and the Palace. They had a twelve-piece Negro orchestra and at Hammerstein's the musicians wouldn't let them play in the pit, so Vernon Castle put them on the stage (the first time a Negro orchestra played on the stage for any other kind of an act). It became a craze and many dancing acts used Negro musicians.

That same year the Palace ran the Harry Lauder picture and billed the name Lauder very big and the word picture very small. This is the same Lauder to whom the Keith Circuit had refused to pay $500 a week before he came over when he was booked by K. & E. for their Advanced Vaude for $2,500; he later received four and five thousand a week for William Morris.

Hammerstein's was feeling the Palace opposition. They ran twenty-two-act bills and gave out mint gum which the manufacturer gave to Hammerstein (2,000 packages) at each performance in return for a mention of the product on the picture sheet at the finish of the show. The Palace served free lemonade at the matinees.

The Palace decided that during the warm weather, when theatergoers are mostly transients, holdover acts would be O.K. An act would be signed for a four- to six-week run, but was announced from week to week as having been such a hit that it was being held over for another week. The acts would take these contracts because they figured a run at the Palace would give them prestige in the other houses and with the other circuits. They would naturally accept a low summer salary. Adelaide & Hughes had the longest run at the Palace, twelve weeks. Frank Fay stayed for eight weeks, Kate Smith for eleven, Eddie Cantor and George Jessel for nine, Lou Holtz and William Gaxton for eight. Ruth Roye was held for six weeks; so was Sylvester Schaffer; Nora Bayes stayed four; Molly Picon, three.

Belle Baker was the first single woman to close the show at the Palace, and Bert Fitzgibbons the first male single to do it. Savoy & Brennan were the first male team to be held over (1917). In 1915 the Palace ran a style show of women's fashions from leading dressmakers. It made quite a hit and was held over. This show later was copied by other metropolitan theaters and even by the small time.

In 1918 the Palace was tops for big shows; nothing even approached it in the other houses. They paid top prices for talent, but that doesn't always make for a good show. There were other large theaters that also called for big high-priced programs, like the Riverside, the Brooklyn Orpheum, the Majestic and Palace in Chicago, the Keith houses in Philly, Boston, Washington, Detroit, etc. The Palace played to capacity, and the few weeks it didn't were due to the weakness of the featured turns, often the headliner, but that didn't often happen at the Palace!

In 1920 the Palace was still the kingpin vaude house moneymaker, with a $2.00 top scale on week days. It was the Palace that overclassed vaude. It had been predicted long before that it would set styles, and it did. Acts began to build for the Palace; but then they had to take the same act over the circuit, and out of New York the audiences didn't go very much for the "class" acts or the ones that pulled "nifties" that the "smarties" at the Palace would howl at. Even there, the gang out front was getting a bit tired of too much "class"; they would have hugged an old-time tramp comedian.

There have been many acts that claimed to have played the Ace House more times than anyone else. A good standard act would play it sometimes three and four times a year. York & King claim the championship, as do the Mosconi Bros.; the latter played it with many acts—their own double act, the Bessie Clayton act, their family act, etc. Belle Baker, Sophie Tucker, Van & Schenck, Nora Bayes, and Jack Wilson are certainly way up there on the "most times" list. It is very hard to check.

By 1925 there were claques working on Monday matinees (opening show) at the Palace. Acts were getting receptions on their entrance and applause at the finish beyond their due. This was accomplished through agents distributing tickets to friends with instructions to applaud for their act (maybe their first appearance at the Palace; if they made good they would naturally get more bookings, etc.). Music publishers also gave out tickets for someone who was using their songs on the show, and the acts would give out tickets to their friends and relatives. It didn't fool the smart bookers, critics, or actors, but the audience thought the act was a hit. Claques are not good for any part of show biz (they have been using them at the opera for years). It tends to slow up a show. It certainly wasn't good for the Palace.

You would never believe that an egg was thrown at a performer in the classiest house in the world. The actor was one of the nicest guys in the sports world, Benny Leonard, the champion. Benny did a great act, and it was said the egg was thrown by an enemy of his. I never knew he had one.

It was 1925 when they tried "timetable billing"; the acts were listed according to the time they went on, but of course even in this billing some acts were in larger letters than others. Georgie Price got double billing (the first time that ever happened) because he was doing two acts, his own single and an afterpiece, "Joe's Blue Front."

For years the Palace had a sidewalk patrol whose business it was to watch the specs and stop the people at the door who bought from them. In 1926 things got a bit tough for the Palace, so they laid off the patrol, as there weren't many specs around anymore, and they started to bolster business by selling large blocks of tickets at reduced prices to lodges, societies, clubs, etc.

It must have been tough getting headliners for the Palace in 1926, because they booked Eva Tanguay, who earlier in the season had played Loew's State (just a few blocks down the street). Loew's top was fifty cents while the Palace was getting $3.00. Eva broke all records at the State and did very well at the Palace. I guess Mr. Albee had a bit of the jitters that year too, because he again issued an order not to take more than two bows (which again was soon broken), and he also gave orders to cut out the spotlight and the drum crashes, claiming, "There's too much noise in vaudeville theaters." The spotlight had become a part of practically every act. Where years ago an act would use a spotlight only to call attention to a certain number, the acts later began using a spot even with full lights up; they certainly did abuse it, but that rule too was broken as soon as Albee got back to his office. Toward the end of the year Albee really did get nervous because the opposition of the films was definitely being felt, so the Palace cut salaries of all employees and dismissed porters and cut everything down. Nobody gets panicky quicker than show people.

The handwriting on the wall for the Palace showed up in 1929 when on March 10 it started three shows a day on Sundays, and upped the budget to $12,000-a-week bills. They even published a small magazine, *Magazine of Vaudeville*, which was a giveaway (no charge), but that didn't help either. (They didn't know that a panic was in the making for everybody in and out of show biz.)

Some sort of a first was established by the Four Small Bros. (white boys) when they doubled at the Palace and Loew's State on the same day, opening the show at the Palace and closing the show at the State, where they complained to the management for putting them in the Louis Armstrong act. (The Small brothers were Southerners, but there were very few incidents of this kind in all of vaudeville.) They were trying everything at the Palace to get biz; they played the Roxy Ballet with Patricia Bowman and Leonide Massine. They also played Heywood Broun, who in my opinion was a fine monologist.

Everybody was going in each other's acts. (This originally started years ago as a "gag.") On closing nights, when we all had to make trains and were all going in different directions, we had no time to wait around to say good-by to each other, and so for a laugh we would walk out in the middle of some guy's act, dressed in street clothes and carrying our grips, and say good-by. Some of these things turned out to be very funny with ad-lib kidding. This was nothing like the afterpieces, which were rehearsed.

It was funny to see the Palace now playing acts direct from opposition houses. They were also playing acts from radio, which they had barred for a long time, and found that they were their best drawing cards, and they were also playing picture actors.

Talking pics were beginning to cancerize vaude; the doctors ordered the Palace to be wired for sound. It was the beginning of the end. Talking pictures were the noise that chased vaudeville.

The Palace was beginning to drip red ink, with losses of $4,000 a week. The house was being used as a "flash" for stockholders and bankers, because by now it was big business—not in the theater, but on the stock market, making $150,000 to $200,000 a year profit, with weekly grosses about $20,000 to $25,000, and bills costing $10,000 to $13,000 a week. In the old days bills cost $8,000 a week and showed $800,000 a year profit. Now they had to pay big salaries to acts because of the big pic-house opposition, but even the Palace could offer them only three or four weeks, and the other houses on the circuit couldn't pay those salaries at all. The Palace found that to play and pay them was just a whim and a very expensive flash! In 1930 Eddie Cantor was booked at the Palace for $7,700 a week (alone). The next year Cantor and George Jessel were the first in Palace history to be booked for an eight-week run, that is, to get an eight-week contract in advance. The show cost $16,000, Cantor getting $8,000, which was the tops for anyone in vaude up to that time. They broke all Palace records, but even the great Eddie Cantor and Georgie Jessel on their eighth week lost $3,000, doing $25,000 on the week. On their seventh week they did $28,000, which missed by $100 being an even break. They had a nine-week run. After the Cantor-Jessel show, the house went to straight pics with Cantor's picture, *Kid from Spain*.

They tried everything that year at the Palace. To keep people in the house, the headliners were closing the shows. There was a big eight-week run with Lou Holtz, William Gaxton, and Kate Smith. Ethel Merman was in for the first week and was replaced with Kate Smith, who stayed eleven weeks. They did $30,000 grosses and were a big hit (the first entire show to be held over at the Palace). Walter Winchell got $3,500 for his week there, his first pro booking on a stage in ten years. He was a big draw and really did a good act, working with everybody on the show.

In 1932 they used plenty of microphones for the radio acts, and had a Radio Week. They tried a stage-band-presentation style for the first time in September, with a four-act show and pic. Acts stretched out to eight, counting specialties of the Waring Band. Fred did M.C. In November they tried a Film Name Week for the last full week of vaude-film policy, with Arthur and Florence

Lake, Lina Basquette, Nick Stuart, Sue Carol, Stuart & Lash, M. C. Dolinoff, and the Raya Sisters (dancers), all silent-pic people.

Dennis King headlined during a hot July week and did $8,000, which was $1,000 under the Palace low for eighteen years.

January 19 saw Milton Berle for his first time at the Palace. He did his act and also M.C. He was a terrific hit and the talk of the town for months, creating a lot of resentment among actors because he was saying on the stage that he took for material everything he remembered. But the guy certainly wowed 'em! It was his springboard to fame and fortune.

The Palace was not then Big Time but continuous performances. Martin Beck came back to his office with no title or salary but just to be there in an advisory capacity (no advice could help the Palace now). York & King announced that they were playing their fiftieth engagement at the Palace.

Frank Fay, with Barbara Stanwyck, came back to the house of his early triumphs and had a struggle as M.C. Fay dropped out and Barbara Stanwyck finished the third week alone. Gus Van replaced Fay.

On July 12 Louis Sobol, the noted columnist, was the headliner, doing his first stage appearance, and did a $8,000 gross. May saw the last two-a-day at the Palace, with a loss of $14,000. On May 17 a new grind policy was introduced, with ten acts doing four and five shows a day. They put a new box office in the street (à la pic house). The show was Phil Baker, June and Cherry Preisser, the Gus Edwards Act (with Gloria Gilbert, the Human Top, and Hildegarde), Von Grona's dancers, King Bros. & Cully, Will Oakland, Joe Laurie, Jr., & Nephews, Eddie Garr (also doubled in Edwards' act), Ethelind Terry, and the Jack Denny Orchestra. Show went into the red for $11,000. Martin Beck issued an order: no speeches! Four acts made them. The loss at the Palace since January was now $100,000.

That year there was a new all-time low in salary at the Palace. "Glad Rags," a nine-person hoofing act with John Convey and eight gals, received $100, which made it 45 cents a show! (The great wondrous Palace!)

It got so bad that on January 17, 1933, the Palace played "freak acts" (anything to make a buck and satisfy the stockholders). They booked Prince Mike Romanoff, who was enjoying much publicity (and who now in his swank Hollywood Restaurant makes more dough in a night than they took in the week he played at the Palace), Mrs. Freddie Rich (wife of the band leader), and Jack De Ruyrer with a twelve-piece band; just imagine the beautiful divorcee and her Park Avenue playboy playing the Palace! The only noise they heard was Willie Hammerstein's laugh from Heaven. He wasn't laughing at them, but at the Palace, which had put him out of business. On February 7 the bill was Felovis, the Arnaut Bros., Benny Leonard with Eddie Moran, Bob Murphy, and the Walter Powell Orchestra. The picture was *The Bitter Tea of General Yen*. It was bitter tea for the Palace too, because they went into straight pics again.

It was the eighth policy change since straight vaude was dropped in 1932. The Palace reversal of vaude-film to film was a flop (couldn't get good pics). Sydney S. Cohen, a well-known picture operator, took over the Palace for three weeks, showed a profit of $7,500, of which he got a third, but RKO asked for the house back. I guess they figured anybody that could make dough with the Palace at that time was too smart, so they wanted the house back before he took that too!

In 1934 the Palace hit a new low. Timmy & Freddy Sepia (hoofers) set a precedent for the theater by using it as a break-in; they lasted two shows. By now the Palace was playing at 40 cents to 65 cents top. Ray Conners, the manager, a good showman, had buses stop there and the guide say, "And now, ladies and gentlemen, on your right is the famous Palace. This is the theater every vaudeville actor aspires to play." And many of the "pop-eyes" (sightseers to you) believed him! Because they had read so much about this Magic Palace.

In 1935 it really got worse. The Palace played straight pictures, with double features (no vaude), plus a preview of coming pics on Thursday nights. Again a change of policy to vaude and pics, and the last show of that was September 25, 1935, with Clara Barry and Orville Whitledge, Carl Freed and His Harlequin Harmonicans, Helene Reynolds and Her Skating Sweethearts, Clyde Hager, and Dick and Edith Barstow. *Page Miss Glory* and *Top Hat* started the final pic policy.

And just for the record, in 1950 there was a revival of vaudeville at the Palace, which showed that vaude pays off on Broadway, but not generally.

As you see, there were many changes at the Palace after 1913, when it opened with top-notch two-a-day. The real two-a-day went out when the Lou Holtz-Billy Gaxton and the Cantor-Jessel type show came in, and when Frank Fay did bits with acts—that wasn't what I would call the real pure vaudeville show that the Palace started with. It was great entertainment, but it wasn't vaudeville.

But when the two-a-day died, then the Palace on Broadway and Forty-seventh Street, New York City, was just the same as a pic house named the Palace in Broadlooms, North Dakota. It was like a dame in the *Follies* who lost her shape, like a fine Shakespearean actor who just mumbles his lines, and like a dancer who couldn't find the rosin box!

Yop—you can write a book just about the Palace, because it was a theater with a personality. It made millionaires and bums! It was the "hope chest" of many vaudevillians. It paid off many an act for struggling years through the tank towns, and it shattered the hopes of many more that just couldn't "make it."

And yet, did you know there were a number of acts that were offered dates at the Palace and wouldn't take them. Because they would get nervous about it. It meant new wardrobe, touches from old friends who figured when you played the Palace you were loaded, the missus had to have her hair done and would get into a nervous breakdown worrying about her wardrobe.

Amos 'n' Andy feared playing the Palace, claiming that actors didn't like their stuff and the Palace catered to actors. They appeared in all the other theaters. (I knew more actors that listened to Amos 'n' Andy than to anyone else—but as I told you some performers had a phobia about playing the Palace.)

The youngsters took a chance with a heartful of hope. Playing the Palace helped fill up your scrapbook and your ego. Sometimes it boosted the salary and, again, sometimes it knocked you out of a route if you flopped. Anyway, it was a great Fairyland for many of us. Even if it turns into a garage, it will still be the Palace of great memories to many of the boys and girls who went through that stage door twice a day.

The State Theatre

"He shall return no more to his house, neither shall
his place know him any more."—Job 7:10

On Tuesday, December 23, 1947, I saw Vaudeville laid out in
state, or maybe I should say, laid out at the State! It was the last
vaudeville show for the State Theatre after a continuous run of
twenty-six years. They hung the closing notice on the Christmas
Tree!

These wakes were nothing new to me. I was at the closing of
Hammerstein's, the New York Theatre, and the Palace (as M.C.,
if you can picture a wake having an M.C.). It wasn't a surprise
when they went; we knew they were ailing for years before the
finish came. But with the State it was different, it all came so
suddenly. The doctors in the main office (who count the heart-
beats of the box-office till, claimed that death was caused by high
blood pressure (too much red ink).

In memory, twenty-six years is just a short step. To me it seems
like only yesterday that the State Theatre opened with great fanfare. What a day that was for show biz in general and for Marcus
Loew in particular. Loew had watched this dream child of his grow
from his office window in the Putnam Building until the day of
August 29, 1921, when the doors were opened. All of show biz
came to pay tribute to this fine man, Marcus Loew. It was not a
phony Hollywood opening, even if E. F. Albee, whose Palace was
just up the street, did send his Keith Boys' Band to serenade the
opposition. They played in front of the State, and what's more,
they played good!

Inside the theater, Will Morrisey, one of Broadway's wittiest
children, acted as M.C., introducing great stars of vaude, musical
comedy, and pics. There was also a great finale with all the
Ziegfeld Follies girls led by David Warfield and Marcus Loew!
How proud Nils T. Granlund (N.T.G.) was, for it was he who
masterminded all the publicity and arrangements. Joe Vogel, now
one of the top execs (V.P.) of the Loew organization, was the first

manager of the house, then came Joe Emmett (ex-yodeler), following him was Ken Behr (ex-war aviator), then George Miner (one of the famous Miner theatrical family), and then Al Rosen, who stayed for over fifteen years and left to become an independent producer. (He brought Mae West back to the stage.) He was one of the best-liked managers in the business. Joe Jordan was the first leader and was followed by Ruby Swerling, who shook his baton at actors and musicians for nearly twenty years at the State, and at the closing there were many men in the pit who had started with him. Nick Massa took over the stage management even before the house was finished and retired when the house went into straight pictures. Richard Block was the first doorman (after working at the American for eighteen years), and the stage doorman was Louis Samelson, a grand guy who is still at the State. The booker, of course, was lovable Jake Lubin.

They ran four shows a day with the acts doing three, using five acts each show. Loew put long pants on small-time vaude. Vaudeville actors smiled; it was another week added to the fast-growing small time!

A funny thing about the State, on opening day they found that they had forgotten to build dressing rooms! (This has happened a number of times in show biz. The Savoy on Thirty-fourth Street and Madison Square Garden both had no dressing rooms when they opened.) The actors would go across the street to the New York Theatre, get dressed and made up, and come back to do their acts at the State. Loew bought the building on 160 West Forty-sixth Street, built dressing rooms, and had a bridge inside connecting the building with the back stage; the building also had offices for the franchised agents of the Loew Circuit.

I was sitting that Tuesday night of the last show wondering what Marcus Loew was saying to his cronies "upstairs." I imagined they were all kinda sad up there, where now there were no jealousies, opposition, or blacklists. I am sure they all felt badly to see vaudeville on Broadway become only a memory. B. F. Keith, E. F. Albee, Tony Pastor, Percy Williams, F. F. Proctor, Oscar and Willie Hammerstein, Martin Beck, William Morris, Mike Shea, Pantages, Poli, Sullivan & Considine, the great giants and pioneers of vaudeville, must have shed a tear when they saw the passing of vaudeville from the State Theatre—the poor man's Palace!

In past days when an actor stopped filling his scrapbooks with

glowing notices from the two-a-day and decided to fill his bankbooks with memorabilia for a future day, he began to play the
State. The topnotchers of the two-a-day slowly yielded to the
smaller money but steadier routes of the Loew Circuit, of which
the State was the show window. Van & Schenck, Eva Tanguay,
Amelia Bingham, Jim Barton, Jack Norworth, Imhof, Conn &
Corinne, Clark & Verdi, Lillian Shaw, Sophie Tucker, and so many
more vaudeville greats would shuttle back and forth between the
Palace and the State when the barriers were broken down by the
shortage of talent. The actors saved their small-time dough; they
were tired of being stalled, kicked around, blacklisted, and salary-
sliced. So they played for Loew, and Loew was happy; he was
building a great circuit.

From my seat on the mourner's bench that Tuesday night, I
watched the last rites given to my favorite love, Vaudeville. They
were administered by the children of Vaudeville. Jack & Charlie
Brick said a few words in the only way they knew how, with a
fine routine on the trampoline. They were followed by George
Andre Martin, who spoke for Vaudeville with his dancing fingers
and tapped out a eulogy. Then out came a little gal who has
been a great part of vaudeville all over the world, Molly Picon,
who on this last show sang with an honest catch in her throat; as
one of Vaudeville's favorite children she was a true mourner. She
was followed by Dave Apollon, another favorite of the Vaudeville
family; he played "The Requiem" on his magic mandolin. Then
came one of Vaudeville's younger children, Jack Carter, who paid
his tribute as a youngster should, with laughs! Laughs, the foundation of vaudeville! He didn't feel the closing of the State to
vaudeville as a great loss. He is young and talented and has many
places to go. He was followed by Harold & Lola in their novelty
snake dance. Lola represents a snake while Harold is a snake
charmer, and finally the snake bites the charmer and he dies. That
was a very fitting closing act for the occasion.

Then out on the stage stepped the one and only George Jessel,
dressed in black tails and white tie, matched with a black toupee
with white sides. He sort of gave the funeral a touch of "class."
He got a big reception. I thought, well, here is where George will
tell them in his own inimitable way about the heart of vaudeville
and what these closings mean to the old-timers who still carry a
song and dance in their hearts. What a great job of reminiscence

he could have done. But he just said, "I wasn't invited here. I heard vaudeville is finished here tonight. So I thought I'd drop in and tell you folks that talent never can die." With that George bowed and walked off. Maybe George was right, why talk about something which very few seemed to care about? The only one interested was our own little Vaudeville family circle.

But while George was talking I was thinking of the Broadway I knew when the State opened. Memories of 1921 rose like partridges. On the site of the present State Theatre was the old Bartholdi Inn, also the *Variety* office, and Mack, the tailor, who designed those large elk lapels for his actor clientele. O'Hearn, the cleaner, was also a tenant in the building. He was an ex-Irish tenor of vaudeville and maybe didn't like his spot on the bills, because the catch line in his ads read, "We remove that spot!" And there were many gravy spots on actors' clothes in those eating days of vaudeville. O'Hearn always wore a white carnation in his buttonhole. There were a number of carnation wearers in those days; Ted Marks, Jules Delmar, James K. Hackett, Arthur Levy, Jackie Osterman, and Arthur Caesar never missed the lapel decoration.

I remembered the Loew Booking Office in the American Theatre Building, where Joe Schenck was the head booker and Jack Goldberg his office boy. In a short time, Jack became the head booker and Joe Schenck became the big man in pics. It was Jack Goldberg's good judgment and knowledge of acts that helped Loew give such good shows. There was N.T.G. (Nils T. Granlund) as a press agent who revolutionized vaude and picture exploitation. He was followed by Terry Turner, Arthur Schmidt, Oscar Doob, and Ernst Emerlin—all great. There was Charlie Moscowitz, a young bookkeeper, who now is V.P., and Marvin Schenck, an office boy, now producer at M-G-M.

I recall the tops of the old-time Loew managers, Gene Meyers, Vic Morris, Larry Beatus, and Charlie Potsdam. There were kids in the office like Leo Cohn and Jesse Kay who became assistant bookers; Sydney Piermont, another kid raised by the organization, was the last booker the circuit had, a very competent one. A great bunch of guys who reflected the head of the organization—Marcus Loew!

Thirty-two years ago, when the State had its housewarming, Broadway was much different than it is today. Prohibition had most of the night spots closed, but there still remained some of the old places for the gang that weren't going to speak-easies. Joel's, Anselmo's, Blue Hour, Maxim's on Thirty-eighth Street, the Ted Lewis Club, Reisenweber's, where Sophie Tucker took over the top floor and was doubling in vaude dates with an act written for her by Jack Lait. Scotch was selling at $115 a case, rye for $100, and gin for $60—and all of it bad! There was Shanley's Café de Paris, the Little Club, Palais Royal, and Folies Bergere, all running without booze, and in a short time they too had to fold. People were complaining that one-step and waltzes were "morgue stuff"; fox trots were the rage. The most-played pop dance tunes were "Yoo-hoo," "Ka-Lua," "Blue Danube Blues," "When Buddha Smiles," "In Old Granada," "April Showers," and "Say It with Music."

"Zit" had the Casino in Central Park, Eva Tanguay advertised about her $5,000 job of face-lifting, Minsky was still at the National Wintergarden on Second Avenue, John Golden had seven hits including Frank Bacon in *Lightnin'*, Sam Harris had nine shows on the road and in New York and six theaters in Chicago. Billy Grady, now M-G-M casting director, was a vaude agent, Jack Benny was doing a single, Paul Ash was playing with his orchestra in Frisco and Al Lewis and Max Gordon were vaude agents and producers of sketches. Mae Murray did *Peacock Alley* for Metro, D. W. Griffith had *Orphans of the Storm*, Harry Lauder was making his farewell tours under management of William Morris, Joe LeBlang was selling cut-rate tickets, Mollie Williams was one of the stars of burly, Mitzi was in *Lady Billy*, *Irene* had three touring companies, and Al Jolson was breaking records in *Bombo*.

Broadway those days was hot summer and winter, and Loew's State was certainly part of it all. It kept a candle burning on the altar of Vaudeville long after the Palace blew theirs out!

The Big Parade

Dear Joe,

This is the last letter I'm going to write you for a while because me and Aggie are going for a little vacation to see our grandchildren, if you can call that a vacation. We are gonna check up on 'em, as they are now at the age where they are singing, dancing, and making faces like Jerry Lewis. So me and Aggie are gonna give them a sort of an audition, and if they show any talent, we'll "pencil 'em in" for 1965; we figure by then people will be tired of Cinerama, three-dimension pictures, radio, and TV and the "Vaudeville Cycle" will start again. We don't figure to be around then, but if you happen to pass a marble orchard and see the dirt moving, you will know it's the old vaude vets applauding the new kids!

The other afternoon I fixed me and Aggie a couple of highballs, and sitting at the window we saw one of the finest parades we ever saw.

The parade started way down on the Bowery from a honky-tonk, then it passed Tony Pastor's, Keith's Union Square, Proctor's Twenty-third Street, then Proctor's Fifth Avenue, the Greeley Square, then up to Eighth Avenue and Forty-second Street passing Loew's American, across to Broadway to Hammerstein's, then they passed the State and finished at the Palace!

The sidewalks were jammed with people from all over the country who saw many of these marchers in their home-town theaters when they were young, and there were a few real old people that saw the beginning of the parade and followed it up to the finishing line, at the Palace!

There was a special reviewing stand at Duffy Square (facing the Palace) which was filled with the owners, managers, bookers, and agents. They rated these good seats because they did a lot for (and to) vaudeville. We saw seated there William Morris and Marcus Loew, B. F. Keith and E. F. Albee, J. J. Murdock, F. F. Proctor, Tony Pastor, P. G. Williams, Mike Shea, Oscar and Willie Hammerstein, Martin Beck, Sullivan and Considine, Alex Pantages,

William Fox, Eddie Darling, Dan Hennessy, S. K. Hodgdon, Max Hart, Gene Hughes, Harry Weber, M. S. Bentham, Harry Jordan and Elmer Rogers—these were just a few of 'em. Me and Aggie were kinda wondering what they were thinking of when they saw the children of Lady Vaudeville passing by. Many must have felt proud and a few ashamed, I am sure.

On the northwest corner of Forty-sixth Street and Broadway (where the White Rats' club used to meet, above Churchill's) there stood a small loyal group of White Rats, who tried to do so many good things for these marchers years ago. They made mistakes, but they were honest ones, and they had the satisfaction of knowing that it was through their fighting that many things didn't happen to the actor that could have. They were invited to sit in the special stand, but they couldn't sit with some of the managers who had had them on their blacklists for years and deprived them of a living. So they all stood at that sacred corner and watched the parade (and even pointed to the few that were disloyal—those turned their heads away when passing). There was George Fuller Golden, the founder of the White Rats, with nearly all of his original gang, Jim Dolan, Dave Montgomery, Tom Lewis, Sam Ryan, Sam Morton, and Mark Murphy, and of course Harry Mountford. They were singing the White Rats' fighting song, loud enough for the managers and agents in the stands to hear.

> "And this shall be our battle cry,
> Be Brave, Be Brave, Be Brave.
> Fight for the White Rats 'till you die,
> And never be a slave or knave
> And when the fight is over, boys,
> Be proud of your stars,
> For the Rats that live in Ratland
> Are the real White Stars!
>
> (Shouted)   Rats! Rats! Rats! *Stars!*"

Even the bands couldn't drown them out!

On the northeast corner of Broadway and Forty-fifth Street, outside Loew's State Theatre where the *Variety* office was for many years, there stood Sime, Chicot, Jack Conway, Jolo, and Jack Pulaski from *Variety*, William H. Donaldson from the *Billboard*, "Zit" from *Zit's Weekly*, Frank Queen from the *Clipper*, and reporters and editors from the *Morning Telegraph*, New York

Star, the *Player*, *Dramatic Mirror*, and many other theatrical trade papers. They knew all the marchers, because for many years they bathed them in printer's ink, and some of them in red ink (those who never paid for their ads).

The parade was led by Eva Tanguay, swinging a diamond baton —as the Spirit of Vaudeville!

She was followed by bands led by John Philip Sousa, then there were Creatore, Arthur Pryor, Ben Bernie, Six Brown Brothers, Dixieland Jazz Band, House of David Band, Kiltie's Band, Boston Fadettes, and you could hear the golden notes from the cornet of Jules Levi. All the great musical acts were playing their favorite instruments; it was a sensation.

Then came the monologists and entertainers led by Harry Lauder, Al Jolson, Will Rogers, and Bert Williams, followed by Fred Niblo, Ezra Kendall, J. C. Nugent, Clifton Crawford, Gus Williams, Jim Thornton, Honey Boy Evans, Nat Wills, Cliff Gordon, Ernest Hogan, Herb Williams, Albert Chevalier, George Lashwood, Leon Errol, Raymond Hitchcock, Bill Fyfe, and Wilkie Bard!

They were followed by the "single women" (as they always have been through the centuries). Right in the front line were Nora Bayes, Maggie Cline, Marie Dressler, Vesta Victoria, Gertrude Lawrence, and Fannie Brice. Then came Irene Franklin, Florence Moore, Alice Lloyd, Marie Cahill, May Irwin, Bonnie Thornton, Cissie Loftus, Lottie Gilson, Mme. Schumann-Heink, Mme. Calvé, Dorothy Jardon, and Vinnie Daly.

The clowns were great, led by Slivers Oakley, Toto, and Marceline. They were followed by our lovable "talking clowns," you know, our "bad boys" that were so good: Frank Tinney, Bert Fitzgibbons, Jimmy Duffy, Jack Inglis, Harry Breen, Joe Towle, Arthur Rigby, Frank Van Hoven, Neil McKinley, Roy Cummings, Jackie Osterman, Chappie Aveling, Jack Rose, Sid Lewis, and Ted Healey, and those lovable guys, Johnny Stanley and Big Jim Morton!

The two-man acts, with the straight man carrying a newspaper in one hand, came next: Smith & Campbell, Gallagher & Shean, Haines & Vidoq, Conroy & LeMaire, Raymond & Cavalry, the Klien Bros., Fields & Wooley, Bert Swor and Charlie Mack; this contingent was led by Weber & Fields and McIntyre & Heath!

They in turn were followed by the mixed acts and sister acts.

Some marched singly while others were together: Charlie King (Brice & King), Hal Skelly (Groody & Skelly), Mabel McCane (Howard & McCane), Cecil Lean (Lean & Holbrook), Cooper & Ricardo, Dooley & Sales, Mike Donlin & Mabel Hite, George Felix & Lydia Barry, Harriet Lee (Ryan & Lee), Billy Gould (Gould & Suratt), Melville & Higgins, Peter Donald, Sr. (Donald & Carson); then there were Pauline & Marie Saxton, Yanci Dolly (Dolly Sisters), McCarthy Sisters, Elinore Sisters, Nieholl Sisters, and so many many more.

The dramatic acts were all riding in open barouches and taking bows. They were led by a white coach carrying Sarah Bernhardt, who received a terrific ovation. Following came barouches with Lillian Langtry, Mrs. Campbell, Nance O'Neill, Amelia Bingham, Leslie Carter, and Mme. Nazimova. Then came Maurice and Jack Barrymore, Nat Goodwin, Frank Keenan, James O'Neill, and Tyrone Power, Sr. But the ones who got the laughs, riding in hansom cabs, were Willard Simms, Ryan & Ritchfield, Cressy & Dayne, Murphy & Nichols, Bert Baker, James & Sadie Leonard, John C. Rice, Mr. & Mrs. Sidney Drew, and Gardner & Vincent.

The professional athletes were led by James J. Corbett and John L. Sullivan, with Babe Ruth, Hackenschmidt, Jack Johnson, Dorando and Hayes, Weston, Walthour, James J. Jeffries, Jack Sharkey, and Bob Fitzsimmons.

The "family groups" were led by the Four Cohans, Jerry, Helen, Josephine, and George M. Right behind them were Sam and Kitty and their daughter Clara Morton, with Eddie Foy and his sons Dick and Irving. The Dooleys, Bill, Johnny, and Gordon, all received an ovation.

The "hoofers" came dancing up the street led by George Primrose. It was great to see Barney Fagan, Bill Robinson, Pat Rooney, Sr., Jack Donahue, Hiram Brazil (Boyle & Brazil), Jack Doyle (Doyle & Dixon), Phil Cook, Lulu Beeson, Bunny Granville, Laddie Cliff, Tom Dingle, Patsy Doyle, Al Leach, Needham & Kelly, and waltzing behind them came Bryan & Broderick, Vernon Castle, dancing with Marilyn Miller, Lester Shean & Pearl Regav, Sawyer & Jarrott, and Moss & Fontana. Maurice danced with Florence Tamara, and Kosloff danced with Ulasta Maslova.

Then came the bicycle acts led by Joe Jackson, and behind him came flocks of jugglers, magicians, acrobats, wire acts, boomerang throwers, rope and casting acts. They were just wonderful.

The parade finished up with the greatest bunch of animal acts you ever saw, from ponies and dogs to elephants: Powers' Elephants, Adgie's Lions, Brandenberg's Bears, Meehan's Leaping Dogs, Howard's Ponies, Consul the Monk, Barnold and his Drunken Dog, trying to understand Don the Talking Dog—cats, dogs, birds, and the rest all doing great routines. The kids went wild about them.

When the parade came to the finishing line at the Palace, most of it broke up. Some of the marchers kept right on going to join other parades, like radio, pics, night clubs, and TV. Other acts just dropped out; their feet and hearts hurt; they just couldn't go any further. Quite a few never even reached the finishing line; they just couldn't make it—and dropped out en route.

Toward the finish of the parade, we heard great shouting and cheering and applause. This came mostly from the younger folks in the crowd. When I asked what all the cheering was about, someone said that a big crowd of youngsters had joined the tail end of the parade and were cutting up and had the crowds wild. They were led by Danny Kaye, Sid Caesar, Imogene Coca, Herb Shriner, Red Buttons, Jackie Miles, Bob Crosby, Jane & Betty Keane, George Goebells, Frank Sinatra, Alan Young, Judy Garland, Martha Raye, Betty Hutton, Morey Amsterdam, Steve Allen, Robert Q. Lewis, Sam Levenson, Danny Thomas, Jan Murray, Peter Lind Hayes and Mary Healy, Frank Fontaine, Jack Carter, Willie Shore, Marie Wilson, Lucille Ball and Desi Arnaz, Buddy Hackett, Larry Storch, Lenny Kent, Jackie Gleason, Danny O'Connor, Jackie Leonard, Gary Moore, Art Carney, Wally Cox, Dennis James, Cliff Arquette, Ward Wilson, Orson Beane, Jack Carson, Perry Como, Peter Donald, Dagmar, Phil Foster, Phil Harris, Ernie Kovac, Pinky Lee, Henry Morgan, Jimmy Nelson, Ozzie and Harriet Nelson, Jack Parr, Carl Reiner, Joe Silver, Paul Winchell, Jean Carroll, also a personality kid by the name of Arthur Godfrey, and two of the craziest and most talented guys in show biz, Dean Martin and Jerry Lewis!

Me and Aggie heard a lot about these fresh, talented youngsters, but we couldn't wait, because it would be some time before they would pass the finishing line, but I hope to write you about them in the very near future. Me and Aggie like these kind of kids who are full of vim, vigor, talent, and hopes with star dust in their eyes. We are sure they will find the trail with such vaude-trained veteran guides showing them the way as Ed Wynn, Eddie Cantor, Jack Benny, Jimmy Durante, Bob Hope, Groucho Marx, Fred Allen, Milton Berle, Ritz Bros., Bing Crosby, Fibber McGee & Molly, Joe E. Brown, Ken Murray, Ben Blue, Abbott & Costello, Joe E. Lewis, George Jessel, Patsy Kelly, Guy Kibbee, Judy Canova, Jack Kirkwood, Jerry Lester, Mary Livingston, Walter O'Keefe, Olsen & Johnson, Red Skelton, Edgar Bergen, Jerry Bergen, Jimmy Savc, Joan Davis, Bea Lillie, Bobby Clark, Jack Pearl, Smith & Dale, Amos 'n' Andy, Hildegarde, Burns & Allen, Pat Henning, Lulu McConnell, Victor Moore, Fred Stone, Leo Carrillo, William Gaxton, Bert Lytell, Mary Margaret McBride, Fred Waring, and Paul Whiteman, and the greatest Girl Scout of 'em all, Sophie Tucker!

Anyway, in my letters to you I want to tell you that when I said the Palace, me and Aggie meant all the first-class two-a-day houses in America. We figured the Palace was a symbol of all of them and there were plenty of them, and believe me, they meant more in the vaude picture than the Palace, New York, because they were paying the bills. Without them there would have been no vaudeville.

We tried to tell you about the children of Lady Vaudeville who helped blaze the trail from the honky-tonks to the Palace.

Hope you enjoyed it as much as me and Aggie enjoyed thumbing our memories of the most fascinating part of show biz—*vaudeville*!

SEZ

Your pal,

LEFTY

P.S. Thanks for the use of the hall.

INDEX

Index

A

Givot, George, 102
Glason, Billy, 198, 328
Glass, Montague, 209-210
Gleason, Bill, 125, 126
Gleason, Jackie, 256
Glenn & Jenkins, 82, 85
Glenroy, James Richmond, 193
Glissando, Phil, 66
Glockers, The, 25
Glover, Lyman B., 349
Glyn, Elinor, 225
Godfrey, Arthur, 73, 256
Godfrey, George, 485
Godwin, Jack, 75
Goldberg, Jack, 502
Goldberg, Phil, 327
Goldberg, Rube, 211
Golden, Claude, 108
Golden, George Fuller, 123, 136, 173-174, 311-312
Golden, Horace, 106, 107
Golden, John, 49, 310
Golden Gate Professional Club, 298
Golden Gate Quartette, 205
Goldie, Robert, 326
Goldman, Pete, 132
Goldsmith, Mose, 293
Goldsmith & Hoppe, 68
Golfers, 129
Gomez, Vernon "Lefty," 126
Gompers, Samuel, 312
Goodell & Nora Williams, 488
Goodman, Jules Eckert, 210
Goodwin, Nat, 100, 103, 251
Gordon, Bert, & Gene Ford, 230
Gordon, Cliff, 192
Gordon, Harry & Bert, 153
Gordon, Max, 192, 234, 485, 503
Gordon & Lord, 247
Gordon and Richards' Comique, Butte, Mont., 14
Gordon Bros., 164
Gordon Highlanders, 68
Gordoni, Arthur, 57
Gorman, Rev. Frank, 220
Gotch, Frank, 128
Gotham Theatre, Harlem, 240
Gouge, Jim, 116

Gould, Billy, 211, 298, 323
Gould, Frank, 393
Gould, Jay, & Flo Lewis, 233
Gould, Venita, 99
Gould & Lewis, 229
Goulding, Edmund, 326
Goulette & Fogler, 130
Gowdy, Hank, 126
Gowongo, The Great, 108, 204
Graces, Three, 148
Grady, Billy, 503
Graggar Bros., 32
Graham, Lillian, 387
Grahams, Four Novelty, 121
Grandi, Lou, 327
Grange, Red, 130, 256
Granlund, Nils T., 210, 247, 499, 502
Grant, Alf, 136
Grant, Cary, 21
Grant, Fred Bula, 87
Grant, Sydney, 100; & Charlotte Greenwood, 229
Grant Hotel, Chicago, 281
Granville, Bernard, 46, 102, 198, 295; & Dorothy, 154
Granville, Taylor, 137, 232
Grapewin, Charley, 21
Grauman, Pop, 242, 245
Grauman, Sid, 245, 260
Gray, Gilda (May), 42, 102, 252
Gray, Harry, 327
Gray, Tommy, 49, 130, 231, 268
Gray & Graham, 70
Greasy Front club, 297-298
Greater New York Film Exchange, 240
Greb, Harry, 122
Greeley Square Theatre, N.Y.C., 383
Green, Burt, 61-62, 328
Green, Clay M., 49
Green, Cora, Ada Smith & Florence Mills, 204
Green, Harry C., 51, 136, 231, 234
Green, Mitzi, 147
Green, Phil, 306
Green, McHenry & Dean, 80
Green Room Club, 293-294

Horse acts, 160
Hot Air Club, 304
Hotels, 276-286
Houdini, Harry, 21, 37, 112-113, 138, 386
House of David, 72
"Housewarmers," 233-234
Houston, Belle, 15
Howard, Bill, 485
Howard, Bronson, 210
Howard, Fred, 114
Howard, The Great, 114
Howard, Joe E., 13, 80
Howard, Sam, 154
Howard, Wille, 100, 102; & Eugene, 83, 85, 86, 154
Howard & Heck, "The Kugelwalker Twins," 216
Howard & North, 82-83
Howard & Shelton, 87
Howard & Thompson, 319
Howard Bros., 64
Howard Theatre, Boston, 335
Howard's, Mother, Baltimore, 281
Howard's Dog and Ponies, 161
Howe and Scott, 204
Howell, Harry, 127
Hoyt, Wait, 126, 127, 328
Hubbard, Elbert, 211-212
Huber, Fred H., and Kitty Alyne, 226
Huber, Otto, 356
Huber's Museum, N.Y.C., 16, 237
Hubert's Museum, N.Y.C., 121
Hudson, Mable, 116
Hudson, "What a Man," 221-222
Huehn, Billy "Musical," 66
Hufford & Chain, 142
Hughes, Gene, 78, 150, 268, 294-295.
Hughling's Seals, 165
Hume, Charles, 203
Humphries, Joe, 124
Humphries, "Tink," 351
Hungarian Boys' Band, 345
Hunt, Zelland, 66
Huntley, J. P., 134
Hurgon, August, 487
Hurley House, Philadelphia, 281

Hurst, Watts & Hurst, 80
Hurtig and Seamon, 242
Hussey, George W., 114
Hussey, Jimmy, 121, 198, 258-259, 300
Hussey & Boyle, 87
Hutton, Betty, 256
Hyams, Johnny, & Leilia McIntyre, 148
Hyams, Leilia, 148
Hyatt, Dan, 84; & Jessie, 137
Hyde, Victor, & Sister, 154
Hyde and Behman, 356, 417-418
Hymack, 98
Hyman, Harry, 111
Hyman, Joe, & Franklin, 324
Hymer, John B., 51
Hypnotists, 110-111; sample dialogue, 480
Hyson, Carl, & Dorothy Dickson, 45

I

Ichi, Ten, 109
Illusionists, 107
Imhof, Roger, 22; Conn, & Corinne, 22, 51, 501
Imitators, 99-104
Imperial Chinese Trio, 79
Imperial Gardens, N.Y.C., 385
Imperial Theatre, N.Y.C., 240
Impersonators. See Female impersonators; Male impersonators
"In Self Defence," 97
Inge & Farrel, 95
Inglis, Jack, 199
Inglis & Reading, 230
Ink Spots, 205
Inman, Henry, 306
Innes & Ryan, 229
Inter-State Circuit, 127, 235, 349
"Into the Light," 97
Ioleen Sisters, 35, 151
Irish acts, 319-321; double, sample script, 452-454
"Irish Servant Girls, The," 85, 88

Tunney, Gene, 121, 254, 256, 407
Turelly, 68
Turner, Terry, 502
Twain, Mark, 211
Twelfth Night Club, 303
Twelve Pound Look, 51
"Twelve Speed Maniacs, The," 489
Twenty-third Street Theatre, N.Y.C.,
 365-367
"Two Black Crows." *See* Moran &
 Mack
Two-man act, 82-87; sample scripts,
 445-458, 461-464, 474-478; *see also*
 Brother acts
Two-woman act, sample script, 458-
 461; *see also* Sister acts
Tyler, George, 210

U

U.B.O. *See* United Booking Office
Ukulele Ike, 73
"Unexpected," 51
Union organized by White Rats, 312-
 316
Union Hotel, N.Y.C., 305
Union Square Hotel, N.Y.C., 18, 305
Union Square Theatre, N.Y.C., 240,
 248, 322, 336, 366-367, 404
Unique Theatre, N.Y.C., 121, 240,
 241
Unique Theatre (National), San
 Francisco, 242
United Booking Office (Keith Vaude-
 ville Exchange), 241-242, 248, 340,
 344, 345-346, 357, 361-363, 372,
 398-399, 420; opposition of White
 Rats to, 310-316
"Unknown, The," 51
Upholders, Benevolent Order of, 298
Uplifters Club, California, 300
Urma, Hetty, 94
Urso, Camilla, 404
Usher, Claude and Fannie, 52
Usher, Harry & Frances, 110
Usher, May, 54, 60, 229

V

Valadon, Don & Lora, 30
Valadon, Paul, 109
Valdos, The, 109
Vallecita's Leopards, Dolores, 157
Vallee, Rudy, 253
Van, Billy B., 84, 142, 151, 198
Van, Gus, 496; & Joe Schenck, 8o
 138, 254, 493, 501
Van Allen, Will, 67
Van & Belle, 34
Van Biene, 69
Van Bros., 153
Vance, Clarice, 59, 324
Van Cello and Mary, 25
Vancos, The, 112
Vanderbilt, Gertrude, 54
Vandioff & Louise, 212
Vane, Sybil, 79
Van Horn, Harriet, 213
Van Horn & Inez, 32
Van Hoven, Frank, 108, 137, 199-200,
 408
Vannis, Four, 487
Van Siclyn, 322
Vanvards, Six Flying, 31
Varden, Perry & Wilbur, 8o
Vardman, 89
Variety, 152, 237, 274-275, 280, 313,
 351, 374
Variety Artists League, 298
Variety Clubs of America, 373
Varroll, Kaye, 116
Varvara, Leon, 68
Vasco, "The Mad Musician," 219
Vaterland Band, 71
Vaudeville, history of, 9-16
Vaudeville Comedy Club, 294-295
Vaudeville Managers Protective Ass'n,
 248, 314
Vaudeville News, 316
Vaughn, Sara, 205
Vavarra, Leon, 327
Veiller, Bayard, 209
Veloz & Yolanda, 45
Vendig Hotel, Philadelphia, 281